MW00779940

Get a Running Start

Your Comprehensive Guide to the First Year Curriculum

David C. Gray
Professor of Law
University of Maryland, Francis King Carey School of Law

Donald G. Gifford
Edward M. Robertson Professor of Law
University of Maryland, Francis King Carey School of Law

Mark Graber
Jacob A. France Professor of Constitutionalism
University of Maryland, Francis King Carey School of Law

William M. Richman
Distinguished University Professor of Law (Emeritus)
University of Toledo School of Law

David Super
Professor of Law
Georgetown Law

Michael P. Van Alstine
Professor of Law and Co-Director of the International and Comparative Law Program
University of Maryland, Francis King Carey School of Law

444 Cedar Street, Suite 700
St. Paul, MN 55101
1-877-888-1330

Printed in the United States of America

ISBN: 978-1-63459-683-1

To our students—past, present, and future—who provide the inspiration for this work.

DCG, DGG, MAG, WMR, DAS, & MPV

To my parents, who taught me how to learn.

DCG

To Nancy, Caroline and Michael, Rebecca and Jonathan, and Madeline and her (expected) brother.

DGG

To JB.

MAG

To Carol.

WMR

To Lisa.

MPV

FOREWORD

Welcome to your study of the law. Whether you are starting law school, thinking about starting law school, or just interested in the topic, this is likely to be a lifelong pursuit. Law is regarded as a "learned profession" which attorneys "practice." These are not instances of semantic happenstance. Lawyers are learning constantly. Each new case brings with it new facts, new issues, and new challenges that require new investigations and new learning about people, procedure, the substantive law, and institutions.

The law is also not static. New statutes are passed and courts issue new rulings on a daily basis, changing the substance and trajectory of the law, sometimes by tiny increments, and sometimes in historic leaps. All of this means that lawyers are always on a learning curve, and seldom bored.

Legal issues also pervade our society. In contexts ranging from popular culture to policy debates, the law often is a central character. Thus, even if you are just a casual consumer of crime dramas or a devoted reader of the New York Times opinion pages, there will always be new invitations to learn about the law.

With this book, we hope to provide you with a platform for a lifetime of legal learning. The substantive chapters in this volume offer overviews of the main courses taken by all first-year law students: criminal law, torts, civil procedure, constitutional law, property, and contracts. The individual lessons offered in each of these courses cover core concepts, rules, and areas of doctrine that all first-year law students are expected to learn. The lessons themselves are brief. Designed to be read in ten minutes or so, they offer a concise overview of material that first-year students explore at greater depth during the course of a day or week of classes. The lessons in this book do not offer a substitute for law school or a legal education. They instead offer a basic introduction and foundation for further exploration.

Our principal audiences for this book are pre-law students and first-year law students. In these courses and lessons, we therefore aim to offer a resource we wish we had when we were in school; one we believe will give law students a jump on their classes and a competitive advantage over their peers. In an effort to help students maximize the potential of these lessons, we have included an introductory chapter that offers advice on how to use this book as part of deliberate study and preparation process. We have also included a short chapter that offers advice from some of our successful students and alumni. Although all students need to find their own ways through law school and their careers, we hope this advice, along with the substantive course materials, will provide students with a head start on their ways to successful careers in law school and beyond.

The list of those who have contributed to this work in ways large and small is long. Although we cannot thank all of those people here, a few deserve special recognition. We therefore thank Charles Austin, Esq., Lindsay DeFrancesco, Trina Eiden, Maggie Grace, Esq., Jonathan Huber, Esq., Michael Jacko, Reshard Kellici, Esq., Daniel Kobrin, Esq., Jessica Kyle, Esq., Frank Lancaster, David McAloon, Esq., Kristin Neubauer, Katherine O'Konski, Esq., Thomas Pacheco, Liz Clark Rinehart, Esq., Clara Saltzberg, Esq., and Samantha Spencer, Esq., each of whom made important contributions during the course of this project. We would also like to thank Professors Stephen Henderson and Oscar Salinas, who provided invaluable expert feedback, and Dr. Gail Gray for his close editing and insightful comments. Finally, we would like to thank Tessa Boury at West for her encouragement and support.

ABOUT THE AUTHORS

David Gray is Professor of Law at the University of Maryland, Francis King Carey, School of Law where he teaches courses on the Fourth Amendment, criminal law, evidence, and jurisprudence. He has published dozens of articles and essays in leading journals on topics relating to criminal law, criminal theory, and criminal procedure. He is also author of The Fourth Amendment in an Age of Surveillance and co-editor of the Cambridge Handbook of Surveillance Law, both with Cambridge University Press. Students at Maryland voted Professor Gray Teacher of the Year in 2012. Professor Gray has also taught at Northwestern University and Duke Law School.

Don Gifford is the Edward M. Robertson Professor of Law at the University of Maryland, Francis King Carey, School of Law. He is the author or co-author of four books, including a torts casebook and a legal negotiation textbook. He has also published numerous articles about topics including mass torts, products liability, comparative fault, and medical malpractice. Along with Oscar S. Gray and Christopher J. Robinette, Professor Gifford prepares semi-annual updates to Harper, James, and Gray on the Law of Torts, the definitive five-volume torts treatise. Professor Gifford has also taught at the West Virginia University College of Law, the University of Toledo School of Law, and the University of Florida College of Law, where he twice received awards for teaching.

Mark Graber is the Jacob A. France Professor of Constitutionalism at the University of Maryland, Francis King Carey, School of Law. He is the author of major monographs and scores of articles on constitutional law, constitutional history, and constitutional politics. He is also co-editor (with Keith Whittington and Howard Gillman) of a two-volume textbook on constitutional law. Professor Graber has also taught at Yale University, Harvard University, Wesleyan University, the University of Virginia School of Law, the University of Texas, and the University of Oregon School of Law.

William Richman is Distinguished University Professor of Law (Emeritus) at the University of Toledo School of Law. He has published major course texts, monographs, and articles on topics relating to civil procedure, appellate court administration, conflicts of law, and constitutional law. Professor Richman is a member of the American Law Institute and has occupied leadership roles in the American Association of Law Schools. Professor Richman has also taught at the University of Michigan School of Law and the University of Maryland, Francis King Carey, School of Law.

David Super is Professor of Law at Georgetown Law. He has published dozens of major articles in top journals on issues relating to property law, administrative law, constitutional law, welfare law, and poverty law. Professor Super has also taught at Yale Law School, Harvard Law School, Howard University School of Law, Columbia Law School, the University of Pennsylvania Law School, the Washington and Lee University School of Law, and the University of Maryland, Francis King Carey, School of Law, where he was thrice honored with teaching awards.

Michael Van Alstine is Professor of Law and Co-Director of the International and Comparative Law Program at the University of Maryland, Francis King Carey, School of Law. Professor Van Alstine specializes in international and domestic private law. He has published widely in both English and German, including the leading course book on international business transactions and numerous articles and book chapters. Prior to joining the faculty at Maryland, Professor Van Alstine taught at the University of Cincinnati College of Law, where he was a four-time recipient of the Goldman Prize for Excellence in Teaching.

TABLE OF CONTENTS

GET A RUNNING START

Your Comprehensive Guide to the First Year Curriculum

CHAPTER 1

HOW TO USE THIS BOOK AS PART OF YOUR LAW SCHOOL PROCESS

Just as there are no shortcuts in the practice of law, there are no shortcuts in law school. The hallmarks of successful law students and successful attorneys are diligence, discipline, attention to details, and a capacity for hard work. You should therefore be skeptical of anyone offering quick or easy alternatives to careful reading and analysis of your assigned course materials and thorough preparation for your classes and exams. This includes many commercial outlines, review books, and hornbooks. That may seem like odd advice from the authors of a book that purports to offer a comprehensive guide to the first-year curriculum. On this point, however, we want to be perfectly clear: success in law school is all about process. That process will take time and will require effort. If you cheat on that process, then you are cheating yourself out of the opportunity to get the most out of your classes, not to mention the opportunity to get the best grades. This book is designed to facilitate that process. It is not a substitute. This book will give you a head start. It will not take you over the finish line.

Based on our experience and observations, we have found that students who excel in law school make a habit of working through class materials in different ways at least five or six times over the course of the semester. That might seem like a waste of time. It is not. To see why, it is important to understand a little bit more about the practice of law and the role of law school in helping you to develop the skills and habits essential to the practice of law.

The hallmark of a good lawyer, one in whom you would be willing to trust your property, your future, or your life, is analytic rigor. It is surely true that experienced lawyers tend to have deep funds of knowledge and good judgment based on years of practice, but knowledge alone is not enough. Good lawyers must also be thoughtful, careful, and deliberate. Good lawyers therefore take their time to listen and gather all the relevant facts. When considering those facts, they deploy a series of mental checklists to identify potential issues, problems, and solutions. They never make assumptions or jump to conclusions. Instead, they ask questions and withhold judgment until they have had the opportunity to gather all the facts and to think things all the way through. These habits sometimes earn lawyers a reputation for being obtuse, argumentative, or contrarian. That is a misperception. Good lawyers are just careful.

It is often said that one of the primary goals of law school is to train you to think like a lawyer. This is one old saw that is true. Particularly in your first-year courses, your professors will help you to develop and strengthen new neural pathways, installing a series of analytic checklists and instilling a commitment to approach legal questions or problems with a high level of analytic rigor. Success in this endeavor requires repeating a process of exposure to new material and concepts through reading and lecture, critical engagement with that new material through discussion and writing, consolidation of your new knowledge into an analytic framework, and application of that framework to new problems. Your professors will structure your assignments and class time with these process steps in mind. They will ask you to read and analyze cases that seem to present the same issues, but come out differently. They will challenge you to explain these apparent disparities. They will demand that you pay attention to details. They will encourage you to think about how you, as an attorney in those cases, might achieve a different result. All the while they will be training your brain by creating and reinforcing new neural pathways. They will also be socializing you into the practice of law by modeling a professional commitment to analytical rigor when confronted with new or even seemingly familiar situations.

From your first day in law school, you should commit yourself to a preparation and study process that will require you to work through your class materials several times with an eye toward the basic steps of exposure, engagement, consolidation, and application. Although you will need to work out the details of that process for yourself, we have observed that the most successful students have processes that feature some combination of ten basic steps, which they adapt to their individual schedules and learning styles:

1. Pre-semester preparation for their courses.
2. Weekly preparation for their courses.
3. Daily preparation for their classes.
4. Attending classes.
5. Daily review of their classes.
6. Weekly review of their courses.
7. Outlining materials for their courses.
8. Exam review.
9. Practicing final exams.
10. Final exam review.

Below we describe each of these steps and make recommendations for when and how you might use this book to facilitate your own study and preparation process. We will also offer some advice on taking exams. You will need to find your own way, of course. Your versions of these various steps may involve more or less time and investment than others. You may even find one or more of these steps unnecessary over time. It may also simply be impossible for you to do all of these things for every class and all of your courses every day and every week. You should therefore not treat this as a prescription. You should, instead, treat it as what it is: a set of recommendations and ideas that invite you to be conscious and thoughtful about your study and preparation process.

PRE-SEMESTER PREPARATION FOR YOUR LAW SCHOOL COURSES

It is important to start each semester of law school rested, energized, focused, and engaged. We therefore recommend that you try not to spend your pre-law summer worrying too much about school. You should instead focus on doing something relaxing, or at least unrelated to academics. Spend a few weeks hiking the Appalachian Trail. Get a job at a summer camp, ice cream parlor, or bowling alley. Sit by the pool. Whatever you do, just try not to worry about law school.

We do not mean to imply that you should turn your brain off during your pre-law summer. Quite to the contrary, we recommend that you spend as much time as you can reading and writing. What you read is up to you, but you should put a premium on well-written prose and good editing such as you might find in the novels of Ernest Hemingway, essays in the *New Yorker*, or stories in the *New York Times*. You should also write. This need not be serious, academic writing. Keep a journal. Write letters (real letters; not e-mails!). Writing is a skill that requires practice and maintenance. The goal of your pre-law summer writing should be to maintain and hone that skill by regularly constructing well-formed sentences into organized paragraphs that communicate ideas or events. You should also get into the habit of editing what you write. If you keep a journal, then reread your entries from prior days with an eye toward spotting grammatical mistakes, ambiguities, or inelegant phrasing. If you use e-mail, commit yourself to never jotting off an e-mail and sending it. Instead, reread and edit your e-mails several times before you send them. This is not only good practice but will also help you to develop important professional habits.

As the first days of classes approach, plan on sorting out your practical living arrangements. If you are moving, then try to get into your new housing a week or so before orientation begins. This way you can settle in, arrange furniture, stow pans and plates, find the local grocery store, locate the gym, and generally take care of all the necessaries before school starts. If you plan to prepare your own meals, it is also a good idea to get into the habit of planning menus and shopping for the week ahead. This will save considerable time and mental energy while also ensuring that you keep yourself properly fed. Be sure to keep your meals simple but well-balanced. If you live with others, you might also think about negotiating away your culinary responsibilities for at least some of the week.

The best time to start reading the substantive chapters in this book is toward the end of your pre-law summer. At some point during the week or two before classes begin, set aside time to read all the lessons for each of the courses you will be taking that semester. Go course by course, allocating a morning or an afternoon to each class, but try not to cover more than one course per day. There is no need on this first reading to get bogged down in details. You should devote real attention to your reading (turn off the television!), but focus on the big picture rather than the fine details. Having this global view of your courses will be invaluable as you get into the semester. It will help you to organize and understand your weekly and daily readings and discussions. It will also open the door to insights you otherwise might not reach until the end of the semester.

Once you have finished reading the chapters for a course, find someone to teach. This should be someone who is neither a lawyer nor a law student. Call a parent, corner a spouse, or invite a friend over for dinner. Spend some time during your conversation explaining to them some of the highlights of what you learned in your reading. Focus on the bits you found interesting, surprising, or confusing. Again, you should avoid getting bogged down in the details. The point of this exercise is for you to engage and consolidate some of what you have just been exposed to by recalling, repackaging, and communicating. In the process, you will begin to build a conceptual superstructure for your first-year courses while also modeling some of the important study habits that will serve you well during the semester.

WEEKLY PREPARATION FOR YOUR COURSES

As you get into the semester, you will need to plan a weekly schedule that affords you ample time to skim and then read carefully all the materials assigned for each of your courses. As a prelude to your weekly course preparations, we recommend that you read the lessons in this book addressing topics on your syllabus for the week. Your textbook's table of contents should provide you with the necessary guidance. You will spend a lot of time during your first year reading cases and dense editorial notes. Amidst your efforts to dig through sometimes difficult prose, it is easy to lose track of the basic legal questions and rules. Having a high-level overview in mind before wading into the tall weeds can be very helpful in navigating a clear path for the rest of the week and beyond.

After reviewing the relevant lessons in this book, conduct a quick skim of your assigned readings to get a basic sense of the major topics and cases. You should immediately see some connections. You are now ready to dig into the materials in earnest. Be an active reader. Underline, but sparingly (excessive underlining or highlighting can inhibit comprehension). Take short notes in the margins of your books summarizing or rephrasing key concepts. Look up from your reading at significant junctures, such as the end of a case, note, or section, and try to recall and review what you have just read. Try to avoid the temptation to create separate documents such as case briefs and reading notes at this point. This breaks the flow of your reading process and inhibits comprehension.

After you have finished the assigned readings for a particular course, you may find it helpful to create separate documents such as case briefs or reading notes. Case briefs are short summaries of the main components of a case (procedural posture, facts, question presented, rule applied, analysis, and holding). Reading notes are brief summaries or overviews that may include some of your own thoughts and analysis. These efforts may be particularly helpful during your first few weeks of law school as you become accustomed to reading unfamiliar materials like judicial decisions. Just keep in mind the purpose and benefit of creating case briefs and reading notes. The goal is not to produce documents for the ages. In fact, the product is an artifact. The primary benefit of creating these kinds of summary documents is in the process. By reviewing, consolidating, and summarizing cases and readings, you will enhance your comprehension and retention. You should therefore not waste too much time on formatting or stating rules and holdings with absolute precision. Your views and understanding of the material will develop and evolve in the course of class discussions, after class reviews, weekly reviews, outlining, and exam preparation. You want to leave space for those parts of your learning process.

DAILY PREPARATION FOR YOUR CLASSES

Before each of your classes, you should make a habit of reviewing the material assigned for the day. Try to do this as close to the time of your class as you can. Take ten minutes to flip through the assigned reading, focusing on your underlining and margin notes. If you created case briefs or separate reading notes, then this is a good time to glance through those materials so the facts, analysis, and basic holdings of each case assigned for the day will be fresh in your mind. As part of this process, you might also review the summary notes at the end of the relevant lessons from this book. This may help focus your thinking before class begins.

ATTENDING CLASSES

Go to your classes. There are lots of reasons why you should, but three should suffice. First, class provides you with an early opportunity to test your understanding of the course material in a live, interactive environment. There is simply no substitute. Recorded lectures can be useful for some purposes, such as summarizing doctrinal rules, but very little of your time in first-year courses will be devoted to covering and summarizing the rules. You will, instead, be engaged in uncovering, analyzing, engaging, and applying those rules. For these tasks, recorded lectures cannot recreate the live, in-class experience. Second, going to class is often the most efficient use of your time. In the span of an hour or two in class, you will make connections and gain insights that would require hours, days, or even years for you to achieve on your own—if ever. Third, your professors will be writing and grading your exams. They inevitably will show their hands during class, emphasizing the issues and concepts that are most important or most intriguing, giving you considerable insight as to what is likely to be on your final exam. You will also become familiar with your professors' expectations, and therefore how your exams will be evaluated.

Participate in class. Do not merely observe. This means that your focus during class should be on the flow of ideas and the application of analytic processes. Most of your law school classes will feature some version of the Socratic Method. This is a model of engaged learning that seeks to explore and expose concepts, ideas, and analytic processes through dialogue. Whether or not you are "on call," you should be engaged. Try to answer for yourself the questions posed by the professor. Try to identify the major concepts or insights that emerge from the conversation. Feel free to jot these down as they come up, but do not try to transcribe everything that happens in class. We cannot emphasize this enough. Almost without exception, the students who have done the best in our courses over the years have their eyes up during class. They are looking at us or their fellow students. They do not have their heads down, buried in their books, their notebooks, or their computers.

This last point deserves emphasis. Although portable electronic devices, such as laptop computers, tablets, and the like, have incredible potential, they can also be very damaging to your learning process. They provide a constant temptation to distraction during class. Some students succumb to these temptations fully, and simply tune out in favor of games, web surfing, chatting, or shopping. Others fool themselves into thinking they can multitask. They cannot. Nobody can. The scientific consensus is that "multitasking" is really rapid shifting among multiple focuses. Each switch requires a few moments' reorientation. So, when you try to multitask during class, you inevitably miss important material, lose the flow of ideas and analysis, and build inefficiencies into your learning process. Even when students avoid temptation, limiting themselves to taking notes during class, computers frequently tempt them to act as stenographers, trying to thoughtlessly capture everything the professor says rather than engaging in class discussions. Electronic devices also erect physical barriers between you and the classroom experience. Finally, screens offer an immersive universe unto themselves, pulling you away from the shared space of the classroom into a private world. For these reasons and others, we routinely recommend that students think carefully about bringing electronic devices and laptops into the classroom.

If you decide to use a laptop or other electronic device during your classes, then we recommend closing your e-mail program, games, and web browsers for the duration of class. As a matter of precommitment, you might even consider installing software that will allow you to block access to specified programs and even the Internet. Although this may seem silly, these sorts of hedges against temptation are common habits among effective students and professionals.

DAILY REVIEW OF YOUR CLASSES

It is a good idea to take a few moments after class ends to jot down a few summarizing notes or thoughts about the material you have just covered. Later on, with the opportunity of some remove, it is a good idea to review and consolidate what you learned in class with your notes and your reading. You may find that revising your reading notes or creating a new summary document will help facilitate this process. It need not be anything too formal. Something in the mode of a journal or running outline is perfectly sufficient. The point is to take some time to sit with your readings, your notes from class, and the relevant lessons from this book in order to start pulling things together for yourself in a provisional fashion.

As part of this daily review process, you should also try to test what you have learned by applying it to new circumstances. For example, you might think about how the outcome of a case you read for class might or might not be different if certain facts changed. You might also construct new hypotheticals for yourself. One good way to do this is to put yourself in the role of your professor. Imagine that you are trying to test students' understanding of the material for that day. Try to construct a fact pattern that would confirm their basic understanding while also challenging their grasp of the nuances. This process of self-testing is extremely useful for your learning process and may also yield considerable insights as you get to the end of the semester.

WEEKLY REVIEW OF YOUR COURSES

On a weekly basis, you should reserve a block of time to review the materials you covered that week in each of your courses and to think about how it links up with what you have learned so far in the semester. As part of this process, you will want to extend and refine the notes you wrote as part of your daily reviews, incorporating all the materials from your reading and class notes for the week. You should also make a point of working through a few questions or problems from the book, or perhaps from a third-party text. The goal is to consolidate and apply. This process of creative repetition will solidify your understanding of the material and reinforce your new neural pathways. The lessons in this book may be helpful to you as a prelude to this process by focusing your attention on the major conceptual points for the week.

As part of your weekly review process, consider working with a study group of three to five people (fewer limits your group's resources while too many more can make the group unwieldy). You should have a regular structure for your meetings. For example, you might have each person do a five or ten minute summary of one of your courses, effectively "teaching" the rest of the group. If you do this, then switch things up every week so everyone has several chances to lead the group's discussion of every class. After this initial presentation, you might open the floor for other members of the group to supplement the summary, ask questions, pose hypotheticals, and suggest connections to topics covered earlier in the course. You might also just start out with questions and hypotheticals. However you choose to structure your meetings, keep the conversation open rather than having any particular person on point. Try to devote at least 30 minutes to each of your courses.

There is often a lot of pressure associated with study groups in law school. Many students think it is imperative to be in a group with the "best" students. Study groups can also start to look like high school cliques, complete with perceived hierarchies. Try to avoid falling into this trap. The most important criteria in selecting members of your study group are perspectives, personalities, and schedules. You should therefore pick people you like, respect, who share your commitment and work ethic, and with whom you will be able to meet on a regular basis every week.

Some students eschew study groups altogether. If this is your instinct, then we recommend at least giving it a try. There is simply no way, working on your own, to recreate the benefits of peer dialogue in the learning process. Study groups are also important to your professional development. Most law practice involves team efforts. This requires an ability to work productively and cooperatively in groups. Even solo practitioners maintain a close network of colleagues with whom they discuss cases and bounce around ideas. Working with a study group is therefore an important part of your socialization process. Noninstrumentally, it is also a great way to make close, lasting friendships. Keep in mind that your study groups need not always be physically in the same place at the same time. Although it is great to meet face-to-face, Internet chats using text or video, e-mail chains, or other means may provide the same or different benefits.

One note of caution on study groups is in order, however. These are not opportunities for free-riding. In order for you to get the most out of your study groups, you need to come to your group sessions having done your own work. Timing of group sessions in your overall study process is therefore critical. You will need to decide these matters with your group, but we recommend meeting a few hours after your last class for the week. By this point, everyone in the group will have had the opportunity to do their pre-class preparations. They will have gone to class. They will have done their daily reviews. And they will have started their weekly reviews. This is the perfect juncture for a two- or three-hour discussion covering all the material for the week. Feel free to reward yourselves with some pure socializing after your session is over.

As you think through scheduling various steps in your daily and weekly course work, we recommend keeping three priorities in mind. First, you should try to work on each of your courses every day. Doing at least a little bit of work for each of your courses every day will keep you primed on that subject. Spreading out your work for each course will help you to avoid burnout. Second, you should vary your work tasks so you are engaging in different process steps every day—reading for one class, reviewing for another, consolidating for a third. With a little careful planning, meeting the first priority should take care of the second. Finally, you must reserve inviolable time for sleep. Learning experts and neurobiologists agree that adequate sleep is essential to learning and effective thinking. You should therefore make sure to get seven or eight hours of sleep every night.

In addition to meeting with your peers, you should make a point of going to your professors' office hours several times over the course of the semester. At some point early in the semester, visit each of your professors to introduce yourself and to get general advice on the course and law school. If you find a course particularly difficult or challenging, do not hesitate to visit that professor during office hours every week to ask questions and seek clarification. For other courses, you should visit office hours at least once every three weeks or so to make sure you on the right track. Do not worry that you may be bothering them. For the most part, professors love the topics they teach and love to interact with students. We certainly do!

OUTLINING MATERIALS FOR YOUR COURSES

At some point during your first semester, you will start to hear people talk about outlining. Outlining is the process of consolidating the material for an entire course into a coherent and comprehensive document. This process is called outlining because most students find that the outline format, which utilizes headers, subheaders, and brief supporting text, provides the most intuitive structure. The ultimate format is secondary, however. The primary benefit of outlining is the process of consolidating, not the final product.

Views vary on when it is best to start outlining. Some argue for outlining from the beginning of the semester. Others argue for reserving your outlining process until the waning weeks of the semester, when you will have a better global grasp of your courses. We recommend something between these two extremes. Each of your courses will be divided into parts and sections. These represent conceptual chunks that are ripe for consolidation. We therefore recommend that you start outlining each of your courses once you have completed a section or two, or when you otherwise see a set of concepts or ideas coming together as a distinct unit. For example, a natural time to start outlining criminal law might be when you have finished your discussions of *mens rea* and *actus reus*. In civil procedure, you might start outlining at the end of your discussion of personal jurisdiction. Once you have started outlining for a course, you should try to update your outline as new conceptual chunks come into focus.

As a preliminary to outlining, we recommend that you reread all the relevant lessons from this book. This should facilitate your outlining process in at least two ways. First, it will help refresh your memory of materials covered earlier in the semester. Second, it will help you develop a holistic perspective on the course, drawing your attention to connections and intersections that frequently get lost in the day-to-day and week-to-week process of keeping up with your classes. You may also want to review a past exam for each of your classes in order to get a better sense of the scope and form of the exams you will be taking. We also recommend that you make a point of visiting your professors in office hours before beginning your outlines. There is no reason to hide your purpose for such a visit. Simply tell your professor that you are thinking about starting your outline and would like to spend a few minutes reviewing and asking questions about the relevant materials. You should lead the conversation, however. Do not go to your professors with the expectation that they will give you an impromptu mini-lecture covering weeks or months worth of material.

Given our emphasis on process, it should come as no surprise that we do not recommend relying on outlines from others or using commercial outlines in lieu of making your own outlines. You may use these third-party materials as references to help you think about how to put an outline together. They may also be helpful as a way to double-check your work. The real benefit from outlining is in the process, however, not the product. Students who do well on their exams do not do well because they have the best outlines. They do well because they take the time to make those outlines.

This leads us to a frequent mistake students make in understanding the role of outlines in test-taking. Many of your law school exams will be "open-book," meaning that you will be allowed to use your books, notes, and outlines during the course of your exam. This marks a departure from most undergraduate classes, where exams are closed-book. Many students think the open-book format requires less preparation or that they will be able to get by using a superior outline as a reference during the exam. This is a terrible mistake. Law school exams do not test rote knowledge. They test comprehension and analytic acumen by asking you to apply what you have learned to new situations and to communicate your thought processes in clear, organized, and concise prose. The only way to do well on these exams is through a deliberate process of disciplined learning over the course of the semester. You cannot accomplish that goal or perform well on exams if all of your knowledge is in external reservoirs. It needs to be part of you. Having your outlines next to you during your exams will provide you with some reassurance. It will also allow you to look up a few details or to double-check a fact or two. In general, however, if you need to rely on your outlines during your exams then you are in trouble.

EXAM REVIEW

During the final weeks of the semester, you will want to turn your attention to your exams. As with other steps in your semester-long study and review process, your exam review process should involve opportunities to revisit, engage, consolidate, and apply what you have learned. As a first step, you will want to finish your outlines. You may then find it helpful to reread the lessons from this book covered in your classes, paying particular attention to any topics you may still find mysterious or confusing. You may also want to reread some sections of your textbooks, again focusing on topics you find difficult.

As another means of review and consolidation, you might also consider condensing your outlines, creating flowcharts, or developing checklists. For example, you might create a flowchart documenting the steps you take in assessing whether a contract has been formed or a checklist of the elements of an intentional tort. These exercises may seem like busy work, but they can be very helpful in providing you with a forum for consolidating and organizing the material for a course. Unlike your main outlines, these documents can also be quite useful during your exams, providing you with a ready-made answer outline, a tool for double-checking your work, a way to ensure that you have not skipped issues, or even a means for calming your mind and organizing your thinking if you become nervous or panicked.

In addition to flowcharts and checklists, you may want to create a document containing clear, concise statements of some major rules of law central to each of your courses, perhaps borrowing from your outline. Time is a very limited commodity during your exams. There is no reason to fuss over prose or to worry about how best to phrase a particular rule during the exam if you can do this work ahead of time and simply copy it onto your exam paper. For example, it might be helpful to have a clear, concise statement of the rule against perpetuities during your property exam or the rule governing diversity jurisdiction in civil procedure.

Your study groups should also play an important role in your exam review process. We recommend that you dedicate at least one extended session to each of your exams. During that time, you should work together to understand difficult issues, test your knowledge by discussing hypotheticals, and get feedback on your checklists, flowcharts, and rules lists. You might also consider going to office hours or scheduling appointments with your professors as a group to ask questions or to confirm your answers.

PRACTICING FINAL EXAMS

Once your exam review process is well under way, it is time to start taking practice exams. There are two goals here. First, you need to get comfortable with organizing and writing answers under time pressure. Second, you need to practice applying your knowledge to new questions and problems.

The first goal is best achieved by taking exams under real test conditions. Reserve three or four hours in your schedule at the same time of the day as when your exam is scheduled. Find a quiet place in the library or a vacant classroom. Lay out the materials you plan to bring into your exam, and nothing more. Put in a set of earplugs. Open a model exam or past exam for your course that you have not seen before, read the questions, outline answers, and write your answers, all within the time allotted for the exam.

Although this is a time-consuming process, it is the only way to get comfortable with the actual mechanics of taking a law school exam. Fortunately, it is probably not necessary for you to take multiple practice exams under real test conditions for each of your classes. You certainly can take a timed practice exam for each of your courses, but the basic mechanics carry over. For this same reason, it is probably not necessary to take any practice exams under real conditions once your exams have begun. After you have walked the gauntlet once, there is little to be gained by doing it again under artificial conditions during that exam period.

You should still take practice exams after you feel comfortable with the basic mechanics of writing timed exams. Instead of writing out full answers, however, you should limit yourself to setting up your answers. Find practice problems or past exams and work through the questions, creating outlines for your answers using your knowledge, checklists, and flowcharts. As you outline your answers, try to avoid the temptation to skip steps in your analyses. Much can be lost in ellipses and "yadda, yadda, yaddas," including key issues that may mark the difference between a good grade and a mediocre grade. It is therefore important that you practice good habits during these last stages of your exam preparations.

Your best resources when practicing exam outlining and writing are past exams given by your professors. These are always in short supply, however, so you should use them wisely. On this score, we highly recommend against looking at past exams too early in the semester. If you are only halfway through a course, then a substantial portion of any past exam will be a complete mystery. It is far better to reserve looking at past exams until later in the semester, when you completed most of the course material and have had the opportunity to work through most of your outlining process.

FINAL EXAM PREPARATIONS

The most important thing you can do in terms of final preparations for your exams is to get some exercise, eat well, and, above all else, get some rest. Every credible source we have found in the neuroscience and pedagogical literature supports the simple truth that you will perform much better on your exams after a good night's sleep than you will by sacrificing sleep for a last-minute cram session. We therefore recommend that you take the evening before each of your exams off to exercise, eat a good meal, read a book, and get to bed early. Some light reviewing the day of your exam is fine. As part of this final warm-up, you may find it helpful to review the summary notes for the lessons in this book and perhaps even skim some of the lessons just to center your thinking. If you have managed your study process properly, however, then there should be very little left to do other than to go in and do your best work.

EXAMS

Our first and most important advice for taking law school exams is to arrive relaxed, confident, and well-rested. If you have committed yourself to a thoughtful and thorough study and preparation process all semester long, then you will have every reason to feel relaxed and confident on exam day. All that preparation may matter very little, however, if you arrive exhausted by several nights of cramming. To do your best, you simply must get enough sleep in the days leading up to your exam. You should also eat good meals during the days leading up to the exam. It is also a good idea to bring a bottle of water and a snack or two into the exam with you. All of these efforts to take care of your body will pay off.

Law school exams are designed to test the quality, depth, and clarity of your analytic process. Because they are timed, law school exams also test your organization, time management, and ability to communicate in clear, concise prose. Most first-year exams consist of a hypothetical case that you will analyze by applying the relevant rules, principles, and policies discussed during the course. The questions usually begin with a fact pattern meant to mimic something a client might bring to you in practice. Your task is to analyze those facts in light of the relevant law and then offer your appropriately qualified assessment of the parties' rights and liabilities. First-year exams do not test your rote memory. Your professors may include a few short questions to test your basic understanding of a few rules or concepts but, for the most part, simply parroting back the rules, doctrines, and policies you learned in a class by itself will not lead to good grades on a law school exam. That is as it should be. Lawyers are not parrots. They are counselors, problem solvers, and advocates. It is therefore fitting that law school exams test your ability to perform the careful, thoughtful, and thorough analysis of facts and legal issues necessary to giving effective advice, identifying solutions, and defending your clients' rights.

Given the goal and structure of law school exams, we advise that you approach your exams as an attorney rather than a student. In keeping with that orientation, your first task is to read both the fact patterns and the questions very carefully. In our experience, students often do poorly because they miss key facts or ignore important directions and constraints set forth in the questions. As a result, they miss key issues or spend valuable time opining about matters that are not at issue. We do not necessarily advocate reading the whole exam from the get-go. Exams frequently include multiple discrete fact patterns, each with their own set of questions. You may find it most helpful to go fact pattern by fact pattern. Just make sure you read all the questions associated with a fact pattern before you begin to write your answers.

After you have read through the fact pattern and questions, we recommend that you outline your answers. These outlines need not be detailed, but they should provide you with a well-structured and complete overview of the answer you intend to write. This serves several important purposes. First, it helps you to avoid missing issues. Many important issues raised in your exams will not be apparent on a surface reading of the facts. They will, instead, reveal themselves only as you get into the thick of your analysis. If you jump straight to writing rather than taking the time to outline your answers, then you may miss these issues entirely or, perhaps worse, find them only as time is running out. This suggests a second reason you should outline before you write: it shows you how much territory you will need to cover, allowing you to assess how much time you should dedicate to each issue. By outlining, you will avoid spending inordinate time writing up the first issue and then find yourself with little or no time as you get to important issues that naturally come later in your analysis. A third reason you should outline before writing is that it will help you to organize and structure your answers. Scattered prose that jumps from thought to thought with no apparent coherency or continuity in thought or analysis is a recipe for disaster on law school exams. Outlining your answers before you write will help you to avoid this outcome while keeping you in control of your writing process.

In the course of constructing your outlines, you may find it helpful to refer to checklists or flowcharts you may have developed as part of your study process. These tools can sometime save considerable time during the outlining process itself, allowing you to simply check off issues you need to discuss while crossing out those you do not. They can also be useful in double-checking your answer outlines to make sure you have not missed anything.

For the writing process itself, focus on keeping your prose concise, declarative, and to-the-point. Do not waste time on flowery imagery or extended exegesis of particular cases (unless the question specifically asks you to opine at length on, say, *Palsgraf*). Structure is critical. In this regard, you may find it helpful to use reliable law school standards like IRAC (Issue, Rule, Analysis, Conclusion). It is also a good idea to keep your paragraphs short, inserting a carriage return or line break every time you change issues or otherwise want to emphasize a point. Above all, do not skip steps in your analysis. Show your work. Even if the point seems obvious to you, it is not obvious to your professor that you have spotted and addressed an issue unless you write it out. Being thorough also shows that you are careful, disciplined, and thorough in your analysis—the hallmarks of a good attorney.

In addition to writing clearly and concisely, you should also make sure your presentation makes it easy for your professor to read your essays and hard to miss your discussion of key issues. Using strong topic sentences at the beginning of each paragraph helps a lot. You might also consider making judicious use of bolded text, underlining, and numbered lists. To see why these tools are important, put yourself in your professor's shoes, faced with dozens or scores of exams to grade in a short period of time. You should make it as easy as possible for your professor to give you points. If you expect her to spend hours upon hours digging through your essays in the hope of finding points to give, then you will be disappointed with the outcome. Also important is the fact that most law school exams are graded on a curve. Papers that are structured, organized, coherent, and concise tend to come out at the top.

Law school exams are timed. Time management is therefore important. The best way to get comfortable with writing exams under pressure is to take several practice exams under real testing conditions. In the course of your practicing, you will notice something important: some issues are rather straightforward, and therefore require nothing more than a few sentences to state the rule, apply the facts, and come to a relatively clear conclusion. Other issues are more complicated in that they involve disputes of fact, lie in an unsettled or controversial area of the law, or require you to work with competing precedent cases covered in class. These are the issues that offer you the best opportunity to show off your analytic acumen by drawing analogies and spotting distinctions. You should therefore make sure you reserve sufficient time to show off.

As you address each issue raised in your exams, be sure to include the rule or doctrine relevant to that issue. Most of the points lost on law school exams result from failures to recognize issues or instances of stating rules or doctrines in a manner that is substantially incorrect. Simply identifying an issue and the governing rule or doctrine will therefore put you way ahead. This is another juncture where some advanced work during your study process will pay off. If you come to your exams with a list of major rules and doctrines condensed into clear, concise prose, then you can simply copy your work into your exam answers without spending time fussing over phrasing during the exam period.

The analytic portions of your exams are your opportunities to shine. By repeatedly engaging, analyzing, consolidating, and applying material for your courses during the semester, you will have developed a flexible set of neural pathways that allow you to spot connections and explain the relevance of material differences in light of the law. You are now thinking like a lawyer. Put your new cognitive skills to good use. Highlight facts that link the problem presented by the exam to particular cases and doctrines covered in your readings or discussed in class. Point out facts that suggest dissonance or a potential exception. Explain the significance of these facts and, if the question calls for it, suggest what result you might predict and why.

AFTER EXAMS

When you walk out of your exams, we advise you to resist the urge to discuss the questions and issues with your classmates. There is no upside to this practice. You will have additional learning opportunities when you meet with your professors to review your exams, but that can wait. You should also set aside any feelings you may have about how well the exam went. We have found that good students who were convinced that they bombed an exam often end up at the top of the curve. The exam is over. Let it go and move on. In this effort, it is helpful to keep some perspective. Your performance on any single exam will end up comprising about 3 percent of your final grade-point average at graduation. It will not make or break your career as a lawyer. The same is true of first-year grades more generally. They may help with some early career opportunities but do not, by and large, predict the rest of your career. We have all had students who got C's in our classes or ended up in the bottom quintile of the class after their first years but nevertheless went on to successful and fulfilling careers. Some of us fit this bill, earning quite forgettable first-semester grades before going on to successful careers in practice and teaching. Far more important than your grade in any particular class are your knowledge, skills, and relationships with your colleagues and professors.

This last point deserves particular emphasis. No matter what your final grades, you should make a point of visiting your professors after grades come out to review your exams and to seek advice on your classes and your career. Whether you did well or poorly, reviewing your exams can help you to reinforce what you did right and diagnose what you did wrong, allowing you to adjust your study and preparation processes going forward. Asking your professors for advice can also help solidify potential mentorship relationships while providing those professors with more fodder for letters of recommendation or phone calls to potential employers. Above all, however, you should look at your exams as one step in a lifelong relationship with your professors. You should therefore approach these post-exam review sessions as an investment in that relationship.

CHAPTER 2

SOME ADVICE FROM SUCCESSFUL STUDENTS

Despite our best efforts, we find that students routinely ignore or discount our advice. Sometimes this is because the advice seems remote or even impossible to implement. We therefore solicited advice from some of our most successful current and past students. We asked them about the best and worst advice they had received as first-year students and what advice they wish they had received. Here are some of their answers:

TAKE IT SERIOUSLY

- Take your classes as seriously as you want your professors and future colleagues to take you. Always be prepared for class. Professors pay attention and you never know who may be a valuable champion for your cause (whatever that may be) down the line.
- I think the best advice I got was essentially that short term pain equals long term gain. Law school is hard. You have to be willing to sacrifice some of the leisurely aspects of your life during your first year in order to devote enough time to the rigorous study necessary to succeed. Law school is not like college. You cannot get by on your innate intelligence like you could in college because you are now surrounded by people who succeeded just like you did in college.
- Don't mistake first year of law school for college. I think many of my colleagues treated the first semester of the first year of law school as an extension of college. Go out and drink after finals, not before.

- Too often I felt like I saw people who seemed to believe they had an inalienable right to going out on the weekends. Anything that infringed on that was simply invalid and merited no consideration. It's not to say that you can't find time for friends and to relax, but you have to recognize the work comes first.
- Don't be misled about how hard you should work for a writing course based on the number of credits it is worth. It is really important that you learn to write well and that someone can speak to your writing abilities.
- These three years are short, busy, and can be great fun. Make the most of every conversation and interaction.

MENTORSHIP AND ADVICE

- Find a professor (or more than one) to mentor you, and take advantage of office hours. I really think this is the most important factor to success in law school. I would not have been successful in law school, would not have been Editor-in-Chief of Law Review, would not have gotten my clerkship, and would not have the opportunities I now have without the guidance and support of my mentor professors.
- I think the best thing I did in law school was establish relationships with professors. I have a lot of friends now (other 3Ls) who didn't do that and they really regret it. I'm not close with every professor I have ever taken a class with, but I do have a few in my corner who have been unbelievably supportive. It is just really nice to know you have that.
- Never be afraid to ask someone for help: professors, 2Ls, 3Ls, and even your classmates; but also understand that while that advice/technique/supplement worked well for them

and they got an A in some class, it might not work for you.

- Take everyone's advice, hints, tricks, and tips with a grain of salt. What works for everyone else may not work for you.

STUDYING AND CLASSES

- For preparation, this sounds facile, but I think that it is crucial to have the reading done and to take notes in advance of class. I would also suggest that the notes happen after the reading is done. Both those students who take notes as they are reading (often copying down lots of extraneous details) and those who take no notes at all seem equally likely to lose the big picture. Above all, read to understand.
- Study at the library. Study in a different library once exam season hits.
- If you can, continue to brief even when everyone else seems to stop. For someone who doesn't remember what he read unless he writes it down, I needed to brief if I was going to survive a cold call. And overall that helped me remember cases come exam time.
- Try color-coding cases and writing notes in the margins as a tactic to deal with cold calls. It makes it easy to glance down and see what you were thinking about any particular part of a case.
- Go to class and take good notes. It sounds small and silly, but I think one of my keys to success was consistently attending class, actively listening and participating (when warranted), and taking good notes.
- As for participation in class, there is a balance that needs to be struck. On the one hand, I continue to be dumbfounded by the number of students who think they can chat/read the

news/shop online during class and still follow the discussion. Perhaps it is a generational thing to attempt it, but all the research I know of says that human beings are much worse at multitasking than we think we are. On the other extreme are those students who type every word the professor says. They never have time to think about what (s)he is saying because they are too busy transcribing. For me, the magic balance is that during class I follow along with the notes I took prior to class and supplement/correct myself when I missed a relevant point. If I prepared well, I don't have to write much during class at all. The result is that I get exposed to the material three times (reading, taking notes, lecture.)

- Be respectful of your fellow students in class. Don't subject those sitting behind you to tons of game playing or surfing. It's distracting to them and bad for you. Also try to avoid the temptation to show off. This goes double when someone else is on call. Keep your hand down until the professor asks for volunteers. Waving your hand around while someone else is struggling is demeaning to them and distracting for everyone.
- A good tactic to stay on top of your classes is to go back through your notes and reading at the end of each week and try to make sense of it and state it more succinctly. Then, at the end of the semester, you can go back to this condensed version of your notes and more easily make an outline.

EXAM PREPARATION

- I ended up taking a step before jumping into outlining where I tried to condense class notes with briefs maybe about a month after learning the information. This saved a lot of time when I started outlining and just added another layer of reviewing the information.

- Smart has absolutely nothing to do with doing well on the exams. Practice, practice, practice! We are all smart and can take exams but you need to learn how to take law school exams. The only way to get comfortable is to practice. Also, most of the exams are time crunched, so you need to learn how to get your answers out quickly and efficiently.
- Doing practice exams is key. And asking your professors about what they are looking for in an answer is even more important.
- Lawyers read and write. Practice reading and writing whenever you can. Don't worry about making a beautiful outline to prepare for exams. Your time is better spent taking timed practice exams and learning how to write effectively under pressure.
- There may come a time in the semester when you realize you can't write or speak as well as you could before law school. This is a function of your brain having too much to process. It will pass. The best way to get through it is to talk to people about what you are learning. Talk to professors and classmates, but also talk to non-law students. If you can explain proximate cause to your friend before the friend gets bored, you can probably explain it on an exam.

STUDY GROUPS

- Study with someone else, but make your own outline. I studied in several groups throughout law school, but my most productive was one where one other student and I would meet together to go over a specific portion of the class after we had outlined it. We could talk through issues we were having and supplement our understanding of the material.
- When preparing for exams, find one or two friends to bounce hypotheticals around with. It's fun and

you'll actually understand what you have in your outline.

- Talking with other students about the cases and what is important to take away from them can be extremely effective. Working with others can alert you to nuances in the law you hadn't thought of and it's more fun than working by yourself. But work with the right people. You need someone who is engaging with the material as much as you are.
- Don't feel obligated to stay with a study group if it's not working for you.

COURSE SELECTION

- Take lots of doctrinal classes that force you to analyze a statute or complex case law (i.e., tax, fed courts, criminal procedure, etc.). If you know you want to be a litigator, you will be more practice ready having taken classes that involve procedure, evidence, etc. Taking "Law and _______" courses can be a great supplement if you know that you'll only ever be practicing environmental law or health law one day, but there are two problems with these classes. First, you'll almost certainly forget everything (or nearly everything) you learned in those classes, making their practical use to you of minimal value. Second, in this environment, it's better to be flexible in your training than rigidly adhere to what you think your future career will hold. You'll learn (or re-learn) most (if not all) of the substantive law you'll need to do your job, but being able to spot that a given case is removable will put you miles ahead of your colleagues.
- Try to keep in mind your career goals and the reasons you came to law school when you decide what classes to take or what extracurricular activity to sign up for. Law school is more enjoyable if you can make it your own, and if you

keep in mind how it can further your goals and vision for the future.

- When/if you get to choose a class the second semester of 1L, take a class with a small number of people. You will get to know the teacher and your colleagues.
- Learn to write well. Take advantage of classes in which you have the opportunity to write and seek out those classes after first year.
- Get involved with trial advocacy or moot court. Even if you don't think they want to be a litigator, these are unique and fleeting opportunities to practice writing and public speaking, both of which are critical skills no matter what kind of lawyer you end up being.

GRADES

- 90% of the time you will not get the grades you received in college, but that is normal. You were probably one of the smartest people in your class at college, but now you are amongst people who were all the smartest in their classes. Even worse, you are now graded against them. Don't be discouraged. Don't constantly compare yourself to everyone. Do your best. But push yourself. If you get a bad grade (and the likelihood is you will at some point) take a second to think about why you got it, what you can do to improve, learn from it, and move on.
- Try to get the highest grades you can because it will open doors in terms of firms and clerkships later on. But also keep things in perspective. If you work hard toward the career that you want, a B or even a C on your transcript isn't going to stop you, though it may mean you have to work a little bit harder than you would have had to otherwise to get the early career opportunities you want.

- Do your best, or at least do what you can. It is tempting to look for meaning in grades, like as if they should determine your career path. Grades are important, but they aren't everything.
- Talk to your professors after you get your grades, but don't try to get them to change your grade. They won't and they shouldn't. Use the time to learn a little about the subject and get advice.
- Networking. Networking. Networking. First semester grades are important, but a lot of times it is who you know, your reputation, and your demeanor that are critical in landing you the job you want.

MAINTAINING PERSPECTIVE AND BALANCE

- Be kind. It is the right thing to do and easier than the alternative. Don't worry about fitting the mold of law school or being competitive. Don't worry at all. Study the material, meet with professors, and get to know your classmates. The days of being a faceless associate are over. Employers want someone pleasant and knowledgeable. The best way for them to find that person is through someone else who is pleasant and knowledgeable. Associate with those people. Be that person.
- Do whatever works best for you. Do not get wrapped up in what everyone else is doing. If you are behind in writing a paper, reading, outlining, or prepping for exams, just keep pushing. If you compare yourself to what others are doing you will just stress yourself out.
- Avoid the competitive atmosphere. I never understood the people who zealously guarded their outlines and treated study groups as some advanced interrogation, carefully parsing out their information while fishing for your thoughts. The best work I did came after sharpening my

thoughts through an open exchange of ideas. You can't control how others will do, but you will greatly improve how you do through collaboration.

- Do not let law school consume you. Pursue one or two passions outside of school. Pursue extracurricular activities that take you outside of your comfort zone. Law school is a time to grow, even more so than college. In addition to developing a working knowledge of the law you have to develop your speaking skills, your networking skills, and your confidence in order to become a truly successful attorney. Take advantage of the opportunities you're given.
- Take care of your body. It is very easy to give up on a workout routine because you're exhausted from the day and studying, but when you're fit and healthy it is much easier to handle the stress of law school. That being said, you don't have to be a gym rat. Just do some type of physical activity for 30 minutes a day and you will notice the difference. At the very least, it gives you a much needed break.
- Pizza is not a food group. There will be a lot of pizza (and just unhealthy food in general) served at the beginning of the school year during different club meetings and social events. It's fine to indulge once in a while but try and balance it out with food that actually has nutrients.
- Sleep schedule. Sleep schedule. Sleep schedule.
- Find time to do something you enjoy, even during finals, or before a deadline. For me, this was going to the gym. I made sure I always had time for a gym break and this kept me sane!

CAREER

- Lately I have come across quite a few 3L students who perform well in class but have zero employment prospects. When I ask why, the answer keeps coming back to "I focused on schoolwork and didn't pay much attention to applying for jobs." Until you can eat grades or use them as currency to pay bills, please give proper attention to your career path.

- Always double-check advice before acting. I was offered advice on how to make certain changes in my resume. When I forwarded my changed resume to a family friend who is a recruiting partner for a firm, it was his opinion that my resume would have ended up at the bottom of the pile. Based on my technical background, I was also "tracked" by our career development office into intellectual property work. After telling them that most of that work not only did not interest me and was also out of [city A] and I was looking to stay in [city B], the response that came back was "sometimes we all have to make certain sacrifices." Then I talked to one of my professors who advised me to consider using my technology background to work for the Department of Justice prosecuting child pornography crimes. That conversation gave me a whole new perspective on what I wanted to do with my law degree. It wasn't the specific area he suggested so much as the faith he had that I could be successful in an organization as prestigious as DOJ. Another professor with a background in BigLaw told me she could see me working in that environment based on my performance in class and personal skills. It is hard to express the impact these conversations had on me, my life, and my career. I will always be grateful to them and thankful that I didn't stop with the first career advice I received.
- Pick the proper audience for your questions. If you want to know about life in a law firm, don't ask someone who has never been in private practice. If you want to know about life working in the public sector, don't ask the adjunct professor who is a

partner at his law firm. Learn from those who have done what you aspire to do.

- Don't assume that the answer is "no" until you ask. During my 1L year, I was told that, because of the economic downturn, nobody was hiring 1L summer associates and that I should either consider clinic or doing some sort of public sector work/internship. I decided to spam every law firm in town with my resume, transcripts, and writing sample and asked my mentor professors to make a few calls on my behalf. In March/April I was sitting on two offers. The rest is history!
- Consider getting an internship in state or federal government or an internship with a judge after your first year. I wish I had worked at the Federal Public Defender or in the United States Attorney's office after my first summer. This experience would have helped me figure out, if I'm ever lucky enough to have the opportunity, whether I want to work in either office and, if so, which.
- When selecting internships and externships, look for a couple of experiences outside the scope of what you think you want to do. You may be surprised. If nothing else, you will confirm that you are heading in the right direction.
- Do something fun, unexpected, meaningful, and that you couldn't/wouldn't ordinarily be able to do once out in the real world during your pre-law summer and maybe even your first summer after your first year. I was very concerned with getting a job that was going to put me in a good position for the next year's hiring season. While I enjoyed my time [with employer A], I wish I had taken the advice to travel or do service that first summer.
- Talk with other lawyers to figure out what they do on a daily basis. When interviewing at a job, try to figure out things such as:

- Will I be working with a collegial group of people, or are things more "buttoned up" here?
- How much feedback will I receive and when will I receive it?
- For firms, what types of assignments will I have in my first year here? Will I be doing document review 50% of my time? What is the mix between the mind-numbingly boring and the stimulating? Don't ask a partner these questions—if possible, ask to speak to someone who's closer to your level. They're more likely to give you a candid answer.
- For firms with more than one practice area, ask whether there is flexibility in moving practice groups or getting work from a practice group to which you are not assigned.
- For litigators, ask how often they spend time in state court versus federal court. How often do they go to trial versus settle? Where are most of their trials?

* This one is a no-brainer but I must include it because I saw way too many friends of mine go wrong during recruitment events: control your drinking! The drinks might be free but the impression you leave behind will cost you.
* When faced with choosing whether to pursue [Firm A] for my whole second summer or to split with another firm in town, one professor's advice was so simple and yet so brilliant at the same time: (1) Always go where they love you and show you support; and (2) Dig around and find out about the firms' financials and business models. That made my choice easy.

FINANCES

- Become financially educated. Know how much you will owe by the time you graduate and factor that into your spending and career planning.
- Find out who does the financial exit interviewing at your school and make an appointment to see that person early in your first year. They can help you better understand your options when it matters. Also consider seeing a professional financial advisor. Lots of them are willing to meet and give advice to law students in the hope that you will come back as a paying client once you are out in practice.
- Control your budget (there are apps on your phone that can track your spending). Watch how much you spend on eating out, going out, etc.
- Factor summer expenses into your financial planning.

CHAPTER 3

CRIMINAL LAW

LESSON 1: INTRODUCTION AND OVERVIEW

Everything we really need to know we learned in kindergarten. Don't hit. Don't steal. Don't touch others without their permission. These are foundational moral rules with near-universal appeal. Why, then, if the lessons are so basic, would we need a whole branch of the law dedicated to dealing with assault, homicide, theft, and sexual assault?

The answers are complex, but come down to this: some people can't or won't follow the rules. It's not just, as Justice Oliver Wendell Holmes might describe them, the "bad men" who cannot behave themselves. We all have violent thoughts from time to time. We all have fantasized about stealing something or perhaps pulling off a daring heist. Given these dark impulses, the philosopher Thomas Hobbes suggests that, without a state apparatus to keep us in line, fear and competition would set us against one another in a constant war of all against all. The criminal law is there to mark and guard the line between civilization and this fearsome world where, Hobbes promises, our lives would be "nasty, brutish, and short."

The criminal law is not alone in this role. As Professor Gifford tells us in the materials on tort law, many assaults and homicides can give rise to civil lawsuits as well as criminal charges. Despite this overlap, the criminal law is unique in at least two important regards. First, the criminal law belongs to a branch of law often referred to as "public law" as opposed to "private law." That is evidenced by the fact that prosecutors bring criminal actions on behalf of the state or the people. By contrast, most tort suits are brought by private attorneys representing individual clients. Second, the principal question in any criminal action is whether the defendant will be punished. The remedies in private actions brought in tort or contract seek instead to ameliorate or compensate for harm.

There are five main sources of law in the American system: constitutions, statutes, judicial opinions, regulations, and regulatory opinions. **Most criminal law comes from statutes and judicial opinions.** Although most American jurisdictions now have criminal codes, this statutory approach to the criminal law is relatively new. The American legal system is constructed on foundations we inherited from English common law. "Common law" describes the iterative process by which a body of legal rules and principles is developed through years and centuries of judicial opinions resolving individual cases. The "blackletter law" is the settled set of rules and principles that emerge through the common-law process. The blackletter criminal law is, then, the body of well-settled rules and principles describing the conditions that must be met before a defendant can be convicted and punished.

In most jurisdictions, the common law of crime has been displaced in whole or in part by statutes. It is nevertheless important to study the common law when studying the criminal law. That is because all criminal law statutes incorporate the common law, depart from it in some meaningful way, reject it altogether, or do some combination of all three. Law students therefore study the common law so they can better understand the problems and issues that criminal statutes are addressing and the solutions they propose. In the lessons that follow, we will look at some examples of criminal law statutes from various jurisdictions in order to explore and explain the different approaches they take.

One of the most influential criminal codes is not attached to any jurisdiction at all. The American Law Institute (ALI) is a group of judges, practitioners, and scholars that studies various areas of law in an effort to describe the state of the law and to propose reforms. Starting in 1952, the ALI began working on a Model Penal Code (MPC) under the leadership of Professor Herbert Wechsler of Columbia University. The ALI adopted the first complete text of the MPC in 1962. In the intervening years, legislators and judges have often referred to the MPC, sometimes adopting it, sometimes departing from it in meaningful ways, and sometimes rejecting it altogether. Given its broad influence, most law students will study the MPC alongside the common law. In the lessons that follow, so shall we.

What You Need to Know:

1. The criminal law is a branch of public, as opposed to private, law.
2. Even though many crimes involve a victim, criminal charges are brought by the state on behalf of the people as a whole rather than by or on behalf of a particular person.
3. The principal question in any criminal action is whether, how, and to what degree the defendant should be punished.
4. The criminal law has its roots in the common law, but most jurisdictions now have statutory criminal codes that incorporate, depart from, or reject the common law.
5. The Model Penal Code is a widely influential set of proposed reforms to the criminal law developed by the American Law Institute.

LESSON 2: PUNISHMENT

As we learned in Lesson 1, the criminal law is concerned primarily with punishment. Any study of the criminal law must therefore engage important questions about the nature of punishment, when it is justified, in what form, and how much. Although views vary widely, most answers to these questions draw from one of two theoretical perspectives: retributivism and consequentialism.

Retributivism is committed to the proposition that punishment should only be inflicted if it is deserved and only to the extent it is deserved. When assessing whether punishment is deserved, most retributivists are concerned primarily with an offender's blameworthiness (often referred to as "culpability") and the nature of his crime. Thus, offenders who intentionally commit the most serious offenses deserve the most severe punishments, while offenders who cause slight harms out of inattention deserve very little punishment. This may seem so obvious that it hardly merits mention, which many retributivists count as good reason to be a retributivist.

Consequentialism, which you may also see referred to as "utilitarianism," is committed to the proposition that punishment should only be inflicted if and to the extent it can produce more benefit than harm. The principal good that can justify punishment on this calculus is prevention of future crime. Punishment can achieve this goal by deterring an offender from committing future crimes, by incapacitating him, or by rehabilitating him. Punishment might also deter others from committing crimes by showing them the consequences of lawlessness or by educating them about what the law demands.

To see how retributivism and consequentialism might lead to different results, consider the following hypothetical:

> Beelzebub commits a vicious rape and then murders his victim in a brutal and sadistic fashion. Fortunately, there is a pill we can give Beelzebub that will guarantee that he will never break the law again. We also know that punishing Beelzebub will serve no other good, including general deterrence or public education.

On these facts, a retributivist would maintain that Beelzebub must be punished because he has intentionally committed a serious crime. By contrast, a consequentialist would see no point in punishing him. After all, that would not do any good. To the contrary, it would just cause Beelzebub hardship while also drawing limited public resources from other worthy efforts to promote the public good.

Both retributivism and consequentialism have their adherents and critics. Rather than choose between them, most legislatures and courts draw from both traditions when elaborating the substantive law, setting sentencing policy, and determining the sentences to be applied in individual cases. Take, for example, 18 U.S.C. § 3553(a)(2), which is the federal law governing sentencing decisions in federal courts, which provides that:

> The court, in determining the particular sentence to be imposed, shall consider . . . the need for the sentence imposed—
>
> (A) to reflect the seriousness of the offense, to promote respect for the law, and to provide just punishment for the offense;
>
> (B) to afford adequate deterrence to criminal conduct;
>
> (C) to protect the public from further crimes of the defendant; and
>
> (D) to provide the defendant with needed educational or vocational training, medical care, or other correctional treatment in the most effective manner.

As you might imagine, taking all of these potentially conflicting factors into account is no simple task. Of course, that is probably as it should be. Sending someone to prison or inflicting other forms of punishment is a very serious matter, and certainly a decision that deserves careful thought from multiple perspectives.

What You Need to Know:

1. Because criminal law is defined by the possibility of punishment, theories of punishment play an important role at all levels of criminal law and practice.
2. There are two major schools of punishment theory: retributivism and consequentialism.
3. Retributivists are committed to the proposition that a person should be punished only if, and only to the extent, punishment is deserved.
4. Consequentialists hold that a person should be punished only if, and only to the extent, punishment produces more benefit than harm.
5. Most criminal codes adopt a hybrid theory of criminal punishment that incorporates elements of both retributivism and consequentialism.

LESSON 3: THE LEGALITY PRINCIPLE

Imagine that you are an outspoken critic of your local mayor, city council, and law enforcement officials. In order to exact political revenge, these powerful enemies arrest you, convict you of unnamed secret charges, and throw you into jail. Does this seem right? Would it make you feel better if, after noting that, during your arrest, you were wearing a checked shirt and striped tie, the sheriff urged your city council to pass a law punishing those who mix patterns and then you were prosecuted for violating this brand-new law? What if they instead found an ancient statute prohibiting the consumption of meat on Fridays and used that statute to arrest and prosecute you even though it had not been enforced in over 200 years and Friday nights were locally celebrated as "Steak Night" at every restaurant in town?

If these hypotheticals strike a note of unfairness for you, then you are not alone. As we learned in Lesson 2, there are two main theories of criminal punishment: retributivism and consequentialism. Despite their different approaches, retributivists and consequentialists agree on many things. Among the most important is that punishment should only be inflicted when an offender has violated the law. This may seem like an obvious point, but it reflects a fundamental tenet of criminal law: the legality principle.

The **legality principle** holds that both fundamental fairness and crime prevention goals require that states provide citizens with fair warning that certain conduct and actions are subject to criminal punishment. In order to provide this warning, the law must meet certain demands, which are embedded in the United States Constitution, most state constitutions, many states' criminal codes, and the common law.

1. The law must be promulgated and publicly accessible. Thus, a state would violate the legality principle if it never wrote or recorded the law or if it promulgated laws in secret. These requirements are enforced by the "due process" clauses of the

Fifth and Fourteenth Amendments to the United States Constitution.

2. The law must be prospective. It would violate the legality principle if a state were to create a legal prohibition and then enforce it retroactively. This prohibition on retroactive enforcement of the criminal law is enshrined in Article I, Sections 9 and 10 of the United States Constitution, which prohibit "ex post facto" laws.
3. The law must be general in application. Laws written to target individuals, including bills of attainder, are also prohibited by Article I, Sections 9 and 10 of the United States Constitution.
4. Laws must be clear. Where criminal laws are ambiguous, courts may apply the "**rule of lenity**," which bars conviction if a reasonable person could have read the law as allowing the defendant to do what he did. Both the requirement for clarity and the rule of lenity draw force from the due process clauses of the Fifth and Fourteenth Amendments to the United States Constitution.
5. The criminal law as a whole must be internally consistent. It is both unfair and pointless to put someone in a position where he is "damned if he does and damned if he doesn't." The requirement for consistency is also linked to the due process clauses of the Fifth and Fourteenth Amendments to the United States Constitution.
6. The law must be regularly and consistently enforced. Haphazard, inconsistent, or discriminatory enforcement of the law is pointless, unfair, and also violates the due process clauses of the Fifth and Fourteenth Amendments, the equal protection clause of the Fourteenth Amendment to the United States Constitution, or both.

The legality principle's fundamental commitment to fair warning is widely noted as a necessary feature of legitimate criminal systems. For example, Professor Lon Fuller has argued that the legality principle is part of the basic moral character of the law and that failure to abide by the demands of legality amounts to a failure to make law in the first place. *See* Lon Fuller, *The Morality of Law* (1964). Looking internationally, the Universal Declaration of Human Rights also maintains commitments to legality, *see, e.g.*, Article 11 (prohibiting ex post facto enforcement of the law), as does the International Covenant on Civil and Political Rights, *see, e.g.*, Article 9 (ensuring the right to be informed of, and bring challenges against, criminal charges).

What You Need to Know:

1. According to the principle of legality, the government may only punish someone if that person has engaged in conduct that is explicitly forbidden by law.
2. Many features of the legality principle, including the prohibitions on bills of attainder and retroactive enforcement of laws, and the requirements for publicity, clarity, and consistency, are incorporated into the United States Constitution, most state constitutions, many states' criminal codes, and the common law.
3. The legality principle's basic commitment to fair warning as a prerequisite to punishment has deep roots in moral theory and international law.

LESSON 4: COURTS AND PRECEDENT

Imagine that your client is on trial for theft. The charge is based on a "dumpster diving" incident in which he retrieved a very nice armchair from a garbage bin next to a local apartment complex. Fortunately for him, you have found a prior decision by the highest court in your state which says that any property left out for trash pickup has been "abandoned," and is therefore available for anyone to claim as if it were in the "state of nature." In that earlier case, the court specifically rejected a theft charge based on facts almost identical to those in your client's case. Relying on this decision, you move to dismiss the charges against your client.

Unfortunately, the trial judge refuses to grant your motion. It seems that he has a particular antipathy for dumpster divers, whom he regards as a scourge on the community. He therefore allows the charges to go forward in the hope that he can make an example of your client.

In our legal system, this trial judge has erred in this hypothetical case. That is because he ignored binding **precedent**. Precedents are prior judicial decisions wherein courts have discussed and applied legal rules. Attorneys and courts often rely on precedents to guide their understanding and analysis of cases before them. In doing so, they usually invoke one of two principles:

The first is **stare decisis**, a Latin phrase often translated as "let the decision stand." When considering what the law is, and how it applies in a particular case, stare decisis requires courts to consider and give due respect to the decisions of prior courts that have addressed and decided the same or similar issues.

The second is **res judicata**, a Latin phrase often translated as "a thing decided." Sometimes referred to as the law of the case, res judicata requires a court to respect its own prior decisions, and those of higher courts, made during the course of a particular case.

There are **two main categories of precedent: binding precedent and persuasive precedent**. Binding precedents are prior opinions that a court is institutionally obliged to accept and apply. Persuasive precedents are prior court opinions that a court should respect, but may reject or accept based on its own considered views. To understand whether a precedent is binding or merely persuasive requires understanding the hierarchy of trial and appellate courts in American jurisdictions.

Most American jurisdictions have at least **three tiers of courts: trial courts, intermediate appellate courts, and courts of final appeal**. For example, in the federal system there are district courts, which are the trial courts, circuit courts of appeals, which are the intermediate appellate courts, and the Supreme Court, which is the court of final appeal.

Many jurisdictions also have specialized courts, including small claims courts, drug courts, housing courts, juvenile courts, family courts, tax courts, and bankruptcy courts.

As a general matter, any decision issued by a court is binding upon all inferior courts within its jurisdiction and persuasive with respect to its peer courts and courts outside its jurisdiction. So, cases decided by the United States Supreme Court bind all federal circuit courts of appeals and all federal district courts. Cases decided by the Second Circuit Court of Appeals bind federal district courts in Vermont, Connecticut, and New York but are merely persuasive with respect to other federal circuit courts of appeal and federal district courts in other circuits. Likewise, decisions issued by a federal judge in the Southern District of New York are merely persuasive with respect to other federal district judges, including those in the Southern District of New York.

Precedent is one of the most powerful arrows in the quiver of a practicing attorney. If a lawyer can persuade a court that a prior decision of a superior court in the jurisdiction where the case is being considered binds the court to favor her client, then she wins. Faced with binding precedent that appears to prejudice her client's interests, a lawyer will work hard to distinguish that prior decision by arguing that there are material differences between the precedent case and the case at bar. Where she has only persuasive authority, an attorney will try to convince the court that these prior decisions demonstrate a consensus, or at least that the precedents upon which she relies have been issued by particularly thoughtful judges on highly regarded courts for compelling reasons.

The research, reading, and analysis that go into finding and using precedents are among the most important skills of successful attorneys. They are therefore a focus for law students from the first day of class. By reading multiple cases, and challenging students with hypothetical situations, law professors train their students to be careful readers, to think creatively, to draw analogies, and to spot material distinctions. These engagements are intellectually thrilling, but also provide the best opportunities for aspiring attorneys to develop the skills that will make them worthy trustees of their clients' interests.

What You Need to Know:

1. Courts in United States jurisdictions are arranged hierarchically.
2. Decisions issued by "higher" courts bind lower courts within their jurisdictions according to the principle of stare decisis.
3. Decisions issued by peer courts or courts in other jurisdictions may provide persuasive authority.
4. Much of what attorneys do when advising and advocating for their clients entails finding precedential decisions and arguing about whether those decisions are binding, merely persuasive, or simply irrelevant.
5. The centerpiece of the 1L year for most law students is learning to find, analyze, and use precedents to construct legal arguments.

LESSON 5: BURDENS OF PROOF AND ELEMENTS OF THE CRIME

We have learned that states generally cannot assert a right to punish unless they have met the basic demands of fair warning encompassed by the legality principle. The burdens of the state in a criminal action do not stop with the legality principle, however. The state also carries the burden of proving that a defendant broke the law. Under the common law and the Fifth, Sixth, and Fourteenth Amendments to the United States Constitution, defendants are entitled to a **presumption of innocence** and **the prosecution bears the burden of proving guilt**. Looking internationally, Article 11 of the Universal Declaration of Human Rights provides similar guarantees.

In the United States, the prosecution bears the burden of proving guilt beyond a reasonable doubt in all criminal trials. This "**beyond a reasonable doubt standard**" has ancient common-law roots. For example, in his famous and influential

Commentaries on the Laws of England, William Blackstone justifies this requirement on the grounds that "[i]t is better that ten guilty persons escape than that one innocent suffer." More recently, the United States Supreme Court has held that demanding proof beyond a reasonable doubt in criminal trials is an "axiomatic and elementary principle whose enforcement lies at the foundation of the administration of our criminal law." *In re Winship*, 397 U.S. 358, 363 (1970).

Asserting that the government has the burden of proof leads to the obvious question of what must be proved. The answer is the **elements of the crime**. Elements are the acts, circumstances, and results that comprise legal prohibitions. They are therefore central to the analysis of any criminal law problem and guide every major decision in the criminal justice process. Courts elaborate the elements of crimes through the common-law process and legislatures describe the elements of crimes in statutes. Arrests and indictments are governed by preliminary assessments of whether the facts as they appear to a police officer or a grand jury fulfill the elements of a crime. The elements of the crime also govern the admission of evidence at trial. Evidence is only admissible if it is relevant; and it is only relevant if it tends to prove or disprove one of the elements of the crime or of an affirmative defense. Finally, when juries are sent out to deliberate at the end of a trial, judges instruct them on the elements of the crime so they can properly hold the state to its burden of proving each element beyond a reasonable doubt.

Elements fall into one of three broad categories: acts, facts (sometimes called attendant circumstances), and results. It is important when assessing any criminal case to assign each element of the crime charged to its proper category. That is because the burden of what must be proved and corresponding opportunities to raise reasonable doubt vary depending upon whether an element is, for example, an act, such as "breaking and entering," or an attendant circumstance, such as "a dwelling place." We will spend considerable time in later lessons identifying these differences.

Legislatures and common-law courts have broad authority to shape the elements of crimes. Take as examples two murder statutes:

> **Statute #1**
>
> A person is guilty of murder when, with intent to cause the death of another person, he causes the death of such person.
>
> **Statute #2**
>
> A person is guilty of murder when, with intent to cause the death of another, and without considerable provocation, he causes the death of such a person.

Do you see the difference between these two statutes? By adding the phrase "and without considerable provocation," the second statute adds an element, which means that a prosecutor must prove beyond a reasonable doubt that the defendant was not acting under the influence of "considerable provocation." A prosecutor would have no such burden under the first statute. Furthermore, evidence of provocation offered by a defendant would be relevant in a trial where murder was charged under the second statute, but it would not be relevant in a trial governed exclusively by the first statute. In order to establish the relevance of provocation in a trial governed by the first statute, a defense attorney would therefore need to appeal to another source of law, such as a statute or a precedent case.

In subsequent lessons, we will investigate different kinds of elements and how a prosecutor might go about proving them. We will then discuss the elements of different crimes, including homicide, sexual assault, theft, attempt, and conspiracy. As we go forward, you should focus on the power wielded by legislatures and common-law courts to define the elements of crimes and how their choices reflect different views on social policy, the proper role of the criminal law, and competing theories of punishment.

What You Need to Know:

1. The components of crimes are called "elements."
2. There are three categories of elements: acts, facts, and results.

3. Legislatures have broad discretion to define the elements of crimes.
4. In order to fulfill its burden of proof in any criminal case, the prosecution must prove each element of the crime beyond a reasonable doubt.

LESSON 6: A SHORT PRIMER ON LEGAL ANALYSIS

One of the main tasks in any first-year law class is for students to hone their legal analysis skills. The centerpiece of legal analysis is the **simple syllogism**. A syllogism is a form of deductive argument composed of a major premise, a minor premise, and a conclusion. Major premises often take the form of a conditional "If . . . then . . ." statement. The first clause of a major premise in this conditional form (the clause starting with "if") is called the antecedent. The second clause (the one starting with "then") is called the consequent. Take, for example:

If James is a human (antecedent), then he is mortal (consequent).

A minor premise usually describes a particular state of affairs. Take, for example:

James is a human.

A conclusion is a statement that can be deduced by applying a rule of logic to the major premise and the minor premise. One commonly used rule of logic is modus ponens. Modus ponens allows us to conclude the consequent of a major premise if we can affirm the antecedent. Thus:

Major Premise:	If James is a human, then he is mortal.
Minor Premise:	James is a human.
Conclusion:	Therefore, James is mortal.

Modus tollens, another rule of logic that appears frequently in syllogisms, allows us to conclude that the antecedent is not true by denying the consequent. Thus:

Major Premise:	If James is a human, then he is mortal.
Minor Premise:	James is not mortal.
Conclusion:	Therefore, James is not a human.

The basic work of law students and lawyers relates in one way or another to formulating and defending or identifying and critiquing syllogisms. Most of the time, the major premises in legal arguments are rules of law. Contests over major premises are therefore most often resolved—or not—by appeal to constitutions, statutes, judicial opinions, regulatory codes, or regulatory opinions. The minor premises in legal arguments usually are drawn from the facts in any given case. Contests over minor premises therefore are most often resolved—or not—by appeal to evidence or common knowledge. Contests over conclusions explore whether or to what degree the facts in a given case fulfill the conditions described by a rule of law.

Many law students learn about this process of legal analysis by memorizing the mnemonic **IRAC**, which stands for **Issue, Rule, Application (or Analysis), and Conclusion**. The "Issue" is simply the question to be answered. The "Rule" often takes the form of a major premise. The "Application" usually involves applying facts to the rule using logical operations. The "Conclusion" is, well, the conclusion. Consider some examples:

Example #1

Issue:	Should Bart be punished?
Rule:	If a person steals a candy bar, then he should be punished.
Application:	Bart stole the candy bar.
Conclusion:	Therefore, Bart should be punished.

Example #2

Issue:	Should this evidence be admitted at trial?
Rule:	If evidence is admitted at trial, then it must be relevant.

Application: This evidence is not relevant.

Conclusion: Therefore, this evidence should not be admitted at trial.

Example #3

Issue: Should juvenile defendants be subjected to the death penalty?

Rule: If juvenile defendants can be subjected to the death penalty then it must be true that putting juvenile defendants to death does not violate the Eighth Amendment prohibition of "cruel and unusual" punishment.

Application: Putting juvenile defendants to death violates the Eighth Amendment prohibition of "cruel and unusual" punishment.

Conclusion: Therefore, juvenile defendants should not be subjected to the death penalty.

The first task for a lawyer or law student when engaged in legal analysis is to suss out the syllogisms or chains of syllogisms that might lead to a particular conclusion. Only by carefully conducting this first step can she plan and organize her research, develop her strategy, advise her client, draft the best brief, or make her most effective arguments. It is no surprise, then, that almost every task in almost every first-year law course traces back in one way or another to identifying, critiquing, and constructing syllogisms.

What You Need to Know:

1. One of the primary goals in any first-year law school class is to teach legal analysis.
2. Legal analysis is the process of examining, criticizing, and constructing legal arguments by focusing on their underlying logical structure.
3. Most legal arguments can be broken down into a series of simple syllogisms.

4. Syllogisms are composed of a major premise, a minor premise, and a conclusion.
5. Many first-year law students learn to work with syllogisms using the mnemonic "IRAC," which stands for Issue, Rule, Application (or Analysis), and Conclusion.

LESSON 7: THE ACTUS REUS REQUIREMENT

Imagine two cases of untimely death:

Example #1

While driving down a city street, John sees his arch rival sitting in a crowded sidewalk café. Seizing upon the opportunity, John pushes the gas pedal of his car to the floor and steers into the group of diners, killing several customers, including his target. Should John be punished?

Example #2

While driving down a city street, Jane is seized by a sudden spasm that causes her right foot to extend violently and her hands to jerk to the right. As a consequence, her foot pushes the gas pedal to the floor and her hands turn the steering wheel, causing her car to turn into a crowded sidewalk café, killing several customers. Should Jane be punished?

According to the common law and statutory codes in most jurisdictions, John should be punished, but Jane should not. That is because, with very few exceptions, the criminal law will punish only voluntary acts. This is known as the **voluntary act requirement**. Here, John's hitting the accelerator and turning his steering wheel were voluntary acts. By contrast, Jane's depressing her accelerator and turning her wheel were the results of involuntary spasms.

The voluntary act requirement has a number of important consequences. Perhaps the most obvious is that every crime will include at least one act element. These act elements are often referred to using the Latin phrase "**actus reus**." To meet its burden in any criminal case, the prosecution must therefore prove beyond a reasonable doubt that the defendant engaged in at least one voluntary act.

If we are going to limit criminal liability to circumstances of a voluntary act, then the next natural question is "What is a voluntary act?" Despite the best efforts of philosophers, theologians, lawyers, psychologists, and neuroscientists, we still do not have a clear answer to this apparently simple, yet deeply complicated question.

For example, the philosopher J. L. Austin has suggested that a voluntary act is a "willed bodily movement." Critics find this definition unavailing, in part because it is too atomistic—focusing on distinct parts rather than accounting for the holistic nature of action. When you pick up a book, do you "will" each of the incremental muscle flexes and extensions entailed in picking up a book, or do you just pick up the book?

Perhaps more problematic is the concept of a will and its relationship to voluntary action. Very little of what we do on a daily basis is the result of any deliberate decision making. Rather, most of what we do is automatic or preconscious. Take walking, for example. We seldom, if ever, consciously will each step we take or even a series of steps taken from one location to another. Does that mean that I act "involuntary" by walking down the hall?

Modern neuroscience has even thrown some doubt over the core concept of the will. Advanced brain imaging techniques reveal that the action centers of our brains frequently fire before the areas responsible for reason and decision making. Thus, it seems that, even when we have the experience of making a deliberate decision, much of the time it is our actions shaping our wills rather than the other way around.

The common law and the Model Penal Code avoid all of these thorny questions by focusing on cases and examples of involuntariness rather than seeking to define voluntariness. Thus, a voluntary act for criminal law purposes is simply an act that is not involuntary. Among the most commonly cited examples of involuntary action are:

1. Reflex.

2. Convulsions, spasms, or seizures.
3. Unconsciousness for which the defendant is not responsible, such as being drugged.
4. Hypnosis.
5. Sleepwalking.
6. Physical control by another person.

With those examples in mind, consider the facts in *Martin v. State*, 31 Ala. App. 334, 335 (1944), which is cited by many courts and textbooks:

> Appellant was convicted of being drunk on a public highway . . . Officers of the law arrested him at his home and took him onto the highway, where he allegedly . . . manifested a drunken condition by using loud and profane language. The pertinent provisions of our statute are: "Any person who, while intoxicated or drunk, appears in any public place where one or more persons are present, and manifests a drunken condition by boisterous or indecent conduct, or loud and profane discourse, shall, on conviction, be fined."

Should the conviction stand? The Alabama Court of Appeals held that it could not because:

> Under the plain terms of this statute, a voluntary appearance is presupposed. The rule has been declared, and we think it sound, that an accusation of drunkenness in a designated public place cannot be established by proof that the accused, while in an intoxicated condition, was involuntarily and forcibly carried to that place by the arresting officer.

Id. Thus, the prosecution could not meet its burden of proving an act element because the conduct was "involuntary."

What You Need to Know:

1. The criminal law maintains a voluntary act requirement.
2. Among the elements of all crimes there will be at least one act, which is often called the *actus reus*.

3. To meet its burden of proof with respect to any act element, the prosecution must prove beyond a reasonable doubt that the defendant engaged in a voluntary act.
4. For purposes of the criminal law "voluntary act" is usually defined in the negative as an act that is not involuntary.
5. Actions commonly regarded as involuntary include reflex reactions, spasms, convulsions, acts done during a state of sleep or unconsciousness, and acts performed under hypnotic suggestion.

LESSON 8: OMISSIONS

Consider this hypothetical:

> Dexter is a serial killer. He has set his sights on Jimmy. Despite the fact that he cannot swim, Jimmy spends his afternoons relaxing at the end of a dock that extends over a deep ocean bay. Dexter decides to kill Jimmy by pushing him off the dock to drown. When Dexter arrives to do the deed, he finds that Jimmy has already fallen off the dock and is now struggling to survive. Jimmy pleads with Dexter, "Save me! I'm drowning! Throw me that life buoy!" Of course Dexter does not save Jimmy. Instead, he sits back and enjoys the show, grinning to himself as Jimmy drowns.

Do you think that Dexter is guilty of a crime? There is no doubt that he is a bad man. Moreover, he went to the dock with the intention of seeing Jimmy drown; and drown Jimmy did. Shouldn't that be enough? If you are inclined to say yes, then consider another case:

> Watching television late one night, you see an advertisement for "Save the Children." A famous spokesperson tells you that the children standing in the background behind her are starving and desperately in need of your help. For only a few pennies a day, you can provide much-needed food, shelter, and education for these desperate souls.

> Despite these pleas, you decide not to donate. A few weeks later you read that these children have all died.

Are you guilty of a crime? If you think you are not, then how would you draw the line between you and Dexter? You both had a reasonable chance to save innocent people in peril with minimal effort. Granted, Dexter wanted Jimmy to die, whereas you merely knew there was a significant risk the needy children would die, but your lack of intent to kill only means Dexter is guilty of murder and you are guilty of involuntary manslaughter, which is still a very serious offense.

These are thorny problems indeed. The common-law solution is to draw a sharp distinction between acts and omissions. As a general matter, a prosecutor can fulfill her burden of proving *actus reus* by showing that the defendant engaged in a voluntary act. By contrast, a prosecutor generally cannot fulfill her burden of proving *actus reus* by showing that the defendant engaged in a voluntary omission. Thus, both you and Dexter go free because neither of you acted. Rather, you failed to act.

As is often the case in the law, there are exceptions to the general rule that omissions cannot provide grounds for criminal punishment. Most of these exceptions fall into one of five categories, all of which describe special circumstances where a defendant has a legal duty to act.

First, a defendant can be punished for failing to take action when she has a statutory obligation to act. For example, 26 U.S.C. § 7203 requires that income earners pay estimated taxes, file tax returns, and keep certain tax records. In the event someone fails to perform any of these duties, she can be prosecuted and fined up to $25,000.

Second, a defendant can be punished for failing to take action when he has a special relationship with someone that imposes special duties. For example, parents have special relationships with their children that impose special duties of care, including duties to feed, clothe, and generally protect their children from harm. In the event that a parent fails to perform on one of these duties, he may be held criminally liable if his child suffers from neglect or harm as a result.

Third, a defendant can be punished for failing to take action when he has assumed a contractual duty to act. For example, doctors, nurses, and other caregivers in hospitals, physical therapy centers, and nursing homes assume duties to care for their patients as part of the contracts they enter into with their patients. Thus, a nurse who ignores obvious signs of respiratory distress in his patient can be prosecuted for homicide if that patient dies.

Fourth, the criminal law will allow those who voluntarily assume a duty to care for another person to be prosecuted for failing to act if the person to whom that duty is owed is also secluded from the public. Imagine, for example, that John and Sally meet at a bar, have a few drinks, hit it off, and decide to go back to John's apartment. If, in her drunken state, Sally slips, falls, and strikes her head violently on a coffee table and John then decides to go to bed rather than seek medical help for Sally, then he can be prosecuted for homicide if Sally dies insofar as his taking her into his home entails a duty of care and her being in his home means she is secluded from the public.

Fifth, a defendant can be prosecuted if he is involved in the creation of a perilous situation and then fails to take reasonable action to avert harm to those who are put at risk. Thus, if John is involved in a car accident where the other driver is hurt badly, then John has a duty to call for help. In some jurisdictions, that is true even if the accident was not John's fault. Others require that John act negligently in creating the risk before imposing on him a duty to act. By whichever rule, once John has the duty to act, he may be guilty of homicide if he drives away from the accident without calling for help and the other driver dies.

What You Need to Know:

1. The criminal law generally will not punish for omissions or failures to act.
2. That rule is subject to five important exceptions:
    a. Where the defendant is under a statutory duty to act;

b. Where the defendant has a special relationship with another person that imposes upon him a duty to act;

c. Where the defendant is under a contractual duty to act;

d. Where the defendant has voluntarily assumed the duty to care for another person and that person is secluded from the public; and

e. Where the defendant is involved in the creation of a dangerous circumstance that puts another person in peril, even if the defendant was not at fault in his creation of the peril.

LESSON 9: THE MENS REA REQUIREMENT

Imagine that a defendant is driving 30 m.p.h. over the speed limit in a school zone during morning hours when students traditionally arrive at school. As he passes the school, a child attempts to cross the road, is struck, and killed. The defendant immediately stops, jumps out of the car, and, when confronted with what he has done, exclaims, "I didn't mean to kill her! I'm not a bad person!" Is the driver guilty of homicide?

Most of us looking at this case would say "yes." We may be sympathetic with his representation that he did not intend to kill anyone. We therefore do not hold him to blame to the same degree as, say, a cool, calculating serial killer who stalks his victims over the course of several days before running them over with his car. But we still have the sense that the accidental killer is a killer nonetheless, and therefore deserving of blame and punishment (at least insofar as he cannot provide some justification for his actions).

Distinguishing between levels of blameworthiness or culpability in the criminal law is the office of **mens rea** or **scienter**. "*Mens rea*," which is a Latin phrase often translated as "guilty mind," limits criminal liability to circumstances where a defendant is blameworthy or culpable. As a general rule, defendants will only be punished if they have some level of mental connection to each element of a crime, be it act, fact, or result.

The *mens rea* requirement raises a number of questions. Two are particularly important:

1. What sort of mental connection must a prosecutor prove between a defendant and the acts, facts, and results that make up the elements of a crime?
2. How can a prosecutor prove what is in a defendant's head?

The level of *mens rea*, culpability, or *scienter* that a prosecutor is obliged to prove depends on the crime, the jurisdiction, and the type of element at issue, be it act, fact, or result. Among the most common of these are:

1. Intent: To prove intent, prosecutors generally must prove that a defendant acted with the goal of engaging in the prohibited conduct or of bringing about a particular result. When required to prove intent with respect to fact elements, however, it is generally sufficient to prove knowledge.
2. Purpose: Like intent, purpose usually requires proof of a specific design. When defining "purpose," many courts take guidance from the Model Penal Code, which defines "purpose" as acting with the "conscious object to engage in conduct of that nature or to cause such result." When applied to fact elements, however, the MPC defines "purpose" as awareness of the existence of such facts or belief or hope that they exist.
3. Willfulness: When statutes prohibit "willfully" acting in some way or "willfully" producing a particular result, prosecutors generally must prove intent or purpose. When applied to fact elements, however, prosecutors can meet their burdens of proving willfulness by proving knowledge.
4. Knowledge: Under the MPC, and in most jurisdictions, "knowledge" with respect to act

elements requires conscious awareness. For fact elements, either conscious awareness or awareness of a "high probability of its existence" will do, "unless [the defendant] actually believes that it does not exist." For result elements, it is sufficient if the defendant is "practically certain that his conduct will cause such a result."

5. Recklessness: Recklessness is usually defined as engaging in conduct despite awareness of a substantial and unjustified risk that a fact exists, that a result will occur, or that his act constitutes the kind of conduct prohibited by law. It is important to note that recklessness is a **subjective standard**. To meet her burden of proving recklessness, a prosecutor must therefore prove that the defendant was *actually* aware of the risk. That she *should* have been aware is not enough.

6. Malice: Malice is a common-law standard of *mens rea* that you may also see in some criminal statutes. Malice does not necessarily imply spiteful ill will. Rather, it is a term of art that describes a range of mental states including purpose, intent, knowledge, and sometimes recklessness.

7. Negligence: In contrast to intent, purpose, willfulness, knowledge, and recklessness, negligence is an **objective standard** that describes circumstances where a defendant *should* have been aware that a fact exists, a result might obtain, or her act constituted the kind of conduct prohibited by law. When judging negligence, juries usually apply the **reasonable person** standard, asking what a reasonable person would have known.

Returning to our hypothetical, we can now give some precision to our instincts about the driver's culpability. Assuming that he is being truthful, he is not guilty of any crime that requires proof of purpose, intent, or knowledge. He is pretty clearly guilty of negligence, however, insofar as any reasonable person would have been aware of a substantial and unjustified risk that driving at an excessive speed through a school zone might result in the injury or death of a child. The tougher question is whether he might also be guilty of a crime requiring recklessness, which would require proving that he was actually aware of that risk.

It can be quite difficult for prosecutors to prove *mens rea* because mental states are, by definition, private and subjective. Sometimes defendants oblige by sharing their thoughts with others, by recording their intentions in diaries, or by confessing. More often, however, prosecutors must resort to circumstantial evidence. In these cases, jurors are left to use their experience and common sense to infer what a defendant was thinking based on the circumstances, what happened, and what he did. In the case of our driver, it would be up to the jury to determine whether, all things considered, they believe the defendant was aware of the risk he was creating.

In aid of proving *mens rea*, the criminal law sometimes allows for **permissive presumptions**. For example, judges often instruct juries that they may presume that a defendant intended the natural consequences of his actions. Thus, a jury may presume that a defendant intended to kill his victim if the facts show that he pointed a loaded gun at his victim's chest and pulled the trigger three times. In contrast with permissive presumptions, mandatory presumptions are unconstitutional in most cases. Returning to our hypothetical, this means that the judge could not instruct juries that they *must* presume intent to kill, only that they *may*. Presumptions can also be rebutted. For example, this defendant might rebut the presumption of intent to kill by suggesting that he thought the gun was merely a toy. The prosecutor would then need to prove beyond a reasonable doubt that the defendant knew he was holding a loaded gun or, perhaps, that he knew that there was a substantial risk that he was holding a loaded gun, but pulled the trigger anyway.

What You Need to Know:

1. The criminal law maintains a *mens rea* or *scienter* requirement.

2. To meet its burden of proof for *mens rea*, the prosecution must prove beyond a reasonable doubt that the defendant had a sufficient mental connection to each element of the crime.
3. Some common standards of *mens rea* are purpose, intent, willfulness, knowledge, recklessness, malice, and negligence.
4. "Malice" is a term of art that encompasses intent, purpose, knowledge, and, in some cases, recklessness.
5. Most *mens rea* standards are subjective, which means that the prosecutor must prove what was in the defendant's mind. By contrast, negligence is an objective standard, which merely requires proof of what a reasonable person would have known.
6. Prosecutors usually use a combination of circumstantial evidence and permissive presumptions to prove *mens rea*.

LESSON 10: A SHORT PRIMER ON STATUTORY INTERPRETATION

Although criminal law is a field with deep common-law roots, contemporary criminal law is largely governed by statute. This is true of both crimes regarded as **mala in se** (or "wrong in itself"), such as murder, rape, and theft, and crimes considered **mala prohibita** (or "wrong because it is prohibited" by law), such as drug possession, catching and keeping undersized fish, and driving on the left-hand side of the road. Most *mala in se* crimes have a long common-law history that precedes statutory codes. Today, much of that common law has been displaced by statute. This means that criminal lawyers must have the ability to interpret and apply statutes as well as case law.

There are three main tasks criminal lawyers face when reading a statute. The first is to identify the elements of the crime. The second is to assign each element to a category: act, fact, or result. As we saw in our discussions of *Martin v. State* in Lesson 7, the results of this effort can dramatically affect a prosecutor's burden of proof and the excuses available to a defendant. The third interpretive task is to determine what *mens rea* is required for each element. This too is a question that affects prosecutors' burdens and defendants' opportunities. For example, it is much easier for a prosecutor to prove negligence than intent or purpose.

Despite the importance of these questions, statutes seldom list the elements of particular crimes, much less designating them as acts, facts, or results. Statutes sometimes designate a *mens rea* by using words such as "intentionally," "willfully," or "recklessly," but they seldom specify whether that *mens rea* applies to one of the elements, some of the elements, or all of the elements of the crime. Just as often, statues are completely silent on the question of *mens rea.* All of this leaves considerable room for prosecutors and defense attorneys to argue about the best interpretation of a statute.

Like all questions lawyers face, statutory interpretation entails an analytical process that uses the same syllogistic logic that we learned about in Lesson 6. The main sources for major premises in statutory interpretation are **canons of construction** and other factors that may bear on determining the best interpretation of a statute, including policy considerations. Like most legal analysis, the process of statutory interpretation seldom leads to determinate results. To the contrary, there often are several plausible ways to interpret most statutes. From an advocacy point of view, statutory interpretation is therefore as much about persuasion as it is hard logic.

There are dozens of canons of construction that have been recognized and applied by courts in the United States. There are a few that deserve special attention here because they are so commonly applied or because they are particularly relevant to the interpretation of criminal statutes:

1. **Plain Meaning:** The first, and sometimes last, canon of construction courts apply when interpreting criminal statutes gives primacy to the plain meaning of the text. If a statute is neither ambiguous nor incomplete, and the facts of the case do not implicate other canons of construction,

then this canon requires that courts apply the statute according to the plain meaning of its text. Because the meaning of words can change over time and context, applying this canon raises questions about whether plain meaning should be assessed by contemporary standards or by the original meaning of the words when the law was adopted. You may be familiar with a version of these debates in the context of constitutional law where originalists, such as Justices Antonin Scalia and Clarence Thomas, routinely do battle with living constitutionalists, such as Justices Ruth Bader Ginsburg and Stephen Breyer.

2. **Legislative Intent:** Although not all judges think it is proper, most courts strive to interpret statutes in such a way that they best effect the intent of the legislature. *See, e.g.*, *United States v. Balint*, 258 U.S. 250, 252 (1922) ("[The meaning of a statute] is a question of legislative intent to be construed by the court."). Divining legislative intent often requires appeal to resources outside the text of the statute, including committee reports and transcripts of floor debates. Justice Antonin Scalia is critical of legislative intent as a canon of construction because these outside resources often create rather than resolve ambiguity.

3. **Avoid Absurdity:** Courts should avoid interpreting a statute in such a way that it would lead to absurd results. Absurdity may be logical. For example, if a court is considering two possible interpretations of a statute, and one of those interpretations creates a direct conflict with the Constitution or another law, then that interpretation should be disfavored. The absurdity may also be practical. For example, if a court is considering two possible interpretations of a statute, and one of those interpretations would compromise important public policy goals or lead to undesirable results, then that interpretation

should be disfavored. In their efforts to persuade courts on questions of statutory interpretation, attorneys frequently appeal to this canon of construction by describing the "parade of horribles" that will come to pass if one interpretation is selected over another.

4. **Ejusdem Generis:** Often translated as "of the same class," this canon is applied in circumstances where a statute contains a generic phrase and a list of examples. *Ejusdem generis* asks that courts limit the meaning of the generic phrase to cases that are similar to the specific examples. For example, in *McBoyle v. United States*, 283 U.S. 25 (1931), the Supreme Court applied *ejusdem generis* to hold that "motor vehicles" as it was used in a federal statute did not include airplanes because the specific motor vehicles named in the statute—"automobile, automobile truck, automobile wagon, motorcycle, or any other self-propelled vehicle not designed for running on rails"—all travelled on the ground.
5. **The Rule of Lenity:** Out of respect for due process and the legality principle, courts faced with an ambiguous statute may resolve the ambiguity in favor of the defendant if that ambiguity has not been resolved by a court of competent jurisdiction prior to the defendant's conduct. This does not mean that a court applying the rule of lenity is obliged to endorse the interpretation of the statute that absolves the defendant. Rather, the rule of lenity requires that, if the "guilty" interpretation of an ambiguous statute is preferred, then that interpretation should only be enforced prospectively.

What You Need to Know:

1. Although it maintains roots in the common law, the criminal law increasingly is governed by statutes.

2. To best advise clients, develop legal arguments, and advocate in court, criminal lawyers must be able to interpret statutes.
3. Statutory interpretation is a process of legal analysis that uses various canons of construction to determine the meaning and application of statutory texts.
4. According to the rule of lenity, courts faced with an ambiguous statute may resolve the ambiguity in favor of the defendant if that ambiguity has not been resolved by a court of competent jurisdiction prior to the defendant's conduct.

LESSON 11: MISTAKES THAT NEGATE MENS REA

Imagine that a traveler waiting for his baggage at the airport sees a black suitcase come around on the carousel. The suitcase is the same make and model as his suitcase and, by all outward appearances, is his suitcase. In the full and honest belief that this is his suitcase, he picks it up, carries it out to his car, drives home, and opens it only to discover that it is not his at all. Is he guilty of theft?

Most of us looking at this case would say "no." Rather, it seems that our traveler has made an honest and reasonable mistake. He did not intend to steal the bag, and only picked it up by accident. We might prefer that he had taken more care to avoid his mistake, but he is not a thief. This same instinct is embodied in the criminal law requirement for *mens rea* or *scienter*, which we discussed in Lesson 9. In a famous passage from *Morissette v. United States*, 342 U.S. 246, 250–52 (1952), Justice Jackson defended this *mens rea* requirement in powerful terms:

> It is as universal and persistent in mature systems of law as belief in freedom of the human will and a consequent ability and duty of the normal individual to choose between good and evil. A relation between some mental element and punishment for a harmful act is almost as instinctive as the child's familiar exculpatory

> "But I didn't mean to," . . . . Crime, as a compound concept, generally constituted only from concurrence of an evil-meaning mind with an evil-doing hand, was congenial to an intense individualism and took deep and early root in American soil.

On this point retributivists and consequentialists agree with Justice Jackson: punishment is neither deserved, nor does it serve crime control purposes in most cases, if a defendant is not culpable by reason of a simple mistake. In keeping with this principle, defendants will be found not guilty in circumstances where they make a mistake that has the effect of negating *mens rea*. The facts in *Morissette* provide a good example.

The defendant in *Morissette* was a junk dealer who gathered discarded metals and other materials, which he then sold for scrap. He thought he'd found a rich source of scrap metals on an Air Force testing range, where bomb casings and other cast-off materials were left in the open, unclaimed, sometimes for years. Based on these circumstances, Mr. Morissette believed that the casings had been abandoned by the government, effectively thrown away, and therefore were available to anyone who wanted to collect them. He turned out to be wrong in this belief and subsequently was prosecuted under a federal statute making it unlawful to steal government property. At trial, Mr. Morissette sought an instruction that would allow the jury to acquit based on his mistake. That request was denied; he was convicted; and he then appealed to the Supreme Court, which reversed. According to the Court, the prosecution was required to prove *mens rea* with respect to every element of the crime, including knowledge as to the fact that the casings belonged to the United States. Because Mr. Morissette's mistake negated that *mens rea*, the Court held that he was entitled to a jury instruction that would have required the prosecution to prove that he knew the casings belonged to the government when he gathered them and carried them away.

In order to provide an excuse, a defendant's mistake must actually negate the required *mens rea* of the offense. It is therefore important when analyzing any criminal law problem to determine the elements of the offense and what level of *mens rea* the prosecution is required to prove with respect to each one of those elements. For example, a mistake as to a fact element of a crime will provide an excuse if the required *mens rea* is knowledge, or perhaps even recklessness. It likely will not provide an excuse if the required *mens rea* is negligence, however. That is because negligence only requires the prosecutor to prove what a reasonable person would have known, not what the defendant actually knew.

It is important to note that mistake as an excuse is not an affirmative defense. This means that the defendant is not required to prove that he made a mistake. Rather, all a defendant needs to do is raise the possibility that the prosecution's evidence does not exclude the possibility of a mistake that would negate *mens rea*. It is then up to the prosecution to prove beyond a reasonable doubt that the defendant did not make a mistake or otherwise had the required *mens rea*. As we have seen in prior lessons, this is often accomplished by reference to circumstantial evidence. For example, a prosecutor might point to the defendant's conduct and relevant facts to suggest that he could not have made an honest mistake, and therefore must have had the required *mens rea*. Alternatively, a prosecutor might point to the defendant's conduct and the surrounding circumstances to argue that no reasonable person could have made the mistake defendant claims to have made and that the defendant therefore did not make the mistake he claims to have made.

In some circumstances prosecutors may be able to defeat a claim of mistake by arguing that any such mistake must have been willful. This is sometimes referred to as the **ostrich defense**. If the evidence shows that a defendant willfully avoided acquiring knowledge that would make his conduct illegal—akin to an ostrich's hiding its head in the sand—then that may be sufficient to demonstrate that he had the required *mens rea*. For example, if a defendant is offered $5000 to carry a briefcase full of cocaine from Columbia to the United States, but specifically avoids learning what is inside, then that intentional ignorance may be enough to establish the *mens rea* for possession and importation of narcotics. That is because, in the language of Model Penal Code § 2.07, he was "aware of a high probability" that the briefcase contained some kind of contraband.

What You Need to Know:

1. The criminal law maintains a *mens rea* or *scienter* requirement.
2. Mistakes that negate *mens rea* demonstrate that the prosecution has not met its burden of proof with respect to *mens rea,* and therefore provide an excuse.
3. In order to provide an excuse, a mistake must negate *mens rea.* It is therefore important to identify what level of *mens rea* is required for each element of an offense.
4. Prosecutors may challenge alleged mistakes by pointing to evidence that the defendant did not honestly believe what he claims to have believed.
5. Willful ignorance generally will not provide an excuse in circumstances where a defendant's mistake is solely attributable to his own efforts to avoid acquiring critical knowledge.

LESSON 12: STRICT LIABILITY

We have learned that prosecutors must prove some level of mental connection between a defendant and the acts, facts, and results that define the elements of a crime. This *mens rea* requirement allows the criminal law to distinguish between those who are truly culpable, and therefore deserve punishment, and those who make understandable mistakes, but do not warrant legal condemnation. Thus, mistakes that negate the *mens rea* of a crime will provide a full excuse.

There is a class of crimes for which this general rule does not seem to apply. These are called **strict liability crimes**. Strict liability crimes excuse the prosecutor from alleging or proving *mens rea* with respect to one or more elements of the offense. Strict liability crimes also bar defendants from claiming mistake as grounds for exculpation. For example, speeding is a strict liability offense in most jurisdictions. Thus, when prosecuting a case of speeding, the state need not prove that the defendant knew he was speeding. Moreover, the defendant cannot escape punishment by claiming that he honestly believed he was not speeding.

The concept of strict liability is found elsewhere in the law as well. For example, as Professor Gifford teaches us in the materials on torts, tortfeasors may sometimes be held strictly liable when damage is done as a result of their dangerous activities, even if they take extraordinary measures to prevent harm. So, if a farmer chooses to keep an aggressive animal on his property, then he may be held strictly liable if the animal escapes and causes harm, no matter what he did to prevent the beast from escaping.

How might we justify strict liability as a matter of law and policy? The predominate justification for strict liability in tort is economic. In certain circumstances, it is just more efficient to put the entire burden of risk associated with some activities on one party. Returning to our farmer, if he is forewarned that he bears the full risk of harm caused by his animal, then he can buy insurance. This economic justification for strict liability is less convincing in the criminal law context. That is because the consequences of criminal convictions are not limited to injunctions and monetary damages.

As we have learned here, the criminal law is primarily concerned with the distribution of punishment. It is one thing for a court to impose upon a defendant the duty to pay tort compensation. This usually does not entail moral condemnation. Furthermore, there are morally neutral ways to bear the risk of having to pay compensation, such as insurance. It is quite a different matter for a court to find that a defendant did a bad thing and deserves to be punished. The very essence of punishment is moral condemnation. There is also no insurance in the world that can help ease the burden of a prison sentence. Thus, strict liability in the criminal law seems to require moral, rather than merely economic, justification.

In *United States v. Balint*, 258 U.S. 250 (1922), the United States Supreme Court described how strict liability can be morally justified in the criminal law context. In that case, the defendant sold derivatives of opium and cocaine in violation of the Narcotic Act of 1914. Before trial, Balint argued that the indictment against him should be dismissed because the prosecution failed to allege *mens rea* with respect to the fact that the substances he sold were derivatives of opium and cocaine. Relying on the common-law rule, Balint argued that it would violate his right to due process if the prosecution was not required to prove beyond a reasonable doubt that he knew the substances he was selling contained opium or cocaine.

Writing for the Court, Chief Justice Taft held that legislatures have broad discretion to remove from prosecutors the burden of proving *mens rea* in circumstances where the criminal law is used to advance public policy. The common law traditionally deals with crimes that are *mala in se*, or wrong in themselves. As the twentieth century ushered in a world of expanding industry and commerce, legislatures started creating a new class of criminal offenses addressing conduct that is *mala prohibita*, or wrong solely because it is against the law. These new criminal prohibitions were designed to assist in the enforcement of new regulations that sought to advance important public policy goals, including the protection of consumers from dangerous or adulterated products. Chief Justice Taft was familiar with many of these efforts because he had helped to promote them, first as a principal advisor and cabinet secretary to Theodore Roosevelt, and then as President of the United States.

Courts often face the question whether a particular statute creates a strict liability offense. Like many questions of statutory interpretation, there is seldom a clear answer. Courts must instead consider a number of canons of interpretation and other relevant factors to determine whether, on balance, it appears that the legislature has created a strict liability offense. This multifactor analysis starts with a presumption in favor of preserving the *mens rea* requirement. Courts will only impose strict liability where it is clear that the legislature has, in fact, created a strict liability crime. As part of this analysis, courts look to the public interests at stake on the assumption that the legislature would only resort to strict liability if those interests are particularly weighty.

Courts are particularly reluctant to impose strict liability for *mala in se* offenses or other crimes that have a long common-law history, preferring instead to reserve strict liability for purely regulatory offenses. Courts are also reluctant to impose strict liability when there are stiff penalties at stake, preferring to reserve strict liability for crimes with relatively light punishments. There is one important exception to these general rules, which is statutory rape. Despite the misleading name, statutory rape is a common-law crime that prohibits intercourse with minors, even if the minor is a willing participant. When prosecuting statutory rape, prosecutors do not need to prove *mens rea* as to the age of the minor. Furthermore, a defendant charged with statutory rape cannot claim mistake of fact as to the age of his sexual partner. That is true no matter how reasonable his mistake may have been. Some jurisdictions have moved away from this strict liability approach to statutory rape, requiring instead that the defendant act negligently with respect to the age of his paramour.

When determining whether a statute creates a strict liability offense, courts also look at the barriers of entry into the regulatory field governed by the statute. Courts are more likely to impose strict liability if defendants go out of their way to enter a closely regulated field of activity, passing high barriers of entry along the way because these hurdles provide substantial warning of potential dangers ahead. For example, the Court in *Balint* thought it was important that pharmaceutical distribution is a highly regulated field of activity, limited to a small number of people, who are well-apprised of the dangers and responsibilities associated with their businesses.

What You Need to Know:

1. Strict liability offers prosecutors the opportunity to convict defendants of certain crimes without needing to allege or prove *mens rea*.
2. Defendants cannot argue mistake as an excuse if the crime charged is a strict liability offense.

3. Most strict liability crimes are regulatory offenses that are *mala prohibita*, or created by statute, rather than *mala in se*, or wrong in themselves.

4. The only strict liability crime recognized by the common law is statutory rape, which makes it a crime for an adult to have sexual intercourse with a minor, whether or not he knows that the minor is underage.

LESSON 13: MISTAKES OF LAW

My first appearance in court was on my own behalf to contest a traffic ticket. I had been pulled over by a patrolman after executing a perfect left-hand turn one morning while driving a friend to work. Unfortunately, I did not know that left-hand turns were illegal at that intersection during the morning rush hours. Relying on an undergraduate course in the philosophy of law, I argued in court that I did not know my conduct was illegal and therefore did not have a guilty mind. The presiding judge was remarkably indulgent in letting me make my case. When I was done he said, "Ignorantia legis neminem excusat," struck his gavel, and directed me to the window where I could pay my fine.

Ignorantia legis neminem excusat, which is often translated as "ignorance of the law does not excuse," is a core principle of the criminal law. Although it seemed deeply unfair to me at the time, it is easy to understand why the judge did not want to recognize my mistake as grounds for an excuse. After all, if ignorance of the law did provide a general excuse, then there would be good reason to avoid knowing what the law prohibits and requires. By contrast, maintaining respect for the principle of *ignorantia legis neminem excusat* creates a powerful incentive for people to ask whether their proposed course of conduct is legal before they act and, if necessary, to hire an attorney to provide legal advice.

As with many rules and principles governing criminal law, the general rule that mistakes of law do not excuse is subject to some important exceptions. The first of these applies where one of the elements of the crime requires proof of intent to act unlawfully or proof that the defendant knew his conduct was against the law. For example, in *Liparota v. United States*, 471 U.S. 419 (1985), the United States Supreme Court confronted an alleged violation of 7 U.S.C. § 2024(b)(1), which provided that " 'whoever knowingly uses, transfers, acquires, alters, or possesses [food stamps] in any manner not authorized by [the statute] or the regulations' is subject to fine and imprisonment." Writing for the Court, Justice Brennan held that, as written, the statute required that the prosecution allege and prove beyond a reasonable doubt that Mr. Liparota knew he was violating the law when he took possession of several hundreds of dollars' worth of food stamps. Thus, if Mr. Liparota was ignorant as to the law governing possession of food stamps, then he could not be convicted.

A second important exception to the general rule that ignorance of the law does not excuse applies in cases where one of the elements of a crime is determined by law. In these circumstances, an honest mistake that negates *mens rea* will excuse. Take as an example 26 U.S.C. § 7203, which provides that anyone who willfully fails to pay taxes on income is guilty of a misdemeanor. As the Supreme Court pointed out in *Cheek v. United States*, 498 U.S. 192 (1991), "income" has a specific legal meaning under the internal revenue code. Because the question whether income is "income" for tax purposes is determined in part by law, the Court held in *Cheek* that an honest mistake of fact as to the legal status of the money identified in the indictment would negate *mens rea*, providing Mr. Cheek with an excuse. Mr. Cheek also argued that he honestly believed that the income tax was unconstitutional, and that his mistake of law on this point should provide grounds for an excuse. Applying the principle of *ignorantia legis neminem excusat*, the Court rejected that argument.

The third exception to the general rule that ignorance of the law does not excuse applies in cases that implicate the legality principle discussed in Lesson 3. As we learned there, in order to earn its right to inflict punishment, the state must provide fair warning as to what conduct is prohibited. If the state fails to fulfill this duty, then a defendant may be able to argue that an honest mistake of law should provide an excuse.

For example, in *Lambert v. California*, 355 U.S. 225 (1957), the Supreme Court was asked to consider a criminal statute—quite novel and rare at the time—requiring all convicted felons who entered and remained in Los Angeles, California, to register with law enforcement. Because registration laws were so uncommon and unexpected, and because local authorities did not sufficiently publicize this duty to register, the Court held that Los Angeles officials had failed to meet their responsibility to provide fair warning to Ms. Lambert and others covered by the statute. In that circumstance, the Court held, Ms. Lambert's ignorance of the law could provide an excuse.

Whether a mistake of law falls within any of these exceptions raises questions of statutory interpretation. Attorneys often are called upon to interpret statutes when formulating a defense strategy for a client who has already been arrested and charged. That is not always the order of events, however. Sometimes a lawyer is retained to provide legal advice in advance. In these cases, a lawyer may advise a client that his proposed course of conduct appears to be legal as the lawyer reads the statute. If the client follows that advice, and a court later disagrees, then the client might hope that his lawyer's advice would provide some grounds for a defense. Unfortunately, it does not—at least in most jurisdictions. When clients act on the advice of their attorneys, they do so at their own risk. You can imagine, then, that giving advice to a client in these circumstances is a heavy burden to bear. After all, bad advice might land that client in jail!

What You Need to Know:

1. According to the principle of "*ignorantia legis neminem excusat*," mistakes of law generally will not provide an excuse.

2. That general rule is subject to several important exceptions:

    a. Mistakes of law will provide an excuse where the *mens rea* of the crime requires intent to act unlawfully and a defendant's mistake negates that *mens rea*.

b. Mistakes of law will provide an excuse where one of the elements of the crime is determined by law and a defendant's mistake negates the *mens rea* of the crime.

c. Mistakes of law will provide an excuse where conviction and punishment would violate the legality principle.

3. Determining whether one of these exceptions applies requires interpreting statutes.

4. Attorneys sometimes provide prospective advice to clients on the legal status of a proposed course of conduct. If an attorney providing this kind of advice makes a mistake, and his client acts on that bad advice, then the client will not generally be able to rely on his attorney's mistake as grounds for an excuse.

LESSON 14: MURDER

Most first-year criminal law courses focus on the conditions of criminal responsibility and prepare students to use cases and statutes in order to identify the elements of crimes and analyze fact patterns. This leaves very little time to examine specific crimes in any depth. No criminal law course is truly complete without a discussion of homicide, however.

"Homicide" is defined as the killing of one human being by another human being. Homicide is not necessarily criminal. There are many circumstances where killing is permissible or even celebrated. For example, uniformed soldiers engaged in open armed conflict are permitted to kill one another. Soldiers returning from war often receive praise and awards for their heroic efforts to kill enemy combatants. In states where the death penalty is enforced, executioners kill as part of their jobs. Thus, when we talk about homicide in the criminal law, we are interested in unlawful rather than lawful killing.

The most commonly discussed homicide crimes are murder, voluntary manslaughter, involuntary manslaughter, and negligent homicide. Under the common law, and the statutory law of most jurisdictions, the most serious homicide crime is **murder**. The elements of common-law murder are:

1. Unlawful
2. Killing
3. Of Another
4. With Malice Aforethought

As a fact element, "**unlawful**" seems fairly straightforward. After all, most of us are not soldiers engaged in armed conflict or executioners carrying out a death sentence, so it is hard to see how a normal citizen might be able to claim a lawful right to kill. As we will see later on, however, defendants sometimes claim the lawful right to use deadly force out of necessity or in self-defense. Moreover, where a defendant makes a mistake as to his legal authority to kill, that mistake may negate the required *mens rea* for this element, excusing him from liability, in whole or in part.

"Killing" is really two elements rolled into one. The first element is an act. The second element is a result. In order to meet her burden of proving an act of killing, then, a prosecutor must show that the defendant engaged in a voluntary act. She must also prove that this act caused the victim's death. We will discuss the special burdens associated with proving cause in the next lesson.

The *mens rea* of murder under the common law is "malice aforethought." Just as we saw in our discussion of malice, "malice aforethought" should not be read for its colloquial meaning. That is because it is a term of art that describes a range of different theories a prosecutor might present to a jury in order to meet her burden of proving the *mens rea* for murder. Among the most widely recognized theories of malice aforethought for murder are:

1. Intent to kill the victim.
2. Intent to kill another person (transferred intent).
3. Knowledge that death will occur.
4. Intent to cause grievous bodily harm.
5. Knowledge that grievous bodily harm will occur.

6. Intent to commit a felony.
7. Intent to interfere with law enforcement.
8. Wanton recklessness demonstrating depraved indifference to the value of human life.

Although the common law does not distinguish between grades of murder, many states have passed homicide statutes describing different degrees of murder. Jurisdictions vary widely according to where they draw the lines between first-degree, second-degree, and third-degree murder, but one common approach is to define first-degree murder as "**premeditated**." "Premeditation" suggests a cool, calculated, or cold-blooded killing that is the culmination of careful planning—the sort of murder that might find its way into an episode of *Perry Mason* or *Colombo.* In most jurisdictions, however, "premeditation" is used to describe nothing more than intentional killing. In these jurisdictions, even if a defendant only forms the intent to kill at the moment of the act, that will be enough to show premeditation.

The seventh theory of murder listed above is commonly called **depraved-heart murder**. Depraved-heart murder is a theory of malice aforethought that shows how fluid the criminal law can be when it is developed through the common-law process. As we will see in our discussion of manslaughter, the traditional *mens rea* for involuntary manslaughter is recklessness. Nevertheless, wanton recklessness is sufficient to prove malice aforethought, and therefore murder. The differences in sentencing between murder and manslaughter can be dramatic—decades of prison time or even death. Many first-year law students therefore search for a clear line of demarcation between wanton recklessness, which would make a defendant guilty of murder, and ordinary recklessness, which would make a defendant guilty of involuntary manslaughter. Unfortunately, that effort is in vain. Whether a defendant's recklessness warrants a conviction for murder or merely manslaughter is, ultimately, a question left to the judgment of a jury or judge at trial.

What You Need to Know:

1. Homicide is the killing of one human being by another human being.
2. Homicide crimes include murder, voluntary manslaughter, involuntary manslaughter, and negligent homicide.
3. Murder is defined as the unlawful killing of one human being by another human being with malice aforethought.
4. "Malice aforethought" is a term of art that describes a range of different theories sufficient to prove the *mens rea* of murder including intent to kill, intent to cause grievous bodily harm, and wanton recklessness demonstrating depraved indifference to the value of human life.
5. Many jurisdictions grade murder according to different degrees. First-degree murder often is defined as a "premeditated" killing, which often requires nothing more than intent to kill.

LESSON 15: CAUSE

As we learned in Lesson 5, the elements of crimes fall into one of three categories: acts, facts, and results. A prosecutor's burden of proof with respect to any element of a crime is determined in part by its category. For example, we have learned that act elements require proof of a voluntary act. Defendants will not be convicted or punished for conduct that is involuntary. Result elements also come with special burdens. Foremost among these is the prosecution's responsibility to prove a causal connection between a defendant's voluntary act and any result elements of the crime. To see the role played by this cause requirement, consider this hypothetical:

> Jake is in desperate financial straits. He sees only one way out. His Aunt Bea is quite wealthy and has named Jake in her will. If she dies, then Jake can use the proceeds of his inheritance to save himself. Unfortunately for him, Jake neither has a stomach for

> violence nor does he know how to go about hiring a hit man. Then a vague memory crosses his mind of a movie he once saw in which one of the characters used a Voodoo doll to kill his enemy. Inspired, Jake uses some rags and buttons to make a crude doll. He puts a nametag on it that reads "Bea." Finally, he drives a needle through the left side of the doll's chest. The next day, he hears that Aunt Bea has suffered a fatal heart attack.

Is Jake guilty of murder? All of the elements (unlawful, killing, of another, with malice aforethought) seem to be there. He does not have grounds to claim a legal authority to kill, so his "killing" looks to be unlawful. It does not appear that he suffered a spasm, acted under hypnosis, or that his conduct was otherwise involuntary, so his act of "killing" seems to be voluntary. His victim was Bea, who is another person. Finally, he acted with intent to kill, which is sufficient to show malice aforethought. Nevertheless, he is not guilty of murder. That is because his conduct—poking a needle into the doll—was not a **cause in fact** of Bea's death.

To meet her burden of proof for any crime that involves a result element, a prosecutor must prove beyond a reasonable doubt both that the defendant's conduct in fact caused the result and that his act was the proximate or legal cause. Proving cause in fact does not present a very high hurdle. All the prosecutor needs to show is that, but for the defendant's actions, the result would not have occurred when it did and in the way that it did. In Jake's case, however, even this minimal requirement is not met. His conduct, though ill-willed, simply did not contribute to the chain of causation leading to Bea's death. She died of a heart attack. His playing with the doll just before she died was mere coincidence.

Now consider a variation on our Jake hypothetical. He is still broke and still wants to kill Bea in order to get access to his inheritance. This time, however, Jake has a different plan: he decides to max out his credit card in order to buy Bea an all-expense paid trip to Tahiti in the hope that her plane will crash. Delighted with her nephew's generosity, Bea goes on the trip, arrives safely, and has a wonderful time. Unfortunately, her plane does crash on the return flight. Is Jake guilty of murder? Again, all the elements are there. He engaged in a voluntary act with the intent of killing Bea; he does not appear to have any ground for claiming a lawful privilege to kill her; and now she is dead. Furthermore, we can say without difficulty that his conduct was a cause in fact of her death. After all, but for his actions, she would not have been on that plane, and therefore would not have died at the time or in the manner that she did. Despite all of this, Jake is still not guilty of murder. That is because his conduct was not a proximate or legal cause of Bea's death.

Assessing **proximate cause** is a complex matter that requires judges and juries to consider three questions. First, was the result an **objectively foreseeable** consequence of the defendant's conduct? "Objective foreseeability" is determined using a reasonable person standard. In Jake's case, Bea's death probably was not objectively foreseeable. As a subjective matter, Jake hoped that Bea's plane would crash. That hope was entirely unreasonable, however. No reasonable person in his position would have thought that there was any real risk that her flight would crash. Flying is among the safest modes of travel, and there was no reason to think that Bea's flights were particularly risky or dangerous.

The second question judges and juries ask when assessing proximate cause is whether the defendant's conduct is an **efficient cause** of the criminal result. Here, lawyers frequently use the metaphor of links in a chain. If there are too many links in the chain of events between a defendant's conduct and the result, or if the chain is otherwise too long, then punishment usually is not deserved. There is no hard rule to be applied here. Rather, the question is whether the defendant's conduct is close enough to the result to warrant holding him criminally responsible.

The third question judges and juries ask when assessing proximate cause is whether any independent, free-willed agents have intervened, effectively **breaking the causal chain**. This question played a prominent role in the early prosecutions of Dr. Jack Kevorkian, who was famous for contriving a "suicide machine" that would allow his patients to self-administer lethal doses of intravenous medications by pushing a button. Dr. Kevorkian was prosecuted for murder when several of his patients successfully used his device; but the charges ultimately were dismissed because those patients appeared to be of sound mind and they pressed the buttons as an act of independent free will. On those facts, their conduct broke the causal chain leading from Dr. Kevorkian's design, manufacture, and installation of his machine to his patients' deaths. The controversy around Dr. Kevorkian led many states to pass assisted suicide laws in order to work around this instance of the proximate cause requirement.

What You Need to Know:

1. For all result elements, a prosecutor must prove beyond a reasonable doubt that the defendant's conduct caused that result.
2. To meet her burden of proving cause, a prosecutor must show both that:
   a. The defendant's conduct was a cause in fact of the result; and that
   b. The defendant's conduct was a proximate cause of the result.
3. Cause in fact is measured by the "but for test," which often is described using the metaphor of a causal chain.
4. Proximate cause is determined by looking at three factors:
   a. Objective foreseeability, as measured by the reasonable person standard;
   b. Efficiency, as measured by the length or attenuation of the causal chain; and
   c. The role of independent, free-willed agents whose conduct might break the causal chain.

LESSON 16: FELONY MURDER

Harold is a very considerate and careful bank robber. He is always courteous and respectful to patrons and bank tellers. To limit the risk of injury to others, he never carries a real gun. Instead, he uses a very realistic looking toy gun. Despite his thoughtfulness and care, tragedy struck during one of his recent robberies. As he pulled out his toy gun and announced loudly, "This is a robbery . . ." a grandmotherly lady named Bea, who was standing in line to see the teller, suffered a sudden heart attack brought on by the fright of being caught in the middle of the robbery. Harold saw her collapse and rushed to her side. He administered expert CPR, but his efforts failed and Bea died. Is Harold guilty of murdering Bea?

As we have learned, the elements of murder are:

1. Unlawful
2. Killing
3. Of Another
4. With Malice Aforethought

Harold certainly did not have legal authority to kill Bea. There is no doubt that his actions were voluntary. It seems pretty clear that, but for his actions, Bea would not have died when and in the manner that she did die. Harold's conduct was the immediate and efficient cause of Bea's death. There do not seem to be any intervening acts or actors to cut the causal chain. Harold might argue that no reasonable person could have foreseen the possibility that a patron might die from the stress and fright of being subject to an armed robbery, but that is not an argument likely to succeed. So, we are left with the question of *mens rea*. Harold killed Bea; but did he do it with malice aforethought?

If we take malice aforethought to mean what it appears to mean in common parlance, then it seems unlikely that Harold could be convicted of murder. He did not want to kill anyone. Quite to the contrary, he took great care to avoid even the possibility that someone would get hurt during one of his heists. He even tried to save Bea, ensuring his capture and arrest in the process. All of this suggests that Harold is a robber, but certainly is not a killer.

Unfortunately for Harold, "malice aforethought" is a term of art that encompasses at least seven different theories that a prosecutor can use to meet her burden of proving the *mens rea* for murder. One of these theories is felony murder. The felony murder rule provides that, if a death occurs during the course of a felony, and all the other elements of murder are present, then the intent to commit that felony is sufficient to prove malice aforethought. In Harold's case, he intended to commit robbery, which is a felony, and Bea died in the course of that robbery. Under the common law, that makes Harold guilty of murder on a theory of felony murder.

At common law, felony murder was an absolute rule that did not admit of exceptions. If a defendant was guilty of a felony, and someone died during the course of that felony, then it was murder—period. This strict approach to felony murder may have made sense during an era when there were relatively few felony crimes and most felonies involved violence or otherwise created a risk of death. Robbery, for example, was defined at common law as using force of violence to achieve a larceny. Obviously this is a risky business. So too rape, arson, and burglary. In the modern era, however, expanding criminal and regulatory codes have created a whole range of felony offenses that pose little danger—some are even called "victimless" crimes. Both in response to the expansion of felony crimes, and out of more general concerns about the fact that the felony murder rule allowed for people like Harold to be punished just as severely as cold-blooded killers, courts and legislatures have imposed a range of limitations on the scope of felony murder.

The **merger doctrine** is among the most important limitations on the felony murder rule. Under the merger doctrine, prosecutors cannot use crimes like assault and battery as predicates for felony murder because the elements of these crimes "merge" completely into the course of conduct leading to death. For example, if Fred commits an assault and battery against Bill by stabbing him 20 times in the chest, then the merger doctrine would bar the prosecutor from charging felony murder. She would need to proceed instead on a theory of intent or knowledge.

Many jurisdictions also apply the **inherently dangerous felony** rule. Under this rule, felony murder can only be charged if the underlying predicate felony is a crime of violence or otherwise is so dangerous that it demonstrates a depraved indifference to the value of human life. The Model Penal Code has adopted a version of this rule, providing that "recklessness and indifference [to the value of human life] are presumed if the actor is engaged . . . in . . . robbery, rape or deviate sexual intercourse by force or threat of force, arson, burglary, kidnapping or felonious escape."

There are many more limitations on the felony murder rule that are important, but less common. For example, some jurisdictions only allow felony murder charges where the death occurred in the course and in furtherance of the felony. Under this rule, Harold could not be charged with felony murder because Bea's death did not advance his felonious agenda. Some jurisdictions also apply the co-conspirator rule, which provides that felony murder charges will not stand if the person who died was a participant or co-conspirator in the felony. All of these, and the many other rules governing felony murder that have been promulgated by courts and legislatures, seek in one way or another to hold prosecutors to their burdens of proof and to limit felony murder charges to circumstances where the defendant deserves the condemnation and punishment reserved for the most serious of crimes: murder.

What You Need to Know:

1. If someone dies during the course of a felony, then the defendant can be charged with murder under the felony murder rule, even if there is no intent to kill.
2. Under the common law, the felony murder was applied quite strictly.
3. In the modern era, courts and legislatures have sought to limit the extension of the felony murder rule.
4. The merger doctrine and the inherently dangerous felony rule are among the most common ways to limit the use of felony murder.

LESSON 17: INVOLUNTARY MANSLAUGHTER

Stan recently started his new job as an associate at a law firm. Over the past several weeks, he has been putting in very long hours on a major case that is coming to trial. After being at work for 36 straight hours, he is looking forward to driving home, taking a shower, and finally getting some sleep. He knows he is exhausted. In fact, he has fallen asleep sitting at his desk several times in the past few hours. He also knows it is dangerous to drive when sleep deprived. But he decides to risk it and drive home anyway. Unfortunately, due to his fatigue, he loses concentration while driving, drifts into the opposite lane, and collides with a car driven by Lisa, who dies on the scene.

Did Stan murder Lisa? Common-law murder is the unlawful killing of another with malice aforethought. Stan had no lawful authority to kill Lisa. His driving was a voluntary act insofar as it was not the result of spasm or otherwise involuntarily done. But for his hitting Lisa, she would not have died when and in the manner she did die. An accident is certainly an objectively foreseeable result of driving on the wrong side of the road. There were no intervening events attenuating the causal chain. Neither were there any intervening acts by others that might break the causal chain. So, all the act, fact, and result elements for murder seem to be present. That leaves only *mens rea*.

Malice aforethought is a term of art that describes a range of theories prosecutors might use to prove murder, including intent to kill and intent to cause grievous bodily harm. Stan did not mean to hurt anyone. That might make it difficult for a prosecutor to convict him of murder. Far more likely to succeed would be a charge of involuntary manslaughter.

Despite its title, involuntary manslaughter is distinguished from murder on the basis of *mens rea*, not *actus reus*. In this regard, involuntary manslaughter is a **lesser, but included, offense** of murder. It is easy to see what this means by comparing the elements of involuntary manslaughter and murder. The elements of involuntary manslaughter under the common law are:

1. Unlawful
2. Killing
3. Of Another
4. With Malice

The first three elements should be very familiar. They are also the first three elements of murder. In fact, the only difference between murder and involuntary manslaughter lies in the defendant's *mens rea*. The *mens rea* for murder is malice aforethought. The *mens rea* for involuntary manslaughter is simple malice. Like malice aforethought, malice is a term of art that covers a range of theories including recklessness and gross negligence. Thus, involuntary manslaughter is a lesser, but included, offense of murder because they share the same act, fact, and result elements, and the *mens rea* for involuntary manslaughter is less demanding than the *mens rea* for murder. If a prosecutor can prove murder then he can, by definition, meet his burden of proving involuntary manslaughter as well.

Recklessness, for the purpose of involuntary manslaughter, is defined as acting with the knowledge that one's conduct poses a substantial and unjustified risk of causing death or grievous bodily harm to another. That certainly seems to describe Stan. He knew he was exhausted. He also knew there was a serious risk he would cause an accident if he drove in his sleep-deprived condition. Despite this knowledge, he decided to drive anyway. It therefore looks like Stan is guilty of involuntary manslaughter.

This is not to suggest that a murder charge is out of the question. That is because one of the theories recognized by the common law as sufficient to show malice aforethought is wanton recklessness demonstrating depraved indifference to the value of human life. A prosecutor in Stan's case might therefore charge him with both murder and the lesser, but included, offense of involuntary manslaughter. It would then be up to the jury to decide whether Stan acted recklessly and, if he did, whether his recklessness was sufficiently wanton to justify a murder conviction. If the jury returned a guilty verdict on the "top count" of murder, then the lesser, but included, charge of involuntary manslaughter would merge into the murder conviction. Stan would then be sentenced for murder.

Most serious offenses encompass multiple lesser, but included, offenses. For example, distribution of narcotics includes the lesser, but included, offense of possession with intent to distribute narcotics, which, in turn, includes the lesser, but included, offense of possession of narcotics. This graduated structure reflects the fact that some actions and some offenders are more dangerous, harmful, or odious than others. It also allows prosecutors to be aggressive in their charging decisions without risking the possibility of a complete acquittal. So, a prosecutor in Stan's case might charge murder knowing that she had the fallback position of involuntary manslaughter.

Lesser, but included, offenses also play an important role in plea negotiations. Trials are expensive and inherently risky for both the prosecution and the defense. In a case like Stan's, a prosecutor might prefer a murder conviction, but offer to accept a plea of involuntary manslaughter in order to avoid the expense of a trial and the possibility that the jury could acquit Stan on all counts. Stan, who would prefer no conviction at all, might be inclined to accept such an offer in order to avoid the possibility of a murder conviction.

What You Need to Know:

1. Involuntary manslaughter is the unlawful killing of another with malice.
2. "Malice," for purposes of involuntary manslaughter, includes recklessness and gross negligence.
3. Recklessness for purposes of involuntary manslaughter is defined as acting with the knowledge that one's conduct poses a substantial and unjustifiable risk of causing death to another.
4. Involuntary manslaughter is a lesser, but included, offense of murder.
5. Lesser, but included, offenses play an important role in the both the substantive criminal law and

the procedural dynamics of charging decisions, jury instructions, and plea negotiations.

LESSON 18: VOLUNTARY MANSLAUGHTER

Like clockwork, Sarah starts to feel that "itch" after seven years of marriage to Owen. One afternoon, she decides to scratch it by inviting a coworker, Lloyd—on whom she's long had a crush—to come to her house for an interlude at a time when Owen is scheduled to be at work. Unfortunately for everyone, Owen decides to leave work early that day and catches his wife *in flagrante delicto* with Lloyd. Inflamed by rage, Owen reaches for the loaded gun he keeps in his bedside table, points it at Lloyd, and pulls the trigger. Lloyd dies as a result of his wounds.

Is Owen guilty of murder? Looking purely at the elements, it certainly seems that he is. Cuckolds do not have lawful authority to kill libertines. Owen's shooting the gun seems to constitute a voluntary act. His act was both the "but for" and proximate cause of Lloyd's death. Lastly, it seems that Owen acted with malice aforethought. His actions certainly bespeak intent to kill, or at least intent to cause grievous bodily harm.

Despite the fact that Owen's conduct meets all the elements of murder, there is a good chance his crime will be **mitigated** from murder to voluntary manslaughter because he acted in the heat of passion. As opposed to involuntary manslaughter, where a defendant acts recklessly, voluntary manslaughter describes a range of cases where a killing that would otherwise be murder is mitigated to manslaughter because of some extenuating circumstance. Provocation is the quintessential example.

Under the common law, a killing that would otherwise be murder is treated as manslaughter if the defendant is provoked by his victim, the nature of that provocation is such that a reasonable person in that defendant's same circumstances might be expected to act in the heat of passion, and there has been no opportunity for the defendant to "cool off." In Owen's case, he can claim to have been provoked by seeing Lloyd engaging in intercourse with his wife. This is the kind of provocation that, a jury might find, would cause an otherwise reasonable person to act out of heat of passion. Finally, Owen acted immediately rather than, say, leaving the house, buying a gun, and coming back to kill Lloyd.

The reasonable person standard serves an important role in this context by excluding acts of belligerence or cases of overreaction or short temper. Whether a defendant's response to a provocation is objectively reasonable is a question usually left to a jury. Jurors are invited to apply common sense, their own experiences, and the standards of the community to determine whether a defendant claiming mitigation is guilty of murder or voluntary manslaughter. Sometimes, however, established legal standards govern the reasonableness of a defendant's response to provocation. For example, verbal insults and taunts that fall short of threats of physical harm almost never provide sufficient provocation to mitigate murder to manslaughter as a matter of law.

Voluntary manslaughter is also a common charge in cases where death occurs in the course of **mutual combat**. "Mutual combat" in this context contemplates informal confrontations rather than licensed events such as boxing matches, martial arts tournaments, or ultimate fighting events. The most common contexts for voluntary manslaughter charges based on mutual combat are bar fights and street altercations. So, if two people get into an argument at a bar or on a street corner, decide to settle their differences by fisticuffs, and one of them ends up dead, then the survivor may be convicted of voluntary manslaughter rather than murder.

A conviction for voluntary manslaughter may also result if a defendant charged with murder claims an affirmative defense but is unable to "perfect" that defense for some reason. We will discuss affirmative defenses in later lessons. For now, it is enough to know that affirmative defenses have elements and that defendants usually bear the burden of production or persuasion with respect to these elements. If a defendant fails to meet his burden on one or more elements of an affirmative defense, then he cannot claim a full defense but may still qualify for a partial defense. For example, a defendant who claims that he killed in self-defense has the burden of showing in the first instance that he was in reasonable fear of death or severe bodily harm. If he cannot fulfill that burden, perhaps because his fear was unreasonable, then the jury cannot grant him a full defense. It may nevertheless grant him a partial defense, resulting in a voluntary manslaughter conviction.

Because voluntary manslaughter contemplates mitigation or partial defense, it raises important questions about burdens of proof. If a prosecutor decides to charge voluntary manslaughter, then she obviously carries the burden of proof. But consider a case where the prosecutor charges murder, but the defendant claims that he was acting in the heat of passion, and therefore should be convicted of voluntary manslaughter, not murder. Does the defendant in this case have the burden of proving provocation or does the prosecutor have the burden of proving absence of provocation? Under the common law, the defendant may be required to raise the question, but the final burden remains with the prosecutor to prove the absence of legally sufficient provocation. Some jurisdictions have departed from this common-law model by putting the full burdens of production and persuasion on the defendant. *See, e.g., Patterson v. New York*, 432 U.S. 197 (1977). In these jurisdictions, provocation is, in effect, an affirmative defense.

What You Need to Know:

1. In some cases where a defendant commits murder, extenuating circumstances may provide grounds to mitigate his crime to voluntary manslaughter.
2. Adequate provocation that causes a defendant to act in the heat of passion may provide grounds for mitigating murder to voluntary manslaughter.
3. Mere insults or taunts cannot, as a matter of law, provide adequate provocation to mitigate murder to voluntary manslaughter.
4. Other common theories of voluntary manslaughter are mutual combat and "imperfect" affirmative defense claims, including imperfect self-defense.
5. Under the common law, the prosecutor in a murder trial has the burden of proving that the

defendant should be convicted of murder rather than voluntary manslaughter.

LESSON 19: RAPE AND SEXUAL ASSAULT

Rape and sexual assault are among the most challenging topics in any criminal law course. These are very serious crimes, of course, combining physical violations with profound emotional trauma. The physical and psychological effects of rape and sexual assault often persist for years, decades, or a lifetime, altering survivors' senses of themselves, their places in the world, and their abilities to trust others.

Rape and sexual assault law also intersects with a host of complicated social norms and expectations relating to gender, sex, and sexuality. These public dimensions can magnify the harm caused by rape and sexual assault. For example, many survivors of rape and sexual assault may feel, or be made to feel, ashamed, stigmatized, or partially culpable. Due in part to these social consequences, sexual assault is dramatically underreported. Estimates vary, but it is likely that 60–80 percent of sexual assault crimes are never reported. This means that rape and sexual assault are much more common than most of us know. In fact, experts estimate that between one quarter and one half of women will be raped or sexually assaulted during their lifetimes.

Sexual assault also presents unique problems of proof for prosecutors. This is due in large part to the fact that many defendants in rape and sexual assault cases admit that there was sexual contact, but maintain that it was consensual. This makes the credibility of the complaining witness a central question at trial, opening the door to aggressive cross-examination and potentially invasive investigations of survivors' personal histories. **Rape shield laws** passed in most jurisdictions limit the scope of cross-examination to some extent, but survivors very often report feeling that they are the ones on trial rather than their assailants.

Given these challenges, police sometimes are reluctant to make arrests in rape and sexual assault cases and prosecutors often are willing to accept lenient plea agreements. Among the cases that go to trial, conviction rates can be very low. By some estimates, the cumulative result of all these challenges is that less than 4 percent of rapes lead to a felony conviction—much lower than the rate for other violent crimes like murder, robbery, and assault.

Criminal laws dealing with rape and sexual assault have changed dramatically since the mid-twentieth century. The elements of traditional common-law rape are:

1. Vaginal Penetration
2. By a Man
3. With his Penis
4. Of a Woman not his Wife
5. Against her Will
6. Accomplished by Force or Threat of Violence
7. That is Sufficient to Overcome the Resistance of a Woman of Ordinary Resolution

Almost all of these elements have been altered, augmented, or eliminated from contemporary criminal statutes and case law. Consider, for example, the first element: vaginal penetration:

Why would the common law focus on vaginal penetration, excluding a host of other sexual acts that might be just as harmful to victims if accomplished by force and against their wills? The surprising, and horrifying, reason is that, historically, rape was not considered a crime against women, but against the fathers and husbands who had the right to control women's reproductive capacities. Sexual assaults that could not result in pregnancy were less concerning in this highly patriarchal world.

Although modern rape law properly identifies the true victim, heated debates persist about which other forms of sexual violation should be called "rape." Some jurisdictions have responded to these contests by expanding the scope of "rape." Others have preserved a limited definition of "rape" and have instead created a range of other sexual offenses. In most jurisdictions, however, "rape" requires some act of penetration.

Assaults that do not include an act of penetration usually are categorized as sexual battery rather than rape.

Common-law rape could only imagine men as perpetrators and women as victims. Modern rape law has expanded outside these constraints to encompass sexual assaults perpetrated by men against men, by women against men, and by women against women.

Again tracing to a time when rape law was concerned primarily with preserving exclusive control over women's reproductive capacities, it was legally impossible under the common law for a man to rape his wife. Although this marital exception has been abandoned in most jurisdictions, it is still quite common for courts and legislatures to presume consent to sex within marriage or long-term domestic relationships.

The common-law requirement that intercourse be against a woman's will may seem unproblematic, but is regarded as too narrow by contemporary courts and legislatures. The law in most jurisdictions focuses instead on absence of consent. This shift has given rise to a variety of new issues relating to *mens rea*. For example, must a perpetrator intend to have intercourse without the consent of his victim, or will knowledge or recklessness suffice? The answer to this question leads to others, including whether consent can be assumed absent a clear protest, or, alternatively, whether absence of consent must be assumed unless there is a clear and unequivocal declaration of consent.

The common-law requirement that a perpetrator use force to commit a rape is preserved in most jurisdictions, although in a weakened form. For example, the law in many states now provides that force requirements can be met by the minimal force necessary to accomplish penetration. Some courts have even held that unlawful threats that do not involve violence, such as blackmail, can give rise to rape charges. By contrast, the duty to resist has all but disappeared, although some jurisdictions do require a clear and unequivocal expression that sexual advances are unwanted and unwelcome.

Conversations about rape and sexual assault law often get entangled with complicated questions about the nature of intimacy, romance, and sex that are both highly private and linked to broader social norms relating to gender and relationships. The questions are particularly confusing in cases of acquaintance rape, where alcohol or other drugs often play a role. In these circumstances, the question often is not whether consent was given—it was not—but whether, given all the circumstances, a prosecutor can prove that the defendant knew consent had not been given. Because the prosecutor must prove *mens rea* beyond a reasonable doubt, miscommunications or misunderstandings often lead to acquittal. Some commentators have described these as cases of rape without a rapist.

What You Need to Know:

1. Rape and sexual assault are serious crimes that are underreported.
2. Rape and sexual assault law has changed dramatically since the mid-twentieth century, tracking progress in women's rights movements.
3. Even with these reforms, rape and sexual assault cases present serious challenges for police and prosecutors, particularly in cases where the victim and the perpetrator are acquainted.
4. The main questions in most rape and sexual assault cases relate to consent: whether consent was given, or whether a defendant reasonably believed that consent was given.

LESSON 20: THEFT

Theft, as a category of crimes, includes a long list of offenses. As Professor Super teaches us in the materials on property law, conceptions of property and ownership are always evolving to accommodate expansion and innovation in the economy. Each of these changes creates new opportunities for dishonest activity relating to property, which often requires changes in theft law. The result is a body of law that can be esoteric and highly technical.

To get a feel for how complicated the distinctions between various theft crimes can be, let's start with the paradigmatic theft crime: larceny. The elements of common-law larceny are:

1. Unlawful
2. Appropriation (Taking)
3. And Asportation (Carrying Away)
4. Of Personal Property
5. In the Possession of Another
6. With Intent to Permanently Deprive

Thus, if Sam reaches into Jane's book bag, removes her very expensive criminal law textbook, and walks away intending to keep the book for himself, then he has committed larceny.

Seems simple enough, but now imagine that Sam has title in the book, which means that he owns it. To make a little extra money, he has rented the book to Jane for the semester and her rent is all paid up. So, even though Sam owns the book, it is lawfully in Jane's possession. Larceny is a crime against possessory rights, not ownership rights. So, Sam is still guilty of larceny, even if he has title in the book, because he unlawfully violated Jane's possessory rights.

Returning to our original hypothetical, imagine that, instead of reaching furtively into Jane's bag to get that textbook, Sam yanks the bag from her shoulder, pulls out the book, and runs away. This is **robbery**, which is defined in the common law as larceny accomplished by force. This means that larceny is a lesser, but included, offense of robbery insofar as robbery includes all the elements of larceny with the added element of "accomplished by force." If Sam uses a weapon in the course of his robbery, then he has committed **armed robbery**.

What if Sam chooses deviousness over stealth or force? For example, imagine that he offers to buy the book and promises that he will pay Jane twice what the book is worth next week if she gives it to him today. Of course, he has no intention of paying her anything at all. Because Sam has used an artifice to acquire title in the book, he has committed the crime of

obtaining property by false pretenses. If he instead asks to borrow the book, but never intends to return it, then he only gains possession, not title. In that case, he would be guilty of **larceny by trick**.

If your head is not already spinning, then consider another twist on our Sam and Jane saga. This time Jane tells Sam that she is going to sell her textbook back to the bookstore. Sam is heading to the bookstore to sell some of his own books, so he offers to sell Jane's book and promises to bring her the proceeds. Grateful for the extra study time, Jane gives Sam her book. At this point, Sam has possession of Jane's book so that he can carry it to a third party. The name for this type of possession is a **bailment**. As the possessor, Sam is the bailee. As the donor, Jane is the bailor. If, on his way to the bookstore, Sam decides not to sell Jane's book after all, but to keep it for himself instead, then he has committed **embezzlement** by converting Jane's book to his own use instead of selling it as promised. If, however, his original promise was false, and he intended to keep Jane's book for himself all along, then he has committed **larceny by trick** because no bailment was formed. To add further complexity, if Sam takes possession of Jane's book in good faith, but decides on his way to the bookstore to remove and keep the last two chapters from Jane's book, then he has probably committed larceny, not embezzlement, under the common-law doctrine of "**breaking the bulk**."

The law of theft is not done with you yet. Now imagine that Sam knows something about Jane, which, if revealed, would cause her embarrassment. In exchange for maintaining his silence, Sam demands that Jane give him the textbook. This is **blackmail**. If, instead, Sam threatens to kill Jane's cat unless she gives him the textbook, then he has committed **extortion**. The difference between the two lies in the lawfulness of the threatened action. Although it is uncouth, there is nothing illegal about revealing embarrassing information. By contrast, it is unlawful to kill someone's innocent pet.

Just to add one more headache, now imagine that Jane accidentally leaves her book sitting on her usual study table in the library when she runs off to class. Sam happens upon it a few minutes later, picks it up, and decides to keep it. Taking and keeping **mislaid property** is a form of larceny because mislaid property is still in the constructive possession of the owner. By contrast, taking and keeping **lost or abandoned property** is not a crime. Distinguishing between property that is lost or abandoned and property that is mislaid can be quite difficult, but usually is a function of whether there is a reasonable possibility of identifying the owner or lawful possessor. So, a wallet that contains identification is mislaid, but a random penny sitting on the sidewalk probably has been lost. In our hypothetical, Jane seems to have mislaid her book, which makes Sam guilty of larceny.

At this point, you should be ready to throw up your hands. It is nearly impossible to keep track of all the various theft offenses, much less the often subtle differences between them. In order to avoid confusion and reduce the potential that defendants who clearly have committed some sort of theft will avoid punishment by exploiting technicalities in the law, many jurisdictions have adopted **consolidated theft statutes**. These laws define theft in very general terms in order to encompass a wide range of traditional common-law offenses.

What You Need to Know:

1. Theft covers a broad range of offenses including larceny, robbery, armed robbery, obtaining property by false pretenses, larceny by trick, embezzlement, blackmail, and extortion.
2. Distinctions among theft crimes can be quite technical, often turning on whether the thief gains possession or title, and how.
3. Many jurisdictions have adopted consolidated theft statutes that eschew the distinctions between common-law theft crimes.

LESSON 21: ATTEMPT

Consider two men with murder in their hearts: Jerry and Greg. Jerry wants to kill Frank. So, he pulls out a gun, aims it at Frank, and squeezes the trigger. A bullet flies out, strikes Frank in the chest, and Frank dies. Greg wants to kill Harry. So, he pulls out a gun, aims it at Harry, and squeezes the trigger. A bullet flies out, narrowly misses striking Harry in the chest, and Harry walks away unharmed.

Jerry has committed murder, but Greg has not. You cannot have a murder unless someone dies. But this seems to present the criminal law with a moral quandary. After all, Jerry and Greg both had the *mens rea* for murder. They both engaged in exactly the same conduct. Greg just got lucky—or unlucky, depending on your point of view—when he missed Harry. It does not seem right or fair to have the possibility of potentially severe criminal punishment hang on nothing more than luck.

The law of attempt fills this moral gap by punishing people who try, but fail, to commit a crime. Attempt is often called an "**inchoate offense**" to emphasize the fact that it is an imperfect or incomplete version of a target offense. This means that attempt is not a freestanding crime like murder or larceny. Rather, attempt is always defined in relation to a substantive crime or target offense. In Greg's case, he is probably guilty of attempted murder.

Like all crimes, attempt requires both *mens rea* and *actus reus*. The *mens rea* of attempt is purpose or intent. In order to convict a defendant of attempt, a prosecutor must therefore prove beyond a reasonable doubt that the defendant intended to complete the target crime. Although it is helpful for prosecutors to have direct evidence of a defendant's intentions, it is not necessary. Prosecutors can meet their burdens of showing *mens rea* by appealing to circumstantial evidence, including a defendant's own actions, and allowable presumptions. In Greg's case, his actions speak for him. Applying the familiar presumption that a person intends the natural consequences of his actions, it seems clear that Greg intended to kill Harry.

The *actus reus* of attempt is determined by the crime being attempted. So, the *actus reus* of attempted murder is very different from the *actus reus* of attempted larceny. Setting these differences aside, it is important to distinguish between harmless fantasy and criminal attempt. We all have evil thoughts. On occasion, we've all taken preliminary action on at least some of these thoughts. But relatively few of us ultimately follow through by committing a crime. In order to avoid being overinclusive by punishing people who do not deserve punishment and in order to encourage all of us to listen to our better angels, the criminal law distinguishes between conduct that is sufficiently advanced and dangerous so as to warrant punishment from our common struggles with everyday demons. Regardless of the target offense, the *actus reus* of attempts therefore is determined by a function of three factors: **proximity, equivocality, and likelihood of success**.

To understand **proximity**, it is helpful to think about crimes not as discrete, eruptive events, but as courses of conduct that follow a timeline. The timeline begins when a defendant is first struck with an evil thought and ends when the crime is completed. The question for proximity is where, along this timeline, we should mark the boundary between mere preparation and criminal attempt. Under the common law, criminal responsibility for an attempt will not lie until the defendant has taken the "**final step**" toward completing the target crime. On this standard, Greg would be guilty of an attempt. After all, he pulled the trigger. There was nothing else for him to do.

In place of the "final step," the Model Penal Code sets the proximity threshold for criminal attempt much earlier: when a defendant has engaged in a **substantial step** toward his criminal goal. In order to encourage aspiring criminals who have passed that substantial step threshold to abandon their criminal ways before it is too late, the Model Penal Code provides an affirmative defense based on renunciation, which requires affirmatively abandoning the course of criminal conduct and disclaiming any intent to commit the crime. There is no renunciation defense available under the common law, of course, because any defendant who has taken the final step toward his criminal goal has no more opportunities to abandon his crime. All he can do is hope for the best.

Equivocality as a factor of attempt crimes highlights the link between *actus reus* and *mens rea*. In general, a defendant will not be found guilty of an attempt if his course of conduct is equivocal as to his intent to commit the target crime. On the facts of our hypothetical, there does not seem to be anything equivocal about Greg's conduct because he came so close to hitting Harry. But imagine that Greg missed Harry by five feet. In that case, Greg might have a credible claim that his conduct was equivocal as to whether he meant to kill Harry or merely to scare him.

The final factor, **likelihood of success**, tries to avoid punishing would-be criminals who really do not pose any danger to anyone. Consider, for example, a hypothetical that we discussed in an earlier lesson: Jake wants to kill his aunt Bea because he hopes to inherit money from her estate. Jake does not have much of a stomach for violence, however, so he makes a primitive doll, puts a piece of tape on it labeled "Bea," and sticks the doll with needles hoping that this will result in her death. If his plan fails, then it is unlikely that Jake could be charged with attempted murder. There is no doubt that he wanted to kill Bea. He also took the final step described by his murderous plan. His plan is just too unlikely to succeed to warrant criminal punishment.

Many of the complexities in attempt law trace to moral, social, and policy concerns that are often at odds with one another. On the one hand, it is good policy to encourage would-be criminals not to even start down the road to a completed crime. It therefore might make sense to impose liability for attempts at the first step. On the other hand, it seems both immoral and undesirable to punish people for their thoughts. If we set the threshold for attempt liability too early, then we come very close to punishing people for their thoughts. It is also good policy for police to take action to prevent crimes rather than waiting until after the fact to make an arrest. We might therefore prefer to set the threshold for attempt liability quite early so that police can make an arrest well before the public is in danger. But we also want to encourage people who start down a criminal path to stop, backtrack, and take a different path. If we set the threshold for attempt liability too early then those incentives start to disappear.

What You Need to Know:

1. Whenever a defendant tries, but fails, to commit a crime, he may be guilty of an attempt.

2. The *mens rea* for attempt is intent to commit the target crime.
3. The *actus reus* for attempts is determined by the target crime and a function of three factors: proximity, equivocality, and likelihood of success.
4. In applying these factors, the criminal law tries to strike a reasonable balance between competing moral, social, and policy concerns.

LESSON 22: CONSPIRACY

All of the crimes we have discussed so far require a physical act of some kind. There are some crimes, however, that can be perpetrated with mere words. Conspiracy offers a prime example. The elements of conspiracy under the common law are pretty straightforward:

1. Two or more people
2. Agree
3. To perform an unlawful act, achieve an unlawful goal, or achieve a lawful goal by unlawful means.

The *actus reus* for conspiracy is the agreement, which can be explicit or implicit. The *mens rea* for conspiracy is intent to commit the target crime. Knowledge alone usually is not sufficient. So, if a telephone company knows that some of its customers use their phones to facilitate drug transactions, then that would not automatically make the telephone company party to a drug conspiracy. The prosecutor would instead need to prove that the telephone company intended to advance the drug conspiracy by providing communications services.

Like attempt, conspiracy is an inchoate offense defined by its relationship to a target crime. Unlike attempt, however, conspiracy does not require that the target offense be completed. This has two important consequences. First, a conspiracy is complete once the agreement is reached. Even if the conspirators take no additional steps in pursuit of their criminal goal, they can be prosecuted and punished for their agreement. Second, if conspirators manage to complete their target offense, then they can be prosecuted, convicted, and sentenced for both the conspiracy and for the target crime. Under the common law, at least, conspiracies do not merge into their target crimes. By contrast, attempt crimes merge into their target crimes if those target crimes are completed. For example, a two-man drug dealing team who sells narcotics to a customer can be tried, convicted, and punished for both conspiracy to distribute narcotics and distribution of narcotics. They cannot, however, be punished for both attempt to distribute narcotics and distribution of narcotics.

In addition to being a crime in itself, conspiracy is also a source of vicarious liability under the **Pinkerton doctrine**, which takes its name from the famous Supreme Court case *Pinkerton v. United States*, 328 U.S. 640 (1946). The Pinkerton doctrine holds that parties to a conspiracy are liable as principals for the criminal acts of their co-conspirators when done in the course and in furtherance of the conspiracy. The scope of Pinkerton liability can be quite broad, encompassing dozens or hundreds of crimes perpetrated by participants across the globe who have never met. Take, for example, the average drug conspiracy. The dealer who sells a baggie of heroin on a street corner is tied by conspiratorial threads to hundreds or thousands of co-conspirators engaged in crimes as diverse as growing poppy plants, manufacturing heroin, smuggling, bribery, murder, and money laundering. Under the Pinkerton doctrine, that dealer can be prosecuted and punished for every one of those crimes as if he committed them himself.

Conspiracy charges can also toll or extend statutes of limitation, which usually bar prosecution of crimes after a statutorily defined period of time has passed. Given that many conspiracies can last for years or decades, this can extend significantly an individual's period of exposure to criminal charges. This tolling of statutes of limitation can also expand further the number of crimes encompassed by the Pinkerton doctrine.

Conspiracy also has important procedural consequences. For example, charging a conspiracy can dramatically expand the scope and length of a trial by linking dozens of co-conspirators and hundreds of individual crimes. Conspiracy also affects evidentiary rules, and particularly the admissibility of hearsay evidence. ("Hearsay" is an out-of-court statement offered at trial to prove the truth of the matter asserted. A classic example of hearsay is a witness at a murder trial who testifies that he was told by a third party that the third party witnessed the defendant committing the crime.) Hearsay evidence generally is not admissible. Under Federal Rules of Evidence 801(d)(2)(e), however, testimony relating to statements made by a co-conspirator during the course and in furtherance of a conspiracy are admissible. The governing rules of evidence in most jurisdictions have similar exceptions to the hearsay rule. Moreover, prosecutors generally are allowed to avail themselves of this exception before proving the existence of a conspiracy. In fact, evidence that otherwise would be excluded as hearsay is admissible to prove the existence of a conspiracy in the first place.

The expansive scope of conspiracy law, Pinkerton liability, and the procedural consequences of conspiracy charges are all controversial. Defenders point to the benefits to law enforcement and prosecutors. Because conspiracy is a crime in itself, police officers have the authority to intervene and make arrests at a very early stage, perhaps preventing crime and protecting the public from danger. The threat of expanded liability under the Pinkerton doctrine also allows officers to leverage relatively minor participants to "flip" on their co-conspirators. The Pinkerton doctrine may also encourage co-conspirators to keep closer tabs on one another lest they find themselves liable as principals for crimes they did not approve.

On the other hand, the expansive nature of conspiracy law can create some problems. Many conspiracy trials are long and unwieldy, involving dozens of defendants, thousands of pieces of evidence, and months or years of testimony. The individual crimes contemplated in these trials also vary widely from cold-blooded murders to money laundering to smuggling. These features of conspiracy trials can make juries' jobs nearly impossible. There are also concerns about whether relatively minor participants sitting at the defense table next to kingpins and murderers can receive a fair trial. Critics maintain particular concerns about conspiracy trials conducted under the auspices of the federal Racketeer Influenced and Corrupt

Organizations Act (RICO). Originally designed to combat the mob, RICO has been put to much broader use, leading some critics to call for its abolishment.

Despite the controversies posed by conspiracy, reform efforts have been few and modest. For example, some jurisdictions require at least one affirmative act in support of a conspiracy; but, even here, the most trivial acts will suffice. Some jurisdictions bar conviction for both conspiracy and a target crime. In these jurisdictions, the conspiracy merges into the target crime. But these merger rules do not prohibit charging both conspiracy and a target crime, preserving all of the evidentiary and procedural issues that accompany conspiracy trials. The Model Penal Code has led the way on some of these reforms and also proposes severe limits on vicarious liability rules. This sort of reform, which would dramatically reduce the impact of Pinkerton liability, has so far failed to take hold in most jurisdictions.

What You Need to Know:

1. Conspiracy is an agreement between two or more parties to commit a crime.
2. Once an agreement has been reached, the crime of conspiracy is complete.
3. Under the Pinkerton doctrine, conspirators are liable as principals for crimes committed by their co-conspirators in the course and in furtherance of the conspiracy.
4. Conspiracy charges dramatically expand the scope of criminal trials and also allow for the admission of hearsay and other evidence that would not otherwise be admissible.

LESSON 23: COMPLICITY

Al has had a very frustrating day at the bank trying to secure a loan to purchase his dream house. After hours of bureaucratic run-around and more broken promises than he can count, Al's application is refused. Angry and bitter, he is leaving the bank just as Slim arrives to rob the bank. Al does not know Slim. Neither does he have any aspirations to be a bank robber. He is just mad at the bank. So, when he sees what's happening, he cheers, claps, and shouts, "Stick it to them—they're all dirty capitalist pigs!" He cheers even louder when Slim pistol-whips the loan officer who refused Al's loan application. Slim makes off with several bags laden with cash. Al returns home.

Is Al guilty of a crime? It is hard to see how he could be. He did not take the money, so did not commit larceny or robbery. He did not hit the loan officer, so did not commit assault or battery. There was no agreement between him and Slim, so there is no conspiracy and therefore there are no grounds for holding him responsible for robbery or assault under the Pinkerton doctrine. It therefore appears that Al cannot be prosecuted as a principal in any of the crimes related to the bank robbery. He may, however, be guilty of a crime of complicity.

Complicity offenses are crimes of support and encouragement. Complicity is distinct from the Pinkerton doctrine and other forms of vicarious liability, however. This can cause some confusion because the fact elements of complicity offenses include at least one crime perpetrated by someone other than the defendant. Vicarious liability also contemplates criminal conduct by someone other than the defendant. The difference is that, under vicarious liability, a defendant is held directly responsible for the criminal conduct of another person as if she were the principal perpetrator. By contrast, defendants who commit complicity offenses are held responsible for their own conduct *in relation* to the criminal conduct of another person. In other words, a crime committed by another person is a fact element of all complicity crimes.

The common law generally recognizes three complicity offenses:

1. Aiding and abetting or acting as an accomplice during the crime,
2. Accessory before the fact, and
3. Accessory after the fact.

Accordingly, Al may not be responsible as a principal in the first degree for robbery or assault, but he may well be guilty of aiding and abetting robbery and assault.

Under the common law, the traditional *mens rea* for all complicity crimes is intent that the principal complete the target crime. To prevail at trial, a prosecutor would therefore need to prove beyond a reasonable doubt that the defendant "associate[d] himself with the venture, that he participate[d] in it as in something that he wishe[d] to bring about, [or] that he [sought] by his action to make it succeed." *United States v. Peoni*, 100 F.2d 401, 402 (2d Cir.1938). This traditional requirement may be loosened, however, in cases where the principal's crime is particularly serious. For example, in *United States v. Fountain*, 768 F.2d 790 (7th Cir. 1985), Judge Posner held that knowledge is sufficient to meet the *mens rea* requirement for aiding and abetting murder because it supports a strong inference of intent. As the Supreme Court recently made clear, that knowledge must precede the act of support or encouragement. Otherwise, the inference of intent is defeated. *See Rosemond v. United States*, 134 S. Ct. 1240 (2014).

The *actus reus* for aiding and abetting, accessory before the fact, and accessory after the fact entails some form of support or encouragement. The main differences between these offenses has to do with physical presence and timing.

If a defendant is present at the scene of a crime and provides assistance or encouragement to the principal during the course of the crime, then he is an accomplice guilty of aiding and abetting. There is no requirement for this support or assistance to be necessary, effective, or even received. It is enough if the accomplice offers his support or encouragement with the intent that the principal engage in the crime. By this standard, Al seems to be an accomplice to Slim's bank robbery and assault. Al was there. He yelled his encouragement. By all appearances, he wanted Slim to succeed. That makes Al an accomplice, regardless of whether his encouragement provided necessary assistance to Slim. The Model Penal Code takes one step further. Under § 2.06(3)(a)(ii), Al would probably be guilty of aiding and abetting even if Slim was deaf, and therefore did not hear any of Al's shouts of encouragement.

If a defendant provides assistance or encouragement to a principal before the crime, then he is an accessory before the fact. For example, if Slim asks his friend George to provide a gun and mask for the robbery and George complies, then George could be charged as an accessory before the fact. As in the case of aiding and abetting, the support or encouragement provided by an accessory before the fact need not be necessary or determinative. Some courts do require, however, that it be at least minimally effective. So, if Slim's mother wrote him a note reading, "Have a good day robbing the bank!" and left it on the kitchen table, but Slim never received it, then she may be able to avoid a charge of accessory before the fact in some jurisdictions.

Some jurisdictions recognize a crime closely related to accessory before the fact called solicitation, which entails recruiting or hiring someone to commit a crime. Murder-for-hire is a classic case of solicitation. Solicitation requires something more than mere support or encouragement, however. To be found guilty of solicitation, a defendant usually must initiate the crime and procure the participation of the principal.

If a defendant provides support or encouragement to a principal after the crime, then he is an accessory after the fact. Returning to Slim and his mother, imagine that Slim flees to his mother's house with police hot on his tail. If his mother tells officers that Slim has been home with her all morning, then she has made herself an accessory after the fact to his bank robbery.

Although complicity crimes do not involve a meeting of the minds between an accomplice (or an accessory) and the principal, the facts in any given case may sit on the border between complicity and conspiracy. Returning to Al and Slim, imagine that Slim and Al made direct eye contact just as Slim was entering the bank, Al immediately divined what Slim was about to do, uttered his words of encouragement, and Slim responded by saying, "Thanks man!" In this circumstance, a prosecutor might be able to argue that there was a meeting of the minds between Al and Slim and that they therefore formed a conspiracy. Al would then be guilty of conspiracy and as a principal to the bank robbery and the assault under the Pinkerton doctrine. He could not be convicted of both conspiracy and complicity, however. In these circumstances, the complicity charge would merge into the conspiracy.

What You Need to Know:

1. Defendants who support or encourage the criminal activities of others may be guilty of complicity.
2. The three main complicity crimes are aiding and abetting, accessory before the fact, and accessory after the fact.
3. Complicity generally requires intent, but knowledge may suffice for particularly serious crimes like murder if that knowledge precedes the acts of support or encouragement.
4. The main differences between aiding and abetting, accessory before the fact, and accessory after the fact relate to when the support or encouragement was given and whether the defendant was present for the principal's crime.

LESSON 24: AFFIRMATIVE DEFENSES

All of the preceding lessons have focused on prosecutorial burdens in criminal trials. Although, defendants can avoid conviction by raising questions that offer grounds for reasonable doubt, our main task up to now has been to identify what the prosecutor must prove. For the lessons that remain, we will be shifting perspectives to discuss affirmative defenses.

As a prelude to this discussion, it is worth emphasizing that defendants in criminal trials are under no obligation to call witnesses, offer evidence, or otherwise put on a case. The burden of proving each element of every criminal charge beyond a reasonable doubt lies with the prosecution. A defendant can therefore avoid conviction by raising doubts in the mind of jurors about the reliability of witnesses and physical evidence, or simply by pointing out that evidence offered by the prosecution, when taken in its totality, is not enough to eliminate reasonable, alternative, and innocent theories of events.

If a defendant chooses to offer his own witnesses or evidence, then he may have one of two goals. First, he might offer evidence that raises doubt in the minds of the jury as to his guilt. For example, he might present evidence that he was someplace else at the time of the crime, and therefore could not have been the perpetrator. Second, he may offer an affirmative defense.

When a defendant offers an affirmative defense, he all but admits that the prosecution has met its burden of proving each element of the crime. He nevertheless argues that he should be fully or partially exonerated due to some extenuating circumstance such as necessity, self-defense, duress, intoxication, or insanity. Like crimes, affirmative defenses have elements. Unlike crimes, however, it is the defendant, not the prosecution, who has the primary burden of production. This means that the defendant must offer sufficient evidence to present the affirmative defense to the jury or judge as trier of fact. The defendant may also have the burden of persuasion. Depending on the defense and the jurisdiction, a defendant bearing the burden of persuasion on affirmative defenses may be required to prove the elements of that affirmative defense by clear and convincing evidence or by a preponderance of the evidence. The final burden of persuasion may also fall on the prosecution on a preponderance standard, on clear and convincing evidence, or even beyond a reasonable doubt. The allocation of burdens of persuasion and the degree of certainty required varies between jurisdictions.

Affirmative defenses generally fall into one of two categories: **justification defenses** and **excuse defenses**. Defendants claiming justification admit that they committed the crime, but argue that, all things considered, they did the right thing. The two predominate justification defenses are necessity and self-defense. Defendants claiming excuse defenses admit that the prosecution has met its technical burden of proof, including its burden of proving *mens rea,* but argue that there is more to the story on culpability. The most common excuse defenses are duress, intoxication, and insanity. In the lessons that remain, we will discuss each of these defenses.

What You Need to Know:

1. Although defendants are never under any obligation to put on a case of their own, they have the option to plead affirmative defenses.
2. If a defendant pleads an affirmative defense, then he carries the burden of production on each element of that defense and may also bear the burden of persuasion as well.
3. Affirmative defenses fall into one of two categories: justification defenses and excuse defenses.
4. Justification defenses provide that, in some circumstances, committing a crime is the right thing to do, all things considered, such as in cases of self-defense.
5. Excuse defenses recognize that, in some circumstances, a defendant may not be completely culpable, even if he had the *mens rea* required for the crime, such as in cases of duress or insanity.

LESSON 25: NECESSITY

Imagine that Don is standing next to a trolley track at a point where the main track splits into two side tracks. There is a switch where the track splits, which is used to divert trolley cars coming down the main track onto one or the other of the side tracks. Fifty yards down the track on the right, Don observes five workmen engaged in track repairs. Fifty yards down the left track, Don observes one workman engaged in track repairs. He also observes that the switch is set to direct oncoming trolleys down the right track. Now imagine that Don sees a runaway trolley car barreling down the main track toward the junction. The car is out of control, and there is no way to stop it and no time to warn any of the workmen. Don therefore has a choice. If he does nothing, then the five workmen on the right track will die. Alternatively, if he flips the switch, directing the car down the left track, then the lone workman on that track will die. Don decides to flip the switch despite knowing that the lone workman will die as a result. As a consequence of Don's actions, the workman is hit by the trolley and dies.

Based on these facts, Don seems to be guilty of murder. Setting aside the extenuating circumstances for the moment, he does not have lawful authority to kill the lone workman. There is no reason to think that his flipping the switch was an involuntary act. But for his flipping the switch, the lone workman would not have died when or in the manner that he died. There are no intervening events between Don's flipping the switch and the workman's death that could serve to break the causal chain. Finally, Don knew that, if he flipped the switch, then the lone workman would die, which is sufficient to show malice aforethought. It therefore appears that a prosecutor would have no trouble at all meeting her burden of proof as to each element of a murder charge.

Despite the fact that all the elements of murder are present, most of us would feel uncomfortable sending Don to prison as a murderer. Although it is true that he killed one person, he also saved five people in the process. On a purely consequentialist calculus we might even say that, all things considered, he did the right thing. After all, as one notable logician famously remarked, "The needs of the many outweigh the needs of the one." Fortunately, the criminal law provides an outlet for these instincts in the form of the affirmative defense of necessity.

Although the specific elements may vary depending on the jurisdiction, the necessity defense generally provides that, if:

1. By virtue of circumstances not of the defendant's intentional or reckless creation,
2. There is an immediate, and
3. Emergent threat of harm, and
4. The defendant commits a crime

5. That is reasonably likely to prevent that harm, and
6. The harm caused by his crime is substantially less than the harm averted, and
7. There was no lawful or reasonable alternative,

   Then the defendant will be excused,

8. Unless the defense has been excluded by law.

Applying these elements, Don has good reason to hope that he will be excused. He did not create the situation. The five workmen were under immediate threat that arose as an emergency. Flipping the switch was the only way to save them. Although one person died as a result of Don's actions, five were saved. Finally, there are no legal exclusions that would prohibit a necessity defense in these circumstances.

As with all affirmative defenses, necessity raises questions about burdens of production and burdens of persuasion. Although it is characterized as an affirmative defense, necessity operates as a claim of lawful privilege. Given that most crimes include an element of unlawfulness, it usually falls on the prosecutor in the final analysis to disprove necessity. This means that a defendant may not have the final burden of persuasion but may instead only be required to provide sufficient grounds to put the issue of necessity in question. Here, jurisdictions vary.

The necessity defense implicates thorny moral and policy issues, many of which have come to the fore in the context of the war on terror. Confronted with the possibility of large-scale terrorist attacks using weapons of mass destruction, legislators, judges, policy makers, and commentators have opined at length about what should be done in the event of a "ticking time bomb." In a set of infamous memoranda issued by the Office of Legal Counsel (OLC) during the administration of George W. Bush, officials relied in part on the necessity defense to justify broader policies allowing for enhanced interrogation techniques. More recently, the basic conditions of necessity were used in a controversial OLC memorandum written by officials in the Obama administration to justify missiles launched from aerial "drones" against suspected terrorists.

What You Need to Know:

1. The criminal law offers defendants who commit crimes in order to avoid greater harm a defense based on necessity.
2. The burden of production for necessity defenses usually falls on defendants, who must offer sufficient foundation to put the issue in question.
3. Jurisdictions vary as to who has the final burden of persuasion in cases where defendants plead necessity.
4. The necessity defense has played an important role in the war on terror, where it has been used to justify policies of enhanced interrogation and remote killing of terrorist suspects.

LESSON 26: SELF-DEFENSE

On December 22, 1984, Bernard Goetz shot four teenagers on a subway train in lower Manhattan. All four survived, but Goetz was prosecuted for attempted murder. At trial, Goetz sought to justify his actions by claiming that the four young men, Troy Canby, Darryl Cabey, James Ramseur, and Barry Allen, had threatened him. His use of deadly force, he argued, was in self-defense. Goetz was acquitted.

On February 26, 2012, George Zimmerman shot and killed 17-year-old Trayvon Martin on a suburban street in Sanford, Florida. Zimmerman, who was associated with a citizen watch group, observed Martin walking in the neighborhood after dark. Suspicious, Zimmerman called the police, who advised him not to follow or confront Martin. Zimmerman ignored that advice, approached Martin, a confrontation ensued, Zimmerman shot Martin, and Martin died. Amidst nationwide controversy, Zimmerman was charged with murder and the lesser, but included, offense of manslaughter. At trial, Zimmerman claimed that Martin attacked him and that he used deadly force in self-defense. Zimmerman was acquitted.

Cases like these spark vociferous debates in law school classrooms and the public at large. The core question in these conversations is whether and when a person is justified in killing another person in self-defense. Under the common law, a person is justified in using deadly force to defend himself if:

1. He actually, and
2. Reasonably believes that such force is
3. Necessary to prevent imminent death or great bodily harm
4. To himself or another person, and
5. There is no reasonable opportunity to escape, or the defendant honestly and reasonably failed to recognize an opportunity to escape, and
6. The defendant was not the initial aggressor, and
7. The force used was reasonable and
8. Necessary to terminate the threat.

Like necessity, self-defense is an affirmative defense of justification. A defendant claiming self-defense admits that he has committed an intentional killing, but maintains that, all things considered, it was the right thing to do.

There are three predominate rationales for self-defense as an affirmative defense. The first arises from our fundamental right of self-preservation. Faced with a threat, we have a basic right to defend ourselves. The second recognizes the effects of our limbic systems on our mental processes and physical responses. The drive to survive is primal and the instinct to defend oneself is hard-wired. As Justice Oliver Wendell Holmes once wrote, "Detached reflection cannot be demanded in the presence of an uplifted knife." *Brown v. United States*, 256 U.S. 335, 343 (1921). The third rationale focuses on the aggressor. By initiating a violent confrontation, the argument goes, an attacker compromises his moral standing and renders himself subject to counterattack.

Objective reasonable person standards play an important role in self-defense claims. The law of self-defense does not require that a defendant actually be under threat of imminent death or severe bodily harm or that the force used in self-defense is actually necessary. Rather, all that is required is that a defendant reasonably believes he is under attack, and reasonably believes that his use of force is necessary. Mistakes can be forgiven, as long as they are reasonable.

Questions about reasonable perception of threat and reasonable use of force become particularly complicated when issues of race, gender, and class are implicated. For example, Bernard Goetz was a middle-aged white man when he shot his four victims, all of whom were young black males. In the wake of that incident, many wondered whether Goetz would have reacted as he did if he had been approached by four teenaged girls or four young white men. Those questions have just as much life today as they did in 1983, having come to the fore again in the wake of the Trayvon Martin shooting (Martin was black and Zimmerman is light-skinned).

If a defendant is unable to meet his burden as to one or more elements of a self-defense claim, then we say that he has failed to perfect his claim of self-defense. Where this occurs, a defendant may still be able to secure a partial defense. For example, if a defendant uses deadly force in the honest, but *unreasonable*, belief that he is under attack, then he cannot perfect his claim of self-defense. He can nevertheless seek mitigation to a lesser, but included offense, such as voluntary manslaughter.

Under the common law, deadly force is only justified as a last resort. A defendant claiming self-defense would therefore be obliged to show that he had exhausted all nonviolent means of avoiding or terminating an attack, including retreating or running away, before resorting to deadly force (under the "castle doctrine," this duty to escape generally does not apply when a defendant is attacked in his own home). This traditional requirement was modified or abandoned in many American jurisdictions, most recently by "stand your ground" laws. In these jurisdictions, there is no obligation to retreat or escape before using deadly force. Florida is among the states that have adopted stand-your-ground laws. That decision was the source of considerable nationwide controversy in the wake of the Trayvon Martin shooting when many commentators argued that Zimmerman should have retreated rather than engaging in a confrontation.

What You Need to Know:

1. The common law provides a right to use force in order to terminate threats of violence.
2. The right to use force in self-defense is limited by objective reasonableness as to the need to use force and the amount of force used.
3. Imperfect self-defense claims may provide grounds to mitigate a murder charge to voluntary manslaughter.
4. Under the common law, the right to use deadly force is justified only as a last resort if there is no opportunity to escape or terminate an attack by nonviolent means.
5. The common law duty to retreat has been modified or abandoned in many American jurisdictions by "stand-your-ground" laws.

LESSON 27: DURESS

Mary lives in a small mountain village in a region of Columbia notorious for cocaine production. The area is under the effective control of a paramilitary group designated as a terrorist organization by the United States Department of State. One day, a local commander in the group approaches Mary and asks her to smuggle a load of cocaine into the United States. Mary refuses. The commander then tells her that she can either do as he asks or he will kill her and her entire family. Given this highly credible threat, Mary agrees to smuggle the cocaine. Unfortunately, she is detected at customs, arrested, and prosecuted for attempting to import illegal narcotics, conspiracy, and providing material support to a terrorist organization.

Cases like Mary's should inspire empathy. Through no fault of her own, she was caught in a truly unfortunate circumstance. It seems, nevertheless, that she has committed the crimes with which she is charged. Fortunately, Mary may have a credible affirmative defense based on the excuse of duress.

Under the common law, duress can provide a complete defense against any crime other than murder, if the defendant:

1. Acts out of an honest and
2. Reasonable fear of
3. Immediate harm,
4. Posed by another,
5. To use unlawful force,
6. So long as the defendant is not at fault for putting himself in the situation, and
7. The nature of the threat would have overcome the will of a person of average fortitude in the defendant's circumstances.

Although duress does not offer a full defense against a charge of murder under the common law, it can provide grounds to mitigate a murder charge to voluntary manslaughter.

Based on these standards, it seems that Mary has a good argument to make for duress. Her crimes did not involve murder. She was in actual fear that, unless she smuggled the cocaine, she and her family would be killed. Given the history of the people making threats, her fear was perfectly reasonable. She had no hand in making herself vulnerable to those threats. Perhaps most importantly, it is hard to imagine that anyone could resist such a threat.

Mary is not home free, however. Courts reviewing claims of duress routinely interpret the immediacy requirement as imposing an obligation on defendants to report threats made against them to law enforcement or, alternatively, to turn themselves in to law enforcement at the first reasonable opportunity. In Mary's case, she would need to persuade the jury that she did not have a reasonable opportunity to seek the protection of law enforcement or that law enforcement could not provide sufficient protection for her or her family.

In addition to domestic law, duress is an important topic in international criminal law. Particularly in the context of war crimes, genocide, and other mass atrocities, it is routine for perpetrators to recruit others into their violent campaigns using threats of "kill or be killed." Many child soldiers are recruited by such means and then directed to participate in the killing of innocent civilians.

In recent years, several defendants facing criminal charges in international tribunals have raised duress as a defense. Among them is Drazen Erdemovic, who was a soldier in a unit of the Bosnian Serb Army responsible for the massacre of several hundred civilians at Srebenica in 1995. Asked to consider his duress claim, a majority of the Appellate Chamber of the International Criminal Courts for the former Yugoslavia and Rwanda held that "duress does not afford a complete defence to a soldier charged with a crime against humanity and/or a war crime involving the killing of innocent human beings." *Prosecutor v. Erdomevic*, Case No. IT–96–22, para. 19 (7 October, 1997).

The Appeals Chamber in *Erdomevic* did not have occasion to consider whether a civilian faced with the threat of "kill or be killed" could claim a defense based on duress. Article 31 of the Rome Statute of the International Criminal Court (ICC), which was adopted in 1998 and went into force in 2002, states that duress can be used as a defense in cases before the ICC. The ICC Statute makes no mention, however, of any limitations in cases of murder. This suggests that, in principle, at least, duress may be available as a full defense against a charge of murder under international law in some circumstances.

What You Need to Know:

1. Under common law, duress can provide a defense against any charge other than murder.
2. Although duress cannot provide a complete defense to murder, it can mitigate a murder charge to manslaughter.
3. Like necessity and self-defense, duress requires that a defendant be under immediate threat and have no reasonable, lawful alternatives.

4. Duress is a significant issue in international criminal law, particularly in the context of war crimes, genocide, and crimes against humanity.

LESSON 28: INTOXICATION

Bob and Jane are at a bar one night having a few drinks with friends. At some point in the evening, after his fourth cocktail, Bob makes an off-color remark about Jane. Jane rightly takes offense and immediately leaves. The next day, Bob calls Jane and explains that he was "just drunk" and that it was "the booze talking," not him. Should Jane excuse Bob and hold him blameless for his behavior? Would you?

Most people in Jane's situation might cut Bob a little slack, but would still hold him responsible for his conduct. After all, the effects of alcohol on judgment and self-control are well known. Despite being aware of these facts, Bob decided to drink, and therefore should be held responsible for his conduct. Moreover, his claim that it was the alcohol talking, not him, is simply inaccurate. Intoxication may affect perceptions and inhibitions, but does not—except in extreme cases—alter character or leave people completely incapable of controlling their conduct. So, although it may be true that Bob would not have said what he said if he had been sober, we would not blame Jane in the slightest if she held him responsible.

The common law follows these general instincts in cases where a defendant commits a crime under the influence of alcohol or some other intoxicating substance. Except in extreme cases, such as where the defendant is so intoxicated that he suffers permanent neurological consequences, voluntary intoxication will not provide an excuse if the crime charged does not require a high level of *mens rea* such as sophisticated planning. If the crime charged requires a high level of *mens rea*, and the defendant's intoxication renders him incapable of forming that *mens rea*, then voluntary intoxication may provide a partial excuse, mitigating the defendant's crime to a lesser but included offense. For example, if a prosecutor charges first-degree murder against a defendant who was intoxicated when he committed his crime, and first-degree murder requires cold, calculated premeditation, then the defendant may have grounds to argue that he should be convicted of second-degree murder instead.

Now consider a slightly different version of our Bob and Jane story, this time with Ron and Amy. Ron doesn't drink alcohol—at least not anymore. He had some bad experiences back in college. Out with friends at a bar one night, Ron is drinking nothing but ginger ale. Having heard stories about his past drunken antics, Ron's friends decide to spike his ginger ale with a colorless, flavorless liquor. None the wiser, Ron drinks four glasses and is soon quite drunk. In his inebriated state he insults Amy. Chagrined, Ron's friends admit what they have done. When Ron calls the next day and explains everything to Amy, should she be more forgiving than Jane was of Bob?

Most people in Amy's situation would be willing to cut Ron more slack than Jane cut for Bob, but would still reserve some blame for Ron. Again, the effects of alcohol are the key. Ron's inhibitions were affected, but he was still capable of forming thoughts and expressing those thoughts out loud. Since that is the conduct that hurt Amy, she probably will not find too much solace in knowing that Ron would have kept his insulting thoughts to himself if his friends had not slipped him the mickey.

Here again, the law traces our basic moral instincts. Involuntary intoxication will not provide a defense under the common law unless the defendant is so intoxicated that he cannot form the requisite *mens rea* for the crime charged or is so profound so as to cause temporary insanity. The common law is therefore slightly more forgiving of involuntary intoxication than it is of voluntary intoxication because the potential excuse is not limited to cases where the crime charged entails a high level of *mens rea*. That makes good moral sense. After all, a defendant who is involuntarily intoxicated is not responsible for his intoxication, so we cannot carry forward any claim of responsibility derived from his decision to drink. On the other hand, he did the deed, so may not be entitled to a complete excuse.

What You Need to Know:

1. The common law provides very limited excuses based on intoxication.
2. Voluntary intoxication will not provide any excuse if a defendant is charged with a crime that does not require a high level of *mens rea* unless his level of intoxication is so profound that it renders him incapable of voluntary action and results in permanent neurological damage.
3. Voluntary intoxication can provide a partial excuse in some cases if the defendant is charged with a crime that requires a high level of *mens rea*, his intoxication makes it impossible for him to form the required intent, and there is a lesser, but included, crime for which he can be charged.
4. The common law is slightly more forgiving of defendants who commit crimes in states of involuntary intoxication, providing an excuse in any case where the defendant's intoxication renders him incapable of forming the requisite *mens rea* for the crime charged.

LESSON 29: MENTAL ILLNESS AND THE INSANITY DEFENSE

Mental disease plays a prominent role in the criminal-justice system at almost every level. According to a 2006 study by the Bureau of Justice Statistics, over half of the inmates housed in United States prisons and jails suffer from some form of mental illness. Depression is by far the most common. In addition, three-quarters of prisoners have substance abuse problems. Pointing to the fact that many mentally ill prisoners are incarcerated for relatively minor crimes, reform advocates argue that some of the public resources committed to criminal law enforcement would be more effective if allocated to public health programs focusing on mental health and substance abuse.

Public policy relating to mental health, addiction, and law enforcement priorities raise serious and important questions that any student of the criminal law should keep in mind. In addition to these general, policy-level concerns, there are at least four occasions when a defendant might raise the issue of mental disease or disorder during the course of his individual engagement with the criminal-justice system.

First, mental disease may delay, perhaps indefinitely, a criminal prosecution. If, by virtue of mental disease or disorder, a defendant is not capable of understanding the nature of a criminal proceeding, or is not able to provide effective assistance to his attorney, then he cannot stand trial. *See Dusky v. United States*, 362 U.S. 402 (1960). It is unlikely that a defendant in this circumstance would be released, however. Rather, he would remain in state custody, likely in a mental health facility, until such time that he is able to stand trial.

Second, the Eighth Amendment to the United States Constitution bars the execution of any inmate who, by virtue of mental disease or disorder, is unable to understand the nature of or reasons for his punishment. *See Ford v. Wainwright*, 477 U.S. 399 (1966). Here again, insanity serves as a delay, not a permanent bar. A convict in this circumstance would remain in prison. In the event his mental health was restored, he would be eligible for execution.

Third, a convict who suffers from mental illness may have access to special services or facilities while incarcerated. Eligibility and availability of these services varies greatly between jurisdictions.

Fourth, mental illness may provide grounds for an affirmative defense based on insanity. Insanity is an excuse defense, which, if successful, leads to complete exoneration. This does not mean that a defendant who successfully argues insanity as a defense will be released immediately. Rather, most successful insanity defenses lead to indefinite civil incarceration until such time that the defendant no longer poses a danger to himself or others. Because civil incarceration is indefinite, and tied to risk assessment, it is not at all uncommon for defendants who successfully plead insanity defenses to spend more time incarcerated in a mental health facility than they would have spent in prison had they been convicted.

Like other affirmative excuse defenses, insanity has elements. Under the common law, a defendant will be excused if,

1. At the time of his offense,
2. He was laboring under a defect of reason,
3. Caused by a mental disease or disorder,
4. That rendered him unable to understand the nature of his conduct or to distinguish between right and wrong.

These elements trace directly to the famous *M'Naughten's Case*, decided by the English House of Lords in 1843.

The fourth element of the M'Naughten test contemplates two effects that a mental disease may have on a defendant's culpability. First, mental disease may affect a defendant's capacity to appreciate reality. The classic example used in most law school classrooms is a defendant who suffers from severe hallucinations that cause him to believe that he is squeezing a lemon when, in fact, he is strangling his wife. Second, mental disease may affect a defendant's ability to appreciate the illegality of his conduct. For example, a defendant may have compelling command hallucinations that tell him to kill his victim because his victim is trying to kill him. A defendant suffering from these kinds of hallucinations would believe that he is killing in self-defense when, in fact, he is not. These cases should be distinguished from those where a defendant's mental disease inclines him to believe in an idiosyncratic view of right and wrong such that he knows his conduct is against the law, but acts on the basis of his commitment to a "higher" law. Courts almost universally reject claims of insanity in these circumstances.

The M'Naughten test focuses on the effects that mental disease can have on cognition. Some jurisdictions, inspired by § 4.01(1) of the Model Penal Code, have expanded the scope of the insanity defense beyond *M'Naughten* to encompass cases in which a defendant's mental disease or disorder renders him incapable of conforming his conduct to the requirements of the law by resisting his criminal impulses or desires. This volitional approach is controversial, and remains by far the minority rule. The principal concern cited by courts and legislatures is that it is often hard for professionals, much less juries, to distinguish between an irresistible impulse or desire and an impulse or desire that has not been resisted. *See, e.g.*, *United States v. Lyons*, 731 F.2d 243 (1984).

The insanity defense came under considerable scrutiny in the wake of the attempted assassination of Ronald Reagan by John Hinckley, Jr., on March 30, 1981. Hinckley, who had a long history of psychosis, was found not guilty by reason of insanity. Subsequent public outcry led legislatures and courts to adopt stricter approaches to and interpretations of insanity as an affirmative defense. In partial response to that backlash, courts and legislatures have begun to allow juries to return verdicts of "guilty, but mentally ill." A defendant who is adjudicated guilty, but mentally ill, is guilty, but may qualify for special treatment or other consideration while incarcerated.

What You Need to Know:

1. Mental illness plays a prominent role in the criminal-justice system, with more than half of all inmates in U.S. prisons and jails suffering from some form of mental illness.
2. Mental illness may provide grounds for excuse based on the affirmative defense of insanity.
3. The predominate standard for the insanity defense is the M'Naughten rule, which focuses on the cognitive effects of mental disease on a defendant's ability to appreciate the nature of his conduct or the illegality of his conduct.
4. Some jurisdictions extend the insanity defense to volitional disorders that affect a defendant's ability to resist his impulses or desires.
5. Successful insanity defenses do not result in immediate release but, rather, lead to indefinite terms of civil incarceration in mental health facilities.

CHAPTER 4

TORTS

LESSON 1: INTRODUCTION

When most beginning law students receive their class schedule for the first semester, they probably have some notion about what will be covered in Criminal Law, Contracts, and Civil Procedure. However, when they see they are scheduled for a course entitled "Torts," their response is likely to be "What's that?" The word "torts" is not self-defining. For our purposes, it is not an Austrian pastry, although both "torts" and "torte" share a common Latin root—*tortus*, meaning twisted. As you study tort law, from time to time you will find that derivation appropriate!

Perhaps you've had a little more exposure to the law and understand that "Torts" covers the question of whether someone whose person or property has been injured in an accident should be compensated by the party that "caused" (whatever that may mean—stay tuned!) the accident. As the semester continues, you will come to understand that Torts covers everything from an auto accident to global climate change litigation; from a slip-and-fall in the grocery store to punitive damage claims against tobacco manufacturers. Tort principles also underlie many of the topics you will consider in your advanced courses in law school. For example, the tort of nuisance played an important role in the development of environmental law, and the tort of misrepresentation lies at the heart of modern law governing corporate securities.

When nonlegally educated people talk about accidents and say that someone "caused" the accident, they usually mean that that person was "at fault" as well. In torts, however, **the distinction between "cause" and "fault" is critical**.

> Assume that Amanda just purchased a brand-new luxury sedan. As she drove down the street immediately after leaving the dealership, she pushed her foot on the brake pedal to stop her new car in the

> usual manner. However, on this occasion, nothing happened and Amanda failed to stop at the red light. Unfortunately, one of her law professors was driving his eight-year-old compact economy car on the intersecting road. He had a green light, but Amanda's sedan collided with his car, severely damaging it.

Were Amanda's actions a "cause" of the accident? Was she at fault?

> Dr. Kayla Klein, an oncologist, treated her new patient Zachary for a severe and, until very recently, incurable form of leukemia. She was able to offer Zachary a new drug that clinical trials had shown results in an instantaneous cure for leukemia without any side effects or any possibility of remission in 999 cases out of 1,000. In the one-thousandth case, however, the drug results in agonizing side effects that always result in a prolonged, horrible, painful death. Dr. Klein fully and accurately explained the possible outcomes to Zachary, and he decided to take the drug. Unfortunately, he was the unlucky one and died after experiencing excruciating suffering.

Were Dr. Klein's actions a "cause" of Zachary's death? Was she at fault?

If, in each example, you identified Amanda or Dr. Klein's actions as a "cause" of the accident, but concluded that neither was "at fault," you are already thinking like a torts lawyer! In torts, when we use the term "cause," we mean nothing more than the defendant (here, Amanda or Dr. Klein) is a necessary factual antecedent of the harm experienced by the plaintiff (the victim who files suit) and is closely enough connected to the harm that a court might decide to hold the defendant (the party sued) financially responsible ("liable") for the harm. "Fault," on the other hand, usually refers to "negligent" or "intentional" conduct.

Perhaps the most important issue that you will explore in your Torts course is the distinction between when the plaintiff must prove either intentional conduct or negligence on the part of the defendant in order to recover and when the plaintiff will be able to recover on a strict liability basis without a showing of fault. Most of the specific, individually defined torts (theories of recovery) that you will study will be classified as belonging to one of **three basic categories of torts: intentional torts**, **negligent torts**, and **strict liability torts**, depending on how egregious the defendant's conduct must be in order to justify recovery.

Not all Torts courses follow the same sequence. We encourage you to begin by reading Lessons 1–4 that cover some basic concepts in Torts. It is most likely that, perhaps after an introductory chapter, you will begin your study of torts with intentional torts. If so, proceed directly to Lessons 5–7. However, if your professor begins with negligent torts, we encourage you to defer reading Lessons 5–7 until later and instead begin with Lessons 8–21. Finally, a few courses (including the one I teach) begin with traditional strict liability torts. If you are a student in one of those courses, after the introductory material, proceed to Lessons 21–26.

What You Need to Know:

1. Torts can best be defined as the body of law that determines when the costs of an accident should be shifted from the party that originally sustained the loss to the party who "caused" the harm.
2. Cause and fault mean two different things. A cause in tort law is a necessary factual antecedent closely enough connected to plaintiff's harm for the court to consider imposing liability. Fault is usually either intentional conduct or negligence.
3. Most individual torts are classified according to how culpable the defendant must be in order for the plaintiff to recover. We will study intentional torts, negligence, and strict liability torts.

LESSON 2: OBJECTIVES OF TORT LAW

What are the purposes and objectives of tort law? Torts scholars and judges often disagree. Most laypersons probably believe that someone who has caused injury (the "tortfeasor") to the victim should pay when the tortfeasor's conduct was wrongful and caused the victim's harm: "She was wrong. I'm worse off. She should pay." This idea lies at the heart of the **corrective justice** and **civil recourse** theories of tort law. Although these two conceptions of tort liability differ modestly, these distinctions should not worry you during the first few weeks of law school—unless, of course, your professor is a strong proponent of one theory or the other! The basic idea is that doing wrong to another and injuring him creates a moral or ethical disequilibrium that requires the tortfeasor to pay damages to the victim in order to restore the *status quo ante.* The origins of the corrective justice and civil recourse theories lie in moral philosophy.

The other major conception of tort law is generally referred to as the **instrumental approach**, a form of what philosophers call **consequentialism**, played out in the tort arena. This approach identifies the objectives of tort law as reflecting the consequences of tort law on society and the economy. The leading instrumental approach to tort law is **law and economics**, which treats economic self-interest and rationality as the motivating principles of human behavior.

Two instrumental objectives in tort law are most important: loss distribution and loss minimization. It is often said that "**compensation**" is an objective of tort law. However, compensating the tort victim for his loss does not make the loss go away, it simply shifts it to another party. Because the costs of litigating tort claims (in this context, "transaction costs") are substantial, the traditional view has been that financial responsibility for a loss should not be shifted from one party to another without good reason. For example, most studies show that of every one dollar spent on liability insurance premiums, victims of accidents receive only approximately forty cents. The rest is spent on fees for attorneys and expert witnesses, court costs, and the operating expenses and profits of insurance companies.

Most often tortfeasors who are worth suing are either insured or are businesses. Insurance companies have the ability to spread or distribute losses to other insured parties who pay premiums, and businesses distribute losses to their customers through modest increases in the price for goods and services. The theory behind the ***loss distribution*** objective of tort law is that it is less disruptive to society when numerous policyholders or customers pay a tiny amount than it is when an accident victim must pay all the costs resulting from his accident.

The second of the instrumental objectives of tort law is ***loss minimization*** or, if you prefer, **deterrence** or **regulation** of an activity likely to cause harm. The basic idea is that if a tortfeasor must pay for the damages it causes as a result of harm-producing activity, it will either conduct its activities more carefully or will reduce or stop its harm-producing activities.

Deterrence of harm-producing activity obviously is also a goal of administrative regulation and the criminal-justice system. Why then do we need the loss minimization function of tort law? For one thing, busy prosecutors and regulators often lack sufficient resources to prosecute many examples of conduct likely to produce harm. In other instances, regulated interests have cozy relationships with administrative regulators that inhibit effective regulation.

The corrective justice/civil recourse and instrumental theories of tort law are not mutually exclusive. Judges probably simultaneously consider both sets of objectives in torts cases, often without realizing it.

In many cases you will study, the corrective justice and instrumental approaches to tort law will be in tension with each other. Assume, for example, that Dave's Dynamite Co. is in the demolition business. Dave's demolition efforts damage Michael's mansion two blocks away. Dave's employees did everything they were supposed to do and therefore they were not at fault. Should Dave's Dynamite be liable to Michael? Corrective justice principles arguably suggest that it should not be, because Dave's employees have acted without fault. However, Dave's Dynamite is the party better able to distribute the costs of the accident through either the purchase of insurance or modest increases in the prices it charges for demolition services. Further, if Dave's Dynamite is forced to pay for damages to Michael's mansion, it might minimize future losses by stopping the use of dynamite near residential areas or even switching to a different business entirely, such as selling supplemental study guides to beginning law students! In short, the instrumental approach to tort law might argue in favor of liability even when the corrective justice/civil recourse perspectives do not.

Historically and traditionally, tort law also served other functions. For example, the ability to seek compensation for injuries through tort litigation served as a substitute for retaliatory violence. Second, judicial decisions in tort cases helped establish norms for what society regarded as acceptable conduct.

What You Need to Know:

1. The corrective justice and civil recourse objectives of tort law suggest that a person whose wrongful conduct injures another is ethically obligated to compensate the victim for his loss.
2. The instrumental approach to tort law focuses on loss distribution and loss minimization. Law and economics is the most important instrumental approach.
3. Loss distribution as a goal of tort law, whether accomplished through insurance or an increase in the prices charged by a business causing the harm, assumes that having many people pay a little bit for the victim's losses causes less disruption to society than having the victim alone pay all the costs resulting from her accidental injury.
4. Loss minimization reflects the idea that a defendant's obligation to pay tort judgments provides an incentive to avoid harm-producing activity in the future.

LESSON 3: THE HISTORY OF THE COMMON LAW AND THE DEVELOPMENT OF NEGLIGENCE

Most tort law is **state law**. It is also predominantly **judge-made or "common law."** In some jurisdictions, appellate court judges are elected; in others, they are appointed.

Regardless, the legitimacy of the exercise of power by common-law judges does not rest on electoral accountability. Even if elected, judges are prohibited from making campaign promises such as "I promise always to favor injured plaintiffs and to rule against corporations." Instead, **the legitimacy of common-law decisions** rests on the idea that courts will honor the rules established by their own prior decisions, or "**precedents**," as well as those decided by higher courts in the same jurisdiction. Following precedents assures at least a certain degree of consistency and fairness among litigants. This legal principle is known as ***stare decisis***.

If a court departs from one of its prior precedents, it usually justifies the overruling by explaining its reasons—a process that sometimes is referred to as "**reasoned elaboration**." However, more often than overruling a precedent that would lead to a seemingly unfair outcome in a particular case, the court "**distinguishes**" the unwelcome **precedent** by explaining how the legally relevant facts of the instant case differ from those of the precedent, thus justifying a different result.

If common-law courts in the United States begin their decision-making processes by considering precedents, what did they do when our country first became independent from the United Kingdom and there were no American precedents? Bizarrely enough, most state constitutions of the original 13 states expressly adopted "the common law of England as it existed on July 4, 1776" (thus giving new meaning to the term "revolution"!). Accordingly, you may study **old English precedents** in Torts. Further, American courts often regard the **decisions of the courts of England and other British Commonwealth countries, even after our independence, as "persuasive authorities."** Although persuasive authorities are not binding on an American court, they may influence the court's reasoning in the same way that a New York appellate court might regard the reasoning of decisions of the Supreme Court of California as persuasive.

In order to recover in merry olde England, the attorney for the victim of a tort needed to plead and prove facts that fit within any one of a limited number of existing ***writs***. Each writ carried with it not only its own body of substantive law, but also its own distinctive process and procedure. If the victim's lawyer chose the wrong writ, unlike in modern times, the plaintiff's case was dismissed "with prejudice," meaning the plaintiff was unable to file under a different and presumably correct writ. Think of the legal malpractice implications!

For purposes of what we now call tort law, the two most important writs were "**trespass**" and "**trespass on the case**," sometimes abbreviated as "on the case" or even "case." The distinction between the two was that to qualify for the writ of **trespass,** the plaintiff's harm was required to be the "**immediate**" or "**direct**" result of defendant's conduct, while liability for **trespass on the case** would lie for **indirect and consequential harms.** For example, on one hand, if the defendant threw a log onto a highway and it hit the driver of a carriage on the head, the action would be one "sounding in" trespass. On the other hand, if the log fell onto the roadway and sometime later, the plaintiff's horse that was drawing a carriage tripped, overturned the carriage, and threw the plaintiff to the ground, the proper writ for this indirect sequence of events would be trespass on the case.

In the **earliest English personal injury cases, the plaintiff was not required to plead and prove that the defendant's conduct which caused the plaintiff's harm was intentional or negligent, or that the defendant was otherwise at fault**. Instead, the gist of the action in trespass was that defendant's action directly produced the injury.

In the casebooks that some of you will be studying, you will carefully trace a series of old English cases (decided during the period extending from the seventeenth century through the early nineteenth century). In each case, the defendant argued that he was "utterly without fault"—language originating in *Weaver v. Ward*, [1616] Hobart 134, 80 Eng. Rep. 284 (Eng.), where the court suggested that the defendant would not be liable under such circumstances. However, each time the defendant raised the "not my fault" defense, he lost—almost always on procedural grounds, thus theoretically leaving open the possibility of a defense based on the defendant's total lack of fault.

Finally, during the **mid-nineteenth century** (1812–1871), in a series of cases of which *Brown v. Kendall*, 60 Mass. 292, 6 Cush 292 (1850), is the most famous, **American courts began to require that the plaintiff prove that the defendant acted with fault**—*at least* **negligence**—in order to recover. These same decisions required the plaintiff to prove that he acted without fault or contributory negligence on his own part. In other words, the pre-existing law—under which a plaintiff was not required to prove that the defendant acted with fault—was turned upside down.

Why this dramatic change in the law of torts during the mid-nineteenth century? It is important to remember that **accidental injuries were relatively few and far between until the mid-nineteenth century advent of railroads and other new activities that characterized the Industrial Revolution**. Most states rarely, if ever, had more than two or three torts claims filed per year. One explanation of the change from the no-fault standard of the English common law to the requirement of negligence is that without such a change, emerging industries and railroads would have paid enormous damages to workers and consumers, rendering them unprofitable. In effect, **the change from a no-fault standard of liability to a negligence regime avoided breaking the backs of newly emerging industries**. An alternative but not mutually exclusive explanation for the emergence of negligence is that the **change from no-fault liability to negligence law echoed a new focus on *moral wrongdoing*** that occurred simultaneously in both philosophy and American culture during the first half of the nineteenth century. In any event, by 1870, American tort law required negligence (or intent) in most—but not all—cases.

What You Need to Know:

1. The legitimacy of common-law decisions rests on the idea that courts should presumptively follow the reasoning of precedents or past decisions.

2. The American colonies adopted the common law of England at the time they declared their independence from the United Kingdom. American courts continue to regard decisions of the courts of

the United Kingdom and other common-law British Commonwealth countries as persuasive.

3. Until the mid-nineteenth century, a plaintiff could recover without showing that the defendant had been negligent or otherwise at fault. At that time, state courts adopted a series of decisions requiring plaintiffs to prove negligence or intent in order to recover.

LESSON 4: SOURCES OF COMPENSATION: VICARIOUS LIABILITY AND INSURANCE

Because the objective of most tort actions is the recovery of damages, uninsured individuals without substantial assets are rarely, if ever, defendants in tort actions, even if their actions were extremely egregious and caused considerable harm. Instead, defendants in tort actions are usually either individuals or corporations that are insured, or corporations or other business entities that are vicariously liable for the harm caused by their employees. **Vicarious liability is the idea that one party will be held liable for torts committed by another.**

Liability of the employer. With the exception of claims arising from automobile accidents, a high percentage of tort claims involve vicarious liability. When an employee of a corporation or other business commits a tort while working within "**the scope of employment**," the employer as well as the employee is liable—even if the employer's supervisors did nothing wrong, under the doctrine of "***respondeat superior***." Often this concept is expressed using the antiquated language that "**the master**" (the employer) must answer for the torts of his "**servant**" (the employee).

Traditionally, the question of whether the acts of the employee were within the scope of employment was determined by **whether the acts of the employee were intended to profit or benefit the employer**. In recent decades, however, many **courts have expanded the scope of vicarious liability**. Holding the employer liable provides a source of funds to compensate the plaintiff because the employer can either obtain insurance or pass the costs of the accidents on to its customers by charging slightly higher prices (loss distribution). In addition, employers are arguably in a better position to prevent similar accidents in the future than are the employees themselves (loss minimization). Some courts now provide that employers will be held vicariously liable for **losses resulting from risks that are typical of the kinds of enterprises undertaken by the employer**. For example, if an employee drinks too much at an employer-sponsored party and causes an automobile accident after he leaves the celebration in an inebriated state, the employer likely would be held vicariously liable.

Liability for torts committed by independent contractors. Sometimes the person doing work for a business is an **independent contractor** instead of an employee. In this case, **usually the business will not be held vicariously liable**. Obviously, the important question is whether the tortfeasor is an employee or an independent contractor. On one hand, **a servant or employee** is someone hired by an employer to perform services and who is **subject to the right of physical control by the employer**. On the other hand, **an independent contractor is someone hired to accomplish a task or to achieve a result, but who is not subject to the right of control** by the employer. Certain factors sometimes assist courts in distinguishing employees from independent contractors. Employees typically work for one employer, while independent contractors work for many employers. Further, independent contractors are more likely than employees to be specialized and possess expertise in completing their work.

However, even those who hire independent contractors sometimes can be held liable for the damage they cause. For example, if a homeowner hiring a plumber fails to exercise reasonable care in selecting the plumber, she may be found to be **negligent** in her own right **in selecting an incompetent independent contractor**. If the negligently chosen plumber screws up, causing a leak in a water line that floods the basements of the neighbors, the neighbors probably can successfully sue the homeowner for her negligence in selecting the plumber.

Further, courts regard some duties as **"nondelegable" duties**. If, for example, Caustic Chemicals, Inc. hires Joe Schmo to haul away its toxic wastes and Joe negligently disposes of the wastes in an unreasonably unsafe manner, Caustic Chemicals will be vicariously liable for Joe's negligence despite the fact that Joe is an independent contractor. A party cannot avoid liability by hiring an independent contractor when the task to be performed is regarded as "**inherently dangerous**." Similarly, the owner of **premises open to the public**, such as a retail store, remains liable for damages caused by negligently conducted repairs, even if the store owner had hired an independent contractor to perform the repairs.

Insurance. When a tort is committed by an individual who is not acting within the scope of her employment, the damages are often paid by her liability insurer. Liability insurance pays damages to someone injured as a result of the tortious (usually accidental) conduct of the insured party. For example, all states require that automobile owners purchase a minimal level of liability insurance coverage.

Under the terms of the **insurance contract**, known as a "policy," **the insurer is obligated to pay damages arising from a covered claim up to the contracted-for limits of the policy**, for example, $50,000. In addition, the **insurer is obligated to provide** the insured party **with an attorney** to defend the claim. In most jurisdictions, neither the plaintiff nor the defendant is allowed to tell the jurors (or even hint to them) that the defendant is insured.

Corporations and other businesses also purchase insurance. The prevalence of insurance often is credited (or blamed) as a major factor that led courts to expand the circumstances under which defendants could be held liable during the second half of the twentieth century.

What You Need to Know:

1. Almost always, damages recovered by plaintiffs in tort actions are paid for by either the employer of

the person who actually caused the harm or the tortfeasor's insurance company.

2. An employer is held vicariously liable for torts committed by an employee within the scope of his employment. Traditionally, the act of an employee was regarded as within the scope of employment when it was intended to benefit or profit the employer. More recently, some courts have expanded the notion of vicarious liability, often by holding the employer liable for damages caused by risks typical of the enterprise in which the employer is engaged.

3. Those who hire independent contractors usually are not vicariously liable for the torts they commit. Independent contractors are hired to accomplish a specific task, but the person retaining them does not have a right of physical control over how they accomplish that task.

4. Those who hire independent contractors are held liable when they negligently select the contractor. In addition, they may be held vicariously liable if they hire an independent contractor to perform a "nondelegable duty."

5. Insurers are often obligated to pay the damages tortiously caused by their insureds that are covered under the contract (policy) between the parties. Insurers also provide legal representation to defend against a covered claim.

LESSON 5: BATTERY AND INTENT

Most tort courses begin with intentional torts to the person, usually including battery, assault, intentional infliction of emotion distress, and false imprisonment. The most common intentional tort is a prototypical battery: a punch in the nose. However, you almost certainly will spend your time studying the unusual intentional tort cases, the ones that test the limits of the definitions of battery and other intentional torts. The law governing intentional torts arguably is more dependent on the application of rule-like doctrines than is the law governing either negligent or strict liability torts. You probably will practice both working from specific cases to formulate rules and definitions governing liability for intentional torts (inductive reasoning) and applying these general rules and definitions to sometimes bizarre hypothetical fact patterns, as well as case opinions presenting varied fact patterns (deductive reasoning).

Courts and professors use a variety of definitions of battery and, of course, you should use whatever definition your professor prefers. A logical starting point, however, is to say that someone will be held liable for **battery** when she **(1) causes unconsented to, harmful, or offensive contact with the person of another (2) with the intent to cause either (a) such bodily contact or (b) the apprehension of such contact**.

To cause contact with another person requires that the defendant's act must be **voluntary**. It is perhaps easiest to explain a voluntary act by explaining what it is not. If a strong person seizes your hand and forces it to strike against the shoulder of the victim and the victim sues you for battery, you will not be liable. Your act in striking the victim was not voluntary. Similarly, if the defendant is in the midst of a seizure and cannot control her muscular movements and she strikes the victim, her actions are not voluntary and she will not be liable.

For battery, the defendant must cause "unconsented to," harmful or offensive bodily contact. You already know what harmful is: **harmful** is something that causes injury, physical impairment, pain, or illness. However, what does offensive mean? **Offensive contact** is contact that a person of ordinary sensibilities would not consent to. It is the "unconsented to" kiss or the pervert's grope on the bus or the subway. Again, whether something is offensive depends upon an objective standard—whether the person of ordinary sensibilities would consent to the contact, not whether the particular victim would. For example, if Victoria Victim has an aversion to being touched, and Annie Aggressive incidentally and lightly brushes against her in a crowded subway car, Victoria probably will not be able to recover from Annie for battery.

Even if the defendant causes bodily contact with the plaintiff that is harmful or aggressive, the plaintiff still must prove that he **did not consent** to the contact. For example, if Cody agrees to box against a former world heavyweight boxing champ for a single round as part of a Las Vegas casino act, he cannot later sue the boxing champ claiming battery because of the harmful contact. Further, (and this hypothetical may cause this book to lose its PG rating), if Adam is a masochist and consents to engage in sexual activities that most of us would not engage in, that may be offensive, but it is not "unconsented to," there is no liability for battery. Properly speaking, most courts regard the lack of consent as an element of the battery that must be proved by the plaintiff. However, in practice many courts handle consent as an affirmative defense that must be proved by the defendant.

The harmful or offensive bodily **contact** must be **with the person of the victim or with something closely connected to her**, such as a purse or wallet, a piece of clothing, or an umbrella. The plaintiff need not know that the battery is taking place. For example, imagine that a surgeon proceeds to unnecessarily touch his patients in inappropriate places while they are under the effect of anesthetics. Even if one of the patients does not realize this is happening at the time, she can still recover for battery.

The contact **need not be direct contact** between the body of the victim and the defendant. The defendant who throws a snowball or a rock or fires a bullet at the plaintiff may be liable for battery.

Battery and all other intentional torts require the plaintiff to prove that the defendant acted with intent. However, courts disagree on what it is that the defendant must intend in order to be found liable. Must the defendant intend only to cause the contact that the plaintiff finds offensive or harmful (the "single-intent rule"), or must the defendant intend the offensive or harmful nature of the contact, as well as the contact itself (the "double-intent" rule)? There is judicial authority subscribing to each of these two positions.

Intent can be proved in either of two ways. First, as one would expect, the defendant acts with intent when she acts with a **purpose or a subjective desire** to cause the harmful or offensive bodily contact. The second way to prove intent is subtler. If the defendant acts "**with knowledge to a substantial certainty**" that the bodily contact will occur, this satisfies the intent requirement. For example, assume that smokestacks at the defendant's factory emit particulates that the wind carries onto the properties of downwind landowners. The landowners complain to the factory owner, but she does nothing and the factory's emissions continue to cause respiratory and other illness and damages to the aluminum siding of the property owners. The factory owner knows to a substantial certainty that the particulates are causing harmful or offensive contact with those who live on nearby plots, and therefore the defendant has acted intentionally.

In your torts class, you may study one other aspect of intent—the doctrine of **transferred intent**. Let's assume that Dylan and Ryan are high school students and rivals for the attentions of Ashley. In our first hypothetical example, Dylan throws a punch, intending to strike Ryan, but instead hits Ashley. When Ashley sues Dylan for battery, Dylan's response is "I did not intent to commit any intentional tort on Ashley. I had no intent to strike her. Indeed, when it comes to Ashley, I would rather make love than make war." Will Dylan's argument prevail? No. Although Dylan had no intent to strike Ashley, he did intend to strike Ryan. His intent to strike Ryan "transfers," and, when coupled with the harmful contact he caused Ashley, completes the tort of battery. In a second example, assume that Dylan shoots a gun at Ryan, intending to miss him but to scare the heck out of him. However, Dylan is stoned and he hits Ryan instead of missing him. Again, Dylan might argue that he did not intend to strike Ryan. However, he will be liable for the tort of battery, because the intent to commit one tort on the victim (here, assault—to scare Ryan) suffices to establish the required intent element of a different intentional tort, battery. In our third and final hypothetical, we combine "the different victim" and "the different tort" situations. If Dylan intends to scare Ryan, but hits Ashley, his intent to commit an assault on Ryan will transfer to complete the tort of battery on Ashley.

In order to recover for battery and the other intentional torts causing harm to persons, the victim, unlike with negligent and strict liability torts, **is not required** to prove that he suffered **actual harm**. Battery protects the victim from violation of her or his bodily integrity. In the absence of actual damages, the plaintiff can recover so called **"nominal" damages**, a minimal amount of damages that nevertheless recognizes violations of the plaintiff's rights. Of course, the plaintiff also can recover **compensatory damages**, including damages for emotional distress. Finally, because intentional torts often involve an intent to injure or malice, the plaintiff in an intentional tort case often is able to recover **punitive damages**.

What You Need to Know:

1. To recover for battery, the plaintiff must prove that the defendant (a) caused unconsented to, harmful, or offensive bodily contact with the person of another with (b) the intent to cause either such harmful or offensive bodily contact or the apprehension of such contact.
2. Offensive bodily contact is contact that a person of ordinary sensibility would not consent to.
3. Intent can be shown by proving either (a) purpose or (b) knowledge to a substantial certainty.
4. The plaintiff need not prove actual harm in order to establish liability for an intentional tort.

LESSON 6: DEFENSES TO INTENTIONAL TORTS

In the next lesson (Lesson 7), we will consider three additional intentional torts involving personal harm. First, however, we turn our attention to affirmative defenses to intentional torts, also known as privileges or justifications. Obviously, the defendant will prevail if the plaintiff fails to prove any of the elements of battery—for example, that the defendant did not act with intent. Also remember that even though the lack of consent is technically regarded as an element of battery, many courts handle it as an affirmative defense that the defendant must raise and prove.

The most important of the affirmative defenses is **self-defense**. The general rule is that the defendant may use ***reasonable*** **force** to defend herself against bodily harm or offensive contact that she ***reasonably*** **believes is necessary** to prevent her from being intentionally harmed. However, the defendant may use **deadly force** only if she has a ***reasonable*** **belief** that **force sufficient to cause serious bodily injury or death** is about to be inflicted upon her.

Note the number of times that the word "reasonable" or one of its variants appears in the previous paragraph. Torts professors often say that the most interesting issues in intentional torts arise in the context of privileges. Consider the facts of a famous case, *Courvoisier v. Raymond*, 23 Colo. 113, 47 P. 284 (1896). If you do not study *Courvoisier*, it is likely that you will read a case with facts at least somewhat similar. The defendant in *Courvoisier*, a jewelry store owner who lived upstairs from his store, was awakened by thieves or vandals who were trying to break into his store and who threw rocks at him. After chasing the intruders from his building, he fired a shot to scare them away. The shot attracted the plaintiff, a police officer. The plaintiff started to walk toward the defendant, calling out that he was a police officer and telling the defendant to stop shooting. The defendant testified that he thought the plaintiff was approaching him in a threatening manner. He fired at the police officer, believing it was necessary in his own self-defense, and the officer was seriously wounded.

The trial court instructed the jury that in order for the self-defense privilege to exonerate the defendant, the plaintiff must actually have been assaulting the defendant. In other words, if the defendant claiming self-defense was wrong and he injured someone who did not pose a threat of death or grievous bodily harm to him, the defendant would be liable even if his mistake was a reasonable one. A similar issue arises when the defendant fires in self-defense and injures an innocent bystander. Roman law provided that in this situation, the defendant would be liable. Both the trial judge's instruction to the jury and Roman law correspond with a strict liability standard—if the defendant makes a mistake, even a reasonable one, which harms someone, he will be held liable. In *Courvoisier*, however, the Colorado Supreme Court found that the trial court's instruction was in error, and that the proper standard to apply was whether the defendant reasonably believed that the use of deadly force was necessary. If he acted reasonably, he cannot be held liable even if he was mistaken. In other words, **defendants in self-defense cases will be held liable only for *unreasonable* mistakes**, a rule that parallels a negligence standard. (We will discuss negligence in Lesson 8.) So here, in a case about self-defense, an affirmative defense to intentional torts, your Torts professor is likely to bootstrap in one of the most important issues in the law of torts: Should we hold people liable under a strict liability standard or only when they are negligent?

Note that the test for whether the use of force in self-defense is allowed is an objective one, requiring a **reasonable belief** that harm is about to be inflicted on the defendant (or, in the case of deadly force, that grievous bodily harm or death is threatened)—**not** a subjective one, requiring that the defendant have **an honest (but perhaps unreasonable) belief** that harm to him is imminent. In some older criminal law cases, an "honest belief" was enough to justify self-defense, but this has never been the rule in torts cases. In torts, courts are concerned about the compensation needs of the victim, not just the moral culpability of the defendant. The subway passenger who is trigger-happy and honestly but unreasonably believes that several youths on the train are going to seriously harm him may not justifiably draw his gun and fire.

Another issue is whether the defendant must attempt to retreat before using force. The traditional rule was that the defendant was not required to retreat before using force. During the past 50 years there was a trend toward requiring retreat before using *deadly force.* In many states, there was an exception to this trend: under the so-called **castle doctrine**, the defendant who is in her own home and fears death or grave bodily injury is not required to retreat before using deadly force. During the past decade, many state legislatures adopted so-called **stand-your-ground** statutes that extend the "no retreat" concept of the castle doctrine so that it now applies not only in the home in these states, but to anyplace the defendant might legally be.

Self-defense is an affirmative defense. In *Courvoisier,* for example, the jewelry store owner *did commit a battery* on the police officer. However, if the defendant acted reasonably, the privilege of self-defense precludes his liability to the police officer. Because self-defense is an affirmative defense, the **burden is on the defendant** to both raise the defense and prove the facts necessary to establish the defense.

The next privilege to consider is the **defense of others**. A defendant is entitled to use reasonable force to defend others when it reasonably appears to be necessary to protect them from bodily harm. At one time, courts generally allowed the defense only when the person in jeopardy was a member of the defendant's family, but that is no longer necessary. The tough cases involving this privilege are ones where the defendant reasonably believes that the third party is in jeopardy of bodily harm but, in reality, he is not. For example, the plaintiff and the third party on whose behalf the defendant intervened may simply have been engaged in horseplay.

The third affirmative defense to intentional torts is one involving the **defense of property**. One can use force that appears to be reasonable under the circumstances to defend property. Assume that Brittany and Zachary break off their romantic relationship. Shortly thereafter, Brittany parks her Mercedes, and Zachary raises a sledgehammer over its hood and says, "I'm going to bash in your hood." Brittany throws a punch and knocks Zachary out cold. If Zachary sues Brittany for battery, Zachary will not prevail because of Brittany's privilege to use reasonable force to protect her property. However, let's change the facts and assume that Brittany sets a spring gun so that it will fire automatically if someone enters her garage where she parks her Mercedes. In fact, shots from the spring gun do hit Zachary when he enters the garage to vandalize the car. When Zachary sues for battery, can he recover? Yes; the privilege to use reasonable force to protect property will not help Brittany because **one can never use force likely to inflict death or great bodily harm to protect property**.

What You Need to Know:

1. The defendant has the burden to plead and prove affirmative defenses to intentional torts, often called privileges.
2. Under the privilege of self-defense, the defendant may use reasonable force to defend herself if she reasonably believes it is necessary to prevent her from being intentionally harmed.
3. The defendant may use deadly force only if she has a reasonable belief that force sufficient to cause grievous bodily harm or death is about to be inflicted on her.
4. The defendant is privileged to use reasonable force to protect others when it reasonably appears to her to be necessary to do so.
5. The defendant is entitled to use reasonable force, but never deadly force, to protect property.

LESSON 7: OTHER INTENTIONAL TORTS TO THE PERSON

In this lesson, we will consider three additional intentional torts to the person: assault, intentional infliction of emotional distress, and false imprisonment.

If we think of the prototypical case of battery as the defendant's fist hitting the plaintiff's jaw, then assault compensates the plaintiff for the fright he feels before the punch connects. **Assault is (1) a victim's apprehension of imminent harmful or offensive bodily contact caused by the defendant's action or threat, coupled with (2) the defendant's intent to cause either the apprehension of such contact or the contact itself.**

It is sometimes said that an assault is an attempted battery, and often this is the case, but this statement is not always true. Assume that as a practical joke, Zachary comes up behind Amanda in a dark alleyway and says, in a menacing voice, "Your money or your life." Amanda is terrified. This is not an attempted battery: Zachary did not intend to hit Amanda. However, Amanda did experience apprehension, and Zachary will be liable for assault. Note that Zachary's benign motive—his acts were intended as a practical joke—does not mean that he is not liable for assault. On one hand, the defendant must have acted with intent: Zachary must either have acted with a purpose to scare Amanda or with knowledge to a substantial certainty that his acts would scare her. However, it is not required that he acted with malice or ill will.

The victim's **apprehension must be reasonable**. If, for example, Nicole is overly squeamish as she watches Tyler stare at her from the other side of the classroom and believes that he is going to cause her offensive bodily contact during the class break, she probably is not going to be able to recover for assault. On the other hand, what if Tyler is aware of Nicole's squeamishness and intentionally plays upon it to cause her apprehension? As of this writing, this issue is one that is causing considerable controversy within the American Law Institute (ALI) as its members decide how to address this issue in the *Restatement (Third) of Torts*.

It is often said that "mere words alone do not constitute an assault." Ordinarily this is true, because typically words alone do not cause a person of ordinary sensibilities to experience apprehension, but this statement is only a guideline. As the dark alleyway hypothetical illustrates, sometimes "mere words" are enough for assault.

Suppose Amber receives a telephone call from Brandon who identifies himself as a professional assassin who has been hired by Tyler, whose advances Amber recently spurned. Brandon tells Amber that he expects to be in her neighborhood the next day. He threatens to kill Amber and informs her that he has previously made 100 similar phone calls and there are now 100 dead law students. Amber is terrified. Is there an assault? No. There is no assault because the threatened harmful contact is not of **"imminent" contact**. So what? Presumably, Amber has the opportunity to call the police or otherwise protect herself. **Liability for assault is most often circumscribed within its traditional definition.** Without this strict interpretation of the definition of assault, every threat would be an assault and courts would have time for little else.

Also, liability for assault requires that the defendant possess the **apparent ability** to cause the harmful or offensive bodily contact. If Nicole threatens Roberto with a realistic looking toy gun, Nicole may be liable for assault. Even though there is no *actual ability* to cause harmful contact, there is the *apparent ability* to do so and therefore Roberto's apprehension is reasonable.

Now let's turn our attention to the tort of **intentional infliction of emotional distress**, which requires proof of three elements: (1) The defendant must engage in extreme and outrageous conduct, (2) either intentionally or recklessly, which (3) causes the plaintiff to experience severe emotional distress. Extreme and reckless misconduct is really nasty stuff. Courts sometimes define it as conduct "**exceeding all bounds of human decency**" or that would cause ordinary people to scream "OUTRAGEOUS." An example would be calling the family of a soldier serving in combat to tell them, falsely, that their daughter had been killed in combat. The classic film *The Godfather* provides another example—namely, when the movie producer wakes up to find a bloody, severed horse head in his bed.

Finally, intentional infliction of emotional distress requires the plaintiff to experience **severe emotional distress**. Again, the purpose of this requirement is to weed out trivial complaints. Regrettably, life is full of emotional distress, which is far too often intentionally inflicted. However, most courts do not require that the emotional distress be characterized by a medically diagnosed condition or physical illness. In contrast, courts often require evidence of physical harm in order to establish liability under the tort of *negligent* infliction of emotional distress. In other words, as the level of egregiousness of the defendant's conduct increases, the severity of the plaintiff's harm necessary to establish liability decreases. When the defendant's conduct is sufficiently atrocious, this factor alone helps legitimate the severity of the victim's emotional distress as an element of intentional infliction of emotional distress.

The fourth and final intentional tort to the person is **false imprisonment**. False imprisonment is conduct by the defendant that is intended to, and does in fact, **confine the victim within boundaries** fixed by the defendant, if, in addition, the victim is either conscious of the confinement or is harmed by it. What does it mean to be confined within boundaries? A plaintiff's freedom of movement must be limited in all directions—a roadblock preventing the plaintiff from proceeding in the direction she wants to go is not sufficient. The bounded area may be large or even in motion. Assume Kenny Convict's probation officer tells Kenny that if he leaves the city, the officer will send bail bondsmen to hurt him. False imprisonment? Probably—courts have found liability in similar fact patterns. If the defendant stuffs the plaintiff in the trunk of his car, a court will impose liability even though the area in which the victim is confined is mobile, not stationary.

The **means of confinement** used by the defendant to confine the plaintiff may include **physical barriers, physical force, threats,** or the **wrongful assertion of lawful authority**. If Carlos, a store detective, tells a customer that she must come with him, this assertion of lawful authority is probably enough. Of course, if the customer asks if she must go with him and Carlos says "no," there is no false imprisonment.

What interests of the plaintiff are protected by the tort of false imprisonment? If the victim is conscious of the false imprisonment, the victim probably experiences emotional distress. In some instances, such as when a diabetic in the midst of an insulin reaction is incarcerated while unconscious, it is possible that she experiences physical harm. Most courts would find that there is a claim for false imprisonment when the victim, even if unconscious, experiences such harm. Finally, a few courts find the "dignitary harm" to the plaintiff caused by the false imprisonment to be sufficient to impose liability, even if the plaintiff is neither conscious nor harmed.

A "**shopkeeper's privilege**" enables retail store personnel to restrain a suspected shoplifter for a reasonable period of time to investigate in a reasonable manner. However, when store personnel today restrain someone suspected of shoplifting on a previous visit to the same store, the privilege does not apply.

What You Need to Know:

1. To recover for assault, the plaintiff must prove that the defendant's action or threat resulted in the plaintiff experiencing apprehension of imminent harmful or offensive bodily contact and that the defendant intended to cause either the apprehension of such contact or the contact itself.
2. Intentional infliction of emotional distress occurs when the defendant intentionally engages in extreme and outrageous conduct, which causes the plaintiff to experience severe emotional distress. Extreme and outrageous misconduct is really nasty stuff.
3. False imprisonment is conduct by the defendant that is intended to, and does in fact, confine the victim within boundaries fixed by the defendant, where, in addition, the victim is either conscious of the confinement or is harmed by it.

LESSON 8: NEGLIGENCE: BASIC ELEMENTS AND DUTY

Only a small portion of real-world tort actions involve punches and kisses without consent. The bulk of tort litigation seeks compensation for **accidental personal injuries** that are the **unintended consequences of legitimate activities**—for example, injuries resulting from automobile accidents, patrons who "slip and fall" on the slippery floors of grocery stores, medical malpractice, and the use of consumer products.

Perhaps the most important issue throughout most of the history of American tort law has been whether victims of such accidental harms are required to prove that the defendant acted with fault (negligently or intentionally) in order to recover. Today, one of the largest categories of accidental injuries, workplace injuries, is handled by **state-based workers' compensation systems** instead of within the common law of torts. The workers' compensation system does not require the injured worker to prove that the employer was negligent in order to receive compensation from the employer. In other categories of injuries that we will consider later, notably strict products liability and injuries arising from abnormally dangerous activities, the victim also is not required to prove fault in order to recover. However, the **baseline tort** that covers most accidental injuries today is **negligence**.

Torts teachers use the term "negligence" in two different ways. First, it sometimes refers to the ***defendant's conduct*** that poses an **unreasonable risk of harm to others**. For example, negligence occurs when the driver exceeds the speed limit by 20 miles per hour at the same time that he is texting. Second, the word "negligence" is also used to describe the **plaintiff's cause of action or claim**.

Because negligence has been the predominant tort for more than a century, one would expect that all the main issues have been decided but that is far from the case. For example, how is negligence (here referring to the defendant's conduct) defined? The traditional rule, which most courts continue to follow, is to define negligence as **doing something that the ordinary, reasonably prudent person (the "ORPP") would not do, or failing to do something that the ORPP would do, *under all the circumstances*.** In other words, under this approach, whether the defendant is negligent depends upon whether her activity lives up to the standard of conduct of the ordinary, reasonably prudent person. However, the emerging trend, as reflected in the *Restatement (Third) of Torts*, defines negligence as the failure to exercise **reasonable care under all the circumstances and then uses an economic or cost-benefit analysis** to determine whether reasonable care has been exercised.

In order to recover under a negligence claim, the plaintiff and his counsel must plead and prove **four elements: (1) a duty of care owed by the defendant; (2) a breach or violation of that duty of care; (3) causation, including both cause in fact and proximate causation; and (4)**

actual harm. In most negligence cases, **actual harm means either a physical injury or property damage**. Only under unusual circumstances will the plaintiff be able to recover for emotional distress in the absence of physical injury or for purely economic or commercial loss. Note the contrast with intentional torts where the plaintiff is not required to prove actual harm in order to recover but instead can recover nominal damages and, where appropriate, punitive damages, even if he is not able to prove actual harm.

When is a duty of care owed by a defendant to a plaintiff? Let's assume that Sarah L. Student was injured when the walls of the library building in which she was studying, located in the northeastern United States, collapsed during a major earthquake and injured her. Assume that there had never been a significant earthquake in this part of the country and that no one could have reasonably foreseen such an event. Can Sarah successfully sue anyone, for example, the owner and operator of the building, the architect who designed it and supervised construction, or the contractor who constructed the building, for negligence in failing to make the building earthquake proof? The answer is no. In order for any of these possible defendants to be liable to Sarah, that defendant would need to have foreseen that its actions posed a risk of harm, at least to someone. In other words, if it was **not unreasonable for the defendant to fail to foresee harm to someone—anyone—there is no negligence**.

The next issue in a negligence case is whether in order for the plaintiff to recover, she must prove that it was foreseeable to the defendant that if the defendant did not exercise reasonable care, some harm would occur to the plaintiff or at least to someone within a class of people among whom the plaintiff was a member. In other words, must the plaintiff be a foreseeable victim to the defendant? This is one of the most basic issues in all tort law, and you would expect it would have a well-established answer. Again, it does not. The **majority rule** is that a **duty of care is owed to** the plaintiff only if she is a member of the class of persons who might be foreseeably harmed (sometimes called "**foreseeable plaintiffs**") as a result of the defendant's negligent conduct. The **minority**

view is that if the defendant can foresee harm to anyone as a result of his negligence, a **duty is owed to everyone** (whether or not a foreseeable victim) **who is harmed** as a result of the defendant's breach of a duty of care. However, this **does not mean that the injured party will necessarily be able to recover**; her injury may not be closely enough connected to the defendant's conduct ("proximately caused" or "within the scope of liability") to hold him liable. It is possible that when studying "duty" in your Torts course, you will read the great case of *Palsgraf v. Long Island Railroad*, 248 N.Y. 339, 162 N.E. 99 (1928) where the judges duel over this issue. We will consider *Palsgraf* in Lesson 16, "Proximate Causation (aka Scope of Liability)."

Let us briefly address the issue of whether a defendant ever can be held liable for a **failure to act**. Assume that Natalie Narcissist, an Olympic medal-winning swimmer, is relaxing on the shores of a lake, reading a book, and guzzling a beer. No lifeguard is on duty. A teenager, swimming in the lake without his parents, begins to drown and screams for help. Natalie sees him and recognizes his plight, but reaches for her beer and continues to read. Assume Natalie could have save the boy without any risk and minimal inconvenience to herself. Instead, she lets him drown. His parents sue Natalie for negligence. Can they recover? No. Why? The courts would say that Natalie **owed no duty of care** to the boy. Why such a harsh rule? Probably because of strong resistance among Americans to the idea that the government (including the judicial branch) should be allowed to tell us that we have to act affirmatively in any way (think taxes, the once-upon-a-time military draft, and, more recently, the Affordable Care Act). Further, where would courts draw the line? Would you be negligent and liable for a wrongful death if you failed to donate the $1 per week that could have saved the life of a child in a poor, underdeveloped country? Of course, the rule that ordinarily the defendant does not owe a duty to act affirmatively, even when a cost-benefit analysis suggests that she should, often yields harsh results. Accordingly, it is riddled with exceptions usually not discussed in first-semester Torts.

What You Need to Know:

1. Most torts cases involve accidental, not intentional, harms. Most cases are governed by the law of negligence.

2. Negligence is doing something that the reasonable person would not do or failing to do something that the reasonable person would do.

3. In order to recover for negligence, the plaintiff must plead and prove: (1) a duty of care, (2) a breach of duty; (3) causation; and (4) injury.

4. In order for the defendant to be found negligent, it must have been reasonably foreseeable to the defendant that his failure to use reasonable care would cause harm to someone (anyone).

5. In addition, a majority of courts holds that in order for a duty of care to be owed to the plaintiff, it must be reasonably foreseeable to the defendant that if he fails to use reasonable care, some harm will occur to the plaintiff or at least to someone within a class of people among whom the plaintiff is a member.

6. A strong minority of courts holds that the harm to the plaintiff need not be foreseeable in order for the defendant to owe a duty of care to the plaintiff. Under this view, once the defendant reasonably should foresee harm to someone, a duty of care is owed to anyone who in fact is injured. However, just because a duty is owed does not necessarily mean that the victim can recover for her injuries.

7. The general rule is that the defendant does not owe a duty to others to act affirmatively, even if his failure to do so is unreasonable.

LESSON 9: THE ORDINARY, REASONABLY PRUDENT PERSON

In the last lesson, we began to consider when a defendant engaged in active conduct can be held liable for negligence.

Under the traditional (and still the majority view) of negligence, **negligence is defined as doing what a reasonable person would not do or failing to do what a reasonable person would do *under all the circumstances*.** With a few exceptions, this is the standard or level of care owed by a defendant who owes a duty to the plaintiff. Who, then, is this masked man or woman known as the reasonable person? The reasonable person is a **hypothetical** being who represents an "**objective standard**." We do not judge a particular defendant's conduct by whether she is acting in good faith, or even to the best of her abilities.

Let's assume that our defendant is Mitch Miami, who lives in a warm, southeastern city where it never snows but where there is (hypothetically, of course) significant access to certain illicit drugs. Mitch is visiting his grandparents in Minnesota in January, driving his Porsche. He sees glistening white powder on the roads. He has never seen snow, but he always gets excited when he sees glistening white power. He speeds up, skids, and hits a police cruiser. When sued for his alleged negligence in damaging the police cruiser, Mitch testifies, "I did the best I could. Mom and Dad always said to do the best you could and don't worry about it." Will his argument prevail? Definitely not. Mitch will be held to the standard of the ordinary, reasonably prudent person. **The ordinary, reasonably prudent person standard does not make allowances for differences in intelligence, education, or temperament.** Mitch will be held to the standard of what an ordinary person in the community, here Minneapolis, would know—namely that the glistening white powder was snow, not cocaine.

Note that in some cases, this objective standard means that a person of limited intelligence might be held liable in negligence even if he could not do any better. Why? First, the law of negligence, through the objective standard of the ORPP, strives for a world in which members of society, when interacting with one another, do not need to constantly evaluate the level of intelligence of the people they encounter—for example, the driver of the oncoming car (of course, they still might want to do this to avoid an accident!). In addition, the

ORPP standard does not require that the decision makers in the courtroom evaluate the intelligence or the temperament of the defendant and evaluate his liability by that uncertain and variable standard of whether he is acting in good faith or to the best of his ability. We will leave this impossible task of mind-reading to juries determining *mens rea* in criminal cases.

However, what about defendants with physical infirmities? Here the law takes a different approach. The **person with a physical disability is held to the standard of how a reasonable person with the same disability** would act. Obviously, this does not mean that the blind person can drive a car. The blind person who decided to get behind the wheel of the Porsche would be acting unreasonably, even taking into account all the circumstances—including his blindness. However, we would expect the blind person with a white cane and a guide dog to act differently on a sidewalk than we would a fully sighted person. Why do we take into account a physical disability when we previously established that the ORPP was an objective standard, not taking into account differences in intellect, education, and temperament? First, there is little chance that a sighted person would successfully feign blindness in the courtroom in order to fool the jury in a negligence case. Second, as suggested by the pedestrian example, most often, other people can detect parties with identifiable physical disabilities and modify their behavior accordingly. Obviously, a physical disability is one that is significant and ascertainable. If a defendant in an auto accident calls his tennis partner as a witness to testify as to his total lack of coordination in order to lower the standard of care to which he will be held, such a gambit would be unsuccessful.

To what standard will courts hold a child? First, remember that most of the time, when the conduct of a child is evaluated against a negligence standard, the question is whether the child as a plaintiff is contributorily negligent (negligence in failing to protect herself that either bars or reduces her own recovery). Judges, apparently none of whom are parents, appear to operate under the assumption that children are rarely defendants because they cannot cause much harm to others! As the reasoning goes, holding children to a lesser standard will not cause significantly greater risk to others, but will enable them to recover when the negligence of others, combined with their own contributory negligence, results in them being harmed. Accordingly, the general rule is that in deciding whether a child is negligent, we hold her to the **standard of a child of similar age, experience, and education**. The standard remains an objective one—not based on whether a particular child has acted in good faith or to the best of her ability. However, the class of people against whom the child's conduct is evaluated is much smaller and more focused: children of a similar age with similar education and experience. As with persons with physical disabilities, the justification for treating children differently is that childhood is a status easily detected both by judges and jurors and by other members of society with whom the child interacts. There is an important exception, however: children engaged in "**adult activities**" are held to the reasonably prudent adult standard. Courts disagree as to how far this exception extends. Obviously the licensed driver of a car or motorboat is held to the adult standard, but what about the child who is hunting or golfing? Finally, states usually provide that **young children below a certain age**, often 3, 4, or 5, **are conclusively presumed to be incapable of negligence**.

What You Need to Know:

1. The traditional standard for measuring whether the defendant's conduct is negligent is the standard of the ordinary, reasonably prudent person. This standard is objective and hypothetical. The defendant cannot avoid liability for negligence by proving he acted in good faith or to the best of his ability.
2. Even if the defendant is of lower intelligence, has less education, or has a particularly volatile temperament, he will be held to the standard of someone with average intelligence, ordinary knowledge, or a typical predisposition.
3. A party with a physical disability is held to the standard of a reasonable person under the same

circumstances, including one with the same disability.

4. Children are held to the standard of children with similar age, experience, and education, except that children engaged in an adult activity, for example, a 16-year-old driving a car, are held to an adult standard.

LESSON 10: COST-BENEFIT ANALYSIS, PRECEDENTS, AND THE STANDARD OF REASONABLE CARE

With the exception of automobile accidents, a high percentage of tort cases involve claims against businesses. The reason is simple: plaintiffs' counsel, usually paid on a contingent fee basis, is rarely interested in investing her own time if the defendant cannot pay a court judgment.

Cost-benefit analysis. Not surprisingly then, whether a defendant is negligent is increasingly viewed through the prism of whether the defendant has exercised **cost-justified precautions** to avoid harm. If the defendant fails to do so, it is negligent. However, if the precautions are expensive and the risk of harm is quite small, the defendant is not negligent. The *Restatement (Third) of Torts* calls for courts, when determining whether a person has acted without reasonable care to **weigh** (a) the **foreseeable likelihood** that the conduct **will be harmful**, (b) the **foreseeable severity of any resulting harm**, and (c) the **burden of precautions** (including both costs and opportunity costs) necessary to eliminate or reduce the risk of harm. Obviously, the *Restatement* approach reflects the influence of the **law and economics** school on tort law.

Let's consider an example. Assume Courtney, a professional truck driver, is driving a specific route in a rural area for the first time. She approaches a railroad grade crossing of the B & F Railroad displaying the familiar crossbuck sign providing warning of a "railroad crossing." However, the railroad has not erected any flashing red signal lights to warn when a train is coming. Buildings near the tracks and overgrown shrubbery make it difficult or impossible to see an oncoming train. Courtney is seriously injured when a locomotive strikes her truck. Her lawyers discover that the cost of erecting automatic red-flashing lights is $50,000 with annual operating costs of $5,000. Three previous drivers have been hit by trains at this crossing within the past 20 years, and each of them is now paralyzed. Is the defendant B & F Railroad liable for negligence under a cost-benefit analysis test? Probably: the foreseeable likelihood of an accident times the foreseeable severity of the resulting harm appears to exceed the costs of preventing the accident.

Sometimes experts testifying in cases such as these use a cost-benefit analysis, often called the "Learned Hand formula" after Judge Learned Hand, who articulated the cost-benefit analysis as an algebraic formula in *United States v. Carroll Towing Co.*, 159 F.2d 169, 173 (2d Cir. 1947). The difficulty with cost-benefit analysis, of course, is that it is often difficult, if not impossible, for the prospective tortfeasor to ascertain the likelihood and severity of any harm that might occur as a result of its negligence.

More important than the use of cost-benefit analysis in any particular case, the idea that negligence consists of the failure to take cost-justified precautions looms over modern tort law. Obviously, the issue of which precautions a defendant is required to take to avoid liability is an important issue affecting what we previously referred to as the loss minimization objective of tort law. Moreover, one of the issues that **law and economics scholars debate** is **whether a negligence standard—requiring the potential tortfeasor to take only cost-justified precautions—or a strict liability standard—holding the defendant liable for all the harms caused by its conduct—leads to the lowest sum of costs of accidental injuries and accident prevention**. The resolution of this issue is complicated by the fact that the plaintiff may be able to prevent the harm to herself if she exercised reasonable care for her own safety. Traditionally, and in a few states today, the doctrine of **contributory negligence** prevents the plaintiff from recovering if she failed to exercise reasonable care to protect herself.

In your course, you may encounter the "**Coase Theorem**," named after its author, the late economist Ronald Coase. Coase realized that **in a world without significant transaction costs, the liability rule will not ultimately affect the level of safety precautions taken by the parties**. Instead, the potential tortfeasor and those who might be affected by its conduct would bargain over which safety precautions should be taken, and by whom, to most efficiently prevent the harm, regardless of which party initially is assigned the costs of the accident by the legal system. Of course, as Coase recognized, the world is full of transaction costs, such as the costs of knowing what harms will occur as a result of the tortfeasor's conduct, identifying potential victims, and bargaining with them. Potential tortfeasors and their foreseeable victims often do not foresee the harms that might occur and generally do not have the ability to bargain with each other over what safety precautions should be taken. At the end of the day, in a world *with* transaction costs, it probably is impossible to determine whether a negligence or strict liability regime is most socially efficient (that is, results in the lowest sum of accident and accident prevention costs).

Specific standards governing defendants' conduct derived from past judicial precedents. Finally, we turn to another means of establishing the standard of care in a negligence case, the one that probably is both most important in the real world and will be least discussed in your Torts course. In handling any negligence claim, the attorneys and judges typically look first at how courts in their own and other jurisdictions have decided cases with similar facts in the past. If the state supreme court has previously decided a case regarding the alleged negligence of a railroad company in failing to erect flashing warning lights, that decision will be an important, often the most important, factor in determining the standard in the current case.

When a court's **precedents establish a specific, judicially created rule** that a defendant's conduct is not negligent across an entire category of cases, courts sometimes say that a defendant owes "no duty" or only a "limited duty" to a plaintiff.

Lawyers and judges usually assume that the ordinary citizens who comprise the jury are more likely to be sympathetic to the injured plaintiff than they are to the defendant, usually either a business or another defendant that jurors suspect is insured. The attorney representing the **plaintiff usually wants her case to be heard by the jury**. On the other hand, more often than not, the lawyer representing the defendant wants the case to be decided by the judge. Accordingly, **defendants typically favor specific rules** governing tort cases that enable judges to "take the case from the jury," while **plaintiffs prefer** extremely **vague** statements of what constitutes negligence in a specific case—for example, **the reasonable person standard**—so that the case will be sent to the jury to decide whether the defendant's conduct was negligent.

It is often said that juries decide "matters of fact" and judges decide "matters of law," but what does this mean? The **jury has two roles**. First, it must decide what the **primary facts** are: when the parties disagree about the facts leading to the accident, the jury must evaluate the competing evidence. Second, the jury then **applies the law** contained in the jury instructions **to the facts** of the case to decide whether the plaintiff has proved the elements of the tort and whether the defendant has proved the elements of any affirmative defense. **Judges decide whether there is enough evidence for the jury** to find the defendant negligent through rulings on motions for summary judgment and directed verdicts. They also rule on the **admissibility of evidence** and other matters regarding the conduct of the trial. Finally, they read "**instructions of law**" to the jury explaining the law that is to be applied to the case.

What You Need to Know:

1. Determining whether the defendant has taken cost-justified precautions to avoid harm is another important standard for determining whether a defendant is negligent.

2. The cost-benefit analysis requires the defendant to balance the product of the likely frequency of harm caused by its activities multiplied by the likely

severity of such harms against the burdens—all costs, including opportunity costs, of avoiding the harms.

3. Law and economics scholars debate whether a negligence system or a strict liability system produces the lower sum of accident costs and accident prevention costs.

4. The Coase Theorem provides that in a world without transaction costs, the choice between a negligence or strict liability standard will not affect the level of safety precautions that are actually taken. However, we do not live in a world without transaction costs. It probably is impossible to answer the question as to whether a negligence regime or a strict liability system leads to the lower sum of accident prevention and accident costs in the real world in which tort law operates.

5. Precedents often establish judicially established rules for when a defendant will be held liable in a particular factual situation.

6. Believing that juries favor victims and not defendants that are likely to be either businesses or insured parties, plaintiffs typically want their cases decided by juries. Defendants favor specific rules defining negligence in particular cases that enable judges to "take the case from the jury."

7. Judges decide "matters of law." Juries typically decide "matters of fact"—that is, establishing what really happened and whether the facts that are proved are sufficient to find negligence.

LESSON 11: THE ROLE OF CUSTOM IN NEGLIGENCE LAW

If the traditional measuring rod for determining whether the defendant's conduct is negligent is what the **ordinary**, reasonably prudent person would or would not do, it should not surprise you that what businesses and individuals ordinarily or

customarily do plays an important role in deciding whether the defendant has been negligent.

The role played by custom in ordinary negligence cases (other than professional malpractice) has changed dramatically since the late nineteenth century. At that time, if a defendant was able to prove that its conduct that caused the plaintiff's injury corresponded with custom, the defendant was held not to be negligent as a matter of law. In other words, customary care was reasonable care. By the 1930s, however, the winds shifted: a business's correspondence with custom no longer necessarily meant that the defendant was not negligent. In the leading case of *The T.J. Hooper*, 60 F.2d 737 (1932), Judge Learned Hand stated, "[I]n most cases reasonable prudence is in fact common prudence; but strictly it is never its measure; a whole calling may have unduly lagged in the adoption of new and available devices. . . . Courts must in the end say what is required. . . ." What accounts for this dramatic change? Courts during the late nineteenth century trusted the free market to determine the socially optimal level of safety precaution. The Great Depression shook faith in the free market system. Judge Hand and other judges were no longer willing to give the marketplace *carte blanche* to set the standard of care in negligence cases.

Even though **court**s generally **no longer allow industry custom to determine the standard of reasonable care**, this does not mean that custom is irrelevant to the jury's negligence determination. **Evidence of the custom** in a trade or industry, or among individuals, **is still admissible** and may be considered by the jury in deciding whether the defendant has acted with reasonable care. Similarly, safety codes promulgated by industry associations for the guidance of its members are also admissible.

What happens if following an accident, the defendant makes repairs to prevent a reoccurrence of the accident? Is evidence of the subsequent repair admissible to show the defendant's negligence in failing to make the repairs earlier? Certainly such evidence appears relevant for purposes such as showing the feasibility of making the defendant's operations safer. However, the general rule is that evidence of post-accident repairs is not admissible. Why? Because the admissibility of such evidence would likely lead at least some defendants to delay making repairs because they would anticipate that evidence of repairs would weaken their exposure to liability in pending cases. This rule, however, is riddled with exceptions and qualifications. Plaintiffs' attorneys often find ways to introduce evidence of post-accident repairs.

Turning to professional liability cases—the liability of physicians, lawyers, architects, and other professionals—custom plays a more important role. In contrast to its limited effects in negligence cases against nonprofessionals, **correspondence with custom is usually a defense as a matter of law if the defendant is engaged in professional practice**. Why should professionals be able to establish their own standard of care as expressed by professional custom? Courts reason that it is more difficult for laypersons on the jury to determine what constitutes a reasonable standard of care for professionals. Accordingly, greater deference is owed by the jury to professionals because of their expertise. Additionally, professions tend, at least in theory, to engage in self-regulation. Obviously, these justifications for the distinction between the role of custom in cases against nonprofessional businesses and in litigation against professionals are not entirely convincing. Often the choices made by nonprofessional industries regarding which safety precautions are justified require considerable expertise. Further, at least in a few instances, professional expertise appears unnecessary to establish that a professional's conduct, such as a lawyer missing a filing deadline, is negligent.

While it is well established that the correspondence between a defendant-physician's conduct and professional custom establishes a defense to medical negligence (medical malpractice) as a matter of law, it is less clear which group of physicians will be used to determine medical custom. Until the 1960s or 1970s, the general standard of customary care in medical malpractice cases typically was how the physician in the **same or a similar locality** would have practiced. Beginning at that time, many courts reasoned that improvements in medical education, continuing medical educational programs, and greater communication and interaction among physicians justified that all physicians should be held to a single standard, the degree of skill and care possessed by the "**average qualified practitioner**"—sometimes called the "**national standard**."

The most obvious consequence of the choice between a "same or similar locality" standard of care and the national standard is how the trial judge defines the standard of care in her instructions to the jury to guide its consideration of whether the defendant-physician's conduct was negligent. However, in the real world, the more important consequence is **which physicians** are able to offer their **opinions as experts** to the jury as to whether the defendant acted negligently under the facts of a particular case. Can an expert specialist from the Johns Hopkins Hospital or the Mayo Clinic testify that in her opinion, the general practitioner in a small town failed to conduct himself in accordance with an applicable customary standard of care? The adoption of the national standard enables physicians from all over the country to appear as expert witnesses against defendant-physicians practicing in small, rural communities. This factor, among others, has contributed to the development of a new industry: physicians who earn their livings largely through appearing as expert witnesses in malpractice cases.

During the period extending from the 1970s through the 1990s, cultural changes affecting both juries and claims rates against physicians, as well as changes in the legal system, resulted in significant increases in both the frequency of claims against physicians and the size of the resulting claims payments. Accordingly, under pressure from physicians and their insurers, many state legislatures enacted a wide variety of "medical malpractice" reform measures. In some jurisdictions, these medical malpractice reform statutes caused the standard of care to revert from the national standard to that of the "same or similar locale" standard. Today, some jurisdictions follow this older standard, and others the national standard. Many states today split the difference and apply the "same or similar locale" standard to general practitioners and the national standard to board-certified specialists.

Although correspondence with customary practice generally establishes a complete defense as a matter of law in medical malpractice cases, there are a number of situations where at least some courts hold that the standard of care should be one of reasonable care under all the circumstances rather than the customary standard of care. For example, consider the standard of care to be applied in "**informed consent**" cases—the standard governing the level of disclosure of the risks of treatment that should be explained to a patient before the patient chooses to elect the surgery or other treatment. A **substantial minority** of courts holds that the level of disclosure required in informed consent cases should be determined by the risks that the jury believes are "**material**," that is, the **risks that a reasonable person would take into account in deciding whether to have surgery**, and not by the level of disclosure determined by medical custom.

What You Need to Know:

1. In most cases, the defendant in a negligence action is able to introduce evidence that its conduct corresponded with the custom in its trade or industry, but such correspondence with custom does **not** establish a defense as a matter of law.

2. For a physician or other professional, correspondence with custom establishes a defense to a negligence action.

3. In some jurisdictions, the customary standard of care for physicians is determined by custom in the same or a similar locality. In other states, the customary standard of care is a "national" standard—the custom among average, qualified practitioners. In still another group of states, the conduct of general practitioners is judged against the custom of physicians in the same or similar localities, while the conduct of board-certified specialists is judged against the standard of similar specialists on a nationwide basis.

4. Some courts, in specific instances, reject custom as a defense in medical malpractice cases. For

example, in informed consent cases, a strong minority of jurisdictions require the physician to disclose the risks of surgery the jury deems "material," that is, risks that the reasonable person would take into account in deciding whether to proceed with the surgery.

LESSON 12: NEGLIGENCE PER SE

It may surprise you to learn that ordinarily, **even if a business or other defendant is in compliance with all statutes and regulations, a court may still find it liable for negligence**. In the American common-law system, unlike the civil-law system in place in most countries of the world, state legislatures do not comprehensively prescribe when a defendant will or will not be held liable. State legislatures usually act against a background of the existing common law and know that, even if they do not act, common-law courts can still hold defendants liable for unreasonable conduct resulting in injury.

There is one important exception to this general idea that has become increasingly important during the last decade or two. In some instances, federal regulation may "**preempt**" a state common-law tort action. This can happen if: (1) Congress explicitly states that tort actions are preempted; (2) it is impossible for defendants to comply with both the federal regulations and the rule emanating from the state tort action; or (3) Congress has comprehensively regulated in a particular field. So, for example, comprehensive regulation of prescription drugs by the federal Food and Drug Administration is sometimes found to preempt a negligence claim by a patient harmed by the ingestion of the drug.

Legislatures, of course, **can change or modify the common law** if they decide to do so, as long as their statutory enactments are not unconstitutional. They can also explicitly provide a civil cause of action for the violation of a criminal or regulatory statute.

The concept of **negligence per se**, which you will no doubt encounter in your Torts class, is different. State and federal statutes that regulate conduct or impose criminal penalties for prescribed conduct often do not mention civil liability at all. Yet, courts borrow the standard contained in the statute or regulation and use it to define what reasonable care means in a negligence action. The use of criminal and regulatory statutes to define what reasonable care means is known as "negligence per se."

The basic rule of negligence per se contains five elements:

1. Where a **criminal** or **regulatory statute** imposes upon any person a specific duty for the protection or benefit of others;
2. The defendant **neglects to perform** that duty;
3. Her **violation** of the statute **proximately causes** an injury;
4. To any member of the class of people **intended to be protected** by the statute; and
5. The harm is of the type against which the statute **intended to protect**.

See Osborne v. McMasters, 40 Minn. 103, 41 N.W. 543 (1889).

Why should courts decide that a criminal or regulatory statute sets the standard of care in negligence cases even when the legislature could have said so and did not? First, because the legislature knows that courts have applied the negligence per se doctrine for the past 150 years, it may have anticipated and intended that the criminal enactment would set the standard of care for a negligence action even if it did not explicitly say so. Second, negligence per se may reflect deference to the legislative judgment of how a reasonable person would act or not act. Third, the court might believe that reasonable people do not violate the law.

Let's assume that a legislature has passed a statute that says that minors cannot be employed as waiters or waitresses in bars where liquor is served. A company known as Family and Frolic operates a restaurant, located in a midwestern state, with both a family dining room where alcohol is not served and a bar. Seventeen-year-old Dudley Do-Right is employed as a waiter in the family section, but when two servers scheduled to work in the bar area fail to show up for work because of a severe thunderstorm, the manager assigns young Dudley to work in the bar area. Without warning, a tornado strikes the bar, severely injuring Dudley, but the family portion of the restaurant is left untouched. Can Dudley's parents sue Family and Frolic for Dudley's injuries under a negligence per se theory, asserting that the defendant's violation of the liquor statute was the cause of Dudley's injuries? No. The statute presumably was enacted to protect minors from being corrupted or harmed by the influence of alcohol or those who are under the influence of alcohol. This is a different type of harm from the natural disaster that injured Dudley.

One of the subtopics you will discuss in your class when you consider negligence per se is what the **effect of the defendant's violation** of an appropriate statute should be. In some jurisdictions, the violation of a statute is, as famous jurist Judge Benjamin Cardozo once said, "more than some evidence of negligence . . . [it] *is* **negligence in itself**." *Martin v. Herzog*, 228 N.Y. 164, 168, 126 N.E. 814, 815 (1920). In other states, the violation of the statute creates a **"presumption" of negligence**—that is, the violation of the statute is enough for the jury to find that the defendant acted negligently unless the defendant presents evidence that its conduct was reasonable. Finally, in a few states, the defendant's violation of a statute is **merely evidence of negligence**, which a jury can ignore if it wants to. *Tedla v. Ellman*, 280 N.Y. 124, 131, 19 N.E.2d 987, 990–91 (1939). The contrast between *Martin* and *Tedla* illustrates a basic choice that occurs not only in tort law, but in other fields of law and in management: Is society better served by general rules or by allowing individuals and juries to make their own decisions on an ad hoc basis, taking into consideration all the surrounding facts?

Your first encounter with the doctrine of negligence per se will probably involve a **statute** enacted by a state legislature. As you proceed in your study of negligence per se, you may consider what impact a **municipal ordinance**, a law enacted by a city council or county commission, has on a negligence action. How about **regulations** enacted by administrative agencies within the executive branches of state or federal governments? Most jurisdictions give ordinances and regulations the same effect in negligence per se actions that they give statutes, but some courts treat ordinances and regulations only as evidence of negligence.

What You Need to Know:

1. Correspondence with statutes and regulations usually is not a defense for defendants in negligence actions.
2. Statutes sometimes provide the standard of care in negligence actions under the doctrine of negligence per se.
3. Negligence per se requires that the statute be designed to protect against the type of harm that in fact injured the plaintiff.
4. Most jurisdictions hold that a violation of the statute creates either negligence "as a matter of law" or a presumption of negligence. In a few states, violation of a statute is only evidence of negligence.
5. The doctrine of negligence per se also applies to local ordinances and administrative regulations.

LESSON 13: PREMISES LIABILITY AND OTHER NO-DUTY OR LIMITED-DUTY RULES

In certain categories of cases, courts hold that the duty of care owed by the defendant is **less than a reasonable standard of care**, **or even** that the defendant owes **no duty** to the plaintiff.

Premises liability. Under the **traditional common law**, **the duty of care owed by the possessor of land to a visitor** injured while on the land was in many cases something less than a reasonable standard of care. The standard of care of the land possessor **depended upon whether the injured visitor fell into the classification of an invitee, a licensee, or a trespasser**. Only **the invitee**, either someone on the defendant's land for a purpose related to business dealings of the land possessor or as a member of the public for a purpose for which the land was held open to the public, was **owed a duty of reasonable care**. The prototypical example of an invitee is obviously a store customer, but the category also includes others such as visitors to a park or library, or a plumber completing repairs on the owner's premises.

A **licensee** is someone visiting the land **with the consent of the owner who is not an invitee**. Included within this group are social guests, children who routinely pass over the property on the way to school and whose presence is tolerated by a homeowner, or police or fire personnel visiting the premises. In most jurisdictions, the landowner or tenant owes the licensee **the duty to repair or at least warn of any hazards that she knows about or has "reason to know" about but that would be concealed from the licensee**. Assume, for example, that Samantha, a homeowner, invited friends over to her place for a backyard picnic. Samantha is a busy professional who neither performs her own lawn maintenance nor spends much time in her backyard. She is unaware of the nest of yellow jackets buried in the ground, even though she would have found them if she had used reasonable care to inspect her yard. Her friend Jeremy is attacked by a swarm of yellow jackets, repeatedly stung, and hospitalized. The last sting is perhaps the one that hurts the most: in a jurisdiction that retains the traditional distinction between liability to invitees and licensees, he will not be able to successfully sue Samantha. On the other hand, if Jack, the young man who routinely mows Samantha's lawn, is attacked by the yellow jackets, he would be able to recover, because Jack is an invitee.

Finally, the third category of land visitor is the **trespasser**. The land possessor owes the trespasser only the duty **to refrain from intentional or "willful, wanton, and reckless" conduct** that harms the trespasser.

Thus, the standards of care owed to licensees and trespassers, less than the "ordinary, reasonably prudent person" standard of care, are known as **"limited-duty" rules**. The origins of the traditional trichotomy for classifying land visitors lay in the courts of nineteenth-century England. The judges feared that jurors who most often were not themselves landowners would be able to empathize with the injured land visitor but not the landowner, and thus would unfairly favor the plaintiff under the open-ended "reasonable care" standard usually applied. The more restrictive rules enabled judges to rule for land possessors as a matter of law and keep the cases from juries.

Within the past generation, **almost exactly one-half of all American jurisdictions have discarded the traditional trichotomy** and **now apply a standard of reasonable care in cases brought against land possessors by either invitees or licensees**. A few states even apply a reasonable standard of care under all the circumstances in cases brought by trespassers, but a substantial majority of even those courts that apply the "unitary standard" of reasonable care to claims brought by invitees and licensees continues to require that trespassers prove intentional or willful, wanton, and reckless misconduct in order to recover.

Negligent infliction of emotional distress. The next **two categories of no-duty or limited-duty rules are based on the type of harm suffered by the plaintiff**. Traditionally, of course, if the plaintiff suffered a physical injury, she was allowed to recover for emotional distress resulting from the physical injury. However, courts were extremely reluctant to award damages for emotional distress in the absence of a tangible physical injury. They apparently feared that allowing recovery for emotional distress alone would lead to both fraudulent claims and to "difficult-to-measure" awards of damages. Under the traditional law, it was sometimes said that **the plaintiff could not recover without a "physical impact" or at least a physical illness** resulting from the defendant's negligence. In recent decades, courts that continued to follow these rules sometimes interpreted them generously, such as where an airline passenger who experienced "sweaty hands" and "elevated blood pressure" when his plane suddenly plunged 34,000 feet in a tailspin was allowed to recover. In addition, even under the traditional common law, courts allowed plaintiffs to recover for emotional distress in tightly circumscribed situations, such as when a telegraph company negligently informed a mother and father that their child had been killed in combat or when the corpse of a family member was negligently mishandled.

More recently, courts have loosened the requirements for recovery of emotional distress to a greater or lesser extent. Most states now allow a plaintiff to recover in a situation where he experiences emotional distress because he is standing on the sidewalk in the "**zone of danger**" when a car negligently driven by the defendant careens off the street and onto the sidewalk, striking and killing a nearby family member and nearly missing him. **Some states** have gone further, and allow the recovery when a defendant's negligence results in **the death of (1) a close family member of the plaintiff, (2) where the plaintiff is present at the accident** (but not necessarily in the "zone of danger") **and perceives the victim's injury at the time when it occurs, and (3) suffers severe emotional distress**. Note, however, that even this liberalized standard represents a substantial limitation on the ordinary rule that plaintiff is able to recover for foreseeable consequences of the defendant's negligence. Suppose the plaintiff was present when her closest friend was negligently killed? Or was listening on a cell phone when her daughter was fatally struck by a negligently driven automobile? In either of these circumstances, few if any courts would allow recovery.

Recovery for purely commercial loss. Most jurisdictions do not allow a plaintiff to recover for a **purely economic or commercial loss** in the absence of either personal injury or property damage, even if such losses are foreseeable. For example, assume that as a result of negligence on the part of the employees of the Copper Plate Railroad Co., one of its trains derailed and ruptured tank cars containing toxic fluids that forced the evacuation of the surrounding area. Terrapin Travel, a local travel agency, was forced to close shop for a week, and lost $180,000 as a result of the negligence of the Copper Plate Railroad Co. Will Terrapin Travel be able to recover from Copper Plate? Assuming that there is neither damage to the property of Terrapin Travel nor personal harm to any of its employees, the answer is no. Courts fear that allowing recovery for purely commercial losses would result in a proliferation of claims from innumerable parties suffering economic losses that would be difficult to accurately value.

No-Duty and Limited-Duty Rules in Other Contexts. In countless factual situations other than those involving premises liability and recovery for emotional distress or commercial losses standing alone, courts—some more frequently than others—hold that the defendant owes the plaintiff no duty of care even if the identity of the plaintiff and the type of risk are foreseeable. In these situations, judges create specific rules indicating when a defendant can or cannot be found liable. For example, some states still hold that even if a tavern continues to sell alcoholic drinks to a patron who is obviously intoxicated and who then foreseeably drives and harms someone in an accident, the tavern owes no duty to that victim. Similarly, when a psychiatrist's patient credibly threatens violence and the psychiatrist unreasonably fails to warn the victim of the threat, many courts find that the psychiatrist owes no duty to the victim.

Courts sometimes justify no-duty and limited-duty rules by stating that **judges** and not juries **should formulate these restrictions on liability because** the justifications for these restrictions on liability **depend on policy factors and not on the determination of facts in a specific case**.

What You Need to Know:

1. In certain categories of cases, which vary considerably from one jurisdiction to the next, courts establish "no-duty" or "limited-duty" rules that limit liability far more than would a general rule that plaintiffs can recover whenever their harms are the foreseeable consequences of the defendant's negligence.

2. Traditionally and still in about one-half of all jurisdictions, the liability of the owner or lessee of premises depends on whether the injured land visitor is an invitee, a licensee, or a trespasser. Only the invitee is owed a duty of reasonable care. The licensee can recover only when the land possessor fails to correct or warn of a concealed

danger of which the defendant is aware. The trespasser recovers only when the defendant's actions are intentional or willful, wanton, and reckless.

3. About half of all states have altered the traditional rules governing the land possessor's liability. Lawful visitors to land, including both invitees and licensees, are owed a duty of reasonable care under the circumstances. However, even among these states adopting the unitary standard of liability, most continue to handle the issue of liability to the trespasser under the traditional standard.

4. Limited-duty rules also prevent victims from recovering for certain types of harm. For example, traditionally a plaintiff suffering only emotional distress in the absence of personal harm was usually able to recover only if he were personally in the zone of danger created by the defendant's conduct. Today, many states allow a plaintiff to recover when he personally observed harm to a close family member, resulting in severe emotional distress.

5. The plaintiff who suffers purely economic or commercial loss is generally not able to recover in the absence of either personal injury or property damage.

6. In many other situations, some courts create no-duty or limited-duty rules limiting liability that apply to a category of cases and depend on policy factors and not the facts of a specific case.

LESSON 14: BREACH OF DUTY AND *RES IPSA LOQUITUR*

In this lesson, we turn to the second element of negligence, **the breach (or violation) of duty, which is usually a matter of proving facts**: What is it that the defendant did or did not do that was negligent? Most lawyers will tell you that facts are more important than the law in torts cases. However, one specific legal principle, now generally regarded as a substantive legal doctrine and not merely as a rule of circumstantial evidence, sometimes assists the plaintiff in proving that the defendant violated a standard of care. This doctrine is known by the Latin phrase *res ipsa loquitur*, which, roughly translated, means "the thing speaks for itself."

Res ipsa loquitur begins with the notion that it provides **a form of circumstantial (indirect) evidence** that the defendant violated a duty of care. **Traditionally**, the plaintiff needed to prove **three foundational elements**, articulated in the *Restatement (Second) of Torts*, in order to invoke *res ipsa loquitur*: (1) **the accident must be of a kind which ordinarily does not occur in the absence of someone's negligence**; (2) it must be **caused by an agency or instrumentality within the exclusive control of the defendant**; and (3) the evidence must **eliminate other possible responsible causes of the accident, including any voluntary action of the part of the plaintiff**. If the plaintiff can prove these requirements, it makes sense to allow the jury to find that the defendant violated a duty of care without direct proof. For example, when a barrel falls from the second floor of the defendant's warehouse, cracking the victim's skull, the defendant can be held liable even in the absence of direct testimony as to the careless conduct of the defendant's employees within the warehouse.

The requirement that the instrumentality that caused the plaintiff's injury was within the exclusive control of the defendant often posed a problem, particularly in products liability cases. For example, assume that a customer of a restaurant suffered physical harm when he realized that the bottle of cola from which he had been drinking also included a dead cockroach. Regrettably, cases like these were all too common. The plaintiff lacked evidence of any specific negligent acts by employees of the bottling company, so he invoked the magic phrase, *res ipsa loquitur* (today, of course, he probably also recovers under a strict products liability claim). The defendant bottling company responded that the "instrumentality" that caused the plaintiff's harm was not within the exclusive control of the defendant, but instead had passed through the hands of the distributor and the restaurant before the plaintiff took possession. Because of cases like these, many states and the *Restatement (Third) of Torts* have now eliminated the exclusive control requirement.

These new versions of the *res ipsa loquitur* doctrine also delete the requirement that the plaintiff's own conduct must not contribute to the harm. Although this traditional requirement is consistent with the rule that plaintiff's own contributory negligence total bars recovery for negligence, it is inconsistent with the comparative fault system now followed by most states. Thus, *Restatement (Third)* § 17 **allows the use of *res ipsa loquitur*** to find a breach of duty **"when the accident causing the plaintiff's physical harm is a type of accident that ordinarily happens as a result of the negligence of** a **class of actors of which the defendant is the relevant member."** However, the common law of many states continues to track the traditional requirements articulated in the *Second Restatement*.

Students habitually over-identify *res ipsa loquitur* issues on their Torts examinations. For example, **the doctrine rarely if ever applies in a case arising from a two-vehicle collision**. Applying the *Second Restatement's* version of the requirements, if you believe that the defendant's car was the instrumentality that caused the accident and that the plaintiff did not contribute to the accident, you have already assumed that the defendant was at fault (breached a duty of care) and therefore you do not need *res ipsa loquitur* to prove what you've already assumed were the facts! Similarly, under the *Third Restatement*'s version, it cannot be said that the defendant is the "relevant member" of the class of actors (drivers) usually responsible for collisions because automobile accidents often result when either the plaintiff is at fault or the accident occurs through the fault of neither driver (such as in cases involving a brake failure on a borrowed or rented car or skidding on impossible-to-detect ice).

What is the consequence if the plaintiff is able to prove the requirements for *res ipsa loquitur*? Ordinarily, if the jury finds that the doctrine applies, it merely means that **the jury can,**

but is not required to, find that defendant violated a duty of care without direct proof of the breach of duty. In a small number of cases, courts have held that plaintiff's satisfaction of the requirements of *res ipsa loquitur* shifts the burden to produce evidence of nonnegligence to the defendant in order to avoid having the court direct a verdict against it on the issue of breach of duty. In even fewer opinions, the courts not only shift the burden of production of evidence to the defendant, they also shift the burden of persuasion to the defendant. In other words, if *res ipsa loquitur* applies, the defendant must prove by a preponderance of evidence that it did not breach a duty of care in order to prevail.

You may study *Ybarra v. Spangard*, 25 Cal.2d 486, 154 P.2d 687 (1944), which is a case often used by business and conservative critics as "Exhibit A" to show what is wrong with the tort system. Following surgery during which he was anesthetized, the plaintiff woke up with significant pain in his neck and back that later became disabling. A number of doctors, nurses, and medical technicians attended to him during his surgery. Obviously, the plaintiff could not testify as to negligent acts on the part of any of the defendants. The Supreme Court of California allowed him to use *res ipsa loquitur* to hold all of the defendants jointly and severally liable unless one or more of them proved to the jury that they had not violated a duty of care. The court reasoned that the control of the patient had passed to each of the defendants at one point or another during the surgery. What can justify the plaintiff's recovery despite his inability to prove either that anyone violated a duty of care or even who it was that caused his injury? The most superficial rationale is that the court shifted the burden of proof to the defendants because they, unlike the patient, were not unconscious and possessed greater information regarding who had been negligent. However, this seems unconvincing because, as it turned out, none of the co-defendants was able to identify a negligent party! The second justification is that the defendants had "concurrent" control over the patient and therefore should be held jointly and severally liable. But ask yourself if each of the defendants, for example, any of the nurses or medical technicians, was really in a position to control the activities of the other medical professionals (*i.e.*, the physicians), who were present during surgery. The most honest explanation for the decision probably is that the court functionally employed a strict liability standard while purporting to apply a traditional negligence standard, presumably on the grounds of loss minimization and loss distribution. In any event, *Ybarra* appears to be at odds with the traditional requirement that the plaintiff loses unless he can establish all the elements of negligence, including both violation of duty and the identity of the person causing the harm.

What You Need to Know:

1. Proof of the second element of negligence, breach of duty, usually is a matter of proving facts that establish what it is that defendant did that violated the standard of care.
2. *Res ipsa loquitur* is a substantive torts doctrine that sometimes enables the plaintiff to prove the defendant's violation of duty in the absence of direct evidence.
3. The traditional version of *res ipsa loquitur* requires plaintiff to show that (1) the accident was of a type that usually does not occur without negligence, (2) the instrumentality that caused the accident was within the exclusive control of the defendant, and (3) the plaintiff did not contribute to the accident. In comparison, the modern approach to *res ipsa loquitur* requires the plaintiff to prove that the plaintiff's harm ordinarily results from the negligence of "a class of actors among whom the defendant is the relevant member."
4. Ordinarily, the application of *res ipsa loquitur* merely allows the jury to infer that the defendant has been negligent.
5. In a controversial decision, the Supreme Court of California used *res ipsa loquitur* to hold all members of a surgical team jointly and severally liable where the plaintiff could prove neither that any particular defendant breached a duty of care

nor which defendant caused the accident. The case is probably best understood as a decision that functionally imposes strict liability.

LESSON 15: CAUSE IN FACT AND CAUSAL LINKAGE

Proving causation in a tort claim involves establishing two separate things. The first, discussed in this lesson, is **"cause in fact"—proving the connection between the defendant's violation of a duty of care and the harm that plaintiff suffered**. The other component of causation—traditionally called "proximate causation," but increasingly referred to as "scope of liability"—involves placing boundaries on the scope of liability for things that would not have occurred without the negligence of the defendant.

But/for causation. In most cases, the **"but/for" test** applies to establish cause in fact: Can it be said that but for (without) the defendant's negligence, the plaintiff would not have been injured? Would the collision at the intersection that injured José have occurred if Courtney had not run the red light? Today, courts generally hold that the plaintiff must prove but/for causation **by a preponderance of the evidence**. Some older cases and a few cases today require that the plaintiff eliminate all causes of the accident other than the defendant's negligence.

Multiple and indeterminate tortfeasors. In a few situations, it is logically impossible for the plaintiff to be able to prove but/for causation. Either more than one tortfeasor causally contributed to the plaintiff's harm ("multiple tortfeasors"), or the person who caused plaintiff's harm can be identified as belonging to a group of tortfeasors but the plaintiff cannot identify which specific defendant caused his harm. In these situations, particularly common in cases involving toxic diseases caused by products, the plaintiff resorts to alternative tests of causation.

First, if the plaintiff proves that **independent tortfeasors concurrently contributed to plaintiff's indivisible injuries**, then the court will hold these defendants jointly and severally liable. For example, imagine that Alyssa is simultaneously struck by two automobiles driven negligently by Joshua and Jessica. The experts agree that the negligence of both Joshua and Jessica combined to contribute to Alyssa's injury, a broken hip. Traditionally, Joshua and Jessica will be held **jointly and severally liable** for Alyssa's injury. On the other hand, if the facts show that the impact of Joshua's negligently driven car impacted with and caused harm to Alyssa's right arm at the same time that Jessica's negligently driven car impacted with Alyssa's left leg, then the injury is not an indivisible one, and the rule does not apply. Instead, Joshua will be held liable only for the damages resulting from Alyssa's right arm, and Jessica will be held liable only for the damages to Alyssa's left leg.

A second situation in which multiple tortfeasors contribute causally to the plaintiff's harm involves **concert of action**. If two or more tortfeasors act pursuant to a **common plan or design** and the acts of one or more of them tortiously causes the plaintiff's harm, again, all the tortfeasors are held jointly and severally liable. For example, if two defendants agree to a drag race on a public highway and one of them injures the plaintiff, the driver of a third car, both the racing drivers will be held jointly and severally liable.

A third alternative causation doctrine, **alternative liability**, originated in the case of *Summers v. Tice,* 33 Cal.2d 80, 199 P.2d 1 (1948). The plaintiff was hunting with two companions who simultaneously shot in his direction, hoping to hit a quail. Instead, the plaintiff was struck in the eye. A single shot caused the harm, but the plaintiff could not prove which defendant fired the shot that injured him. The Supreme Court of California held that both defendants were jointly and severally liable unless one of them was able to prove that the shot that harmed the plaintiff's eye came from the gun of the other. The court reasoned that (1) the defendants were in a better position to establish whose tortious act in fact caused the harm and (2) as between two negligent defendants and an innocent victim, the defendants should pay even in the absence of proof as to which defendant caused the accident. Remember, however, that two defendants were held liable despite the fact that only one caused the harm. The other defendant was held liable even though he did not in fact cause the harm!

Identifying which specific tortfeasor in fact caused a particular plaintiff's harm is a particularly important problem in products liability cases. Manufacturers sometimes produce identical or similar products that cause illnesses in consumers that do not manifest themselves until decades later, making it difficult or impossible for a victim to prove which manufacturer(s) produced the product causing her harm.

To address this situation, in *Sindell v. Abbott Laboratories*, 26 Cal.3d 588, 607 P.2d 924 (1980), the Supreme Court of California adopted the controversial doctrine known as **market share liability**. The plaintiff was a victim of cancer caused by her mother's ingestion of DES, an anti-miscarriage drug, which causes cancer in the daughters of those who consume the drug. The DES manufacturers were negligent but, a generation later, the plaintiff could not establish which manufacturer produced the drug that her mother consumed. The court held that where (a) multiple defendants manufacture fungible products and (b) the plaintiff is injured by the products of one or more manufacturers, but she cannot prove which one, each manufacturer is liable for the proportion of her damages that is equivalent to the manufacturer's share of the market for the product. The plaintiff also must file suit against manufacturers who together produced a substantial portion of the market share of the drug.

Market share liability addresses the kinds of tortious harms that are all too common in the modern era. However, only about one-third of all states apply market share liability even in DES cases, and only a handful of courts apply it in other situations. Why? First, most products produced by numerous manufacturers are not **fungible**, that is, they are *not in*distinguishable from one other (pardon the double negative!). Second, the passage of a considerable period of time between product distribution and the plaintiffs' harms often makes it impossible to determine the defendants' **respective market shares** with a meaningful degree of accuracy.

Loss of chance of recovery. The traditional but/for test for cause in fact also does not work in many cases involving a

negligent failure to diagnose a disease that later causes the patient's death. Assume that at the time when Dr. Garten negligently failed to diagnose Cynthia's cancer, she had a 40 percent chance of survival. Because of Dr. Garten's failure to diagnose the cancer, Cynthia's treatment was delayed until she changed physicians two years later and her chances of survival had decreased to 10 percent. Even so, because Cynthia probably would have died even if Dr. Garten had diagnosed her cancer in a timely fashion, Cynthia's survivors cannot prove by a preponderance of evidence that Dr. Garten's failure to diagnose was a but/for cause of her death. Therefore, under the traditional test of but/for causation, they would not be able to successfully recover from Dr. Garten.

Assuming that Dr. Garten negligently failed to diagnose cancer in 100 similarly situated patients and the survival chances for each fell from 40 percent to 10 percent, his negligence would be the cause in fact of the death of 30 of them. However, as previously explained, no particular patient would be able to prove causation under the traditional but/for test of causation, and none of them would recover. This is unfair. Further, requiring proof of cause in fact in any particular case would not yield the socially efficient level of financial disincentive (he should pay for 30 of the 100 deaths) to induce Dr. Garten to exercise the appropriate degree of greater care in diagnosing cancer in his patients.

Today, a growing number of courts allow the plaintiff to **recover *partial damages*** under a doctrine known as **loss of chance of recovery**. If prior to a physician's negligent misdiagnosis, the patient's chances of recovery were less than 50 percent, then the survivors can recover damages equal to (1) the total damages attributable to the decedent's death multiplied by (2) the percentage chance of survival lost as a result of the negligent misdiagnosis. If, for example, the jury determined that the entire damages resulting from Cynthia's death were $1 million and that Dr. Garten reduced Cynthia's chances of survival from 40 percent to 10 percent (in other words, 30 percent),then Cynthia's survivors will be able to recover $300,000 (30 percent x $1 million).

Substantial factor as a test of cause in fact. In some cases where the traditional test of but/for causation does not work, such as one involving a negligent failure to diagnose, some courts substitute another test of cause in fact, **the "substantial factor" test.** The jury is simply asked whether the defendant's tortious conduct was a substantial factor in producing the plaintiff's harm.

The problem with the substantial factor test is that courts use it in multiple contexts, and the meaning of the test is unclear in all of them. As discussed here, substantial factor is **sometimes used as a test of cause in fact**. Other courts sometimes use it as a **test of proximate cause;** in other words, is a cause in fact "substantial" enough that it should also be treated as a proximate, or legally responsible, cause? Finally, courts sometimes use "substantial factor" as **a shorthand expression encompassing both cause in fact and proximate cause**. Indeed, the instructions to the jury in routine tort cases often merely ask the jury to decide whether the defendant's negligence was a substantial factor in causing the plaintiff's injury as a proxy for both cause in fact and proximate cause. The substantial factor language originated in the *First and Second Restatements of Torts*. In an unusual move, **the *Third Restatement* explicitly disavows the use of the term in any context**. If you use the phrase "substantial factor," be sure to explain both the context in which you are using it and its meaning.

Causal linkage. **Sometimes**, even though it is literally true that "but/for the defendant's negligence, the plaintiff's harm would not have occurred," **but/for causation results from mere coincidence**. For example, assume the defendant Acme Trucking Company negligently delayed the shipment of Banana, Inc.'s computers. As a result, the computers happened to be in a warehouse that was struck by a tornado, destroying them. Acme's negligence in shipping the computers is a but/for cause, if the test is literally applied, of the destruction of the plaintiff's property. Accordingly, some courts and scholars have astutely suggested that **in order for the defendant's negligence to be a cause in fact, it must increase the probability that the plaintiff will be harmed**. Sometimes this is expressed by saying there must be a **"causal link"** between defendant's negligence and the plaintiff's harm. Most of the time, establishing that the defendant's negligence was a but/for cause of plaintiff's harm means it increased the probability of that event, thus implicitly satisfying the requirement of causal linkage. However, as the tornado hypothetical demonstrates, this is not always true.

What You Need to Know:

1. In order for the plaintiff to recover, the defendant's tortious conduct must be both a cause in fact and a proximate cause (within the scope of liability) of the plaintiff's harm.
2. In most cases, the plaintiff establishes cause in fact by showing that, but for the defendant's tortious conduct, the plaintiff would not have been harmed.
3. But/for causation fails as a test of cause in fact when multiple defendants contribute to the plaintiff's harm. In these cases, the plaintiff may be able to establish cause in fact under the doctrines of either "independent tortfeasors concurrently contributing to an indivisible harm" or "concert of action."
4. But/for causation also fails as a test of cause in fact when it is known that the specific defendant(s) who caused a particular plaintiff's harm were one or more members of a larger group whose members acted tortiously, but it cannot be established which defendant caused the plaintiff's harm. Under specific circumstances in some jurisdictions, the plaintiff may be able to recover employing either alternative liability or market-share liability.
5. A growing number of jurisdictions allow plaintiffs to recover under a loss of chance of recovery theory in negligent failure to diagnose cases, but limit damages to the percentage of total damages

proportional to the reduction in the patient's chances of recovery.

6. The "substantial factor" test is sometimes used as an alternative test of cause in fact in cases where but/for causation does not work. On other occasions, it also is used as a test of either proximate causation or the combination of both cause in fact and proximate cause. The phrase has proved to be unsatisfactory, and you probably should avoid using it.
7. Cause in fact also requires causal linkage—that the defendant's tortious conduct increased the probability that plaintiff would be injured.

LESSON 16: PROXIMATE CAUSATION (AKA "SCOPE OF LIABILITY")

There must be limits on the scope of liability for the defendant's negligent acts—liability cannot extend indefinitely. Even if Mrs. O'Leary was negligent in allowing her proverbial cow to kick over the lantern that caused the Great Chicago Fire, she will not be held liable to all the owners of property destroyed by the fire. Scope of liability poses two analytically separate issues: (1) Which victims harmed by the defendant's negligence will be able to recover? and (2) Must the particular type of risk that resulted in the harm to the plaintiff be foreseeable to the defendant in order for the plaintiff to recover?

Which victims can recover? In *Palsgraf v. Long Island Railroad Co.*, 248 N.Y. 339, 162 N.E. 99 (1928), a man carrying a package covered in newspaper tried to board a moving train. He seemed unsteady, so two employees of the defendant tried to assist him. The package, which unbeknownst to the defendant's employees contained fireworks, was dislodged and fell onto the tracks, causing the fireworks to explode. The blast toppled some scales at the other end of the platform, which struck the plaintiff, injuring her. She sued the railroad, alleging that the defendant's employees were negligent in assisting the passenger in boarding the moving train.

To Judge **Cardozo**, writing for the majority, the issue was whether or not the defendant owed Mrs. Palsgraf a duty of care. He held that **no duty was owed** to her because she was **not a foreseeable victim** of the defendant's negligence. According to Judge Cardozo, **negligence is a relational tort**: the defendant must breach a **duty of care to a particular victim or at least to a class of people** among whom the plaintiff is a member.

Judge **Andrews**, dissenting, disagreed. He reasoned that the tort of negligence was not relational: "Due care is a **duty imposed on each one of us to protect society** from unnecessary danger, not to protect A, B, or C alone." However, even under Judge Andrews's understanding of negligence, it does not follow that any victim harmed by the defendant's negligence necessarily should be able to recover. To recover, the **plaintiff** must show that her injury was ***proximately* caused** by the defendant's negligence. Unlike Judge Cardozo, Judge Andrews reasoned that whether or not a particular plaintiff should recover does not turn solely on foreseeability. Instead, proximate causation is a matter "**of convenience, of public policy, of a rough sense of justice**." In deciding whether the defendant's negligence proximately caused the plaintiff's harm, the jury should consider factors such as whether there was a **natural and continuous sequence**, a **direct connection without too many intervening causes**, the **likelihood** and **foreseeability** of the result, and **remoteness in time and place**.

Today, a majority of states follows Judge Cardozo's opinion and hold that defendants owe a duty of care only to foreseeable victims, but a substantial minority of jurisdictions follows Judge Andrews's approach.

Type of risk. The second issue under scope of liability is **whether the defendant must be able to foresee the particular type of risk that causes harm to the plaintiff**. At least on this issue, courts agree that the issue is one of proximate causation. In *In re Polemis*, [1921] 3 K.B. 560 (Court of Appeal), a longshoreman negligently dropped a plank into the hold of a ship. Obviously, the shipowner was a foreseeable plaintiff under *Palsgraf*: The defendant could foresee that some harm, such as a dent, would occur to the ship. However, during the ship's voyage, part of its cargo, tins containing benzine (a highly flammable liquid distillate of petroleum, not to be confused with benzene) had been damaged, causing highly flammable gases to escape into the ship's hold. When the plank dropped, the ship burst into flames. The result was unforeseeable, but the court held the defendant liable for **all the damages directly caused** by the dropping of the plank, **even if they were unforeseeable**. The court stated that defendants would **not** be **liable for remote causes**.

Forty years later, in *Overseas Tankship (U.K.) Ltd. v. Morts Dock & Engineering Co., Ltd.*, [1961] A.C. 388 (Privy Council) (often called "*The Wagon Mound No. 1*"), the Privy Council rejected the test applied in *Polemis* and reached a conflicting conclusion. In *Wagon Mound*, the defendant's ship discharged fuel oil into Sydney Harbor. The plaintiff, who owned a wharf, proceeded with its welding activities after being assured by "experts" that the floating fuel oil would not burn. Molten metal set afire cotton waste or rags floating in the oil, and the resulting flames destroyed the dock. The court explicitly rejected the "direct causation" test of *Polemis* and instead held that a defendant **was liable only for damages caused by foreseeable types of risks, not unforeseeable ones**. The dock owner was a foreseeable plaintiff under Judge Cardozo's test in *Palsgraf* because some harm to the dock, for example, the mucking of the dock with fuel oil, was foreseeable. However, the fire was not a foreseeable type of risk and therefore the shipowner was not liable.

Note the way in which the foreseeability test in *Wagon Mound* on the issue of the foreseeability of the type of risk parallels the foreseeability test of Cardozo's opinion regarding the foreseeability of the victim. At the same time, Judge Andrews's opinion in *Palsgraf,* which does not require that the plaintiff necessarily be foreseeable in order to find liability, parallels the reasoning of *Polemis* to some degree, but outlines a far more policy-oriented test of proximate causation than the linguistic distinction between "direct" and "remote" causes in *Polemis*.

A majority of American courts today follows *Polemis*, not *Wagon Mound*. A defendant may be held liable for *direct* results, even if they are unforeseeable.

Intervening and superseding causes. Scope of liability issues often arise in the context of intervening and superseding causes. An **intervening cause** is a cause that occurs after the defendant's negligence and combines with it to produce plaintiff's harm. A **superseding cause** is an intervening cause that "breaks the chain of causation" between the original defendant's negligence and the plaintiff's harm and thus precludes the original defendant from being held liable to the plaintiff. The critical issue, of course, is when is an intervening cause also a superseding cause? As a general guideline, courts frequently state that if the original defendant can foresee the intervening cause, it is not a superseding cause, and the defendant remains liable to the plaintiff.

Usually intervening causes that consist of a third party's negligence are regarded as foreseeable and therefore not superseding causes. For example, the negligent driver who causes an automobile accident will be liable not only for the victim's broken leg resulting from the accident, but also for the amputated leg resulting from the attending physician's negligence. An older rule, sometimes not followed today, is that an intervening cause consisting of a third party's intentional or criminal wrongdoing is regarded as a superseding cause.

What You Need to Know:

1. Scope of liability, often called proximate causation, consists of (a) whether the harm to a particular victim is closely enough connected to the defendant's negligence that she can recover, and (b) whether the particular type of risk that harms the victim is closely enough connected to defendant's negligence to allow plaintiff to recover.

2. A majority of courts holds that a duty of care is owed only to foreseeable victims. In contrast, a substantial minority of courts regards the issue as one of proximate causation and holds that a

plaintiff can recover if the harm is closely enough connected to defendant's tortious conduct.

3. Judge Cardozo and some courts regard the issue of which plaintiffs are able to recover as a question of duty, not a question of proximate cause. To Judge Andrews and many courts today, the issue is one of proximate causation.

4. Most courts hold that a plaintiff can recover for harms directly, but not remotely, caused by the defendant's conduct. A substantial minority of courts holds that a plaintiff can recover only when the type of risk that harmed him was foreseeable to the defendant.

5. Many proximate cause cases involve whether an intervening cause is also a superseding cause, thereby cutting off the liability of the original defendant.

LESSON 17: DAMAGES AND CONTINGENT FEES

In **negligence** cases, the plaintiff must prove **actual harm, usually personal injury or property damage**, in order to recover. In other words, as basketball commentators sometimes say, "No harm, no foul." Unlike in intentional torts cases, nominal damages are not recoverable. Further, in most situations, the victim who suffers only economic damages ("purely commercial loss") or emotional distress without any physical harm is not able to recover in a negligence action.

Most damages in negligence cases are **compensatory damages**. The general measure of compensatory damages is that the jury should award the plaintiff the amount of money that would "**make the victim whole**, as if she had never suffered an injury." Obviously, this is a total legal fiction. The jury cannot turn back the clock and undo, for example, the victim's paralysis. The first type of damages recoverable by the victim is damages for the **loss of earning capacity**, whether the victim would have decided to work or not. The second type of damages includes **past and future medical and rehabilitative expenses**. The third category of damages is often called "**pain and suffering**." This is a rather imprecise label that encompasses damages for things such as physical pain and suffering resulting from the accident; emotional distress; the loss of enjoyment of life for a victim denied the pleasure of things such as holding her child, dancing, playing soccer, or having sex; and the emotional distress resulting from the death of or injury to a close family member. The inherently imprecise nature of valuing such items and the occasionally very large awards for these noneconomic damages make them a target for critics of the tort system. Many state legislatures have **limited or "capped" recovery of noneconomic damages** at a designated amount, for example, $300,000.

Under the so-called **doctrine of avoidable consequences**, the accident victim must take reasonable measures to "mitigate" his damages. If he fails to do so, he will not be able to recover damages for the "aggravated" portion of the injury. For example, if the victim is injured in an automobile accident and he *unreasonably* fails to seek treatment for his broken leg, which then becomes gangrenous and must be amputated, he will be able to recover damages for the broken leg, but not for the results of the amputation.

At common law, the amount of damages that the defendant owed the plaintiff was not reduced by any compensation the plaintiff received from "**collateral sources**," such as his health insurer. However, most often the plaintiff would not receive "double recovery," because under the subrogation clause of the contract between the health insurer and the victim, the health insurer was entitled to be reimbursed by the victim for any benefits it had paid that the plaintiff later recovered from the defendant or his liability insurer. Many states have now modified the collateral source rule, at least in some circumstances, and in these states, the plaintiff's recovery may be reduced by amounts received from first-party insurers and other collateral sources.

Another extremely controversial aspect of damages is **punitive damages**. Punitive damages are separate and distinct from pain and suffering damages (which are a type of damages intended to compensate the plaintiff). Punitive damages begin with the proposition that compensatory damages are sometimes inadequate to punish the defendant for its wrongdoing or to deter it from similar wrongdoing in the future. The plaintiff is entitled to punitive damages if she proves by clear and convincing evidence that the defendant acted "willfully, wantonly, and recklessly" or with malice. Like the collateral source rule, punitive damages have been very controversial during the past generation, and many states have enacted legislation to limit them. In fact, punitive damages remain relatively rare in tort litigation, and most punitive damage awards occur in specific contexts such as intentional or business torts. This also is one of the few areas of tort law that the U.S. Supreme Court has frequently addressed in recent years. The court has struck down punitive damage awards on due process grounds in a few cases, such as where the ratio of punitive damages to compensatory damages was too great.

Wrongful death and survival statutes. Under the traditional common law, when the injured victim of tortious conduct died, so did his cause of action. Today, **all American jurisdictions have adopted "wrongful death and survival statutes,"** which enable survivors of the decedent to pursue claims resulting from his tortiously caused death. Each state's statutes differ from those of other states, so it is important to read the applicable statutes carefully. Most states continue to recognize two separate actions, a "survival" action and a "wrongful death" action, but the two are sometimes merged.

Typically, **survival actions** are **brought by the legal representative of the decedent's estate** (usually known as the "executor," "executrix," "administrator," or "administratrix") and pursue recovery for **any claims that the decedent had at the time of his death**, such as compensation for any medical expenses incurred between the time of the accident and the time of his death, any loss of income during this period of time, any pain and suffering he suffered during the same interval, and any damages to property he owned, such as his automobile. Survival statutes also typically allow for recovery of the decedent's funeral expenses.

Wrongful death actions are brought by the **family members of the decedent who are specifically identified**

in a state's wrongful death statutes, most often the decedent's spouse, children, or parents. The recoverable **damages are those that the decedent's family members sustained as a result of his death**, notably his loss of income from the time of his death until the time that he otherwise would have retired (less his anticipated living expenses), the loss of companionship that the survivors experienced, and compensation for the household tasks that the decedent performed before his death.

Contingent fees. In most other countries of the world, attorneys are paid through a "loser pays" system. If the plaintiff sues to recover damages for her personal injury and prevails, she is entitled to recover not only her damages, but also her reasonable attorney's fees. Similarly, if the defendant prevails, it is entitled to collect its attorney's fees from the plaintiff but, in reality, most plaintiffs have few resources to be tapped for this purpose.

The **American system, where each party pays its own attorney**, poses a problem for most victims of personal injuries who are unable to pay "up front" for substantial attorney's fees and other litigation expenses—often tens of thousands of dollars or more. Accordingly, in almost all tort actions, the plaintiff's attorney is compensated on a "**contingent fee**" basis. If the plaintiff recovers from the defendant, her attorney is entitled to a **percentage of the recovery** agreed upon by the client and her attorney as compensation for his services. This percentage is often one-third of the recovery, but sometimes is a somewhat lower percentage if the case settles significantly before a scheduled trial date or a higher percentage if the case is appealed or retried. In addition, the plaintiff's attorney generally fronts the litigation expenses, including, for example, expert witness fees, deposition costs, and filing fees, and typically recoups these expenses only if the plaintiff recovers.

Contingent (sometimes called "contingency") fees are a highly controversial aspect of the American tort system. Critics point to the huge fees earned by plaintiffs' attorneys in some cases, particularly the litigation brought by state governments against tobacco manufacturers in the late 1990s, where plaintiffs' attorneys collectively earned over $13 billion in fees. In this unusually immense litigation, individual attorneys sometimes earned tens of thousands of dollars per hour of work. Critics also allege that the contingent fee system sometimes results in compensation that does not reflect the amount of time invested in a case but instead only the strength of the case. Occasionally the defendant's insurer quickly settles a "slam dunk" case against its insured for "policy limits" of $50,000 before it is necessary for the plaintiff's attorney to invest a substantial amount of time in the case, thus earning an extremely hefty hourly rate.

However, the contingent fee system aligns the interests of the plaintiff and her attorney. If it is worthwhile for the attorney to spend substantial hours on a case, he has an incentive to do so; otherwise, he will not. Most victims of personal injuries have little experience in dealing with attorneys. If they were billed on an hourly basis for the attorney's time, they would lack the experience necessary to determine whether they are being overbilled. In contrast, most defendants either are businesses or have their attorneys provided and monitored by insurance companies. These attorneys generally are compensated on an hourly basis. Perhaps surprisingly, the few available studies on the compensation of attorneys in tort actions show that in the aggregate, across a range of cases, the compensation paid to defense attorneys is nearly as great as that received by plaintiffs' attorneys.

What You Need to Know:

1. In order to recover for negligence, but not intentional torts, the plaintiff must prove actual harm—usually a personal injury or property damage.

2. The general measure of compensatory damages in tort cases is the amount of damages designed to make the victim whole.

3. Punitive damages are intended to punish the defendant for his unusually egregious wrongdoing

and deter him from committing similar acts in the future.

4. Today, all jurisdictions have adopted wrongful death and survival statutes that enable recovery for both damages that the decedent sustained during her lifetime and those that her family will experience in the future as a result of her death.
5. Plaintiffs' attorneys typically work under contingent fee agreements that provide that they will receive a designated percentage of their clients' recoveries as compensation for their legal services.

LESSON 18: CONTRIBUTORY NEGLIGENCE AND COMPARATIVE FAULT

We have finished considering what the victim of an accident must plead and prove in order to establish a *prima facie* case of negligence—that is, the elements sufficient to establish liability unless rebutted by the defendant. Sometimes the defendant will prevail by presenting evidence showing that the plaintiff cannot prove one or more of the elements of negligence. Under the traditional common law, the defendant could also prevail by pleading and proving the requirements of an **affirmative defense** to negligence—usually contributory negligence, assumption of risk, or an immunity.

Contributory negligence consists of **conduct on the part of the plaintiff in which she fails to exercise reasonable care to protect herself from harm, and her failure to exercise reasonable care is a contributing cause of her own injury**. Under the traditional common law, if the plaintiff is contributorily negligent, even if the defendant is far more negligent, the plaintiff cannot recover any damages. For example, assume that Victoria Victim, while driving through an intersection with a traffic light, momentarily looked down to adjust her radio. As a result, she did not notice that Mickey Moran, who is driving on an intersecting road and runs a red light, is also entering the intersection. Under the traditional rule of contributory negligence, although Mickey is negligent, Victoria is also contributorily negligent and she will not be able to recover. It does not matter that Mickey's negligence is far worse—that is, significantly more egregiously culpable, than Victoria's contributory negligence.

Several justifications have been offered for the **traditional rule** that the plaintiff's contributory negligence, even if modest, was a **total bar to plaintiff's recovery**. First, it was sometimes said that plaintiff's contributory negligence was a superseding cause breaking the chain of causation between defendant's negligence and plaintiff's harm, but this notion does not conform to the usual rule governing intervening and superseding causes, which provides that another party's negligence is viewed as foreseeable and therefore not superseding. Second, it was argued that contributory negligence encouraged plaintiffs to be more careful, but one would expect that avoiding serious personal injury is incentive enough by itself. Also, contributory negligence as a total bar to recovery lowers the defendant's (often a business's) incentives to use reasonable care to avoid injury to others, because the defendant's liability is precluded by the doctrine of contributory negligence. Third, it was sometimes said that a plaintiff needed to come to court "with clean hands" and that courts did not believe they were competent to apportion or divide liability between the parties. However, most legal historians believe that the most important reason for contributory negligence as a total bar to recovery was to reduce the liability exposure of emerging industries and railroads during the nineteenth century so that their liability would not thwart the Industrial Revolution.

The traditional common-law rule of contributory negligence as a total bar to recovery, once applied in all jurisdictions, now applies in only four states and the District of Columbia.

The other 46 states, either through judicial decisions or legislation, have adopted some form of what is known as **comparative fault** or **comparative negligence**. In a comparative fault jurisdiction, the jury compares the respective degrees of fault of the plaintiff and the defendant and expresses each party's fault in percentage terms. The **plaintiff** then **recovers a judgment equal to the product of her total damages times the defendant's degree of fault**. So if the jury found that Victoria's damages were $100,000, Mickey was 90 percent at fault, and Victoria was 10 percent at fault, Victoria would be able to recover $90,000 in a comparative fault state. Remember, under the traditional rule of contributory negligence, she would recover nothing!

How does the jury determine the respective degrees of fault of the plaintiff and the defendant? There are three approaches used in various jurisdictions. Under the first approach, the jury assigns percentages of liability according to the relative culpability of each of the parties—how far did the plaintiff and the defendant(s) deviate from the standard of the ordinary, reasonably prudent person? In other states, the jury is asked to weigh the respective "causal contributions" of the parties, that is, how closely the harm that occurs falls within the scope of the risk created by each party's conduct. Finally, an increasingly popular approach is that the jury considers both the parties' respective levels of culpability and the extent that their respective acts of negligence causally contributed to the accident.

What happens when the plaintiff is more at fault than the defendant? Twelve states apply "**pure comparative fault**." Under this approach, **even the more-at-fault party can recover partial compensation from the less-at-fault party**. So, for example, assume Victoria was injured in an automobile accident in which her car collided with Mickey's, and she sustained $20,000 in damages. Mickey was severely injured in the same accident. If Victoria sued Mickey in the first instance, Mickey could "counterclaim" against Victoria to recover for his injuries. If Mickey's total damages from the accident were $1,000,000 and the jury found Mickey to be 90 percent at fault and Victoria to be 10 percent at fault, Victoria would recover $18,000 on her claim, but Mickey could recover $100,000 on his counterclaim. Note that even when Mickey is far more at fault, he ends up recovering more from Victoria than Victoria does from him because he is the far more seriously injured victim.

Outcomes like this under a pure comparative fault regime were a factor leading at least 33 states to adopt a form of comparative fault known as "modified comparative fault." In most **modified comparative fault** jurisdictions, the **plaintiff is not able to recover if her degree of fault is greater than that of the defendant** (or, in a small number of states, if plaintiff's degree of fault is equal to the defendant's degree of fault). When legislatures, not courts, adopt comparative fault, they have almost always adopted modified comparative fault.

Contributory negligence was never a bar to recovery for intentional torts or "willful, wanton, and reckless" behavior—conduct on the part of the defendant that was far worse than negligence. Today, most comparative fault states hold that comparative fault analysis should apply when defendant's conduct is willful, wanton, and reckless, but not when it is intentional.

Imputed contributory negligence. In Lesson 4, "Sources of Compensation: Vicarious Liability and Insurance," we considered when one *defendant*, usually the employer, could be held liable for the tortious acts of another party, usually the employee. However, it is rare for a *plaintiff* to be precluded from recovery under the doctrine of contributory negligence because of the negligence of another party. Today, **the doctrine of "imputed contributory negligence" is largely discredited**. Under the traditional common law, if a passenger in an automobile was injured as a result of the negligence of both the driver of her car and the driver of a second automobile, she was unable to recover in an action against the driver of the other automobile because the fault of the driver of her car was **imputed** to her and thus barred her action against the other driver at a time when contributory negligence was a total bar to recovery. This is no longer the case.

Consider also an example where the driver of a car in a suburban development exceeded the speed limit and was therefore negligent per se. He struck a two-year-old child who was playing in the street, severely injuring him. The child's father, who was responsible for taking care of him at the time, was distracted by a radio report that his favorite football team had just scored a touchdown. He did not see his child go into the street and did nothing to prevent him from doing so. The father's negligence in failing to use due care to watch the child will not be attributed to the child as contributory negligence. In addition, of course, because of the child's young age, he is not capable of being held contributory negligent in his own right. Accordingly, the child would be able to recover against the speeding driver even in a jurisdiction that recognizes contributory negligence as a total bar to recovery; similarly, his recovery would not be reduced by his own negligence in a comparative fault jurisdiction.

What You Need to Know:

1. Contributory negligence consists of the plaintiff's failure to use reasonable care to protect herself from an accident for which her lack of due care, combined with defendant's negligence, was a contributing cause.
2. Under the traditional common law, and still in a few jurisdictions, plaintiff's contributory negligence is a total bar to recovery.
3. Most states now apply comparative fault, which apportions responsibility for plaintiff's damages to the defendant and the plaintiff according to their respective degrees of fault.
4. Depending on the rules of the jurisdiction where the accident occurs, the defendant's and the plaintiff's respective portions of financial responsibility for the plaintiff's harm are determined by comparing the level of egregiousness of each party's conduct, their respective causal contributions to the accident, or both.
5. Some states apply "pure" comparative fault, but most states apply modified comparative fault. In a modified comparative fault system, the plaintiff recovers nothing if his fault is greater than that of the defendant, but he recovers a reduced amount if his fault is less than that of the defendant.

6. Under modern law, the plaintiff's recovery is rarely barred or reduced by the negligence of a third party imputed to her.

LESSON 19: APPORTIONING LIABILITY AMONG JOINT TORTFEASORS

Often the negligent conduct of multiple defendants combines to cause the plaintiff's harm. How then do we **assign financial responsibility to each defendant for the damages owed after the plaintiff obtains a judgment against multiple defendants**?

Joint and several liability. In Lesson 14 discussing *res ipsa loquitur* and in Lesson 15 on cause in fact, we already encountered the doctrine of **joint and several liability**. To review briefly, when two or more defendants are held jointly and severally liable, the plaintiff has the choice of collecting the entire judgment from one defendant, the entire judgment from another defendant, or recovering portions of the judgment from various defendants—as long as the plaintiff's entire recovery does not exceed the amount of the judgment. Even if one of the co-defendants is insolvent, immune, or beyond the jurisdiction of the court, the plaintiff is entitled to collect her entire judgment. The risk and consequences of one co-defendant's inability to pay falls on the remaining co-defendant(s) and not on the plaintiff.

In some cases, joint and several liability appears to produce arguably unfair results. Consider, for example, the case of *Walt Disney World v. Wood*, 515 So. 2d 198 (Fla. 1987). The plaintiff was injured at Walt Disney World when the bumper car she was driving was rammed by another bumper car driven by her fiancé, Daniel Wood. The jury found that both Daniel and Walt Disney World were negligent, but that the plaintiff was also contributorily negligent. Asked to assign percentages of fault to each party under Florida's rule of comparative fault, the jury assigned 85 percent of the fault to the defendant Daniel, 14 percent of the fault to the plaintiff, and 1 percent of the fault to the defendant Walt Disney World. However, prior to trial, the plaintiff and the defendant Daniel were married, so Daniel was now immune from liability under interspousal immunity. The judge reduced the total judgment by the 14 percent attributable to the plaintiff's degree of fault and held the co-defendant Walt Disney World (WDW) liable for the remaining 86 percent. In other words, even though the jury attributed 14 times as much fault to the plaintiff as it did to the defendant WDW, WDW was responsible for 86 percent of the damages!

Traditionally, in the days before comparative fault and contribution among tortfeasors (discussed later in this lesson), joint and several liability could be justified on several grounds. First, as between a co-defendant whose negligence was a necessary "but/for" cause of the accident and an "innocent" plaintiff (because under the traditional rule of contributory negligence as a total bar to recovery, if the plaintiff were contributorily negligent, she would recover nothing), it made sense to assign the unpaid share attributable to the insolvent or immune co-defendant to the remaining defendant whose tortious conduct caused the accident. However, after comparative fault replaced contributory negligence, under a rule of joint and several liability, the plaintiff was able to recover from the remaining defendant even when she was contributorily negligent. Second, in the past it was sometimes said that courts would not apportion liability among parties and that courts should not settle disagreements "among wrongdoers." Of course, once comparative fault arrived on the scene, neither of these reasons remained valid. A third reason justifying joint and several liability is that the party left holding the bag is most likely a business or an insurance company. This outcome may be an advantage to those such as Judge Guido Calabresi, who regard "loss distribution" as an important objective of tort law, but not to the Chamber of Commerce that probably views it as a "liability tax."

Joint and several liability was the traditional rule at common law, and today approximately fifteen states continue to employ joint and several liability. A majority of states now employs one of several alternatives to joint and several liability that will be discussed later in this lesson, but first let's consider how a co-defendant who has paid the plaintiff's judgment might be able to recover some or all of what it has paid from its fellow co-defendants.

Indemnity. Even under the traditional common law, if a defendant paid a judgment only because it was vicariously liable for the tort committed by another party, it could sue the party that actually committed the tort for **indemnity** and recover the **entire amount** it had paid. The most common example was that if an employer was held vicariously liable for a tort committed by an employee and paid the judgment, it could then turn around and sue the employee who had actually committed the tort. Of course, in most cases this did not happen, presumably because either the employee was judgment-proof or suing the employee was regarded as being bad for workplace morale or likely to cause union problems!

Contribution. At common law, if two or more defendants were held jointly and severally liable to the plaintiff, and one defendant paid more than its fair share of the entire judgment, it could not sue the other co-defendants for "**contribution**." By the 1980s, all or virtually all states had adopted some variant of the *Uniform Contribution among Tortfeasors Act*. The basic idea of the act is that where one defendant has paid more than its "fair share" of a judgment owed to the plaintiff, it could sue the other co-defendants **to collect anything in excess of its fair share**. Most often, each co-defendant's "fair share" of a judgment is determined by its relative culpability, in much the same way as the respective shares of fault of the plaintiff and the defendant are determined under comparative fault. The *Uniform Contribution among Tortfeasors Act*, by itself, did not change the common law rule that the co-defendants remain jointly and severally liable to the plaintiff.

Alternatives to joint and several liability. Once most states adopted both comparative fault (apportioning liability between the plaintiff and the defendant) and contribution among tortfeasors (apportioning liability among co-defendants even while they remain jointly and severally liable to the plaintiff), the traditional justifications for the "all or nothing" approach of joint and several liability were no longer as compelling as they had been in the past. Beginning in the 1980s, **approximately**

35 states abrogated joint and several liability and replaced it with one of several alternatives.

Several or proportionate liability. This approach, favored by businesses that are likely to be defendants and by insurers, leaves **a co-defendant liable to the plaintiff for only the portion of the plaintiff's total damages that is proportionate to its percentage share of fault**. So, for example, in a proportionate liability jurisdiction, Walt Disney World would be held liable for only 1 percent of the plaintiff's damages. Superficially, this sounds fair. However, **several or proportionate liability** is unfair to the plaintiff in the same way that joint and several liability is unfair to the defendant. The jury found that the plaintiff in *Walt Disney World v. Wood* should be responsible for only 14 percent of the damages, but under several liability 99 percent of her damages will be uncompensated. Approximately 15 states now apply several or proportionate liability.

Compromise alternatives for the handling of the liability of joint tortfeasors. Because both joint and several liability and proportionate liability appear to be unfair to either the remaining defendant(s) or the plaintiff, many state legislatures enacted **compromise alternatives**. Because the resulting rules reflect the balance of power in each state among powerful lobbying groups such as plaintiffs' trial lawyers, the business community, and insurers, there are dozens of different variations. However, most enactments are variants or combinations of one of the following three approaches.

The **first alternative** provides that all co-defendants are held **jointly and severally liable for economic damages** (such as medical expenses and lost income), but **only severally liable for noneconomic damages** (damages for pain and suffering).

The **second alternative is that a co-defendant will be held jointly and severally liable if its respective share of liability exceeds a threshold level of fault defined by statute**. However, if its share of liability is less than the threshold, it will be held only severally liable. In some states, this threshold is as low as 15 percent, but in other states, it is as high as 60 percent.

The **third alternative** is to **reallocate the share of liability of the co-defendant that is not collectible** because of its insolvency, its immunity, or the lack of jurisdiction over the co-defendant, **to the remaining co-defendants proportional to their respective shares of liability**. In other words, in *Walt Disney World*, Daniel's unpaid share would be reallocated to the plaintiff and the co-defendant Walt Disney World, with the plaintiff taking most of the hit because the jury found her to have a much greater degree of fault in the accident than did Walt Disney World.

What You Need to Know:

1. At common law, co-defendants were held jointly and severally liable to the plaintiff. About 15 states continue to follow this rule.
2. Even at common law, a defendant who paid a judgment only because of its relationship with the party who actually caused the harm (such as vicarious liability), could seek indemnification (reimbursement) from the party who actually caused the harm.
3. Approximately 16 states today follow a rule of several liability, in which each defendant is liable only for the same percentage of the judgment that reflects its percentage allocation of fault. The plaintiff takes the hit if one of the co-defendants is insolvent, immune, or beyond the jurisdiction of the court.
4. The remaining states have adopted compromises for allocating the share that is not collectible from a co-defendant among the plaintiff and remaining defendants.
5. Today all states allow a defendant who has paid more than its fair share of a judgment to sue any co-defendants for contribution.

LESSON 20: ASSUMPTION OF RISK

The second affirmative defense to negligence based on the plaintiff's conduct is "assumption of risk." Traditionally, courts used this label in three distinct contexts. First, it is sometimes said that when a defendant and a plaintiff sign a contract that **disclaims liability** for the defendant's negligence, the plaintiff has "assumed the risk" of any subsequent injury. This is known as **express assumption of risk**. For example, assume Amelia enrolls in a parachute school. Her contract with the school provides that she will not hold the school liable for any injuries she sustains, including those caused by its negligence. Amelia is then injured on her first jump as a result of the school's negligence. Is her negligence action barred by the disclaimer of liability?

The general rule is that parties can agree to disclaim liability for negligence. However, there are three exceptions: the parties cannot agree to disclaim defendant's liability (1) for intentional torts or willful, wanton, and reckless conduct; (2) where there is a gross disparity of bargaining power between the parties; or (3) when the transaction involves "a matter of public interest." For example, defendants cannot disclaim liability for negligence if they are common carriers (planes, boats, and trains, etc. for hire), innkeepers, or employers requiring disclaimers of liability as a condition of employment. Some courts require the parties to be very explicit when disclaiming liability for negligence. For example, the contractual provision cannot simply disclaim liability "for all injuries," but must make clear that injuries resulting from the defendant's "negligence" or "fault" are disclaimed. A few courts hold that any business holding itself open to members of the general public cannot disclaim liability for negligence.

Today, better-reasoned opinions recognize that express assumption of risk is really **not an affirmative defense** at all. Instead, when the parties agree by contract that the defendant does not owe a duty of care to the plaintiff in the first place, there is **no duty** on the defendant's part and therefore the plaintiff cannot prove the first element of negligence—a duty of care owed by the defendant to the plaintiff.

The second type of "assumption of risk" can best be explained by understanding its historical context. In the case of workplace injuries during the nineteenth century, the employee was said to have assumed the risk of injury from any **inherent risks** that remained after the employer had provided a reasonably safe (but not perfectly safe) place to work. The employer had no duty to eliminate the inherent risks of the workplace. This background helps explain why today assumption of risk continues to be regarded as a "**disfavored**" **defense**. However, a spectator attending a professional baseball game and choosing to sit in an unscreened area of the ballpark is sometimes said to have "assumed the risk" of thrown and batted balls that end up in the stands through no fault of the ballpark operator. Again, the defendant ballpark operator does not owe a duty of reasonable care to protect against the inherent and incidental risks of the game, and therefore, he is not negligent in the first place.

The third type of "assumption of risk" really is a true affirmative defense. Traditionally, when a plaintiff "**voluntarily assumed a known risk**," the defendant had a valid affirmative defense of assumption of risk. In its original incarnation, the plaintiff's conduct was not required to be unreasonable in order for the defendant to prevail under this affirmative defense.

For the defense to apply, the plaintiff must be aware of and appreciate a **specific risk**. Just because you know that there is always a risk of a careless driver on a busy highway does not mean that you have assumed the risk of a traffic accident and that therefore the negligent driver who hits you has an affirmative defense!

Consider the following examples, posed in *Blackburn v. Dorta*, 348 So. 2d 287 (Fla. 1977). Assume that a landlord negligently caused a fire to occur in the tenant's premises. In the first hypothetical, the tenant returns to find his apartment in flames. Knowing that his young child is still in the apartment, he goes rushing into the flames in order to save the child's life and is severely burned in the process. A literal application of the assumption-of-risk doctrine might prevent the tenant-plaintiff from recovering from the landlord-defendant, because he has "voluntarily encountered a known risk." Today, however, few if any courts would apply the doctrine in such a harsh manner. Most courts that still recognize assumption of the risk as a separate and independent affirmative defense apply it only in situations in which the plaintiff's conduct is unreasonable.

On the other hand, assume that the tenant arrives home, finds his apartment in flames, and remembers that his favorite hat, a fedora, is inside. In an attempt to save his fedora, he rushes into the burning apartment and is injured. Here the tenant has "**unreasonably, voluntarily encountered a known risk**." This sounds like an appropriate occasion for applying the affirmative defense of assumption of the risk. However, because the tenant's conduct is unreasonable, it also fulfills the requirements for contributory negligence. In other words, in jurisdictions where contributory negligence continues to totally bar recovery, either assumption of risk or contributory negligence standing alone precludes plaintiff's recovery. Accordingly, it is not necessary to preserve both affirmative defenses in these jurisdictions.

In addition, approximately half of comparative-fault jurisdictions no longer recognize assumption of risk as a separate defense. In modified-comparative-fault jurisdictions, the jury probably will find that if the plaintiff unreasonably and voluntarily encountered a known risk, the degree of fault attributable to her exceeds 50 percent, thus barring her recovery entirely. Thus, just as in contributory-negligence jurisdictions, a separate affirmative defense of assumption of risk is generally redundant. Finally, in pure-comparative-fault jurisdictions, the actions of the plaintiff in unreasonably and voluntarily encountering a known risk merely reduce her recovery under comparative-fault analysis. However, even here, the degree of fault attributable to the plaintiff probably is very high, so she would recover only a small portion of the damages she sustained.

To recap, traditionally assumption of risk encompassed three situations. The first involved contractual disclaimers of liability, but a separate and independent affirmative defense of assumption of risk is not necessary there because the defendant owed no duty of care to the plaintiff in the first place. In the second situation, where the plaintiff sues the defendant for harms caused by the inherent risks of an activity that could not have been prevented by the exercise of reasonable care, this also is a "no duty" situation, and a separate affirmative defense is not needed. In the third category, the plaintiff's conduct in encountering a known risk is either reasonable or unreasonable. In the "reasonable" assumption of the risk situation—a rare case—most courts find that they do not want plaintiff's reasonable conduct to bar recovery for his injuries. On the other hand, where plaintiff "unreasonably" assumes the risk, the plaintiff is already contributorily negligent. **Many courts**, therefore, **have abolished assumption of the risk as a separate defense**.

Assumption of risk itself does not apply to **intentional torts**, but its close analog—**consent—does bar recovery**.

What You Need to Know:

1. Contractual disclaimers of liability are valid in a majority of jurisdictions provided that (a) the defendant does not try to disclaim liability for intentional torts or willful, wanton, or reckless conduct, (b) there is not a gross disparity of bargaining power between the parties, and (c) the matter is not one involving the public interest.
2. Contractual disclaimers are best understood as negating the existence of a duty of care owed by defendant to the plaintiff, thereby preventing plaintiff from proving negligence in the first place.
3. In many cases, such as those involving injuries resulting from the inherent risks posed by the workplace or watching a ballgame, the defendant does not owe a duty of care to prevent harm from inherent risks of the activity if the defendant is not otherwise negligent. Again, this is best handled as a "no duty" situation and not by the application of the assumption of risk doctrine.
4. The affirmative defense of assumption of risk requires that the plaintiff voluntarily encounter a

known risk. The known risk must be of a specific risk.

5. Today, most courts, either explicitly or implicitly, require that the plaintiff's assumption of risk be an *unreasonable*, voluntary encountering of a known risk.
6. Because the plaintiff's unreasonable conduct in encountering a known risk also satisfies the requirements for contributory negligence, many courts have abolished assumption of risk as a separate affirmative defense.

LESSON 21: "IMMUNITIES" AND GOVERNMENTAL LIABILITY

Traditionally, **immunities** constituted a distinct set of **affirmative defenses**: even if certain defendants inflicted tortious harms, they could not be held liable because of either (1) the **identity of the defendant** or (2) the nature of the **defendant's relationship with the plaintiff**. One of the greatest changes in tort law during the past 50 years has been the total or partial **"abrogation" (elimination) of such immunities**. Even today, however, the liability of family members, charitable institutions, and governments and their officers and employees generally continues to be governed by different—and generally more restrictive—rules than those governing the liability of other defendants.

Interspousal Immunity. **Interspousal immunity**, the doctrine that prevented one spouse from suing the other, originated in the pre-twentieth-century notion that the husband and the wife constituted a single legal entity. It was later justified on the grounds that a tort action by one spouse against another would create marital disharmony. One wonders whether it was the tort liability or the incident giving rise to the filing of the plaintiff's complaint that created the disharmony! Further, in the modern era, it can be assumed that usually one spouse would not file an action against the other unless the judgment would be paid with the proceeds of insurance, usually either an automobile or homeowner's policy.

This possibility, of course, raises another objection to the abrogation of interspousal immunity—that liability between spouses would facilitate the filing of collusive lawsuits designed to defraud the defendant-spouse's insurer. However, is the risk of insurance fraud by an unscrupulous married couple any greater than that posed by dishonest close friends?

Against this historical and policy background, a few jurisdictions have eliminated interspousal immunity in all cases, while others have eliminated it only in the cases of litigation arising from automobile accidents where the judgment presumably will be paid by the liability insurer. Other states abrogate the immunity only in the case of truly "outrageous" intentional torts. Still another set of states, the largest group, allow recovery for torts arising from both traffic accidents and from outrageous intentional torts, but not for other torts.

Parent-Child Immunity. Like spouses, **parents** were once **immune from tort actions filed by their minor children**, and children were immune from tort actions filed by their parents. Today, these immunities also have been abrogated in many states but at a somewhat slower pace than interspousal immunities. Increasingly, parents and children are liable to one another in cases involving automobile accidents (where the family members usually are insured) and in cases of outrageous intentional torts, such as the sexual abuse of a child by a parent. However, courts still do not allow parents to be held liable for negligence in parenting. For example, a child's lawsuit against a parent alleging that "Mom, Dad, but/for your negligence in restricting me to a vegetarian diet that stunted my growth, I would have been an NBA-star" is not going to survive a motion to dismiss.

Charitable Immunity. Traditionally, **charitable institutions were immune** from liability. The purported justification was that holding charitable institutions liable would divert funds contributed by donors from the purposes for which they were contributed to the payment of plaintiffs and their lawyers. However, when for-profit hospitals faced competition from charitable hospitals, they understandably argued that charitable immunity gave charitable hospitals an unfair economic advantage. Today, **courts and legislatures have abrogated the immunity of charitable institutions either wholly or, more often, partially—often by capping the limits of recovery from charitable institutions**.

Sovereign (Governmental) Immunity. **Historically, governments were immune from tort liability.** The pre-modern rendition of the concept was that "the King or Queen can do no wrong." Others explained that because all rights come from the sovereign, it logically followed that the sovereign could not be sued without its consent. During the early decades of the twentieth century, courts proffered more policy-oriented justifications for sovereign immunity. For example, imposing tort liability on governments would penalize them for performing functions they alone were able to fulfill, such as law enforcement functions. However, beginning in the early twentieth century, the federal and state governments became much larger entities than they once had been. Immunity in the face of burgeoning harms inflicted by government employees conflicted with the public's growing sense of an entitlement to redress of tortious harms and access to courts.

Looking first at the liability of state governments, most state legislatures passed **"state torts claims acts" waiving the defense of sovereign immunity** and, **with exceptions**, providing that the state government could be held liable in the same way as a private defendant. However, because the state was waiving its common-law sovereign immunity, it could do so under the terms and conditions it prescribed. So, for example, state torts claims acts typically limit the amount of damages recoverable by a plaintiff, prohibit punitive damages, provide a shorter statute of limitations in which to file the claim, and exclude liability for damages arising in specified contexts. Each state torts claims act is different.

Federal Tort Claims Act. The United States government, also a sovereign, has waived its immunity to liability in the **Federal Tort Claims Act** (FTCA). The FTCA allows recovery against the United States for any wrongful act or omission of a U.S. government employee if a private defendant would be liable if she had committed the wrongful act or omission under the law of the state where the accident occurred. In other words, this federal act incorporates and applies the state common law of torts with, of course, statutory exceptions. The most important exception is that the FTCA **does not waive the government's immunity** for harms caused by the exercise of a **discretionary function**, that is, a judgment by a government employee involving public policy. The FTCA also includes a variety of limitations on the claims *process*. There is neither a right to a jury trial nor punitive damages, and all plaintiffs must first file an administrative claim before filing a claim in court.

Personal Liability of Government Employees and Officers. The issues of when governmental employees and officers can be held personally liable can best be described as extremely complex, with answers varying greatly from one jurisdiction to another. When **judges, legislators, and high executive department officials** act within the scope of their responsibilities, they often are **absolutely immune** from tort liability. Imagine, for example, a judge who recognizes a witness as someone who had dumped her after they had dated in high school. For the worst of reasons, the judge tells the jury that the witness is a "liar." Can she be successfully sued for defamation? Probably not, her immunity is absolute. Other state officials benefit from only a "qualified" immunity to personal liability and may be held liable if their acts are particularly egregious.

What You Need to Know:

1. Traditionally, immunity from liability protected family members from tort actions filed by other family members. Today, most states allow one spouse to sue another for particularly outrageous intentional torts, injuries arising from automobile accidents in which a family member is driving, or both.

2. Today, charitable institutions usually do not benefit from total immunity from liability. However, the amount of damages that plaintiffs can recover is often capped or limited.

3. Traditionally, governments were immune from liability under the doctrine of sovereign immunity. Today, both the federal government and the state governments have waived their respective sovereign immunities by statutes. They can be sued, but their substantive liabilities are limited in a variety of ways, and plaintiffs face specified procedural hurdles.
4. The liability of state and federal employees and officials is also severely restricted by immunities created by the common law, statutes, or both.

LESSON 22: TRESPASS TO LAND

A trespass to land occurs when the **defendant's intentional act causes a physical invasion of the land of another**.

Is trespass to land an intentional tort? A strict liability tort? In our first hypothetical, let's assume that Danica is driving her car and all of a sudden, through no fault of her own, the car's steering fails and she ends up in William's front lawn. Is Danica liable to William for trespass? Before answering that question, let's consider a second hypothetical. Assume that an erroneous survey of George's property (it was not his fault that the survey was wrong) leads him to believe that an annoying cherry tree is on his property. In fact it is on the property of his neighbor Tom. George intentionally enters the space where the tree is located and cuts it down.

Will either Danica or George be liable for trespass? Danica will not be. She did not intend for either her or her car to end up at the location where it was when she violated William's property rights. In this sense, trespass to land is an intentional tort. On the other hand, what about George? It might be argued that he did not intend to violate Tom's property rights. However, neither the **knowledge that the defendant was violating someone else's property rights nor any intent to violate the plaintiff's property rights is required for trespass**. Viewed in this context, trespass is a strict liability tort.

Trespass does not require the defendant herself to enter the land of another. If the defendant shoots artillery shells onto the land of her neighbor or—at least in some states—emits particulates into the air over the land of another, these acts are sufficient for liability in trespass.

Is harm or damages required for trespass? Assume that I hosted a picnic in my backyard last weekend. Because of the number of people attending, the picnic flowed over onto my neighbor Carl's property. Carl was away for the weekend. He had previously told me never to enter his property without his permission. At the end of the picnic, my guests and I cleaned up everything. Not a single blade of grass was out of place. I even left Carl a six-pack of his favorite brew. Have I committed a trespass? Yes. **Liability for trespass by things of normal size does not require proof of damages**. Liability for trespass without proof of damages has its origins in the need of the plaintiff to be able to vindicate the ownership of his land.

Assume, however, that the trespass occurs when the defendant's factory emits **particulates** onto Old MacDonald's farm. Is the presence of particulates enough to make the defendant liable to Old MacDonald for trespass? Most courts would say that **something more is required—either harm or appreciable harm or perhaps that the invasion was significant enough to be likely to cause conflict among the neighbors**. Otherwise, when I shout at my neighbor, if air molecules travelled across the property boundary, I would be liable for trespass! In addition, an increasing number of courts would hold that the intrusion of particulates is never a trespass and instead must be addressed under the law of nuisance.

The Privilege of Necessity. At some point in the first semester, many students will study the classic case of *Vincent v. Lake Erie Transportation Co.*, 100 Minn. 456, 124 N.W. 221 (1910). The defendant's steamship, for purposes of unloading, had been moored to the plaintiff's dock. It remained there, even after the unloading had been completed, because of a severe storm. As the lines securing the boat to the dock became damaged, the defendant's employees replaced them. Wind and waves lifted the boat and threw it against the dock, damaging it. The dock owner alleged that the damages resulted from the defendant's trespass to land. The court held that there was no trespass because the defendant's employees were acting under necessity. **Necessity is an affirmative defense or "privilege" to** the tort of **trespass to land. A defendant who acts to prevent a threatened injury from some source of nature or other independent cause** not connected with the plaintiff **is said to be acting under necessity**. Defendants acting under necessity have the right to use property of others in order to save life or more valuable property.

The *Vincent* court accepts that the defendant boat owner is acting under necessity and is therefore not a trespasser. Further, the court finds that the defendant is not in any way at fault or acting negligently. Nevertheless, **the plaintiff is allowed to recover damages** for the harm to his dock. This holding appears inconsistent with the prevailing principle in 1910, when the case was decided, which required that a defendant must be at fault before he could be held liable. The court's reasoning appears to rest on the concepts of **unjust enrichment** and **restitution**. In other words, it would not be fair to allow the defendant boat owner to damage the plaintiff's dock in order to save his own property without reimbursing the plaintiff.

What You Need to Know:

1. A trespass to land occurs when the defendant's intentional act causes a physical invasion of the land of another.
2. The defendant need not know he is violating the plaintiff's property rights.
3. Trespass involving normally sized persons or objects does not require damages in order to complete the tort.
4. For liability for trespass caused by particles, most courts require the plaintiff to prove some degree of harm or be able to show that the invasion was of sufficient magnitude that it was likely to cause conflict with the plaintiff.

5. Necessity is an affirmative defense or privilege that applies to the tort of trespass to land. A defendant acts under necessity when he trespasses on the plaintiff's land in order to save human life or more valuable property. However, according to the *Vincent* court, when a defendant acting under necessity damages the property of another, he must still compensate the plaintiff for the damage.

LESSON 23: NUISANCE

Sometimes, two neighboring landowners want to use their properties in ways that are incompatible with each other. For example, assume that for many years, Kelly has operated the Kindercare Childcare Center for families of service members and others associated with a navy base. Only a few months ago, XXX, Inc. responded to "other market demands" in the community by opening a store that sells adult movies, magazines, and other assorted goodies. Because no other property was available near the navy base, XXX opened its porn shop immediately adjacent to the Kindercare Center. Does Kelly have any legal recourse?

The tort of nuisance (private nuisance) may provide Kelly with a remedy. She may be able to either obtain an **injunction** (court order) "abating" (terminating) the nuisance posed by XXX or recover **damages**.

A **nuisance is a substantial invasion of the use or enjoyment of another's property**. Nuisances usually are continuous. Unlike recovery for the tort of trespass to land, a nuisance **does not *require* a physical invasion** of the plaintiff's property. However, sometimes, such as when defendant's factory sends particulate emissions onto plaintiff's pastureland, making grazing of animals on that land impossible, the defendant's conduct may satisfy the elements of both nuisance and trespass (at least in some states).

Traditionally, nuisance was a strict liability tort, even after courts began to require negligence in most personal injury cases. Today the situation is a bit more complicated. Under the *Restatement (Second) of Torts*, a **plaintiff may recover** for a substantial interference with the use and enjoyment of her land **if the defendant's conduct is (1) intentional and unreasonable, (2) negligent, or (3) actionable under the principles of strict liability for abnormally dangerous activities**. (The portions of the *Restatement (Third)* covering private nuisance have not yet been adopted at the time I write this.) An example of a negligent nuisance would be if the defendant, the operator of a chemical plant, fails to employ reasonable care in the maintenance of pipes that carry chemical byproducts and, as a result, the effluent escapes and flows onto the plaintiff's property. After you read the next lesson, examples of abnormally dangerous nuisances should be readily apparent to you—for example, harm to the use and enjoyment of land caused by a neighboring landowner's storage of toxic wastes.

However, it is the "intentional and unreasonable" category that encompasses a majority of private nuisances and causes most of the complexities and fun in untangling this category of tort liability. Let's start with the term "intentional." As was the case with battery, intention does not always require that the defendant act with a **purpose** to cause substantial interference with the plaintiff's use and enjoyment of her land. It is sufficient, for example, if Kelly had complained to XXX that its porn shop was driving away her customers and scaring the children. If XXX continues to operate the porn shop after Kelly has complained to XXX, it is acting with **"knowledge to a substantial certainty"** that its conduct is interfering with Kelly's use and enjoyment of her property, thus satisfying the intent requirement.

The next issue is what is required for the interference with the plaintiff's use and enjoyment of her land to be "**unreasonable**." In the first instance, courts typically evaluate whether the activity is regarded as **harmful or annoying to the reasonable person**. Just because the plaintiff is a legal scholar who values silence while he works at home does not render his neighbor's use of a lawn tractor to mow her lawn a nuisance (I wonder where this "hypothetical" came from???). Further, in deciding whether the defendant's use of its property is unreasonable, **the court weighs the**

social utility of the defendant's conduct against the harm caused to the plaintiff. For example, assume that emissions from a large coal-fired power plant, despite its compliance with all environmental regulations, make it impossible for a neighboring landowner to commercially raise orchids. It is likely that the importance of the power plant to the regional economy means that the orchid grower will not be successful in a nuisance suit.

Also, in deciding whether the defendant's interference with plaintiff's land is unreasonable, the court can consider whether the defendant began using its land before the plaintiff moved to the adjoining plot. However, the plaintiff's "coming to the nuisance" does not conclusively establish that the defendant's activity is not a nuisance. Why? Should the orchid grower, just because her family began its business in 1817, be able to prevent the use of surrounding land by industrial enterprises for decades or even centuries to come? Instead, the court considers "coming to the nuisance" only as one factor to be weighed against others in deciding whether the plaintiff has established that the defendant's activities constitute a nuisance.

Separate and distinct from the tort of private nuisance, which creates liability for interference with the plaintiff's use and enjoyment of her land, is public nuisance. **Public nuisance** is limited to **interference with rights that members of the public hold in common with one another**, such as the right of safe passage on a highway or a navigable stream or the right to an adequate level of air quality (air pollution) or water quality (water pollution). Also, **state legislatures** exercise wide discretion in **declaring various annoyances to be public nuisances by statute**, including, for example, houses where illegal drugs are sold, gambling, disorderly taverns, and allowing certain kinds of particularly thorny bushes (multi-flora roses) to grow. There are three remedies for public nuisances: (1) criminal prosecution; (2) abatement of the public nuisance through injunctive relief when requested by either an appropriate public official or a private person who has suffered "special damage," that is, damages of a type above and beyond those sustained by members of the general public; and (3) actions for damages by those who have sustained special damages.

What You Need to Know:

1. A nuisance (private nuisance) is a substantial interference with the plaintiff's use and enjoyment of her land.
2. In order to recover for nuisance, the plaintiff must prove that the nuisance was (a) intentional and unreasonable, (b) negligently maintained, or (c) actionable under the strict liability principles governing abnormally dangerous activities.
3. An intentional nuisance usually is one where the defendant has been informed of the harm he is causing and he continues to inflict the harm.
4. In judging whether a nuisance is unreasonable, courts consider both (1) what would be annoying to the reasonable neighboring land possessor, and (2) the social utility and social harm resulting from the defendant's activity, as well as the social utility of the plaintiff's use of her land. Priority in time is considered as a factor under the doctrine of "coming to the nuisance," but is not conclusive.
5. The remedies for nuisance may include either damages or injunctive relief.
6. A public nuisance is the interference with the use and enjoyment of a right held in common by members of the general public.

LESSON 24: STRICT LIABILITY FOR ABNORMALLY DANGEROUS ACTIVITIES

As we have seen, most often a plaintiff must prove that the defendant acted either negligently or with intent in order to recover—but not always. In some instances, the nature of the defendant's harm-producing activity is regarded as so dangerous that courts allow the plaintiff to recover without proving fault. Typical examples include harms caused by explosives, hazardous waste disposal, the storing of large quantities of liquids (particularly ones that are flammable or toxic), fumigation, and excavation.

The origins of this so-called "**strict liability for abnormally dangerous activities**" lie in an 1868 English case, *Rylands v. Fletcher*, [1868] L.R. 3 H.L. 330. The defendant owned a reservoir that powered his mill. Through no fault of his own, water leaked from the reservoir into old coal-mine shafts beneath it. The water travelled through the mine tunnels into mines located beneath the surface of plaintiff's land. Despite the plaintiff's inability to prove negligence on the part of the defendant, the Exchequer Chamber ruled for the plaintiff and the House of Lords affirmed. Justice Blackburn, in his opinion in the Exchequer Chamber, held that a person who lawfully brings onto his land something that will do mischief if it escapes is liable to his neighbor for any damage caused. During the late nineteenth century, some American courts followed this holding but others did not.

The holding in *Rylands v. Fletcher* led those who drafted the *Second and Third Restatements of Torts* to recognize liability without fault for abnormally dangerous activities. The *Third Restatement* provides that a defendant should be held strictly liable if (a) its **activity creates a highly significant risk of physical harm even when she exercises reasonable care and** (b) **her activity is not one "of common usage."** In addition to these requirements, in evaluating whether an activity is abnormally dangerous, courts often consider the following factors identified in the *Restatement (Second) of Torts*: **(a) the gravity of the harm resulting from the activity, (b) the inappropriateness of the place where the activity is being conducted, and (c) the limited value of the activity to the community**.

The focus in deciding whether an activity is abnormally dangerous is on the **inherent nature of the activity**, not on how careful the defendant may or may not be in conducting the activity (*i.e.*, unreasonable conduct or negligence). Students often make the mistake of believing that anything done in an unreasonably dangerous manner is abnormally dangerous—that situation, of course, describes negligence, not strict liability for abnormally dangerous activities.

Strict liability for an abnormally dangerous activity exists **only if the harm that actually occurs results from the risk that made the activity abnormally dangerous in the first place**. For example, if Lance Laborer drops a heavy package of explosives, hitting Victoria Victim's head and causing a concussion, Victoria's claim is for negligence, not strict liability for abnormally dangerous activities.

What You Need to Know:

1. The defendant will be held liable without proof of negligence if she is engaged in an abnormally dangerous activity.
2. In deciding whether the defendant's activity is an abnormally dangerous one, the focus is on the inherently abnormally dangerous nature of the activity in which the defendant engages, not on how carelessly she is in performing the activity.
3. Under the *Restatement (Third) of Torts*, an activity is regarded as abnormally dangerous if (a) it creates a significant risk of physical harm even when the defendant is not negligent and (b) the activity is not a common one. Under the *Second Restatement*, courts also considered (a) the gravity of the harm resulting from the activity, (b) the inappropriateness of the place where the activity is being conducted, and (c) the limited value of the activity to the community.
4. The defendant is strictly liable only for harm resulting from the type of risk that causes the activity to be classified as an abnormally dangerous one.

LESSON 25: STRICT LIABILITY FOR POSSESSORS OF ANIMALS

In some circumstances, the liability of the possessor of animals is another example of "traditional" strict liability. At least in the first instance, the liability rules governing animals turn on whether the animal that caused the harm was **wild** or **domesticated.**

A wild animal is an animal that, **as a species or a class**, has not been domesticated. For example, even a particular wild elephant that has been tamed and exhibited as part of a circus remains **categorized as a wild animal**. The possessor of a wild animal is **strictly liable** for harm done by that animal (a) in spite of any precautions the possessor has taken to confine the animal or prevent the harm, if (b) the harm arises from a **dangerous propensity** that is **characteristic of such wild animals** or of which the owner **has reason to know**. For example, assume Robert Reptile keeps rattlesnakes in secure cages in his backyard. A rattlesnake escapes when the cages are destroyed by a hurricane of unprecedented ferocity, the likes of which no one could have predicted. Two days later, three-year-old Jaylen, while playing in the street of the same suburban cul-de-sac where Robert lives, trips over the rattlesnake and breaks his arm. Will Jaylen be able to sue Robert on a strict liability basis? No. The harm to Jaylen did not arise from the dangerous propensity that is characteristic of rattlesnakes.

The possessor of a **domesticated animal** is strictly liable for injuries caused by that animal only if he **knows** of the animal's **dangerous propensities**. In other words, as a starting point, "every dog is entitled to one free bite." However, this is not always true. For example, imagine that Jennifer's dog Fido is a pit bull. Assume, as does the *Restatement (Third) of Torts: Liability for Physical and Emotional Harm* § 23, comment e (2010), that pit bulls as a variety are known to be particularly prone to bite and attack. Assume further that when pit bulls do bite, the harm is likely to be significant. If Fido mauls Jason, Jennifer is strictly liable to Jason even if this was Fido's first bite.

At common law, if the animal is neither by nature wild, nor domesticated but known to have dangerous propensities, the injured victim, in order to recover, is required to prove that the owner of the animal was negligent. However, you can imagine what happens when a child is bitten by a dog and the parents cannot prove negligence. They run to state legislators and other public officials! As a result, many states have enacted "**dog-bite statutes**" that hold owners of dogs and/or other domesticated animals designated in the statute strictly liable for damages resulting from personal injuries.

At common law, the owner of any animal, wild or domestic (other than household pets), was **strictly liable for any reasonably foreseeable damage caused by his animal while trespassing on the land of another, including both property damage and personal injury**. However, not surprisingly, in some states where ranching is prevalent, this rule has been changed.

In most jurisdictions, the **plaintiff's contributory negligence will not reduce his recovery** in a comparative fault state or bar recovery in a contributory negligence jurisdiction in a case alleging **strict liability against a possessor of animals**,. However, if the plaintiff is aware of the dangerous propensity of an animal and **taunts the animal**, he may be prohibited from recovering under the doctrine of **assumption of the risk**.

What You Need to Know:

1. The owner of a wild animal, other than one that is by nature harmless, is strictly liable.
2. Courts determine whether the animal has dangerous tendencies by looking at an entire class of animals, not by looking at the specific animal that caused the harm.
3. Strict liability applies only when the harm that occurs results from the dangerous propensity that created strict liability in the first place ("scope of risk").
4. Under the common law, there is no strict liability for domesticated animals unless the owner is aware of the animal's dangerous propensities.
5. Many states have enacted "dog-bite statutes" that make owners of dogs and other domesticated pets strictly liable for the personal injuries they cause.
6. Ordinarily, the owner of any animal is strictly liable for any property damage it causes while the animal is trespassing on another's property.

LESSON 26: STRICT PRODUCTS LIABILITY

Products liability proves the lesson that in modern American tort law, unlike in the old English writ system, a single fact pattern can create many causes of action. Suits against product manufacturers often allege negligence for (a) failure to inspect, (b) inadequacies in the design of the product, or (c) failure to warn. They also frequently feature contract-based claims, such as violations as express and implied warranties leading to consequential damages resulting from personal injuries. In this lesson, however, our focus will be on the development of the independent, tort-based cause of action traditionally known as "**strict products liability**."

In order to recover under nineteenth-century common law, the victim needed to prove both that he was in contractual privity with the defendant—namely, the supplier of the product that injured him—and that the defendant was negligent. You may read *MacPherson v. Buick Motor Co.*, 217 N.Y. 382, 111 N.E. 1050 (1916), another opinion by Judge Cardozo and one regarded by many torts scholars as the greatest of all American tort opinions. In it, Judge Cardozo holds that **privity**—a contractual relationship between the victim and the supplier of the product that injured him, **is not required in order to establish a duty of reasonable care**. Instead, a duty exists whenever it is reasonably foreseeable to the product supplier that someone would be injured.

After *MacPherson*, the victim injured by a product was no longer required to prove privity with the manufacturer, but he still needed to prove negligence on its part. It often was difficult for the plaintiff's lawyer to prove specific negligent acts within the operations of the typically large, faceless manufacturer. In *Escola v. Coca Cola Bottling Co.*, 24 Cal.2d 453, 150 P.2d 436 (1944), a young Justice of the California Supreme Court, Roger Traynor, wrote in a concurring opinion that the manufacturer should be held to a standard of "absolute liability when an article that he has placed on the market . . . proves to have a **defect** that causes injury to human beings." To justify this proposition, Justice Traynor explicitly cited the objectives of **loss minimization**—the manufacturer can prevent product-caused harms in ways that users cannot, and

loss distribution—"the cost of an injury . . . may be an overwhelming misfortune to the person injured . . . [but] can be insured by the manufacturer and distributed among the public as a cost of doing business." Nineteen years later, after Traynor had become the Chief Justice of the California Supreme Court, the court adopted strict products liability, at about the same time that several other influential state supreme courts did. Shortly thereafter, in 1965, the American Law Institute (ALI) adopted *Restatement (Second) of Torts § 402A* (1965) and recommended that courts recognize a cause of action for strict products liability. Without question, this *Restatement* provision was to become the single most influential section included in any of the ALI restatements. From the time of its enactment through the mid-1980s, many jurisdictions simply "adopted § 402(A)." All suppliers of the product in the chain of distribution—the retailer, the distributor, and the manufacturer—could now be held strictly liable.

The key to strict products liability is that the victim's harm must have been caused by a product defect. A "defect" is to liability under a strict products liability claim what "unreasonable conduct" is to liability for negligence. The courts now recognize three distinct types of product defects. First, a **manufacturing defect** is present when the product is in a substandard condition compared to the manufacturer's own design or specifications.

The second type of product defect is a **design defect**. Depending on the jurisdiction, there are two basic tests of whether a product contains a design defect: the **consumer-expectation test** and the **risk-utility test**. Under the consumer-expectation test, a product is defective if it contains a condition that was not anticipated by the consumer that is unreasonably dangerous to her. The risk-utility test asks whether the risks of the product outweigh its benefits. This test obviously is a close relative of the cost-benefit analysis used for determining whether the defendant's conduct is negligent. In the early years of strict products liability, most courts followed the consumer-expectations test. Today, however, most courts and the *Restatement (Third) of Torts: Products Liability* (1998) apply either the risk-utility test or a variety of hybrids that combine elements from both tests. A key question in design defect cases is whether the plaintiff is required to prove that there was a **reasonable alternative design** available to the manufacturer that would have made the product safer. The *Restatement (Third)* requires the plaintiff to prove such a reasonable alternative design. Although the jurisdictions split, the trend is to follow the *Third Restatement* on this issue.

The third and final type of product defect is a failure-to-warn defect. The manufacturer must warn the consumer of the risks of using a product, for example, cigarettes or prescription drugs, so that she can make an informed choice as to whether to use the product. The other type of product warning is the warning that instructs the consumer on the safe use of the product, for example, "Do not consume alcoholic beverages when using this medication."

What about affirmative defenses related to the plaintiff's conduct in strict products liability cases? Courts have typically held that the type of **contributory negligence** that consists of the plaintiff's unreasonable encountering of a known product risk is a defense to strict products liability. In some jurisdictions, this same behavior bars the plaintiff's claim but passes under the label of assumption of risk. The more difficult issue is whether the plaintiff's unreasonable conduct in failing to discover a product risk qualifies as contributory negligence. A variety of opinions following the initial adoption of strict products liability held that it did not, because the underlying rationale of strict products liability placed the burden of discovering such risks on the manufacturer. Today, however, the emerging trend, at least among the 46 states that have adopted comparative fault, is for all forms of plaintiff's contributory negligence to reduce (but, of course, not to eliminate) the plaintiff's recovery.

Finally, the plaintiff's conduct also may preclude recovery under the doctrine of **product misuse**. When an injury results from the use of the product in a manner neither intended nor foreseeable to the manufacturer, courts typically hold that an injured victim cannot recover. For example, when partying teenaged girls decided to "scent" a candle by spraying perfume on it, resulting in one of them being burned, she was not able to recover in an action against the perfume manufacturer.

What You Need to Know:

1. Strict products liability now enables a plaintiff to recover even if the plaintiff is not in privity with the product supplier and is unable to prove fault on the part of the product supplier.
2. The key to recovery in a strict products liability claim is a product defect. There are three types of product defects: manufacturing defects, design defects, and failure-to-warn defects.
3. The emerging trend is that all forms of contributory negligence reduce plaintiff's recovery in comparative fault states. Earlier, and still today in at least most contributory negligence states, the plaintiff's fault that consists of an unreasonable failure to discover a product defect does not bar recovery.
4. A plaintiff will not be able to recover if she misused the product in an unintended and unforeseeable manner.

CHAPTER 5

CONSTITUTIONAL LAW

LESSON 1: JUDICIAL REVIEW

In the beginning, there was *Marbury v. Madison*, 5 U.S. (1 Cranch) 137 (1803).

Marbury v. Madison is the case in which the Supreme Court first explicitly declared that federal courts have the power to declare laws unconstitutional. This is known as the power of judicial review. A few dissenters aside, almost all constitutional law classes begin by studying Chief Justice John Marshall's opinion in *Marbury*. Constitutional law exists because the Supreme Court has the power to declare laws unconstitutional.

Marbury arose during a political conflict between Federalists and Jeffersonians over the structure of the federal court system that had initially had little to do with judicial review and even less to do with William Marbury. During the long interval between the election in 1800, in which Thomas Jefferson was elected president and Jeffersonians gained control of Congress, the lame duck Federalist Congress created federal circuit courts and President John Adams appointed members of the Federalist Party to serve on those courts. During this time period, the Federalist Party with much less controversy provided a judicial system for Washington D.C., and Adams pursuant to that statute nominated Marbury to be a local Justice of the Peace. On his last day in office, Adams signed and sealed Marbury's commission. He gave the commission to his Secretary of State, John Marshall, to be delivered, but Marshall and his brother were unable to deliver the commission by the end of the day. Jefferson upon assuming the presidency immediately ordered his Secretary of State, James Madison, not to deliver the commission. Marbury promptly asked the Supreme Court of the United States to issue a writ of mandamus, a judicial order requiring Madison to deliver the judicial commissions that Adams had signed and sealed. Once the Jeffersonian majority in Congress was seated, the Congress repealed the Judiciary Act of 1801, putting the Federalist justices Adams had appointed out of a job. The political universe braced for a judicial decision on whether Congress could, consistent with the constitutional requirement that justices enjoy life tenure, eliminate judicial offices. That decision never came.

The bulk of *Marbury v. Madison* is devoted to technical legal questions. Chief Justice Marshall first ruled that Marbury had a right to the commission once the commission was signed and sealed. Marbury's right to a commission, Marshall continued, entailed that a judicial remedy existed for that right and that a writ of mandamus was the right remedy. Marshall then interpreted Section 13 of the Judiciary Act of 1789 as giving the Supreme Court original jurisdiction over Marbury's case. This meant that federal law authorized Marbury to bring his case in the Supreme Court, rather than in a federal district court. Marshall, however, insisted that Section 13 was unconstitutional because Article III of the Constitution forbade Congress from passing laws that added to the original jurisdiction of the Supreme Court.

Marbury derives judicial review, the judicial power to declare laws unconstitutional, from the constitutional commitment to limited government, from the writtenness of the Constitution of the United States and from the higher law status of the Constitution. Marshall begins with the American commitment to limited government. Justices may declare laws unconstitutional only if there are some laws government may not constitutionally pass. *Marbury* then establishes a relationship between limited government and written constitutions. Writing, Marshall declares, makes the constitutional limits on government definite and demonstrates the constitutional commitment to limited government.

> The powers of the legislature are defined, and limited; and that those limits may not be mistaken, or forgotten, the constitution is written. To what purpose are powers limited, and to what purpose is that limitation committed to writing, if these limits may, at any time, be passed by those intended to be restrained?

Marshall insists that the Constitution is "superior, paramount law." Marshall's claim that the Constitution is "law" is important because we normally consider courts as being responsible for interpreting the law. The most famous sentence in *Marbury* asserts, "It is emphatically the province and duty of the courts to say what the law is." Marbury's assertion that the Constitution is "superior" is important because the Constitution is not the sort of law that a legislature can change. Ordinary law is governed by the principle "last in time, first in line." When a conflict between two laws occurs, the most recently enacted law ("last in time") governs ("first in line"). If there is a conflict between a law enacted yesterday and a law enacted last week, the law enacted yesterday governs. Constitutional law is a higher law than ordinary statutory law (or common law, or state law, etc.). If there is a conflict between a statute enacted yesterday and a constitutional provision enacted last week, the constitutional provision governs. Congress cannot change the Constitution because the Constitution is the higher law that both empowers and limits Congress.

Every constitutional law book and every constitutional law class studies *Marbury*. No other case, not even *Brown v. Board of Education*, 347 U.S. 483 (1954), is so prominently featured in the constitutional law canon. Every judge before whom you might practice is committed to the principle that courts have the power of judicial review. Do not argue in a court of law that *Marbury* was wrongly decided. That is malpractice. Feel free to make those arguments in class and at history, philosophy, or political science conventions. A fair case can be made that the arguments Chief Justice Marshall makes for judicial review are not sound. A fair case can be made that no good reason justifies giving nine lawyers the power to declare unconstitutional laws made by elected officials. Those arguments appear in the law reviews with some frequency and, if you make law review, you may enjoy reading them or even writing one yourself. Nevertheless, *Marbury* is not going away. You will not be taken seriously as a lawyer if you ask a court to foreswear the power to declare laws unconstitutional.

Shortly after deciding *Marbury v. Madison*, the Supreme Court in a series of cases established the judicial power to declare state laws unconstitutional. *Fletcher v. Peck*, 10 U.S. (6 Cranch) 87 (1810), is the first case in which the Supreme Court clearly declared a state law unconstitutional. Justice Joseph Story in *Martin v. Hunter's Lessee*, 14 U.S. (1 Wheat.) 304 (1816), provided the canonical justification of this power. Judicial review of state legislation, he noted, was necessary to ensure uniformity throughout the nation and to prevent biased state justices, many of whom were elected, from warping basic constitutional norms. Most commentators believe judicial review of state legislation stands on even stronger foundations than judicial review of federal legislation. "I do not think the United States would come to an end if we lost our power to declare an Act of Congress void," Justice Oliver Wendell Holmes once wrote, but "I do think the Union would be imperiled if we could not make the declaration as to the laws of the several states."

What You Need to Know:

1. *Marbury v. Madison* establishes that the Supreme Court has the power to declare federal laws unconstitutional.
2. This power to declare federal laws unconstitutional is derived from the constitutional commitment to limited government and the Constitution's status as higher law.
3. *Martin v. Hunter's Lessee* establishes that the Supreme Court has the power to declare state laws unconstitutional.
4. This power to declare state laws unconstitutional is derived from the need for uniformity throughout the nation and a fear of local bias.

LESSON 2: CONSTITUTIONAL AUTHORITY

The Constitution does not explicitly allocate constitutional authority (or sanction judicial review). Article VI, paragraph 2, the "Supremacy Clause," plainly states that the Constitution is superior to all other forms of federal and state law. The

Supremacy Clause does not state what governing institution or institutions determine whether a conflict exists between the Constitution and a federal or state law.

Judicial Supremacy

The Supreme Court insists that the federal judiciary is responsible for settling most disputes over the meaning and application of the Constitution. Justices maintain that they enjoy the powers associated with judicial review and judicial supremacy. Judicial review is the power to declare laws unconstitutional in an ordinary lawsuit. Constitutional or judicial supremacy is the power to decide how other governing officials must interpret the Constitution. Courts in ordinary lawsuits decide only the rights and duties of the parties before the court. When a court sides with Flintstone in a contract dispute with Rubble, Rubble is the only party legally bound to obey the judicial order in that case. Other people might be well advised to be guided by the court's opinion, but they have no legal obligation to do so until they lose a similar lawsuit. The Supreme Court nevertheless claims that when the justices declare a law unconstitutional, all governing officials have legal obligations to obey the judicial decree, even those governing officials who were not parties in the case before the court. When the justices rule that an affirmative action program adopted by legislators in Kansas is unconstitutional, lawmakers in Colorado and the other 48 states have obligations to abandon similar programs.

Cooper v. Aaron, 358 U.S. 1 (1958) is the canonical citation for the proposition that the Supreme Court is the institution that determines how all governing officials interpret the Constitution. The case arose in the wake of *Brown v. Board of Education*, 347 U.S. 483 (1954), when southern states attempted various forms of resistance to judicial decrees ordering them to desegregate their public schools. Arkansas officials insisted that they were not bound by the decision in *Brown* that racially segregated schools violated the Equal Protection Clause of the Fourteenth Amendment because no Arkansas school district was a party to the *Brown* litigation. Chief Justice Earl Warren, in an opinion signed by every member of the Supreme Court, quickly disabused state officials of that conceit. He condemned this and any assertion of independent state authority to interpret the Constitution. Warren interpreted *Marbury v. Madison*, 5 U.S. (1 Cranch) 137 (1803), as empowering courts both to declare laws unconstitutional and to establish the constitutional rules for other government officials. The most important passage in *Cooper v. Aaron* states,

> Article VI of the Constitution makes the Constitution the "supreme Law of the Land." In 1803, Chief Justice Marshall, speaking for a unanimous Court, referring to the Constitution as "the fundamental and paramount law of the nation," declared in the notable case of *Marbury v. Madison*, that "It is emphatically the province and duty of the judicial department to say what the law is." This decision declared the basic principle that the federal judiciary is supreme in the exposition of the law of the Constitution, and that principle has ever since been respected by this Court and the Country as a permanent and indispensable feature of our constitutional system. . . .
>
> No state legislator or executive or judicial officer can war against the Constitution without violating his undertaking to support it. Chief Justice Marshall spoke for a unanimous Court in saying that: "If the legislatures of the several states may, at will, annul the judgments of the courts of the United States, and destroy the rights acquired under those judgments, the constitution itself becomes a solemn mockery."

Alternatives to Judicial Supremacy

The Supreme Court's authority to interpret the Constitution has not gone unchallenged. Several challenges occurred shortly after the Constitution was ratified. The Virginia and Kentucky Resolutions of 1798 insisted the states are the parties to the Constitution and as the parties to the compact, have the power to determine the meaning of constitutional provisions. Thomas Jefferson, who authored the Kentucky Resolutions of 1798, wrote, "[T]o this compact each State acceded as a State, and . . . as in all other cases of compact among powers having no common judge, each party has an equal right to judge for itself, as well of infractions as of the mode and measure of redress." Several years later, President Jefferson raised a departmentalist challenge to judicial authority. Departmentalists believe that every branch of the national government has an equal right to interpret the Constitution, that no branch of the national government is constitutionally superior to another. When explaining why he pardoned persons convicted under the Alien and Sedition Acts of 1798 after federal courts declared those persons constitutionally convicted, Jefferson stated,

> The judges, believing the law constitutional, had a right to pass a sentence of fine and imprisonment; because that power was placed in their hands by the Constitution. But the Executive, believing the law to be unconstitutional, was bound to remit the execution of it; because that power has been confided to him by the Constitution. That instrument meant that its co-ordinate branches should be checks on each other. But the opinion which gives to the judges the right to decide what laws are constitutional, and what not, not only for themselves in their own sphere of action, but for the Legislature & Executive also, in their spheres, would make the judiciary a despotic branch.

Abraham Lincoln invoked the distinction between judicial review and judicial supremacy when claiming that the Republican Party would not be bound by the Supreme Court's declaration in *Dred Scott v. Sandford*, 60 U.S. (19 How.) 393 (1856) that the national government could not prohibit slavery in American territories. Lincoln accepted that *Dred Scott* established that Dred Scott was legally a slave, but he insisted that governing officials who were not a party to that case remained free to act on their best understanding of constitutional norms.

These sporadic challenges have not left a strong enduring mark on American constitutional law. Compact theory failed to survive the Civil War. Constitutional law at present is what the Supreme Court says constitutional law is.

Beyond Judicial Supremacy

States and federal elected officials may not act inconsistently with Supreme Court decisions, but they may interpret their constitutional powers more narrowly or constitutional rights more broadly than the justices. Existing constitutional law prohibits government officials from taking actions the justices have ruled constitutionally forbidden. When the justices say the Fourteenth Amendment guarantees women the right to terminate their pregnancies, states may not ban abortion. Existing constitutional law does not require government officials to take action that is constitutionally permitted. When the justices declare that persons have no constitutional right to a government-funded abortion, Congress is permitted as a matter of constitutional law to give persons a statutory right to a federally funded abortion and states are permitted as a matter of federal constitutional law to create a state constitutional right to a state-funded abortion. Judicial decisions create floors rather than ceilings.

What You Need to Know:

1. Judicial supremacy is the judicial power to determine authoritatively what constitutional provisions mean. Judicial review is the power to declare laws unconstitutional in a particular case.
2. The contemporary Supreme Court exercises the power of judicial supremacy and judicial review. The justices vigorously insist that governing officials must be guided by judicial interpretations of constitutional provisions.
3. Elected officials may interpret their powers more narrowly and constitutional rights more broadly than the Supreme Court, but they may not act in ways forbidden by Supreme Court precedent.

LESSON 3: CONSTITUTIONAL LITIGATION: JURISDICTION

Article III, Section 2, paragraph 1 vests the federal courts with jurisdiction over all cases "arising under this Constitution, the Laws of the United States, and Treaties made, or which shall be made, under their authority." Article III, Section 2, paragraph 2 details when the Supreme Court exercises original jurisdiction and when the Supreme Court exercises appellate jurisdiction. The sentence detailing appellate jurisdiction declares, "In all the other Cases before mentioned [the cases in which the Constitution vests the Supreme Court with original jurisdiction] the Supreme Court shall have appellate Jurisdiction, both as to Law and Fact, with such Exceptions, and under such Regulations, as the Congress shall make."

Supreme Court precedent establishes that federal courts may exercise appellate jurisdiction only when Article III and a federal law vests the court with appellate jurisdiction. All cases must have constitutional and statutory foundations. This rule dates from *Wiscart v. D'Auchy*, 3 U.S. (3 Dall.) 321 (1796). Chief Justice Oliver Ellsworth's opinion stated, "If Congress has provided no rule to regulate our proceedings, we cannot exercise an appellate jurisdiction." This view interprets the exceptions clause as requiring Congress to act affirmatively before the Supreme Court exercises jurisdiction. If Congress has not passed a law that vests the Supreme Court with appellate jurisdiction over appeals from decisions denying Sixth Amendment rights, then the Supreme Court may not exercise federal jurisdiction. Justice Joseph Story in *Martin v. Hunter's Lessee*, 14 U.S. (1 Wheat.) 304 (1816), asserted that Congress had a constitutional obligation to vest the federal courts with full federal questions jurisdiction, jurisdiction over any case making a claim based on the Constitution of the United States or federal law. That constitutional obligation, however, is not judicially enforceable. If no statute vests a federal court with jurisdiction, courts may not adjudicate the case.

Ex parte McCardle, 74 U.S. (7 Wall.) 506 (1868), tested the limits of the congressional power to determine when the Supreme Court may adjudicate cases raising constitutional issues. During Reconstruction, William McCardle was arrested by the military for inciting insurrection. McCardle filed for a writ of habeas corpus under the Habeas Corpus Act of 1867. After oral argument was finished in his case, but before the

Supreme Court announced a decision, Congress repealed the provision in the Habeas Corpus Act that vested the Supreme Court with jurisdiction over McCardle's case (the justices self-consciously delayed their vote to give Congress the time to override President Andrew Johnson's veto of the Repealer Act). After the Repealer Act became law, Chief Justice Salmon Chase promptly announced that the Repealer Act had deprived the court of the jurisdiction in the case. He wrote, "Jurisdiction is power to declare the law, and when it ceases to exist, the only function remaining to the court is that of announcing the fact and dismissing the cause."

The last paragraph of *McCardle* muddied the jurisdictional waters in ways that the Supreme Court has never clarified. Chase stated:

> Counsel seem to have supposed, if effect be given to the repealing act in question, that the whole appellate power of the court, in cases of habeas corpus, is denied. But this is an error. The act of 1686 does not except from that jurisdiction any cases but appeals from Circuit Courts under the act of 1867. It does not affect the jurisdiction which was previously exercised.

Under one interpretation, this paragraph is dicta that has nothing to do with the actual resolution of case. Chief Justice Chase merely observed that a different jurisdiction path existed for bringing habeas corpus claims to the Supreme Court. On another interpretation, this paragraph is essential to the holding of *McCardle*. On this view, Congress may choose the path cases take to the federal court system, but may not exclude claims of federal constitutional right from the federal court system altogether. The justices could deny jurisdiction in *McCardle* only because McCardle had some other means of having a federal court adjudicate his claim of federal constitutional right. Scholars have debated the meaning of this paragraph for more than 100 years. The Supreme Court has never determined which interpretation is correct.

Political Questions

Contrary to the apparently clear mandate of Article III that federal courts adjudicate all controversies "arising under this Constitution," the Supreme Court has carved out a class of so-called "political questions" that federal courts may not consider. Political questions concern constitutional issues that for various reasons Supreme Court justices believed should not be litigated. Justice William Brennan set out the basic criteria for political questions in *Baker v. Carr*, 369 U.S. 186 (1962). He wrote:

> Prominent on the surface of any case held to involve a political question is found a textually demonstrable constitutional commitment of the issue to a coordinate political department; or a lack of judicially discoverable and manageable standards for resolving it; or the impossibility of a court's undertaking independent resolution without expressing lack of the respect due coordinate branches of government; or an unusual need for unquestioning adherence to a political decision already made; or the potentiality of embarrassment from multifarious pronouncements by various departments on one question.

Brennan pointed to questions about when a declared war was over as an example of a political question. The Constitution provides a court with few guidelines for determining when a war has terminated and good reason exists for not questioning a presidential decision that a war has (or has not) ended.

The basic standards for political questions are more easily stated than applied. *Baker v. Carr* concerned whether legislative reapportionments raised political questions. Previous decisions held that challenges to legislative apportionments under the Guarantee Clause of Article IV raised nonjusticiable political questions. *Baker* held that legislative apportionments could be challenged in court under the Equal Protection Clause of the Fourteenth Amendment. [another] *Nixon v. United States*, 506 U.S. 224 (1993), is the only case in more than 50 years in which the Supreme Court invoked the political questions doctrine. In that case, the justices ruled that the Supreme Court could not determine whether Senate procedures for impeaching a federal judge met constitutional standards. That constitutional issue was entrusted to the Senate. *Zivotofsky v. Clinton*, 132 S. Ct. 1421

(2012), is more typical. The Supreme Court ruled that the justices could determine whether the President or Congress could decide whether Jerusalem was the capital of Israel. Roberts Court justices who think determining the capital of Israel is not a political question are unlikely to find many other constitutional matters to raise nonjusticiable political questions for the foreseeable future.

What You Need to Know:

1. The Supreme Court may exercise jurisdiction only when authorized to do so by Congress and by federal law.
2. Congress may have a constitutional obligation to vest the Supreme Court, or at least federal courts, with some form of jurisdiction over all federal questions, but that constitutional obligation is judicially enforceable.
3. Justices will not resolve constitutional issues raising political questions that are constitutionally entrusted to other governing institutions, but the set of political questions has been steadily decreasing.

LESSON 4: CONSTITUTIONAL LITIGATION: STANDING

Article III, Section 2 mandates that federal courts may adjudicate only "**cases** arising under this Constitution." That people disagree over the meaning of a constitutional provision or whether proposed legislation in Congress violates the First Amendment is not sufficient to invoke judicial authority. The Supreme Court may not be authorized to weigh in even after Congress or a state legislature pass a law many people think is unconstitutional. Litigants must have what is known as "standing" to challenge a claimed constitutional wrong. Constitutional adjudication takes place only when adversarial parties are contesting whether one caused the other to suffer a legal injury. Federal and state courts make constitutional decisions only when adjudicating lawsuits where the parties have met the requirements for bringing and defending an ordinary lawsuit.

Plaintiffs in the United States have standing to challenge the constitutionality of a federal or state law in the United States only if they meet three conditions.

1. They must claim that they have suffered a particularized injury.
2. They must claim their injury was caused by some action they claim violates the Constitution.
3. Their claimed injury must be redressable by the court.

Plaintiffs need not establish either their injury, causation, or a legal wrong at the pleading stage. As you may remember from the Civil Procedure lessons, John does not have to prove at the pleading stage that his computer was broken when the police searched his apartment or even that the search was unconstitutional. That is for the actual trial. All John must do at the pleading stage is allege a particularized injury was allegedly caused by the allegedly unconstitutional actions of the government. Whether John suffered an injury or the government acted unconstitutionally can be determined only after John makes a sufficiently plausible claim to meet the standing requirements.

The constitutional requirements for standing are easy to understand in theory. Consider persons who file a lawsuit claiming that the president violated Article II, Section 3 by delivering an inadequate State of the Union address. This claim fails to meet the particularized injury requirement for standing. All Americans suffer the same harm to the same degree when the president delivers an inadequate State of the Union Address. Undaunted, several litigants claim their proposal of marriage was turned down because the president delivered an inadequate State of the Union Address. This claim fails the causation requirement for standing. Even if the president's speech actually caused a marriage proposal to be rejected, this consequence was almost certainly unforeseeable. Plaintiffs who somehow demonstrate the president was aware of this consequence will not be able to overcome the redressability requirement for standing. Federal courts, like the genie in *Aladdin* (Robin Williams's best role), do not have the power to make people love each other.

Standing doctrine in practice is generally considered to be a mess. More often than not, you may find yourself memorizing results that seem incoherent. Consider the line of precedents in cases concerning when taxpayers have standing to make constitutional challenges, none of which have been overruled. *Frothingham v. Mellon*, 262 U.S. 447 (1923), ruled that taxpayers do not have standing to challenge the constitutionality of a federal law that funded state efforts to reduce infant mortality. Justice George Sutherland's opinion declared, "The party who invokes the power [of judicial review] must be able to show not only that the statute is invalid but that he has sustained or is immediately in danger of sustaining some direct injury as the result of its enforcement, and not merely that he suffers in some indefinite way in common with people generally." *Flast v. Cohen*, 392 U.S. 83 (1968), determined that taxpayers do have standing to challenge whether federal spending policies violate the establishment clause. The judicial majority thought a particularized injury had occurred because the First Amendment was intended to prevent the "taxing and spending power" from being "used to favor one religion over another or to support religion in general." *Hein v. Freedom from Religion Foundation*, 551 U.S. 587 (2007), decided that taxpayers do not have standing to challenge a presidential decision allocating some federal funds to faith-based organizations. Justice Samuel Alito's majority opinion found a constitutional distinction between a specific congressional appropriation to a religious group and a presidential decision to allocate general funds to a religious group. You are welcomed to try to reconcile these and related decisions.

Congress by statute may ease but not eliminate standing requirements. The degree to which standing requirements may be eased is uncertain and controversial. In *Massachusetts v. Environmental Protection Agency*, 549 U.S. 497 (2007), a 5–4 Supreme Court majority ruled that Massachusetts had standing to challenge the decision of the Environmental

Protection Agency not to regulate greenhouse gases. Justice John Paul Stevens found the standing requirements met because increased greenhouse gases threatened climate change, rising sea levels were damaging state coasts, and better regulation might reduce to some degree that damage. Chief Justice Roberts in dissent claimed that no standing existed because global warming threatened everyone on the planet and that regulation in the United States would reduce only by a tiny fraction the greenhouse gases in the atmosphere.

What You Need to Know:

1. Courts in the United States make constitutional decisions only when adjudicating a traditional lawsuit.
2. Plaintiffs meet the standing requirements only if they have suffered a particularized injury caused by the illegal or unconstitutional conduct of the defendant that is redressable by the courts.
3. Congress by statute may weaken but not eliminate standing requirements.

LESSON 5: NATIONAL POWERS: BASICS

The Congress of the United States may exercise only enumerated powers. When justifying any national action, lawyers for the federal government must point to a specific constitutional provision enumerating a relevant power. They must say that "the commerce power in Article I, Section 8 vests Congress with the power to inspect potatoes being shipped in interstate commerce" or "Section 5 of the Fourteenth Amendment vests Congress with the power to prohibit states from adopting a particular affirmative action plan."

This concern with enumerated powers distinguishes federal power from state power. States possess a "general police power." This power authorizes state legislatures to pass any legislation that promotes the public health, safety, morals or welfare. State lawyers need not make explicit the state constitutional basis for state legislation when defending state laws from constitutional attack in federal court. They must demonstrate only that the state statute is in the public interest and does not violate any federal constitutional restriction on state power. Federal lawyers must point to specific federal constitutional language authorizing Congress to pass that law under constitutional challenge as well as demonstrate that the federal statute does not violate federal constitutional restrictions on federal power.

The national government may exercise implied powers as well as powers plainly stated by the constitutional text, as long as the implied powers are derived from the enumerated powers. The Constitution does not include a provision that explicitly declares, "The Congress shall have power to . . . issue postage stamps." Nevertheless, the implied power to issue postage stamps can be implied from the enumerated power in Article I, Section 8 "to . . . establish Post Offices and post Roads." The enumerated power to establish the post office implies other powers, such as the power to punish people who rob postal inspectors and the power to issue postage stamps. The necessary and proper clause, Article I, Section 8, paragraph 18, sanctions the exercise of implied powers. That provision states, "The Congress shall have Power . . . To make all Laws which shall be necessary and proper for carrying into Execution the foregoing Powers, and all other Powers vested by the Constitution in the Government of the United States, or in any Department or Officer thereof." Congress under the necessary and proper clause may pass various laws not enumerated in the Constitution as long as those laws can be traced to an enumerated power and do not violate an explicit constitutional restriction on federal power.

McCulloch v. Maryland, 17 U.S. (4 Wheat.) 316 (1819), is the foundational case for interpreting national powers. The main issue in *McCulloch* was whether Congress could constitutionally incorporate a national bank. The Constitution of the United States neither explicitly gives Congress the power to give corporate charters nor specifically the power to create a national bank. Indeed, the framers rejected a proposal to add such a provision to Article I, Section 8. Nevertheless, the Supreme Court in a unanimous opinion written by Chief Justice John Marshall sustained the federal law that incorporated a national bank.

Marshall's opinion provided constitutional foundations for implied federal powers. *McCulloch* insisted that constitutions speak in general language, leaving specific powers to be deduced from general constitutional principles. Marshall wrote:

> A constitution, to contain an accurate detail of all the subdivisions of which its great powers will admit, and of all the means by which they may be carried into execution, would partake of the prolixity of a legal code, and could scarcely be embraced by the human mind. It would, probably, never be understood by the public. Its nature, therefore, requires, that only its great outlines should be marked, its important objects designated, and the minor ingredients which compose those objects, be deduced from the nature of the objects themselves.

The most famous passage in *McCulloch* declares that "we must never forget that it is a constitution that we are expounding." A constitution whose enumerated powers were too strictly construed, Marshall contended, would not last. When government is explicitly given the power to declare war or regulate interstate commerce, the enumerated power entails all other powers that are necessary to fight wars effectively or regulate interstate commerce efficiently. Congress had the power to incorporate a bank, in this view, because the implied power to incorporate a bank was one means for exercising the enumerated power to regulate interstate commerce.

Marshall interpreted the necessary and proper clause broadly. He rejected claims by Jeffersonian strict constructionists that Congress could exercise only those powers that were strictly necessary for the exercise of an enumerated power. Instead, Marshall maintained that the best synonyms for "necessary" as used in the necessary and proper clause were "convenient or useful." *McCulloch* concluded, "Let the end be legitimate, let it be within the scope of the constitution, and all means which are appropriate, which are plainly adapted to that end, which are not prohibited, but consist with the letter and spirit of the constitution, are constitutional."

McCulloch introduced the rational basis test to American constitutional law. This test has historically been used to determine whether an exercise of national power is constitutional. The Supreme Court first examines the end government is trying to achieve. That end must be explicitly stated by the Constitution. Congress must be attempting to regulate interstate commerce or raise an army. The justices then consider the means Congress is using to achieve that end. These means must be a rational way of achieving the government end. The means do not have to be perfect or even wise. All the government lawyer must demonstrate is that some probability exists that the policy under constitutional attack will achieve some constitutional end to some degree. Judges who hate progressive taxation nevertheless recognize that taxing rich people at higher rates than poor people is one reasonable means for obtaining government revenue. Judges who support progressive taxation nevertheless recognize that taxing all people at the same rate is another reasonable means for obtaining government revenue.

Great debate continues to exist over whether, in light of the numerous enumerated powers, the necessary and proper clause, and *McCulloch v. Maryland*, the requirement that all national legislation be derived from an enumerated constitutional power has bite or is a mere ritual. The five most conservative justices on the Roberts Court insist that a constitutional enumeration of national powers articulates a constitutional commitment to limited government. They believe judicial scrutiny of national legislation is necessary to ensure that Congress does not assume powers that belong to the states. The four more liberal justices on the Roberts Court insist that the broad coverage of the constitutional text implies a constitutional commitment to providing a national solution to national problems. Because Congress is a representative body, they insist, the Supreme Court should not interfere when Congress identifies a national problem and passes national legislation reasonable people might think will alleviate that national problem.

What You Need to Know:

1. The federal government may exercise only enumerated powers. Unlike the states, Congress may not exercise a general police power.

2. Congress may exercise implied powers.
3. The standard for whether Congress may exercise an implied power is derived from *McCulloch v. Maryland.* The end must be legitimate and the powers exercised must be an appropriate or reasonable means for achieving that end.

LESSON 6: NATIONAL POWERS: THE COMMERCE CLAUSE

Article I, Section 8, paragraph 3 of the Constitution of the United States vests Congress with the power "To regulate Commerce with foreign Nations, and among the several States, and with the Indian tribes." The commerce clause was the least controversial national power granted in 1789. Both Federalists and anti-Federalists agreed that the federal government should have the power to regulate commerce between the states and foreign nations. No one thought that New York should be empowered to ban goods shipped from Connecticut or that Virginia should have the power to make commercial treaties with France. Nevertheless, what constitutes interstate commerce or a regulation of interstate commerce was not clear at the time of the framing and has been the subject of controversy for more than 200 years. The least controversial provision in the original Constitution has been the subject of the most constitutional debate ever since.

In the Beginning

Gibbons v. Ogden, 22 U.S. (9 Wheat.) 1 (1824), is the canonical Marshall Court decision interpreting the commerce clause. Chief Justice John Marshall in that case declared that commerce was not limited to "buying and selling," but included all navigation and other forms of "commercial intercourse." Congress was constitutionally authorized to give Gibbons a license to operate steamships between New York and New Jersey because transporting goods and people between states was interstate commerce. The New York monopoly was unconstitutional under the Supremacy Clause because state laws may not conflict with valid exercises of federal power (We will discuss preemption in a later lesson).

Marshall in *Gibbons* made three other points that structured future debates over the commerce power. First, he stated that Congress was free to regulate interstate commerce throughout the United States and was not confined to state borders. If a train is travelling from New York to Boston, Congress may determine whether that train will stop for refueling in New Haven, which is near the middle of Connecticut. Second, Marshall declared that congressional power over interstate commerce is plenary. Congress can regulate interstate commerce in any way Congress pleases, subject to explicit limits on federal power. Congress may prohibit items from being shipped in interstate commerce and may have noncommercial reasons for regulating interstate commerce. Congress may, for example, forbid shipping cigars in interstate commerce if the national legislature concludes that smoking cigars is a health hazard. Third, Marshall noted that states retain considerable power to make various laws that do not regulate interstate commerce, such as inspection laws. What Marshall did not explicitly consider is whether Congress could regulate activities that *Gibbons* declared did not involve interstate commerce if the national legislature determined such regulation was necessary to achieve certain interstate regulatory goals.

Commerce clause doctrine has evolved substantially from *Gibbons* to the present. For approximately 100 years, the Supreme Court attempted to maintain a line between interstate commerce and intrastate commerce. The justices ruled that a difference existed between production and commerce. Congress could regulate the transportation of goods, but not the creation (or consumption of goods). During the New Deal, those precedents were abandoned. From 1937 until 1995, the Supreme Court sustained every law but one that Congress claimed was an exercise of the power to regulate interstate commerce. Then in 1995, the justices began imposing limits on federal power to regulate interstate commerce.

The Modern Commerce Clause

Wickard v. Filburn, 317 U.S. 111 (1942), is the first modern commerce clause case that every student must know. Roscoe Filburn violated a federal law limiting how much wheat farmers could grow on their land, even if they consumed all the wheat they grew on their farm. Justice Robert Jackson's unanimous opinion upholding the federal law relied on the substantial effects test. This test permits Congress to regulate any activity that substantially affects interstate commerce, even if the participants in that activity are not directly involved in interstate commerce. That test had previously been used in *NLRB v. Jones & Laughlin Steel Corp.*, 301 U.S. 1 (1937), when the justices sustained a federal law requiring major steel companies to recognize unions on the theory that a strike in a steel plant would have an effect on interstate commerce even if the workers were engaged only in producing steel and shipping steel. Getting the commerce power to reach *Wickard* was trickier. Jackson did so by adding aggregate effects test to substantial effects. When determining whether Congress may regulate a particular activity under the commerce clause, his opinion declared, judges must consider whether that actor when combined with similar situated actors has a substantial effect on interstate commerce and not whether an individual actor is having a substantial effect on interstate commerce. If all farmers imitated Filburn and met their needs by homegrown wheat, that might destroy the interstate wheat market.

United States v. Lopez, 514 U.S. 549 (1995), is the second core precedent for contemporary commerce clause doctrine. When overturning a federal law passed under the commerce clause that forbade persons from bringing weapons to school, Chief Justice Rehnquist's majority opinion announced a new three-part test for determining whether Congress could regulate interstate commerce.

1. Congress may regulate the instrumentalities of interstate commerce.

2. Congress may regulate goods that will be, are being, or have been shipped in interstate commerce.

3. Congress may regulate commercial activities that have a substantial effect on interstate commerce.

The first two categories are uncontroversial and restate accepted doctrine. Congress may regulate at any time and in any place things that are used in interstate commerce. Highways are a good example of an instrumentality of interstate commerce. Because highways are regularly used to ship goods in interstate commerce, Congress may regulate in any way any road that might be used to ship a good from one state to another. Congress may also regulate any good that has a connection with interstate commerce. Had the law at issue in *Lopez* forbade persons from bringing to school a gun that had moved in interstate commerce, that law would have been constitutional. The third category is new. *Lopez* limited *Wickard* to economic or commercial activities. Congress could regulate Roscoe Filburn, even though he was not engaged in an interstate activity, because he was engaged in commerce. Congress could not regulate Alfonso Lopez because he was not engaged in commerce.

The Supreme Court subsequently handed down three decisions that somewhat clarified the distinction between in-state commercial activities that Congress may regulate under the commerce clause and in-state noncommercial activites that Congress may not regulate under the commerce clause. *United States v. Morrison*, 529 U.S. 598 (2000), held that Congress had no commerce clause power to provide rape victims with a civil remedy because rape is not a commercial activity. *Gonzales v. Raich*, 545 U.S. 1 (2005), held that Congress could forbid home-grown marijuana because the production of marijuana is a commercial activity. *National Federation of Independent Business v. Sebelius*, 132 S. Ct. 2566 (2012), held that Congress under the commerce clause could not require persons to purchase health insurance because the failure to buy or sell goods is not a commercial activity.

What You Need to Know:

1. Congress under the commerce clause may regulate the instrumentalities of interstate commerce, goods that will be, are being, or have been shipped in interstate commerce, or in-state commercial activities that have a substantial effect on interstate commerce.

2. When determining whether an activity has a substantial effect on interstate commerce, we consider the activity in the aggregate and not whether any particular instance of the activity has a substantial effect on interstate commerce.

3. Congress is not required to have an economic or commercial motive when regulating interstate commerce, as long as the regulation satisfies the above two conditions.

LESSON 7: NATIONAL POWERS: TAXING AND SPENDING

Article I, Section 8, paragraph 1 of the Constitution of the United States declares, "The Congress shall have Power To lay and collect Taxes, Duties, Imposts and Excises, to pay the Debts and provide for the common Defense and general Welfare of the United States." This clause was designed to provide the United States with an independent source of revenue. Under the Articles of Confederation, the Continental Congress relied solely on contributions from the states. This was not a big success. By granting Congress the power to collect taxes and impose tariffs, the framers sought to ensure that Congress would have the financial resources necessary to exercise other federal powers.

The precise powers Article I, Section 8, paragraph 1 gives Congress are controversial. One controversy is over whether Congress may use the taxing power to achieve goals other than raising revenue. Another controversy is over whether the power to provide for the general welfare is a distinct enumerated power or merely enables Congress to spend money when exercising such powers as the power to regulate interstate commerce.

The Tax Power

Under contemporary constitutional law, a tax is constitutional if that tax will raise some revenue and does not violate some other constitutional provision. If a 10 percent tax on beer raises revenue, a court will not ask whether the government might raise more money by taxing soda (or taxing beer and soda) or whether the real purpose of the law is to raise revenue or to reduce beer drinking. As long as the tax is likely to raise some revenue, the tax is constitutional. No constitutional problem exists when government taxes a good primarily to make that good more expensive.

The Supreme Court's recent decision in *National Federation of Independent Business v. Sebelius*, 132 S. Ct. 2566 (2012), highlights the broad scope of the contemporary tax power. *Sebelius* concerned the constitutionality of a tax on persons who did not purchase health insurance. As noted in Lesson 6, Chief Justice Roberts's majority opinion first concluded that Congress could not under the commerce clause require people to purchase health insurance. He nevertheless concluded that the tax was constitutional because the tax would raise revenue and no clause in the Constitution forbade Congress from taxing persons who do not purchase health insurance. *Sebelius* also establishes the principle that Congress need not describe a measure as a tax in order for the measure to be a constitutional tax. The Affordable Care Act declared that persons who did not purchase health insurance would have to pay a penalty, not a tax. Nevertheless, Roberts ruled, the measure was really a tax partly because the money was collected by the Internal Revenue Service and partly because Congress did not intend to treat as criminals the millions of persons who did not purchase health insurance. In short, if it looks like a duck or a tax, and quacks like a duck or a tax, it is constitutionally a duck or a tax, even if it is not labelled a duck or a tax.

The Spending Power

Under contemporary constitutional law, Congress may spend money for the general welfare, even when that spending is not an exercise of any other enumerated power. Many framers disagreed with this interpretation of Article I, Section 8, paragraph 1. James Madison and James Monroe were among the early presidents who thought that the power to "provide for the general welfare" was limited to spending when exercising other enumerated powers, such as the power to regulate interstate commerce. Americans over time became more committed to Alexander Hamilton's belief that the power to provide for the general welfare gives Congress the power to spend money on matters Congress cannot directly regulate. This creates what many students find an anomaly in federal powers. There are matters that Congress cannot regulate directly, but can influence through spending (and taxing). Congress can pay for actors who wish to study Shakespeare, but may not require adults to read Shakespeare.

Conditional federal spending presents tricky constitutional problems. Congress often provides states or individuals with money on the condition they perform particular actions. Instead of giving you a five-dollar rebate every time you purchase a salad, Congress gives you five dollars on the condition that you have salad for lunch (as this example suggests the line between spending and conditional spending can be obscure). The present test for conditional spending was laid out in *South Dakota v. Dole*, 483 U.S. 203 (1987). That case ruled that the federal government may use the spending power to induce behavior that Congress could not compel if and only if:

1. The spending program was for the general welfare.
2. The condition was unambiguous.
3. The condition was related to the spending program.
4. The condition did not violate some other constitutional provision.
5. The condition was not coercive.

The issue in *Dole* was whether the federal government could condition a portion of federal highway funds on a state's willingness to raise the state drinking age to 21. The Supreme Court ruled this spending constitutional, even though the possibility exists that under the Twenty-First Amendment Congress could not directly regulate drinking in a state.

1. The spending program was designed to promote highway safety (general welfare).

2. The spending program clearly informed states what they had to do to obtain their maximum share of federal highway funds.
3. Bans on teenage drinking are directly related to highway safety.
4. Teenagers have no constitutional right to drink.
5. The percentage of highway funds involved was sufficiently small that states had a realistic choice as to whether to take the money or run.

The conditions attached to the spending need not be attached to the particular way federal funds are spent. A Congress wanting to promote healthy habits is not limited to paying for salads or gym memberships. Instead, Congress may say that the federal government will pay for your salads providing you join a gym. The program is constitutional because the spending (purchasing salads) is relevant to the overall program (health).

The Supreme Court reinvigorated the coercion requirement in *Sebelius*. *Sebelius* concerned whether the federal government could cut off all federal Medicare funds to states that refused to adopt the conditions of those grants declared by the Affordable Care Act. Seven justices maintained this law was unconstitutional on the ground that, given the crucial role federal Medicare funds presently play in states, the federal government had made the proverbial offer that could not be refused.

What You Need to Know:

1. The federal government may use the taxing and spending power to influence behavior the federal government may not directly regulate.
2. A federal tax is constitutional if the tax raises some revenue and does not violate an independent restriction on congressional action.
3. Conditional federal spending is constitutional if the program advances the general welfare, the condition is unambiguous, the condition is related to the program, the condition does not violate an

independent restriction on congressional power, and the condition is not coercive.

LESSON 8: NATIONAL POWERS: THE POST-CIVIL WAR AMENDMENTS

The last clauses of the Thirteenth, Fourteenth, and Fifteenth Amendments declare, respectively, "Congress shall have the power to enforce this article by appropriate legislation," "The Congress shall have power to enforce by appropriate legislation, the provisions of this article," and "The Congress shall have power to enforce this article by appropriate legislation." General agreement exists that the slight wording differences are legally insignificant and that these provisions give Congress the power to remedy violations of the post-Civil War Amendments. General agreement also exists that Congress can do more than make such declarations as "any person held as a slave has a right to habeas corpus." Substantial disputes exist over what Congress can do other than remedy constitutional violations.

Provide Remedies

The post-Civil War Amendments authorize Congress to punish violations of the post-Civil War Amendments and to provide remedies for victims of unconstitutional actions. The Enforcement Act of 1871, now Section 1983 of Title 42 in the United States Code, exercised this power when declaring:

> Every person who under color of any statute, ordinance, custom or usage, of any State or Territory or the District of Columbia, subjects, or causes to be subjected, any citizen of the United States or other persons within the jurisdiction thereof to the deprivation of any rights, privileges, or immunities secured by the Constitution and laws, shall be liable to the party inured in an action at law, suit in equity, or other proceeding for redress.

Section 1983 does not state what constitutes a violation of the Constitution. That is left entirely to the courts. Section 1983 declares only that if state actors violate your constitutional rights, as those rights are determined by a court, you can sue them for damages.

Fact-Finding

Congress may make the fact-findings necessary for determining when a constitutional violation has taken place. If the constitutional status of a law depends on particular facts, Congress may determine whether those facts exist and, if Congress determines they do not, Congress may prohibit that law. This congressional power to make fact-findings played a crucial role in the legislation outlawing literacy tests for voting. The Supreme Court in *Lassiter v. Northampton County Board of Elections*, 360 U.S. 45 (1959), ruled that literacy tests per se did not violate the Constitution if, but only if, they were not designed to prevent persons of color from voting. Congress when passing the Voting Rights Act subsequently prohibited literacy tests in many southern states after finding that those tests were being implemented in ways that discriminated against persons of color. The Supreme Court sustained those provisions of the Voting Rights Act in *South Carolina v. Katzenbach*, 383 U.S. 301 (1966). That decision ruled, "Congress may use any rational means to effectuate the constitutional prohibition of racial discrimination in voting." Five years later, on the basis of additional fact-finding, the Congress suspended literacy tests throughout the United States. The Supreme Court unanimously sustained that prohibition in *Oregon v. Mitchell*, 400 U.S. 112 (1970).

Deterrence

Contemporary constitutional law permits Congress to prohibit otherwise constitutional laws and practices when doing so is likely to deter or prevent unconstitutional behavior. The congressional power to deter unconstitutional behavior provided one underlying basis for the Supreme Court's decision in *Katzenbach v. Morgan*, 384 U.S. 641 (1966). That case concerned the constitutionality of a provision in the Civil Rights Act of 1964 that forbade states from denying the ballot to persons who had been educated in Puerto Rico. The judicial majority reasoned that Congress may have feared that if many Spanish-speaking American citizens were denied the right to vote, state legislatures would be far more inclined to discriminate against Hispanic-Americans.

Interpretation

Contemporary constitutional law does not permit Congress to pass legislation that challenges the Supreme Court's interpretation of various provisions in the post-Civil War Amendments. When passing legislation under the post-Civil War amendments, Congress must be faithful to Supreme Court rulings on constitutional law. If the Supreme Court declares that the Fifteenth Amendment forbids states from passing laws that deny the ballot to persons of color, but does not forbid states from passing the laws that deny the ballot to people who have not taken a class in constitutional law, then Congress may prohibit state laws that require voters to take a constitutional law class only if Congress finds that these laws are implemented in ways that discriminate against persons of color or if Congress finds that prohibiting these laws will prevent or deter discrimination against persons of color. Congress may not declare that the Supreme Court wrongly interpreted the Constitution when sustaining state laws requiring voters to take classes in constitutional law.

Distinguishing Interpretation from Prevention

The Supreme Court uses a "proportionate and congruence" test for distinguishing unconstitutional congressional efforts to interpret the Constitution from constitutional efforts to remedy, prevent, or deter constitutional violations. *City of Boerne v. Flores*, 521 U.S. 507 (1997), the case that announced the "proportionate and congruence" test, provides an instance of how the justices employ that standard. The issue in that case was whether Congress could require in the Religious Freedom Restoration Act of 1993 (RFRA) that states give religious believers an exemption from state laws unless a compelling reason existed for not having an exemption. The first part of the Court's opinion noted that Congress was trying to reverse the Supreme Court's decision in *Employment Division v. Smith*, 494 U.S. 872 (1990), which held that the religion clauses of the Constitution forbade only laws that explicitly discriminated against religious believers. Congress, the justices agreed, could not challenge the Court's understanding of free exercise. The second part of the Court's opinion discussed whether a ban on laws that made no exemption for religious believers might be interpreted as preventing states from passing laws that were motivated by religious discrimination or implementing neutral laws in ways that discriminated against religious believers. Justice Anthony Kennedy's majority opinion observed that RFRA would prohibit numerous state laws, but that Congress had provided no evidence most of the prohibited laws were motivated by religious prejudice or were being implemented in ways that intentionally discriminated against religious believers. For this reason, RFRA was declared unconstitutional.

Preclearance, National Power, and State Sovereignty

Congressional power under the Fifteenth Amendment to require states to preclear changes in voting laws presents thorny problems of national power, state sovereignty, voting rights, and race discrimination. The Voting Rights Act of 1965 required all states in which less than 50 percent of the adult population voted in the 1964 election to gain approval (preclearance) from either the Justice Department or the Court of Appeals for the District of Columbia before changing most voting practices. The Supreme Court with only Justice Hugo Black dissenting sustained this measure in *South Carolina v. Katzenbach*, 383 U.S. 301 (1966). Chief Justice Warren's opinion stated, "As against the reserved powers of the States, Congress may use any rational means to effectuate the constitutional prohibition of racial discrimination in voting." Nearly 50 years later, a narrow 5–4 majority in *Shelby County v. Holder*, 133 S. Ct. 2612 (2013), declared unconstitutional the provision in the Voting Rights Act of 2006 that relied on the same formula when determining which states had to preclear changes in voting laws. After noting that preclearance "was justified by 'exceptional' and 'unique' conditions," Chief Justice John Roberts concluded, "Congress must ensure that the legislation it passes to remedy that problem speaks to current conditions." Whether *Shelby* held that maintaining the same formula for preclearance was irrational or announced state sovereignty limits on congressional power under the Fifteenth Amendment is for the future to determine.

What You Need to Know:

1. Congress under the post-Civil War Amendments has the power to remedy, deter, and prevent constitutional violations. Congress may also make fact-findings that establish constitutional violations.
2. Congress may not independently interpret the Constitution.
3. The Supreme Court uses a proportionate and congruence standard for determining whether Congress is unconstitutionally interpreting the Constitution or constitutionally enforcing the provisions of the post-Civil War Amendments.
4. Whether state sovereign limitations exist on congressional power to implement the post-Civil War Amendments is presently not clear.

LESSON 9: FEDERALISM

The Tenth Amendment declares, "The powers not delegated to the United States by the Constitution, nor prohibited by it to the States, are reserved to the States respectively, or to the people." This language differs from the analogous provision in the Articles of Confederation, which states, "Each state retains its sovereignty, freedom, and independence, and every power, jurisdiction, and right, which is not by this Confederation expressly delegated to the United States, in Congress assembled." Unlike the Articles, the Constitution does not explicitly speak of state "sovereignty, freedom, and independence." The Tenth Amendment speaks of powers "not delegated" rather than powers "not expressly delegated" when describing the powers reserved to the states.

Whether and the extent to which these textual differences make a constitutional difference are subjects of ongoing constitutional debate. Contemporary constitutional liberals think the Constitution of the United States substantially changed the relationship between the federal government and the states under the Articles of Confederation. Their Constitution does not recognize states as independent sovereigns. Their Tenth Amendment does not limit in any way the powers delegated to the federal government. Congress when regulating interstate commerce may treat the states no differently than ordinary persons. Contemporary constitutional conservatives think that the Constitution merely modified the sovereignty states enjoyed under the Articles of Confederation. Their Constitution recognizes the states as sovereign entities. Their Tenth Amendment or underlying principles of federalism limit in important ways the powers of the federal government. Congress when regulating interstate commerce must acknowledge state sovereignty and state sovereign immunity. This means some federal regulations that are constitutional when applied to individuals are not constitutional when applied to states or state officials. At present, conservatives have one more vote on the Supreme Court than liberals, so with the exception of the occasional case in which Justice Kennedy defects, the conservative understanding of federalism is the constitutional law of the land.

Sovereign Immunity

Seminole Tribe of Florida v. Florida, 517 U.S. 44 (1996), and *Alden v. Maine*, 527 U.S. 706 (1999), are the two most important contemporary precedents on state sovereign immunity. *Seminole Tribe* ruled that Congress when exercising the commerce power may not permit any individual to sue any state in federal court. States enjoyed sovereign immunity in federal courts from lawsuits brought by state residents, as well as residents of other states. *Alden* held that Congress when exercising the commerce power may not subject states to lawsuits in state courts. Both decisions went beyond the Eleventh Amendment by extending state sovereign immunity to suits brought by state residents and suits brought in state courts. Justice Anthony Kennedy's majority opinion in *Alden* explained that state sovereign immunity derives from basic constitutional principles and not from any particular constitutional amendment. He wrote:

> the sovereign immunity of the States neither derives from nor is limited by the terms of the Eleventh Amendment. Rather, as the Constitution's structure, and its history, and the authoritative interpretations by this Court make clear, the States' immunity from is fundamental aspect of the sovereignty which the States enjoyed before the ratification of the Constitution, and which they retain today . . . except as altered by the plan of the Convention or certain constitutional Amendments.

Both *Seminole* Tribe and *Alden* adopt the conservative position on state sovereign immunity. Both hold that the Eleventh Amendment merely codifies one aspect of state sovereign immunity, but is not the only source of federalism limits on federal power to subject state governments to lawsuits. Both hold that federalism is an affirmative limitation on federal power. Consider a federal law forbidding age discrimination in employment. After *Alden*, you can sue General Motors (a private corporation) if they insist you retire at age 65, but not the state of New York.

The Supreme Court has permitted the federal government to subject states to lawsuits when exercising some federal powers. Existing doctrine holds that the federal government may abrogate state sovereign immunity when exercising power under the post-Civil War Amendments, which were passed after the Eleventh Amendment. The Supreme Court has also ruled that Congress may abrogate state sovereign immunity when exercising power under the bankruptcy clause of Article I. With that exception, the rough rule of thumb is that Congress may not abrogate state sovereign immunity when exercising powers granted to the federal government by the original Constitution, but may abrogate state sovereign immunity when exercising powers granted to the federal government by constitutional amendments.

Commandeering

Contemporary disputes over constitutional federalism also rage over whether and the extent to which Congress may "commandeer" states by mandating that state governments and state officials implement federal programs. Both liberals and conservatives agree that state justices must enforce federal laws when adjudicating lawsuits. Conservatives insist that the federal government under the Tenth Amendment may not force states to pass legislation or require state employees to implement federal laws. Liberals disagree.

New York v. United States, 505 U.S. 144 (1992), and *Printz v. United States*, 521 U.S. 898 (1997), are the most important contemporary cases on commandeering. The Supreme Court in *New York* ruled that the federal government could not require state legislatures to pass particular laws. *Printz* extended *New York* to members of the state executive branch. The issue in that case was whether the federal government could require state police officers to perform the background checks necessary to implement federal gun control legislation. The Supreme Court by a 5–4 majority declared that regulation violated basic principles of federalism. Justice Antonin Scalia's majority opinion observed,

> By forcing state governments to absorb the financial burden of implementing a federal regulatory program, Members of Congress can take credit for "solving" problems without having to ask their constituents to pay for the solutions with higher federal taxes.

Justice John Paul Stevens in dissent took the liberal position that a federal power trumped Tenth Amendment defenses. He wrote, "When Congress exercises the powers delegated to it by the Constitution, it may impose affirmative obligations on executive and judicial officials of state and local governments as well as ordinary citizens."

The Constitution, liberals and conservatives agree, does not prohibit state officials from voluntarily implementing federal laws. The federal government may purchase state cooperation through the spending power (see Lesson 7). A federal law that paid police officers to conduct the background checks necessary to implement federal gun control legislation is constitutional, provided all states are free to refuse the deal.

What You Need to Know:

1. Federalism presently (and by one vote) limits federal power under Article I.
2. Congress when exercising Article I powers may not compel states to defend lawsuits (except in bankruptcy) in federal and state courts or commandeer state officials to implement federal policies.
3. Congress may provide states with financial incentives to waive sovereign immunity, but such waivers must be voluntary.

LESSON 10: PREEMPTION AND THE DORMANT COMMERCE CLAUSE

The Supremacy Clause in Article VI mandates that when federal and state laws conflict, the federal law governs. That clause declares, "The Constitution, and the Laws of the United States which shall be made in Pursuance thereof; and all Treaties made, or which shall be made, under the Authority of the United States, shall be the Supreme Law of the Land." If the United States signs a treaty with Mongolia which requires the United States to sell Idaho potatoes to Mongolia, then Idaho cannot forbid farmers from growing potatoes. More difficult questions arise when determining when state laws should be declared unconstitutional because they unduly conflict with federal policy.

Preemption and the dormant commerce clause are the two judicially developed doctrines that courts use when determining whether states have unconstitutionally entrenched on federal power. A state law is preempted when that law interferes or is in some way inconsistent with federal law. If Congress prohibits the importation of elephants, then Kansas may not authorize the organizers of the Kansas State Fair to import elephants from Kenya. Courts invoke the dormant commerce clause when prohibiting some state laws that interfere with interstate commerce, even when Congress has passed no law and made no policy on the subject matter. Kansas may not insist that all public roads in the state be constructed with yellow bricks manufactured in Kansas, even if Congress has passed no law on the subject because that state law discriminates against and unduly interferes with interstate commerce.

Preemption and the dormant commerce clause differ in one vital way from every matter of constitutional law. Elected officials may normally reverse Supreme Court decisions only by passing a constitutional amendment. If the Supreme Court declares that state bans on flag burning violate the First and Fourteenth Amendments, elected officials committed to that prohibition must change the constitutional text. Supreme Court decisions on preemption and the dormant commerce clause are the only constitutional decisions by federal courts that Congress may reverse by ordinary statute. The logic of this exception is simple. When the Supreme Court declares a state law is preempted by a federal law, the court is declaring only that the justices believe the state law is inconsistent with federal law. Congress may therefore pass a federal law denying that inconsistency. Similarly, a judicial decision under the dormant commerce clause can be interpreted as identifying a federal policy that states should not be allowed to regulate interstate commerce in this way. Congress may therefore by statute indicate that such regulations are consistent with federal policy.

Preemption

Preemption comes in three flavors: express preemption, conflict preemption, and field preemption. Express preemption occurs when Congress explicitly declares that no states may regulate a particular subject matter that Congress is constitutionally empowered to regulate. A federal law stating that states may not regulate the forests in national parks is an example of express preemption. Conflict preemption occurs when the Supreme Court determines that a state law is inconsistent or interferes with a federal law. The Supreme Court's decision in *McCulloch v. Maryland*, 17 U.S. (4 Wheat.) 316 (1819), is a famous example of conflict preemption. No federal law prohibited state taxes on the national bank, but the justices determined that a state tax on the national bank would thwart the congressional policy of incorporating a national bank. Field preemption occurs when the Supreme Court determines that a pervasive scheme of federal regulation necessarily excludes any state regulation. During the McCarthy Era, the Supreme Court in *Pennsylvania v. Nelson*, 350 U.S. 497 (1956), declared that congressional laws regulating Communists were intended to be the only regulatory measures in that area. Express preemption and conflict preemption raise few difficult legal issues, at least where the congressional intent or the conflict is clear. Far more debate occurs when the justices are considering whether state laws interfere with federal laws and whether field preemption has occurred.

The Dormant Commerce Clause

The Supreme Court has declared some state laws unconstitutional that interfere with interstate commerce even when the federal government has made no relevant law. The so-called "dormant commerce clause" treats the interstate commerce clause as a grant of federal power and a simultaneous denial of state power. In particular, the Supreme Court has interpreted the commerce clause as prohibiting state regulations that discriminate in favor of the home team's commerce. In other cases, dormant commerce clause decisions reflect a judicial sense that the lack of congressional regulation reflects a congressional policy that the matter not be regulated. These dormant commerce clause rulings are close cousins to preemption decisions.

State laws that discriminate against interstate commerce are constitutional only if they are justified by a compelling state interest. Such discriminatory laws either limit state goods from being shipped outside the state or restrict the goods that may be shipped into a state. A good recent example is *City of Philadelphia v. New Jersey*, 437 U.S. 617 (1978). New Jersey passed a law forbidding out-of-state waste to be deposited in New Jersey landfills. The Supreme Court declared the state law unconstitutional. After noting that states are "without power to prevent privately owned articles of trade from being shipped and sold in interstate commerce on the ground that they are required to satisfy local demands or because they are needed by the people of the State," Justice Potter Stewart's majority opinion concluded, that a state may not "isolate itself in the stream of interstate commerce from a problem shared by all." Not all state discriminations are declared unconstitutional. In *Maine v. Taylor*, 477 U.S. 131 (1986), the Supreme Court sustained a Maine law prohibiting out-of-state baitfish on the ground that such fish might significantly damage delicate state ecosystems.

State laws that do not discriminate against interstate commerce are evaluated on the basis of a balancing test. *Pike v. Bruce Church Inc.*, 397 U.S. 137 (1970), is the canonical statement of this standard. Justice Stewart's opinion declared that "where the statute regulates evenhandedly to effectuate a legitimate local public interest, and its effects on interstate commerce are only incidental, it will be upheld unless the burden imposed on such commerce is clearly excessive in relation to the putative local benefits." As with most balancing tests, results tend to vary with consistency only in the eyes of the individual justice.

What You Need to Know:

1. State laws may not conflict with federal laws nor unduly interfere with interstate commerce.
2. State laws are preempted if existing federal law prohibits state regulation, if the state regulation interferes with existing federal law, or if the federal law was clearly intended to cover the entire area being regulated.
3. State laws violate the dormant commerce clause, even in the absence of federal regulation, if the law discriminates against interstate commerce without a compelling reason or if the burdens on interstate commerce outweigh the benefits to the state.

LESSON 11: SEPARATION OF POWERS: BASICS

Americans are committed to the separation of powers. James Madison declared, "The accumulation of all powers, legislative, executive, and judiciary, in the same hands, whether of one, a few, or many, and whether hereditary, self-appointed, or elective, may justly be pronounced the very definition of tyranny." Americans nevertheless find a complete separation to be impossible. Madison in *Federalist* 48 noted that the framers rejected a constitutional design in which "the legislative, executive and judiciary departments" were "wholly unconnected with each other." Instead, they preferred that "these departments be so far connected and blended as to give to each a constitutional control over the other." What the Constitution prevents is unilateral action by any government institution. Presidents may veto bills that pass Congress. Courts may declare laws and presidential actions unconstitutional. Congress may impeach the president and members of the federal judiciary. These arrangements are often referred to as "checks and balances" rather than a strict separation of powers.

The Unitary Executive and Presidential Power

Whether the Constitution provides for a unitary executive is at the heart of many constitutional conflicts. Supporters of broad presidential powers insist that, unless the Constitution declares otherwise, executive powers can be exercised only by the president and executive branch officials supervised and controlled by the president. If President Rubble cannot tell Flintstone how to perform his job and fire Flintstone at will, then Flintstone may not exercise executive power. Opponents of the unitary presidency insists that, in light of such constitutional provisions as the requirement that the Senate confirm most presidential appointments and the constitutional antipathy to unilateral action by any branch of the national government, the Constitution does not contemplate a unitary executive. Permitting President Rubble to fire Flintstone at will, in their view, inhibits the checks and balances necessary to prevent arbitrary rule by one person.

Supporters of broad presidential powers also insist that Article II vests the president with substantial unenumerated powers. These powers have two sources. First, Article II declares, "The executive Power shall be vested in a President of the United States." This contracts to Article I, which declares, "All legislative Power herein granted shall be vested in a Congress of the United States." Proponents of presidential power interpret the absence of "herein granted" as entailing that the president may exercise any executive power, even if that power is not specified elsewhere in Article II. Presidents, for example, need not point to a specific provision in the Constitution that empowers them to make executive agreements with foreign leaders because that is an inherently executive power. Second, some presidents and their supporters interpret the provision in Article II, Section 2 which declares that the president "shall take care that the Laws be faithfully executed" as enabling the president to take unilateral action without congressional approval when doing so is necessary to enforce federal laws already on the books. President Lincoln relied in part on the take-care clause when at the outbreak of the Civil War he suspended habeas corpus, blockaded southern ports, and issued a call for soldiers, all without congressional permission. Opponents of these broad presidential powers insist that the framers were committed to limiting the powers exercised by members of all branches of the national government. Vesting the president with broad undefined powers, in their view, is particularly troublesome because no single person should be able to determine whether to suspend habeas corpus, send troops abroad, or make other decisions that affect many fundamental rights and interests.

Formalism or Functionalism

Neither Americans nor the Supreme Court have agreed on any particular approach to determining the extent to which the Constitution blends legislative, executive, and judicial powers. Some judicial opinions take a formalist approach that emphasizes the importance of clear lines between the powers of the different branches. Other judicial opinions take a functionalist approach that emphasizes the need for a workable government.

Youngstown Sheet & Tube Co. v. Sawyer, 343 U.S. 579 (1952), is the canonical case that structures many contemporary judicial opinions on the separation of powers. The Supreme Court in that case by a 6–3 vote declared that President Truman had unconstitutionally seized steel mills during the Korean War when he acted in the absence of a federal law. Justice Hugo Black, who delivered the opinion of the Court, issued the canonical expression of constitutional formalism. He wrote:

> The President's order does not direct that a congressional policy be executed in a manner prescribed by Congress—it directs that a presidential policy be executed in a manner prescribed by the President.

Notice the way in which Black reasons. He first determined whether the president had made policy (a legislative function) or executed policy (an executive function). Once he determined that the President had made policy (a legislative function), he declared President Truman's actions unconstitutional because a president (an executive officer) cannot exercise a legislative function unless the Constitution explicitly vests the president with that power.

Justice Robert Jackson disagreed with Justice Black's claim that the Constitution neatly divided powers between the national legislature and national executive. His opinion explored three different circumstances in which presidents might make policy.

1. The President was making policy pursuant to a directive from Congress.
2. The President was making policy in the absence of any directive from Congress.
3. The President was making policy inconsistent with Congressional policy.

If a presidential action is in category 1, Jackson concluded, then the president may make policy as long as the national government as a whole may make the policy in question. If a presidential action is in category 3, presidential power "is at its lowest ebb" and may be justified only if the Constitution clearly gives the president independent policy-making authority on that matter. If a presidential power is in category 2, Americans are in a "zone of twilight" in which "any actual test of power is likely to depend on the imperatives of events and contemporary imponderables" or, in short, who knows. Jackson then stated that Truman had acted unconstitutionally because Congress had previously disapproved of presidential seizures, thus putting the seizure of the steel mines in the third category.

Justice Jackson's concurring opinion in *Youngstown* is the central text for those who adopt a functionalist understanding of the separation of powers. Rather than begin with the text of the Constitution, Jackson begins with the actual relationships between the executive and legislative branches of the government. If the elected branches of the national government have established a relationship that is acceptable to them, Jackson and other functionalists would have the court not interfere. The justices look to the formal boundaries established by the Constitution only when a clear dispute over power has arisen between the Congress and the president or, perhaps, when Congress has not approved or disapproved the presidential action in controversy.

What You Need to Know:

1. The Supreme Court throughout American history has oscillated between more formalist and functionalist theories of the separation of powers.
2. Formalists tend to view the Constitution as clearly dividing power between the national executive and national legislature.
3. Functionalists tend to defer to the president and Congress when the two reach agreement on a workable division of powers.

LESSON 12: SEPARATION OF POWERS: ISSUES

The case law on separation of powers ranges from simple (delegation) to close to incoherent (appointments and removals). Some doctrines have been settled for almost a century. Others change by the judicial term.

Delegation of Legislative Authority

The constitutional rules that determine when Congress may empower administrative agencies or regulatory commissions to make rules and regulations are simple in theory and even simpler in contemporary practice. Congress may not transfer the legislative power wholesale to another branch of government, but may seek assistance in making policy. *J.W. Hampton Jr. & Co. v. United States*, 276 U.S. 394 (1928), states the relevant principle of constitutional law. Chief Justice William Howard Taft declared, "If Congress shall lay down by legislative act an intelligible principle to which the person or body authorized" to make rules or regulations "is directed to confirm, such legislative action is not a forbidden delegation of legislative power." During the 1930s, the Supreme Court declared that several New Deal statutes did not meet that standard. No such decision has been handed down since 1936. No matter how vague the delegation, the Supreme Court has always found "an intelligible principle." A federal law that authorized the Federal Elections Committee to make campaign finance regulations that "respect the value our society places on free speech and fair elections" under present constitutional law would no doubt be found to articulate "an intelligible principle," even though all proposed campaign finance reforms purport to respect the value our society places on free speech and fair elections.

Appointing and Removing Executive Officials

The extent to which Congress may participate in the removal of executive branch officials is the oldest constitutional debate in the history of the United States. Article II, Section 2, paragraph 1 details how various officers of the United States may be appointed, but no constitutional provision specifies how these officers may be removed from office, short of impeachment. The First Congress debated removals at length when considering a bill that gave the president the power to remove cabinet officials at will. President Andrew Johnson was almost impeached for violating a federal law that forbade the president from removing certain executive branch officials without congressional permission.

The Supreme Court over the last hundred years has handed down three decisions that clarified some, but not all the constitutional questions about removals. *Myers v. United States*, 272 U.S. 52 (1926), held that the president "has the exclusive power of removing executive branch officers of the United States whom he has appointed by and with the advice and consent of the Senate." Later decisions interpreted *Myers* as giving the president the sole power to remove any purely executive branch official from office. Chief Justice Taft declared that such a rule reflected the constitutional practice of keeping the executive and legislature "separate in all cases in which they were not expressly blended" and ensuring that the president had control over subordinates charged with implementing laws. *Humphrey's Executor v. United States*, 295 U.S. 602 (1935), confined *Myers* to "purely executive officials." The Supreme Court in that case ruled that Congress could require the president to have good cause when removing a member of an independent regulatory commission. *Morrison v. Olson*, 487 U.S. 654 (1988), ruled that Congress may require that some executive branch officials be removed only on good cause when "the removal restrictions are [not] of such a nature that they impede the President's ability to perform his constitutional duty." For this reason, the justices sustained a statute providing that the independent counsel be removed only for good cause. What executive branch officials fit this description of officials whose removal will not impede presidential abilities is for the future to determine.

Making Laws

The Constitution requires that all laws be passed by both the House and Senate and signed by the president (or if vetoed by the President overridden by a two-thirds majority in both Houses of Congress). The Supreme Court in two recent decisions has limited how elected officials may tinker with that process. *INS v. Chadha*, 462 U.S. 919 (1983), declared unconstitutional the legislative veto. This device permitted Congress to delegate power to make regulations or other decisions to an administrative agency or independent regulatory commission subject to those decisions being rejected by a majority in one house of Congress or even by a committee chair. Proponents claimed that legislative vetoes passed constitutional muster because they were put in bills that passed both the House and Senate. The Burger Court rejected this position. When Congress takes action that has "the purpose and effect of altering the legal rights, duties, and relations of persons," Chief Justice Warren Burger declared, the bill must pass both houses of Congress (bicameralism) and be signed by the president (presentment) or a presidential veto must be overridden. Presidents are not permitted to sign only parts of federal bills. *Clinton v. City of New York*, 524 U.S. 417 (1998), declared unconstitutional a federal law that gave the president a "line-item veto," the power to approve some appropriations in a single bill but not others. Justice John Paul Stevens's majority opinion declared that presidents do not have "the unilateral power to change the text of duly enacted statutes."

Foreign Policy

United States v. Curtiss-Wright Export Corp., 299 U.S. 304 (1936), is the second most important Supreme Court case on the basic principles underlying the separation of powers, particularly with respect to presidential power in foreign affairs. The case arose after President Roosevelt prohibited arms sales to Bolivia and Paraguay. Roosevelt based this action on federal legislation permitting the president to decide whether to suspend arms sales to several South American nations. The Curtiss-Wright Export Corporation challenged the legality of that presidential order, claiming that this was an unconstitutional delegation of power. The Supreme Court by a 7–1 vote declared President Roosevelt's actions constitutional. Justice Sutherland's opinion for the court declared that presidents had substantial power to act unilaterally in foreign affairs. He spoke of "the very delicate, plenary and exclusive power of the President as the sole organ of the federal government in the field of international relations—a power which does not require as a basis for its exercise an act of Congress."

The precise interpretation of *Curtiss-Wright* remains controversial. A general consensus exists that presidents have far greater power to act unilaterally in foreign affairs than in domestic affairs. Nevertheless, debate exists over whether the president is "the sole organ of the federal government in the field of international relationships." Many presidents and their advisors claim that control over foreign policy (and military engagements) is an executive power and, hence, under Article II is vested in the president even if not specifically enumerated.

There is an adage in the Office of Legal Counsel to the effect "*Curtiss-Wright* means we must be right." Many members of Congress, particularly those of a different party than the incumbent president, insist that the president may exercise only the powers specifically enumerated in Article II.

What You Need to Know:

1. Distinctive rules exist for most distinctive separation of powers issues.
2. Congress may delegate rule-making power to the executive branch or a regulatory commission as long as the delegation contains "an intelligible principle."
3. Congress may not participate in the removal of any purely executive branch official, but may play some role in removing a member of an independent regulatory commission. Congress may condition some executive removals, but only when doing so does not interfere with fundamental executive powers.
4. Presidents have more power to act unilaterally when making foreign policy than when making domestic policy, but the degree of that independence remains contested.

LESSON 13: THE BILL OF RIGHTS AND THE STATES

Whether, when, and how states must respect the liberties set out in the Bill of Rights is another longstanding dispute in American constitutional law. Congress in 1791 rejected James Madison's proposal that the Constitution be amended to declare, "No state shall violate the equal rights of conscience, or the freedom of the press, or the trial by jury in criminal cases." The Supreme Court in *Barron v. Baltimore*, 32 U.S. (7 Pet.) 243 (1833), ruled that the first ten amendments to the Constitution limited only federal power. John Bingham, the Congressperson who drafted Section 1 of the Fourteenth Amendment, thought the privileges and immunities clause required states to respect the liberties set out in the Bill of Rights, but the Supreme

Court in *The Slaughter-House Cases*, 83 U.S. (16 Wall.) 36 (1873), rejected this interpretation of the post-Civil War Constitution. The tide began to turn during the early twentieth century when the Supreme Court interpreted the Due Process Clause of the Fourteenth Amendment as protecting some rights that were also protected by the Bill of Rights. What was a trickle became a wave when Earl Warren became Chief Justice. At present, the Supreme Court interprets the due-process clause of the Fourteenth Amendment as requiring states to protect almost all the liberties enumerated in the Bill of Rights.

The process by which states became obligated to respect the liberties enumerated in the Bill of Rights is known as "incorporation." Constitutional lawyers speak of the Due Process Clause of the Fourteenth Amendment as incorporating the free exercise clause of the First Amendment when they are claiming that state governments must respect the same rights to religious freedom under the Fourteenth Amendment as the federal government must under the free exercise clause of the First Amendment. The process by which provisions of the Bill of Rights are incorporated is known as selective due process. The Due Process Clause in this view incorporates those liberties set out in the Bill of Rights that are "fundamental principles of liberty and justice which lie at the basis of all our civil and political institutions" or are "basic to our system of jurisprudence" or are the "very essence of a scheme of ordered liberty." A fair case can be made that every liberty enumerated in the Bill of Rights is a "fundamental principle of liberty and justice" (otherwise why would the liberty have been included in the original Bill of Rights) and an equally fair case can be made that no liberty enumerated in the Bill of Rights is of "the very essence of a scheme of ordered liberty" (each of those liberties is omitted or significantly modified in some constitution of a reasonable just constitutional democracy). The word "selective" hardly describes the process by which the states have been required to respect the liberties enumerated in the Bill of Rights. During the first third of the twentieth century, selective incorporation was selective. One new right (takings, free speech, right to counsel) was incorporated every ten to fifteen years. For the last 60 years, selective incorporation has been selective in the sense, dare we say it, that the admissions process for most for-profit law schools is selective. In every case in which the issue has been raised, the Supreme Court has ruled that the Fourteenth Amendment requires the states to respect the provision of the Bill of Rights in question.

Contemporary justices follow a two-step procedure when applying selective incorporation. They first determine whether a particular provision of the Bill of Rights is essential to liberty and freedom. If they do, and they always do, then the Due Process Clause of the Fourteenth Amendment requires that states obey the same standards as the analogous provision in the Bill of Rights requires of the federal government. If a federal law violates the Eighth Amendment, then the identical state law violates the Due Process Clause of the Fourteenth Amendment. Should the Supreme Court rule that the First Amendment does not prohibit the federal government from punishing people who yell "Fire" in a crowded theater, then the court will rule that the Due Process Clause permits state governments to punish people who yell "Fire" in a crowded theater.

The Supreme Court recently reaffirmed selective incorporation with a slight twist in *McDonald v. City of Chicago*, 561 U.S. 742 (2010). In that case, the justices by a 5–4 majority held that the Due Process Clause of the Fourteenth Amendment incorporated the individual right to bear arms that the Supreme Court in *District of Columbia v. Heller*, 554 U.S. 570 (2008), held was protected by the Second Amendment. Incorporation was constitutionally required, the majority opinion stated, because "the right to keep and bear arms is fundamental to our scheme of ordered liberty." The slight twist is that the five justices in the majority were the more conservative justices whose ideological ancestors had historically been opposed to incorporation while the four justices in the minority were the more liberal justices whose ideological ancestors had historically favored incorporation.

The Supreme Court has incorporated every provision of the Bill of Rights but the Third Amendment, the grand jury provision of the Sixth Amendment, the Seventh Amendment, and the excessive fines clause of the Eighth Amendment. For your practice, you should know that no lawyer has lost an incorporation case in a very long time, so expect that in the appropriate case, the remaining provisions of the Bill of Rights are likely to be "selectively" incorporated.

What You Need to Know:

1. The Due Process Clause of the Fourteenth Amendment incorporates almost all the provisions in the Bill of Rights.
2. When a clause of the Bill of Rights is incorporated by the Due Process Clause, state governments are held to the identical standard as the federal government.

LESSON 14: STATE ACTION

The second sentence of the Fourteenth Amendment, Section 1 declares, "No State shall" violate particular rights. This phrasing provides the foundation for the "state-action doctrine." Persons claiming Fourteenth (and Fifteenth) Amendment rights must demonstrate that action they claim is unconstitutional can be imputed to a state actor. State actors who engage in racial discrimination violate the constitutional commandment that "No State shall deny to any person within its jurisdiction the equal protection of the laws." Non-state actors who engage in racial discrimination may violate federal laws passed under Article I, but their conduct does not violate any provision of the Fourteenth Amendment. Government officials performing official duties are obviously state actors. More difficult constitutional questions arise when private persons perform actions that have some connection to the state.

The state-action doctrine often seems to make common sense. Private actors routinely engage in conduct that is forbidden to state actors. Students may discriminate on the basis of race, religion, ethnicity, and gender when choosing friends and romantic partners, but the federal government may never prefer members of one race or a particular gender per se. Many parents create religious theocracies in their residence. Only one religion is allowed to be practiced in their living room, mandatory prayers are said before meals, and children are forced to have religious education. These actions are constitutionally protected, even though analogous actions by the state violate the First and Fourteenth Amendments.

Distinguishing between state and private action is not simple and Supreme Court doctrine has not run a steady course. Present judicial doctrine requires plaintiffs to establish one of three circumstances when claiming that a private party is a state actor.

1. The private party was engaged in a traditional state function.
2. The state encouraged the unconstitutional action.
3. The private actor was entwined with the state.

More often than not, the contemporary court does not find any of these elements. Being heavily regulated, for example, is not a sufficient basis for finding state action. No matter how heavily regulated a private actor, if the regulations do not encourage unconstitutional action, then the private actor is not a state actor.

Jackson v. Metropolitan Edison Co., 419 U.S. 345 (1974), illustrates the three tests used to determine state action and the fairly narrow way in which they have been recently interpreted. The issue was whether Metropolitan Edison could cut off utility services without the hearings and notice that might be necessary if that utility company was a government institution. Justice William Rehnquist first explored whether Metropolitan Edison was serving a public function. In his view, this prong of the state-action test could be satisfied only if the service in question was "traditionally the exclusive prerogative of the state." Since states had historically not had a monopoly on utility services, Rehnquist concluded that this prong of state action was not satisfied. He then explored whether the state of Pennsylvania had encouraged Metropolitan Edison to take the actions in question. Rehnquist noted that state law required Pennsylvania to approve the procedures of a regulated utility, but he insisted that approval was not encouragement. "Respondent's exercise of the choice allowed by state law where the initiative comes from it and not from the State does not make its action in doing so 'state action' for purposes of the Fourteenth Amendment," he wrote. Finally, Rehnquist looked to see if there was a "symbiotic relationship" between Metropolitan Edison and Pennsylvania. While he admitted that the utility was "subject to a form of extensive regulation by the State in a way that most other business enterprises are not," what was more important to Rehnquist was that the utility did not "lease its facilities from the State of Pennsylvania" and was "alone . . . responsible for the provision of power to its customers."

A few recent plaintiffs have successfully demonstrated state action. In *Brentwood Academy v. Tennessee Secondary School Athletic Ass'n*, 531 U.S. 288 (2001), the Supreme Court by a 5–4 vote ruled that the Tennessee Secondary School Athletic Association (TSSAA) was a state actor because the TSSAA "entwined" public and private functions. The judicial majority noted that public schools composed five-sixths of the membership of that association, public school principals and faculty members chose the TSSAA board, and all these schools were in Tennessee. A few years earlier, the Supreme Court had ruled that the National Collegiate Athletic Association (NCAA) was not a private actor because many private schools were NCAA members and the NCAA encompassed every state in the Union. These distinctions were obvious only to Justices Stevens and Blackmun, the only two justices in the majority in both cases.

The Thirteenth Amendment

The state action requirement applies only when persons are making claims under the Fourteenth and Fifteenth Amendments, not when they are making claims under the Thirteenth Amendment. The declaration that "Neither slavery nor involuntary servitude . . . shall exist within the United States" permits Congress to prohibit private as well as public actions that the national legislature believes are forms of enslavement. *Jones v. Alfred H. Mayer Co.*, 392 U.S. 409 (1968), concluded that Congress under the Thirteenth Amendment could prohibit housing developments from refusing to sell to persons of color. Justice Potter Stewart's majority opinion stated that a federal law that "bars all racial discrimination, private as well as public, in the sale or rental of property . . . is a valid exercise of the power of Congress to enforce the Thirteenth Amendment." Housing discrimination, he reasoned, was one of the badges and incidents of slavery that Congress could prohibit. *Jones* concluded that "when racial discrimination herds men into ghettos and makes their ability to buy property turn on the color of their skin, then it too is a relic of slavery."

What You Need to Know:

1. Persons making constitutional claims under the Fourteenth and Fifteenth Amendments, as well as federal legislation enforcing the Fourteenth and Fifteenth Amendments, must demonstrate state action or regulate only state action.
2. Private persons are state actors under the Fourteenth and Fifteenth Amendments only if they are performing a traditional state function, if their actions were encouraged by the state, or if they are entwined with the state.
3. The Thirteenth Amendment has no state action requirement.

LESSON 15: PROPERTY: CONTRACTS CLAUSE AND THE FREEDOM OF CONTRACT

The Constitution enumerates three protections for property rights. Article I, Section 10, paragraph 1 declares, "No State shall . . . pass any . . . Law impairing the Obligation of Contracts." This provision is commonly referred to as the "contracts clause." The Fifth Amendment (incorporated by the Due Process Clause of the Fourteenth Amendment) declares, "[N]or shall private property be taken for public use without just compensation." This provision is commonly referred to as the "Takings Clause." The Due Process Clauses of the Fifth and Fourteenth Amendments forbid the federal government and the states from "depriv[ing] any person of life, liberty, or property, without due process of law." The protections these rights offer have ebbed and flowed over time. During the early nineteenth century, property holders relied on the contracts clause. By the turn of the century, the Due Process Clause emerged as the provision of choice for those committed to property rights. At present, both contacts clause and due process protections for property rights are largely moribund, while Takings Clause protections for property rights are being revived.

The Contracts Clause

The contracts clause forbids states from interfering with vested contract rights. If Mary sells a cow to John for $50, payable in $10 increments every month, the state of Georgia cannot declare John's obligation complete after John pays three installments. The purpose of the contracts clause is to prevent states from requiring creditors to forgive all or part of the debts they were owed.

Two important restrictions exist on contract clause litigation. The contracts clause limits only state power. The federal government when exercising the bankruptcy power is authorized to discharge debts owed to creditors. The contract clause limits only state power to interfere with existing contractual relationships. No contract clause issue arises when a state forbids future uses of installment contracts. What states may not do under the contracts clause is relieve people of debts they contracted under an installment plan before the ban on installment plans was passed.

Two Supreme Court decisions played a crucial role in the process by which the contracts clause ceased to be a strong protection for property rights. The first was *Stone v. Mississippi*, 101 U.S. 814 (1879). Mississippi in 1867 gave a company a charter to operate a lottery for the next 25 years. State voters the next year passed a constitutional amendment outlawing lotteries. The Supreme Court held that the state law trumped the lottery charter. The key holding of that case was that future state legislatures retain the power to pass legislation in the public good. "All agree," Chief Justice Waite wrote, "that the legislature cannot bargain away the police power of the state." The second case was *Home Building & Loan Ass'n v. Blaisdell*, 290 U.S. 398 (1934). That case concerned the constitutionality of the Minnesota Moratorium Law (1932), which forbade lenders from foreclosing mortgages until 1935 if the mortgagee paid the fair rental value of the house. Chief Justice Charles Evans Hughes when declaring the law constitutional stated that "the reservation of essential attributes of sovereign power is . . . read into contracts as a postulate of the legal order." All contracts after *Blaisdell* have an implicit clause declaring "the parties agree that the state may regulate the manner in which this contract is implemented when doing so is necessary for the public welfare." The end result of *Stone* and *Blaisdell* is that states now have substantial power to interfere with existing contracts.

The Freedom of Contract

During the late nineteenth and early twentieth centuries, the Supreme Court and many state courts interpreted the Due Process Clause of the Fourteenth Amendment and similar clauses in state constitutions as protecting the freedom of contract. "Liberty," in the federal and state constitutions, one state judge declared, "means the right, not only of freedom from actual servitude, imprisonment or restraint, but the right to use his faculties in all lawful ways, to live and work where he will, to earn his livelihood in any lawful calling, and to pursue any lawful trade or avocation." This right, the Supreme Court maintained, encompassed "the general right to make a contract in relation to his business."

Lochner v. New York, 198 U.S. 45 (1905), is the most famous instance of the freedom of contract and substantive economic due process, the view that the Due Process Clause of the Fourteenth Amendment protects certain economic rights. The Supreme Court in that case declared unconstitutional a New York law forbidding bakers from working more than ten hours a day or sixty hours a week. The case is presently famous as one of the two most important examples of a judicial mistake and for Justice Oliver Wendell Holmes's dissent, which rejected the liberty of contract altogether. Holmes insisted that "The Fourteenth Amendment does not enact Mr. Herbert Spencer's *Social Statics* [a prominent libertarian treatise of the time]," that the constitution "is made for people of fundamentally differing views" and that "the word liberty in the Fourteenth Amendment is perverted when it is held to prevent the natural outcome of a dominant opinion, unless it can be said that a rational and fair man necessarily would admit that the statute proposed would infringe fundamental principles as they have been understood by the traditions of our people and our law."

Justice Holmes's understanding of the freedom of contract soon became the constitutional law of the land. Chief Justice Hughes, when sustaining a state law prescribing minimum wages for women, bluntly declared, "The Constitution does not speak of freedom of contract." "Liberty under the Constitution," he continued, "is thus necessarily subject to the restraints of due process, and regulation which is reasonable in relation to its subject and is adopted in the interests of the community is due process." The justices soon made clear that they had a very deferential notion of reasonableness. *Williamson v. Lee Optical, Inc.*, 348 U.S. 483 (1955), concerned the constitutionality of an Oklahoma law that required opticians to obtain a prescription when making frames or lenses, even when replacing lost glasses or repairing broken frames. Justice William O. Douglas admitted that "the Oklahoma law may exact a needless, wasteful requirement in many cases," but he insisted that the legislature was entitled to decide whether the circumstances in which prescriptions were useful justified imposing a burdensome requirement in circumstances where the prescription was useless. "The law need not be in every respect logically consistent with its aims to be constitutional," he wrote. "It is enough that there is an evil at hand for correction, and that it might be thought that the particular legislative measure was a rational way to correct it."

What You Need to Know:

1. Both the contracts clause and the freedom of contract are largely dead or dead as a source of constitutional protections for property rights.

2. The Supreme Court interprets all contracts as having an implicit provision that permits states to adjust contract obligations when doing so is required for the public good.

3. The Supreme Court no longer recognizes the freedom of contract and uses a weak rationality

standard when considering the constitutionality of most economic and social policies.

LESSON 16: PROPERTY: TAKINGS

Courts when determining whether government has violated the Takings Clause ("nor shall private property be taken for public use without just compensation") of the Fifth Amendment (as incorporated by the Due Process Clause of the Fourteenth Amendment) consider three issues.

1. Did a compensable taking occur?
2. Was the property taken for public use?
3. Did the government offer just compensation?

Both constitutional law and constitutional law classes focus on the first two questions. Whether the government offered just compensation is fact specific and usually decided by lower courts. The Takings Clause is the only constitutional protection for property that presently provides substantial protections for property holders.

Compensable Takings

A compensable taking always occurs when government takes possession of formerly private property. If government takes title to any part of a private possession, that is a compensable taking. Both personal and real estate are subject to this rule. *Horne v. Department of Agriculture*, 135 S. Ct. 2419 (2015), ruled that a taking occurred when Congress required farmers wishing to sell raisins on the interstate market to give a percentage of their crop to the federal government.

A compensable taking also occurs when a government invasion of private property causes substantial damage or is relatively permanent. A taking occurs when government diverts a river that causes your property to be flooded. *Loretto v. Teleprompter Manhattan CATV Corp.*, 458 U.S. 419 (1982), ruled that a compensable taking occurs when government establishes a permanent physical presence on private property, even if title is not transferred. The issue in this case was whether New York could require landlords leasing apartments to install cable television wires. Justice Thurgood Marshall's opinion for the court ruled, "When faced with a constitutional challenge to a permanent physical occupation of real property, this Court has invariably found a taking."

Regulatory takings are more complex and are generally not compensable. Regulatory takings occur when government passes some restriction on the use of property that reduces the value of that possession. A government regulation forbidding buildings above a certain height reduces the value of your home, since you have lost some capacity to make improvements. In most cases, the Supreme Court relies on an "ad hoc" balancing test that considers the economic impact of the regulation on the defendant and the justification for the taking. This test is heavily biased against persons making takings claims. Justice Oliver Wendell Holmes, Jr., in *Pennsylvania Coal Co. v. Mahon*, 260 U.S. 393, 413 (1922), observed, "Government hardly could go on if to some extent values incident to property could not be diminished without paying for every such change in the general law." Every change in the building code affects to some degree the value of every house. Moreover, you are partly, if not fully compensated for the loss you suffer when your town limits the height of your home because no one else can build a house that blocks your view of the sky.

The Supreme Court permits compensation for regulatory takings under two conditions. First, if the regulation "goes too far," destroying reasonable "investment-backed expectations" while providing little benefits in return for the property owner. Such a regulation took place in the *Pennsylvania Coal* case, when the state law forbade a mining company from excavating coal under houses the company had sold to buyers on the condition that the company retain the right to mine under the surface. Second, if the regulation destroys the entire value of the land, a compensable taking will have occurred, unless the regulation merely forbade the owner from using the property in ways previously banned by state common law. *Lucas v. South Carolina Coastal Council*, 505 U.S. 1003 (1992), is the leading contemporary case which stands for this proposition. South

Carolina passed a law forbidding all development on certain beachfront properties. Justice Antonin Scalia's majority opinion requiring compensation maintained that "where regulation denies all economically beneficial or productive use of land," compensation is necessary unless the restrictions are consistent with "the background principles of the State's law of property and nuisance already place upon land ownership." If Lucas's effort to develop his beachfront property would cause other homes to collapse, South Carolina could forbid the development. If, however, development did not violate the preexisting rights of other landowners, then South Carolina could not forbid all development without paying compensation (alert readers may have noted that the land in question was hardly worthless after regulation, since Lucas could always sponsor sleep-outs on the beach).

Public Use

General agreement exists that public use occurs when the government takes title to condemned property or gives the condemned property to a private person who opens the property to the public. The public use requirement is met whenever government takes title to property, no matter how government uses the property. If government takes title to your property and builds a condo for law professors, that is a public use because government has taken title. The public use requirement is also met whenever government gives title to a private party who opens the property to the public. If government takes title to your property and gives that property to Mr. Moneybags, who uses the land to build a railroad, a baseball stadium, or a public park, that is a public use as long as the railroad, stadium, or park is open to the public. Mr. Moneybags may attach reasonable conditions to the use, including charging admissions fees. Nevertheless, the public use requirement is satisfied whenever members of the public are regularly invited to use the private property.

Federal constitutional law also regards a public use as occurring when government gives condemned private property to a private owner for a public purpose. This issue arose in *Kelo v. City of New London*, 545 U.S. 469 (2005), after New London gave condemned property to the Pfizer Corporation, which promised to build a plant that would substantially increase the number of jobs in a distressed part of the community. Justice John Paul Stevens's majority opinion concluded that "because that plan unquestionably serves a public purpose, the takings challenged here satisfy the public use requirement of the Fifth Amendment." The dissents pointed out that the logic of the majority opinion might permit government to condemn my house and give the land to McDonald's if that would increase employment and tax revenues. For this reason, many states have enacted laws and state constitutional provisions forbidding condemnation for economic development. Those who support *Kelo* think the requirement that states must provide just compensation deters truly trivial condemnations.

What You Need to Know:

1. Compensable takings occur when government takes title to private property or permanently occupies private property, even if only a portion of the property is invaded.
2. Compensable takings also occur when government regulations destroy the entire value of property, unless the regulation merely codified existing restrictions on property rights.
3. The public use requirement of the Fifth Amendment is satisfied when the public takes title to property, the condemned property is given to a private owner who opens the property to the public, or the condemned property is given to a private owner who promises to use the property in ways that promise public benefits.

LESSON 17: RELIGION: BASICS

The Constitution of the United States got religion, or at least religion clauses, in 1791. The First Amendment declares, "Congress shall make no law respecting an establishing of religion, or prohibiting the free exercise thereof." The first part of this provision is the "Establishment Clause." The second part is the "Free Exercise Clause." The Establishment Clause was incorporated by the Due Process Clause of the Fourteenth

Amendment in *Everson v. Board of Education*, 330 U.S. 1 (1947). The Free Exercise Clause was incorporated by *Cantwell v. Connecticut*, 310 U.S. 296 (1940).

When Americans consider the constitutional meaning of the religion clauses, they often turn to the debates in Virginia during the 1780s over religious assessments. Patrick Henry in 1784 proposed a bill that would require all Virginians to pay a tax to support the Christian teacher of their choice. Presbyterians could earmark their taxes for Presbyterians. Baptists could earmark their taxes for Baptists. The few Jews and atheists in the state were stuck. In response to this proposal, James Madison penned his "Memorial and Remonstrance against Religious Assessments." The crucial passage of that pamphlet declared, "The Religion then of every man must be left to the conviction and conscience of every man; and it is the right of every man to exercise it as these may dictate." With specific respect to state assessments for religious teaching, Madison wrote:

> Who does not see that the same authority which can establish Christianity, in exclusion of all other Religions, may establish with the same ease any particular sect of Christians, in exclusion of all other Sects? That the same authority which can force a citizen to contribute three pence only of his property for the support of any one establishment, may force him to confirm in all cases whatsoever.

Madison and his friend Thomas Jefferson defeated religious assessments in Virginia. Rather than pass Henry's proposed bill for the support of Christian teachers, the Virginia legislature in 1786 enacted "An Act for Establishing Religious Freedom" that Jefferson drafted. The measure declared:

> No man shall be compelled to frequent or support any religious worship, place, or ministry whatsoever, nor shall be enforced restrained, molested, or burdened in his body or goods, nor shall otherwise suffer on account of his religious opinions or belief, but that all men shall be free to profess, and by argument to maintain, their opinions in matters of Religion, and that the

> same shall in no wise diminish, enlarge, or affect their civil capacities.

Jefferson later declared that this measure, along with the analogous provisions in the Bill of Rights, "buil[t] a wall of separation between Church & State."

Madison and Jefferson's principles provide the foundations for interpreting the religion clauses of the Constitution, but their application is contestable. Consider the Supreme Court's 5–4 decision in *Everson v. Board of Education*. The issue in that case was whether the town of Everson, New Jersey, could pay the transportation costs of students attending parochial schools as part of a more general program to pay transportation costs for all students attending public and nonprofit private schools. Justice Hugo Black's majority opinion began with a statement of fundamental principles that both paraphrased and quoted Madison and Jefferson.

> The "establishment of religion" clause of the First Amendment means at least this: neither a state nor the Federal Government can set up a church. Neither can pass laws which aid one religion, aid all religions, or prefer one religion over another. Neither can force nor influence a person to go to or to remain away from church against his will or force him to profess a belief or disbelief in any religion. No person can be punished for entertaining or professing religious beliefs or disbeliefs, for church attendance or non-attendance. No tax in any amount, large or small, can be levied to support any religious activities or institutions, whatever they may be called, or whatever form they may adopt to teach or practice religion. Neither a state nor the Federal Government can, openly or secretly, participate in the affairs of any religious organizations or groups, and vice versa. In the words of Jefferson, the clause against establishment of religion by law was intended to erect "a wall of separation between church and State."

Black nevertheless concluded that Everson Township had not breached the wall between church and state. He interpreted the transportation program as a general program aimed at all persons whose children attended nonprofit schools. Just as we would expect the fire department to put out a blaze in a church, so Black reasoned, children attending private parochial schools had the right to the same benefits as children attending private secular schools. Justice Robert Jackson disagreed. He believed that a law funneling tax money to parents who sent their children to nonprofit religious schools unconstitutionally discriminated against parents who sent their children to for-profit private schools.

The practical distinction between establishment and free exercise usually depends on whether religious belief and practice is being benefitted or burdened. Government provisions of benefits to religion and religious believers are generally analyzed under the Establishment Clause. *Everson* was an Establishment Clause case because the issue was whether government could provide a benefit to parents who sent their children to religious schools. Government impositions of burdens on religious belief are generally analyzed under the Free Exercise Clause. *Everson* would have been a free exercise case had the Board of Education excluded parents who sent their children to religious schools from a law reimbursing the transportation costs other parents incurred sending their children to nonreligious schools.

The Supreme Court confronted the potential conflict between the Establishment and Free Exercise Clauses in *Locke v. Davey*, 540 U.S. 712 (2004). The issue in that case was whether a state scholarship program could exclude students whose degree was in "devotional theology." The Supreme Court sustained the measure by a 7–2 vote. Chief Justice Rehnquist's majority opinion insisted that "there is room for play in the joints between" the two religion clauses. When deciding whether to include religious believers and activities in programs that provided benefits (or burdens) to many, but not all, other citizens, he claimed, states may exercise their best judgment. Rehnquist wrote that "there are some state actions permitted by the Establishment Clause but not required by the Free Exercise Clause." Had Washington included "devotional theology" in the state's scholarship program, that action would not have violated the Establishment Clause because the state could have chosen to extend a benefit granted to most citizens to religious citizens (though Washington could not have denied a benefit to persons just because they are religious. The law could not have given scholarships only to nonreligious students majoring in chemistry).

What You Need to Know:

1. The religion clauses forbid government actions that benefit or burden religious belief or religious organizations.
2. Establishment litigation concerns whether laws unconstitutionally benefit religion. Free exercise litigation concerns whether laws unconstitutionally burden religion.
3. There exists a middle ground in which government officials may choose whether to include or exclude religious believers or practices in programs that provide benefits to or burdens on many citizens.

LESSON 18: RELIGION: ESTABLISHMENT

The contemporary Supreme Court adjudicates three kinds of Establishment Clause questions. The first concerns religious displays on public property. The second concerns prayer exercises in public schools and at public events. The third concerns the extent to which government can fund religious activities as part of a more general funding program.

Many justices refer to the three-part test the Court announced in *Lemon v. Kurtzman*, 403 U.S. 602 (1971), when resolving Establishment Clause issues.

1. "The statute must have a secular legislative purpose."
2. "Its principal or primary effect must be one that neither advances nor inhibits religion."
3. "The statute must not foster an excessive entanglement with religion."

The *Lemon* test has never been overruled, but no justice uses the above criteria with any consistency.

Religious Displays on Public Property

Religious displays on public property are presently constitutional if they have a secular purpose. Justice Souter in *McCreary County v. ACLU of Kentucky*, 545 U.S. 844, 870 (2005), rejected the display of the Ten Commandments in a local courthouse because "[t]he display's unstinting focus was on religious passages, showing that the Counties were posting the Commandments precisely because of their sectarian content." Chief Justice Rehnquist in *Van Orden v. Perry*, 545 U.S. 677, 691 (2005), had no constitutional problem with a monument displaying the Ten Commandments in state park because "Texas has treated its Capitol grounds monuments as representing the several strands in the State's political and legal history." Justice Breyer, the only justice in the majority in both cases, concluded that, based on the particular details of the particular settings, the religious message of the Ten Commandments in the courtroom predominated, but religious messages did not predominate when the Ten Commandments display was placed with other monuments in a park.

Several justices have proposed more general tests aimed at clarifying when religious displays may be placed on public property. Justice Scalia insists that government may display the Ten Commandments because the Constitution permits government to show respect for religion in general, rather than any specific religious sect. Justice Sandra Day O'Connor proposed an endorsement test, which looks at whether government "by endorsing religion or a religious practice make[s] adherence to religion relevant to a person's standing in the political community" or "identifies nonadherents as outsiders." Neither commands a majority of the Court.

Public Prayer

The Supreme Court prohibits official prayer exercises during normal hours at public schools. *Engel v. Vitale*, 370 U.S. 421 (1962), ruled that school officials may not write prayers for public school children to recite, even when recitation is voluntary. *Abington School District v. Schempp*, 374 U.S. 203 (1963), forbade schools from beginning the day with a reading from the Bible or the Lord's Prayer. Justice Clark's opinion stated, "These are religious exercises, required by the States in violation of the command of the First Amendment that the Government maintain strict neutrality, neither aiding nor opposing religion." The school prayer decisions are controversial and often ignored, but they are the official law of the land.

The Supreme Court muddied the waters in two cases decided long after *Engel v. Vitale*. The first, *Lee v. Weisman*, 505 U.S. 577 (1992), concerned the constitutionality of prayer at a middle school graduation. Justice Anthony Kennedy began with the traditional concern that state officials were "direct[ing] the performance of a formal religious exercise at promotional and graduation ceremonies for secondary schools." This suggests that any official prayer exercise in a school is unconstitutional. Kennedy then pointed out that "attendance and participation" at graduation are "in a fair and real sense obligatory." Perhaps a state-sponsored prayer exercise before a chess club meeting is constitutional (a later case decided that, for many students, attendance at a football game was obligatory). Kennedy further noted that prayer at graduation carries "a particular risk of indirect coercion" because young adolescents might conform rather than refuse to exercise their right not to stand during the benediction. Perhaps prayer at high school or college graduations is constitutional, because of less peer pressure. No one knows the precise significance of *Lee*, except Justice Kennedy. Twenty years later in *Town of Greece v. Galloway*, 134 S. Ct. 1811 (2014), Justice Kennedy speaking for a 5–4 majority found nothing wrong when a local town invited local clergy to deliver invocations to start town meetings. Although most prayers were sectarian, Kennedy noted that the court should not generally police prayer and that members of the community had no obligation to participate in this activity. Perhaps the bottom line is that the present status of public prayer is whether Justice Kennedy thinks anyone is coerced.

Public Funds

The constitutional law of public funds under the Establishment Clause, after an erratic history, has become relatively stable, if still controversial. General agreement exists that public benefits may find their way into religious institutions if they do so as the result of "true public choice." The federal government is not barred from giving every American 100 dollars, merely because some people will donate that money to the local church or use the cash to pay for Hebrew lessons. What federal and state governments may not do is structure programs in ways that encourage persons to use the public benefit for religious rather than secular purposes. Unsurprisingly, liberals are more likely to see encouragement than conservatives.

Zelman v. Simmons-Harris, 536 U.S. 639 (2002), is the most important contemporary precedent on when states may provide indirect financial assistance to religious institutions. The issue in *Zelman* was whether Cleveland could provide parents with vouchers that they could use for tuition assistance at private schools, when 46 of the 56 private schools that participated in the state program were religious schools. The Supreme Court sustained the voucher program by a 5–4 vote. Chief Justice Rehnquist's majority opinion stated the relevant constitutional test.

> Where a government aid program is neutral with respect to religion, and provides assistance to a broad class of citizens who in turn, direct government aid to religious schools wholly as a result of their own genuine and independent private choice, the program is not readily subject to challenge under the Establishment Clause.

Rehnquist concluded the Cleveland program met these standards. Every private school in the Cleveland area was invited to participate in the program. Parents had their choice of using vouchers for private religious schools, private secular schools, or community schools, which had more state funding. Justice Souter dissented, noting that the vast majority of state funding in practice went to religious schools.

What You Need to Know:

1. Religious displays on public property are constitutional only if the secular purpose predominates.

2. Schools may not sponsor voluntary prayer during the school day or have prayer exercises that might indirectly coerce younger students, but town councils may have a prayer exercise as long as no one is sanctioned for not participating.

3. Government funds may be directed toward religious institutions as long as the program is neutral as to whether the funds go to religion and private persons make the choice to direct the funds to religious purposes.

LESSON 19: RELIGION: FREE EXERCISE

The constitutional law of free exercise focuses on two questions. The first concerns discrimination against religious believers. On this, near unanimity exists. Neither the federal government nor the states may pass a law that discriminates against religious believers as a whole or a particular group of religious believers. The second concerns whether the federal and state governments must sometimes exempt religious believers from general laws that burden their religious practices. This matter has been controversial since the colonial era.

Discriminations Against Religious Belief, Practices, or Believers

Government may discriminate against religions, religious belief, or religious practices only when such discriminations are justified by a compelling interest. Government cannot forbid people to attend religious services on Thursday, worship a golden calf, or play trumpets in a religious ceremony. Although official constitutional law theoretically regards such discriminations as constitutional when government demonstrates a compelling interest, thinking of a compelling interest that justifies discriminating against a religion or a religious practice is difficult. Consider the example of a law banning playing trumpets in a religious ceremony. If government has a compelling reason to ban trumpet playing during a religious ceremony, then surely government has a compelling reason to ban trumpet playing more generally.

Church of the Lukumi Babalu Aye v. Hialeah, 508 U.S. 520 (1993), is the most recent instance when the Supreme Court reaffirmed the practical ban on laws that explicitly discriminate against religion or religious practices. That case concerned a local edict that prohibited animal sacrifices in rituals. Justice Kennedy's opinion for the Court noted that states could not "regulate or prohibit conduct because it is undertaken for religious reasons." The local edict was unconstitutional because, although the locality forbade killing animals in a ritual, they permitted persons to kill animals in the exact same way as long as the purpose for the killing was not religious.

Exemptions from General Laws

Whether religious believers should enjoy exemptions from general laws that require them to behave in ways inconsistent with their religious duties has been an ongoing controversy throughout American history. Benjamin Franklin and James Madison believed that religious pacifists should not be required to bear arms. Other framers as vigorously insisted that all persons had the same obligation to defend their country, state, and neighbors. The Supreme Court of the United States for most of American history refused to grant religious believers exemptions from general laws. *Reynolds v. United States*, 98 U.S. 145 (1878), which sustained the conviction of Mormon polygamists who insisted the federal ban violated their free exercise rights, is the canonical citation for the proposition that government need not grant exemptions to religious believers. Chief Justice Morrison Waite stated, "Congress was deprived of all legislative power over mere opinion, but was left free to reach actions which were in violation of social duties or subversive of good order."

The pendulum swung towards mandating exemptions for religious believers during the 1960s and 1970s. When declaring unconstitutional a law that denied unemployment to a Seventh-Day Adventist who would not work on Saturday, Justice Brennan's majority opinion in *Sherbert v. Verner*, 374 U.S. 398 (1963), declared that state officials must demonstrate a compelling interest whenever a state law burdens a person's religious freedom. The Supreme Court applied this compelling interest test a decade later in *Wisconsin v. Yoder*, 406 U.S. 205 (1972), when declaring unconstitutional as applied to Amish children a law requiring all children under 16 to attend a public or private school. Chief Justice Burger's majority opinion insisted that Wisconsin "show with more particularity how its admittedly strong interest in compulsory education would be adversely affected by granting an exemption to the Amish."

The pendulum swung away from exemptions in *Employment Division v. Smith*, 494 U.S. 872 (1990). That case held that the Free Exercise Clause did not require states to give exemptions to religious believers unless, as in *Yoder*, the plaintiffs might base their claim on an independent constitutional right (such as the right to raise their children) or the case concerned unemployment compensation (*Sherbert*). Justice Antonin Scalia's majority opinion stated, "To make an individual's obligation to obey such a law contingent upon the law's coincidence with his religious beliefs . . . permitting him to become a law unto himself . . . contradicts both constitutional tradition and common sense." *City of Boerne v. Flores*, 521 U.S. 507 (1997), confirmed *Smith*. That case declared unconstitutional as applied to states the Religious Freedom Restoration Act of 1993 (RFRA), a federal law that restored the compelling interest test announced in *Sherbert*. "Legislation which alters the meaning of the Free Exercise Clause cannot be said to be enforcing the Clause," Justice Anthony Kennedy wrote.

The Supreme Court presently interprets the Free Exercise Clause of the Constitution as not mandating that the federal government or states exempt religious believers from generally applicable laws that burden their religious practices. Persons who have religious obligations to drink have no constitutional right under the Free Exercise Clause to an exemption from a state law raising the drinking age to 104. Nevertheless, persons might have a state constitutional or state law right to an exemption if the state in question has passed a law similar to RFRA or the state court has interpreted the state constitution as mandating exemptions for religious believers. Similarly, RFRA is still good federal law. Thus while the federal government had no constitutional obligation to give religious employers exemptions from laws requiring them to provide contraception coverage for their employees, *Burwell v. Hobby Lobby Stores*, 134 S. Ct. 2751 (2014), ruled that RFRA mandated that exemption.

What You Need to Know:

1. Neither the federal government nor the states may prohibit particular religions, particular religious practices, or conduct performed for religious reasons.
2. The Free Exercise Clause as presently interpreted does not require the federal government or states to provide religious believers with exemptions from general laws that require them to engage in conduct prohibited by their religion.
3. The federal government and states may by law grant exemptions to religious believers.

LESSON 20: THE RIGHT TO BEAR ARMS

The Second Amendment declares, "A well regulated Militia, being necessary to the security of a free State, the right of the people to keep and bear Arms, shall not be infringed." That provision was incorporated by the Due Process Clause of the Fourteenth Amendment in *McDonald v. City of Chicago*, 561 U.S. 742 (2010). The right to bear arms is unique among the rights examined in constitutional law. The Second Amendment is the only rights provision with a prefatory clause. The First Amendment declares, "Congress shall make no law . . . abridging the freedom of speech," not "Public debate on matters of public interest being necessary to a democratic society, Congress shall make no law abridging the freedom of speech." The Second Amendment both enumerates a right and explains why that right is enumerated. Whether and how that prefatory clause influences the correct interpretation of the right to bear arms is controversial.

Judges and constitutional commentators advance two different interpretations of the Second Amendment. The standard or collective interpretation limits Second Amendment rights to militia service. The preface, on this view, states the scope of the right. Proponents of the standard interpretation think the Second Amendment is a federalism provision that ensures state governments will control state militias. The Constitution may grant persons a right to be in the state militia, if one exists, but no one has a constitutional right to bear arms for self-defense or hunting. The individual rights interpretation insists the right to bear arms encompasses activities outside the militia. The preface, on this view, states the purpose, but not the scope of the right. Proponents of the individual rights interpretation think that citizens have a constitutional right to keep guns for self-defense and perhaps for hunting, even when those activities are not connected to a state militia.

Neither the constitutional text nor the relevant texts of state constitutions ratified during the late eighteenth century conclusively settle the debate between proponents of the collective and individual rights interpretations of the Second Amendment. The prefatory clause supports the collectivist model. That the Constitution speaks of "a right of the people" supports the individual rights model (although some scholars think the reference to "the people" supports a collectivist reading).

History provides almost no help in determining the meaning of the Second Amendment. Most state decisions before the Civil War indicated that persons had a state constitutional right to bear arms. Most state court decisions immediately before and after the Civil War limited the right to bear arms to militia service. The framers of the Fourteenth Amendment thought freed persons of color had a right to bear arms, but whether they meant that former slaves had a specific right to bear arms or merely the same right to bear arms as white persons is not certain.

Supreme Court decisions on the Second Amendment handed down before the twentieth century were not entirely clear or helpful. The justices in *United States v. Miller*, 307 U.S. 174 (1939), appeared to side with the collectivist interpretation of the Second Amendment when sustaining a federal law prohibiting persons from transporting a sawed-off shotgun. Justice James McReynolds's opinion for the court declared:

> In the absence of any evidence tending to show that possession or use of a "shotgun having a barrel of less than eighteen inches in length" at this time has some reasonable relationship to the preservation or efficiency of a well regulated militia, we cannot say that the Second Amendment guarantees the right to keep and bear such an instrument.

Virtually all commentators in the twentieth century interpreted *Miller* as limiting the right to bear arms to militia service. Nevertheless, *Miller* might be read, perhaps straining a bit, to hold that the Second Amendment protects the right to keep and bear a weapon that might be used for militia service, even when the owner is putting that weapon to other uses.

The Supreme Court finally settled the debate over the constitutional status of the Second Amendment when the justices in *District of Columbia v. Heller*, 554 U.S. 570 (2008), held that the Constitution protects an individual right to bear arms. Justice Antonin Scalia's opinion for the Court concluded that the "right to bear arms" encompassed "the individual right to possess and carry weapons in case of confrontation." He reached this conclusion by noting that the Second Amendment spoke of "the right of the people," a phrase he maintained referred to "individual rights." "The prefatory clause," Scalia emphasized, "does not suggest that preserving the militia was the only reason Americans valued" the right to bear arms. The four dissenters defended the standard model. Justice Stevens insisted, "The Second Amendment was adopted to protect the right of the people of each of the several States to maintain a well-regulated militia."

Heller declared a complete ban on handguns in the home unconstitutional, but did not specify the proper standard to be used when courts are evaluating more common gun control regulations. Scalia indicated that "longstanding" gun control measures were constitutional, but did not indicate the appropriate standard for judging more recently enacted measures. In the absence of a subsequent Supreme Court decision specifying that standard, lower federal courts have interpreted the Second Amendment in various ways. Most rely on an intermediate-scrutiny test. Gun control laws must be substantial means of achieving important government ends. Everyone agrees that public safely is an important end, but whether restrictions on carrying weapons out of the house and the precise weapons that can be in the house are substantial means to that end remains contestable, although most courts have sustained most gun control measures.

What You Need to Know:

1. Americans have debated for more than 200 years whether the Second Amendment protects an individual right to bear arms or merely prohibits the federal government from disarming state militias.
2. The Supreme Court has determined that the Second Amendment protects an individual right to bear arms.
3. The precise scope of this individual right to bear arms remains undetermined.

LESSON 21: FUNDAMENTAL RIGHTS: BASICS, BIRTH CONTROL, AND ABORTION

The Due Process Clauses of the Fifth and Fourteenth Amendments prohibit government actions that "deprive any person of life, liberty, or property, without due process of law." Throughout American history these provisions have been used to protect certain fundamental rights ranging from slaveholding in American territories to same-sex marriage. Unsurprisingly, whether the Due Process Clauses protect fundamental rights and how to identify those rights is perhaps the most controversial question of constitutional interpretation in the United States.

Americans interpret "due process" in two different ways. "Due process" might refer only to the process necessary for finding persons guilty of criminal or civil offenses. On this view, known as procedural due process, the Due Process Clauses leave government free to regulate all human activities that are not protected by some other constitutional provision, subject to the proviso that a person can be penalized for the offending conduct only after they are given a fair opportunity to contest charges that they have broken the law in question. Government is free to prohibit first cousins from marrying each other, but must give a married couple a fair opportunity to prove they are not first cousins. History has rejected this position in favor of what is known as substantive due process. On this view, the Due Process Clauses protect certain fundamental rights that are not otherwise enumerated in the Constitution. Government may not normally violate those fundamental rights, no matter what procedures are in place to identify rights violations. If first cousins have a constitutional right to marry, government may not penalize first cousins who marry, no matter what procedures are in place for proving the offense.

Judges disagree over the best method for identifying fundamental rights. General agreement exists that the fundamental rights protected by the Due Process Clauses must be rooted in longstanding traditions, but identifying and applying those traditions is controversial. Justice Antonin Scalia insists that traditions be defined narrowly. He maintains, "We refer to the most specific level at which a relevant tradition protecting, or denying protection to, the asserted right can be identified." The traditional right to marriage, in this view, is limited to those persons that American law has historically permitted to marry each other. Other justices insist that traditions be interpreted in light of the fundamental principles that best explain and justify historical practices. If the best justification of the fundamental right to marry is that persons have a right to marry the persons of their choice, then same-sex couples should have a constitutional right to marry, even if that right was not previously recognized by the American people.

The modern era of substantive due process began in *Griswold v. Connecticut*, 381 U.S. 479 (1965). That case concerned the constitutionality of a Connecticut law that banned married persons from using contraception. The Supreme Court by a 7–2 vote declared the state law unconstitutional. Justice William Douglas's majority opinion, while insisting that the court would not use the Due Process Clause to "determine the wisdom, need and propriety of laws that touch economic problems, business affairs, or social conditions," maintained that the "intimate relation of husband and wife" was a different kettle of constitutional fish. That relationship was "within the zone of privacy created by several fundamental constitutional guarantees." He famously asked:

> Would we allow the police to search the sacred precincts of marital bedrooms for telltale signs of the use of contraception? The very idea is repulsive to the notions of privacy surrounding the marriage relationship.

Justice Hugo Black issued a blunt dissent that noted this right to privacy was not enumerated in the Constitution.

> I like my privacy as well as the next one, but I am nevertheless compelled to admit that government has a right to invade it unless prohibited by some specific constitutional provision.

The differences between the two justices are instructive. Douglas noted a broad American commitment to privacy. He then deduced a right to use birth control from the best justification for that right to privacy. Black asked what specific privacy rights had Americans protected. He rejected a right to use birth control, because American law had never protected that specific right.

Roe v. Wade, 410 U.S. 113 (1973), brought the culture wars to the Supreme Court. That 7–2 decision interpreted the Due Process Clauses as protecting the fundamental right to terminate a pregnancy. Justice Harry Blackmun's majority opinion claimed this right to an abortion could be derived from past cases interpreting the Due Process Clause of the Fourteenth Amendment as protecting various privacy rights. He stated that past decisions:

> make it clear that the right [of personal privacy] has some extension to activities relating to marriage procreation, contraception, family relationships, and child rearing and education. This right of privacy, whether it be founded in the Fourteenth Amendment's

> conception of personal liberty and restrictions upon state action, as we feel it is, or in the Ninth Amendment's reservation of rights to the people, is broad enough to encompass a woman's decision whether or not to terminate her pregnancy.

Blackmun then divided pregnancy into three trimesters. During the first trimester, states could not regulate abortion. During the second trimester, states could regulate abortion, but only in ways that promoted maternal health. Abortion could be prohibited only in the third trimester, when fetuses were viable.

Justices William Rehnquist and Byron White dissented. Their dissents insisted that the court had illegitimately revived substantive due process. They pointed out that bans on abortion existed in most states when the Fourteenth Amendment was ratified and when *Roe* was decided. These facts, in their view, demonstrated that the framers did not intend the Due Process Clause to prohibit bans on abortion and that abortion was not a longstanding right of the American people.

The Supreme Court sustained and modified *Roe* in *Planned Parenthood of Southeastern Pennsylvania v. Casey*, 505 U.S. 833 (1992). Justice Sandra Day O'Connor, Justice Anthony Kennedy, and Justice David Souter issued a joint opinion declaring that "the essential holding of *Roe v. Wade* should be retained and once again reaffirmed." The justices did not, however, retain the trimester system. Instead, the justices announced a new "undue burden test" that they believed better balanced the interests of the pregnant women and the "State interest in potential life." Under this test, states may pass laws that demonstrate respect for the unborn and help inform a pregnant woman's decision, but those laws may not place "a substantial obstacle in the path of a woman seeking an abortion of a nonviable fetus."

What You Need to Know:

1. The Supreme Court interprets the Due Process Clause of the Fourteenth Amendment as protecting certain substantive rights.

2. These rights include the right to use birth control and the right to have an abortion.

3. States may not ban abortion until the third trimester, but may regulate abortion in any way that does not unduly burden the pregnant woman.

LESSON 22: FUNDAMENTAL RIGHTS: LBGT RIGHTS AND THE RIGHT TO MARRY

The Supreme Court's recent decision in *Obergefell v. Hodges*, 135 S. Ct. 2584 (2015), interpreting the Due Process Clause of the Fourteenth Amendment as prohibiting state laws limiting marriage to opposite sex couples was an outcome of two lines of precedent. The first line was a series of decisions holding that the Fourteenth Amendment protected a fundamental right to marry. The second line was a series of decisions declaring that the Fourteenth Amendment protected certain fundamental rights of LGBT individuals.

The Right to Marry

The Supreme Court in *Loving v. Virginia*, 388 U.S. 1 (1967), held that the Due Process Clause of the Fourteenth Amendment protected the fundamental right to marry. *Loving* invalidated a Virginia law that prohibited a person of one race from marrying a person of another race. Although much of the decision focused on the racial discrimination, Chief Justice Warren's unanimous opinion maintained that the statute also violated the independent right to marry. He stated, "The freedom to marry has long been recognized as one of the vital personal rights essential to the orderly pursuit of happiness by free men."

Zablocki v. Redhail, 434 U.S. 374 (1978), confirmed that the Constitution protected the fundamental right to marry when no independent equal protection right was alleged. When declaring unconstitutional a Wisconsin law that restricted the marriage rights of people with child support obligations, Justice Thurgood Marshall wrote that "it would make little sense to recognize a right of privacy with respect to other matters of family life and not with respect to the decision to enter the relationships that is the foundation of the family in our society." Giving equal time to those with less successful marriages, the Supreme Court in *Boddie v. Connecticut*, 401 U.S. 371 (1971), struck down laws requiring impecunious people to pay fees before legally ending their marriage.

The Right to Same-Sex Intimacy and LBGT Individuals

The Supreme Court did not initially provide LBGT individuals with the same protections as heterosexuals. *Baker v. Nelson*, 409 U.S. 810 (1972), curtly dismissed as not presenting "a substantial federal question" a challenge to state laws limiting marriage to a man and a woman. *Bowers v. Hardwick*, 478 U.S. 186 (1986), refused to extend the right of privacy to same-sex intimacy. Justice White's opinion for the Court stated, "No connection between family, marriage, or procreation on the one hand and homosexual activity on the other has been demonstrated."

The judicial tide in favor of LBGT rights turned within a decade. In *Romer v. Evans*, 517 U.S. 620 (1996), the Supreme Court declared unconstitutional a Colorado constitutional amendment forbidding any governmental unit in the state from prohibiting discrimination on the basis of sexual orientation. Rather than point to a fundamental right protected by the Due Process Clauses, Justice Anthony Kennedy's majority opinion maintained that the law violated the Equal Protection Clause. The Colorado state constitutional amendment, he held, was motivated by unconstitutional animus (see Lesson 27). *Romer* nevertheless provided precedential foundations for the Supreme Court's 6–3 decision in *Lawrence v. Texas*, 539 U.S. 558 (2003), which relied on the fundamental rights strand of due process law when declaring unconstitutional bans on homosexual sodomy. Justice Kenney's majority opinion defined constitutional privacy broadly. He declared, "Liberty presumes an autonomy of self that includes freedom of thought, belief, expression and certain intimate conduct." From this principle, *Lawrence* deduced a due process right to same-sex intimate behavior. Kennedy continued, "These statutes do seek to control a personal relationship that, whether or not entitled to formal recognition in the law, is within the liberty of persons to choose without being punished as criminals." The end result of *Lawrence* is that two (and maybe more) consenting adults are free to engage in intimate behavior without state interference, whether that intimate behavior is an enduring relationship or a one-night stand.

The LBGT movement initially enjoyed mixed success when claiming that such cases as *Lawrence* provided precedential support for a right to same-sex marriage. Some states, most notably Massachusetts in *Goodridge v. Department of Public Health*, 440 Mass. 309, 798 N.E.2d 941 (2003), recognized a state constitutional right to same-sex marriage, but successful litigation efforts in other states were overturned by state constitutional amendment. Many other states passed state constitutional amendments limiting marriage to a man and a woman in order to forestall litigation under state law. The tide turned when the Supreme Court in *United States v. Windsor*, 133 S. Ct. 2675 (2013), declared unconstitutional a provision in the Defense of Marriage Act forbidding the federal government to recognize same-sex marriages that were legal in the couple's state of residence. As was the case in *Romer*, the judicial majority relied on unconstitutional animus under the Equal Protection Clause rather than on a right to privacy under the Due Process Clause. As was the case in *Romer*, litigants immediately interpreted *Windsor* as nevertheless providing the constitutional foundations for their due process attack on laws prohibiting same-sex marriage. They were almost universally successful. With rare exception, every lower federal and state court that adjudicated a constitutional attack on same-sex marriage in the fall of 2013 and in 2014 ruled that same-sex couples had a constitutional right to marry.

Obergefell

Obergefell v. Hodges, 135 S. Ct. 2584 (2015), merged the constitutional right to marry declared in *Loving* with the constitutional right to same-sex intimacy declared in *Lawrence*. Justice Kennedy's majority opinion insisted that what constituted a traditional marriage did not remain constant over time. The principles that best justified the contemporary right to marriage, his opinion maintained, justified extending the right to marriage to same-sex couples. In his view, the right to marry was fundamental because that right "is inherent in the concept of individual autonomy," "supports a two-person union unlike any other in its importance to the committed individuals," "safeguards children and families," and "is a keystone of our social order." "There is no difference between same- and opposite couples with respect to th[ese] principles," Kennedy continued. Given, for example, that most states permitted same-sex couples to adopt, those families had the same right to official recognition of their relationship as heterosexual couples.

All four dissenting justices issued dissenting opinions. Chief Justice John Roberts spoke the language of judicial restraint. He claimed, "The people of a State are free to expand marriage to include same-sex couples, or to retain the historic definition." Justice Samuel Alito worried about the consequences of expanding understandings of marriage. He claimed that "by officially abandoning the older understanding" of marriage, the majority "may contribute to marriage's further decay."

What You Need to Know:

1. The Supreme Court interprets the Due Process Clause of the Fourteenth Amendment as protecting a constitutional right to marry.
2. The Supreme Court interprets the Due Process Clause of the Fourteenth Amendment as protecting a constitutional right to intimate behavior, no matter what the gender of the intimates.
3. The Supreme Court has combined the first two lines of precedent into a constitutional right to same-sex marriage.

LESSON 23: FREE SPEECH: BASICS

The First Amendment declares, "Congress shall make no law . . . abridging the freedom of speech, or of the press, or the right of the people to peaceably assemble, and to petition the Government for a redress of grievances." Federal and state laws that restrict speech are subject to the same standards. The Supreme Court in *Gitlow v. New York*, 268 U.S. 652 (1925), held that the Due Process Clause of the Fourteenth

Amendment incorporated the freedom of speech. The justices in *Near v. Minnesota*, 283 U.S. 697 (1931), incorporated the press clause and in *DeJonge v. Oregon*, 299 U.S. 353 (1937), incorporated the right to peaceably assemble and petition the Government for a redress of grievances.

Thomas Emerson, the leading civil libertarian of the late twentieth century, observed that constitutional protections for free speech serve four purposes.

1. Free speech is a central element of a democratic system.
2. Free speech is necessary for the discovery of truth.
3. Free speech is important for individual self-expression.
4. Free speech provides a vital way for political losers to let off steam.

These purposes are sometimes reinforcing and sometimes conflicting. A speech criticizing the president's economic policy promotes democracy and the search for truth. An abstract landscape painting is a form of individual self-expression, but less important for the discovery of truth or a democratic system.

When freedom of speech may be restricted is contested. Justice Hugo Black insisted that the freedom of speech is absolute. In a widely publicized interview, Black pointed out that the First Amendment "says Congress shall make **no law** ['abridging the freedom of speech or of the press']." From this text, Black concluded that " 'no law' means no law." Government could not abridge the freedom of speech no matter what the consequences. Free speech minimalists prefer "the bad tendency test". On this view, government may prohibit speech whenever speech threatens a harm that government is constitutionally authorized to prevent. If handing out pamphlets risks an increase in litter and government is entitled to prevent litter, then government may forbid people from handing out pamphlets. More commonly, justices take the position that government may restrict speech when really important government interests are immediately at stake, but not when harms caused by speech are relatively minor or distant.

General agreement exists that the First Amendment forbids prior restraints and the common-law crime of seditious libel. Prior restraints refer to government efforts to censor speech before publication. In seventeenth-century England, no one could publish a manuscript unless they had a license from the government. Publication without the literal seal of government approval was illegal, no matter how inoffensive the book. Seditious libel is the crime of speaking ill of the king or of the government. Under the common law, criticism of the government was a crime no matter how true the criticism. "The greater the truth, the greater the libel," common-law lawyers insisted. England abandoned prior restraints by the end of the seventeenth century. By the time the First Amendment was ratified, legal commentators agreed that the freedom of the press at a minimum meant that speech could be punished only after publication. Americans abandoned seditious libel in the eighteenth century. In *Zenger's Case*, 17 Howell's St. Tr. 675 (1735), Andrew Hamilton argued that the jury in a libel case should determine whether the defendant spoke the truth about government. Although the judge charged the jury that truth was not a defense of a libel charge, the jury verdict of not guilty in that case is generally considered to signal the beginning of the end of seditious libel prosecutions in the United States. Even the hated Sedition Act of 1798 declared that true criticisms of government were constitutionally protected.

The modern constitutional law of free speech begins with a series of cases decided during and immediately after World War I. Concerned with German-American and Socialist opposition to the war effort, Congress passed the Espionage Act of 1917 and the Sedition Act of 1918. The former prohibited "false statements with intent to interfere with the operation or success of the military or naval forces of the United States." More than 1,000 people were convicted under these statutes. Their convictions gave the justices their first substantial opportunity to discuss the constitutional meaning of free speech. The initial decisions were unanimous and sustained restrictive federal laws. Justice Oliver Wendell Holmes, Jr.'s opinion in *Schenck v. United States*, 249 U.S. 47 (1919) (which made famous the metaphor about falsely crying fire in a crowded theater) declared, "The question in every case is whether the words used are used in such circumstances and are of such a nature as to create a clear and present danger that they will bring about the substantive evils that Congress has a right to prevent." Political dissidents could be punished, he concluded, because their efforts to persuade people not to do military service interfered with American military efforts.

Without a few years, Holmes and Justice Louis Brandeis moved into the dissenting ranks, issuing opinions that became foundations for the contemporary constitutional law of free speech. The Holmes dissent in *Abrams v. United States*, 250 U.S. 616, 624 (1919), detailed the philosophical foundation for American civil libertarians.

> But when men have realized that time has upset many fighting faiths, they may come to believe even more than they believe the very foundations of their own conduct that the ultimate good desired is better reached by free trade in ideas—that the best test of truth is the power of the thought to get itself accepted in the competition of the market, and that truth is the only ground upon which their wishes safely can be carried out.

Brandeis articulated the civil libertarian position on when free speech could be regulated in his concurring opinion in *Whitney v. California*, 274 U.S. 357 (1927). He insisted that government could forbid only incitement to an imminent serious evil. "Kill the umpire" might be punishable if said before a mob furious at a strike call, but not at a baseball game or an academic seminar.

The Brandeis and Holmes opinions did not immediately become good constitutional law. During the McCarthy Era, the federal government successfully prosecuted Communists with the blessing of the Supreme Court. *Dennis v. United States*, 341 U.S. 494 (1951), held that clear and present danger might be satisfied, even if no immediate danger existed of a Communist revolution, if the harm caused by such a revolution was substantial in light of the probability that the harm might occur over time. As the 1950s wore on, the Court became less sympathetic to government efforts to limit communist speech. With the ebbing of anti-Communism and the rise of the civil rights movement, the Brandeisian/Holmes vision triumphed. That is the subject of the next lesson.

What You Need to Know:

1. Free speech is considered a vital means for spreading truth and is central to democratic government.
2. General agreement exists that the First Amendment prohibits prior restraints and seditious libel, the crime of making any criticism of the government.
3. The precise standards of free speech protection have varied throughout history, with the libertarian vision articulated by Justices Brandeis and Holmes gaining currency only during the last half-century.

LESSON 24: FREE SPEECH: ADVOCACY

The contemporary constitutional law of advocacy rests on three pillars. *New York Times Co. v. Sullivan*, 376 U.S. 254 (1964), established the foundations for the contemporary constitutional law of libel, the conditions under which public figures may sue those who defame them. *Brandenburg v. Ohio*, 395 U.S. 444 (1969), established the foundations for the contemporary constitutional law of subversive advocacy, the connections between speech and crime. *New York Times Co. v. United States*, 403 U.S. 713 (1971), established the foundations for the contemporary constitutional law of prior restraint. Together, these three decisions largely ended traditional government efforts to prohibit commentary on public affairs.

Libel

New York Times Co. v. Sullivan is the leading case on the constitutional law of libel. L.B. Sullivan, an official in Montgomery, Alabama, sued the *New York Times* after the *Times* published an advertisement by civil rights activists that made false assertions about his conduct during demonstrations for racial equality. Sullivan was eventually awarded $500,000 in damages by Alabama courts, which also awarded similarly high damages in cases where Martin Luther King, Jr., and other civil rights activists were sued directly.

The Supreme Court unanimously declared that the *New York Times* had a constitutional right to print the advertisement in question. Justice William Brennan's majority opinion spoke of a "profound national commitment to the principle that debate on public issues should be uninhibited, robust, and wide-open, and that it may well include vehement, caustic, and sometimes unpleasantly sharp attacks on government and public officials." This commitment means that constitutional protections for free speech may not include "any test of truth." Brennan maintained that too great a risk exists that people would engage in "self-censorship" if forced to demonstrate that every public statement they make is true.

Brennan concluded that "actual malice" was the only standard that properly respects the social interest in robust commentary on public officials. He wrote:

> A public official [cannot recover] damages for a defamatory falsehood relating to his official conduct unless he proves that the statement was made with 'actual malice'—that is with knowledge that it was false or with reckless disregard of whether it was false or not.

This standard has several parts. First, the plaintiff must prove that the speech is factually false. All opinions about public officials are constitutionally protected. Second, the plaintiff must prove "actual malice." "Actual malice" is a legal term that has nothing to do with the speaker's attitude toward the public official. That you intend your criticism to destroy or improve a political career is not constitutionally relevant. "Actual malice" refers to your culpability or mental state. A speaker has actual malice if they know their claims are false or act in reckless disregard of the truth. I would speak with actual malice if I declared that Chief Justice John Roberts consistently supports plaintiffs in death penalty cases because I know that assertion is factually false. I would speak with reckless disregard of the truth if I declared that Chief Justice John Roberts is a secret member of the Communist Party because, although I do not know for certain that this is false, I have no reason to believe the assertion true.

The Supreme Court has sometimes extended and sometimes modified the *Sullivan* rule in cases involving people who are not public officials. The present constitutional rules are as follows:

1. Public officials must demonstrate falsehood and actual malice.
2. Public figure, persons who intentionally seek public notoriety, must also demonstrate falsehood and actual malice.
3. Private figures on matters of public interest must demonstrate falsehood and negligence, but they must demonstrate actual malice to collect punitive damages.
4. Private figures on matters of private interest must demonstrate only what they must demonstrate under state law.

These rules inhibit most, but not all libel suits. Some very prominent businesses and persons have been known to institute libel suits simply because they believe the expense of defending will force their critics either to retract or to settle.

Speech and Crime

Brandenburg v. Ohio is the leading contemporary case on subversive advocacy, advocacy that champions the overthrow of the government or some crime. The per curiam opinion in that case declared that the First Amendment does "not permit a State to forbid or proscribe advocacy of the use of force or of law violation except where such advocacy is directed to inciting or producing imminent lawless action and is likely to incite or produce such action."

The *Brandenburg* standard emphasizes incitement and imminence. Speakers cannot normally be punished for normal advocacy, efforts to persuade some person of some political proposition. If my speech is designed to convince you that "all property is theft" or that "all lawyers should be killed in the most painful way possible," my speech is constitutionally protected. Government may prohibit my speech only when I urge you to act immediately on your new beliefs or seek to incite you by using speech that bypasses your rational faculties. There is a constitutional difference between "Here are five good reasons why all public officials deserve death" and "KILL THE SOB." In the case of the first, time exists for someone else to give five good reasons for not killing public officials, leaving listeners to decide for themselves how to act. In the case of the latter, the speaker is intentionally trying to bypass the deliberative process in order to achieve a result. *Brandenburg* also limits restrictions to speech that is likely to produce immediate action. This is why soapbox orators and professors love the *Brandenburg* test. Given that no one ever listens to us, we can say whatever we want, confident that the government will not be able to demonstrate that our speech has any probability of doing anything other than causing people to laugh at us.

Prior Restraint

New York Times Co. v. United States is the leading case on the constitutional status of prior restraints. The case arose after Daniel Ellsberg, a former Defense Department employee, gave the *New York Times* (and *Washington Post*) a copy of a 47-volume report on the Vietnam War now known as "the Pentagon Papers." Three days after the *Times* started publishing, the Nixon Administration obtained a temporary restraining order prohibiting further installments. Within two weeks, the case was before the Supreme Court and within three weeks the justices issued an order forbidding further restraint on publication.

Nine justices managed to issue ten opinions in the Pentagon Papers case, one for each judge and a per curiam opinion. Fortunately for law students not fond of long reading assignments, the only opinion that has had staying power is the short per curiam opinion which states that there is "a heavy presumption against" the constitutionality of any prior restraint. The standard metaphor is that the danger necessitating the prior restraint must be analogous to a publication that endangers the safety of a transport at sea during wartime.

What You Need to Know:

1. Public officials and public figures may win libel suits only if the offending speech is false and made with actual malice, i.e., the speaker knew the claim was false or the speech was made in reckless disregard of the truth.
2. Subversive advocacy may be punished only when the speaker incites a serious crime and the speech is likely to produce a serious crime.
3. The First Amendment imposes a heavy burden on prior restraints.

LESSON 25: FREE SPEECH: CAMPAIGN FINANCE REFORM AND SPEECH ON PUBLIC PROPERTY

The constitutional law of free speech has shifted focus during the last 50 years. Government efforts to prohibit offensive ideas have largely been abandoned. Opponents of the war against terror spoke far more freely than did American opponents of World War I, members of the Communist Party, or opponents of the Vietnam War. Contemporary free speech fights more often occur over what many constitutional law casebooks had described as "other free speech issues." These include campaign finance reform, commercial speech, speech on public property, speech subsidies, government regulation of the media, speech by government employees, and obscenity.

Campaign Finance Reform

Buckley v. Valeo, 424 U.S. 1 (1976), is the leading case on the constitutionality of campaign finance reform. Three central holdings of *Buckley* are particularly important. First, the Supreme Court ruled that campaign contributions and expenditures are core First Amendment speech. The per curiam opinion stated, "A restriction on the amount of money a person or group can spend on political communication during a campaign necessarily reduces the quality of expression by restricting the number of issues discussed, the depth of their exploration, and the size of the audience reached." Second, the justices maintain that the federal and state legislatures may restrict campaign finance only to prevent corruption or the appearance of corruption. Official policies that attempt to equalize the resources available to candidates are unconstitutional. The justices stated that "the concept that government may restrict the speech of some elements of our society in order to enhance the relative voice of others is wholly foreign to the First Amendment." Third, the justices made a distinction between contributions, which may be regulated, and expenditures which ordinarily may not. Government may restrict within reason the amount that you contribute to a particular candidate, but not any moneys you spend on your own to elect a particular candidate, your contributions to your campaign (you cannot corrupt yourself), or the amount you spend during your campaign. You may not contribute $1,000,000 to the campaign to elect Professor William Reynolds president. You may spend $1,000,000 trying to get Professor Reynolds elected president, provided your efforts are nominally independent (which they almost never are in practice).

The Supreme Court has become stricter when scrutinizing campaign finance regulations during the last decade. Recent opinions have limited corruption to quid pro quo arrangements between candidates and their financial backers. Corruption exists when Mr. Moneybags gives millions of dollars to Sleazy Joe in return for a commitment to be appointed ambassador to Monaco, but not when the public perceives that candidates spend far more time and energy trying to persuade Mr. Moneybags to support them than making appeals to the general public. In *Citizens United v. Federal Election Commission*, 558 U.S. 310 (2010), a narrow majority ruled that corporations have the same constitutional right to make independent expenditures (but not contributions) as more traditional persons (i.e., you and me). Justice Anthony Kennedy declared that government cannot ban political speech "simply because the speaker is an association that has taken on the corporate form."

Speech on Public Property

The First and Fourteenth Amendments protect the constitutional right persons have to speak on certain public properties that are legally considered "public forums." Public streets and public parks are the paradigmatic example of public forums in which persons may speak without fear of official reprisal. Justice Owen Roberts's majority opinion in *Hague v. Committee for Industrial Organizations*, 307 U.S. 496 (1939), is the canonical expression of the public forum doctrine. He wrote:

> Wherever the title of streets and parks may rest, they have immemorially been held for the use of the public and, time out of mind, have been used for purposes of assembly, communicating thoughts between citizens, and discussing public questions.

Governments may designate other areas as public forums in which speech is permitted. Once government creates a public forum, government may not regulate on the basis of content or viewpoint. If State U. declares that the space outside the food court shall be open to all speakers, State U. cannot bar a student group that wishes to talk about tuition increases (content discrimination) or a student organization that advocates the death penalty for professors who give multiple-choice examinations (viewpoint discrimination).

Government can nevertheless regulate the time, place, and manner of speech in public forums in ways that government cannot ordinarily regulate free speech. You do not have to share your house with other people and are free to play music as loudly as you want in your room (as long as you do not disturb your neighbors), but your use of a public forum must recognize that other people may also want to speak and other people may want to use the public property for other purposes. The Supreme Court has adopted the following five part test for determining whether time, place, and manner restrictions on speech in public forums is constitutional.

1. The regulation must be within the constitutional power of government.

2. The regulation must further an important government interest.
3. The government purpose must be unrelated to the suppression of expression.
4. The restriction must restrict no more speech than is necessary to achieve the government purpose.
5. Speakers must have reasonable alternatives for communicating their messages.

Consider a government ban on using amplifiers when speaking on the streets in residential neighborhoods at 2:00 a.m. Government may preserve the peace in neighborhoods. That is an important government interest. Enabling people to sleep is not related to the suppression of expression and the regulation does not restrict any more speech than is essential for permitting people to sleep. Persons are free to communicate their message at 2:00 p.m. when most people can be expected to be awake.

What You Need to Know:

1. The vast majority of contemporary free speech cases focus on what actions are considered speech and the conditions under which persons may speak freely.
2. Campaign finance may be regulated only when doing so prevents quid pro quo corruption.
3. While some contributions may be regulated, personal expenditures and most corporate speech cannot.
4. Persons have a right to speak on public streets and parks, subject to time, place, and manner restrictions.

LESSON 26: THE RIGHT TO VOTE

The Constitution of the United States does not explicitly guarantee anyone the right to vote. Attempts during the drafting convention to specify who could vote in a federal election floundered in light of the different qualifications for suffrage in the different states. Benjamin Franklin was the rare delegate who championed universal (male) suffrage. He was drowned out by the vast majority of delegates who insisted that some degree of property was necessary for persons to demonstrate the capacities and interests necessary to cast ballots for federal officials. Rather than delineate precise qualifications, the framers decided that any person qualified to vote in a state election could vote in a federal election. Article I, Section 2, paragraph 1 states:

> The House of Representatives shall be composed of Members chosen every second Year by the People of the several States, and the Electors in each State shall have the Qualifications requisite for Electors of the most numerous Branch of the State Legislature.

The framers focused on "the most numerous Branch of the State Legislature" because most states had the least restrictive qualifications for voting for members of that institution.

Americans increased access to the ballot in a series of subsequent amendments that prohibited states from making particular kinds of voting discriminations. The Fifteenth Amendment prohibits states from making racial qualifications for voting. The precise text declares, "The right of citizens of the United States to vote shall not be denied or abridged by the United States or by any State on account of race, color, or previous condition or servitude." The Nineteenth Amendment prohibits states from making gender qualifications for voting. The Twenty-Fourth Amendment forbids states from making payment of a poll tax a qualification to vote in federal elections. The Twenty-Sixth Amendment declares that states may not make age a qualification for voting for citizens 18 years or older. Each amendment includes a provision stating "The Congress shall have power to enforce this article by appropriate legislation."

The Right to Vote

The Supreme Court in *Harper v. Virginia State Board of Elections*, 383 U.S. 663 (1966), found a qualified right to vote protected by the Equal Protection Clause of the Fourteenth Amendment. That case concerned the constitutionality of a poll tax for state elections (the Twenty-Fourth Amendment prohibits poll taxes for federal elections). Justice William Douglas, while nominally adhering to the position that no one had a right to vote for any state office, insisted that once states made an office elective, voter discriminations had to satisfy the Equal Protection Clause. He declared, "Once the franchise is granted to the electorate, lines may not be drawn which are inconsistent with the Equal Protection Clause of the Fourteenth Amendment." No one has a right to vote for the dogcatcher of Kalamazoo because Kalamazooians may decide to make dogcatcher an appointive office. Once Kalamazoo makes dogcatcher an elective office, *Harper* holds that any restriction on the franchise must satisfy equal protection standards.

The standards that state restrictions on voting must meet are almost impossible to satisfy. *Harper* was limited to wealth and other classifications previously thought constitutionally obnoxious. "Wealth, like race, creed, or color," Douglas wrote, "is not germane to one's ability to participate intelligently in the electoral process." Later decisions made clear that almost any exclusion from the ballot failed to pass constitutional muster. The crucial case is *Kramer v. Union Free District No. 15*, 395 U.S. 621 (1969). That case declared unconstitutional a local law that limited voting in school board elections to persons who had school-aged children or either owned or leased property in the district. Chief Justice Warren's majority opinion declared all persons had a sufficiently fundamental interest in voting such that any denial of access to the ballot must be "necessary to promote a compelling state interest." With the notable exception of state laws prohibiting convicted felons from voting, this compelling interest test has resulted in almost all restrictions on access to the ballot being declared unconstitutional.

An important constitutional distinction exists between laws that declare a person ineligible to vote and laws that enable a legal voter to cast a ballot. The Supreme Court uses strict scrutiny when determining whether laws of the form "No person of this description may vote in an election" are constitutional. The justices employ a lesser standard when determining whether laws of the form "All persons must prove their eligibility to vote in the follow way" are constitutional. The leading case is *Crawford v. Marion County Election Board*, 553 U.S. 181 (2008). The issue in that case was whether states could require voters to produce photo identification cards before casting a ballot. Three justices sustained that law because the restriction was evenhanded and the state interests in photo identifications outweighed the burden to the voter. Three justices claimed that evenhanded regulations of voting had to meet only a rational-basis test. No justice in the majority suggested that states must demonstrate a compelling interest when passing laws identifying eligible voters.

One Person/One Vote

The Supreme Court insists that the right to vote entails a right to cast an equal vote. States must normally apportion federal and state legislative districts on the basis of population. Chief Justice Earl Warren's majority opinion in *Reynolds v. Sims*, 377 U.S. 533 (1964), stated that "a majority of the people of a State" should be able to "elect a majority of that State's legislators." States are allowed to deviate slightly from one person, one vote when apportioning state legislative districts. Almost no deviation is permitted when states are allocating congressional legislative districts.

The reapportionment revolution did not guarantee that a majority of the voters in any state elect a majority of the representatives to Congress or the state legislature. Many state legislatures routinely gerrymander districts in the ways that skew electoral outcomes. Some gerrymanders are bipartisan. States whose different legislative chambers are controlled by different parties apportion districts to protect incumbents in both parties. Other gerrymanders are partisan. Members of the party that controls the state legislature create a few superdupermajority districts controlled by their rivals, enabling them to create more districts in which representatives of their party are likely to be elected. The Supreme Court has refused to review partisan gerrymanders, but has not yet declared partisan gerrymanders nonjusticiable.

What You Need to Know:

1. The Constitution does not directly give any person the right to vote in any election.
2. The Supreme Court has ruled that whenever a state makes an office elective, all state citizens must be given the right to vote in that election, unless a compelling interest exists for limiting the suffrage.
3. States must apportion federal and state legislative districts primarily on the basis of population.
4. The Supreme Court has refrained from determining when, if ever, partisan gerrymanders are unconstitutional.

LESSON 27: EQUAL PROTECTION: BASICS

The Fourteenth Amendment declares, "No State shall . . . deny to any person within its jurisdiction the equal protection of the laws." Although this provision limits only the power of state governments to treat people unequally, the Supreme Court by a process of reverse incorporation has interpreted the Due Process Clause of the Fifth Amendment as mandating that the federal government in most cases must adhere to the same standards as states are held to under the Equal Protection Clause. The conventional citation for this proposition is *Bolling v. Sharpe*, 347 U.S. 497 (1954), a companion case to *Brown v. Board of Education*, 347 U.S. 483 (1954), that prohibited Congress from mandating school segregation in the District of Columbia.

Equal protection doctrine has two strands; suspect class and fundamental rights. The first question in any equal protection case is whether the law has made a suspect or quasi-suspect classification. Laws that make such classifications must meet a higher standard of scrutiny than laws that do not. Race and ethnicity are suspect classes. Gender and perhaps legitimacy and alienage are quasi-suspect classes. The second question is whether the law burdens a fundamental right. Laws that burden fundamental rights must meet a higher standard of scrutiny than laws that do not. At present, voting is the only fundamental interest that requires heightened scrutiny under the Equal Protection Clause, although the justices have suggested that heightened scrutiny is necessary when states offer education to some persons but deny the privilege to others.

The Supreme Court for the past 40 years has generally refused to find new suspect classes or fundamental interests. *San Antonio Independent School District v. Rodriguez*, 411 U.S. 1 (1973), is the most important instance of this reluctance. That case arose when families living in less affluent school districts in Texas challenged a state law that made extensive use of property taxes to fund public schools. The justices by a 5–4 majority declared the policy constitutional, even though that financing system left poor school districts with very limited capacity to fund education. Justice Lewis Powell's majority opinion first refused to find that persons who lived in property-poor districts were part of a suspect class. Although his opinion did not make the point explicitly, *Rodriguez* came to stand for the proposition that wealth classifications do not merit heightened scrutiny under the Equal Protection Clause. Powell then denied that education was a fundamental interest that warranted heightened scrutiny. He wrote that "the undisputed importance of education will not alone cause this Court to depart from the usual [rational-basis] standard for reviewing a State's social and economic legislation."

Plyler v. Doe, 457 U.S. 202 (1982), is a partial exception to the recent tendency to reject new suspect classes and fundamental interests. The justices in that case by a 5–4 vote declared unconstitutional a Texas law prohibiting the children of illegal aliens from attending public schools. While purporting to use rational basis, Justice Brennan pointed out that the Texas law violated basic equal protection principles by discriminating against children on the "basis of a legal characteristic over which [they] can have little control" and by denying them any access to public education.

Rational Scrutiny

The justices employ rational scrutiny in cases where there is no suspect classification or fundamental right. The rational-scrutiny test requires government to demonstrate that the classification in question is a rational means towards achieving a legitimate government end.

That test ordinarily does not demand much, if anything, from government. Government need not demonstrate the law is particularly intelligent and may even concede the law has many perverse applications. Rational scrutiny normally requires only that a statutory distinction makes sense some of the time. The lawyer for the government may speculate as to why the legislature passed the law. When applying the ordinary rational-scrutiny test, the government need not explain why one particular class was burdened or benefited but not another. Justice William Douglas in *Williamson v. Lee Optical*, 348 U.S. 483 (1955), declared, "Evils in the same field may be of different dimensions and proportions, requiring different remedies. Or so the legislature may think. . . . Or the reform may take one step at a time, addressing itself to the phase of the problem which seems most acute to the legislative mind. . . . The legislature may select one phrase of the field and apply a remedy there, neglecting others."

Not many laws will be declared unconstitutional under this standard. Imagine a state law school that decides that poor performance in morning classes may be caused by law students having an inadequate breakfast. The school decides to combat this problem by serving free orange juice in the constitutional law class Professor Graber teaches every Tuesday at 9:00 a.m. Students taking Professor Gifford's torts class at 9:00 a.m. that day and students taking Professor Gray's criminal law class at 9:00 a.m. on Wednesday complain that they are being treated unequally for no good reason. They will lose their lawsuit. A court citing *Williamson* and using the rational-basis test will note that the state actors who made this distinction might have thought being more alert in constitutional law more important than being alert in torts or criminal law classes. Perhaps they concluded that constitutional law professors as a whole are duller than torts or criminal law professors. Some legislators may have concluded that more students watch Monday night football games and for this reason need more stimulants on Tuesday than on Wednesday. The discrimination may be part of an experimental program where constitutional law classes were selected by a coin flip.

Rational Scrutiny with Bite

The Supreme Court sometimes puts bite into the rational-scrutiny test. This most commonly occurs when judicial majorities determine that a law is based on "animus" against the burdened class. *U.S. Department of Agriculture v. Moreno*, 413 U.S. 528 (1973), is the canonical case for this legal principle. That case declared unconstitutional a federal law that denied food stamps to members of unrelated households. The justices did not declare members of unrelated households a suspect class or access to food stamps a fundamental right. Instead, after noting that the law was aimed at "hippie communes," Justice Brennan declared, "A bare desire to harm a politically unpopular group cannot constitute a legitimate governmental interest." At other times, the justices appear to treat the burdened group as a suspect class without saying so. *City of Cleburne v. Cleburne Living Center, Inc.*, 473 U.S. 432 (1985), concerned whether Texas could discriminate against persons with intellectual disabilities when considering permits for group homes. Counsel for both sides assumed that the issue in the case was whether the justices would use rational scrutiny or treat persons with intellectual disabilities as a quasi-suspect class. Instead, the justices purported to use rational scrutiny, but declared the laws unconstitutional. Although Justice Byron White's majority opinion did not state that the law was motivated by animus or that persons with intellectual disabilities are a quasi-suspect class requiring heightened scrutiny, good reasons exists for thinking some such reasoning motivated the judicial majority.

The contemporary Supreme Court employed the animus test in two major cases involving the rights of LGBT persons. The first was *Romer v. Evans*, 517 U.S. 620 (1996). That case concerned an amendment to the Constitution of Colorado which prohibited the state or any subdivision from passing any law or regulation that prohibited discrimination against gays or lesbians. Justice Kennedy's majority opinion, while purporting to use rational scrutiny, declared the law unconstitutional. He wrote that "its sheer breadth is so discontinuous with the reasons offered for it that the amendment seems inexplicable by anything other than animus toward the class that it affects; it lacks a rational relationship to legitimate state interests." The Supreme Court by a 5–4 vote in *United States v. Windsor*, 133 S. Ct. 2675 (2013), similarly pointed to unconstitutional animus when declaring that a federal law mandating that the federal government recognize only marriages between a man and a woman, even when the same-sex marriage was legal in the state where the married couple resided. Justice Kennedy's majority opinion stated, "The avowed purpose and practical effect of the law here in question are to impose a disadvantage, a separate status, and so a stigma upon all who enter into same-sex marriages made lawful by the unquestioned authority of the States."

What You Need to Know:

1. State governments have a constitutional obligation to treat people equally under the Equal Protection Clause of the Fourteenth Amendment.
2. The federal government has the same obligation, cases involving discrimination against noncitizens aside, under the Due Process Clause of the Fifth Amendment.
3. Courts will use the rational-scrutiny test in equal protection cases unless the law makes a suspect or quasi-suspect classification, or burdens a fundamental right.
4. Government almost always wins under the rational-scrutiny test, unless the court is convinced that the law is based on animus against a group, typically gays and lesbians.

LESSON 28: EQUAL PROTECTION: RACE

The persons responsible for the Equal Protection Clause were primarily concerned with discriminations against former slaves. Conventional wisdom insists that the Fourteenth Amendment was designed to provide secure foundations for federal civil rights laws that prohibited states from denying to persons of color the same rights as "enjoyed by white citizens."

Race remains the paradigmatic example of a suspect class in American constitutional law. Racial discriminations and distinctions are subject to strict scrutiny, the highest standard used for evaluating legislation under the Equal Protection Clause.

Strict Scrutiny

The contemporary Supreme Court applies strict scrutiny when determining whether a discrimination against persons of color is constitutional. The test requires that government use a necessary or, somewhat less strict, narrowly tailored means to achieve a compelling government end. The means must be necessary or narrowly tailored. No other means may exist that are capable of achieving the end in question. A racist community may threaten violence when an African-American couple adopts a white child, but a ban on such adoptions will not survive strict scrutiny because the local government can preserve the public peace by providing protection for the family and teaching the community to be more racially tolerant. The end must be compelling. A high school in a racist community might decide that students would not attend games played by an integrated sports team no matter how hard the teachers promoted tolerance, but increasing attendance at high school football is not a compelling government interest. With the notable exception of *Korematsu v. United States*, 323 U.S. 214 (1944), whenever the Supreme Court has found discrimination against persons of color, that discrimination has failed to satisfy strict scrutiny. *Korematsu* sustained a federal law detaining Japanese Americans living in California during World War II on the ground that detaining all members of a racial group was the only means for ensuring disloyal citizens would not interfere with the American effort to win the war. That decision has been discredited.

Finding Race Discrimination: Segregation

The constitutional law of the late nineteenth and early twentieth centuries often made a distinction between race discriminations and race distinctions. Race discriminations, which gave white persons benefits not granted to persons of color, or which imposed on persons of color burdens not imposed of white persons, were unconstitutional. Race distinctions, which "merely" recognized differences between the races, were constitutional. This distinction between race discriminations and distinctions provided the foundation for *Plessy v. Ferguson*, 163 U.S. 537 (1896). A 7–1 majority in this case found that Louisiana could require white persons and persons of color to sit in separate train cars on the ground that "A statute which implies merely a legal distinction between the white and colored races . . . has no tendency to destroy the legal equality of the two races." Justice John Marshall Harlan wrote a very famous dissent, which included that now often quoted claim, "Our constitution is color-blind, and neither knows nor tolerates classes among citizens."

Brown v. Board of Education, 347 U.S. 483 (1954), brought a fortunate end to the distinction between race discriminations and race distinctions. A unanimous Supreme Court declared unconstitutional laws mandating segregation in public schools on the ground that segregation harmed students of color. A crucial passage in Chief Justice Earl Warren's majority opinion declared, "To segregate them from others of similar age and qualifications solely because of their race generates a feeling of inferiority as to their status in the community that may affect their hearts and minds in a way unlikely ever to be undone." The precise logic (as opposed to the result) in *Brown* remains controversial, but one consensual consequence is that all racial classifications are now constitutionally suspect and merit strict scrutiny, whether they bluntly discriminate against persons of color or are purportedly designed merely to recognize race distinctions. A law prohibiting a white student from dating a student of color is an unconstitutional race discrimination, even if all students are prohibited from dating students of a different race.

Finding Race Discrimination: Impact and Purpose

The Supreme Court is far less likely to find unconstitutional race discrimination when a federal or state statute does not make an explicit racial classification, even though the law in practice burdens persons of color far more than white persons. When claiming that a statute that does not make an explicit race classification nevertheless violates the

Equal Protection Clause, plaintiffs must demonstrate both disparate impact and discriminatory purpose. Discriminatory purpose or disparate impact standing alone is not sufficient to establish a constitutional violation. State law schools may continue to use the LSAT in their admissions process, even though much evidence suggests that many persons of color underperform on that examination (discriminatory impact) in the absence of evidence that state law schools are using the LSAT for the purpose of discriminating against persons of color (discriminatory purpose). If a law school adopts a height criteria for admission to law school because they believe that white students are on average taller than students of color (discriminatory purpose), that rule is constitutional in the absence of any evidence that white students are, in fact, taller on average than persons of color (discriminatory impact).

Two important Supreme Court cases made clear that plaintiffs must establish discriminatory purpose and disparate impact when challenging a statute that does not explicitly make racial classifications. *Palmer v. Thompson*, 403 U.S. 217 (1971), ruled that discriminatory purpose was insufficient to prove unconstitutional race discrimination. Plaintiffs challenged a Jackson, Mississippi, ordinance closing all public pools in the city after a federal court required those facilities to be desegregated. Everybody recognized that Jackson was attempting to forestall racial integration. Nevertheless, a 5–4 majority refused to find any violation of the Equal Protection Clause because the law prevented any one from swimming at a public pool. Justice Hugo Black's majority opinion declared that "no case in this Court has held that a legislative act may violate equal protection solely because of the motivations of the men who voted for it." *Washington v. Davis*, 426 U.S. 229 (1976), ruled that disparate impact was insufficient to prove unconstitutional race discrimination. That case concerned a challenge to the use of a civil service examination in Washington D.C. that African Americans were far more likely to fail than white persons. The Supreme Court by a 7–2 majority ruled the use of this test constitutional, even though no one proved that performance on the test correlated with work performance. Justice Byron White's majority opinion declared that "our cases have not embraced the proposition that a law or other official act, without regard to whether it reflects a racially discriminatory purpose, is unconstitutionally solely because it has a racially discriminatory impact."

The justices do permit evidence of racially disparate impact to prove racially discriminatory motives. If plaintiffs establish a racially disparate impact, the burden falls on the government to demonstrate a plausible race-neutral reason for the racially skewed outcome.

What You Need to Know:

1. Laws that rely on racial classifications must be necessary means to compelling government ends.
2. *Brown v. Board of Education* abandoned the distinction between unconstitutional racial discriminations and constitutional race distinctions.
3. A plaintiff claiming that a law which does not mention race nevertheless makes an unconstitutional race discrimination must prove both racial purpose and racial impact. If the plaintiff proves a racially disparate impact, the burden falls on the state to demonstrate a plausible race neutral reason for the racially disparate outcome.

LESSON 29: EQUAL PROTECTION: GENDER

The persons responsible for the post-Civil War Amendments thought that real differences between men and women justified numerous laws limiting women's civil capacities. Efforts to include women in the civil rights statutes passed after the Civil War were defeated. *Minor v. Happersett*, 88 U.S. (21 Wall.) 162 (1874), declared that women had no constitutional right to vote. *Bradwell v. Illinois*, 83 U.S. (16 Wall.) 130 (1872), held that women had no constitutional right to be attorneys. Justice Joseph Bradley's concurring opinion stated, "The paramount destiny and mission of woman are to fulfill the noble and benign offices of wife and mother." "This is the negro's hour," an influential editorial in the *American Anti-Slavery Standard* declared.

Common law regarded married women as "femme covert." Under the doctrine of coverture, a married woman had no legal identity apart from her husband. *Bradwell* made clear that states were constitutionally free to legislate on the assumption that the vast majority of women were married or intended to be married.

Constitutional standards did not change as fast as social attitudes. For much of the twentieth century, the Supreme Court used a toothless rational-basis test when adjudicating challenges to gender discriminations, even as the justices omitted past references to the "paramount destiny" of women. When sustaining a law providing women workers with minimum wages, Chief Justice Charles Evans Hughes in *West Coast Hotel v. Parrish*, 300 U.S. 379, 398 (1937), wrote, "What can be closer to the public interest than the health of women and their protection from unscrupulous and overreaching employers." As late as *Hoyt v. Florida*, 368 U.S. 57 (1961), Supreme Court opinions declared, "Despite the enlightened emancipation of women from the restrictions and protections of bygone years . . . woman is still regarded as the center of home and family life."

Reed v. Reed, 404 U.S. 71 (1971), began the process by which constitutional law ratcheted up the scrutiny for gender classifications. That case declared unconstitutional a state law that preferred men to women when determining who administered a will. Although Chief Justice Warren Burger purported to use a rational-basis test when rejecting administrative convenience as a justification for the discrimination, observers noted that administrative convenience had previously always been a legitimate reason for discrimination under the rational-basis test. *Frontiero v. Richardson*, 411 U.S. 677 (1973), further muddied the constitutional waters. Four justices insisted that gender classifications merited strict scrutiny. Justice Brennan noted, "There can be no doubt that our nation has had a long and unfortunate history of race discrimination." The justices who cast the deciding votes, however, insisted on deciding the case on the basis of *Reed v. Reed* without addressing the obvious point that the gender classification in question would clearly survive the traditional rational-scrutiny test.

The Supreme Court in *Craig v. Boren*, 429 U.S. 190 (1976), officially heightened the level of scrutiny used when reviewing gender classifications. That case concerned the constitutionality of an Oklahoma law that permitted 18–21-year-old women, but not 18–21-year-old men to purchase 3.2 beer. Justice Brennan declared that all gender classifications would be subject to a new intermediate-scrutiny test. He ruled:

> To withstand constitutional challenge, previous cases establish that classifications by gender must serve important government objections and must be substantially related to achieve those objectives.

Justice Ruth Bader Ginsburg in *United States v. Virginia*, 518 U.S. 515 (1996), described this constitutional standard as requiring states to proffer "an exceedingly persuasive justification." Her opinion mandated that unlike the rational-basis test, the government rely only on the actual legislative rationale for the gender classification and not invent hypothetical post-enactment rationalizations during the litigation. In theory, no difference exists between intermediate scrutiny and the exceedingly persuasive justification standard, although liberal justices are more inclined to the former and conservative justices more inclined to the latter.

The intermediate-scrutiny standard applies to discriminations against men, discriminations against women, and laws that segregate men and women. A public school decision to have only a men's soccer team, only a women's soccer team, or a men's and women's soccer team is constitutional only if each has "an exceedingly persuasive justification" or is a substantial means to an important government end.

The intermediate-scrutiny standard or "exceedingly persuasive justification" text is easier to parrot on an examination than to describe in a coherent fashion. A fair case can be made that Justice Brennan, Justice Ginsburg, and other Supreme Court justices who favored strict scrutiny for gender classifications apply intermediate scrutiny exactly as they apply strict scrutiny. Unsurprisingly most liberal justices have never voted to sustain a gender classification. The best that can be said is that an important government end is not quite as vital as the compelling government end required by the strict-scrutiny standard, but more vital than the legitimate end required by the rational-basis test. A substantial means is not as narrowly tailored as the necessary means required by the strict-scrutiny standard, but more narrowly tailored then the reasonable means required by the rational-basis test.

A simple example will suffice. Imagine your final examination asks you to consider the constitutionality of sex segregated public schools. You might claim that the gender classification is a substantial means to an important government end because much evidence demonstrates that adolescents learn better in sex-segregated environments. You might claim that the gender classification is not a substantial means to an important government end because states have many other ways of improving how teenage boys and girls learn. You should get full credit for both answers, provided you speak of substantial means to important government ends.

Judicial majorities are not inclined to find gender discrimination when a statute does not make an explicit gender classification. In *Geduldig v. Aiello*, 417 U.S. 484 (1974), the justices by a 5–4 vote determined that states do not engage in gender discrimination when they exclude pregnancy from healthcare programs. Justice Potter Stewart pointed out, "There is no risk from which men are protected and women are not. Likewise there is no risk from which women are protected and men are not." Just as Anatole France praised French law for prohibiting both the rich and poor from sleeping in the streets, so you may rest assured that the constitutional law of the United States will make no distinction between pregnant men and pregnant women.

What You Need to Know:

1. Under common law, married women had no legal rights.
2. The framers of the Fourteenth Amendment did not intend to change this aspect of the common law.

3. At present, the Supreme Court requires that gender classifications be substantial means to important government ends or have exceedingly persuasive justifications.
4. Laws treating pregnant people differently than others under present constitutional law do not make gender classifications.

LESSON 30: EQUAL PROTECTION: AFFIRMATIVE ACTION

Affirmative action, programs that make race distinctions in order to promote racial equality, raise controversial equal protection problems. Much constitutional debate over affirmative action is rooted in different interpretations of *Brown v. Board of Education*, 347 U.S. 483 (1954). Proponents believe that *Brown* is best explained by a constitutional commitment to antisubordination. Segregating schools was unconstitutional because states may not adopt policies for the purpose of establishing white supremacy or a racial caste system. Race-conscious policies that are designed to dismantle Jim Crow or the lingering effects of Jim Crow are consistent with the constitutional commitment to equal protection. Opponents believe *Brown* is best explained by a constitutional commitment to anticlassification. Segregating schools was unconstitutional because government should not use race when allocating benefits and burdens or determining a person's legal status. Race-conscious policies are per se unconstitutional unless they are necessary means for achieving a compelling interest.

The Supreme Court by a narrow majority has adopted a modified version of the anticlassification interpretation of *Brown*. Justice Sandra Day O'Connor's plurality opinion in *Adarand Constructors, Inc. v. Pena*, 515 U.S. 200 (1995), highlighted concerns with racial classifications when setting out three basic principles that have guided judicial decision making for the past generation.

1. "Skepticism." Race-conscious measures must be necessary or narrowly tailored means to achieve compelling government ends.
2. "Consistency." Race-conscious measures designed to benefit persons of color must meet the same demanding standard as race-conscious measures designed to burden persons of color.
3. "Congruence." Federal race-conscious measures must meet the same demanding standard as state race-conscious measures.

Consistent with anticlassification, the Court requires strict scrutiny for all racial classifications no matter which race is benefitted or burdened. Nevertheless, although strict scrutiny had historically resulted in offending measures being declared unconstitutional, the justices have permitted government to use race classifications in two instances. Race classifications may be used to remedy federal and state violations of the Equal Protection Clause. State university admissions officers may use race classifications when doing so is a narrowly tailored means to achieve the compelling state interest in a diverse student body.

Remedying Constitutional Violations

Government may use racial classifications when remedying official state race discrimination. Federal courts regularly considered the racial composition of schools after the Supreme Court in *Green v. County School Board of New Kent County*, 391 U.S. 430 (1968), held that school boards that maintained segregated school systems when *Brown* was decided were "clearly charged with the affirmative duty to take whatever steps might be necessary to convert to a unitary system in which racial discrimination would be eliminated root and branch." Lower federal courts self-consciously drew attendance zones with an eye to having the percentage of students in each school in the school system mirror the percentage of students in the entire school system. If all persons in the neighborhood surrounding Robert E. Lee Elementary School were white and all persons in the neighborhood surrounding Frederick Douglass Elementary School were persons of color, then the federal court would draw attendance zones so that half the children in the former neighborhood attended Lee and half the children in the latter neighborhood attended Douglass.

Sharp limits exist on government power to use race to remedy past unconstitutional race discrimination. This remedy is largely, though not exclusively, limited to federal courts and the federal government. The Supreme Court has not looked favorably on local governments that attempt to justify race-conscious measures as a response to past race discrimination in the absence of a judicial finding that those local governments had violated the Equal Protection Clause. Once the constitutional violation is cured, the race conscious measures must cease. In *Parents Involved in Community Schools v. Seattle School District No. 1*, 551 U.S. 701 (2007), the Supreme Court declared that Seattle and Louisville could not use race classifications when assigning students to public schools because the Seattle school system had never been held in violation of the Equal Protection Clause and a federal court had recently declared that Louisville had successfully remedied past equal protection violations.

Supreme Court decisions on racial gerrymanders provide another illustration of the limited use of race classifications to remedy past constitutional violations. States may create majority-minority districts, districts designed to ensure most voters are persons of color, when doing so is necessary to comply with the Voting Rights Act. The Supreme Court in *Shaw v. Reno*, 509 U.S. 630 (1993), and *Miller v. Johnson*, 515 U.S. 900 (1995), nevertheless insisted that racial motives must not "predominate" when the state is under an obligation to remedy past racial discrimination in voting laws. "When a district obviously is created solely to effectuate the perceived common interest of one racial group," Justice O'Connor wrote in *Shaw*, "elected officials are more likely to believe that their primary obligation is to represent only members of that group."

University Admissions

In *Regents of the University of California v. Bakke*, 438 U.S. 265 (1978), the Supreme Court held that universities may make limited use of racial classifications during the admissions process. *Bakke* ruled that racial classifications under restricted circumstances may be a narrowly tailored means for achieving the compelling state interest in achieving a diverse student body. Nevertheless, Justice Powell's crucial plurality opinion held that states may not use race for the purpose of ensuring a fixed percentage of students of a particular race or for remedying general societal discrimination. *Bakke* also held that fixed racial quotas are unconstitutional. Schools may give a "plus" to persons of particular races, but all applicants of all races must be eligible for every seat in the admissions process.

The Supreme Court applied *Bakke* in *Grutter v. Bollinger*, 539 U.S. 306 (2003), and *Gratz v. Bollinger*, 539 U.S. 244 (2003). The crucial factor in both cases was whether the admissions process rejected quotas and considered all students on an individual basis. *Grutter* sustained the admissions program at the University of Michigan School of Law, which sought to achieve a "critical mass" of students of color by requiring all students to write an essay on how they would diversify the student body. The admissions policy placed special emphasis on "students from groups which have been historically discriminated against." Justice O'Connor's opinion declared that "the Law School engages in a highly individualized holistic review of each applicant's file, giving serious consideration to all the ways an applicant might contribute to a diverse student body." *Gratz* declared unconstitutional the undergraduate admissions program at Michigan, which gave all students 20 points for being a member of a historically disadvantaged group. Justice O'Connor declared that the process set up "automatic, predetermined, point allocations . . . ensur[ing] that the diversity contributions of applicants cannot be individually assessed." Seven justices could not figure out the constitutional differences between the law school and undergraduate admissions programs (three thought both constitutional, four thought both unconstitutional), but Justices O'Connor and Stephen Breyer found distinctions, which explains the divergent decisions.

The Supreme Court has never sustained racial classifications in contexts other than education or declared any end other than diversity to be a compelling interest that might justify an affirmative action program.

What You Need to Know:

1. Laws designed to benefit historically disadvantaged racial groups must meet the same constitutional standards as laws designed to burden historically disadvantaged groups.
2. Federal courts and the federal government may use racial classifications when remedying past racial discrimination.
3. Public universities may use racial classifications to achieve diversity, but only if the admissions process does not use quotas and requires individualized consideration for all applicants.

CHAPTER 6

CIVIL PROCEDURE

LESSON 1: JURISDICTION

In most law schools, Civil Procedure is taught in two semester-long courses: one semester on **jurisdiction** of courts (what is the right court to sue in?) and one on **pleading and practice** (the life history of a lawsuit).

Before starting on either semester, you should know that Civil Procedure is usually considered the hardest of the first-year courses for several reasons: (1) it is very abstract, (2) it requires close reading of the Federal Rules of Civil Procedure (a very complex code of rules) and several equally complex federal jurisdictional statutes (laws passed by Congress), and (3) most students have no experience with it (unlike torts, contracts, and criminal law).

The one-semester course on jurisdiction is designed to familiarize you with the federal and state court systems and to allow you to make a legally proper and tactically wise choice of the court in which to bring your client's lawsuit. The first thing you need to know about court selection is: **what are the possibilities?** Each state has a set of trial courts, courts of appeals, and a supreme court and so does the federal court system. A federal court, or perhaps several of them, is headquartered in each of the 50 states. That means you have a lot of choices. The first question to ask is a **tactical one: Which court is the most favorable to your client's case?** The tactical question requires you to think about each court's likely jury prejudices, types of judges, applicable substantive and procedural law, and docket length (how many cases the court will have to hear before it gets to yours).

Once you decide which court you would like to sue in, the next question is: Can you do it? Is the selected court one that you have the right to bring the suit in? Three concepts control that question: **territorial jurisdiction**, **subject matter jurisdiction**, and **venue**. Territorial jurisdiction asks whether the state or federal court can reach out and touch your chosen defendant. If a New York plaintiff drives to California and is injured there in an auto accident, will she be able to sue the California defendant in New York or will she have to travel to California to bring her lawsuit?

The issue for **subject matter jurisdiction** is whether the government that created the court has given it authority to hear the type of lawsuit in question. To continue with our example, some state and federal courts have been given authority (by their respective governments) to hear auto accident cases and some have not. In the first-year course you will spend most of your time on the subject matter jurisdiction of the federal courts, *i.e.*, is your client's suit one that the federal courts can hear or is your only option a state court?

Once you have picked a court that can reach your defendant and has the authority to hear the type of case, you must then tackle the problem of **venue**. In the state systems, venue rules control which county's courts your lawsuit belongs in. In the federal system, venue rules control which is the proper federal district (there are well over 50 of them).

What You Need to Know:

1. The first semester in Civil Procedure is concerned mostly with how to choose the right court for your client's lawsuit.
2. Several variables will affect your tactical choice: each court's likely jury prejudices, types of judges, applicable substantive and procedural law, and docket length (how many cases the court will have to hear before it gets to yours).
3. Once you have picked the court that is tactically most advantageous, you will have to confront the legal question: Is that court available to you? The concepts of subject matter jurisdiction, territorial jurisdiction, and venue will provide the answer to that question.

LESSON 2: TERRITORIAL JURISDICTION

Territorial jurisdiction (sometimes referred to as "personal jurisdiction") refers to the power of a court to **compel the defendant to appear** and defend the lawsuit or **suffer a default judgment** (a judgment rendered in the defendant's absence) that will be recognized and enforced by other courts. Consider this hypothetical:

> A, a resident of Maine, is driving through an intersection in Maine and her car collides with a car driven by B, a resident of Hawaii who is vacationing in Maine. After his vacation, B returns to Hawaii. A would like B to pay for her medical expenses and lost wages, but B refuses. Will A be able to sue B in Maine, or will she have to go to Hawaii to bring the lawsuit?

It is not important to answer the question now, but just to see it as an illustration of the problem of territorial jurisdiction.

A Jurisdictional Basis

In order for a court to exercise personal jurisdiction over the defendant, it will need a jurisdictional basis. That means some kind of connection or relationship with the defendant. In the preceding hypothetical, the connection between B and Maine is obvious; B drove through Maine and caused a car collision there. By contrast, suppose that B had wanted to sue A in Hawaii based on the collision in Maine. The Hawaii court would not have personal jurisdiction over A; there is no jurisdictional basis, no relationship or connection between A and Hawaii.

Throughout the course, you will hear terms like "**personal jurisdiction**," "**in rem jurisdiction**," "**quasi-in-rem jurisdiction**," and "**attachment jurisdiction**." These terms refer to different kinds of jurisdictional bases (connections or relationships between the state and the defendant or his property). Most of the following lessons will consider the territorial jurisdiction of the states' courts; Lesson 18 discusses the territorial jurisdiction of the federal courts.

Notice

The topic of notice will be the subject of a subsequent lesson. For now, all you need to know is that a valid judgment requires not only an adequate jurisdictional basis, but also that the defendant have **adequate notice of the existence of the lawsuit**. Every court system has rules that require that defendants be provided with such notice.

The Impact of the Constitution

The federal Constitution affects a state's right to exercise jurisdiction in two ways. First, a judgment rendered in the absence of a proper basis or proper notice is a violation of the defendant's right to **due process**, guaranteed by the Fourteenth Amendment. Second, the **Full Faith and Credit Clause** does not require the courts of other states to recognize such an invalid judgment. Consider this variation on our earlier hypothetical:

> The basic facts are the same as the first hypothetical, except this time B, after returning to Hawaii, would like to sue A in a court in Hawaii to recover for his medical expenses and lost wages. A does not appear in the Hawaii suit and B wins a default judgment. B is unable to get A to pay the judgment, or to enforce the judgment in Hawaii, so he sues her in Maine (based on the Hawaii judgment), hoping to use some of A's property in Maine to satisfy the judgment. A will object that the Hawaii court lacked a jurisdictional basis and thus that she was deprived of due process in violation of the Fourteenth Amendment; the Maine court will agree, and it will not have to give full faith and credit to the Hawaii judgment.

In this hypothetical, A maintained that B's Hawaii judgment was not entitled to **full faith and credit** in Maine because the Hawaii court lacked jurisdiction over her (no jurisdictional basis). Her assertion of that defense is called a "**collateral attack**." It is collateral in the sense that it was raised in a separate proceeding (in Maine), rather than in the Hawaii proceeding itself. If she had raised her jurisdictional defense against the Hawaii judgment in a Hawaii appellate court, it would have constituted a **direct attack**. Very few defenses can be asserted in a collateral attack. By and large, any deficiency in the Hawaii proceedings must be asserted by appeal in Hawaii. Lack of personal jurisdiction is thus unusual because, unlike other deficiencies, it can be asserted in a direct or a collateral attack.

What You Need to Know:

1. Territorial jurisdiction refers to a court's power to compel the defendant to appear and defend the lawsuit or suffer a valid default judgment.
2. An exercise of jurisdiction must be supported by a jurisdictional basis, some kind of relationship or connection between the state and the defendant.
3. If a court of one state renders a judgment against a defendant in the absence of a jurisdictional basis, it has violated her Fourteenth Amendment right to due process of law, and the judgment will not be entitled to full faith and credit in any other state.
4. The assertion by the defendant in the second proceeding that the first court lacked personal jurisdiction is referred to as a collateral attack.

LESSON 3: ANCIENT HISTORY

The Power or "International Law Theory"

It is very difficult to understand the current Supreme Court opinions on territorial jurisdiction in the United States without knowing some history. Originally in England, the jurisdiction of a court depended on its de facto power over a defendant's person. If a court official could grab the defendant while he was in the court's territory, there was jurisdiction; otherwise not. We can refer to this theory of jurisdiction as the territorial power theory or international law model. The last term is appropriate because it describes fairly well the system of jurisdiction that applies among sovereign nation-states today.

When the English law of jurisdiction was transplanted into the new United States, the judges **treated each state, for jurisdictional purposes, as though it were an independent nation,** and so applied the territorial power theory of jurisdiction. The clearest evidence of this treatment is in the historic case of *Pennoyer v. Neff*, 95 U.S. 714 (1878).

The case arose when Mitchell sued Neff in Oregon for $300 in attorney's fees. Neff was neither domiciled in Oregon, nor was he personally served with process there. Pursuant to an Oregon statute, notice of the action was published in a local newspaper. Neff did not appear, and Mitchell took a default judgment. To satisfy the judgment, a piece of land belonging to Neff was sold at a sheriff's sale to Pennoyer. Neff later sued Pennoyer for the land. Pennoyer's right to the land depended upon the validity of the judgment in *Mitchell v. Neff*; and, therefore, upon the court's jurisdiction to render that judgment. The Oregon court lacked personal jurisdiction over Neff because he was neither domiciled in Oregon nor served with process while present in Oregon. The Supreme Court held that the Oregon court also lacked attachment jurisdiction over the land because it was not attached at the commencement of the action.

Although *Pennoyer* is no longer "good law," its conceptual basis still exerts influence on the opinions of several Supreme Court justices. Today, the important legacy of *Pennoyer* is its famous dictum:

> The several States of the Union are not, it is true, in every respect independent, many of the rights and powers which originally belonged to them being now vested in the government created by the Constitution. But, except as restrained and limited by that instrument, **they possess and exercise the authority of independent States**, and the principles of public [international] law to which we have referred are applicable to them. One of these principles is, that every State possesses exclusive jurisdiction and sovereignty over **persons and property within its territory**. . . . The other principle of public law referred to follows from the one mentioned; that is,

that no State can exercise direct jurisdiction and authority over **persons or property without its territory**.

The result of these two "principles of public law" was that **physical power** over the defendant or his property was necessary for a constitutional exercise of jurisdiction. In other words, an exercise of jurisdiction could not be sustained, no matter how close defendant's ties were with the state, unless the state had some sort of physical power. Further, physical power was **sufficient** for the constitutional exercise of jurisdiction; in other words, power would always justify the exercise of jurisdiction no matter how weak the defendant's ties with the state were.

Traditional Practice

Under this theoretical structure the Supreme Court recognized relatively few adequate jurisdictional bases. For natural persons, jurisdiction would exist if the defendant (1) were **served with process** while in the forum state (think of this as a more civilized analogue for the ancient practice of actually arresting the defendant); (2) were **domiciled** in the forum; or (3) **consented** to the jurisdiction of the forum court. For corporations, the theoretical foundation for jurisdiction was more muddled, but the practical test was clear: the defendant corporation must be "**doing business**" in the forum; that meant "carrying on activity of a systematic and continuous nature."

Modern Inadequacy

The traditional theory and practice proved hopelessly inadequate at the beginning of the twentieth century. The automobile made **interstate travel** routine, and a simple interstate automobile accident could produce a very distressing result under the traditional theory. In *Hess v. Pawloski*, 274 U.S. 352 (1927), for example, a defendant from Pennsylvania drove his car to Massachusetts, injured the plaintiff there, and returned to Pennsylvania. Traditional practice would have left the plaintiff without a remedy in Massachusetts because the defendant was not a domiciliary of Massachusetts, was not served with process in Massachusetts, and had not consented to the jurisdiction of Massachusetts. In the actual case, the Supreme Court did some creative doctrinal stretching and upheld jurisdiction, but the case illustrated the deficiency of the traditional practice.

For corporations, the problem was equally troubling. Under the traditional practice, an out-of-state corporation could send its products into the forum state and derive substantial revenue from the sales, yet not be amenable in a suit by a consumer in the state's courts. As **interstate business became more common**, and local residents sustained harm from out-of-state corporations that were not "doing business," it became obvious that a thorough overhaul of jurisdictional theory and practice was overdue.

What You Need to Know:

1. Ancient English jurisdictional theory depended on de facto power, much as it does today among independent sovereign states.
2. That system was imported in *Pennoyer v. Neff* into the United States even though it was ill-suited to explain jurisdiction among American states.
3. Under the traditional practice, jurisdiction over a natural person existed only when the defendant was personally served in the state, was domiciled in the state, or consented. For corporations, the test was "doing business," which meant "carrying on activity of a systematic and continuous nature."
4. As the automobile and modern business practices rendered traditional practice too restrictive, the Supreme Court stretched the ancient theory and practice, but the fabric had worn very thin.

LESSON 4: THREE LANDMARK CASES

Some professors spend a fair amount of time on the following three cases. Others will proceed directly to the more modern cases discussed in the next lesson. You should be guided by your teacher on the continuing importance of these three landmarks.

Minimum Contacts and Fair Play

International Shoe v. Washington, 326 U.S. 310 (1945), changed the conceptual framework of jurisdiction. It not only changed the factual test that courts apply, but also the way they think and speak about jurisdictional problems. Accordingly, it would be difficult to overstate its importance.

The defendant, a Delaware corporation with its principal place of business in Missouri, manufactured and sold shoes. It employed about a dozen salesmen who lived in Washington and solicited orders for the defendant's shoes from retailers. They transmitted the retailers' offers to purchase to the defendant's offices in St. Louis, where the offers were accepted or rejected. Defendant shipped shoes from Missouri to Washington and received payment in Missouri. Aside from the salesmen, the defendant had little connection with Washington; it did not have an office or factory in the state, nor did it maintain a stock of merchandise there.

When the state of Washington sued the defendant for failure to contribute to the state unemployment compensation fund, the company asserted that Washington lacked personal jurisdiction over it. The Supreme Court's opinion ended almost a century of reliance on physical power as the basis for jurisdiction and announced a new standard: The defendant must have **certain minimum contacts** with the state so that its exercise of jurisdiction does not offend **"traditional notions of fair play and substantial justice."**

The Crucial Ambiguity

The facts of the case fit easily under the new standard. Defendant's activities were much more than required. The *International Shoe* standard contained a crucial ambiguity. Focusing on "**minimum contacts**" suggested that there must be some physical prelitigation connection between the defendant and the forum. Focusing instead on "**fair play and substantial justice**," by contrast, indicated that prelitigation connections were not necessary as long as the exercise of jurisdiction was fair, taking into account the interests of the plaintiff, the defendant, and the forum state and the location of evidence and witnesses.

Fair Play and Substantial Justice

Rather than resolving the ambiguity, subsequent Supreme Court decisions highlighted the tension between the contacts and fairness approaches. In *McGee v. International Life Insurance Co.*, 355 U.S. 220 (1957), the Court seemed to choose the fairness interpretation and upheld California's jurisdiction over a Texas insurer. Franklin, a California resident, purchased a life insurance policy from an Arizona insurance company. The defendant later assumed that company's obligations and mailed to Franklin in California an offer to insure him upon the same terms. Franklin accepted the offer and mailed his policy premiums from California to defendant's offices in Texas. Apart from this one contact, the record revealed no other connection between defendant and California. Plaintiff, Franklin's mother (the beneficiary of the policy), claimed the death benefit after Franklin's death; but the defendant refused to pay on the ground that Franklin had committed suicide.

The plaintiff sued on the policy in California and won a default judgment when the defendant failed to appear. When the plaintiff sued the defendant in Texas to enforce the California judgment, the Texas courts refused to give full faith and credit to the California judgment on the ground that the California court lacked jurisdiction.

The Court held that California's exercise of jurisdiction was proper. There was really only one prelitigation contact between the defendant and the forum (the defendant's mailing the insurance offer to Franklin in California), but the court **relied heavily on the "fair play and substantial justice"** part of the *International Shoe* formula. It cited the difficulty that insurance consumers would face if forced to sue their insurers in a distant state and the interest of their home states in making sure that their citizens were not bilked by foreign insurers. The opinion also noted that the crucial witnesses and evidence on the defense of suicide would all be centered in California.

Contacts and "Purposeful Availment"

McGee's emphasis on fairness and its very plaintiff-favorable holding led many to believe that the federal constitutional limits on state-court jurisdiction were becoming increasingly minimal. The Court, however, proved them wrong in *Hanson v. Denkla*, 357 U.S. 235 (1958), decided only a few months after *McGee.*

In *Hanson*, Mrs. Donner, a Pennsylvania domiciliary, created a $400,000 trust in Delaware, naming a Delaware trustee, and directing that the income be paid to her during her life with the remainder to go to whomever she named in her last power of appointment. She then moved to Florida and executed her will and the power of appointment. The will split about one million dollars of her property between two of her daughters, and she exercised the power of appointment over the $400,000 trust in favor of the children of the third daughter. The result was a relatively even three-way split of her property among her daughters.

After Mrs. Donner's death, the two greedy daughters (think Cinderella's sisters) who were named in the will brought suit in Florida against the third daughter (Cindeigh, herself) and the Delaware trustee, seeking a declaration that the power of appointment was invalid and that they, instead of their sister, were entitled to the assets in the trust. Florida law made the Delaware trustee an indispensable party, and the Florida courts ruled (1) that there was jurisdiction over the trustee and (2) the greedy sisters were correct in their attack on the power of appointment. The result was that nearly all of Mrs. Donner's estate, including the $400,000 trust fund, went to the two greedy daughters.

The Supreme Court held that the Florida courts lacked jurisdiction over the Delaware trustee with the result that Mrs. Donner's estate passed in equal thirds to her three daughters. The Delaware trustee had had some contact with Florida during the eight years Mrs. Donner lived in Florida, almost as much as the Texas insurer in McGee had with California, and so the Supreme Court tried hard to distinguish the two cases.

In retrospect, however, it has become clear that a difference in jurisdictional theory rather than a factual distinction explains the results in the two cases. While fairness, convenience, and state interests preoccupied the *McGee* court, the *Hanson* court cared only about the prelitigation connections between Florida and the trustee. It summarized its approach in a sentence that has become almost as influential as the formula of *International Shoe*: "it is essential in each case that **there be some act by which the defendant purposely avails itself of the privilege of conducting activities in the forum State**, thus invoking the benefits and protection of its laws." That sentence rather than *McGee's* fairness approach has proved much more consistent with the court's later jurisdictional holdings.

What You Need to Know:

1. *International Shoe* expanded the permissible scope of jurisdiction based on contacts with the forum state and notions of fairness.
2. The *Shoe* test contained a crucial ambiguity: Does it require actual prelitigation connections between the defendant and the state; or is it enough that the exercise of jurisdiction will not be unfair?
3. In two subsequent cases, *McGee v. Int'l Life Ins.* and *Hanson v. Denckla*, the Court decided two cases within four months: one favoring the fairness interpretation; the other, the contacts interpretation.
4. In the second, *Hanson*, the court announced a formula that has proved nearly as crucial as the *Shoe* test: The Purposeful Availment Test: "There must be some act by which the defendant purposefully avails itself of the privilege of conducting activities within the forum state, thus invoking the benefits and protections of its laws."

LESSON 5: THE CURRENT TWO-PART TEST

The Supreme Court waited almost 30 years to clarify the ambiguity generated by its holdings in *International Shoe, McGee and Hanson*. In *World-Wide Volkswagen v. Woodson*, 444 U.S. 286 (1980), and subsequent cases, the Court established **a two-part test** requiring an assessment of both minimum contacts and fair play and substantial justice. In order to assert jurisdiction, the defendant must have **purposefully directed its activities** toward the forum state. Exercise of jurisdiction must also be **fair or reasonable**, taking into account:

1. The burden on the defendant.
2. The forum state's interest in adjudicating the dispute.
3. The plaintiff's interest in convenient and effective relief.
4. The interstate judicial system's interest in obtaining the most efficient resolution of controversies.
5. The shared interest of the several states in furthering fundamental substantive social policies.

The content of these two tests will be explored in subsequent lessons, but now it makes sense to ask about the **constitutional source** of the requirements. The Court has always held that the requirements are based on the **Due Process Clauses** of the Fifth and Fourteenth Amendments. It has toyed with and rejected two other constitutional justifications.

In *World-Wide Volkswagen* (facts discussed in Lesson 7), the court stated that fairness to the defendant is not the only reason for the minimum-contacts test. The requirement is also justified by "**principles of interstate federalism** embodied in the Constitution." In the Court's words:

> The concept of minimum contacts perform[s] two related, but distinguishable, functions. It protects the defendant against the burdens of litigating in a distant

> or inconvenient forum. And it acts to ensure that the States, through their courts, do not reach out beyond the limits imposed on them by their status as coequal sovereigns in a federal system.

The passage means that the **relationship of the states *to each other*** (as constituent sovereigns in a federation) places a limit on their adjudicatory jurisdiction that is separate and distinct from any restriction based on fairness to the defendant. In other words, even if the forum's exercise of jurisdiction causes no unfairness to the defendant, it may yet be unconstitutional because of its infringement upon the sovereignty of the other states. Harking back to the territorial theory (discussed in Lesson 3), the Court stated that "the Framers . . . intended that the States retain many essential attributes of sovereignty. . . . The sovereignty of each State, in turn, implied a limitation on the sovereignty of all of its sister States."

The Court's reliance on reasoning of this sort was puzzling. If the restrictions on jurisdiction were based not only on fairness to the defendant but also on the rights of other states, **how could the defendant waive a jurisdictional objection**? Certainly, individuals cannot waive the rights of states. The problem of waiver surfaced quickly and caused the Supreme Court to abandon decisively its reliance on "interstate federalism" as a source of the constitutional limitations on jurisdiction.

In *Insurance Corp. of Ireland v. Compagnie Des Bauxites De Guinee*, 456 U.S. 694 (1982), the defendants objected to the exercise of personal jurisdiction by a United States District Court, and the plaintiff attempted to use discovery to establish defendants' minimum contacts. The defendants refused to comply with the court's discovery orders, and the Supreme Court held that their refusal constituted a waiver of their jurisdictional objections. The Court **abandoned its reliance on interstate federalism** as a foundation for the minimum contracts requirement, focusing exclusively instead on defendant's liberty interest.

The personal jurisdiction requirement recognizes and protects an individual liberty interest. It represents a restriction on judicial power not as a matter of sovereignty, but as a matter of individual liberty. It is **the only source** of the personal jurisdiction requirement and the clause itself makes no mention of federalism concerns.

Only one other constitutional source for the personal jurisdiction requirement has gained any serious attention. Some courts had held that one reason for the requirement was the **First Amendment** (free press) concern that publishers would be deterred from sending their newspapers and magazines to distant states by the prospect of being held amenable to jurisdiction far from home (needless to say, the Internet had not yet been invented by Al Gore or anyone else).

The Supreme Court emphatically rejected that argument in *Calder v. Jones*, 486 U.S. 783 (1984). Shirley Jones (of the Partridge family; Florence Henderson, by contrast, was the lead in the *Brady Bunch*) brought suit in California based on a defamatory article in the *National Enquirer*. They said she was a drunk. There was no question that the *Enquirer* was amenable to jurisdiction in California; that state was its largest market. But Jones also had sued the author and the editor of the article, and they had little contact with California other than their role in producing the offending article. **The Court rejected their contention** that exercising jurisdiction over them would violate the **First Amendment.** For one thing, consideration of First Amendment concerns would "needlessly complicate an already imprecise inquiry." And, for another, the possible chilling effect of defamation actions on protected speech is taken into account already in the elaboration of the constitutional limits on the states' substantive law of libel and slander. "To reintroduce those concerns at the jurisdictional stage would be a form of double counting."

What You Need to Know:

1. In *World-Wide Volkswagen v. Woodson*, the Court established a two-part test for the constitutionality of a state court's exercise of personal jurisdiction. *First*, the defendant must have purposefully established prelitigation connections with the forum state. *Second*, it must

be fair or reasonable to exercise jurisdiction over the defendant.

2. The Court also made it clear that the Due Process Clauses of the Fifth and Fourteenth Amendments are the only source of the personal jurisdiction requirement. The requirement is not based on federalism or the relationship of the states to each other.

3. The personal jurisdiction requirement also is not grounded in First Amendment concerns about deterring publishers from wide dissemination of their magazines and newspapers.

LESSON 6: MEASURING CONTACTS: GENERAL AND SPECIFIC JURISDICTION

In *Helicopteros Nacionale de Colombia v. Hall* (*Helicol*), 466 U.S. 408 (1984), the Supreme Court adopted the distinction between **general jurisdiction** and **specific jurisdiction** as a device for dealing with the "contacts" step of the contacts-plus-fairness test from *International Shoe.*

The distinction between general and specific jurisdiction involves considering (1) the extent of the defendant's contacts with the forum and (2) the relationship between the forum and the events giving rise to the plaintiff's claim. **General jurisdiction** exists when the defendant's contacts with the forum are so extensive that the forum can exercise jurisdiction over the defendant based on any claim, even one that has no relationship with the forum.

Specific jurisdiction exists when the defendant has only minimal connections to the forum, so that the forum can exercise jurisdiction over her only in cases based on claims that are closely related to the forum state. Thus, a defendant will be subject to specific jurisdiction based on a collision in the forum state, even if the collision is the defendant's only contact with that state.

The distinction is difficult, so some examples will help. Each of the following cases involves a lawsuit between the plaintiff (A), domiciled in Ohio, and the defendant (B), domiciled in Hawaii.

A v. B based on an accident in Ohio:

An Ohio court will have specific jurisdiction over B because the accident occurred in Ohio; it will not have general jurisdiction over B because he is domiciled in Hawaii, not Ohio.

A v. B based on an accident in Ohio:

A Hawaii court will have general jurisdiction over B because he is domiciled in Hawaii; it will not have specific jurisdiction over B because the accident occurred in Ohio, not Hawaii.

A v. B based on an accident in Hawaii:

A Hawaii court will have general jurisdiction over B because he is domiciled in Hawaii; it will also have specific jurisdiction because the accident occurred in Hawaii.

A v. B based on an accident in Hawaii:

An Ohio court will have neither general nor specific jurisdiction over B because he is domiciled in Hawaii, and the accident did not occur in Ohio.

General Jurisdiction

The next three lessons treat the constitutional law of specific jurisdiction in some detail, but there is not as much to say about general jurisdiction. It applies in a few clear cases. Defendant's domicile in the forum state is the classic example. Thus, if the defendant **is domiciled** in Ohio, the plaintiff can sue her there even though the events giving rise to the plaintiff's claim (say, a traffic accident) occurred in Hawaii. Large commercial entities that have significant presence in lots of places (think Golden Arches) are other examples; they may be amenable to general jurisdiction wherever they conduct business of a systematic and continuous nature.

Beyond these clear cases, the Court has been **reluctant to find general jurisdiction**; the only case where it was upheld is *Perkins v. Benguet Consol. Mining Co.*, 342 U.S. 437 (1952).

Benguet, a Philippine corporation, operated "in exile" in Ohio during Japanese occupation of the islands. Benguet's president and chief stockholder lived in Ohio, where he kept corporate funds, drew and distributed salary checks, and generally conducted all of the corporation's activities. Plaintiff's claim arose out of the defendant's prewar operations in the Philippines, so Ohio did not have specific jurisdiction. Nevertheless, the Supreme Court upheld the exercise of jurisdiction; Ohio, at least for the war's duration, was Benguet's home, so it could exercise general jurisdiction.

In the two other cases it has decided, the Court has refused to uphold general jurisdiction. In *Helicopteros Nacionale de Colombia v. Hall* (*Helicol*), 466 U.S. 408 (1984), the plaintiffs were the survivors of a crash of one of the defendant's helicopters in South America. They sued in Texas because the defendant had bought its helicopter fleet and spare parts there and had its pilots trained there, as well. The defendant also had sent its president to Texas to negotiate the transport contract that the defendant was performing when the crash occurred. Despite those connections, the Court found the defendant's contacts with Texas to be insufficiently continuous and systematic to support the exercise of general jurisdiction.

Goodyear Dunlop Tire Operations, S.A. v. Brown, 131 S. Ct. 2846 (2011), presented weaker facts for general jurisdiction. The plaintiffs, parents of two boys killed in a bus accident in France, sued Goodyear and two of its foreign subsidiaries in North Carolina. They claimed that tires, manufactured abroad by one of the subsidiaries, had failed and caused the crash. Clearly there was jurisdiction over Goodyear, but the Court found that the subsidiaries were not amenable to general jurisdiction in North Carolina. They conducted no activities there; their only connection with the state consisted of the distribution of a small number of their tires (not the same type that allegedly caused the crash) by other affiliates of Goodyear. The Court concluded that the subsidiaries' activities were not sufficiently continuous and systematic to warrant the inference that the subsidiaries could be "**fairly regarded as at home**" in the forum. The "at-home" test suggests that the Court will rarely if ever permit an exercise of general jurisdiction over a nondomiciliary defendant.

The "Hybrid Case?"

There is little possibility after *Helicopteros* and *Goodyear* that the Court will expand its rigorous standard for general jurisdiction. There is, however, another type of case where the Supreme Court *may* be more generous. Such cases do not fit the paradigms of either general or specific jurisdiction but are a near miss on both. Suppose, for instance, the defendant, a long-distance trucker, domiciled in New York, regularly hauls goods back and forth between New York and California. On one trip, while heading toward California, the defendant collides with the plaintiff, a Californian, in Nevada, one mile east of the California border. The plaintiff sues the defendant in California. California will not have general jurisdiction over the defendant because he is not domiciled in California, and it will not have specific jurisdiction because the collision occurred in Nevada. But should there be jurisdiction anyway? Though not domiciled in California, the defendant regularly conducts business there. Moreover, the collision, although it did not occur in California, occurred only one mile from the border, and California was defendant's ultimate destination. The Supreme Court has not ruled on such a case, so the likely result is still unclear.

What You Need to Know:

1. The Supreme Court has adopted the distinction between general and specific jurisdiction as a device for measuring contacts in the first stage of the two-part, contacts-plus-fairness analysis.
2. General jurisdiction permits the court to exercise jurisdiction over the defendant based on any claim, even one completely unrelated to the forum. General jurisdiction exists only when the defendant has maximal connections with the state; domicile is the classic example.
3. A court can exercise specific jurisdiction over a defendant based on very few contacts, but the

cause of action must be closely related to the state (*e.g.*, an auto accident on the state's roads).

4. Beyond domicile, the Court has adopted a very rigorous standard for general jurisdiction. It will exist only in cases where the defendant's activities are sufficiently systematic and continuous to warrant the inference that the defendant could be "fairly regarded as at home" in the forum.

LESSON 7: MEASURING CONTACTS FOR SPECIFIC JURISDICTION

A common arrangement in our economy is the chain of distribution from component part manufacturer to complete product manufacturer to importer to distributor to wholesaler to retailer to consumer. **What happens when the consumer purchases the product in her domicile, it injures her, and she sues there?** Which of the entities in the chain will be amenable to personal jurisdiction in the forum of the plaintiff's choice? The question turns out to be important because the plaintiff will want to find the deepest pocket. Usually, but not always, the pockets get deeper as you go up the chain.

The Supreme Court has dealt with the problem in three major cases and struggled to produce a clear **stream-of-commerce rule**. In *World-Wide Volkswagen v. Woodson*, 444 U.S. 286 (1980), the plaintiffs had purchased an Audi from Seaway Volkswagen in upstate New York; the car had been manufactured by Audi, imported by Volkswagen of America (Volkswagen), and distributed by World-Wide Volkswagen. Seaway did business only in New York, and World-Wide only in New York, New Jersey, and Connecticut, while both Audi and Volkswagen had nationwide sales. The plaintiffs left New York to establish a home in Arizona. On the way, in Oklahoma, another car struck the plaintiffs' from the rear; their car caught fire, and one of the plaintiffs was severely injured. The plaintiffs brought a products liability action in Oklahoma against all four defendants. Eventually Audi and Volkswagen conceded that they were amenable, so by the time the case reached the Supreme Court the only question was jurisdiction over World-Wide and Seaway.

The Court held that Seaway and World-Wide had essentially no contact with Oklahoma; neither made any sales there either directly or indirectly (through a chain of distribution). Neither defendant advertised, solicited, or carried on any other activity in Oklahoma. Oklahoma could not base jurisdiction "on one, isolated occurrence, the fortuitous circumstance that a single Audi automobile, sold in New York to New York residents, happened to suffer an accident while passing through Oklahoma."

On the way to its holding, the Court adopted **one form of the stream-of-commerce test**. The rule was that a state may exercise jurisdiction over everyone in the chain of distribution if the product was purchased within the state; but that jurisdiction will not necessarily exist when the purchase occurred outside the forum, and the foreseeable action of a consumer brought the product into the state. According to this standard, there was no jurisdiction over Seaway and World-Wide. The chain of distribution of which they were a part ended with the retail sale in New York. Only the independent action of the plaintiff/consumer took the product to Oklahoma.

The Court next considered the stream-of-commerce problem in *Asahi v. Superior Court*, 480 U.S. 102 (1987), and left more questions than it answered. The consumer was injured and his wife killed in a motorcycle accident in California. Alleging that a defective tire valve caused a sudden deflation of the tire, which in turn caused the collision, the consumer brought a product liability claim in California against Cheng Shin, the Taiwanese manufacturer of the tire, who then sought indemnification (via impleader) from Asahi, the Japanese manufacturer of the valve. Cheng Shin settled with the consumer, leaving only the indemnification claim by Cheng Shin, the maker of the tire, against Asahi, the maker of the valve. Asahi moved to quash service, arguing that California lacked personal jurisdiction over it.

The Supreme Court held that the California courts lacked jurisdiction because the case failed the reasonableness step of the two-stage *International Shoe* test, which we will discuss in Lesson 9. The focus now is on the contacts step of the analysis.

The Supreme Court produced a confusing set of three opinions and no majority holding on the stream-of-commerce question.

Justice O'Connor, writing for four justices, concluded that Asahi's mere act of **putting its valve in the stream of commerce,** which then took it to California, where it injured the consumer, was **not enough** to satisfy the contacts requirement of *International Shoe*. She argued that jurisdiction should not exist without **additional contacts**; if the manufacturer had designed the product for the forum's market, or advertised it there, or took some other step *targeted at* the forum, jurisdiction might exist, but merely putting the product into the stream of commerce was not enough.

Justice Brennan, heading another group of four, argued that O'Connor's additional contacts were not required; putting the product into the stream of commerce was enough.

Justice Stevens refused to join either group of four. Thus, the case produced **no majority holding** on the stream-of-commerce test.

Twenty-five years later in *J. McIntyre Machinery, Ltd. v. Nicastro,* 131 S. Ct. 2780 (2011), the Supreme Court again addressed the issue. A New Jersey plaintiff seriously injured his hand in New Jersey while using a metal-shearing machine manufactured by the defendant in England. The defendant had very limited contacts with New Jersey and the United States as a whole. It sold none of its products directly in the United States, using instead an independent American distributor.

Once again the Court was unable to reach consensus on the stream of commerce. Attracting four votes, Justice Kennedy's opinion took the position that **mere placement of a product in the stream of commerce**, which then carried it into the forum, was **not enough**. The opinion reverted to a strongly territorial view of personal jurisdiction, relying heavily on the concept of the defendant's "submission" to the forum's sovereignty. Simply placing the product into the stream of commerce with the expectation that the stream might end in the forum was not sufficient to infer that submission.

Justice Ginsburg's dissenting opinion, in which two of her colleagues joined, favored a return to the unmodified stream-of-commerce test of *World-Wide Volkswagen v. Woodson*, and would have upheld jurisdiction. Justice Breyer, joined by Justice Alito, rejected both Justice Kennedy's and Justice Ginsburg's views. While unwilling to propound a universal rule, he did suggest a pared-down version of the *World-Wide* test. It would produce jurisdiction over a manufacturer if the stream of commerce took its product into the state as part of a regular flow, or the manufacturer established one or more of the additional connections that Justice O'Connor described in her plurality opinion in *Asahi v. Superior Court*: designing the product for the state's market, advertising there, or creating customer advice services in the forum.

Although the Court did not produce a majority opinion, it did produce **a new version of the stream-of-commerce test**. There are now five votes on the current Court for jurisdiction in a stream-of-commerce case where either: (1) the stream consists of a **regular flow** of the defendant's products into the state or (2) the defendant's conduct includes one of the **"something more" factors** laid out in Justice O'Connor's plurality opinion in *Asahi*. Whether that five-vote coalition will hold together in the Supreme Court's next shot at the stream-of-commerce theory, however, is anybody's guess.

What You Need to Know:

1. The stream-of-commerce test was designed to deal with jurisdiction in products liability cases where multiple defendants form a chain of distribution that takes the product into the forum, where the consumer purchases it.
2. The most expansive version of the test would require no more than mere placement of the product into the stream to establish jurisdiction over all commercial actors who formed the links in the chain of distribution.
3. Even under that expansive view, jurisdiction would not exist where the chain of distribution ends outside the forum and the foreseeable action of a consumer brings the product into the state.

4. Several more restrictive versions have been put forward, but the only one likely to garner five votes on the current Court would require placement of the product into the stream and one of the following:
   a. The stream of commerce that took the product into the state was part of a regular flow of the defendant's products into the state, or
   b. The defendant did more than merely place the product into the stream, *i.e.*, it designed the product specifically for the forum state, advertised it there, or established customer advice services there.

LESSON 8: ADDITIONAL CONTACT-EVALUATION THEMES

The stream-of-commerce concept is not the only device that the Supreme Court uses in measuring contacts to meet the contacts portion of the two-step, contacts-plus-fairness test for the constitutionality of an exercise of personal jurisdiction. This lesson considers a few other devices.

Foreseeability ought to be relevant in measuring contacts. If the defendant could not have foreseen that her activities would cause injury in the forum state, she ought not be compelled to defend there. In *World-Wide Volkswagen v. Woodson*, 444 U.S. 286 (1980), the Court made it clear that foreseeability that defendant's activities might cause harm in the forum is not, however, *sufficient* for jurisdiction. The defendants sold a car in New York, which later caused an injury in Oklahoma. The plaintiffs argued that the inherently mobile nature of the product made it foreseeable that, at some point, one of the defendant's cars would pass through Oklahoma and, perhaps, cause injury there. The Court agreed but held that mere foreseeability of injury in the forum was not sufficient to pass the "minimum-contacts" test. Rather the test requires that the defendant purposefully establish some prelitigation connection with the forum.

Although *World-Wide* held that foreseeability is not a sufficient condition for jurisdiction, it did indicate that foreseeability is a relevant concept. The Court said that the foreseeability that is crucial is the defendant's anticipation (given its forum-related activity) that it could be "haled into court" in the forum. In other words, a defendant is amenable to jurisdiction in the forum if it could foresee being amenable to jurisdiction in the forum. That dictum is, of course, a piece of circular reasoning, and it is hard to foresee how it could be helpful either to lower courts or potential defendants. Nevertheless, it has been repeated by the Court and by lower courts, as well.

Who Went to Whom?

If the defendant goes to plaintiff's home state and seeks her business, he ought to be amenable to jurisdiction there. If, instead, the plaintiff initiates the contact, the defendant ought not be amenable to jurisdiction in the plaintiff's home state. The test has figured prominently in some state-court decisions. In *Conn v. Whitmore*, 342 P.2d 871 (1959), the plaintiff, a resident of Illinois, who raised and sold Arabian horses, mailed to the defendant in Utah a list of horses for sale. The defendant purchased a horse, and a dispute developed over its condition. Plaintiff recovered a default judgment against defendant in Illinois, but the Utah court denied that judgment full faith and credit on the ground that the Illinois court lacked jurisdiction over defendant. Said the court: "It is important to bear in mind that it was not the defendant Utah resident who took the initiative by going into Illinois to transact business. Quite the contrary, it was the plaintiff resident of Illinois who proselyted for business in Utah."

Whose Contacts?

The Court has been emphatic that the contacts that count are those of the defendant, not plaintiff or a third party. In *Keeton v. Hustler Magazine*, 465 U.S. 770 (1984), the defendant defamed the plaintiff in a nationally published magazine. The plaintiff sued the defendant in New Hampshire because it was the only state in which the statute of limitations had not yet run. The defendant regularly shipped substantial numbers of its magazine to New Hampshire, but it argued that there should be no jurisdiction because the *plaintiff* had no contact with the state. The Court rejected the argument: "[W]e have not to date required a plaintiff to have 'minimum contacts' with the forum . . . On the contrary, we have upheld jurisdiction where such contacts were entirely lacking." Nor are the forum's contacts with a third party relevant. In *Hanson v. Denckla*, 357 U.S. 235 (1958), a resident of Pennsylvania set up a trust, using a Delaware bank as the trustee. Later she moved to Florida, continuing to have regular dealings with the Delaware trustee. The Court held Florida could not exercise personal jurisdiction over the trustee, explaining that "[t]he unilateral activity of those who claim some relationship with a non-defendant cannot satisfy the requirement of contact with the forum State."

Contract Cases

Most of the Supreme Court's jurisdiction cases have involved torts, not contracts. All other things being equal, however, jurisdiction should be easier in contract than in tort cases. Torts are by their nature unplanned events; no one plans to have an auto accident. Contracts, by contrast, are entered into deliberately, presumably with some thought that litigation might ensue.

The Court made the matter clear in *Burger King v. Rudzewisz*, 471 U.S. 462 (1985). There, the defendant and an associate sought to open a Burger King restaurant in Michigan. They applied to Burger King's Michigan district office, which forwarded the application to headquarters in Miami, Florida. After considerable negotiation with headquarters and with the district office, the defendant and Burger King signed a franchise contract that set up a 20-year relationship during which the defendant agreed to pay $1 million in franchise fees, rent, and advertising and promotional fees and to submit to Burger King's regulation of many facets of the restaurant's operation. When the restaurant failed and the defendant stopped making the franchise payments, Burger King sued him in Miami. The defendant argued that his was a local business and that its size and scope made him unable to defend a lawsuit in a distant forum. The Court rejected the argument, holding that the defendant "had eschewed the option of establishing a local independent restaurant and reached out beyond Michigan to negotiate with a Florida franchisor in hopes of securing the benefits of affiliating with a nationwide organization." His purposeful establishment of that connection to Florida was enough to satisfy the minimum-contacts test.

What You Need to Know:

1. The foreseeability that the defendant's products might enter the forum state and cause harm there is not sufficient to satisfy the minimum-contacts test.
2. Courts are more willing to find jurisdiction in the plaintiff's home forum when the defendant has initiated the contact with the plaintiff than when the plaintiff has initiated the contact with the defendant.
3. The contacts that matter are those that the defendant has purposefully established with the forum. Contacts between the defendant and the forum that have been caused by the activities of third parties do not count.
4. There is no requirement that the plaintiff have minimum contacts with the forum.
5. All other things being equal, a finding of jurisdiction in contract cases is more likely than in tort cases.

LESSON 9: THE SECOND STEP: FAIRNESS OR REASONABLENESS

Since *World-Wide Volkswagen v. Woodson*, the Supreme Court has adopted the two-part, contacts-plus-fairness test for assessing the constitutionality of an exercise of personal jurisdiction under the Due Process Clause. Although the Court has based many holdings on the contacts step, **only one case has turned on the assessment of fairness**: *Asahi Metal Indus. Ltd. v. Superior Court*, 480 U.S. 102 (1987).

While riding his motorcycle in California, Zurcher lost control of the bike because a tire valve failed and caused the sudden deflation of a tire. Zurcher was injured, and his wife was killed. Zurcher brought a product liability claim in California against Cheng Shin, the Taiwanese manufacturer of the tire tube, who then sought indemnification by impleading Asahi, the Japanese manufacturer of the tube's valve. Before the case reached the Supreme Court, Zurcher's claim against Cheng Shin settled, leaving only Cheng Shin's indemnity claim against Asahi.

The Court was unable to reach a majority holding on the contacts issue (see Lesson 7), but the justices agreed that the case failed the fairness portion of the analysis. Justice O'Connor's opinion first enumerated the **five fairness factors**:

1. The burden on the defendant.
2. The forum state's interest in adjudicating the dispute.
3. The plaintiff's interest in convenient and effective relief.
4. The interstate judicial system's interest in obtaining the most efficient resolution of controversies.
5. The shared interest of the several states in furthering fundamental substantive social policies.

According to the Court, the burden on the defendant is "always a primary concern." In *Asahi*, the Court concluded that the "unique burdens" on the **alien defendant** "should have significant weight in assessing the reasonableness of extending personal jurisdiction over national borders."

The Court paid close attention to **the forum state's interests** in *Asahi*. Among the most important of these is the state's interest in providing a forum for its residents to pursue claims against outsiders. Occasionally, the Court has been willing to take account of less pressing interests, such as the state's interest in providing a forum for a non-resident plaintiff injured in the forum. On the other hand, the Court has ignored or discounted some fairly important state interests. For instance, it minimized the forum state's interest in deterring foreign manufacturers from sending defective products or component parts into the forum, as well as the forum's interest in monitoring the affairs of corporations incorporated in the forum. The Court has offered no general principle to explain its seemingly divergent views of the importance of state interests.

The Court assigned relatively little weight to Cheng Shin's (the third party **plaintiff) interests** in securing effective and convenient relief when doing so would mean asserting jurisdiction over an out-of-state insurer. The Court has indicated elsewhere that it might be more sympathetic "when no other forum is available to a plaintiff." Don't take this to the bank. In other cases, the plaintiff's dire necessity was not been enough to make up for a perceived insufficiency of contacts. Moreover, if a plaintiff has access to a ready and convenient alternative forum, then this can count against asserting jurisdiction over a foreign party with relatively few contacts to the host forum.

Neither the Supreme Court nor the lower courts have done much with the **interstate judicial system's interests** in obtaining the most efficient resolution of controversies. Presumably, the proximity of the forum to witnesses, physical evidence, and other forms of proof should matter. Choice of law should be an issue also, with the need for the forum to apply difficult and unfamiliar law counting against jurisdiction. A final concern should be the court's ability to exercise jurisdiction over all parties and all issues in a dispute.

The **shared interests of the states** in substantive social policies have also carried little weight in most jurisdiction cases. It has played a role, however, in cases where the defendant is a foreign entity, such as Asahi. In these cases, the Court has showed concern for national interest in foreign trade and foreign relations.

What You Need to Know:

1. The second part of the Court's two-part test requires measurement of the overall "fairness" of an exercise of jurisdiction.
2. The Court has based only one holding on this step.

3. The factors to be considered are:
   a. The burden on the defendant.
   b. The forum state's interest in adjudicating the dispute.
   c. The plaintiff's interest in convenient and effective relief.
   d. The interstate judicial system's interest in obtaining the most efficient resolution of controversies.
   e. The shared interest of the several states in furthering fundamental substantive social policies.
4. The Court seems to take the defendant's (particularly, alien defendants') inconvenience very seriously, but is not much concerned with whether the plaintiff has an alternative forum.
5. Access to witnesses and other sources of proof may matter at the margins.
6. The Court's discussions of state interests seem conclusory and result-driven.
7. Occasionally the Court mentions the nation's interest in foreign trade and foreign relations.

LESSON 10: STATE-LAW BASES FOR JURISDICTION

The **Due Process Clause** determines the federal constitutional limit on state-court jurisdiction, but it does not and could not *authorize* any state court to exercise jurisdiction. Only state law can do that.

Traditionally the state law that performed that function was judge-made and consisted of the traditional bases for personal jurisdiction for natural persons (service while present, domicile and consent) and corporations (incorporation in the forum and "doing business" in the forum).

The Traditional Bases

Service of Process while the party is present in the state is the oldest and most traditional basis for personal jurisdiction. Personal service gives notice no matter where accomplished, but it serves as a jurisdictional basis only if it is accomplished within the state. Thus, service from a California court upon a New York defendant vacationing in Mexico gives perfectly adequate notice, but it may not be used as a jurisdictional basis; to perform that function, service must be accomplished in California. Service of process within the state gives general jurisdiction over any claim against the defendant regardless of whether it is related to the time, place, or purpose of the defendant's in-state presence.

After *International Shoe* made personal jurisdiction depend on contacts and fairness, some scholars and courts began to doubt the **continued constitutionality of jurisdiction based only on service of process** within the state: in other words, without any calculation of contacts or fairness. In *Burnham v. Superior Court*, 495 U.S. 604 (1990), the Supreme Court upheld the constitutionality of the practice. Some justices relied purely on the practice's traditional acceptance, while others insisted that the practice passed the *International Shoe* test. While the justices could not agree on the reasons for the constitutionality of jurisdiction based on personal service, they agreed unanimously on the practice's continuing validity.

Long before *International Shoe*, **domicile** in the forum state has been considered an adequate basis for personal jurisdiction. Like service, it is a basis for general jurisdiction; the claim asserted against the resident defendant need not have any connection to the state. No one questions the constitutionality of the practice. How could it be unfair to sue the defendant in her own home state?

If the defendant makes a **general appearance** in the forum and agrees to litigate there, the appearance is an after-the-fact consent to the forum state's jurisdiction. But what if the defendant wants to contest jurisdiction? How could a defendant move to dismiss for lack of jurisdiction without first making an appearance, which would constitute consent? The answer to this conundrum was the **special appearance**, which permitted the defendant to appear for the purpose of contesting jurisdiction only, without consenting to the court's personal jurisdiction.

But consent can occur also before the commencement of the lawsuit. Usually this occurs when the defendant has signed a contract with a **consent-to-jurisdiction clause**. These clauses commonly are inserted into form contracts, which are signed by consumers and others, who have not read the clause, did not realize it was in the contract, and have no idea what it means. Nevertheless, the Supreme Court has repeatedly upheld the practice as a constitutionally adequate basis for personal jurisdiction.

Long-arm Statutes

Although the Due Process Clause determines the constitutional limit on state-court jurisdiction, it does not and could not *authorize* any state court to exercise jurisdiction. Only state law can do that. If there is no traditional basis for jurisdiction, the plaintiff therefore must rely on a "long-arm" statute, which is found on the books in every state. Long-arm statutes take two forms:

The **California-Style** statute authorizes state courts to exercise jurisdiction all the way to the limits imposed by the Due Process Clause. Often it will say that "a court of this state may exercise jurisdiction over any defendant as long as the exercise of jurisdiction is not inconsistent with the constitution of this state or the United States."

An **Enumerated Act** statute provides much more guidance for the state's courts. Typically, such a statute will authorize the state's courts to exercise jurisdiction only over defendants who perform one of several enumerated acts. Long-arm jurisdiction is specific jurisdiction; it is limited to claims that arise out of the defendant's performance of the particular enumerated act. The typical enumerated acts are:

1. **Transacting business within the state.** This section can be satisfied by a single transaction,

and the defendant need not physically enter the state.

2. **Contracting to supply goods or services in the state.** The important point here is that the contract need not be *executed* in the state. The requirement is that the goods or services be destined for the state.

3. **Causing tortious injury in the state by an act or omission in the state.** These provisions, sometimes referred to as "local-act-local-injury" clauses, are the descendants of the old "nonresident motorist statutes," and their function is to reach a defendant who enters the state, causes injury there, and leaves before he can be served with process.

4. **Causing tortious injury in this state by an act or omission outside the state.** These provisions, sometimes called "foreign-act-local-injury" clauses are responsible for most of the notorious personal jurisdiction cases. They reach, for example the stream-of-commerce cases and cases where a nonresident publisher sends defamatory material into the state. Because they are so far-reaching, they could easily produce unconstitutional results. To avoid that outcome these provisions almost always contain clauses requiring **additional affiliations** between the defendant and the forum, such as requiring that the defendant regularly conduct some activity within the state or that the defendant derive substantial revenue from goods used or consumed within the state. Most of the cases that have resulted in Supreme Court litigation fit this pattern. You may wish to review them in Lessons 5 and 6 to see that this is so.

What You Need to Know:

1. The Due Process Clause acts only to limit state-court jurisdiction. It cannot act affirmatively to

authorize a state court to exercise jurisdiction. Only state law can do that.

2. Every state recognizes the traditional bases for jurisdiction (service of process while present within the state, domicile, and consent), and the Supreme Court has upheld their constitutionality.
3. In addition, every state has a long-arm statute, which is required to authorize its courts to exercise jurisdiction over defendants who do not fit into one of the traditional bases.
4. California-style statutes permit the exercise of jurisdiction as long as it does not violate state or federal constitutional law. Enumerated Act statutes authorize jurisdiction over defendants who perform one or more of the acts enumerated in the statutes.

LESSON 11: JURISDICTION AND THE INTERNET

Beginning at the turn of the twentieth century, the automobile and the increasing use of chains of distribution stressed the territorial power theory (see Lesson 3) because they minimized distances and nationalized commerce. Similarly, at the beginning of the twenty-first century, the Internet is stressing current jurisdictional theory because it has made state and national boundaries increasingly irrelevant.

Easy Cases

Nevertheless, many Internet cases fit easily within current jurisdiction theory. **E-mail**, for example, is no more problematic than ordinary ("snail") mail or the telephone because the sender is aware of and can limit the geographical target of the message. Although that is not true for cases based on the **World Wide Web**, current doctrine is still adequate for many cases involving websites. In breach of contract and product liability cases, there usually will be contacts between the defendant and the forum beyond defendant's mere construction of a web page that can be accessed in the forum.

Typically, there will be individual negotiations between the plaintiff and the defendant and often the delivery of a product or a service into the forum. While such cases will not always support jurisdiction, the extra contacts make them relatively easy to analyze under current theory.

Even less problematic for current jurisdictional doctrine are assertions of general jurisdiction. **Maintenance of a website** that can be accessed by users in the forum should not render the defendant amenable to general jurisdiction there. Not surprisingly, the few cases that have faced the issue have agreed. In *Weber v. Jolly Hotels*, 977 F. Supp. 327 (D. N.J. 1997), for example, a federal court in New Jersey refused to exercise jurisdiction over an Italian hotel that maintained a website that could be accessed in New Jersey because the plaintiff's claim involved an injury in Italy, not New Jersey, and because the plaintiff's arrangements to visit Italy had nothing to do with the website.

Harder Cases

Cases of specific jurisdiction, where the web page is the defendant's only forum connection, are more difficult. These cases often involve a tort theory or one concerning intellectual property. A very typical fact pattern involves a defendant that has chosen an Internet domain name that allegedly violates the plaintiff's trade name or service mark. Another common case occurs when a defendant defames the plaintiff on his website without knowing the plaintiff's location or even her existence. For instance, the defendant's website might assert that her business is the only one (or perhaps oldest or top-ranked one) that offers a particular service or product.

The clear answer to the question is that the defendant's maintenance of a website accessible from the forum state is not enough, by itself, to generate jurisdiction over the defendant in the forum. A contrary result would expose every web page owner to nationwide (or worldwide) jurisdiction, and threaten to "chill" activity on the web. **Instead, the courts arrange Internet contacts along a continuum.** At one end courts usually find jurisdiction in cases where the defendant regularly does business with forum residents via its website. At the other end of the continuum, courts usually refuse to exercise jurisdiction when the defendant's website, accessible in the forum, just passively advertises the defendant's product or service. In the middle, along a sliding scale, are cases where the defendant's website is "interactive," and the degree of interactivity controls the likelihood of an exercise of jurisdiction.

What You Need to Know:

1. The Internet has challenged current jurisdictional theory just as the increase in interstate commerce and travel challenged the traditional theory a generation ago.
2. Nevertheless, some Internet cases produce clear results:
   a. E-mail presents no special jurisdictional issues. Courts treat it just like snail mail.
   b. The accessibility of a defendant's website in the forum is not sufficient for general jurisdiction.
   c. Jurisdiction over the defendant based only on the accessibility of her website in the forum usually will not be an issue in contract cases or product liability cases because almost always there will be other contacts.
   d. The accessibility of a defendant's website in the forum will be sufficient for jurisdiction if the defendant uses the site to commit a tort targeted at the plaintiff in the forum.
3. Sometimes a defendant can commit a tort via her website without knowing the plaintiff resides in the forum or without knowing that the plaintiff even exists (mostly intellectual property or defamation cases). In these cases the website will be the defendant's only forum contact, and some courts determine jurisdiction according to a sliding scale from highly interactive websites to purely passive ones.

LESSON 12: ANALYTICAL SUMMARY: ATTACKING A PERSONAL JURISDICTION PROBLEM

Prior lessons have discussed the considerations and issues relevant to solving a personal jurisdiction problem. But how should those issues be organized when attacking a particular case? This lesson supplies a plan of attack, a plan that will provide the organization for any personal jurisdiction discussion, whether that discussion occurs in a pretrial memorandum, an appellate brief, or a law school examination.

State Law

First, determine whether jurisdiction over defendant exists because of a **traditional basis**. If defendant is a natural person, was she served with process in the forum, is she domiciled in the forum, did she consent to jurisdiction? If defendant is a corporation, is it incorporated in the forum, is it doing business in the forum, did it consent? If a traditional basis exists, it is quite likely defendant can be constitutionally haled into court.

If no traditional basis exists, examine the forum's **long-arm statute**. If it is a **California-style** statute, it raises no separate issues of statutory construction; proceed to consider the constitutional question. If it is an **Enumerated Act** long-arm statute, determine whether any of its sections provides for jurisdiction over defendant.

Constitutionality

Finally, if there is jurisdiction because of a traditional basis or a long-arm statute use the two-part **contacts-plus-fairness test** to determine whether exercising jurisdiction will violate defendant's constitutional right to due process.

First, does the defendant have minimum contacts with the state? The best place to begin is with the **general/specific jurisdiction distinction**. If the defendant has very substantial contacts with the forum (the defendant is a domiciliary of the forum or a corporation incorporated in the forum), general jurisdiction may exist. If not, the case must fit the specific jurisdiction paradigm, and plaintiff's claim must **"arise out of"** or **"relate to"** defendant's forum contacts.

When assessing contacts, it is helpful to keep at least four considerations in mind:

1. For **general jurisdiction,** a great deal of contact is required. For **specific jurisdiction**, much less will suffice; indeed, one contact may be enough if it is intentionally established by the defendant. Further, the one contact need not involve defendant's physical entry into the forum; purposefully directing her conduct at the forum by mail or telephone, or sending a product into the state may be enough.
2. The contacts that count most are those **purposefully established** by the defendant or her agents. The unilateral activity in the forum of one who claims some relationship to the defendant is not enough. By the same token, the only contacts required are the defendant's; there is no requirement that plaintiff be a forum resident or have minimum contacts with the forum.
3. Are defendant's forum-directed activities such that she should be able to anticipate being "haled into court" in the forum? The mere **foreseeability** that defendant's product will find its way into the forum is not enough. If the case involves dealings between an in-state plaintiff and an out-of-state defendant, apply the **initiation test** to determine who went to whom. Jurisdiction is much more likely if the defendant initially contacted the plaintiff rather than vice versa.
4. Finally, determine whether the defendant's contacts have been established **purposefully**. If a manufacturer purposefully creates a chain of distribution that directs a steady stream of products into the forum, it will be amenable to a products liability action there. If, however, the defendant merely delivers its products into the

stream of commerce with knowledge that a few end up in the forum, jurisdiction probably will not exist.

Fairness or Reasonableness

After measuring a defendant's minimum contacts with a forum, assess the overall fairness or reasonableness of exercising jurisdiction by weighing the various factors identified as relevant by the Supreme Court. Consider first the **burden on the defendant**, particularly if it is an alien. Then determine whether the **forum state has an interest** in adjudicating the case. Usually it will have an interest in providing a forum for state residents to pursue claims against out-of-state defendants. **Plaintiff's interest** in a ready and convenient forum should also be considered, but even plaintiff's dire necessity will not support jurisdiction in the absence of contacts. Finally, factor in the **interstate judicial system's interest** in the efficient resolution of controversies and the **shared interest of the several states** in furthering substantive social policies. Remember, these are factors which must be weighed and balanced together.

What You Need to Know:

When analyzing a personal jurisdiction problem, you may find it helpful to use a checklist or flowchart incorporating the following steps:

1. Does a traditional basis give jurisdiction over defendant?
   a. Natural Persons.
      i. Was defendant served with process in the forum?
      ii. Is defendant a domiciliary of the forum?
      iii. Did defendant consent to jurisdiction?
   b. Corporations.
      i. Is defendant incorporated in the forum?
      ii. Is defendant doing business in the forum?
      iii. Did defendant consent to jurisdiction?

2. If jurisdiction is not available under a traditional basis, consider the forum's long-arm statute.
   a. If it is a California-style statute, proceed directly to the constitutional question (item 3).
   b. If it is an Enumerated Act statute, does one of its sections apply here?
3. If jurisdiction is available under items 1 or 2, is the resulting exercise of jurisdiction constitutional?
   a. Does the defendant have minimum contacts with the forum?
      i. Are defendant's contacts sufficient to support the exercise of general jurisdiction? If not, does specific jurisdiction exist because plaintiff's claim arises out of defendant's forum contacts?
      ii. Are the contacts relied upon to support jurisdiction those of the defendant or her agent?
      iii. Could the defendant anticipate being "haled into court" in the forum?
      iv. Did the out-of-state defendant initiate the contact with the in-state plaintiff or vice versa?
      v. Did the defendant "purposefully establish" contacts with the forum?
      vi. Did the defendant's product enter the state as part of a substantial stream?
   b. Is the exercise of jurisdiction fair or reasonable?
      i. Will the burden on defendant be severe?
      ii. Does the forum have an interest in adjudicating the case?
      iii. Does plaintiff have a convenient alternative forum for the claim?

iv. Will jurisdiction further the interstate judicial system's interest in the efficient resolution of controversies?

v. Will jurisdiction advance the shared interest of the several states in furthering substantive social policies?

LESSON 13: PROPERTY-BASED JURISDICTION: THE TERMINOLOGY

Traditionally, courts have distinguished between **personal jurisdiction** and **property-based jurisdiction.** The best way to understand the dichotomy is to concentrate on the difference between the kinds of judgments the two types of jurisdiction can produce.

A court with **personal jurisdiction** over a defendant can issue a judgment against him for any kind of relief allowed by the substantive law. If the plaintiff's claim is for damages, the court can issue a general money judgment that the plaintiff can satisfy out of any property of the defendant's located within the forum. Further, the Full Faith and Credit Clause permits the plaintiff to sue on the judgment debt in any other state and satisfy it out of the defendant's property there. If, on the other hand, the plaintiff's claim is for equitable relief (for example, an injunction), a court with personal jurisdiction over the defendant can order him to do, or refrain from doing, any act on pain of contempt. Thus, a court with personal jurisdiction can affect the defendant profoundly and can **give the plaintiff any type of relief she desires**.

A court with **property-based jurisdiction can act only in a much more limited way**. It can affect the defendant only by terminating his interest in a particular piece of property. It cannot issue a general money judgment against him, nor can it grant equitable relief against him. From the plaintiff's point of view, the only relief she can get is an order establishing her title to the property or an order requiring the property to be sold and the proceeds paid to her. Thus, if the value of the plaintiff's claim exceeds the value of the property seized, a court with property-based jurisdiction can grant the plaintiff only partial relief. For this reason, the plaintiffs of the world prefer that the court be able to exercise personal jurisdiction.

Courts recognize three kinds of property-based jurisdiction: **in rem** jurisdiction, **quasi-in-rem** jurisdiction, and **attachment** jurisdiction. In an **in rem action**, the court determines the interests of everyone, whether named in the proceedings or not, in the particular res or thing. In essence, the action is one "against all the world."

Examples of in rem actions include admiralty, forfeiture, eminent domain, probate, and land title registration. For these it is crucial that the court be able to extinguish the interests of persons who may be outside the forum's territory or whose interests, or even existence, may be unknown. The captions of such actions may reflect their effect on all the world, since often no parties are named; rather, the case is known by the name of the thing. Thus, a probate proceeding in which a wife contests a husband's will, giving property to his mistress will be captioned "*In re Cheater's Estate*" and not "*Wife v. Mistress.*" Similarly, an eminent domain action (a case where the state seizes private property for a public purpose after paying just compensation) is typically captioned "*In re Blackacre*" rather than "*State v. Owner.*"

In a **quasi-in-rem action**, the plaintiff asserts a preexisting claim to a particular thing against certain named individuals only, and the judgment affects only the interests of the named parties, not those of "all the world." An example of such an action is a suit to remove a cloud on title, an action where plaintiff seeks to establish her right to the land against a particular person's rival claim.

Attachment jurisdiction is quite different. In both an in rem action and in a quasi-in-rem action, the plaintiff has a preexisting claim to the thing, and that claim is the subject of the action. In other words, plaintiff asserts her ownership of the thing, and the court adjudicates that claim. By contrast, in an attachment action, the plaintiff does not assert a preexisting claim of ownership; indeed the claim often has nothing at all to do with the attached property. Rather, plaintiff asserts a personal claim against defendant (a tort or contract claim, for example) and simply uses the property as a device to obtain jurisdiction. The attached property is basically a hostage.

A few examples illustrate the distinction: Suppose the plaintiff purchases a piece of land from owner. The defendant tells the plaintiff that he (defendant) has an easement to haul logs across the plaintiff's land. Plaintiff sues defendant to remove this cloud on her title. The action is a **quasi-in-rem action** because the plaintiff's claim is an assertion of title (free of defendant's purported easement) in the land.

Now consider an ordinary tort claim. The defendant injures plaintiff with his automobile. For some reason, not important here, the plaintiff cannot acquire personal jurisdiction over the defendant in the forum state. However, the defendant owns a piece of land in that state. The plaintiff sues the defendant and the court attaches the defendant's land to gain jurisdiction. The suit is an **attachment action**. The plaintiff does not have a preexisting claim of ownership of the defendant's land. She concedes that the defendant owns the property. In fact, the suit has nothing to do with the land; it is about a completely unrelated tort. The property is used simply as a device (a hostage) to obtain jurisdiction when personal jurisdiction over defendant is unavailable.

In rem jurisdiction and quasi-in-rem jurisdiction have proved relatively uncontroversial. Not so attachment jurisdiction. The next lesson considers the major cases in the development of attachment jurisdiction.

What You Need to Know:

1. A court with personal jurisdiction has a great deal of power over the defendant. It can issue a general money judgment against him, which, because of the Full Faith and Credit Clause, can be enforced against any of the defendant's property. It can also issue an injunction or any other form of equitable relief against him.

2. The power of a court with property-based jurisdiction is much more limited. All it can do is take a particular piece of property from the defendant and give it to the plaintiff, or order the

property sold with the proceeds going to the plaintiff.

3. Plaintiffs will typically prefer a court that can exercise personal jurisdiction over one that has only property-based jurisdiction.

4. Property-based jurisdiction is divided into three types:

   a. In rem jurisdiction: the plaintiff asserts a preexisting claim of ownership of the property "against all the world."

   b. Quasi-in-rem jurisdiction: the plaintiff asserts a preexisting claim of ownership of the property against certain named parties only.

   c. Attachment jurisdiction: the plaintiff does not assert a preexisting claim of ownership; indeed the claim often has nothing at all to do with the attached property. Rather, plaintiff asserts a personal claim against defendant (a tort or contract claim, for example) and simply uses the property as a device to obtain jurisdiction. The property is used as a hostage.

LESSON 14: THE EXPANSION OF ATTACHMENT JURISDICTION

In **an attachment action**, the plaintiff does not assert a preexisting interest in the thing; indeed, the claim often has nothing at all to do with the attached property. Rather, plaintiff asserts a personal claim against defendant (a tort or contract claim, for example) and simply uses the property or res as a device to obtain jurisdiction.

The most well-known statement of the principle appears in *Pennoyer v. Neff*, 95 U.S. 714 (1878). The case arose when Mitchell sued Neff in Oregon for $300 in attorney's fees. Neff was not amenable to personal jurisdiction in Oregon, but, pursuant to an Oregon statute, notice of the action was published in a local newspaper. Neff did not appear, and Mitchell took a default judgment. To satisfy the judgment, a piece of land belonging to Neff was sold at a sheriff's sale to a third party, Pennoyer. Neff later sued Pennoyer for the land. Pennoyer's right to the land depended upon the validity of the judgment in Mitchell's original suit against Neff.

On the way to its decision, the Court announced what has come to be known as the ***Pennoyer* Principle**: A nonresident's land in the forum state can provide the basis for litigating a personal claim against the owner even though the claim was unrelated to the land and even though the court lacked personal jurisdiction over the owner.

Despite this broad language, the Supreme Court held the Oregon judgment invalid. The difficulty was that the trial court had not attached Neff's land at the commencement of the action. Rather, it had treated the case as an ordinary personal jurisdiction action and had seized Neff's land only after rendering judgment against him. The Supreme Court reasoned that the Oregon court's jurisdiction depended on seizing the land, and that a court must have jurisdiction at the commencement. Thus because the land was not seized at the beginning of the action the Oregon court had lacked jurisdiction to proceed.

The actual holding of *Pennoyer* (which is no longer "good law") is less important than its articulation of the *Pennoyer* Principle. The limits on personal jurisdiction were very narrow at the time, which was before *International Shoe* and the advent of long-arm statutes. So, the *Pennoyer* Principle was crucial because it permitted a plaintiff to sue a nonresident defendant as long as that defendant owned land or other tangible personal property located in the forum.

The full impact of the *Pennoyer* Principle became more apparent when courts began to base attachment actions on **intangible property**, like stock in a corporation or a debt owed to a creditor. Exercising jurisdiction over intangible property, such as a debt, generates a question not raised when jurisdiction is asserted over real or tangible personal property: **What is the situs of the intangible?** Or, in plainer terms, where is it? The debtor's residence? The creditor's? Or somewhere else? The question was crucial because the court could exercise jurisdiction only over property that was located within its borders.

The issue provided an opportunity to expand or contract the scope of attachment jurisdiction. In *Harris v. Balk*, 198 U.S. 215 (1905), the Supreme Court opted clearly for expansion. A Maryland plaintiff (Epstein) sued a North Carolina defendant (Balk) in Maryland for $344. The Maryland court acquired jurisdiction by personal service upon Harris, a person who owed Balk a debt from a prior transaction. By serving Harris, the court "attached" the debt ($180) that Harris owed Balk; in other words, the court attached some intangible personal property of Balk's. Pursuant to the court's order, Harris gave up the property (paid the $180 to Epstein) and returned to his residence in North Carolina.

When Balk sued Harris in North Carolina for the $180 debt, Harris answered that he had already paid the money to Epstein and should not have to pay twice. This response raised the issue of the Maryland court's jurisdiction. If the Maryland court had jurisdiction over Balk's property, then Harris gave up the property pursuant to a valid court order and should not have to pay Balk; but if the court lacked jurisdiction, then Harris's payment to Epstein was purely voluntary and did not extinguish his obligation to pay Balk.

The jurisdictional issue turned on the situs of the debt Harris owed Balk; if it was located in Maryland, then the Maryland court, under the *Pennoyer* Principle, had jurisdiction; otherwise not. The Supreme Court announced what has come to be known as the ***Harris* Corollary** to the *Pennoyer* Principle: "[t]he obligation of the debtor to pay his debt clings to and accompanies him wherever he goes." That obligation represents intangible personal property of the creditor (Balk), which can be attached (according to the *Pennoyer* Principle) to provide a basis for attachment jurisdiction, even though the creditor has no connection with the forum state. To picture the holding, it might help to think of Harris actually carrying a piece of Balk's property, say a bag of $180 in cash, into Maryland. There, that property can be attached as could any other piece of Balk's property.

The *Harris* Corollary permitted serious **unfairness to defendants** and seemed to be at odds with the contact-plus-fairness principle of *International Shoe*. Its practical effect was to turn every debtor into his creditor's agent for receipt of service of process. The creditor had to be prepared to defend an attachment action in any forum where the debtor could be found, even though the creditor had no contact with the forum and even though the attached property (the debt) had no relationship to the plaintiff's claim. For example, a person who had a savings account in a bank in a distant state could be forced to defend any cause of action in the distant state. In the commercial context, a supplier was amenable to attachment jurisdiction in the home state of any customer who purchased on credit terms. A defendant caught in that predicament had a choice: she could either default and lose the property or appear to defend and thus subject herself to the court's personal jurisdiction.

Some courts recognized the problem and offered a partial remedy, the **limited appearance**. It permitted the defendant to appear and litigate the merits of plaintiff's claim without submitting to the personal jurisdiction of the court. In other words, defendants could defend their interest in the property that was "held hostage" without risking a personal judgment. Thus, the limited appearance was a valuable dispensation for defendants.

The unfairness of attachment jurisdiction was probably justified before the advent of the contacts-plus-fairness test, when the law of personal jurisdiction was so restrictive. It permitted a plaintiff to reach a defendant, who had injured him in the forum state, but could not be sued there because of the very narrow limits on personal jurisdiction. When the Court expanded those limits in *International Shoe*, the long-arm statutes reduced the need for attachment jurisdiction. Nevertheless, the Supreme Court waited more than 30 years to address the imbalance.

What You Need to Know:

1. In an attachment action, the plaintiff does not assert a preexisting interest in the thing; indeed the claim often has nothing at all to do with the

attached property. Rather, plaintiff asserts a personal claim against defendant (a tort or contract claim, for example) and simply uses the property or res as a device to obtain jurisdiction.

2. The *Pennoyer* Principle: A nonresident's land in the forum state can provide the basis for litigating a personal claim against the owner even though the claim is unrelated to the land and even though the court lacks personal jurisdiction over the owner.
3. In *Pennoyer*, because the land was not seized at the beginning of the action the Oregon court had lacked jurisdiction to proceed.
4. Before the advent of long-arm jurisdiction, the *Pennoyer* Principle was crucial because it permitted a plaintiff to sue a nonresident defendant as long as that defendant owned land or other tangible personal property located in the forum.
5. Exercising attachment jurisdiction over intangible property, such as a debt, generates a question not raised when jurisdiction is asserted over real or tangible personal property: What is the situs of the intangible? Or, in plainer terms, where is it? The debtor's residence? The creditor's? Or somewhere else?
6. The Supreme Court expanded the scope of attachment jurisdiction by specifying that the situs of a debt is wherever the debtor happens to be subject to personal jurisdiction. That definition is known as the "*Harris*" Corollary to the *Pennoyer* Principle.
7. The *Harris* Corollary permitted serious unfairness to defendants and seemed to be at odds with the contact-plus-fairness principle of *International Shoe.*

8. Some courts recognized the problem and offered a partial remedy, the limited appearance. It permitted the defendant to appear and litigate the merits of plaintiff's claim without submitting to the personal jurisdiction of the court.

9. The unfairness of attachment jurisdiction was probably justified before the advent of the contacts-plus-fairness test, when the law of personal jurisdiction was so restrictive. When the Court expanded the limits on personal jurisdiction in *International Shoe*, the long-arm statutes reduced the need for attachment jurisdiction.

LESSON 15: CONTACTS-PLUS-FAIRNESS MEETS ATTACHMENT JURISDICTION

In an attachment action, the plaintiff does not assert a preexisting interest in the thing. Rather, the plaintiff asserts a personal claim against defendant and simply uses the property as a device to obtain jurisdiction over the defendant. Particularly in relation to other means of haling a party into court, **attachment raises some fairness concerns**. The Court addressed some of these in *Shaffer v. Heitner*, 433 U.S. 186 (1977).

The plaintiff in *Shaffer* owned one share of stock in Greyhound, a Delaware corporation with its principal place of business in Arizona. He brought an action in a Delaware court, naming as defendants Greyhound, a subsidiary, and several officers and directors of both corporations. He claimed that these officers and directors had violated their duties to Greyhound and had subjected the corporation to substantial antitrust penalties arising out of corporate operations in Oregon.

The plaintiff in *Shaffer* did not attempt to obtain personal jurisdiction over the officers and directors. Rather, he arranged for the Delaware court to "seize" shares of Greyhound stock belonging to those officers. The "seizure" was only constructive because the stock certificates were not physically present in Delaware. It was accomplished by placing "stop transfer" orders on the books of the corporation. The seizure was possible because of a Delaware statute that made Delaware the situs of all stock in Delaware corporations.

The defendants moved to dismiss, arguing that Delaware's assertion of jurisdiction over their property violated the Due Process Clause. The Delaware courts rejected this contention and held explicitly that minimum contacts between the defendant and the forum were not a prerequisite for the exercise of attachment jurisdiction. The Supreme Court reversed.

The opinion stated that "judicial jurisdiction over a thing is a customary elliptical way of referring to jurisdiction over the interests of persons in a thing." Then it sounded the death knell for the extended use of attachment jurisdiction by concluding that, "**[t]he standard** for determining whether an exercise of jurisdiction over the interests of persons is consistent with the Due Process Clause **is the minimum-contacts standard** elucidated in *International Shoe*."

The importance of the holding would be hard to overestimate. It means, of course, that the presence of defendant's property in the forum is no longer a sufficient condition for exercise of jurisdiction over defendant's interest in that property. That is because, after *Shaffer*, **the contacts-plus-fairness test applies to all exercises of jurisdiction**, whether over people or over their property.

Although *Shaffer* did curtail the excesses of attachment jurisdiction, the opinion was careful to point out the **many uses of property-based jurisdiction would still survive**. First, it rescued *in rem* and *quasi-in-rem jurisdiction.* It reasoned that the:

> [D]efendant's claim to the property suggests that he hopes to benefit from the protection of the state's law. Second, the state has "strong interests in insuring the marketability of property within its borders"; that interest is well served by conducting litigation affecting that property in the state's courts. Finally, the situs of the property will generally be the most convenient place to conduct the litigation. Important

records and witnesses will be found nearby, and the law of the situs is likely to control.

By this reasoning, the Court **saved *in rem* and *quasi-in-rem*** jurisdiction, but what would remain of attachment jurisdiction? One instance where it would survive is in cases where the plaintiff's **claim is closely related to the property**. Injury on land of an absentee owner is an example; the plaintiff concedes that the defendant owns the land, so the action is an attachment action not one *in rem* or *quasi-in-rem,* but the land is closely related to the plaintiff's claim. Permitting attachment jurisdiction makes sense there because of the state's strong interest in the safety of people within its borders.

Another circumstance where attachment jurisdiction would survive is when the defendant has **minimum contacts with the state**. But minimum contacts would support personal jurisdiction, so why would the plaintiff need to resort to attachment jurisdiction? There might be a state-law impediment to personal jurisdiction, such as a weak long-arm statute, and attachment jurisdiction could fill the void.

A third use of attachment jurisdiction that survives *Shaffer* is when it is used **to enforce a sister-state judgment**. The typical case occurs when plaintiff obtains a personal judgment in a state where the defendant has minimum contacts but no property to satisfy the judgment. The plaintiff then sues on the judgment in another state where defendant has property but no other contacts. The Court provided for just this case because otherwise the Full Faith and Credit Clause would be useless in interstate debt collection. To remain judgment-proof, all the defendant would need to do is to move his property to a state where he lacks minimum contacts.

Two additional cases of attachment jurisdiction *may* survive *Shaffer*. In concurring opinions, two justices suggested that attachment jurisdiction should survive **when the property attached is land.** The main unfairness of traditional attachment practice occurred when it was applied to the defendant's *intangible* property. Cases like *Harris v. Balk*, 198 U.S. 215 (1905) and *Shaffer* showed how a defendant could have intangible property with a "situs" in the forum state without having any real connections there. But land is permanently and unalterably sited within the state, and it is rare to have land in the forum but no other contacts there.

Finally, in a footnote, the Court hinted that attachment jurisdiction might survive in cases where **the plaintiff has no alternative forum**. Subsequent cases have not developed this notion of "jurisdiction by necessity," and it is unlikely that the current Court would support it.

What You Need to Know:

1. In *Shaffer v. Heitner*, the Supreme Court overruled *Harris v. Balk* and held that *the contacts-plus-fairness test applied to attachment* jurisdiction just as it did personal jurisdiction.
2. The Court reasoned that "judicial jurisdiction over a thing" really is just judicial jurisdiction over the interests of a person in a thing.
3. Thus all exercises of jurisdiction must be judged by the same contacts-plus-fairness standard.
4. *In rem* and *quasi-in-rem* jurisdiction are still valid after *Shaffer*. Because such actions involve claims of ownership of the attached property, there is no additional contacts-plus-fairness analysis required.
5. Attachment jurisdiction survives when:
   a. The plaintiff's claim is closely related to the attached property;
   b. The defendant has minimum contacts with the forum; or
   c. It is used in to enforce a judgment obtained in a state with which the defendant had minimum contacts;
6. Attachment jurisdiction might survive additionally when:
   a. The attached property is land; or
   b. The plaintiff has no alternative forum.

LESSON 16: THE DUE PROCESS REQUIREMENT OF ADEQUATE NOTICE

The Due Process Clause requires not only an acceptable jurisdictional basis but also adequate notice to the defendant of the action and an opportunity to be heard. No matter what sort of jurisdictional basis exists, and no matter whether jurisdiction is exercised over the defendant's person or property, the judgment will be invalid if defendant has not been given adequate notice. Similarly, no matter how adequate the notice defendant receives, the judgment will be invalid absent a satisfactory jurisdictional basis.

Adequate Notice Under the Due Process Clause

The Supreme Court went a long way toward answering the question in *Mullane v. Central Hanover Bank and Trust Co.*, 339 U.S. 306 (1950). The case involved a New York statute which provided for the existence and administration of common trust funds. Those funds were formed by pooling numerous small trust estates into one fund for purposes of investment administration. The accounts of the common fund were to be settled from time to time by a judicial proceeding called an accounting; beneficiaries of the constituent trusts (some of whose interests, names, and addresses were known to the corporate trustee and others not) were to be notified of the accounting by publication of an ad in a newspaper. The Court held that notification by publication was adequate for the unknown beneficiaries but inadequate for the known beneficiaries and announced this general standard for measuring the adequacy of notice:

> The reasonableness and hence the constitutional validity of any chosen method may be defended on the ground that it is itself reasonably certain to inform those affected or, where conditions do not reasonably permit such notice, that the form chosen is not substantially less likely to bring home notice than other of the feasible and customary substitutes.

The test seems to require a two-part inquiry:

1. Is the method of notice chosen reasonably likely to reach those affected?
2. If conditions do not permit such notice, is the method chosen about as good as any other?

On this standard the result in *Mullane* was clear. Notice by publication failed the first part of the test for both known and unknown beneficiaries. Publication is notoriously ineffective in actually informing its targets. The notice is placed in the back pages of a newspaper that may have limited circulation in a very small geographic area. Further, the names listed in the ad would be those of the settlors (creators) of the trust, which often will differ from those of the beneficiaries, so even seeing an ad would be no guarantee that a particular beneficiary would know her interests were at stake.

For known beneficiaries, publication failed the second test as well, because notice by mail (possible because their names and addresses were known) was clearly more likely to inform them than notice by publication. For the unknown beneficiaries, notice by publication was adequate, not because it was likely to inform them, but because it passed the second part of the test; no other technique was more likely to give them actual notice.

There are numerous ways of giving constitutionally adequate notice. Most are justified because they comply with part 1 of the test; they are reasonably likely to inform the persons affected. The paradigm, of course, is **personal service of process** on the defendant or an agent by an official of the court or a private process server. **Mailed notice**, particularly registered or certified mail, is also very likely to inform the defendant.

Notice by publication is much more troublesome. For the reasons stated in *Mullane*, it is very unlikely to pass the first part of the test. If publication is ever to be considered constitutionally adequate notice, it must be because it satisfies the second part of the *Mullane* test. When the identities, interests, or addresses of persons affected by a legal action are unknown, notice by publication, although not likely to reach them, is no less likely to give actual notice than any other method. It is only in those situations that publication alone is constitutionally adequate.

The measure of adequate notice does not change when the court exercises power over defendant's property instead of her person. There is language in older cases that indicates that, because property is deemed to be in possession of its owner, seizing the property or posting the notice upon it (especially if accompanied by publication) constitutes adequate notice to its owner. In several cases decided after *Mullane*, however, the Supreme Court explicitly rejected this notion.

Posting property and publication in local newspapers will rarely pass part 1 of the test since they are unlikely to give actual notice to defendant. Nor will such forms of notice satisfy part 2 because typically they are not the best means of notice available. The names and addresses of property owners are usually available from public records, and notice by mail (considerably more reliable than posting or publication) often will be possible. Based on this analysis, the Court has rejected notice by publication and posting in a wide variety of contexts.

Before leaving *Mullane* entirely, it is worth shifting gears for a moment and returning to the issue of jurisdictional basis. *Mullane* is the only case in which the Supreme Court approved a very controversial basis for jurisdiction: jurisdiction by necessity. In reviewing the common trust fund legislation in *Mullane*, the Court refused to classify the action as involving either personal or property-based jurisdiction. Instead, it upheld the statute based on the practical necessity for jurisdiction over all interested persons. Without it, common trust funds would be impossible because no trustee would be willing to undertake such an open-ended risk. Although *Mullane* seems to support **jurisdiction by necessity**, it has been a generation since the decision, and the Court, despite several opportunities, has declined to rely on the doctrine again.

What You Need to Know:

1. The Due Process Clause requires not only an acceptable jurisdictional basis but also adequate

notice to the defendant of the action and an opportunity to be heard.

2. In *Mullane*, the Supreme Court adopted a two-part test for determining the constitutionality of a method for giving notice. (1) Is the method of notice chosen reasonably likely to reach those affected? (2) If conditions do not permit such notice, is the method chosen about as good as any other?

3. Personal service of process on the defendant or the defendant's agent will satisfy part 1 of the test. Typically service by mail, especially certified or registered mail, will as well.

4. Notice by publication or by posting of property will almost never satisfy part 1 of the test. If these methods suffice, it will be because they satisfy part 2. In cases where the defendants' identities, names, and addresses are unknown, publication and posting may suffice because they work about as well as any other method.

5. The standard for adequate notice does not differ between personal jurisdiction and property-based jurisdiction.

6. *Mullane* is the only case where the Supreme Court has relied on the doctrine of jurisdiction by necessity.

LESSON 17: SERVICE OF PROCESS

A constitutionally adequate basis and a constitutionally adequate method for providing notice do not guarantee a valid judgment; there are, in addition, **state and federal statutory law requirements** that must be met. We saw in Lesson 10 the limits on the adequacy of jurisdictional basis imposed by state long-arm statutes, and roughly analogous to them are state restrictions on exactly how notice must be given. Those restrictions appear in state codes or rules of court providing the proper etiquette for serving process.

The states differ widely in their requirements for service, but some issues occur regularly enough that all state schemes must address them. First of all, what is process? Here the answer is the same for nearly all systems, state and federal. "**Process**" consists of **a copy of the complaint** prepared by the plaintiff attached to a **summons** issued by the court (usually by the clerk). On other issues the systems may differ. One of these is **who may serve process**. Initially the state and federal systems provided that process had to be served by a court official, but economic constraints on government expense led to provisions that permitted private process servers. A typical limitation is that the process server be of a certain age and not be a party.

To turn the question on its head, **who must receive the process**? Nearly all state systems provide that service may be made on the defendant or on an agent of the defendant; this provision is, of course, the one that will be implicated when the defendant is a corporation or some other form of legal entity. The "agent" may be one actually appointed by the defendant for the purpose (often an attorney) or one created by state law (such as the Secretary of State) as a condition for allowing the defendant to conduct business or perform some other activity within the state. Most systems also provide for special service rules for certain classes of defendants, such as minors, incompetent persons, decedent's estates, and governments, foreign or domestic.

Usually the **"where"** of personal service is easy; it may be accomplished anywhere that the process server can confront the defendant personally. Of course, the service satisfies the basis requirement only if accomplished within the state's boundaries. Nearly all systems also provide for "**residence service**," where the process server must leave the process at the defendant's dwelling place with someone of suitable age and discretion, who lives therein; some also permit process to be left at the defendant's place of work or business. Another common provision controls service on defendants who are outside the state or even outside the country.

The **"how"** of service includes not only personal and residence service, but usually also some form of service by mail, very often certified or registered mail. And finally, most systems provide for some form of process (usually, publication) on defendants whose identity or whereabouts cannot be determined. Provisions for service by publication commonly require repeated failure to serve the defendant by other means or some other proof that the defendant cannot be located.

There are also restrictions on the **"when"** of service, with most systems requiring that service must be accomplished within a set period after the complaint case has been filed. Often these limits can be extended for "good cause."

In the federal system, an elegant **waiver system** has largely replaced the traditional forms of service. Federal Rule of Civil Procedure 4(d) permits the plaintiff to mail to the defendant a request to waive service of process. Enclosed with the waiver request is a waiver form. If the defendant signs and returns the waiver there is no need for service. The rule contains a general provision placing a duty on defendants to "avoid unnecessary expenses" of service, as well as some more specific incentives. If the defendant fails without good cause to return the waiver, the court must impose on the defendant the expenses later incurred in making service as well as the plaintiff's legal expenses. There is a carrot as well as a stick; a defendant who returns a signed waiver form has 60 days to respond to the complaint instead of the usual 20 days.

What You Need to Know:

1. Distinguish service from both notice and basis. The latter two are constitutional requirements. Even if both are satisfied, the statutory requirements for service of process must be met.

2. "Process" consists of a copy of the complaint, prepared by the plaintiff, attached to a summons issued by the court (usually by the clerk).

3. The traditional method required the sheriff or some other public official to place the process in the defendant's hands. Nowadays, private process servers have largely taken over this function. The process server must be of the required age and cannot be a party.

4. Most systems permit "residence" service, where the process is left at the defendant's residence with an adult who lives there.
5. All court systems have restrictions on who must be served, where service can be made, and how service must be made on the typical defendant as well as special provisions for serving particular types of defendants.
6. In the federal courts, a waiver system has largely replaced the traditional forms of service. The plaintiff mails to the defendant a request to waive service of process, including a waiver of service form. If the defendant signs and returns the waiver there is no need for service.
7. If the defendant fails without good cause to return the waiver, the court must impose on the defendant the expenses later incurred in making service as well as the plaintiff's legal expenses. A defendant who returns a signed waiver form has 60 days to respond to the complaint instead of the usual 20 days.
8. If the defendant does not sign and return the waiver, the plaintiff must have the defendant served conventionally, and the defendant must respond to the complaint within 20 days.
9. Waiver of service does not waive the defendant's objections to jurisdiction or venue.

LESSON 18: THE TERRITORIAL JURISDICTION OF THE FEDERAL COURTS

Like a state court, a federal court must have jurisdiction over the person or property of the defendant. Thus there must be an adequate basis for the exercise of jurisdiction, and an appropriate process must be followed. In federal courts, both the basis and the process elements are subject to constitutional and statutory limitations, just as they are in state courts. It might seem that federal courts, being creatures of the federal government, would have nation-wide jurisdiction, but the truth is a bit more complicated.

Congress surely has the constitutional power to confer nationwide jurisdiction on the federal courts. Because that power is constrained by the Due Process Clause of the Fifth Amendment, not the Fourteenth, it is subject only to these limitations: (1) the defendant must have **minimum contacts with the United States as a whole**, rather than with any one state; and (2) the plaintiff's choice of a particular federal court cannot be so inconvenient to the defendant as to constitute a denial of "**fair play and substantial justice**."

In fact, however, Congress generally has not conferred nationwide territorial jurisdiction on the United States District Courts (the federal trial courts). Their jurisdiction is constrained by Rule 4(k) of the Federal Rules of Civil Procedure and stops well short of the constitutional limits.

Rule 4(k)(1)(A) permits a federal court to exercise jurisdiction over the person of a defendant "who is **subject to the jurisdiction of a court . . . in the state** in which the district court is located." Thus under Rule 4(k)(1)(A), state law controls the application of both traditional and long-arm jurisdictional bases to both individual and corporate defendants. Thus the rule confers jurisdiction over a defendant who is served within the state, who would be subject to general jurisdiction in the state courts, or who would be subject to long-arm (specific) jurisdiction in the state courts.

The constitutional test for an exercise of jurisdiction under this provision is also the same as would apply to an action in state court. That standard is the familiar two-part test of *International Shoe,* so the defendant must have the minimum contacts with the **forum state**. It is not sufficient that the defendant has minimum contacts with the United States as a whole.

Rule 4(k)(1)(B) is known as the **"hundred-mile bulge"** provision. It permits the court to exercise personal jurisdiction over certain persons closely related to the lawsuit if they are served (or waive service) in the United States and within 100 miles of the federal courthouse where the action is pending.

What kind of "close relation" is required? The rule is limited to two situations: (1) parties joined pursuant to Rule 19 as persons needed for a just adjudication (that is a very hard standard to meet, and you will learn about it when you study the rules on joinder of parties later on in your civil procedure course), and (2) parties impleaded under Rule 14; those are people who may be liable to the defendant for whatever the defendant may have to pay the plaintiff (think insurance companies). The bulge provision's purpose is judicial convenience, so that an entire dispute can be litigated before one court.

Rule 4(k)(1)(C) provides that service or waiver of service is effective to establish jurisdiction over the person of a defendant "**when authorized by a federal statute**." This provision refers to federal statutes that provide for nationwide or worldwide territorial jurisdiction for particular types of cases. Prominent among these are antitrust and securities cases, which often involve parties whose activities are worldwide in scope. This subsection is satisfied as long as the defendant has minimum contacts with the United States as a whole.

Rule 4(k)(2) provides for jurisdiction in cases that "arise under federal law," over defendants who are **not subject to personal jurisdiction in any state court**, provided that the assertion of jurisdiction is consistent with the Due Process Clause. This gap filler applies principally to aliens who have diffuse contacts with the United States as a whole but lack sufficient minimum contacts with any one state, and to aliens who have sufficient contacts with a state but fall outside the terms of the state's long-arm statute. The other main category of defendants affected is American citizens living abroad, whose national citizenship renders them amenable to jurisdiction in federal court regardless of their minimum contacts with the forum state or the United States as a whole.

The constitutional limitation on an assertion of jurisdiction under Rule 4(k)(2) comes from the **Fifth Amendment,** not the Fourteenth, and thus requires only **minimum contacts with the United States** as a whole, rather than with the forum state. Further, the Fifth Amendment, like the Fourteenth, also prohibits the assertion of jurisdiction if the forum is so inconvenient to the defendant as to **constitute a denial of "fair play and substantial justice"** in spite of the defendant's minimum contacts with the United States.

What You Need to Know:

1. A federal court, like a state court, must have territorial jurisdiction to render a valid judgment. Again, like state courts, federal courts need a proper basis for jurisdiction and must apply proper procedures for notifying the defendant.
2. Congress has the power to confer nationwide territorial jurisdiction on the federal district courts, but it has not done so.
3. Instead, it has placed "statutory" limitations on the territorial jurisdiction of the federal courts, and they appear in Rule 4(k) of the Federal Rules of Civil Procedure.
4. Rule 4(k)(1)(A) permits a federal court to exercise jurisdiction over the person of a defendant "who is subject to the jurisdiction of a court . . . in the state in which the district court is located." Thus under Rule 4(k)(1)(A), state law controls. The defendant must have minimum contacts with the forum state.
5. Rule 4(k)(1)(B) is known as the "hundred-mile bulge" provision. It permits the court to exercise personal jurisdiction over certain persons closely related to the lawsuit if they are served (or waive service) in the United States and within 100 miles of the federal courthouse where the action is pending.
6. Rule 4(k)(1)(C) provides that service or waiver of service is effective to establish jurisdiction over the person of a defendant "when authorized by a federal statute." The defendant must have minimum contacts with the U.S. as a whole, not necessarily with the forum state.

7. Rule 4(k)(2) provides for jurisdiction in cases that "arise under federal law," over defendants who are not subject to personal jurisdiction in any state court, provided that the assertion of jurisdiction is consistent with the Due Process Clause. The constitutional limitation requires only minimum contacts with the United States as a whole, rather than with the forum state.

LESSON 19: LIMITS ON THE EXERCISE OF JURISDICTION: FORUM NON CONVENIENS

The system of jurisdiction outlined in the preceding lessons gives the plaintiff a very wide choice of courts. She can maintain an action against the defendant in any state with which defendant has minimum contacts. Many factors can affect that choice. She may be influenced by geographical convenience, by choice-of-law factors (choosing a forum whose law is hospitable to her claim), and by the likelihood of finding a sympathetic jury. These are all legitimate reasons to pick one forum over another, and our system gives plaintiff the considerable strategic advantage of being able to choose her arena based upon them. On the other hand, that choice might be motivated, not by the legitimate concerns already mentioned, but by a less worthy desire to harass the defendant, provoke a high settlement offer, or force the defendant to default.

Forum Non Conveniens

The doctrine of forum non conveniens, which applies in federal courts and most state courts, permits a court to refuse to exercise jurisdiction if the forum chosen by the plaintiff is seriously inconvenient. The doctrine applies only when the plaintiff's choice is legally correct; if it is not, the defendant is entitled to a dismissal as of right; he is not dependent on the discretionary doctrine of forum non conveniens.

Forum non conveniens does not give the defendant a right to avoid suit in an inconvenient forum; rather, its application depends heavily on the discretion of the trial judge. In *Gulf Oil Corp. v. Gilbert*, 330 U.S. 501 (1947), the Supreme Court indicated the two interests that should be relevant to the trial court's decision. First, the **private interest of the litigants** requires consideration of such factors as: the accessibility of tangible evidence, the availability of compulsory process for unwilling witnesses, the travel costs for willing witnesses, the possibility of viewing the relevant property, and the enforceability of any possible judgment.

The second **interest, that of the public**, requires considering the caseload pressures on the two courts, burden of jury duty on the citizens of a community having no relationship to the cause of action, the local interest in having cases decided where they arose, and the difficulties in having the court decide a case according to unfamiliar principles of substantive law. After identifying the considerations that must be weighed, the court must find that the balance **tilts heavily in favor of the defendant** in order to disturb the plaintiff's choice of forum.

If a state trial judge determines that the balance does favor defendant, what should she do? Although she cannot transfer the case directly to the courts of another state or a foreign country, she does have several options. The simplest option is to **dismiss** the case outright and assume that the plaintiff will bring suit in a more convenient forum. Another possibility is to condition a dismissal upon the defendant's waiver of any objection (jurisdiction over the person, venue, statute of limitations) he may have to bring suit in a more convenient forum. Finally, the court may **stay the action** pending the plaintiff's demonstrated ability to bring suit against defendant in a more convenient forum.

Federal Transfer

Within the federal court system, the doctrine of forum non conveniens has been supplanted largely by transfer. A federal statute, 28 U.S.C. § 1404(a) permits a federal court to transfer the case to any other district where the plaintiff could have brought the action, or any district to which all parties consent. Thus the remedy under the statute is not dismissal, as it is under the common law; rather, the federal court simply **transfers the case** to the more appropriate federal forum. Another difference between the statute and the common-law doctrine is that the statute permits transfer on a lesser showing of inconvenience. Forum non conveniens still exists in the federal system but it applies only when the preferred court is not a federal court (usually the court of some foreign nation).

Choice of Law

A choice-of-law law problem involved in the use of forum non conveniens or the federal transfer statute is that the **new forum may have rules of law less favorable** to the plaintiff's claims than the law of the original forum. Should this problem play a role in the forum non conveniens calculation?

The Supreme Court has dealt with this question three times, twice in the context of federal transfer and once in the context of forum non conveniens. In *Van Dusen v. Barrack*, 376 U.S. 612 (1964), and *Ferens v. John Deere Co.*, 494 U.S. 516 (1990), the Court held that the transferee court was required to **apply the law that the transferor court** would have applied. In the words of the Court, the defendant should not "get a change of law as a bonus for a change of venue."

Piper Aircraft Co. v. Reyno, 454 U.S. 235 (1981), raised the problem of choice of law in the context of forum non conveniens, rather than federal transfer. The suit was based on the fatal crash of a small commercial airplane in Scotland. The plaintiffs, representative of the estates of several passengers (citizens of Scotland) sued two American corporations, Piper, the manufacturer of the plane, and Hartzell, the manufacturer of the propeller, in federal court in the United States.

Both defendants moved to dismiss the action on the ground of forum non conveniens, contending that a Scottish forum would be much more convenient. The plaintiffs opposed the dismissal, contending that it would result in the case being tried under Scots law, which was much less favorable to their claims. The plaintiffs analogized their case to *Van Dusen* and *Ferens,* arguing that if a transfer should not result in a change of governing law, then neither should a forum non conveniens dismissal. The difference between the two contexts is that the Supreme Court can compel the transferee court (a federal trial court) to apply the law of the transferor court whereas it had no power to compel a Scottish court to do anything. Its only options were to permit a trial in an inconvenient forum (federal court in the U.S.) or dismiss with the knowledge that the Scottish court might well apply law less favorable to the plaintiffs. The Court upheld the dismissal, stating that **a change in substantive law ordinarily should not be sufficient to prevent a forum non conveniens dismissal.** It reasoned that plaintiffs will ordinarily choose the forum whose law is most favorable to their claims. Thus, if an unfavorable change in substantive law were conclusive on the issue of forum non conveniens, the doctrine would rarely apply.

What You Need to Know:

1. The doctrine of forum non conveniens permits a court to dismiss an action even though it has jurisdiction.
2. The defendant does not have a right to the dismissal; the decision is left to the trial judge's discretion.
3. The court should exercise its discretion keeping in mind several factors affecting the private interest of the litigants as well as the public interest in the administration of justice. The court should dismiss only if the balance weighs heavily against the plaintiff's choice.
4. The court can dismiss the action outright, issue a dismissal conditioned on concessions by the defendant, or stay the action.
5. In the federal system, a statute permits transferring the case from one federal court to another that is more conveniently located. The transfer statute supplants the doctrine of forum non conveniens when the alternative forum is another federal court. The court has no power to transfer the case to a court of a foreign nation, so the traditional remedy of dismissal for forum non conveniens still survives when a foreign court is the more convenient forum.

6. The Supreme Court has held that a transferee court must apply the law that the transferor court would have applied.
7. The mere fact that the plaintiff would suffer a detrimental change in the governing law is not sufficient to defeat a motion to dismiss for forum non conveniens.

LESSON 20: LIMITS ON JURISDICTION: FORUM SELECTION CLAUSES

Lesson 10, which considered jurisdiction by consent, explained how a consent-to-jurisdiction clause in a contract can operate to confer jurisdiction on the contractually designated court without regard to minimum contacts. A forum-selection clause goes further. The parties agree not only to consent to jurisdiction in the forum but also promise to sue nowhere else. If one of the contracting parties does sue somewhere else, that court, if it recognizes the validity of forum-selection clauses, will dismiss the case.

Two Functions

The contractual designation of a forum, which acts as a consent to jurisdiction, is referred to as "**prorogation**." The exclusion of all other forums is referred to as "**derogation**." At common law, courts were unwilling to enforce the derogation element of a forum-selection clause because private persons could not "oust the jurisdiction of the court." That of course is a conclusion, not an argument. It may be that the initial reluctance to enforce such clauses resulted from the fact that the judges were paid by the case.

Modern courts, which are nearly always overburdened by lengthy dockets, view the matter differently. They see the forum selection clause as a device that reduces uncertainty and helps the parties plan their contractual relationship. It allows them to take the risk of distant litigation into account when they set the other terms of their agreement.

Prima Facie Validity

The Supreme Court adopted the modern position in *The Bremen v. Zapata Offshore* Co., 407 U.S. 1 (1972). The plaintiff, an American corporation, contracted with defendant, a German business entity, to tow plaintiff's drilling rig from the Gulf of Mexico to Italy. The rig was damaged in a storm, and defendant's tug put in at Tampa. The plaintiff sued the defendant there despite a forum-selection clause in the towing contract that required any dispute to be litigated in London.

Relying on current commercial realities and expanding foreign trade, the Supreme Court held that forum-selection clauses are prima facie valid and **should be enforced unless**:

1. The clause is unreasonable or unjust,
2. It was procured by fraud or overreaching,
3. It violates the forum's strong public policy, or
4. Litigation in the designated forum would be seriously inconvenient.

Not explicitly part of the holding but, nevertheless, important for the Court's reasoning, were several key facts in *The Bremen*. The contract was freely negotiated at arm's length by experienced and sophisticated parties from different countries; the forum selected (London) was "neutral"; and the towage contract contemplated performance in international waters and in the territorial waters of several different countries, a circumstance that made forum choice quite uncertain in the absence of a forum-selection clause.

Adhesion Contracts

The rule of *The Bremen* makes good sense; it permits sophisticated parties to plan the resolution of their disputes and to bargain over the risk of inconvenient litigation just as they bargain over the other terms of their agreement. But should a forum-selection clause prevail when one of the parties is not a sophisticated business entity, but rather a consumer, who signed an adhesion contract? The Supreme Court gave a positive answer in *Carnival Cruise Lines v. Shute*, 499 U.S. 585 (1991). Mr. and Mrs. Shute, residents of the state of

Washington, purchased a cruise on one of defendant's ships through a Washington travel agent. In fine print, on the back of their "passage contract tickets" was a clause requiring all disputes to be litigated in Florida. Mrs. Shute was injured on the ship in international waters, and the Shutes sued Carnival in federal court in Washington.

Despite the obvious distinction between the freely negotiated commercial contract in *The Bremen* and the consumer-adhesion contract in *Carnival Cruise Lines*, the Court found three reasons to support enforcement. First, a cruise ship often carries passengers from several different states and foreign nations; so, without a forum-selection clause, a single incident could subject the carrier to litigation in several different forums. Second, a forum-selection clause would save the parties and the courts considerable time and expense by minimizing pretrial litigation over jurisdictional issues. Finally, the Court concluded that "it stands to reason" that *cruise lines save money* by using forum-selection clauses and that the savings are passed on to passengers in the form of reduced fares. Justice Stevens dissented, relying on the hostility of traditional contract law toward forum-selection clauses and adhesion contracts.

The dissent has the better of the argument. The majority's reasons are weak. Litigation in several different forums would not cripple the cruise line, and it was in a position to insure against the risk and to adjust its prices accordingly. The Court was right to note the expense of pretrial jurisdictional litigation, but a forum-selection clause offers no cure; the validity of the clause is tested by a standard that is as subtle and fact-specific as the minimum-contacts formula has turned out to be. Finally, the Court's reliance on law and economics is more a conclusion than an argument. In order to be confident that Carnival would save money because of the clause and that it would pass the savings on to its passengers, the Court would need to know a great deal more about the microeconomics of the cruise industry than is revealed in its brief and conclusory discussion of the issue.

Not only are the Court's reasons weak, but its result is also harsh. Passengers with small and medium-sized claims will not be able to sue the cruise line far from their homes; thus, an entire industry will be able to insulate itself jurisdictionally from the standards of care decreed by the substantive law. Together, *The Bremen* and *Carnival Cruise Lines* reveal the Court's deference to freedom of contract in matters of jurisdiction. That deference makes sense when the parties are sophisticated business actors, but not when one is a consumer, who signed an adhesion contract.

What You Need to Know:

1. A forum-selection clause serves two functions: (1) it confers jurisdiction by consent on the designated forum (prorogation), and (2) prohibits the parties from suing in any other forum (derogation).
2. At common law, forum selection clauses were disfavored as attempts by private persons to "oust the jurisdiction of the court."
3. The modern position is that the clauses make sense because they allow the parties to take the expense of distant litigation into account when they bargain over the rest of their contract.
4. The Supreme Court has approved the enforcement of forum-selection clauses in complicated contracts that involve sophisticated parties on both sides. That result makes sense.
5. Defenses against the enforcement of the clause are:
   a. the clause is unreasonable or unjust,
   b. it was procured by fraud or overreaching,
   c. it violates the forum's strong public policy, or
   d. litigation in the designated forum would be seriously inconvenient.
6. Unfortunately, the Court has also approved of the enforcement of the forum-selection clauses included in an adhesion contract in which one party is a consumer.

LESSON 21: THE ADVERSARY SYSTEM AND THE LIFE HISTORY OF A LAWSUIT

The Adversary System

Among the most important features of our system of procedure is that it is an adversary system. That means that the parties (not the court) are responsible for selecting the issues that will be litigated. This is known as "**party presentation**." Further, at each stage in the litigation the parties are responsible for moving the lawsuit forward (i.e., filing pleadings, motions, producing evidence, etc.) This is termed "**party prosecution**."

The opposite of the adversary system is the "inquisitorial system," used throughout most of Europe. The court takes a much more active role in investigation, issue selection, and production of proof. Arguments for the adversary system are:

1. It places the expense for dispute resolution on those who have caused the dispute.
2. A fairer result will emerge from the opponents' forceful presentation of their positions.
3. It satisfies and channels the parties' atavistic desire for combat.

However, the system also has disadvantages:

1. It is expensive.
2. It results in over-litigation of trivial issues.
3. It increases the advantage of wealthy litigants over poorer ones.

The Life History of a Lawsuit

The "**pleadings**" form the first stage of a lawsuit. The pleadings are documents exchanged by the parties at the start of the suit. These documents state **the propositions each side believes to be true**, and ask the court to reach a certain result.

Historically, the pleadings have been used to a state that the court has jurisdiction, give the parties notice of the opponents' claims and defenses, provide a "table of contents" or "syllabus" for the lawsuit, state the facts each party believes to be true, narrow the issues by disposing of frivolous claims and defenses, and serve as a basis for the preclusion doctrines by showing what was determined and what was not. As we proceed through the lawsuit take notice of which functions the pleadings still perform and which functions have fallen to more modern devices.

Once the plaintiff has stated a claim for relief against the defendant, the defendant has only **a few possible responses:** (1) **Wrong court**. You've sued me in the wrong court; (2) **So what?** Even if everything you say is true, you are not entitled to relief; (3) **Not so**. Your allegations are false or lack proof; (4) **Yes, but** (Affirmative Defense). Although your allegations may be true and the law might ordinarily grant you relief, I have certain defenses under the law that relieve me of liability to you.

The History of Pleading

The common-law system permitted trial **only of a single issue** because the methods for trial were cumbersome, expensive, and dangerous. The earliest method for arriving at a single issue was oral pleading. Later, an official (the Master of the Rolls) would write out each party's pleading after the parties' oral pleading. Still later, the parties began to present written pleadings to the court.

The **Classical System of common-law pleading** was cumbersome. If the defendant demurred (said "so what" to the plaintiff's complaint), the parties were at legal issue; and if the defendant denied one or more of the complaint's allegations, the parties were at factual issue. However, if the defendant asserted an affirmative defense, the parties were not at issue. The plaintiff had to respond to the defendant's plea. This could go on for many rounds.

Before the Norman Conquest, England had a fully competent system of courts. The king set up his own set of courts (the King's Courts) which originally served only to resolve disputes among nobles. In order to file a case in the King's Courts, you had to have a "ticket." These were the "**writs**" or "forms of action." Each writ recited a bare set of facts with blanks for the parties' names and dates and places. If your facts did not fit a writ, the court had no jurisdiction.

The king, his judges, and the parties wished to increase the King's Courts' jurisdiction, so the courts created new writs. The nobles objected and parliament passed a statute forbidding the creation of new writs. **The parties and the courts sidestepped the statute by fiction.** The plaintiff would plead one of the old writs, but prove some new claim that did not fit a writ. The court would simply ignore the discrepancy. The result was that an ordinary person could not read the pleadings and know what the parties' claims and defenses really were.

The first effort at reform was "**Code Pleading**." It required that the complaint contain "**a statement of the facts constituting a cause of action**" in language that a person of ordinary understanding could comprehend. The courts perverted the system by requiring the pleading of "fact, not law" and "fact, not evidence." The result was a requirement for very detailed pleading of facts. Furthermore, the facts had to constitute a "cause of action." This entailed the "Theory of the Pleadings Doctrine," which restricted the plaintiff's proof to the theory of recovery stated in the complaint. This constituted a reversion to the writ system.

In 1934, Congress passed the **Rules Enabling Act**, which gave the Supreme Court the authority to draft rules of procedure. The Court delegated the task to the Rules Advisory Committee, which produced the **Federal Rules of Civil Procedure**. The Rules which were adopted by the Court and Congress (by its failure to object by 1/1/1938) substituted general "notice" pleading for detailed "fact" pleading, requiring only "**a short plain statement of the claim showing that the pleader is entitled to relief**." Note the absence of the words "facts" and "cause of action."

What You Need to Know:

1. Our procedural system is an adversary system.
2. The pleadings can perform many functions. Ask yourself: What function do the pleadings perform under the FRCP?
3. The Logic of Pleading. Faced with a complaint, the defendant can (1) plead that the plaintiff has chosen the wrong court, (2) move to dismiss because the plaintiff has stated no claim recognized by the law, (3) assert that the allegations in the complaint are false, or lack proof, or that (4) the defendant has a legal defense to the claim.
4. The goal of the common-law system of pleading was to narrow the case to a single issue.
5. Originally in England, the king established a set of courts that litigants favored because it featured trial by jury.
6. A litigant could access the King's Court only through a system of writs: a writ was a formulary recitation of facts with blanks that the plaintiff had to fill.
7. Over time the writ system was enlarged by the creation of new writs and the expansion by fiction of the existing writs.
8. Because of these fictions, an ordinary person could not read the pleadings and know what the parties' claims and defenses really were.
9. The first attempt at reform was the Code system of pleading, which required only that the plaintiff allege facts constituting a cause of action.
10. The Codes came to require very detailed recitations of the facts. Hence the term "fact pleading."
11. The FRCP were drafted by the Supreme Court, and its advisory committee, and then adopted by

Congress. They retained the Code reform of abolishing fictions, but improved it by replacing the detailed fact pleading of the Codes with a less rigorous standard, referred to as "notice pleading." It required only that the plaintiff allege a short plain statement of the claim showing the pleader was entitled to relief.

LESSON 22: THE COMPLAINT

Pleading Jurisdiction

In federal court, the plaintiff must include an allegation of subject matter jurisdiction in the complaint. See Fed. R. Civ. P. 8(a)(1). The reason for the requirement is that the federal courts have **limited subject matter jurisdiction**. Because the state courts are courts of general jurisdiction, there usually is no similar requirement. There is no requirement to plead personal jurisdiction or venue. These are defenses that must be raised by the defendant. Otherwise, they are waived.

The kinds of allegations that satisfy subject matter jurisdiction can be found in the Appendix of Forms, Form 7. The following examples indicate the level of detail required:

1. The defendant is a citizen of Maryland and the plaintiff is a citizen of Ohio.
2. The plaintiff is a corporation organized under the law of Ohio having its principle place of business in Ohio, and the defendant is a corporation organized under the law of Delaware and having its principal place of business in a state other than Ohio. (Note the more general allegation of the defendant corporation's citizenship is permitted because principal place of business depends upon facts the plaintiff might not know at the beginning of the lawsuit.)

Pleading the Claim

The level of detail required in the complaint is a sensitive political issue. Plaintiffs typically would like to plead generally because:

1. It allows the plaintiff to recover under any theory of recovery that can be proved.
2. It allows the plaintiff to surprise the defendant.
3. It conceals weaknesses in the plaintiff's claim and thus preserves its settlement value.

In contrast, the defendant would prefer that the plaintiff be required to plead in detail because:

1. It restricts the plaintiff's recovery to the theories the plaintiff has pled.
2. It allows the defendant to eliminate any spurious claims quickly.
3. It saves the defendant from surprise.

More broadly, a principal goal of any legal system should be to **provide substantive justice.** This goal is more compatible with a general pleading requirement because it permits a plaintiff to recover if the facts as shown at trial reveal that the plaintiff has any right to relief. Any dismissal based purely on the lack of detail in the pleading frustrates this goal. Another important goal for any legal system is efficiency. Here, a more detailed pleading requirement might be favored because it allows for the early dismissal of weak claims.

The Codes

The formula used by the Codes, "**facts constituting the cause of action**," required a great deal of detail in the complaint. The requirement could be used to dismiss cases where the complaint probably pled sufficient detail to notify the adversary, but the court believed that the plaintiff would not be able to prevail at trial. The reason courts produced such decisions was that, without a summary judgment procedure, there was no way, other than rigorous pleading requirement, to dispose of weak claims before trial.

One way that the Codes required detail was to prohibit "**pleading law**." The idea was that the plaintiff should not be able to plead pure legal conclusions like "the defendant is liable to plaintiff in negligence." A pleading at that level of generality gives the defendant no notice of what the plaintiff's claim is. Courts got carried away, however, and read the prohibition on pleading law to prohibit the use of any legally conclusory language. We will see this again when we discuss the Supreme Court's most recent decisions on the issue.

The Federal Rules

The drafters of the Rules sought to change the level of factual detail required under the Codes by substituting "**claim showing that the pleader is entitled to relief**" for the code formulation "facts constituting a cause of action." For half a century, the Court was satisfied with this abbreviated requirement, known as "notice pleading." In more recent cases, as we shall see in Lesson 3, the Court has read the crucial standard of Rule 8, "claim showing the pleader is entitled to relief," much more restrictively, more like the Code standard, "facts constituting a cause of action."

Exceptions and Examples

Rule 9(b) requires that **"fraud" and "mistake"** be pled with particularity. The reason for the rule is probably an historical accident. In any case, the cases indicate that 9(b) should be read together with 8(a)(2) and not to require excessive detail. It ought to be sufficient to allege:

1. The content of the representation.
2. Who made the representation.
3. To whom.
4. What was gained thereby.

Rule 9 permits **states of mind** to be alleged generally. The reason is that not doing so would require confusing prolix allegations about why the plaintiff believed that the defendant had a particular state of mind (facial expressions, etc.)

Unlike the common law, Rule 8(e)(2) permits the plaintiff to plead **alternatively or inconsistently** because the plaintiff might not know the truth of the matter. If the plaintiff does know, however, that one of the alternatives is not true, he cannot plead it.

A Prayer for Relief

The complaint must contain **a request for the relief that the plaintiff desires**. It may be legal relief (usually monetary damages) or equitable relief (e.g., an injunction, an order of specific performance). The Federal Rules permit the combination of claims for **legal and equitable relief** in a single complaint. This is possible because the Federal Rules have abolished the distinction between law and equity. Although the complaint must contain a prayer for relief, the plaintiff is not limited to the relief he has requested. Rule 54(c) provides that the plaintiff shall receive the relief he is entitled to even if it is different in kind or greater in amount than he has demanded.

What You Need to Know:

1. The complaint must contain allegations that show the court has subject matter jurisdiction.
2. The detail required in the complaint is a surprisingly sensitive policy and political issue.
3. For several reasons, plaintiffs prefer being allowed to plead generally, while defendants prefer that plaintiffs be required to plead with more factual detail.
4. Society has two opposed goals on this issue: the desire to produce substantive justice, and the desire to pursue efficiency in the judicial system.
5. The Codes required detailed pleading insisting that the plaintiff allege "facts constituting a cause of action." The Federal Rules substituted "claim showing that the pleader is entitled to relief" for the Codes more demanding standard. More recent Supreme Court cases seem to revert to the Code requirement. See Lesson 3.

6. Fraud and mistake must be pled with particularity.
7. States of mind can be alleged generally.
8. Inconsistent and alternative allegations are permitted.
9. A complaint must contain a claim for relief; claims for legal and equitable relief may be combined in one complaint. The plaintiff will receive whatever relief he shows himself entitled to even if it is different in kind or greater in amount than he has demanded.

LESSON 23: RESPONDING TO THE COMPLAINT

Once the plaintiff has stated a claim for relief against the defendant, the defendant has only a few possible responses: (1) **Wrong court.** You've sued me in the wrong court; (2) **So what?** Even if everything you say is true, you are not entitled to relief; (3) **Wrong form.** Your complaint violates one of the rules' formal requirements; (4) **Not so.** Your allegations are false or lack proof; (5) **Yes, but.** Although your allegations are true and the law would ordinarily grant you relief, I have certain legal defenses, which relieve me of liability to you.

Jurisdictional Motions

To entertain an action, the court must have subject matter jurisdiction, personal jurisdiction, and venue. The defendant may assert these by motion under rule 12 as follows:

12(b)(1). Lack of subject matter jurisdiction.

12(b)(2),(4), (5). Lack of personal jurisdiction.

12(b)(3). Improper venue.

Rule 12(g) permits the defendant to **consolidate** or join these motions together. The defendant does not waive any defenses by combining them. Under earlier procedural system the defendant waived the personal jurisdiction defenses by combining them with other defenses.

Timing and Waiver

Rule 12(h)(1) requires that **12(b)(2)–(5)** motions be made in the defendant's first filing, whether that first filing is a motion or an answer. If not, the defense is waived.

Rule 12(h)(3) permits moving to dismiss for lack of subject matter jurisdiction at any time. If the defendant fails to do so, the court is required to note the lack of subject matter jurisdiction on its own and dismiss.

Rule 12(h)(2) applies to all other defenses and requires that they be asserted no later than at the trial and are otherwise waived.

Attacking Form

A Rule 12(f) motion may be used to remove scandalous or immaterial allegations from the complaint, not to challenge the legal sufficiency, in whole or in part. If the defendant wishes to attack the legal sufficiency of part of the complaint, the proper device is a partial 12(b)(6) motion. Rule 12(f) motions are rarely granted and so seldom made.

A 12(e) motion for more definite statement may be used when a pleading is so vague and ambiguous that the opponent cannot respond. Once again this motion is rare. It is not a substitute for discovery.

Attacking Substance

The defendant may believe that there is no legal remedy for the wrong alleged in the complaint. The proper device to assert that defense is a **12(b)(6)** motion (formerly called a demurrer). In ruling on the motion the court considers only the facts alleged in the complaint. This must be so because no other version of the facts is before the court. (Remember that the defendant's answer, her version of the facts, has not yet been filed.)

Until recently, the standard for granting a 12(b)(6) was that the complaint should not be dismissed on a 12(b)(6) motion if there is **any set of facts that the plaintiff could prove in support of the claim that would warrant relief**. *Conley v.*

Gibson, 355 U.S. 41 (1957). The standard was very plaintiff-friendly and promoted access to the courts.

In two recent cases, *Bell Atlantic Corp. v. Twombly*, 550 U.S. 544 (2007) and *Ashcroft v. Iqbal,* 556 U.S. 662 (2009), the Court explicitly overruled *Conley* and announced a new, much more defendant-friendly formulation. The standard requires two steps:

Step One

The court should **disregard any purely conclusory allegations** in the complaint. Thus, it would not be sufficient for a plaintiff to allege a set of facts (in great detail) and then allege that the defendant's conduct violated some common law or statutory rule.

Step Two

The rest of the complaint must contain **allegations of a PLAUSIBLE set of facts** that the plaintiff could prove in support of the claim that would warrant relief.

The Court's motivation for the decisions is to make it harder for plaintiffs to move past the pleadings and into the discovery phase of the case, which can put defendants to great expense.

The new standard gives the court much more discretion to dismiss if it believes that it is highly unlikely (before discovery or any proof) that the plaintiff will be able to *prove* facts that would justify relief.

If the allegations in the complaint make it clear that the defendant would be able to assert a **conclusive affirmative defense** (e.g., the complaint violates the statute of limitations) dismissal is also proper. The motion should be granted only if the defense is conclusive, i.e., no factual showing by the plaintiff could overcome it. Thus dismissal would not be proper if the defendant's conduct was conditionally privileged because the plaintiff might be able to show that the defendant's conduct went beyond the limited privilege. For example, self-defense is an affirmative defense, but the plaintiff might be able to show that the defendant's conduct exceeded the privilege by use of excessive force.

The 12(c) motion is the functional equivalent of the 12(b)(6) motion, but it is made after the answer, not before. Thus if the defendant's answer did not deny the crucial facts and put forward no affirmative defense, a 12(c) motion would be appropriate. The formal standard is that the moving party must show that on the face of the pleadings **no material issue of fact** remains to be resolved and that it is **entitled to judgment as a matter of law**. The motion may be made by either party.

What You Need to Know:

1. Rule 12 motions can be used to attack the complaint.
2. The defendant may file motions under Rules 12(b)(1)–12(b)(5) if the plaintiff has chosen the wrong court.
3. The defendant does not waive any defenses by combining them. The defendant does waive his 12(b)(2)–12(b)(5) motions unless they are made promptly, i.e., before or with the answer. The 12(b)(1) motion is never waived.
4. The defendant may attack the form of the complaint with a Rule 12(e) motion if it is too vague or a Rule 12(f) motion or if it contains any redundant, immaterial, impertinent, or scandalous matter.
5. The defendant may attack the substance of the complaint (if everything you allege is true, you still can't win) by filing a 12(b)(6) motion. Older procedural systems referred to this as a demurrer.
6. The Supreme Court ruled recently that the court's review of a 12(b)(6) motion is a two-step process. In step one, the court should disregard any purely conclusory allegations in the complaint. In step two the motion can be granted if there is no PLAUSIBLE set of facts that the plaintiff could prove in support of the claim that would warrant relief.

7. A complaint that reveals a conclusive affirmative defense may be dismissed by a 12(b)(6) motion.
8. The 12(c) motion differs from the 12(b)(6) motion in timing; it is made after the answer, not before. Either party may file a 12(c) motion.

LESSON 24: THE ANSWER

If the defendant believes that the complaint is not vulnerable to the preliminary motions, or chooses, as a matter of litigation strategy, not to assert them, he must file an **answer**. The answer differs fundamentally from the motions discussed in Lesson 3 in two respects. First, motions usually request that the court take some action (usually dismiss). In contrast, **the answer does not call for an immediate response by the court**; it simply states the facts that the defendant believes to be true. Second, the answer, unlike motions, does not assert that the claim is in some way faulty; again it simply **states the defendant's view of the facts** as opposed to the plaintiff's version alleged in the complaint.

There are two basic possibilities for an answer:

1. **Denials**, which state that some or all of the allegations in the complaint are false; and
2. **Affirmative defenses**, which state that even if all of the plaintiff's allegations are true, there are other legal doctrines that protect the defendant and preclude the plaintiff's recovery.

Denials

Under older procedural systems, the defendant could make a general denial, which denied all of the complaint's allegations or basically said to the plaintiff, "Prove it." The difficulty with this device is that it gives the plaintiff no notice of what will be contested. Without that knowledge, it will be very difficult for the plaintiff to prepare for trial.

The Federal Rules use a different approach. Rule 8(b) requires the defendant to address each of the allegations of the complaint and admit or deny it. If warranted, the defendant can admit part of an allegation and deny the rest, or deny part of an allegation and admit the rest. **Rule 8(b)** lays out several possibilities, but the bottom line is that **the defendant must say yea or nay to each of the complaint's allegations**.

Rule 8(b) does give the defendant some wiggle room. If the defendant **does not know if an allegation is true or false**, i.e., he lacks sufficient information to be able to deny or admit an allegation, he can say just that. That denial for lack of information has the effect of a denial in that it does not count as an admission.

Federal rule 8(b) is much more efficient than the older practice because it lets the parties know early in the lawsuit which allegations they need to muster proof on and which they can assume to be admitted.

Affirmative Defenses

Rule 8(c) controls the pleading of affirmative defenses. An affirmative defense differs from a denial in that it is not a response to an allegation; rather, the defendant's pleading asserts that she **should not be held liable even if plaintiff's allegations are true**. So, for example, if the plaintiff sues the defendant for battery, and the defendant's position is that the plaintiff threw the first punch, the defendant is alleging the affirmative defense of self-defense. The standard for pleading an affirmative defense is the 8(a)(2) standard: a short plain statement.

So, what doctrines are "affirmative defenses," and why should we care whether a concept is labeled as an affirmative defense? The answer, of course, is the **waiver doctrine**: if a concept is considered an affirmative defense and the defendant fails to allege it, she has waived it (unless it is added by the filing of an amended answer). There is an **enumeration** of affirmative defenses in Rule 8(c), "including accord and satisfaction, arbitration and award, assumption of risk, contributory negligence, duress, estoppel, failure of consideration, fraud, illegality, injury by fellow servant; laches, license, payment, release, res judicata, statute of frauds, statute of limitations, and waiver." However, the **list is not exhaustive** as the use of the word "including" makes clear.

So if you encounter some new doctrine, how do you determine whether it is an affirmative defense that must be specifically alleged or not? An example shows the problem. As a result of "tort reform," some states have enacted "statutes of repose," which limit the defendant's liability to a fixed time after the product is *manufactured.* (Contrast a statute of limitations, which limits the defendant's liability to a time period after the *plaintiff's injury.*) Who will bear the pleading burden on the issue of repose? Must the plaintiff plead that the period of repose has not passed in his complaint, or must the defendant (on pain of waiver) allege in the answer that the period of repose has passed. There is no formal test for answering this question. Rather, the court will determine the issue by considering:

1. Fairness (access to proof)
2. Probability (which event is more likely?) and
3. Policy (is the fact one that society would prefer to be true or false?)

The Burdens of Pleading and Proof

The burden of pleading determines who must make allegations concerning a matter. The burden of proof determines who must convince the trier of fact on the question. The two burdens are not always on the same party. The Federal Rules control burden of pleading, but in a diversity case, state law determines burden of proof.

What You Need to Know:

1. The defendant must file an answer to the complaint within a fixed time period.
2. Motions usually request that the court take some action (usually dismiss). In contrast, the answer does not call for an immediate response by the court; it simply states the facts that the defendant believes to be true.
3. There are two basic possibilities for an answer: (1) denials, which state that some or all of the

allegations in the complaint are false and (2) affirmative defenses.

4. Rule 8(b) requires the defendant to address each of the allegations of the complaint and admit or deny it.
5. If the defendant does not know if an allegation is true or false, i.e., he lacks sufficient information to be able to deny or admit an allegation, he can say just that. That denial for lack of information has the effect of a denial in that it does not count as an admission.
6. An affirmative defense differs from a denial in that it is not a response to an allegation; rather the defendant's pleading asserts that she should not be held liable even if plaintiff's allegations are true.
7. There is an enumeration of affirmative defenses in rule 8(c), but it is not exhaustive.
8. How do you determine whether some new legal doctrine is an affirmative defense that must be specifically alleged or not? There is no formal test.
9. The burden of pleading (who must make allegations concerning a matter) is controlled by the Federal Rules. The burden of proof (who must convince the trier of fact on the question) is controlled by state law in a diversity case.

LESSON 25: RULE 11—HONESTY IN PLEADING

Honesty vs. Zeal

Rule 11 is a way of dealing with a fundamental tension in the practice of law. On the one hand, the lawyer is charged with being a zealous advocate for the client. On the other, the advocate is an officer of the court and cannot pursue the client's interest by deceiving the court or the opponent.

It is also part of a much larger debate about how the courts should function as a limit on the unfettered exercise of economic power. On one side **corporate defendants** typically believe that the courts should have very little role in consumer and investor protection and seek to limit the consumer's access to the courts. "**Public interest**" and consumer advocacy groups have the opposite view. There should be few formal obstacles between the public and the courts. Although both the plaintiffs' and defendants' bars have engaged in overly aggressive pleading, the corporate side typically lobbies for more restrictive pleading rules and the plaintiffs' bar takes the opposite view.

The courts don't like overly aggressive pleading any better than the corporate defendants do, but some judges have a good deal of sympathy for powerless litigants, and almost all judges wish to avoid spending much of their time policing attorney conduct.

The Federal Rules give the pleader much more latitude than earlier systems with the paramount goal of achieving substantive justice. Rule 11 is designed **to discourage the pleader from taking excessive advantage** of that liberal provision of the Rules to vex the opponent with sham or unsupportable claims and defenses.

A Little History

The 1938 version of the rule had no teeth; there was very little litigation under its regime. In 1983, the rule was made much more aggressive, but that had the effect of producing a great deal of **"satellite" litigation** (litigation about the conduct of the attorneys in the original lawsuit). The Rule arrived at its current form as a result of the amendments of 1993. The hope was to strike a balance between provisions tough enough to deter abuse of the litigation process, yet not mire the courts in disputes among the lawyers about the lawyers' conduct.

The original rule applied only to pleadings. The current rule applies to **pleadings, motions, and other papers**. In addition, it applies to "later advocating" an item previously filed. This last provision works to restrain advocacy of a paper, justified when filed, but later found by the advocate to be inaccurate.

The Certification Requirements

The rule applies to **attorneys and unrepresented** (*pro se*) litigants as well, requiring the pleader to sign the paper. The signature constitutes a certification to the court about the paper's factual allegations, legal theories, and the motives for filing it.

The **diligence certification** employs an **objective standard**, requiring that the pleader certify that the paper's allegations are true "to the best of the person's knowledge, information and belief, formed after inquiry reasonable under the circumstances."

The **factual certification** is objective as well; it is not phrased in terms of the strength of the pleader's belief in the of the paper's allegations. Rather, it requires the pleader to certify that the paper's factual contentions "**have evidentiary support**" or "will likely have evidentiary support after a reasonable opportunity for further investigation or discovery." The pleader must specifically identify those allegations that meet only the latter standard ("will likely have. . . ."). The objective standard is designed to remove the "pure-heart, empty-head" defense.

The **legal certification** is that the paper's contentions are "warranted by **existing law** or a non-frivolous argument for extending, modifying, or reversing existing law or for establishing new law." The rule **does not limit the pleader to existing law** so that the law can continue to grow and develop. The term "non-frivolous" replaces the earlier version's use of the term "good faith," again choosing an objective rather than subjective approach, and again removes the "pure-heart, empty-head" defense. The rule has been interpreted to require that the certification be made only after reasonable inquiry into standard legal sources.

The **motivation certification** requires the pleader to recite that the paper was not filed for an improper purpose, such as to harass, cause unnecessary delay, or needlessly increase the cost of litigation.

Sanctions for Violation

In an effort to avoid satellite litigation, the rule uses the word "may," thus providing **discretion** to the trial judge. The **severity** of the sanctions imposed is limited to what suffices to deter repetition of the offending conduct. The sanction will usually apply not only to the offending lawyer, but also his law firm. Monetary sanctions usually consist of **a fine paid into court**, but if "imposed on motion and warranted for effective deterrence" can include payment for attorney's fees incurred by opponent. **Non-monetary sanctions** can include professional penalties (attorney discipline, attendance at a continuing legal education course). Monetary sanctions may not be ordered against a represented party for violating the legal certification; the layperson is entitled to rely on her attorney's knowledge and judgment on legal matters.

There are **two procedures** for applying the law: (1) **the opponent** serves the motion on the violator, but does not file it for 21 days, thus giving the offender time to correct the error (the safe-harbor provision); or (2) **the Court**, on its own initiative, imposes a sanction. The court must explain the basis for the sanction but there is no 21 day safe-harbor provision.

What You Need to Know:

1. Rule 11 requires honesty and good faith from anyone filing papers with the court. The rule applies to motions as well as pleadings.
2. The rule requires that the filer certify: (1) The allegation was made only after reasonable inquiry under the circumstances (the diligence certification); (2) the factual contentions "have evidentiary support" or "will likely have evidentiary support after a reasonable opportunity for further investigation or discovery" (the factual certification); (3) the paper's contentions are "warranted by existing law or a non-frivolous argument for extending, modifying, or reversing existing law or for establishing new law (the legal certification); and (4) the paper was not filed for an improper purpose, such as to harass, cause

unnecessary delay, or needlessly increase the cost of litigation (the motivation certification).

3. The court may, but is not required, to impose sanctions.
4. The sanction ordinarily will be imposed on the attorney and her law firm.
5. The sanction must be limited to what suffices to deter repetition.
6. Monetary sanctions usually consist of a fine paid into court but may include payment to the opposing party of his legal expenses incurred by the improper filing.
7. Sanctions may be ordered on motion—the opponent serves the motion on the violator but does not file it for 21 days (the safe-harbor provision)—or by the court on its own initiative (no safe-harbor provision).

LESSON 26: AMENDMENT OF PLEADINGS

In older procedural systems, amendment of the pleadings was very difficult. These systems exaggerated the importance of the pleadings. The result was that many cases turned on pleading errors, rather than the rights of the parties under the substantive law. The Federal Rules seek to **diminish the importance of the pleadings**, the goal being more cases turning on the proven facts and the substantive law and fewer on pleading errors. One way that the rules deemphasize the pleadings is by making them **easy to amend**.

Rule 15(a): Amendment Before Trial

The rules are very generous when a party seeks to amend before trial. Rule 15(a) permits a party to amend its pleading **once as a matter of course** (no permission is required) if she does it soon enough. The right to amend the complaint ends when the plaintiff is served with the defendant's answer. The right to amend an answer ends 20 days after the defendant has served it on the plaintiff.

After that, an amendment is permitted only **by leave of court** or with the written consent of the opposite party. The court should freely grant the leave to amend when justice so requires.

Amendments During and After Trial

Under earlier procedural systems, any difference between a party's pleading and its proof offered at trial was considered a fatal "**variance**." Rule 15(b) is much more liberal. If a party offers evidence on a **new issue** and the opposing party objects, the court will permit the amendment unless doing so would prejudice the opponent. Even then the court may permit the amendment and grant the opponent a continuance to prepare to try the new issue.

Amendment to Conform to the Evidence

If the opponent **explicitly consents** to the amendment, there is no problem. The difficulty arises when the opponent does not object or explicitly consent. The court must determine after the trial whether the opponent **implicitly consented** to try the new issue. The best evidence on that question is whether the opponent responded to the new issue or offered **evidence exclusively relevant to the new issue** but not to any issue that was already in the case. If the court concludes that the parties did try the issue by implicit consent, the pleadings may be amended to conform to the evidence.

An example should help. Suppose the plaintiff's complaint alleges that the defendant injured him negligently and that the answer contains only denials, not the affirmative defense of contributory negligence. At trial, however, the defendant offers evidence on the issue of contributory negligence. If the plaintiff attempts to counter that evidence, then the parties have tried it by implicit consent, and matters stand just as they would if the defendant's answer had explicitly included the defense.

The Statute of Limitations

If the parties try some new claim by implicit consent, the amendment to conform the pleadings "**relates back**" to the date of the original pleading as long as the new claim arose out of the same transaction or occurrence set forth in the original pleading. It does not matter that the statute of limitations has run on the plaintiff's new claim. Suppose, for instance that the plaintiff's complaint alleges negligence, which the defendant's answer denies. At trial, however, both parties offer evidence on negligence but also offer evidence that the defendant struck the plaintiff intentionally. The plaintiff's new claim of battery has been tried by implicit consent, and it does not matter that the time between the incident and the trial by implicit consent exceeds the limitations period. The amendment adding battery to the complaint "relates" back to the date of the filing of the original negligence complaint, which was within the limitations period.

What You Need to Know:

1. Rule 15(a) permits a party to amend its pleading once as a matter of course (no permission is required).
2. The right to amend the complaint ends when the plaintiff is served with the defendant's answer. The right to amend an answer ends 20 days after the defendant has served it on the plaintiff.
3. Later amendment is permitted only by leave of court or with the written consent of the opposite party. The court should freely grant the leave to amend.
4. If a party offers evidence on a new issue and the opposing party objects, the court will permit the amendment unless doing so would prejudice the opponent.
5. If the opponent explicitly consents to the amendment there is no problem.
6. If the opponent of the amendment does not object and does not consent, the proponent of the amendment may claim that it was tried by implicit consent.
7. The best evidence on that question is whether the opponent responded to the new issue or offered

evidence exclusively relevant to the new issue, but not to any issue that was already in the case.

8. If the court concludes that the parties did try the issue by implicit consent, the pleadings may be amended to conform to the evidence.

9. If the parties try some new claim by implicit consent, the amendment to conform the pleadings "relates back" to the date of the original pleading as long as the new claim arose out of the same transaction or occurrence set forth in the original pleading.

LESSON 27: DISCLOSURE AND DISCOVERY

The disclosure and discovery rules are thought by many to be the most important contribution of the FRCP. Their goal is to **minimize surprise**, so the victory goes to the party with the just claim or defense, not to the one with the cleverest lawyer. They do so by a pretrial exchange of information between the parties.

Rule 26(a) requires the parties to exchange certain information **even before it is requested**. A relatively new addition to the discovery rules, it was patterned on the most common interrogatories that parties had demanded of each other before the advent of the disclosure requirement. The rule contemplates several volleys of disclosures.

The rule **requires the parties to disclose initially** (1) the witnesses likely to have information about the case; (2) copies of all documents, as well as other tangible things, that they will use to support their claims or defenses; (3) a computation of each category of damages; and (4) a copy of any insurance policy a party may have to reimburse it for any damages it may be required to pay.

Later, after the parties have prepared their cases, but **before trial**, they must disclose the **witnesses they plan to call**, designation of witnesses the party seeks to present by depositions, and a list of each document or exhibit the party expects to use.

The rule also requires the parties to divulge a list of the **expert witnesses** expected to be called and (among other things) a statement of the experts' opinions, the data used to form that opinion, and the experts' qualifications.

Rule 26(b) Provides for the scope and limitations of discovery. The discovery sought may include any nonprivileged matter relevant to any party's case. The fact that evidence will **not be admissible at trial** does not exempt it from discovery as long as the discovery requested is reasonably calculated to lead to the discovery of evidence that will be admissible at trial. There are several limitations on discovery, but the most important is **proportionality**. The court must limit discovery if the burden or expense of the discovery requested outweighs its likely benefit, considering the needs of the case, the amount in controversy, the parties' resources and the importance of the issue at stake.

The Rules also permit any person from whom discovery is sought to move for a **protective order** from the court specifying that certain matters are not discoverable, including trade secrets and the like. The rule then provides for a wide variety of protective measures that the court may order.

The Discovery Conference

Courts hate to have to make rulings on discovery issues, so rule 26(f) provides that the parties must conduct a discovery conference to **resolve any issues** among them and to **prepare a discovery plan**. The parties must attempt in good faith to resolve their differences and agree on a detailed discovery plan dealing with timing, restrictions, and scope issues.

The Signing Requirement

Analogous to Rule 11, Rule 26(g) requires the parties **to sign every discovery request, response, or objection** certifying that: (1) disclosure is complete and correct; (2) that every request, response, or objection is (a) consistent with the rules and warranted by existing law or a non-frivolous argument for extending, modifying, or reversing existing law, or for establishing new law; (b) is not interposed for purposes of delay, harassment; or to needlessly increase the cost of litigation; and (c) is not unreasonable considering the needs of the case, prior discovery, the amount in controversy, and the importance of the issues at stake in the action.

The Discovery Devices consist of:

1. Oral Depositions.
2. Deposition by Written Questions.
3. Written Interrogatories to Parties.
4. Requests for the Production of Documents or Entry onto Land.
5. Physical and Mental Examinations.
6. Requests for Admissions.

The Work-Product Rule

To be discoverable, an item must be **not privileged**. By and large, the word "privileged" means the same thing that it does in the law of evidence and is outside the scope of this book. But there is one privilege rule that is unique to the area of discovery: the work-product rule. First a definition: Work-product consists of **documents and tangible things** prepared in **anticipation of litigation by a party's counsel**. The rule is part of the determination of how adversarial we want our civil procedure to be. On many issues, the FRCP are less adversarial than older systems.

The work-product rule is one of the areas where the **adversarial dimension of the system still asserts itself**. Imagine a careful attorney preparing for a one-week trial. The attorney will have prepared a large loose-leaf binder, or its electronic equivalent. There will be a tab indicating her opening statement, one for each issue she must prove, each issue where she must counter her opponent's proof, one for each of her witnesses (her direct exam and a forecast of the opponent's cross-examination), one for each opposing witness, one for her impressions of the strengths and weaknesses of different parts of her case, one for the rock-bottom position of her client beyond which he cannot go, as well as potential compromises he might accept. Legal questions will be raised by each of these issues, and the careful attorney will have researched each of these so that she can make arguments "on the spot" at the appropriate point in the trial.

Now suppose her opponent's attorney is not so conscientious. So instead of doing all that work, he simply files a request for the production of documents, which simply says: **"Give me your notebook binder."** If that were permissible, civil litigation would be much less adversarial. Imagine a football game where each coach has a detailed account of his opponent's game plan. Suppose he could watch all of his opponent's practices and chalk sessions and hear on tape the coaches meetings where the game plan was conceived. Now we could have a game with those rules, but it wouldn't be football. So the final justification for the work-product rule is that we are not willing entirely to abandon the adversary system.

The rule is codified in **Rule 26(b)(3)** of the FRCP. It contains both a **qualified privilege** and an **absolute privilege**. The qualified privilege applies when the party is seeking to discover matter that is work-product. He must show that he "has substantial need for the material to prepare" his case and that he "cannot, without undue hardship, obtain their substantial equivalent by other means."

When materials are discovered under that exception, the trial judge must prevent disclosure of the "**mental impressions, conclusions, opinions, or legal theories**" of counsel. For that material, the privilege is absolute.

Discovery Sanctions

As a general rule there are no discovery sanctions without **disobedience to a court order**. The usual sequence for a discovery sanction is:

1. A party makes a discovery request (any of the devices listed above).
2. The opposing party refuses to comply with the request.
3. The party seeking discovery files a motion to compel.

4. The court grants the motion to compel and orders the opponent to comply with the discovery request.
5. The party opposing discovery disobeys the court order.
6. The court orders a sanction to be imposed on the party opposing discovery.

In a few cases, the general rule (no sanction without disobedience) still applies but the process differs from the usual sequence. In these cases, the process begins with a court order. This sequence occurs with a court-ordered mental or physical exam and with the court's denial of a motion for a protective order.

In still fewer cases, there can be **sanctions without disobedience to a court order**. This occurs when:

1. A party puts the opponent to expense by failing to make the required disclosures (Rule 26(a)) or by refusing a request for admission under Rule 36.
2. A party fails to attend his own deposition, fails to respond to interrogatories or a request to inspect premises, or unjustifiably refuses a request for admission under Rule 36.
3. A party fails to participate, in good faith, in framing a discovery plan.
4. A party fails to abide by his ethical obligations under the discovery rules. See Rule 26(g).

The court has at its disposal a considerable range of sanctions, which may be imposed on the party, the party's attorney, or both. Sanctions may include an order to pay the opponent's reasonable expenses (including attorney's fees) caused by the violation.

What You Need to Know:

1. The disclosure and discovery rules require the parties to exchange information before trial. The goal is to avoid surprise and make the result turn on the justice of the case rather than the cleverness of the parties' attorneys.

2. Rule 26(a) requires the parties to exchange certain information even before it is requested.
3. Initial disclosures must be made early in the litigation.
4. A second volley of disclosures (pretrial disclosures) requires the parties to exchange information about the witnesses they will call, the exhibits they will present, as well as information regarding damages, expert witnesses, and their insurance coverage.
5. Discovery on request may include any non-privileged matter relevant to any party's case. The fact that evidence will not be admissible at trial does not exempt it from discovery as long as the discovery requested is reasonably calculated to lead to the discovery of evidence that will be admissible at trial.
6. There are several limitations on discovery, but the most important is proportionality. The court must limit discovery if the burden or expense of the discovery requested outweighs its likely benefit, considering the needs of the case, the amount in controversy, the parties' resources, and the importance of the issue at stake.
7. Any person from whom discovery is sought may move for a protective order from the court specifying that certain matters are not discoverable, including trade secrets and the like.
8. The parties must conduct a discovery conference to resolve any issues among them and to prepare a discovery plan.
9. Analogous to Rule 11, the parties must sign every discovery request, response, or objection certifying that the representations are true, that requests are justified, that the paper is not interposed for delay, and not unreasonable considering the needs of the case, prior discovery, the amount in

controversy, and the importance of the issues at stake in the action.

10. There is a work-product privilege which protects documents and tangible things prepared for a party by her attorney in preparation for litigation. Part of the privilege is qualified and part absolute.
11. With a few exceptions, discovery sanctions are available only for disobedience to a court order.
12. The discovery devices consist of depositions, interrogatories to parties, request for production of things or the permission to enter on property, request for mental or physical examinations, and requests for admissions.
13. The court has discretion to impose a range of possible sanctions, on the party, the party's attorney, or both. Typically, monetary sanctions consist of fines paid into court but may also include an order to pay the opponent's reasonable expenses (including attorney's fees) caused by the violation.

LESSON 28: SUMMARY JUDGMENT

Timing

This lesson address summary judgment after discovery and other motion practice, but it is important to note that the rules are very flexible with regard to the motion's timing. The motion can be filed **as early as 20 days after the commencement** to the action. There is also a limit on how late a summary-judgment motion may be made: **30 days after the close of all discovery**. It is not uncommon, for instance, for a summary-judgment motion to accompany a party's first pleading.

The Basic Idea

In prior procedural systems, the pleadings could not "speak." That expression means that the allegations of the complaint and answer were conceded to be true, at least until trial. Because the complaint and answer were not accompanied by proof, the **first test of the parties' cases came at trial**. That was very wasteful if a few documents or affidavits could have settled the case early on. Thus, while the 12(b)(6) motion says "so what"—"even if everything you say is true, you still can't win"—the summary judgment motion says "put up or shut up." It indicates that the **movant is willing to supply some proof** that its allegations are true and **challenges the non-movant to do the same**, or lose on the spot.

The summary judgment motion can serve other functions in addition to providing an early end to the case. It also can help to pare the case down to those issues actually in dispute. Most useful for this purpose is the language included in Rules 56(a) and (b), providing that either party may move for summary judgment on **all or part of the claim**.

A final way the motion is used is to test some legal theory or defense. The parties file cross-summary judgment motions that agree on a set of facts and leave for the court only the question whether the particular claim or defense is recognized by the law.

Distinguishing Other Motions

The summary-judgment motion is easily distinguished from a **12(b)(6) motion**. The 12(b)(6) motion can test only the **facial validity** of the complaint. The movant must accept, at least for the moment, that all of the nonmovant's allegations are true. By contrast, the summary judgment motion **can be accompanied by admissible evidence**, usually in the form of affidavits. Illustrating clearly the difference, 12(b) provides that if a Rule 12 motion is accompanied by materials outside the pleadings (proof), it converts automatically into a summary-judgment motion.

The summary-judgment motion differs from the directed-verdict motion in two ways. First, **timing:** the summary-judgment motion is made before trial; the directed-verdict motion is made after the plaintiff's case or after all the evidence has been offered at trial. Second, **types of proof**: the summary-judgment motion is usually attacked and supported by documentary evidence. The directed-verdict motion is made and opposed on all the proof, including the oral testimony of witnesses.

The Standard

According to Rule 56(a) the motion should be granted if there is "**no genuine dispute as to any material fact and the movant is entitled to judgment as a matter of law**." An issue is **material** when it matters to the result; the substantive law dealing with the parties' claims and defenses, not any procedural rule, determines whether an issue is "material." A dispute is genuine when both parties are willing to marshal proof on it. Later Supreme Court cases have equated the standards for the summary-judgment motion and the directed-verdict motion: "reasonable minds could not differ" standard.

Relation to Burdens of Proof

The **burden of persuasion**, sometimes spoken of as the risk of nonpersuasion determines who wins when the mind of the trier of fact is in equipoise. In every endeavor there must be a provision dealing with a tie (in baseball it goes to the runner); in the law the tie-breaker is the burden of persuasion. Typically, it rests on the plaintiff and does not shift during the course of the litigation. The most common burden of persuasion in a civil case is "**preponderance of the evidence**." It is very minimal; the slightest difference in the weight of the evidence will suffice. In a very few types of civil cases there is a higher burden, clear and convincing evidence; and in criminal cases the standard is very high: "beyond a reasonable doubt."

The **burden of production** is a very different creature; it is not meant to apply at the end of trial to determine who wins close cases. Rather, it denotes a party's **obligation to produce evidence** or suffer immediate defeat by directed verdict. Imagine, for example, that after his impassioned opening statement, the plaintiff's counsel says portentously to the trial judge, "At this point the plaintiff rests." His client, despite all of the pomp and ceremony, will suffer an immediate directed verdict. At the beginning of the case, **the plaintiff** has the burden of producing evidence on **each element** of her claim, and she has not. The burden of production on **affirmative defenses** falls on the **defendant**, and burdens may shift during the course of the trial.

Why does any of this matter in a discussion of summary judgment? It's easiest to see with the persuasion burden. It is one thing to conclude that reasonable minds must all agree that a proposition has been proved by a preponderance of the evidence, but if we raise the bar to clear and convincing evidence, some reasonable minds might waiver. And so, the Supreme Court has held that the court must **take the plaintiff's ultimate persuasion burden into account** when ruling on a summary-judgment motion.

With the production burden, things get more complex. Suppose the plaintiff has the production burden in a negligence case on the issue of causation, and, so far, discovery has unearthed no evidence on that element. She can produce evidence that the defendant behaved carelessly and that she has suffered injury, but has no evidence that the defendant's negligence was the cause of her injury. Can the defendant file a naked summary judgment motion or must he produce some proof negating one of the plaintiff's elements? The Supreme Court has held that the **defendant can obtain a summary judgment without producing any evidence of his own**. However, he cannot prevail simply by asserting to the court that the plaintiff has no evidence. Instead he must review for the court all of the discovery materials and show that, taken together, they are not sufficient to defeat his motion, i.e., they would not show that a reasonable mind could find for the plaintiff on the issue of causation.

What You Need to Know:

1. Earlier procedural systems provided no way for ending a properly pled case than by going to trial. This was wasteful. The summary-judgment motion provides a solution. It can short-circuit the case by showing that the movant is willing to supply some proof that its allegations are true. It challenges the nonmovant to do the same, or lose on the spot.

2. It can be made as early as 20 days after the commencement to the action and as late as 30 days after the close of all discovery.

3. The summary-judgment motion can produce an early time-saving end to the litigation. It also can save time by removing weak claims and defenses from the case, leaving the parties with just one core problem to solve.

4. If the parties agree on the facts of their case and disagree only about their legal effect, they can file cross-motions for summary judgment leaving only the legal issue to be resolved by the court.

5. The summary-judgment motion differs from the 12(b)(6) motion in that it includes at least some proof. It differs from the directed-verdict motion in timing and the kinds of evidence produced. The summary-judgment motion is made before trial; the directed-verdict motion is made at the end of the plaintiff's case or at the end of the trial. The proof involved in a summary-judgment motion typically will be documentary evidence only; the directed-verdict motion is based on documentary proof as well as oral testimony.

6. The standard for granting the motion is that there is "no genuine dispute as to any material fact and the movant is entitled to judgment as a matter of law." The Supreme Court has equated the summary-judgment and directed-verdict standards: considering the evidence before the court, reasonable minds cannot differ as to the result.

7. When ruling on a summary-judgment motion, the court must take into account the ultimate persuasion burden in the case.

8. The Supreme Court has held that the defendant can obtain a summary judgment without producing any evidence of his own. However, he cannot prevail simply by asserting to the court

that the plaintiff has no evidence. Instead, the defendant must review for the court all of the discovery materials and show that taken together, they are not sufficient to show a genuine dispute of material fact, i.e., they show that reasonable minds could not differ as to the result.

LESSON 29: THE RIGHT TO TRIAL BY JURY

In a civil action in federal court, the parties are guaranteed the right to jury trial by **Rule 38(a)** and the **Seventh Amendment** to the Constitution. The Seventh Amendment contains two clauses: the **Preservation Clause** and the **Reexamination Clause**. The Preservation Clause provides that "in suits at common law . . . the right to trial by jury shall be preserved." The Court has held that the Seventh Amendment is not incorporated in the Due Process Clause of the Fourteenth Amendment, so it guarantees the right to jury trial only in federal court.

The word "preserved" suggests **an historical test**; and subsequent Supreme Court cases have held as much. The main limitation on the right to trial by jury at common law and hence in the Seventh Amendment is that in **equity proceedings** there was and is no such right. Equity proceedings were historically tried to the chancellor, and now are tried to the judge.

There are, of course, cases that contain **both legal and equitable claims**. The classic example is a breach of contract case where the plaintiff demands (1) that the defendant perform his contractual duties, and (2) that the defendant pay the damages already incurred by the plaintiff because of the defendant's breach.

At common law, legal cases were tried by the jury, and equitable claims were tried by the chancellor. When a case contained both legal and equitable claims, the case was tried in the equity courts where the chancellor tried the equitable claims and then resolved any purely legal claims per the **"cleanup" doctrine**.

Now that the Federal Rules have united law and equity, the common-law judge and the equity chancellor are the same person. Actions containing both legal and equitable claims can be tried in federal court with **the jury deciding purely legal claims and the judge deciding purely equitable ones**. There is no longer a need for the "cleanup" doctrine.

In cases where legal and equitable claims turned **on the same factual issues** (did the defendant breach the contract?), batting order became crucial. If the equitable claim were tried first, the common factual issues would be decided by the judge and then by estoppel control those issues in the purely legal claim. If, on the other hand, the legal claim were tried first, the common factual questions would be decided by the jury, and then by estoppel control the outcome of those issues in the purely equitable claim.

The Supreme Court solved this problem; in order to avoid depriving the parties of their right to a jury trial, **the legal claim must be tried first**. That left the question: Which claims were legal and which equitable? Tradition worked fine for claims that were well known historically; the historic classification would hold. But what of new claims based upon newly enacted statutes? The Supreme Court has developed a two-part test to determine whether a new statutory claim was legal or equitable. First, the court should look to history to determine whether the newly created claim **was more similar** to historically legal claims or historically equitable claims. The test produced equivocal results because often the new claim could be analogized both to historically equitable and historically legal claims. The second and more important part of the Supreme Court's test, **the remedy sought**, has produced clearer results. Did the new claim seek legal relief (money damages) or equitable relief (e.g., specific performance, or an injunction)?

The constitutional right to a jury trial is **not self-executing**. According to Rule 38(a), a party must make **a demand** for a jury trial. The demand can be limited to certain claims or issues, with the remainder to be tried by the judge. Failure to make a demand for a jury trial constitutes **a waiver** of the right and the case will be tried by the judge.

What You Need to Know:

1. Rule 38(a) preserves the right to trial by jury "inviolate," and refers to the Seventh Amendment.
2. The Seventh Amendment is not incorporated in the Due Process Clause of the Fourteenth Amendment, so it guarantees the right to jury trial only in federal court.
3. The first clause of the Seventh Amendment is the "Preservation Clause." The second is the "Reexamination Clause."
4. The Preservation Clause test under the Seventh Amendment is historical. At common law, there was a right to jury trial in actions at law but not in equity.
5. At common law, a case stating legal and equitable claims was brought in equity, and the chancellor resolved any purely legal claims per the "cleanup" doctrine.
6. Under the FRCP there is no need for the common-law solution because law and equity are merged. The jury decides legal claim; the judge, equitable claims.
7. If legal and equitable claims turn on common questions of fact, the legal claim must be tried first so that the common questions can be decided by the jury, not the judge.
8. The test for whether new statutory actions are legal or equitable is two-part:
   a. Analogy—What historical claim is the new claim most similar to?
   b. Remedy—Is the remedy sought legal (damages) or equitable (other)?
9. Demand and Waiver.
   a. A party must make a demand for a jury trial and failure to make the demand is a waiver of the right.

b. A party may make a demand for jury trial of some, but not all, of the issues.

LESSON 30: JUDGMENT AS A MATTER OF LAW AND RENEWAL OF THE MOTION

Terminology

The terms used in this context are new ones, recently adopted by the FRCP. The older terms are directed verdict and judgment notwithstanding the verdict. Thus:

Old	New
Directed Verdict	Judgment as a Matter of Law (JML)
Judgment Notwithstanding the Verdict	Renewal of the Motion for JML (Renewal)

There is no functional difference between the new and old terminology. The new terminology was adopted because it clarifies the relationship between the two concepts as we shall see in the discussion of constitutionality below.

The function of the motions is to act as a limit on the jury; there is a fear among the rule makers that jurors may be overcome by emotion and return irrational verdicts. These motions give the judge the power to preempt the jury verdict as a matter of law (JML) or to correct it (Renewal). The basic idea of each is that **the judge takes the case from the jury** entirely and decides it on her own. The difference between the two is timing. The JML motion occurs before the jury gets the case; the Renewal Motion occurs after the jury has returned a verdict.

Constitutionality

The issue is whether these devices violate the Seventh Amendment. The argument would be that the JML violates the Preservation Clause, and that Renewal violates the Reexamination Clause.

The **Preservation Clause** states that "... the right of trial by jury shall be preserved." The Supreme Court has held that the **JML motion is constitutional** because devices very like it were used at the common law, and because, at the time of the Court's ruling, federal courts had been using the directed-verdict procedure for nearly a century.

The **Reexamination Clause** provides that "No fact tried by a jury, shall be otherwise reexamined in any Court of the United States, than according to the rules of the common law." The problem for the Court was that there was no judgment notwithstanding the verdict device at common law. Nevertheless, the Supreme Court upheld the Renewal Motion by **using a fiction**. It affirmed a case where the trial judge had reserved his ruling on the directed-verdict motion at the close of all the evidence, and then granted it after the jury verdict. The Court stated that:

> At Common law there was a well-established practice of reserving questions of law arising during trial and taking verdicts subject to the ultimate ruling on the question reserved.

The Supreme Court reasoned that the Renewal Motion was the equivalent of this time-honored practice of reserving the ruling on the directed verdict motion until after the verdict. The drafters of Rule 50(b), which permitted the Renewal Motion, preserved the fiction by stating that:

> If the court does not grant a motion for Judgment as a Matter of Law, the court **is considered** to have submitted the action to the jury subject to the court's later deciding the legal questions raised by the motion.

The key, of course, is that a litigant who wants to preserve his option to make the Renewal Motion **must** make a motion for JML at the close of all the evidence.

The upshot is that both motions pass muster under the Seventh Amendment, but that making a JML motion at the close of all the evidence is an absolute constitutional prerequisite to the court's granting of a Renewal Motion.

The Current Test

The standard is the same for both granting motions:

> The evidence must be viewed in the light most favorable to the nonmoving party with all doubts resolved in her favor and she must be given the benefit of all legitimate inferences from that evidence. If upon the evidence so viewed, reasonable minds cannot differ, a verdict may be directed.

The rule requires determining (1) **what evidence** the court can consider when ruling on the motions, and (2) whether an inference is "**legitimate**." The caselaw answers both questions. The judge must consider that portion of the movant's evidence that every reasonable person would believe and that portion of the nonmovant's evidence that some reasonable person could believe. An inference is legitimate if it is more probable than not.

What You Need to Know:

1. In both the JML and the Renewal Motion, the court takes the case from the jury entirely. The JML prevents the case form going to the jury in the first place. The Renewal Motion nullifies the jury verdict and substitutes the result the judge would have reached.

2. The JML does not violate the Preservation Clause of the Seventh Amendment.

3. The Renewal Motion does not violate the Reexamination Clause.

4. The current test is the same for both motions: the evidence must be viewed in the light most favorable to the nonmovant party, with all doubts resolved in her favor and she must be given the benefit of all legitimate inferences from that evidence. If upon the evidence so viewed, reasonable minds cannot differ, a verdict may be directed.

5. The judge must consider that portion of the movant's evidence that every reasonable person would believe and that portion of the nonmovant's evidence that some reasonable person could believe.
6. An inference is legitimate if it is more probable than not.

LESSON 31: THE NEW TRIAL MOTION

Constitutionality

Motions for new trials provide another method for courts to control juries. They differ from Judgments as a Matter of Law and Renewal Motions in that the judge does not substitute her own conclusion for that of the jury. Instead, the judge empanels a new jury and the case is retried.

The granting of a new trial motion is **clearly constitutional**; it does not violate the Reexamination Clause of the Seventh Amendment. The constitutional test is historical, and the granting of a new trial motion had been accepted for centuries.

The Standard

It is much easier to say what the standard is not than to say what it is. It is clearly **not as rigorous** as the JML and Renewal Motion standards. The judge need not look at all the evidence in the light most favorable to the nonmoving party, and may grant a motion for a new trial even though reasonable minds could differ.

But it is also not the **thirteenth-juror standard**, according to which the judge could grant a new trial motion whenever he disagrees with the jury's verdict. The current standard, necessarily vague, is that the verdict is against the clear weight of the evidence and would result in a **miscarriage of justice**. When this standard is satisfied, the judge may grant a new trial on all or only some of the issues.

Appellate Review

Appellate courts give great deference to the trial court's decision on the motion. The remaining question is the timing of appellate review. The **denial** of a new trial motion may be appealed immediately. There is a final judgment, the main prerequisite for appeal. The appeal of the **grant** of a new trial motion is different. At the end of the first trial, there is no final judgment, so appeal is impossible. Instead, the appeal of the grant of a new trial motion comes after the second trial, when the trial court has issued a final judgment.

All or Part of the Issues

The rule explicitly permits the trial judge to grant a new trial on part of the issues, including the issue of damages. **Additur** and **remittitur** then are simply variations on the new trial procedure. **Remittitur** is the court's denial of the defendant's new trial motion on the condition that plaintiff consent to a reduction in the amount of damages. By contrast, **additur** is the court's denial of the plaintiff's new trial motion on the condition that defendant consent to an increase in the amount of damages. It is difficult to find any logical differences between the two in terms of respect for the jury. Nevertheless, the Supreme Court, based on incomprehensible reasoning, has ruled that **additur violates the Seventh Amendment, but that remittitur does not**.

Other Grounds

Judges may also grant new trials because of errors or improprieties during trial. The judge may believe that one of his rulings was wrong, or that there has been sufficiently disruptive conduct by a party, attorney, or juror that the verdict cannot stand. When the crucial event occurs the judge has two choices. The court (1) can grant an immediate mistrial or (2) allow the proceedings to continue, and grant a new trial only if the error or impropriety affects the verdict. Judicial economy typically favors the second option.

What You Need to Know:

1. The new trial motion is another method for the court to control the jury.
2. The judge empanels a new jury and the case is retried.
3. The procedure is clearly constitutional under the Reexamination Clause.
4. The current standard: The verdict is against the clear weight of the evidence and would result in a miscarriage of justice.
5. The judge need not look at all the evidence in the light most favorable to the nonmoving party, and may grant a new trial even though reasonable minds could differ.
6. The denial of a new trial motion may be appealed immediately. The grant is appealed after the second trial.
7. Appellate courts give great deference to the trial court's decision.
8. The judge may grant a new trial on all or only some of the issues, and thus may grant a new trial limited to the issue of damages.
9. Remittitur is the court's denial of the defendant's new trial motion on the condition that plaintiff consent to a reduction in the amount of damages. Additur is the court's denial of the plaintiff's new trial motion on the condition that the defendant consent to an increase in the amount of damages.
10. Additur has been held to violate the Reexamination Clause, but remittitur has been held not to. There is no good reason for the distinction.
11. The judge may also grant a new trial because of errors or improprieties during the trial.

LESSON 32: ADDING CLAIMS

Thus far we have considered the life history of a single claim lawsuit, with one plaintiff and one defendant. Real life is seldom that neat and circumscribed. The next few lessons add complications. What happens when there are multiple claims and multiple parties?

Adding Claims by the Plaintiff

Under the FRCP, adding new claims by the plaintiff is relatively straightforward. **Rule 18** provides that the plaintiff may join as many claims as she has against the defendant. They need not arise out of the same transaction or occurrence. It may seem foolish to permit two completely unrelated claims to be joined in the same lawsuit, but that problem is dealt with by FRCP 42(b), which provides: "For convenience, to avoid prejudice, or to expedite and economize, the court may order a separate trial for one or more separate issues [or] claims."

Adding Claims by the Defendant

A **counterclaim** is a claim for relief asserted by the defendant against the plaintiff. It differs fundamentally from a denial (your allegations are untrue) and an affirmative defense (maybe your allegations are true, but there are other legal doctrines which allow me to escape liability). By contrast the counterclaim says: "I may be liable to you, but I have a claim that says you are liable to me."

Counterclaims may be **compulsory or permissive**. If a counterclaim is compulsory, the defendant will lose it if she does not assert it in timely fashion. A counterclaim is compulsory if:

1. It arises out of the **same transaction or occurrence** as the plaintiff's claim;
2. It is not the subject of another pending action; and
3. It does not require adding a party over whom the court cannot acquire jurisdiction.

A counterclaim that is not compulsory is **permissive**, and the defendant does not waive it if it is not asserted during the plaintiff's law suit. A permissive counterclaim need not arise out of the same transaction or occurrence as the plaintiff's claim.

A **cross-claim** is a claim by **one coparty against another**; it does not add new parties to the action. It simply asserts that in cases involving more than one plaintiff or more than one defendant, that one plaintiff is liable to another or one defendant is liable to another. All cross-claims are permissive and all must arise out of the same transaction or occurrence.

Joinder and Jurisdiction

The fact that the FRCP allows the joinder of additional parties or claims does not mean that the court will have jurisdiction over both claims merely because it has jurisdiction over one. That question is determined by the rules on **supplemental jurisdiction.** Joinder is an issue in every court system; supplemental jurisdiction questions arise only in courts of limited jurisdiction where one claim is jurisdictional and one not.

What You Need to Know:

1. Under FRCP 18, the plaintiff may join as many claims as she has against the defendant. They need not arise out of the same transaction or occurrence. The claims will not necessarily be tried together. See FRCP 42(b).
2. A counterclaim is a claim for relief asserted by the defendant against the plaintiff. It should not be confused with a denial or an affirmative defense.
3. If a counterclaim is compulsory, the defendant will lose it if he does not assert it. A counterclaim is compulsory if: (1) it arises out of the same transaction or occurrence as the plaintiff's claim, (2) it is not the subject of another pending action; and (3) it does not require adding a party over whom the court cannot acquire jurisdiction.
4. A counterclaim that is not compulsory is permissive and need not arise out of the same transaction or occurrence as the plaintiff's claim.

5. In a case involving multiple plaintiffs or defendants a cross-claim is a claim by one plaintiff against another or one defendant against another.
6. All cross-claims are permissive and all must arise out of the same transaction or occurrence as the plaintiff's claim.

LESSON 33: ADDING PARTIES

Compulsory Joinder

Rule 19 requires that people be made parties if they meet certain criteria. Typically the defendant raises this issue by a **Rule 12(b)(7)** motion before trial, and the defense is waived if it is not asserted at the proper time.

Rule 19 requires that certain people be made parties if feasible. **"Feasible"** means that the party to be added is subject to the personal jurisdiction of the court and his joinder will not destroy subject-matter jurisdiction (Diversity Jurisdiction). These people fall into three groups:

1. **A person whose absence prevents complete relief among the existing parties.** Suppose O owns some property near a lake, but that two other people, A and B, own properties that block O's access to the lake. O sues only A. B is a party whose absence prevents O from obtaining complete relief. What good would it do him to win an easement across A's land? There would still be the problem of B's land. The plaintiff cannot obtain complete relief unless B is joined.
2. **A person whose absence would prevent her from protecting an interest at stake in the action.** Suppose P and Q are riding on a bus owned by Bus Co. Inc., and there is a collision. Bus Co. Inc. has liability insurance limited to 2 million dollars per accident, and Q sues the bus company for $2.5 million. If he wins, P's ability to recover would be lost, so she is a person whose absence

would prevent her from protecting her interest in the action between Q and Bus Co. Inc.

3. **A person whose absence might leave existing parties subject to multiple or inconsistent liabilities.** Suppose the Fur Store Inc. advertises a free fox jacket to the first customer tomorrow morning. Plaintiff, claiming to be the first, sues Fur Store Inc. for the jacket. Meanwhile A believes that she, rather than the plaintiff, was the first customer. A should be joined in the lawsuit between Plaintiff and Fur Store Inc. because in her absence, Fur Store Inc. might be subject to inconsistent or multiple liabilities. In Plaintiff v. Fur Store Inc., Plaintiff might win and claim the jacket. But A, not a party to the first suit, could later sue the store and win as well, leaving the store subject to multiple and inconsistent liabilities.

If there is a party who fits in one of these categories, but it is not feasible to join him, the court faces a dilemma. If it dismisses, the plaintiff will lose, but if it does not, a nonparty who should have been joined might suffer undesirable consequences. Rule 19 provides a series of considerations that should guide the court's decision **whether to dismiss or proceed** with those parties already present. These are: whether proceeding without the absentee would prejudice an existing party; whether, if her suit were dismissed, the plaintiff would have an adequate alternative forum; and finally whether a judgment rendered without joining the absentee would be "adequate." It is difficult to predict a court's decision (to proceed or to dismiss) in such cases. The result will turn on the individual facts of each case, and it is difficult to find "rules" among decided cases that would help to predict the outcome.

Permissive Joinder

Rule 20 provides for **permissive joinder** of a person who does not fall into one of the Rule 19 categories (persons needed for a just adjudication) as long as the outsider's claims or defenses arise out of the **same transaction or occurrence** as the claim between the plaintiff and the defendant.

Impleader

The principal way that a defendant can add a party is via **impleader**. The basic idea behind impleader is to collapse two lawsuits into one. The main claim is the plaintiff's against the defendant; the impleader claim is a claim by the defendant against an insurer or indemnitor who will have to pay the defendant if the defendant has to pay the plaintiff.

The advantage of impleader is that it avoids the necessity for the original defendant to suffer a judgment first, and then bring a second separate lawsuit against his insurer. The key language is in Rule 14, which provides that a defendant **who is or may be** liable to the plaintiff, may implead any nonparty who would be liable to it for all or part of the plaintiff's claim. The "may be" phrase is the one that permits the defendant to sue the insurer before the defendant has incurred actual liability to the plaintiff.

The original defendant is referred to as the **third-party plaintiff**, and the impleaded party is called the **third-party defendant**. The most typical jurisdictional problem occurs when the plaintiff is diverse from defendant, but the defendant is not diverse from the third-party defendant. The Supplemental Jurisdiction Statute explicitly permits the exercise of jurisdiction over the impleader claim in such circumstances. The third-party defendant is allowed to assert counterclaims against the original plaintiff and the third-party plaintiff (the original defendant).

What You Need to Know:

1. Rule 19 determines whether a nonparty should be joined to an existing proceeding.
2. This issue is usually raised by a defendant in the existing litigation as a reason to dismiss it.
3. Rule 19 defines three groups who should be joined "if feasible." See the text above.

4. "Feasible" means that the party to be joined would be subject to the court's territorial jurisdiction, and would not destroy its subject-matter jurisdiction.
5. If the court determines that it is not feasible to join a person described in (1)–(3) above, it must determine whether to dismiss the action or proceed with those parties already joined.
6. The court should consider: whether proceeding without the absentee would prejudice an existing party; whether, if her suit were dismissed, the plaintiff would have an adequate alternative forum; and finally, whether a judgment rendered without joining the absentee would be "adequate."
7. Rule 14 permits a defendant, who is or may be liable to the plaintiff to implead an outsider, (usually an insurer or indemnitor) who would have to pay the defendant if the defendant has to pay the plaintiff. Rule 14 thus permits a single lawsuit to accomplish what would otherwise require two separate actions.
8. The original defendant is referred to as the third-party plaintiff. The party that has been impleaded is referred to as the third-party defendant.
9. If there is diversity of citizenship between the original plaintiff and the defendant, the Supplemental Jurisdiction Statute will permit the impleader action regardless of the third-party defendant's citizenship.
10. The third-party defendant may assert any counterclaims that it has against the original plaintiff or the third-party plaintiff.

LESSON 34: SUPPLEMENTAL JURISDICTION

What should the federal court do if one claim in a lawsuit meets the jurisdictional requirements, and another does not? And, similarly, what should the federal court do if a claim by or against one party meets the jurisdictional requirements, but a claim by or against another party does not? For convenience sake it is useful to have designations for each of the two claims. The claim that meets the jurisdictional requirements is referred to as the **"anchor"** claim, and its nonjurisdictional companion is referred to as the **"supplemental"** claim.

The problem arises because one of the basic goals of the Federal Rules is to make joinder of claims and parties easy because it is more efficient to try one case rather than two. The leniency of the rules on joinder of claims and parties, however, bumps squarely against one of the most basic principles of federal court jurisdiction: the federal courts are courts of limited jurisdiction and simply cannot hear a case beyond their subject-matter jurisdiction.

The Supreme Court addressed the issue in several major decisions, but was unable to produce a clear solution. Then Congress took its best shot. With the advice of a committee of distinguished scholars, jurists, and practitioners, it passed the **Supplemental Jurisdiction Statute (28 U.S.C. § 1367)**. The intent of the drafters was clear; they wanted to do four things:

1. Permit supplemental jurisdiction where one claim is based on federal law and another is not (joinder of claims) or where a claim by or against one party is based on federal law and a claim by or against another party is not (joinder of parties);
2. Permit supplemental jurisdiction when the plaintiff's claim meets the jurisdictional requirements, but the defendant's counterclaim, cross-claim, or third-party claim does not;
3. Retain the complete diversity rule, which prohibits a plaintiff who is not diverse from the defendant from joining her claim with the anchor claim of a plaintiff who is; and
4. Retain the judge-made rule against allowing a monetarily insufficient claim to ride the coattails of a claim that does meet the jurisdictional amount. (In other words, the rule should require

each of several claims to separately meet the jurisdictional amount.)

The statute was exceedingly complex and technical, but **poorly drafted**. The Supreme Court has interpreted it **literally**, in a way that is consistent with its language, but not all of its four goals. The interpretation tracked the first three goals of the drafters, but hopelessly confused the fourth.

The Court has read the statutory language to distinguish between cases involving **multiple plaintiffs** and those involving **multiple defendants**. According to the Court's interpretation of the statute, when two plaintiffs sue a single defendant and one plaintiff's claim meets the amount, but the other's does not, there will be supplemental jurisdiction over the lesser claim. However, when a single plaintiff sues multiple defendants, and the claim against one defendant meets the amount, but the claim against the other defendant does not, there will not be supplemental jurisdiction over the lesser claim. The interpretation leaves a result that no one could possibly have intended, but is consistent with the literal wording of the statute. Do not despair if you are hopelessly confused. A full understanding of the Supreme Court's opinion on the relation of the language of the statute to its purpose is beyond the scope of these lessons.

What You Need to Know:

1. The Federal Rules permit joinder of two claims, but that does not guarantee that the combination will satisfy the jurisdictional rules of the federal courts. There will always be two questions:

   a. Do joinder rules permit this combination of claims and parties?

   b. Will the federal court, which has jurisdiction over the anchor claim, also have jurisdiction to hear the supplemental claim?

2. To get correct results, follow a few simple rules of thumb:

   a. If the plaintiff's anchor claim against the defendant is jurisdictional, the court will permit any supplemental claim by that same plaintiff against that same defendant.

b. If the plaintiff brings an anchor claim against the defendant, the court will permit any kind of supplemental claim by that defendant against the plaintiff or anyone else.

c. If the anchor claim is a federal question claim, the federal court will permit supplemental jurisdiction over any supplemental claim, including claims adding new defendants or plaintiffs (e.g., joinder of claims, joinder of parties, counterclaim, cross-claim, impleader claim, etc.).

d. The complete diversity rule still holds. The statute does not change the requirement that every plaintiff must be diverse from every defendant.

3. If a claim by one plaintiff against the defendant meets the jurisdictional amount, the court will permit a supplemental claim by a second plaintiff even if does not meet the jurisdictional amount.

4. If a claim by a plaintiff against one defendant meets the jurisdictional amount, the court will not permit addition of a claim by that plaintiff against another defendant unless it independently meets the jurisdictional amount. In other words, two plaintiffs can use supplemental jurisdiction against one defendant, but one plaintiff cannot use supplemental jurisdiction against two defendants.

CHAPTER 7

PROPERTY

LESSON 1: ORIGINS OF PROPERTY RIGHTS

Contracts, Torts, Civil Procedure, Criminal Law, and Criminal Procedure are all about events. Those fields' origins are fairly straightforward: an event occurs that arguably falls within their ambit, and the law must interpret and respond to that event. Property is different. Alone among the usual first-year subjects, it defines a status rather than an event. Someone has property if she or he has a particular kind of relationship with a place, a thing, or an idea. Most Property courses, therefore, begin with an exploration of how people obtain that status.

Different legal regimes answer that question quite differently. Indeed, the rules for how to recognize property rights define a legal regime as much as its political constitution. The rules vary considerably across nations and across time.

These themes and others come through vividly in the early U.S. Supreme Court case of *Johnson v. M'Intosh*, 21 U.S. (8 Wheat.) 543 (1823). *Johnson* involved competing claims to land from two sets of purported owners. One set traced their title to the Native Americans who had originally inhabited the land; the others relied on a grant from the United States Government. Chief Justice John Marshall had to decide who had authority to grant the land.

As Chief Justice Marshall acknowledged, a very important principle in Property is "**first in time, first in right**." By that dictum, those claiming title from the Native Americans should have superior title as their grantors were clearly on the land first, long before the U.S. or any Europeans. But Chief Justice Marshall held that although European nations honored one another's property claims, they did not honor those of the native peoples. In his view, once European settlers conquered Native Americans, therefore, they brought the land in what is now the United States under European control and wiped out any property rights that had existed under the vanquished tribes' law. This is the **conquest** theory of property rights.

Chief Justice Marshall also acknowledged that, even after the European conquest, Britain (and later the U.S.) had allowed Native Americans to remain on the land. That did not, Chief Justice Marshall held, constitute giving property rights to the Native Americans. They were, he ruled, mere occupants of the land rather than its owners. To claim ownership in land, the Court held, one must modify or improve the land to remove it from its natural state. The Native Americans had left the land largely in its natural state and thus, according to Chief Justice Marshall, had not perfected ownership in it.

This latter theme, that property rights reflect efforts made to improve land, is a common and important theme in property law. John Locke, the 17th century English philosopher whose writings provided much of the ideological basis for the American Revolution, wrote that property rights arise when **people mix their labor with the land**, at least as long as enough land remains for others to do the same.

Johnson v. M'Intosh therefore had to resolve a conflict between several important theories of property rights. It rejected first-in-time/first-in-right in favor of the **conquest** and **labor** theories of property. It also rejected any universal definition of property rights in favor of one that is specific to a political regime. And it distinguished between **possession** and **ownership**, two themes that will recur throughout the course. The law often tilts toward possessors in determining ownership rights, but not on this occasion.

Many scholars have criticized *Johnson v. M'Intosh* as racist for its refusal to credit the rights of non-Europeans. Others have argued that the underlying logic of the conquest theory, that might makes right, is inconsistent with the rule of law and a stable regime of property rights. And environmentalists have criticized *Johnson* for its refusal to recognize that living in harmony with the land is a valid choice that may well be superior to "improving" it.

Some law and economics scholars contend that property law regimes adjust to fit the economic system of the day. Thus, although the Native Americans' approach fit the economics of their community—with low population densities and production closely related to the land—the labor theory of property rights better fit the urbanizing, industrializing society of the time when Chief Justice Marshall wrote. If that is correct, we should expect significant new changes in property law in the coming years as this country becomes more firmly ensconced in the Information Age.

What You Need to Know:

1. Property rules define legal regimes and reflect the political and economic preferences of those regimes.
2. Before anyone can buy, sell, give away, or inherit property rights, they must first come into being. Several distinct theories guide courts in recognizing when someone has created property rights.
3. Property law commonly but not uniformly favors those first to assert claims to disputed property.
4. When one political regime conquers another, it often brings its own property rules with it. Similarly, when someone conquers property previously possessed by another, the conqueror may defeat the prior owner's claim to the property.
5. Property law seeks to reward activities it regards as productive by awarding rights to active users over those making more passive use of resources.
6. Although possession of something is often an important step toward gaining legal ownership of property, courts are careful to distinguish ownership rights from possessory ones. Property law covers disputes over both ultimate ownership and current possession.

LESSON 2: OWNERSHIP BY CREATION AND ECONOMIC ARGUMENTS

Before we can consider how property moves among owners, we need to consider from where it comes. Conquest, as discussed in the last lesson (and in Lessons 3 and 5) is one possibility. Another, happier prospect is that a future owner creates the item of value. This Lesson provides a brief introduction to how property law treats one particular kind of creation: intellectual property. It then takes that example as an opportunity to survey some of the kinds of economic arguments that are important in property law.

Statutes and international treaties control most important intellectual property rights. Although countries update these laws and treaties frequently, changes in the nature of intellectual property often outpace those developments. Such was the case in *International News Service v. Associated Press*, 248 U.S. 215 (1918). There, the Associated Press (AP) employed numerous reporters to gather and report the news; it then sold their reports to newspapers around the country. INS did not have reporters or do any newsgathering of its own. But it would get hold of AP stories, copy them, and circulate those stories to its subscribers (presumably for a lower price than AP charged). The Copyright Act at the time did not provide a feasible means of protecting writings whose value was as fleeting as news stories, so if AP had any rights at all, they had to come from the common law. The Supreme Court held AP was entitled to relief against INS. The Court found that INS's activity not only was entirely unproductive but also interfered with AP's ability to obtain a return on its very real efforts. The Court was willing to step in even without statutory authority to prevent unfair, parasitic competition.

Subsequent courts have largely limited *INS v. AP* to its facts. For example, in *Cheney Bros. v. Doris Silk Co.*, 35 F.2d 279 (2d Cir. 1929), Judge Learned Hand rejected a claim by a textile company that one of its competitors was copying the patterns on its fabrics. Judge Hand held that copying was well-established in the fashion industry. He treated *INS v. AP* as dealing only with the special case of news. The copier in *Cheney Bros.* also may arguably have contributed some new value while INS had not. Judge Hand left any additional protection up to Congress to provide.

These cases illustrate the importance of **efficiency**, **fairness**, and **administrability** in property law. Courts seek rules of law that will promote efficient behavior by attaching rewards to the productive activity that created those rewards. Because INS's conduct threatened to make AP's productive news-gathering unprofitable by diverting the rewards, the Supreme Court intervened. Courts also seek rules that are fair by treating like actors alike and meaningfully different actors differently. The Court in *INS v. AP* found the two news organizations operating very differently—one doing the hard work of newsgathering, the other contributing nothing—and announced a rule that accordingly gave them different rights. Finally, courts seek rules of law that will not be unduly costly for the parties to litigate and for the courts to adjudicate. Judge Hand believed that determining which patterns were sufficiently similar for a court to consider them improper copies would be difficult, time-consuming, and error-prone. Attempting to do so also would create costly uncertainty about how the courts would ultimately rule among competing producers. He therefore declined to extend the law in that direction without explicit direction from Congress. Often efficiency, fairness, and administrability all militate in favor of the same result. When they point in different directions, the outcome may depend on how strong and unambiguous the respective arguments are in that case, the leanings of the judges, and which values precedent has favored.

Another important set of economic arguments in property law surround the **right to include** and the **right to exclude**. Put simply, the right to include is the right to do as one wishes with a piece of property; the right to exclude is the right to block others from using a piece of property without one's permission. Both *INS v. AP* and *Cheney Bros.* dealt with the right to exclude. Cases limiting what an owner can do with her or his property (*e.g.*, where a zoning ordinance prohibits a property owner from operating a junk yard in a residential neighborhood) test the limits of the right to include. Both rights are very important.

For example, in *Jacque v. Steenberg Homes*, 563 N.W.2d 154 (Wis. 1997), a company asked a property owner's permission to cross the owner's land to deliver a mobile home to one of the owner's neighbors. After the owner refused, the mobile home company crossed his land anyway. When the property owner sued, the company argued that it had no other feasible way of making delivery and that it had done no harm to the owner's land. The court found this argument unpersuasive, holding that the right to exclude was not limited to instances where the refusal made economic sense and awarded damages against the trespassing company.

The right to exclude is less powerful, however, when it comes into conflict with the right to include. In *State v. Shack*, 277 A.2d 369 (N.J. 1971), the New Jersey Supreme Court reversed the trespass convictions of an attorney and a social worker who had entered a grower's land without his permission to assist migrant farmworkers living in his labor camp. The grower could have kept everyone off of his land completely, but once he partially relinquished his right to exclude by opening it up to farmworkers, they brought with them their right to include those with whom they wished to associate.

The importance of balance between rights to include and rights to exclude is evident in classic stories about the **tragedy of the commons** and the **tragedy of the anti-commons**. In the tragedy of the commons, many people have the right to include but no one has the right to exclude. The likely result is that the property subject to these multiple rights of inclusion will be over-exploited and exhausted, as village greens were when all residents simultaneously grazed their sheep there rather than on the owners' own fields. In the tragedy of the anti-commons, many people have the right to exclude but no one has the right to include. This is likely to lead to the failure to make productive use of the resource. In the former Soviet Union, prime retail locations went unused because too many different arms of the state and party had to agree before a store could open. Closer to home, some properties that Hurricane Katrina damaged or destroyed could not be rebuilt because ownership of the land had become badly fragmented as it was handed down over the generations.

Private property ownership often achieves important efficiencies by concentrating the right to include and the right to exclude for a given piece of property in the same hands. As we will see beginning in Lesson 20, however, this does not always work out perfectly as one neighbor's right to include may adversely affect another neighbor's right to exclude.

Because no one person ordinarily has absolute control over a piece of real property, Professor Wesley Hohfeld suggested that rights in property should be viewed as a **bundle of sticks**, with each stick representing a particular right involving a property. Thus, instead of saying "Felicity owns Blueacre", we would recognize that Felicity holds certain rights (sticks) relating to Blueacre. If Felicity made a binding promise to Gamal not to open a gas station on Blueacre, we would say that Felicity has given away the stick representing her right to include a gas station on Blueacre and that Gamal has acquired a stick representing the right to exclude gas stations.

What You Need to Know:

1. The law seeks to reward creators of valuable items with ownership of those items.
2. Much intellectual property law comes from statutes, but the courts will sometimes intervene in cases not covered by statute to promote efficiency, fairness, and administrable legal rules. These principles permeate property law.
3. Efficient legal rules give parties incentives to engage in productive activities.
4. Fair legal rules treat similar parties similarly and different parties differently.
5. Administrable legal rules avoid costly litigation, especially litigation whose outcome is likely to be wrong or difficult to predict.
6. We can express many property rights in terms of the right to include and the right to exclude.
7. We can view the rights with respect to a property as a bundle of sticks. Owners can surrender some

rights (sticks) without affecting their remaining rights (bundle of sticks).

LESSON 3: ANIMALS AND NATURAL RESOURCES

Although in our everyday lives, almost all of the property we own comes to us in transfers from prior owners, at some point things had to become property in the first place. Either someone needed to create the property from nothing (as with a composer writing a song) or someone needed to convert a place or object that already existed in nature from un-owned to owned status. Each of these processes of property formation pose interesting and difficult questions that have broad implications for the rest of property law. This Lesson will cover the process of obtaining ownership over things in nature; the next Lesson will address how we recognize ownership in something newly created.

Today, the most valuable things in nature that people seek to own are largely inanimate: oil, gas, water, diamonds, metal ores, etc. At the time when the common law was forming, however, animals posed the greatest dilemmas because they were valued but not tied to any one particular plot of land. Several famous cases arose that have become staples of Property curricula and that are helpful in understanding broader questions of property law. And because some natural resources—notably oil, gas, and water—are similarly capable of moving on their own from one piece of land to another, the ideas developed in these animal cases have provided valuable analogies for contemporary natural resources law.

These cases also feature prominently in the early days of most Property courses because they illustrate several of the techniques on which courts rely in deciding property cases:

- One of these approaches is to favor the first person to claim a disputed item as her or his property. This "**first-in-time, first-in-right**" principle offers an easily administered, objective test for resolving competing claims while providing incentives for potential claimants to expedite their efforts.

- Another common approach is to follow **custom**. The original justification for the common law was as a reflection of the traditions of the English.
- Still another goal courts have in deciding property cases is to promote **economic efficiency**, sometimes characterized as putting property in the hands of whomever is likely to put it to its highest and best use. Courts see this as increasing the total well-being of society.
- A fourth principle common in property cases is to promote **good faith** and punish excessively or gratuitously destructive conduct. The subject matter in property disputes typically is so valuable that its loss can devastate an owner; discouraging bad faith avoids the loss.

Probably the most famous property case of all is *Pierson v. Post*, 2 Am. Dec. 264 (N.Y. S. Ct. 1805). Post and his hounds were chasing a fox in a wild, ownerless plot of land when Pierson shot the fox and took it. Invoking the principle of **first-in-time, first-in-right**, Post claimed that the fox should have been his as he had already flushed the animal and was closing in for the kill. The court disagreed. While accepting the first-in-time, first-in-right principle's legitimacy, it held that Post had not done enough with the fox to make himself truly first-in-time. Instead, the court declared that killing the fox, as Pierson did, was the crucial act that converts it from a wild animal to someone's property. Giving people incentives not merely to hunt foxes but to kill them would create incentives for more of this activity, which the court regarded as economically productive.

In *Ghen v. Rich,* 8 F. 159 (D. Mass. 1881), a whaler from Provincetown, Massachusetts, harpooned a whale. As was usually the case, the dead whale immediately sank but subsequently rose again to the surface. After it floated to the shore, Rich found it and claimed it. Ghen, the whaler, sued, claiming that the whale was his. If the court had followed *Pierson v. Post*, it might have concluded that merely sinking a whale in the ocean is not enough to produce any social benefit and awarded the carcass to Rich. Instead, the court held that

Massachusetts custom bound the parties. That custom recognized rights in the whaler and required only a small reimbursement to the finder. Here, established custom, a purer version of first-in-time, first-in-right, and perhaps a different view of which kinds of productive activity to incentivize, prevailed over *Pierson v. Post*'s more literalistic approach to what acts are necessary to render a wild animal's body under firm human control.

In *Keeble v. Hickeringill*, 103 Eng. Rep. 1127 (Q.B. 1707), the plaintiff, Keeble, sued his neighbor, Hickeringill, for setting off noise-makers to scare ducks away from the plaintiff's pond, where the plaintiff had placed decoys and planned to shoot ducks. The defendant responded that he was setting off the noise-makers on his own land and could do as he liked there. The court found for Keeble. It declared that Hickeringill was free to try to out-compete Keeble in luring ducks to his land to be killed there but was not free to disrupt Keeble's duck-hunting as an end in itself. The key, therefore, was not the harm done to Keeble but rather Hickeringill's bad faith. This case also is an early example of a theme that will occupy much of the Property course: how the law regulates harms neighbors can cause one another (intentionally, as in this case, or otherwise).

Courts have applied the lessons of these and other early wildlife cases to natural resources in several ways. Water law provides a good example. Streams and rivers typically flow by many different owners' property, and aquifers commonly lie beneath many owners' plots.

- Western U.S. states typically enforce the first-in-time, first-in-right principle, which courts sometimes call "**prior appropriation**", strictly for surface waters and some groundwater. Thus, for example, if one person begins to extract water from a stream or river (or from some aquifers) and puts it to a reasonable purpose, the law entitles her or him to continued access to that water even if an upstream property owner would like to draw it off—and even if the upstream owner has a more productive use for the water.

- England and Eastern U.S. states are more likely to follow a "**capture**" rule for groundwater extraction similar to the rule in *Pierson v. Post* or *Ghen v. Rich*. Thus, in those states, each landowner is entitled to capture any water beneath her or his land even if that has the effect of drawing water away from aquifers under other owners' lands. In the Eastern U.S., but not in England, wasteful extractions that diminish the water available to neighboring property owners are considered unlawful. This twist on the "capture" rule is reminiscent of *Keeble v. Hickeringill*'s discouragement of bad faith behavior by neighboring property owners.

What You Need to Know:

1. Capturing animals or natural resources is a key method by which people create new property.
2. Courts rely on a variety of methods to decide disputes between rival claimants to natural resources. Among these are the first-in-time, first-in-right principle, custom, the promotion of economic efficiency, and the discouragement of bad faith.
3. Often these principles will support different outcomes. To anticipate how a court might rule in a case for which no precedent controls, a lawyer must apply each of these principles to the facts at hand.
4. Natural resources law has borrowed core principles from early animal law cases, often adapting them to the differences between the ways that people extract water or mineral resources and the ways in which people hunt animals.

LESSON 4: FOUND PROPERTY

"Finders keepers; losers weepers" is the slogan of many a playground bully. But it also is not far from the law's attitude toward lost property. Where property is found and its true owner cannot be ascertained, the law typically moves forward to give ownership of the property to the next-best claimant. Problems with found property are neither terribly common nor terribly important by themselves. But they do provide a nice demonstration of how policy considerations drive property law. Very often, property law awards rights to one person or another based on society's larger interests rather than because the winning party has the most persuasive claim to "own" the item in the conventional sense.

Many Property books make this point with the old case of *Armory v. Delamirie*, 1 Strange 505 (K.B. 1722). A chimney sweep's boy found a jewel, supposedly in the mud. He took it to a goldsmith for an appraisal. The goldsmith refused to give it back to the boy, saying that the jewel obviously was not his. The court, of course, would have preferred to give the jewel back to its rightful owner, but he or she was nowhere to be found. So the court had only a choice between two less-good claimants: the boy and the goldsmith. The court chose the boy because his actions, in finding the jewel, put it back into commerce where it could benefit people again. The goldsmith's actions, on the other hand, would if anything hinder commerce by making the finder of a valuable item reluctant to hand it over to those best in a position to evaluate it and sell it to those that would value it most. (Of course, the chimney sweep's boy might have stolen the jewel in question; if so, letting him keep it would create an incentive for more theft. But that is not what the court found. And even if it was true, the goldsmith was just as dishonest.) This supports application of the principle of **first-in-time, first-in-right**.

Similarly, in *Hannah v. Peel*, 1945 K.B. 509, Major Peel, a soldier stationed in a private house that had been requisitioned for military use, found a cobweb-encrusted brooch on a window sill. The owner of the house had never moved in since buying the place, so the brooch was not his. The court concluded that Major Peel's finding the brooch had brought it back into commerce and that Major Peel should be awarded the brooch on that basis. Again, incentives promoting aggregate efficiency prevailed.

This principle has limits. In *McAvoy v. Medina*, 93 Mass. 548 (1866), a customer found a pocketbook full of money in a barbershop and argued that he ought to be able to keep it if the prior owner remained unidentified. The court instead awarded the money to the barber, reasoning that the true owner would be more likely to come back to the barbershop looking for the money and hence leaving it with the barber was the best way to return it to the true owner. The court might just as well have said that the customer did far less to return the property to commerce than either the chimney sweep's boy in *Armory* or Major Peel in *Hannah*: surely the barber would have found the money soon enough anyway even if the customer had not.

Another exception comes from *South Staffordshire Water Co. v. Sharman*, 2 Q.B. 44 (1896), in which Sharman found two rings in the mud at the bottom of a pool he was cleaning out on orders of the pool's owners. You might argue, on the basis of *Armory*, that Sharman put those rings back into commerce and should be rewarded with their value. The court held, however, that landowners are generally entitled to any property found in their land. It also suggested that Sharman was only on the land at the behest of the landowner and so, when he found the rings, he effectively was doing it on behalf of the landowner. By contrast, the brooch in *Hannah* was not embedded in the property, and Major Peel was not there as a representative of the house's owner.

You can agree or disagree with these individual results. But taken together, they show several important things about the way courts resolve property issues. These insights can be most helpful in other, more common and more important cases.

What You Need to Know:

1. Finders of lost property generally have superior rights to that property against anyone but the prior owner.
2. Courts often rank claimants to property rather than picking a single best claimant and disregarding the rest.
3. Courts value efforts that put property back into commerce.

4. More broadly, courts often award property rights based on what will improve economic efficiency not just in the case at hand but more generally over the broad run of cases.

5. Pragmatism, rather than purist notions of rights and ownership, is often the best guide to the judicial resolution of property law disputes.

LESSON 5: ADVERSE POSSESSION

As little children, many of us loved to hear stories of magical transformations. The kiss of a princess transforms a lowly frog into a fine prince. The touch of King Midas transforms everyday objects (and, alas, loved ones) into gold. A fairy godmother transforms a pumpkin and some mice into a regal horse-drawn carriage. As we grew older, our parents told us that such magical transformations were impossible.

They lied! Through the magic of **prescriptive rights**, a lowly, much-despised trespasser can suddenly be transformed into a powerful (though not necessarily charming) property owner. Each state has a limitations period on actions to remove trespassers. Once the clock strikes twelve on that limitations period—once the prior owner becomes time-barred to assert her or his right to remove the trespasser—the trespasser becomes the new owner and the old owner becomes, well, history. (Sadly, any pumpkins and mice on the premises remain pumpkins and mice.)

Prescriptive rights are a pragmatic response to the problem raised by **statutes of limitations**. Statutes of limitations are important to allow potential parties to disputes to achieve repose and to free the courts from the burden of adjudicating stale claims after relevant evidence may have been destroyed and key witnesses have died or forgotten. Once an owner's action against a trespasser is barred by a statute of limitations, her or his ownership interest would not have much meaning because she or he could no longer regain control of the land from the trespasser. Rather than allow the owner to keep title in name only without the means to regain control of the property, the law transfers ownership to the person who does have the practical ability to stay on the property: the trespasser.

Courts call the ownership interests trespassers gain in this manner "prescriptive rights." The process of taking full ownership of a property in this manner is commonly known as "**adverse possession**." Prescriptive rights can also arise in lesser interests than full ownership of property. For example, someone who routinely trespasses across someone else's land to get to and from the road may eventually gain a prescriptive easement giving her or him the right to continue doing so.

Prescriptive rights are not so much an endorsement of the trespasser as a condemnation of the prior owner for having "slept on" her or his rights by failing to act for so long to secure the property against intrusion. Prescriptive rights also recognize that third parties may have developed beneficial relationships with a long-time trespasser that would be disrupted if a court forced the trespasser to leave.

In order to acquire property by adverse possession, a trespasser must be able to show several things:

1. ***Actual entry*** onto the property now claimed;
2. Possession of the property in a manner that is ***open and notorious***;
3. Possession of the property was ***continuous*** for the period of the statute of limitations;
4. Possession was ***adverse*** or hostile to the interests of the owner; and
5. Possession was under a ***claim of right***.

Some lists put these items in a different order, or group some elements together, but the basic structure remains the same.

Each of these five elements merits a closer look. First, no claim for adverse possession can get off the ground without actual entry. Interfering with the property from the outside, such as by removing locks or "Keep Out" signs, is not sufficient by itself to constitute actual entry onto the land. Some cases hold that you have to occupy the entirety of the land to count as making entry. For example, in *Van Valkenburg v. Lutz*, 106

N.E.2d 28 (N.Y. 1952), the trespasser put chicken coups on part of the land, gardened other parts, and strew the property with junk, but he did not consistently make any one, definable part his own. The court held that he failed to make the requisite entry and occupation. It therefore rejected his claim of adverse possession.

Second, the trespasser cannot conceal her or his presence on the property. The owner does not need to have actual notice of the trespasser's presence. But the trespasser must be occupying the property in such a way that anyone coming by the property could readily see. Sneaking onto the property at night, or hiding out in the woods where only the owls can see you, is not open and notorious occupation and will not get you adverse possession. If the owner does not bother to go to her or his property—or to have an agent do so—throughout the limitations period, she or he is certainly implying that the property is not very important to her or him. On the other hand, if your presence is obvious, the fact that an observer might not realize that it is trespassory does not defeat your claim. If I build my fence four feet inside your property line, I can adversely possess your land even if you do not realize that I have crossed the actual property line.

Third, the occupation of the property must be continuous in a manner appropriate to the property. The trespasser may leave the property for short periods without giving up possession: almost all property owners routinely go out to work, run errands, or go on vacation. The would-be adverse possessor can do likewise. *Howard v. Kunto*, 477 P.2d 210 (Wash. App. 1970), found continuous occupancy in a disputed vacation home despite the adverse possessor's only spending summers there: he was using the home in the same way any owner would. But anything that interrupts the trespasser's occupation of the property sets the statute of limitations back to zero and renders all prior time on the property useless in making a claim for adverse possession.

Fourth, presence on the property only counts if it is in a status adverse or hostile to the owner. Tenants cannot adversely possess property against their landlord because they are present with the landlord's permission. You may have many worries about the house guest who just will not go away, but adverse possession is not one of them (at least not until you explicitly tell them they are a trespasser and they still refuse to go).

Finally, an occupation can only lead to adverse possession if the trespasser claims a right to be there. If you go onto your neighbor Nate's land and occupy it openly and notoriously and continuously for several years without permission, you will not take it by adverse possession if you keep telling people "yeah, I know I am not supposed to be here, but I am hoping Nate will not notice." The claim of right need not be valid—indeed, if it was, the claimant would have no need to assert prescriptive rights—but the trespasser must assert ownership over the property. The courts disagree about the consequences of the purported adverse possessor's mistake as to ownership. Some states follow the "Maine Doctrine" (said to originate in *Preble v. Maine Central Ry. Co.*, 27 A. 149 (Me. 1893)), which holds that someone who mistakenly believes she or he is on her or his own land is insufficiently making a hostile claim to take over ownership through adverse possession. In effect, this rule allows adverse possession only by those consciously trying to seize property that they know does not belong to them. Favoring malefactors in this way offends other courts, which prefer the "Connecticut Doctrine" (traced back to *French v. Pearce*, 8 Conn. 439 (Conn. 1831)). The Connecticut Doctrine which prohibits inquiring into the trespasser's subjective state of mind but only considers whether she or he outwardly asserted title in the disputed property. This split is a classic example of disagreements between courts preferring formal rules (the Maine Doctrine) and those concerned with ease of administration and minimizing bad incentives (the Connecticut Doctrine).

Although seizures of full ownership of entire parcels of land through adverse possession are relatively rare, they do occur. More common are seizures of other property rights through prescription, with the legal test analogous to that for full adverse possession. Many rights to go onto or cross over land (easements, discussed in a later Lesson) are obtained by prescription. Landowners seeking to avoid giving the public an easement over their land may block access to it once a year to prevent any continuous pattern of usage from arising. Prescriptive rights also can move the boundary between adjoining parcels of land where one neighbor erects a fence on the property of the other.

Some special complexities arise when trying to apply prescriptive rights to personal property, such as jewelry, antiques, or artwork. The owner of real estate always knows where to find it and therefore ought to be able to detect any unauthorized intrusions. The owner of stolen personal property, however, may have no idea where it is and hence may have no idea how to assert a claim for its return. Applying the statute of limitations in these situations could be quite unfair and create undesirable incentives to steal. Someone who possesses stolen property in secret in his or her home cannot be said to be possessing it "openly and notoriously," thus failing to meet one of the prerequisites for prescriptive rights. Different states have addressed this problem in different ways. One common approach is to require the owner to make reasonable efforts to find the missing property (such as filing police reports and contacting dealers in the relevant kind of goods) in order to keep the statute of limitations from running (and prescriptive rights from attaching). In *O'Keeffe v. Snyder*, 416 A.2d 862 (N.J. 1980), artist Georgia O'Keeffe claimed that Snyder had three of her paintings that had been stolen from her (apparently not by Snyder). The Supreme Court of New Jersey set aside a judgment in favor of O'Keeffe and remanded the case for a new trial to determine if she had made sufficient effort to get the artwork returned. If she could prove that she had, the statute of limitations would not start running until she discovered that Snyder had her property. But if she had not, the six-year statute of limitations would have run and Snyder would own the paintings. With some reason to believe that O'Keeffe had delayed pursuing the theft for several years, the case settled before trial on remand.

What You Need to Know:

1. Failure to look after your property can result in its loss to trespassers after the statute of limitations has run on any action to remove the intruders.

2. Ownership of property can shift from the established owner to a trespasser if the trespasser makes actual entry onto the property, occupies it openly and notoriously for a continuous period equal to the statute of limitations for trespass actions, and does so adversely to the established owner and while claiming a right to the property (however groundless that claim may originally have been).
3. Prescriptive rights can change ownership of entire parcels of land. They also can change the boundaries of land, can create permanent rights to pass over land, and can change the ownership of valuable personal property such as jewelry, antiques, or artwork.
4. When you wish upon a star, it makes no difference who you are: just make actual entry in an open and notorious manner while asserting a hostile claim of right and, upon the passing of the statute of limitations, your trespassory dreams may come true.

LESSON 6: GIFTS

Whoever it was that said “never look a gift horse in the mouth” clearly was not a property lawyer. The common law has been deeply suspicious of gifts: recipients all too easily hear what they want to hear—or just plain lie—and claim rights in property that the putative donor never meant to give away. In addition, the common law sought to protect property owners from the consequences of short-lived impulses of generosity. This may seem mean-spirited when we imagine the donor as some multi-millionaire who would scarcely notice the absence of property given away. But many a family has fallen into poverty because of a member’s ill-conceived (or skillfully manipulated) generosity.

The common law’s answer was to require putative gifts to pass a two-part test in order to gain legal recognition. Each valid gift needs *both* the **donative intent** of the owner *and* the ritual of **transferring possession** through the donor's presenting the item to the donee and the donee accepting it. Unscrupulous, greedy people might twist the owner's words, but they might have more trouble persuading the court that the ritual took place. In addition, the requirement to hand over the property being gifted may wake up some owners that like to talk a good game about making gifts but are not really prepared to part with their property. Conversely, tricking someone into handing you the property will not make it yours unless you can convince the court that the owner intended it as a gift. This system is far from fool-proof, but the combined effect of these two tests is better than either one of them would have been on its own.

A problem arises when the item conveyed cannot be handed over. Perhaps it is too heavy. Perhaps it is not present where the donor and donee are meeting. Perhaps it is in a form that does not have physical manifestation, such as a copyright or the ownership of some land. In these cases, the law accepts the transfer of a **token** of the property to be given. For example, I might give you the keys to my car rather than try to pick the thing up or I might give you the claim ticket if a suit I want to give you is currently at the drycleaner's. (Of course, if you think my suit is hideous, you can prevent me from giving it to you by refusing to accept the claim ticket.)

Courts have been reasonably patient with parties' attempts to find appropriate tokens as long as the parties are clear what they are transferring—and as long as the ritual of transferring that token confirms the donative intent. Courts' patience, however, has limits. In *Newman v. Bost*, 29 S.E. 848 (N.C. 1898), a dying man had handed his servant the key to a bureau. In the bureau was a valuable life insurance policy. The court honored the gift of the bureau because it was clearly too heavy for the dying man to lift and hand over—and the key was a clear, obvious token for it. But the court would not find a gift of the life insurance: if that had been the dying man's intent, he could have asked someone to bring him the policy so that he could have handed it to the servant.

The court in *Newman*, and courts generally, are particularly cautious about gifts made by dying people. Lying about what now-deceased people said or did is just too easy. Dying people may not be thinking clearly and may be easily manipulated. And courts do not want people using gifts as alternatives to complying with the (considerably more demanding) formalities required for wills.

What You Need to Know:

1. To be legally effective, a gift must both reflect the donor's intent to give and be manifested by a physical transfer at least of a token.
2. Courts are flexible about what sort of token can suffice for the handing over ritual as long as the meaning of the ritual is clear.

LESSON 7: TRUSTS

Over the years, property owners sought legal means to ensure that their property would be used as they intended even if they could not themselves manage that property on a day-to-day basis. The most important means for achieving these ends today is the **trust**. Persons who put their property into a trust are called **settlors**.

Settlors have many reasons for setting up trusts. Most simply, the settlor might wish to control what happens to the property after her or his death. A will can distribute ownership of property among those important to the deceased, but the property owner may wish to constrain the management of property as well as its ownership. This might be because the settlor wishes to benefit some friends or relatives but doubts their ability to manage the property wisely (perhaps because they are still children). This might also be because the settlor has strong views about the best uses of the property, regardless of who gets the property's benefit. For example, the settlor might want to give her house to her niece but not allow the niece to tear it down.

Sometimes a settlor wants to control how their property will be used in future periods even while she or he is still alive. Perhaps the settlor will be busy with other things and unable to attend to the property's management. Perhaps the settlor doubts her or his competence at managing the property (the settlor may lack financial management skills or may anticipate dementia). Or perhaps the settlor wishes to avoid taxes that might be owed if she or he were to own and manage the property directly.

Although much mythology surrounds the world of trusts, the legal principle is quite simple. A trust separates ***legal ownership*** from ***equitable ownership*** in property. A trust may say that Amelia will be the legal owner of some property but that she must use that property to benefit Benjamin. Amelia will be the legal owner (called the "**trustee**") and has all of the powers any legal owner would have. But because Benjamin is the equitable owner (called the **"beneficiary"**), Amelia must manage the property for his benefit. Thus, for example, if the trust property is Blackacre, Amelia can rent it out to local farmers, but she must give Benjamin the rent or spend the rent to meet Benjamin's needs.

A trust can, in principle, be created in a very few, simple words. The trust in the last paragraph might be created by conveying "Blackacre to Amelia, for the benefit of Benjamin." For most significant trusts, however, the settlor will establish more detailed rules for how the legal owner is to manage the trust's property and who is to receive what rights if the first-named beneficiary cannot receive the benefit from the property for whatever reason.

In principle, once a trust separates legal and equitable ownership, they can each travel onward independent of one another. In practice, the legal ownership of a property that you must use for someone else is not particularly attractive. Many trustees charge fees for their services managing the property of others.

Interests in trusts are subject to the **Rule Against Perpetuities**, which Lesson 10 discusses.

What You Need to Know:

1. Trusts arise when an owner conveys property to one person with instructions that that property is to be used to benefit another.

2. Trusts separate legal ownership of the property, which resides in the trustee, from beneficial or equitable ownership, which resides in the beneficiary.

LESSON 8: FEES, LIFE ESTATES, LEASEHOLDS, AND SEISIN

In a simpler world, each piece of property would have a single owner at any one time, with no strings left by those that owned it in the past and no commitments about who might own it in the future. That is not our world. The English common law developed many elaborate devices for dividing up ownership interests in property (called **estates**) over time. Although modern property law has dropped a few of the most arcane—to the everlasting dismay of traditionalist Property professors—the great majority of the common law in this area remains applicable today. As a result, most Property courses spend several classes on these rules.

To build the most elaborate cathedrals, medieval architects had to start with the most basic stone blocks. In the same way, before we explore the more complicated rules, we must start with the basic concepts on which they are built. And nothing in the law of estates in land is more basic than the **fee**. In this context, a fee is not the payment demanded by the doctor, lawyer, or telecommunications company of your choice. Instead, it is an interest in land of *potentially* infinite duration. One person may have the property today, another person may be due to have it next, and still another person may be due to have it after that, but eventually we get to someone who is not guaranteed to lose the property at any point in the future. That person will have a fee interest in the property.

As the common law has come down to us, we recognize two kinds of fees. By far the most common kind—indeed the only kind in forty-six states—is the **fee simple**. This is an estate of potentially infinite duration (fee) with no restrictions on to whom the owner may transfer it (simple). A fee simple that is not subject to any conditions or contingencies is called a **fee simple absolute**, which is the highest form of ownership in the common law system of estates in land. Several other kinds of fee simples exist, as Lesson 9 will discuss.

All states in the past, and four northeastern states today, also recognize the **fee tail**. A fee tail is an estate of potentially infinite duration that (traditionally) the owner could only transfer among the direct descendants of the person who created the fee tail. Today, even the four states that still recognize the fee tail allow the owner to grant it to anyone she or he pleases while the owner is alive but reject provisions in wills that attempt to devise the property to persons other than direct descendants of the original fee tail owner,

Example

> If Oliver, who has children Alison, Benny, and Charlotte, created a fee tail in Blackacre, he can give Blackacre to any one (or more) of his children, or to their children, grandchildren, etc., but he cannot give it to his sister Sue. If Alison comes to own Blackacre, she can give it, sell it, or pass it on her death to her children, grandchildren, etc., to Benny or Charlotte, or to Benny or Charlotte's children, grandchildren, etc., but she cannot convey the property to someone outside the family (or to Sue).

The fee tail arose in feudal times to allow landowners to keep land concentrated in family hands to retain the family name's prominence. In a democratic society such as ours, the fee tail is widely regarded as both obnoxious and inefficient.

What of estates that are not of potentially infinite duration? One of the most important of those is also one of the most generous possible time-limited ownership interests: the **life estate**. The life estate is as its name suggests: full ownership during the life of the person holding it with no rights after death. The life estate holder (known as a "life tenant") can do as she or he pleases with the property—hold wild parties, rent it out for the production of reality TV shows, etc.—as long as she or he does not damage the interests of whomever is scheduled to get the property after her or his life is over. (Such damage is called **waste**, and committing waste can allow those scheduled to own the property after the life tenant to bring suit for an injunction against the injurious activity or even to cut short the life estate prior to the life tenant's death.)

A life tenant can even grant her or his interest in the property to someone else. The duration of the estate, however, remains the same: the life of the original life tenant. Where a life estate is granted, it becomes a **life estate per autre vie** (by the life of another).

Example

> Dennis has a life estate in Greenacre. He sells his interest to Ellen. Ellen now has a life estate per autre vie measured by Dennis's life. As soon as Dennis dies, Ellen loses Greenacre, even if she is alive and well. On the other hand, if Ellen dies while Dennis is still living, Greenacre will go to her heirs or the beneficiaries of her will until Dennis dies.

Other estates in land that are of less than infinite duration are generally referred to as **leaseholds**. Lesson 13 discusses leaseholds in much more detail. For our purposes here, it is worth noting that an interest in land that is scheduled to last a specific length of time is called a **term of years**. A term of years may be less than a year (*e.g.*, 90 days, until your next birthday) and may not be an even number of years (*e.g.*, 3.141598 years). Having a leasehold does not necessarily obligate someone to pay rent for the property unless such an obligation was included in the conveyance of the leasehold.

With ownership of pieces of land split up over time, neighbors interacting with the land had difficulty determining who was in charge. The common law in feudal times had strong needs to be able to point to one person as the principal owner of each property. This person was said to have **seisin** or to be seised of the property. If the property was currently in the hands of a life tenant, that person was considered to have seisin. Persons with mere leaseholds—even very long ones—could not have seisin. In that case, seisin was said to reside in the next person scheduled to take the property as either a life tenant or holder of a fee.

What You Need to Know:

1. Interests in land are commonly referred to as "estates." Property law has elaborate systems for recognizing multiple estates in land across time.
2. An estate of potentially infinite duration is called a "fee".
3. An estate of potentially infinite duration that may be conveyed freely is called a "fee simple."
4. The right to use property as one wishes throughout one's life is called a "life estate." A life estate may be transferred, but it still ends at the death of the original life tenant (or perhaps sooner if someone commits waste on the property).
5. The right to use property for a specific period is called a "leasehold."
6. Only life tenants or holders of fee interests are regarded as having seisin or principal ownership.
7. If you want your child to appear in a Property professor's hypothetical, you should give her or him a name beginning with the letter "O".

LESSON 9: DEFEASIBLE ESTATES AND FUTURE INTERESTS

Most transfers of real estate are quite simple. That pleases the parties, their attorneys, the judges that hear their cases, and pretty much everyone else involved with the transaction. But it infuriates law professors and bar examiners. And fortunately for those two groups, courts and legislatures have proven unwilling to jettison various complex forms of conveying interests in property that originated centuries ago. As a result, many—although by no means all—Property classes include units on these means of dividing ownership of property across time. Some professors teach this material because it has long been part of the Property curriculum, some do so because it is on the Bar examination, some do so because these concepts are important in the upper-level Trusts and Estates course, and some do so because working through these rules gives first-year students practice analyzing legal documents with the precision that is important for all lawyers. (We lawyers don't do "close enough for government work.")

Students down through the ages have rejoiced at the principle of **numerus clausus**, which restricts the number of permissible types of division between **present interests** and **future interests** in property. A detailed rendition of this highly technical area is well beyond the scope of these Lessons. When actually taking this part of the Property course, doing lots of problems and checking your answers is the best way to attain mastery. (Some of my students refer to this area as "legal math.") A broad overview here may, however, make these concepts seem less alien when they come up in class.

The basic concept of present and future interests is dividing up the entirety of ownership across time. If you add up all of the present and future interests in a property, you should be able to account for every ownership right in that property. These rights can, however, be divided in different ways. Each future interest matches up with a particular present interest to encompass all ownership rights.

It might be useful to think of dividing a car into two sets of components. This can be done in different ways. For example, Ahmed could take the wheels off his Ford Focus and give them to Beatrice. Ahmed then has a wheel-less car, and Beatrice has four wheels. Or Chen could take out the engine of his Chevy station wagon and give it to Daphne. Chen then has an engineless station wagon and Daphne has an engine. Each of the four of them has some part of a car, but not enough to drive. Moreover, although the cars can be put back together, this is only possible by combining matching sets of components. Ahmed cannot restore his car's functionality by getting Daphne's components: his car would have power to spare but would still be up on blocks. Indeed, although Ahmed and Chen between them have every part involved in a car, their components probably do not fit together properly.

It is easy to see that a wheel-less car fits together with four wheels and that an engineless station wagon fits together with an engine. The terms property law uses for present and future interests are far less natural, but they fit together in very much the same way to equal the full range of ownership rights across time, known as a fee simple absolute. If you know what present estate you have, you know what future interests are outstanding because, combined, they must create a fee simple absolute. Similarly, if you know what future interests are outstanding, you can infer what present interest would complement them to create a fee simple absolute. (In the same way, if I have the spades and the clubs, I know I need the red suits to complete a standard deck of playing cards, but if I have all of the cards from the twos through the tens, I need the aces, kings, queens, and jacks to complete my deck.) Present and future interests can fit together to account for all of the rights in a fee simple absolute in several different ways, such as:

1. Fee simple subject to an executory limitation + executory interest(s) = fee simple absolute
2. Fee simple determinable + possibility of reverter = fee simple absolute
3. Fee simple on a condition subsequent + right of entry = fee simple absolute
4. Life estate + remainder(s) = fee simple absolute
5. Life estate + reversion = fee simple absolute
6. Fee tail + reversion = fee simple absolute

Once you come to appreciate how these standardized pieces fit together, your next step is to recognize what kind of language splits the ownership interests in each of these ways. This is like knowing that a jack and a lug nut wrench are the main tools required to separate out a wheel-less car and a set of wheels while different equipment is needed to separate out an engineless car and an engine.

A fee simple determinable is an estate of potentially infinite duration that could be cut short if a particular event occurs, with ownership returning to the grantor. If that event does occur, the person with the possibility of reverter (initially the grantor but possibly someone else who got that contingent right to the property from the grantor) obtains fee simple absolute ownership of the property.

Example

> *"To Madeline and her heirs for so long as either a Democrat or a Republican is President of the United States."* Madeline has a fee simple determinable and the grantor has a possibility of reverter. It is possible that no independent or third-party candidate will even win the presidency. As long as none does, Madeline or anyone to whom she conveys her interests will have free use and control of the property. But if that event ever occurs, Madeline loses all rights in the property and the grantor (or whoever then holds the possibility of reverter that the grantor created) will take full ownership of the property.

A fee simple on a condition subsequent is an estate of potentially infinite duration that could be cut short if a particular condition is met, with ownership returning to the grantor. The difference between a fee simple on a condition subsequent and a fee simple determinable is extremely subtle; often the drafter could choose to describe the same contingency either as an event or as a condition. The condition need not be within the control of the person holding the fee simple on a condition subsequent, although it often is.

Example

> *"To Marilyn and her heirs, but if the property is ever used as a tavern, I shall have the right to re-enter and take possession."* Marilyn has a fee simple on a condition subsequent and the grantor has a right of entry. It is possible that no one will ever try to open a tavern on the property. As long as they do not, all ownership rights will be held by Marilyn or whomever receives the property from her. But if a tavern ever does open there, the grantor (or whoever then holds his right of entry) may appear at the property and take back all ownership rights.

A fee simple on an executory limitation is an estate of potentially infinite duration that could be cut short under specified circumstances, with ownership passing to a third party. That third party is said to own an executory interest. A fee simple on an executory limitation is analogous to both a fee simple determinable and a fee simple on a condition subsequent except that the property does not go back to the grantor but on to a third party the grantor named.

Example

"To Miriam and her heirs, but if the property is ever used as a tavern, then to Neena and her heirs." Miriam has a fee simple on an executory limitation and Neena has an executory interest. It is possible that no one will ever try to open a tavern on the property. As long as they do not, all ownership rights will be held by Miriam or whomever receives the property from her. But if a tavern ever does open there, then Neena (or whoever then holds her executory interest) may appear at the property and take back all ownership rights.

A reversion is a catch-all term for the interests the grantor retains in a conveyance (other than interests with more specific names like possibility of reverter or right of entry).

Example

"To Ming for life." Ming has a life estate. Because the grantor did not specify what happens to the property after Ming's life estate ends, the property returns to him or her.

A remainder is a future interest in someone other than the grantor that follows a present interest of less than infinite duration. If it is known who will take the property and any conditions have been met, the remainder is vested. If the identity of the person taking in the future is uncertain or if a condition has not been met, the remainder is contingent.

Example

"To Menachem for life and then to Norman and his heirs." Menachem has a life estate and Norman has a vested remainder in fee simple absolute.

Example

"To Mahmood for life and then to Nancy and her heirs if Nancy has graduated from engineering school by

then." Nancy has not yet graduated from engineering school. Mahmood has a life estate. Nancy has a contingent remainder in fee simple absolute. Her remainder is contingent because it contains a condition that has not yet been met: we do not know if she will graduate from engineering school. Because the conveyance does not specify who gets the property if Nancy does not graduate before Mahmood's life estate ends, the grantor has a reversion. If Nancy later graduates from engineering school, her remainder will change from contingent to vested and the grantor's reversion will fail (disappear).

Example

"To Moses for life and then to whichever of Nicole and Oliver has most recently lived closest to where Moses most recently lived." Moses has a life estate. Nicole and Oliver have alternative contingent remainders in fee simple absolute. Their remainders are contingent because, although they contain no conditions, we do not know which of them will be living closest to Moses at the end of Moses's life estate. Because either Nicole or Oliver will take full ownership of the property after Moses's life estate ends, no possibilities are left unaccounted for and the grantor has no reversion.

What You Need to Know:

1. When owners divide ownership rights in property across time, they create present and future interests.
2. Property law limits the kinds of present and future interests that owners may create.
3. Particular kinds of present interests go with particular kinds of future interests, each of which has a technical, nonintuitive, and all-too-easily forgotten name.

LESSON 10: THE RULE AGAINST PERPETUITIES

Generations of law students have labored mightily to learn a series of rules disallowing or transforming certain kinds of future interests. Much to the irritation of traditionalist law professors, however, merciful courts and legislatures have abolished most of these rules in a great many states. Therefore, odds are that you may be spared the Rule of Worthier Title and the Rule in Shelly's Case, among others. (If your Property course does not require you to learn these rules, and you point that out to an older lawyer relative at the Thanksgiving dinner table, prepare to be swatted.) Still with us, however, is the most famous of all of these rules, the Rule Against Perpetuities. It will never die, both because it gives such joy to sadistic Property professors and Bar examiners and because it serves a genuinely useful social purpose.

Although many conveyances will inevitably be resolved fairly quickly, some property owners try to control events far into the future. Here, the courts have been ambivalent. On the one hand, the courts generally support owners' ability to dispose of their property as they please. On the other hand, property that is subject to outstanding conditions is harder to buy, sell, and develop, reducing its value and creating considerable inefficiency, sometimes referred to as the **dead hand of the past**. The courts' attempt to balance these strong competing considerations is the Rule Against Perpetuities.

The Rule Against Perpetuities disallows **executory interests** and **contingent remainders** that might not become **vested** within **twenty-one years** after the end of a **life in being** at the outset of the conveyance. This allows the grantor to provide for anyone she or he knows and even to provide property to the children of people she or he knows when those children reach the traditional age of legal adulthood. But it generally does not allow the grantor to try to shift property around even farther into the future.

Example

"To Manuela for life and then to any of her children that reach age twenty-five." This purports to create a life estate in Manuela and contingent remainders in

her children. (The remainders are contingent in that both the identity of the children that take ownership and whether they will meet the condition of living to age twenty-five are uncertain.) This violates the Rule Against Perpetuities because Manuela could have another child after the effective date of the grant and then die with that child under the age of four. Twenty-one years after her death, the child might still be alive but would not have met the condition and so the remainder would neither have vested or have failed. The likely outcome is that the life estate to Manuela would be valid, the contingent remainders for the children would be void, and the property would revert to the grantor at the end of Manuela's life estate.

Example

"To Manuela for life and then to any of her children that reach age twenty-one." This also purports to create a life estate in Manuela and contingent remainders in her children. But unlike the last example, this one is valid because the contingencies will be resolved no later than twenty-one years after the death of a life in being (Manuela).

Example

"To Manuela for life and then to any of Noel, Ophelia, and Pauline that reach age twenty-five." Noel, Ophelia, and Pauline are Manuela's infant children. This, too, purports to create a life estate in Manuela and contingent remainders in her three named children. (Even though the identity of the children holding the remainders is known, the remainders are still contingent because we do not know whether they will meet the condition of living to age twenty-five.) This conveyance is valid because its contingencies will have to be resolved within twenty-one years of the end of a life in being. Even though Manuela could die before her children reach age four, meaning that we will not know if they reach age twenty-five within twenty-one years of her death, because they are named in the conveyance we know they are lives in being. We can

test the validity of the conveyance by testing it against their lives. The contingencies will be resolved no later than the end of their lives—giving us twenty-one years to spare! If Manuela had another child, that child would not receive any interest in the property because the conveyance only has grants for the three named children.

The Rule Against Perpetuities does not affect future interests in the grantor: **reversions**, **possibilities of reverter**, and **rights of entry**. Common law judges believed that these rights never left the grantor and so did not have to vest in the future, even long after the grantor was dead.

Example

"To Mikhail and his heirs for so long as the property is not used as a tavern." The property might become a tavern many decades after every life in being at the time of the conveyance has died. But because the future interest is in the grantor—specifically, it is a possibility of reverter—the Rule Against Perpetuities does not block this condition. If someone opens a tavern on the property after the grantor dies, the property will go to whomever owns the grantor's rights.

The Rule Against Perpetuities also does not block future interests in charities.

Example

"To Marcel for two hundred years and then to whichever nonprofit opera company in the U.S. has performed 'Otello' the most times since my death." If the future interest had been in an unspecified natural person, this would clearly violate the Rule Against Perpetuities as the ultimate recipient may not be determined until much more than twenty-one years after the death of all lives in being. Indeed, that is all but guaranteed. But because the beneficiary will be a nonprofit artistic organization, the contingent remainder is allowed.

Many states have modified the Rule Against Perpetuities in various ways to make it easier to apply. For example, some states adopt the "**wait and see**" rule which only disallows a future interest if it *in fact* takes too long to vest, not just if it could theoretically stay unvested for more than a life in being plus twenty-one years.

What You Need to Know:

1. The Rule Against Perpetuities prohibits conveyances that might award property to third parties far into the future.
2. The Rule Against Perpetuities does not affect future interests in the grantor or in charities.
3. Many states have modified the Rule Against Perpetuities to make it easier to apply.
4. Most students spend far too much time worrying about present and future interests, in general, and the Rule Against Perpetuities in particular. Your success in your Property class will depend far, far more on your mastery of the many other concepts and doctrines covered. When future interests come up in class, do a few practice problems to get the hang of it and then go see a good movie.

LESSON 11: CONCURRENT OWNERSHIP OF PROPERTY

Sharing is caring! Also, sometimes, it's suing. Just as property law has developed intricate rules for dividing ownership *across different times*—for example, between life estate holders and reversion-holders—so, too, it has detailed rules for when ownership of property is divided between more than one person *at the same time*. One of the most important ways in which more than one person can have interests in a piece of property is the landlord-tenant relationship. But that is *so* important, it deserves a couple of Lessons all to itself. Also, some other means of co-ownership, such as corporations and partnerships, have their own upper-level courses and are rarely covered in first-year Property. This Lesson looks at other ways in which people can share ownership, ways that *are* commonly taught in the Property course.

The three major means of co-ownership are **tenancies in common**, **joint tenancies**, and **tenancies by the entireties**. (The next Lesson, on marital interests, discusses tenancies by the entireties and another means of co-ownership some states have for spouses.) The default arrangement, and the one that is by far the most frequent, is the tenancy in common. In a tenancy in common, two or more people each owns an undivided fraction of the total property. Their shares of ownership might be equal, but those shares do not have to be. If one of the tenants in common dies, her or his interest in the property passes under her or his will or by intestate succession just like any other property interest she or he may have had.

Example

> Aaron and Benjamin buy Greenacre as tenants in common. Aaron owns two-thirds of Greenacre; Benjamin owns the remaining one-third. A year after they buy Greenacre, Benjamin dies, leaving all of his property to his daughter, Carla. Now Aaron and Carla own Greenacre as tenants in common, with Aaron having a two-thirds interest and Carla having a one-third interest.

A joint tenancy differs from a tenancy in common mainly in what happens when one of the co-owners dies. In a joint tenancy, the deceased co-owner's share is automatically transferred to the other co-owner or co-owners.

Example

> Alice and Beth buy Orangeacre as joint tenants. Alice owns one-half of Orangeacre; Beth owns the remaining half. A year after they buy Orangeacre, Beth dies, leaving all of her property to her son, Charles. Now Alice owns all of Orangeacre under her right of survivorship. Charles has no interest at all in Orangeacre.

A joint tenancy can be a good arrangement for two people who are very close and intend to leave their property to one another. It passes ownership interests upon death without the cost and delay of probating a will. Indeed, at a time when literacy was rare and many property owners could not afford lawyers, joint tenancies served as substitutes for wills. Accordingly, the common law presumed that ambiguous co-ownership arrangements were joint tenancies.

No more. Today, the law regards joint tenancies as anomalies and makes creating them quite difficult. First, unless the grantor creates the co-ownership with specific language—"to A and B, as joint tenants with rights of survivorship" or something quite similar—the law will assume a tenancy in common was intended. In addition, the law only allows creation and continuation of a joint tenancy if all of the "**four unities**" are observed. These are:

1. **Unity of title.** The joint tenants must all have obtained their ownership from the same document.
2. **Unity of time.** The joint tenants must all have obtained their ownership at the same moment.
3. **Unity of interest.** The joint tenants must all have the same fractional share of ownership.
4. **Unity of possession.** The joint tenants must all have the same rights to go anywhere on the property.

Example

"To my sons George, John, and Thomas, as joint tenants with rights of survivorship, with each taking his share upon reaching age 18." If the sons are under 18 (and not triplets), this creates a tenancy in common because the sons will not take ownership at the same time and thus lack unity of time.

Example

"To Antony and Cleopatra, as joint tenants with rights of survivorship, with Antony to own one-third and Cleopatra to own two-thirds." This creates a tenancy in common. Because it violates unity of interest, it cannot be a joint tenancy.

Example

Jack and Beryl Stapleton, brother and sister, purchase a kennel as joint tenants. They wish to add Sir Henry as a third joint tenant. If they try each to convey one-third of their interests to Sir Henry, they will fail to create a joint tenancy with him both because different documents will give them and him title and because he will have taken title later than they did. Instead, their two-person joint tenancy would need to give the property to a new three-person joint tenancy: *Jack Stapleton and Beryl Stapleton, joint tenants, convey the Devonshire Kennel to Jack Stapleton, Beryl Stapleton, and Sir Henry, as joint tenants with rights of survivorship.* If something untoward were to happen to Sir Henry, his share will automatically be divided between the Stapletons as the remaining joint tenants and the property will again be owned by the two of them as joint tenants.

When property is owned by either tenants in common or joint tenants, all co-owners have equal rights to use it even if one tenant in common owns a larger share. Co-owners ordinarily do not owe one another rent for the property even if one of them uses the property disproportionately. None of the co-owners can bar the others from the property by changing the locks, posting guards, or other means.

Courts dislike intervening in disputes between disgruntled co-owners. If one co-owner believes that the arrangement is not in her or his best interest, she or he can try to sell her or his interest. (In the case of a joint tenancy, one co-owner selling will **sever** the joint tenancy and create a tenancy in common.) If that is not feasible—perhaps because no one will pay fair value for only a partial ownership interest—any co-owner can petition the court to **partition** the property. Traditionally, courts would usually order **partition in kind**, dividing the property into smaller segments that would be owned exclusively by the respective former co-owners, which each segment's value proportionate to the ownership interest of the former co-owner who receives it. Even if the acreage of each person's share reflects her or his fraction of ownership, however, disputes arise about which part has more economic value. As a result, the modern practice is to **partition by sale**: the court orders the entire property sold and then divides the proceeds among the former co-owners proportionately to their ownership interests.

What You Need to Know:

1. The law has many devices by which two or more people can divide up ownership in property. Law schools typically do not address some, such as the corporation and the partnership, until upper-level courses.
2. The two most important ways of sharing concurrent ownership of property are tenancies in common and joint tenancies.
3. In ambiguous cases, the law favors the creation of tenancies in common.
4. Joint tenancies can only exist where all co-owners are in identical positions in four key dimensions.
5. When one joint tenant dies, her or his share goes to her or his co-owners. When a tenant in common dies, her or his share becomes part of her or his estate and goes to devisees or heirs.
6. When tenants in common or joint tenants do not get along, courts may order partition of the property, either by dividing up the property or by selling it and dividing up the proceeds.
7. Do not take ownership of property as joint tenants with someone who already wants to kill you.

LESSON 12: MARITAL INTERESTS AND COMMUNITY PROPERTY

Some very special kinds of concurrent property rights exist between spouses. The rules we have today reflect an unusual combination of archaic Anglo-American ideas from a time when the law had little respect for women's agency, contemporary approaches reflecting both aspirations for equality and the reality of continued gender disparities in power, and probably the most important civil law influences in all of property law. These rules are still very much in flux.

A starting point in the common law is the doctrine of **coverture**. This principle regarded a married woman as incapable of holding property independently in her own name. In the eyes of the law, husband and wife were one person, with the husband in complete control. This obviously left married women extremely vulnerable not just to their husbands' malice but also to their husbands' incompetence or irresponsibility. Husbands that grew tired of their wives, those that mishandled their business affairs, and those that drank or gambled excessively could leave their wives destitute.

A partial, although very inadequate, response to this was the doctrine of **dower** rights. Dower gave a widow life estates in one-third of all property her late husband held at any time during the marriage if that property would have been inheritable by his issue. (Some jurisdictions recognized a largely analogous right for men, called curtesy, but that doctrine survives in few if any states.) Even if the husband had sold the property or gambled it away before his death, dower rights still attached. The idea was to give widows some means of support for the remainder of their lives—presumably by renting out the property in which they had dower rights—and somewhere to live. This worked rather badly for several reasons. It made married men's property much harder to sell as buyers would not want to be burdened with dower rights whenever the seller should die. Purchasers therefore often insisted that the wife sign a statement renouncing dower rights. With women having little economic or legal autonomy, many of these waivers of dower rights no doubt were anything but knowing and voluntary.

Eventually, alternatives appeared. States enacted **Married Women's Property Acts** which limited women's liability for their husband's separate debts. In some states, marital property is entirely exempt from creditors' levies for the debts of only one spouse. Thus, if the husband loses heavily at the gambling table, or commits a tort causing injuries, the winners or tort victims will not be able to take property he owns together with his wife. In other states, creditors may levy on the property but must return it to the wife if she outlives her husband. (This so limits what can be done with the property that it often will make levying unattractive.) Some states also void attempts by either spouse to convey away marital property without the signature of the other.

States also enacted inheritance laws giving widows the option to take a fraction of their late husband's estate (often one-third) in lieu of whatever they might have received under any will. Thus, if the deceased husband left his wife half of his property in his will, she would accept the will and renounce her **statutory elective share**. If the husband tried to distribute most or all of his property to his relatives, friends, or favorite charities, the widow could claim her share off the top and the will (apart from any bequests to her) would then govern the disposition of the remaining property. If the husband died intestate, the widow would get her statutory elective share and his heirs would get the rest.

Spouses also have a special form of co-ownership in many common law states called the **tenancy by the entirety**. A tenancy by the entirety closely resembles the joint tenancies discussed in Lesson 11: the rights in each co-owner must have originated at the same time and in the same document, they must be equal (half) shares, and the two co-owners must have equal rights in the property. A tenancy by the entirety, like a joint tenancy, includes a right of survivorship: whichever spouse outlives the other automatically obtains full ownership in any property held as tenants by the entirety no matter what the deceased spouse may have provided in her or his will. A tenancy by the entirety may be created explicitly or by conveying property to the couple and identifying them as being married. For example, conveying Greyacre to "Rachel and Shlomo, wife and husband" would be sufficient to create a tenancy by the entirety in most states that recognize that form of ownership. Unlike joint tenants, however, spouses owning property as tenants by the entirety cannot convey away their interests in the property independently of the other: if Rachel tried to convey her interest in Greyacre to Tran, the conveyance would have no effect. (If she and Shlomo has owned the property as joint tenants, by contrast, her conveyance to Tran would have created a tenancy in common between Shlomo and Tran.) Upon divorce, a tenancy by the entirety automatically ends, becoming a tenancy in common unless the couple provide otherwise.

In about ten states, an entirely different set of rules govern the property rights of married couples. This system is called **community property**. It is derived from the civil law system of continental Europe, a system with very different assumptions and expectations from the common law system that arose in England and spread throughout the English-speaking world. Not surprisingly, then, most of the states with the community property system are in areas once ruled by Spain or France (although Wisconsin adopted what is essentially the community property system legislatively because it makes good policy sense). The community property system has complex rules for special cases, but the basic idea is quite simple. Any property that either spouse acquires during the marriage through labor or through spending other marital resources is half-owned by each of the spouses. Thus, if a spouse works outside of the home, half of her or his wages are owned by the other spouse. If the working spouse buys a business with her or his earnings, half of that business is owned by the other spouse. This means that conveyances generally will be valid only if signed by both spouses.

Each spouse in a community property state is entitled to take her or his half share upon the dissolution of the marriage. In addition, each spouse can will her or his share as she or he pleases upon death: the surviving spouse does not automatically receive the deceased spouse's property (although presumably most spouses designate one another as beneficiaries in their wills).

Some courts in common law jurisdictions have begun to provide somewhat analogous protection to those who helped their spouses succeed by treating degrees or even careers earned by one spouse during the marriage as assets partially owned by the other spouse who provided support for that achievement.

Some early advocacy for legal recognition of same-sex couples sprang from concerns about property rights. If the law did not permit same-sex couples to marry, they could not claim the protection of these various special rules designed to protect the property of partners. When one partner died unexpectedly without a valid will, all of his or her property would go to his or her heirs, potentially leaving the surviving partner destitute or even homeless. Now that the U.S. Supreme Court has recognized same-sex marriages nationwide, many of these problems have a much simpler resolution, although numerous issues remain in flux.

What You Need to Know:

1. At common law, husbands and wives were regarded as one person, with the husband in charge.
2. Common law did give widows dower rights to life estates in one-third of the property their late husband held during their lifetimes. Most states have abolished dower (and related curtesy) rights.
3. Married Women's Property Acts restricted creditors' ability to take marital property for debts that only the husband incurred; some also limited the husband's ability to convey marital property.
4. The tenancy by the entirety allowed married couples to co-own property in a manner similar to joint tenants but without the ability of either spouse to convey away her or his interest alone.
5. Ten states have community property laws that give each spouse a half-interest in all property coming into the marriage, including wages and business income.
6. Some courts are treating educational degrees and even careers as marital assets subject to division upon divorce where one spouse supported the other while she or he was studying or preparing.

LESSON 13: BASIC LANDLORD-TENANT LAW

Property professors approach discussions of landlord-tenant law with considerable trepidation. Because the great majority of students at most law schools are themselves tenants—and a not inconsiderable number have parents who are landlords—class discussions can become quite emotional. Many students find that what they learn in Property class differs considerably from their real-world experiences and are reluctant to believe what they are reading. In addition, landlord-tenant law can be confusing because, perhaps more than any other area of property law, it reflects an uneasy combination of ideas from two very different sources. Some of landlord-tenant law comes to us little-changed from feudal English common law rules developed centuries ago; other aspects of it reflect the modern tendencies of contract law to emphasize mutuality and protect consumers. This Lesson will focus on the traditional aspects of landlord-tenant law derived from old property concepts; the next Lesson explores the influence of contract law (and, to a lesser extent, tort) on landlord-tenant relations.

The first question to ask about a landlord-tenant relationship is what *type of tenancy* the parties have created. These legal labels often are far outside what either the landlord or the tenant were considering when they began their relationship. The law will nonetheless impose one of roughly four names on the tenancy they have created based on the terms under which the tenant holds the property from the landlord. Many arrangements are relatively ambiguous, which leads to considerable litigation (as well as fiendish exam questions!). Although terminology and definitions vary somewhat among the states, four basic types of leaseholds exist. (These are separate from the life tenancy, which generally does not spring from a lease.)

A tenancy for a specified period of time is a "**term of years**." This is true even if the duration is not expressed in years or is much shorter than one year. For example, a lease that runs from now until the end of the month is a term of years. So is one from now until the next election or the next solar eclipse. No notice is required to end a term of years because both parties are presumed to know that it will end on schedule when the term is up.

Examples

1. "To Tamika until August 7."
2. "To Tim until next Thanksgiving."
3. "To Teresa for the next 45 days."

A tenancy that may be renewed at the end of a specified interval is a "**periodic tenancy**." The most common of these are month-to-month and year-to-year tenancies, although a periodic tenancy can be for any interval. Either party may prevent a periodic tenancy from renewing at the end of one of the periods by giving the other party notice equal in length to the period of the tenancy. For example, a week-to-week tenancy requires one week's notice to terminate; a month-to-month tenancy requires one month's notice. In many states, however, only six months' notice is required to prevent a year-to-year tenancy from renewing. The period of a periodic tenancy is the period for which rent is to be paid, not the interval between actual payments. Thus, even if the tenant actually pays rent twice a month (perhaps after receiving each paycheck), if the rental agreement is expressed in terms of a monthly rent, the tenancy is month-to-month.

Examples

1. "To Terrance for June, with this lease to be renewed unless either party gives notice."
2. "To Tomas, who shall pay $500 rent every quarter."
3. "To Tammy, whose rent shall be $600 per month, with half due on the first of each month and the balance due on the sixteenth."

A **tenancy at will** has no specific duration but will end when either landlord or tenant gives notice to the other that she or he is ending the tenancy. For example, if you let me stay in the gardener's cottage in the back of your estate in exchange for helping to keep the place up, I probably am a tenant at will.

Many states have rules specifying the minimum amount of notice required to end a tenancy at will (often thirty days).

Examples

1. "To Trahn for as long as it is convenient for both of us."
2. "To Talat as long as he looks after the place."

A **tenancy by sufferance** exists when the owner allows someone to stay on her or his property without an explicit agreement. It is like a tenancy at will in that it has no specific duration but differs in that the landlord has not explicitly agreed to the tenant's presence but rather acquiesced in it, at least for the moment. For example, if a landlord takes no action to remove a tenant holding over after the end of a term of years, a tenancy by sufferance may arise. Similarly, if a purchaser takes no action to remove the prior owners of a property bought after a mortgage foreclosure, the former owners may become tenants by sufferance. Although some states specify the amount of notice required to remove tenants by sufferance, many do not.

Example

Teddy's lease for a term of years expired March 31. Leonard Landlord comes by on April 4 to check on the place and sees that Teddy's things are still there and that Teddy seems still to have been living there. Leonard does nothing. A tenancy by sufferance arises.

Classifying a tenancy among these types can be challenging. If you rent me your house for one year, is that a term of years or a periodic tenancy (specifically, a year-to-year tenancy)? Although some jurisdictions will have a presumption one way or the other, the usual practice is to look to the parties' intent at the time they created the lease.

Some property owners seek to evade statutes and case law giving tenants rights by claiming that the people living in their units are **licensees** rather than tenants. A licensee is someone who has permission to be in a place but does not have possession of it the way a tenant does. Hotel guests are a common example of licensees. The legal test for who is a tenant and who is a mere licensee varies somewhat across the states, but in general the longer the time the person paying rent is in the property and the more freedom they have to make the place their own (for example, by moving in furniture, by hanging artwork on the walls, or by using it as their mailing address), the more likely the law is to treat them as tenants, notwithstanding whatever the rental agreement may say.

Because the common law regarded the landlord-tenant relationship as a conveyance of a partial estate in land, common law doctrines governing other, more substantial, conveyances of estates in land can apply. For example, although the tenant may use the property in the manner for which it was designed, if she or he does damage that might excessively diminish its value when it is conveyed back to the landlord, the tenant may be liable for **waste**.

What You Need to Know:

1. How a tenancy is classified can affect how much notice is required to terminate the tenancy as well as other rights of the landlord and tenant.
2. Tenancies may be classified as "terms of years" if they are for any fixed term (whether or not exceeding a year).
3. Tenancies may be classified as "periodic tenancies" if they renew every month, week, year, etc.
4. Tenancies may be classified as "tenancies at will" if they have no set duration but just continue as long as both parties agree.
5. Tenancies may be classified as tenancies by sufferance if the landlord tolerates the tenant's presence but has not concluded an agreement with the tenant about an on-going tenancy.
6. People paying to spend time in space that is not fully under their control may be classified as licensees rather than as tenants, although those spending longer periods in a rented property are likely to be seen as tenants.

7. Many common law rules, such as the prohibition of waste, that apply to other conveyances of estates in land may also apply in landlord-tenant law.

LESSON 14: THE LANDLORD-TENANT REVOLUTION

At common law, a lease was just another way in which property owners could transfer some of their rights. The tenant's leasehold was just a relatively transitory estate in land. Accordingly, the grantor of the lease (*i.e.*, the landlord) made the rules just as grantors of other estates in land did. The grantee (*i.e.*, the tenant) could decline the grant, but if accepted, the grant came on the landlord's terms. In addition, in an agrarian society, everyone assumed that the land (rather than any building on the land) was the crucial part of the property being conveyed. Defects in the buildings on the leased property, or even their complete collapse, were not ordinarily grounds for questioning the validity of the lease.

Beginning in the 1960s, however, consumer protection efforts that began in contract law started to spill over into landlord-tenant law. Indeed, courts came to see landlord-tenant law as an aspect of contract law. The analogy made sense: the lease was an agreement between two parties, just as contracts are; leases almost always require performance on both sides, as contracts do; the tenant typically spends more on rent than she or he does on any other single expense; and bargaining power between landlord and tenant is sometimes quite unequal (as it is in some other kinds of consumer transactions). In addition, courts (and some state legislatures) believed that changing the balance of power between landlord and tenant might address broader social problems of urban decay. A series of urban upheavals in numerous U.S. cities between 1965 and 1968 gave these concerns a feeling of urgency.

The result was a series of dramatic changes in the old common law landlord-tenant regime. Some of these came through judicial decisions; others came when state legislatures enacted the Uniform Residential Landlord-Tenant Act or other legislation. Many states have adopted some but not all of these changes or have limited or modified them in various ways.

Perhaps the best-known and most important change was the **implied warranty of habitability**. This is a principle that reads into every residential lease a requirement that the landlord keep the rented property in good condition. Even if the actual lease between the landlord and the tenant says nothing at all about repairs, the courts will treat the lease as if it did. Some jurisdictions describe the implied warranty of habitability as requiring compliance with housing codes; some express it more generally as a duty to keep the premises fit for the use intended; some do both. The most prominent case recognizing an implied warranty of habitability is *Javins v. First National Realty Co.*, 428 F.2d 1071 (D.C. Cir. 1970). *Javins* held that the transformation from an agrarian to an urban society, the rise of consumer protection law, and social concerns about substandard housing all militated in favor of abandoning common law rules limiting landlords' liability for defective conditions.

A second step that most states took was to make the tenant's duty to pay rent **mutual** with, or dependent on, the landlord's duties—including those under the implied warranty of habitability. This follows a familiar pattern of mutual obligation in contract law but is a sharp break from the common law rule that the duties of landlord and tenant were independent. Thus, under the common law the tenant still owed the landlord rent even if the landlord did not perform her or his obligations under the lease, but today in most states the landlord's failure to perform can excuse the tenant's failure to perform (*i.e.*, pay rent). The combined effect of implying a warranty of habitability into leases and making it mutual with the tenant's obligation to pay rent was to create a new remedy for tenants living in dilapidated housing: the tenant can withhold rent, and if the landlord sues or seeks to evict the tenant for nonpayment, the tenant can raise the landlord's failure to repair as a defense. If the court finds that the landlord's failure to repair reduced the property's value by a certain percentage, it can cut the amount the tenant owes by that same percentage. In many states, the tenant also may make repairs her or himself and deduct the cost from her or his rent; courts call this "**repair and deduct**".

Another response to bad housing conditions sprang from *Brown v. Southall Realty*, 237 A.2d 834 (D.C. 1968). *Brown* declared that leases of houses or apartments that were out of compliance with housing codes were **void as against public policy**. The court hoped that this would give landlords an incentive to repair their properties. In practice, its all-or-nothing nature prevented it from conferring much benefit on low-income tenants without anywhere better to move.

Recognizing that these new rights were unlikely to mean much if tenants were afraid of being evicted, some courts and legislatures prohibited landlords from dispossessing tenants as a **retaliatory eviction** for asserting their legal rights. *Edwards v. Habib*, 397 F.2d 687 (D.C. Cir. 1968). Because proving a landlord's intent is so difficult, many jurisdictions established presumptions that evictions begun within a specified period of time of the tenant's assertion of rights were retaliatory (and hence unlawful). A few jurisdictions went farther and required landlords to show "just cause" for evicting tenants. For the most part, however, "just cause" protection is limited to small subgroups of tenants, such as those in trailer parks, public housing, or cities with rent control. To complement and backstop these restrictions on judicial evictions, courts and legislatures also have outlawed landlords' self-help evictions or stiffened the penalties where those evictions already were illegal.

It bears remembering, however, that landlord-tenant law's (partial) embrace of contract law principles helped landlords in some ways, too. Adopting modern contract law's sensitivity to transaction costs, most states gave landlords expedited procedures for evicting their tenants, largely superseding the common law remedy of ejectment in landlord-tenant cases. These rules—called "**summary proceedings**", "summary process", "summary dispossess", or other names in various states—shorten the times for issuance of summonses, for tenants' answer, for scheduling hearings, for appeals, and for executing judgments of possession and may sharply limit the tenant's opportunities to join other claims or conduct discovery.

Although less dramatically than contract law, tort law, too, has eroded common law landlord-tenant principles. At common law, once the property was transferred to the tenant, the landlord generally had no responsibilities for it until the tenant returned the property at the end of the leasehold. If a third party became injured on the property during the tenancy, she or he could sue the tenant but not the landlord; the tenant, in turn, had no more recourse for injuries suffered on leased property than she or he would have on property that she or he owned. Today, tort recognizes that landlords typically have continuing contact with and responsibility for properties that they have rented out. If the **landlord's negligence**—such as leaving exposed electrical wiring or failing to repair decrepit stairs—leads to an injury to the tenant or someone else with permission to be on the premises, the landlord may well owe damages. (Some courts will limit landlords' liability to those defects of which the landlord had actual or constructive knowledge.)

Before the implied warranty of habitability won widespread acceptance, some courts tried to address the issue of repairs within the common law framework. Even at common law, a landlord could not collect rent for land after having evicted the tenant from that land. Courts characterized this as "**actual eviction**" or a breach of an "**implied covenant of quiet enjoyment**" of the property. Courts then broadened this defense of "actual eviction" to cover situations where it was defective conditions for which the landlord was responsible, rather than the landlord's deliberate actions, that forced the tenant from the land. This "**constructive eviction**", too, would excuse payment of rent. Thus, if the landlord failed to maintain the plumbing and a leak filled the tenant's apartment with raw sewage, the tenant could move out in the middle of the lease and owe no further rent. Finally, some courts went further to recognize a defense of "**partial constructive eviction**" in cases where some of the premises remained habitable but some did not.

The problem with all of these approaches is that they implicitly required the tenant to move (or at least to move out of part of the property) to show that she or he had, in fact, been evicted. Yet tenants, especially low-income tenants, may not have anywhere else to go. This drove states to embrace the implied warranty of habitability (although some jurisdictions also recognize constructive eviction). The doctrine of constructive eviction (and sometimes partial constructive eviction) can sometimes complement the implied warranty of habitability in residential properties. Constructive eviction also is important in leases to commercial tenants, where no warranty of habitability applies. For example, in *Reste Realty Corp. v. Cooper*, 251 A.2d 268 (N.J. 1969), Cooper leased some basement rooms to train and meet with the salespeople in a jewelry business. Whenever it rained, however, the offices flooded. The landlord promised to fix the leaks, and in reliance on those promises Cooper entered into a new lease. Eventually, Cooper moved out before the end of the lease. The court held that the flooding sufficiently interfered with Cooper's use and enjoyment of the offices to constitute a constructive eviction and justify her abandoning the lease.

Example

> Putting this all together, consider the case of Terry Tenant, who rents a two-bedroom apartment for her family from Lenny Landlord. Leaking plumbing in the unit above hers drips into her apartment and causes the plaster to sag. Part of the ceiling in her bedroom caves in completely, injuring her in her sleep. This forces her to move out of her bedroom and sleep in her living room.

In some jurisdictions, Terry could move, claiming that plumbing was leaking when she signed the lease and that that constitutes a housing code violation, rendering her lease unlawful and therefore void. Terry also could move and claim that Lenny has breached the covenant of quiet enjoyment or constructively evicted her (if her state recognizes that doctrine).

If she wishes to stay, Terry can stop paying rent to Lenny. Lenny cannot change the locks on her apartment or cut off her utilities without facing liability for an unlawful self-help eviction. Lenny can bring summary proceedings against her, asking a court to remove her for nonpayment of rent. But Terry can argue that Lenny breached the implied warranty of habitability and ask the court to excuse some or all of her rent until Lenny makes repairs. Terry also can argue that the falling plaster—by forcing her to move out of her bedroom—constitutes a partial constructive eviction from her apartment. This would provide a court with an alternative basis for excusing some or all of her rent. Terry also can sue Lenny in tort for her injuries when the plaster fell on her; depending on the jurisdiction, she may or may not be able to join that action as a counterclaim in Lenny's eviction suit. If Lenny then refuses to renew her lease and tries to get a court to evict her, Terry can claim retaliatory eviction and ask the court to let her stay.

What You Need to Know:

1. Understanding landlord-tenant law requires seeing the relationship as *both* a conveyance of a limited estate in the landlord's property to the tenant *and* a contract between landlord and tenant.
2. Most states imply a warranty of habitability in residential leases and make the landlord's duty to maintain the property mutually dependent on the tenant's duty to pay rent. Some jurisdictions give tenants the option to declare their leases void if the rented premises violated housing codes at the beginning of the lease.
3. Many jurisdictions also prohibit landlords from conducting self-help evictions or utility shut-offs and from using judicial eviction in retaliation for tenants' assertion of their rights.
4. Commercial tenants cannot invoke the implied warranty of habitability but may be able to claim that they have been constructively evicted if conditions in the rented premises render them unusable.
5. Tenants and their guests injured because of defects in rented premises may sue their landlords in tort, although some states will require evidence that the landlord knew, or should have known, about the defects.

LESSON 15: CONTRACTS FOR SALE OF LAND AND EQUITABLE CONVERSION

Rome was not built in a day, and valuable real property is rarely sold in a single act, either. Instead, the law has evolved a two-step process. The first part of the process is the **contract for sale**. As its name implies, contract law typically controls most of this stage. The second, and probably more familiar part of the process, is the **deed**. The deed is a conveyance of an estate in land; traditional property law concepts govern this stage to a far greater degree.

Under the contract for sale, the seller agrees to sell the property to the buyer for a stated price. Contracts for the sale of real estate are subject to the **statute of frauds**. They only bind a party who has signed a writing setting out the key elements of the arrangement. (Note that the party *enforcing* the contract does not need to have signed a writing—just the party against whom the court will be enforcing the contract.) Some courts will make limited exceptions where a party who did not sign a writing clearly benefited from the other party's reliance. For example, in *Hickey v. Green*, 442 N.E.2d 37 (Mass. App. 1982), the seller accepted and held a deposit check from the prospective buyer (but did not fill in her name as payee or endorse the back, either of which would have provided a writing to comply with the statute of frauds). She also made no objection when the prospective buyer told her that he was selling his current home so that he could complete the purchase of her property. The seller later received a better offer for her property and told the prospective buyer that she would not go through with the deal. The court held that she could not invoke the statute of frauds to evade her initial agreement to sell the property where she had allowed the prospective buyer to rely on that agreement—and to bind himself by his signature on the deposit check and various correspondence. The prospective buyer was lucky: some courts likely would not have been willing to depart from the statute of frauds in this way.

The contract typically says something about when the sale is to be completed. Often, the contract will require the buyer to make a deposit to an **escrow agent**, who holds the money pending the sale. Many contracts provide that if the buyer does not comply with the contract for sale, the escrow agent shall give the deposit to the seller as liquidated damages for the buyer's breach. Even if the contract does not specify that the deposit is liquidated damages and allows the seller to seek a higher amount as actual damages from the buyer, many sellers will not want to endure the cost and delay of litigation and will be happy to pocket the buyer's deposit. In the same way, if the seller refuses to go through with the transaction, the escrow agent can give the deposit back to the buyer quickly rather than forcing the buyer to go to court to try to retrieve the deposit from the seller.

The contract for sale may contain some **reservations** or **contingencies** that allow one or the other party to void the contract under certain circumstances without being in breach. For example, many contracts are contingent on the buyer being able to obtain financing. If the buyer cannot, despite good faith efforts, obtain a sufficient mortgage, these contracts allow the buyer to back out without paying any penalty or losing her or his deposit. Similarly, the contract may allow the buyer to void the contract if serious defects are discovered in a professional inspection.

The contract for sale commonly will specify a time-line. It will give deadlines for the buyer to either invoke or waive the contingencies in the contract and for the ultimate transfer of the property. Contracts often specify that "**time is of the essence**" so that any delay by one party will be deemed a substantial breach, which in principle enables the other party to suspend her or his performance.

The contract typically will specify what kind of title the seller must provide. If the contract is silent, the law implies into it a promise to convey "**marketable title**." Marketable title need not be free from *all* doubt, but it should be free from reasonable doubts that would cause a buyer well-advised by counsel to refrain from paying fair value for the property. For example, if a property has had recurrent problems with trespassers, one of those trespassers hypothetically could claim prescriptive rights to the property. If this does not appear to be a serious threat, the owner could still convey marketable title. Conversely, if the owner or a prior owner in his chain of title obtained the property by adverse possession, the earlier dispossessed owners might conceivably try to reassert their ownership. If this is not a serious threat, the title may still be marketable.

Some contracts will relax the requirement of marketable title, requiring only that the seller convey "**insurable title**." Insurable title is title that is good enough that a serious, reputable title insurance company would issue a title insurance policy on it. The seller's ownership may be subject to serious challenge, but an established title insurance company would be willing to bet that the challenge would lose. Alternatively, the contract might require the seller to convey good "**record title**", which would require an unbroken chain of recorded deeds back to the government's original grant of the land to its first private owner. If any prior owner claimed title through adverse possession, she or he would have to have won an action to quiet title in her or his name and to have recorded that judgment in lieu of a deed.

The contract for sale typically will specify what kind of deed the seller must execute to the buyer. The types of deeds are discussed in Lesson 17.

Because equity courts regarded each piece of real estate as unique, they traditionally would order **specific performance** of a valid contract for sale. Thus, if the prospective seller refuses to sell, the buyer may seek damages for breach of contract but also may ask a court to order the seller to convey the property as required in the contract for sale. Conversely, if the prospective buyer gets cold feet, the seller may either seek damages for breach of contract or ask the court to order the buyer to pay the agreed-upon sum and accept conveyance of the property.

Traditionally, equity would enforce a contract for sale even if buildings on the property were destroyed after the execution of the contract for sale. In agrarian England and in the United States before the Industrial Revolution, courts presumed the land to be more valuable than anything built on it. Under the doctrine of **equitable conversion**, the courts would deem equitable title to the property to have passed to the buyer as soon as the buyer and seller signed the contract for sale, making it the buyer's problem if buildings were damaged or destroyed unless the destruction was the seller's fault.

In today's urban environment, this doctrine makes little sense: most people buy properties primarily for the buildings on those properties. Some courts have begun to modify it. Well-advised buyers today include in the contract for sale specific provisions about who bears the risk of damage to buildings during the **executory period** before the passing of the deed.

What You Need to Know:

1. Most real estate sales occur in two stages, a contract for sale and a later passing of a deed.
2. Contracts for sale are subject to most usual contract rules, including the statute of frauds' requirement of a writing signed by the party against whom the court is enforcing the contract.
3. Where the contract is silent, the law implies that the seller must convey marketable title to the buyer.
4. Courts will order reluctant parties to go through with valid contracts for sale of real estate that they have signed.

LESSON 16: DUTY TO DISCLOSE DEFECTS AND THE IMPLIED WARRANTY OF QUALITY

Historically, Anglo-American common law adhered strictly to the principle of **caveat emptor**, or "buyer beware", in real estate transactions. The common law arose in an agricultural society where land, not the buildings that might be on it, were the main objects of most real estate transactions. Most prospective buyers presumably could tell whether land could be farmed profitably and did not care much about the condition of any sheds, or even houses, that might stand on the property.

In an urban, industrialized society, defending that rule is increasingly difficult. Sellers typically know much more about a property than buyers do. Keeping the burden to discover defects on the buyer is likely to require considerable inefficient expenditures of money on exhaustive inspections to gather information for the buyer that the seller already has. The parties can, of course, make special arrangements by contract for unusual situations where the seller does not have enough information to take responsibility for informing the buyer, where the buyer does not care about the condition of the building on the property (perhaps because she or he is planning to tear it down), or where the buyer is so anxious to get the property that she or he is willing to take her or his chances on any defects. But the law increasingly places responsibility for disclosing defects in the property on those with the greatest information, typically the sellers. This change is not uniform across the states and it is still a work in progress, but the trend is clear.

One way the law protects buyers is by imposing on sellers a **duty to disclose** known defects. Initially, the requirement was a merely negative one: the seller could be held liable for fraud if she or he falsely asserted that the property had no defects. This might have worked well enough for savvy buyers who knew what questions to ask and how to probe deeper when given correct but evasive answers. But naïve buyers, those most in need of protection, were left out in the cold. Prohibiting only false statements also confronted the courts with difficult cases where they had to interpret precisely what the seller said or where the seller concealed defects nonverbally (*e.g.*, by deploying large numbers of air fresheners in a building with a pervasive bad odor). Increasingly, then, the law imposes an affirmative duty on sellers to disclose **material defects** in the premises. Considerable litigation has arisen about which defects are material; courts generally hold a defect to be material if awareness of it might change what a reasonable buyer would be willing to pay for the property.

Some jurisdictions require disclosure only of **latent defects**—those not readily apparent on a careful inspection. Others find the distinction between latent and patent defects administratively burdensome and require sellers to disclose all defects in the premises. In *Stambovsky v. Ackley*, 572 N.Y.S.2d 672 (App. Div. 1991), the court went so far as to hold a seller liable for failing to disclose that the property was "haunted" where the seller had spread that claim widely in the community (generating extensive drive-by traffic and potentially depressing the house's resale value) and the buyer was from outside the area and had no reason to have heard of the house's reputation before the sale.

States also increasingly are imposing an **implied warranty of quality** on those doing construction and major modifications to property. Here again, the law puts the burden to disclose on the party with the greatest access to information. In addition, many courts now allow **subsequent owners** to enforce the implied warranty even though they had no direct contractual relations, or **privity**, with the construction workers. In effect, the courts hold that purchasers of the property also purchase the contractual rights the prior owner held against bad construction.

Example

> In *Lempke v. Dagenais*, 547 A.2d 290 (N.H. 1988), the prior owner contracted for construction of a garage. After buying the property, the current owners discovered the defect and sued both for negligence and for breach of the implied warranty of quality. Both of these claims might seem to have serious problems: tort law does not routinely award economic damages (*i.e.*, the cost of repairing the garage) and the current owners had no privity of contract with the builders. The court, however, allowed the current owners to recover fully for the defective garage, finding no good reason to cut off the builders' liability just because the property was sold and no good reason to wait for a calamity resulting from the defective garage to award damages.

What You Need to Know:

1. At common law, the principle of caveat emptor generally deprived buyers of any remedy for defects in the property they purchased absent fraud by the seller.
2. Today, most jurisdictions impose a duty on sellers to disclose material defects in the property before

the sale, at least those that are hidden from easy detection.

3. Many jurisdictions also impose an implied warranty of quality on construction work. States increasingly allow subsequent purchasers of the property to enforce the implied warranty against builders that worked for their predecessors in title.

LESSON 17: DEEDS, WARRANTIES OF TITLE, AND TITLE INSURANCE

Many people learned that a **deed** marks ownership of property when they played Monopoly as a child. For every property on the board, one and only one deed exists. They may not give much thought of what a deed is (or perhaps they assume that deeds all contain information about the cost of building houses and hotels on the property). And if they grew up to play Settlers of Catan, they may have come to doubt whether deeds are even necessary to own valuable real estate. So what gives?

Learning real estate conveyancing law from board games is probably about as efficacious as learning criminal law from video games or contract law from bridge. A deed is not so much a token of ownership as a transference of ownership from one person to another. It is much closer to a personal check than it is to a motor vehicle title or a stock certificate. Throughout its history, a piece of real estate is likely to be subject to a series of deeds as ownership passes from one person to another and then on to yet another. In very much the same way, my employer gives me a paycheck—transferring money from it to me—I give a check to the carpenter working on my house—passing on some of the money to her—and she gives a check to the lumber yard—passing on a portion of the money still farther. I do not give the carpenter the check I got from my employer: I write her a new check. But the validity of my new check depends on the effectiveness of my paycheck in transferring money to me.

All valid deeds transfer possible interests relating to ownership in property. But beyond that, they vary considerably. As we saw in Lessons 8 and 9, some deeds may grant only a limited fraction of the ownership interests in a piece of property. In addition, a deed may—or may not—provide the grantee rights against the grantor, generally in the form of the grantor's guarantees (promises) that she or he genuinely owns the property interests conveyed.

A deed that makes no promises at all about the grantor's ownership of the property is called a **quit-claim deed**. You could give someone a quit-claim deed to the Taj Mahal, the Eiffel Tower, or the temple at Angkor Wat without exposing yourself to liability under the deed: a quit-claim deed does not assert that the grantor owns the property but merely transfers the grantor's interests, if any, to the grantee. Your quit-claim deed to me of the Taj Mahal does not make me its owner; the deed merely means that any interests you might have in it now belong to me. (Of course, if you also lied to me and claimed that you *did* own the property that was the subject of your quit-claim deed, you might be liable for fraud.) An owner often seeks a quit-claim deed from holders of implausible claims that they have no desire to assert so that those claims do not cause subsequent purchasers to doubt the soundness of title. If my parents left property to whichever of their sons is the better basketball player, I would give my brother a quit-claim deed to the property to save both of us the trouble of going out to court (or on the court) to demonstrate that he does, in fact, have a better game than I do. I would not expect him to pay for the deed because it is only recognizing what is rightfully his. But because I am not getting anything for the deed—and because I would not, in fact, believe myself to be entitled to the property—I would not give him a deed making any assertions that I own the property.

When real property is bought and sold, however, buyers may want some reassurance that their sellers actually own the property for which the buyers are paying. Although local customs vary, six **warranties** from the grantor to the grantee have become common. Three of these, called **present covenants**, are assertions of fact about conditions at the time of the conveyance:

1. The grantor owns the premises in fee simple;

2. The grantor has the right to convey the premises; and
3. The premises are free from encumbrances except as specifically noted.

Because the present covenants are statements of present fact, they are violated only if the facts at the time the grantor transfers the deed are not as claimed. Nothing that happens after the transfer of the deed can violate the present covenants.

The other three common warranties in a deed, called **future covenants**, are promises about events in the future:

1. The grantor will defend the grantee against anyone lawfully claiming to own the premises;
2. The grantor will assure that the grantee will have **quiet enjoyment** of the premises; and
3. The grantor will, if asked, provide **further assurances**, or execute any additional document, necessary to secure title in the grantee.

"Quiet enjoyment" here is a term of art: it does not protect against loud neighbors or a vociferous screech owl. It only protects against disruptions in the grantee's legal title to the premises. Further assurances are occasionally necessary to make or defeat a claim of prescriptive rights. Because the future covenants are promises about events to come, they may be violated months, years, or even decades after the grantor delivers the deed is delivered. Once a future covenant has been violated, the grantee must move expeditiously to enforce it.

When a deed contains all six of these warranties without qualifications, it is commonly known as a **general warranty deed**. When a deed makes these six warranties only with regard to the grantor's own actions, it is called a **special warranty deed**. If a problem with title to the land later arises due to the something that happened while the property was owned by someone previous to the grantor, the grantor will be liable if she or he conveyed a general warranty deed but not if she or he provided only a special warranty deed (or a quit-claim deed). Warranties in the deed should not be confused with promises in the contract for sale, discussed in Lesson 15.

The value of warranties, of course, depends on the availability and solvency of the person making them. Even if the grantor has a fair amount of money at the time of the transfer—if nothing else, she should have the purchase price—the grantor could lose that money, disappear, or die. Careful buyers therefore are ill-advised to bet their future security on the deed covenants. This has given rise to **title insurance** companies. For a one-time premium at the time of transfer, these companies will issue policies to grantees promising that the grantor's title is good (and agreeing to make good any losses the buyer suffers should this not be true). Here again, these policies typically insure only the legal validity of the title, not the desirability or characteristics of the property purchased.

What You Need to Know:

1. Deeds are conveyances of real property from one person to another. Each transfer of property requires its own deed.

2. Quit-claim deeds transfer any interests the grantor has but do not provide any assurances that that is sufficient to make the grantee the rightful owner of the property.

3. Warranty deeds typically assert that the grantor has good title free of encumbrances and the right to convey it as well as promising that the grantee will have undisturbed legal title and the grantor's help, if needed, in securing that title.

4. A general warranty deed makes these warranties absolute; a special warranty deed warrants only that the grantee will not have difficulties due to events that occurred while the grantor owned the property.

5. Title insurance provides additional protection of the grantor's ownership of the property although not of the quality or desirability of the property.

LESSON 18: RECORDING ACTS AND INQUIRY NOTICE

Most real estate transactions go to completion without any major hitches. The buyers get the property of their dreams, the sellers get the money they need to find joy and contentment elsewhere, and both live happily ever after. Sometimes, however, the real estate transaction fairy tale goes terribly wrong. In particular, sometimes the seller gets so attached to the idea of joy and contentment that he decides to sell the same house again. Because money, unlike real estate, is highly portable, the seller can then find an "elsewhere" to go where the aggrieved buyers (and their large, menacing friends) cannot find him. Property law has made elaborate provisions to try to reduce the opportunities for this particular form of fraud.

With almost any other form of property, analyzing multiple sales by the same seller would be quite easy: after the first sale, the seller had nothing to convey, so the second (and subsequent) buyers would come away with nothing. They could sue the seller—if they could find her—but the first buyer continued to own the item in question. With most forms of personal property, however, multiple sales are not a major problem because possession changes at the time of the first sale. I might want to sell you the bicycle I just sold to Barry, but Barry probably rode off with it after the initial sale and you are unlikely to buy a bicycle that I cannot show you.

At common law, that is just how real estate transactions worked, too: the first buyer got the property, and all subsequent buyers got only causes of action against the sleazy seller—which were probably worthless if the seller was any good at hiding himself or his assets. Multiple sales are much more feasible with real estate because it does not commonly change possession in obvious ways immediately after sale so subsequent buyers may have no way of knowing that the seller has already conveyed the property.

One solution would be to require buyers to move in instantly upon purchasing land. But that is not feasible for many reasons. So the law has looked for other ways to warn off prospective second (and third and . . .) buyers. This was the genesis of the **title recording system**. The system would encourage buyers to record their title as a way of warning off other prospective buyers. But just asking buyers pretty-please to record their titles was not likely to be effective, at least not in every case. And where the buyers did not record timely, unscrupulous sellers would have the opportunity to make fraudulent duplicate sales. So the law had to give buyers a strong incentive to register promptly: the potential loss of their just-purchased property. Thus, **recording statutes** override the common law to provide that the first buyer will not necessarily end up owning the property.

The basic principle is that if the first buyer's failure to record created the possibility for an unscrupulous seller to dupe a subsequent buyer, the loss is partially the fault of the nonrecording first buyer. As between an innocent second buyer and a lazy or irresponsible first buyer who failed to record, the second buyer is less blameworthy and should get the property. Of course, all the negligence in the world on the part of the first buyer does not come close to the culpability of the evil seller, who perpetrated a fraud. So the first buyer has every right to sue the seller—if she can find him. But if, as is usually the case, the seller is in the wind, the property should go to the wholly innocent second buyer over the one who could have prevented the seller's fraud in the first place.

So recording statutes seek to protect the innocent and to encourage prompt recording of title. Much of the time, these two purposes go hand in hand. But occasionally they do not. So which is more important? Different states have answered that question differently. The result is three distinct kinds of recording statutes, commonly known as "**race**", "**notice**", and "**race-notice**":

1. Under a *race* statute, the first buyer to record her or his purchase wins. Period. Full stop. This type of statute gets its name from its reliance on a race to the Recorder of Deeds' office to record the purchase. One might imagine that the first buyer has an advantage in this race, but if she or he tarries, a subsequent purchaser may win the race and hence the property. (Race statutes may not

protect people receiving the property as a gift against a prior purchaser for value even if the donee records first.) A race statute therefore creates the strongest possible incentive to record a purchase. On the other hand, the single-minded focus on recording first can mean that some purchasers who were not innocent at all can prevail over innocent, good faith purchasers who did not record in time. A former colleague of mine refers to a race statute as "the one that lets the crooks win."

2. Under a *notice* statute, the last bona fide (good faith) purchaser of the property without notice of any prior purchases wins. Because a notice statute protects the *last* person to buy without notice of an earlier conveyance, ownership of a property may change hands several times in the course of a series of duplicative sales of a single property, with new buyers displacing their predecessors but then being themselves displaced as later buyers pay for the property. Notice statutes only protect bona fide (good-faith) purchasers for value; the law presumes that anyone who received the property as gift from someone who improperly conveys it multiple times will suffer the least loss if she does not get the property in the end. The merry-go-round only stops turning when one buyer records her or his deed to put all subsequent prospective buyers on notice (making it impossible for them to become bona fide purchasers without notice). Thus, the primary purpose of a notice statute is to protect innocents; as discussed below, recording is part, but only part, of how that is done.

3. Under a *race-notice* statute, the property goes to the first buyer to record *among those bona fide purchasers without notice*. In effect, a race-notice statute is a race statute with those buyers that had notice of prior conveyances excluded from the race. Race-notice statutes typically also only

protect purchasers for value. A race-notice statute places a high premium on recording first but tries to keep the crooks from winning.

Under either a notice or a race-notice statute, notice can come in any of several ways. Notice can be *actual*: if your cousin tells you that she just bought 123 Elm Street, you would of course be foolish to buy the same property from the prior owner. But notice can also be *constructive*: a prior purchaser recorded at the Recorder of Deeds' office. Whether or not the subsequent purchaser actually checked, the law will treat him as having notice of the prior purchase: the first buyer did what she could do to prevent a fraud, and if the second buyer did not take the precaution of checking for a recorded deed, he has no one to blame but himself (and the seller!) for having been taken in. And some buyers may be on *inquiry notice*: they did not actually know of the prior sale, but they knew enough to ask questions that would have led them to learn of the prior conveyance. For example, if you see a moving company unloading furniture at the house you are about to buy, that ought to make you suspicious and demand a good explanation before going through with the purchase.

In any case, notice only matters legally if the prospective buyer had *before the purchase*. Almost everyone involved in a fraudulent transaction eventually finds out about the fraud—but by then, it is too late. Notice only has legal consequences if the buyer receives it in time to call off the transaction. Thus, a prior purchaser who records after you paid for the property but before you recorded your own deed does not give you notice because it does not help you avoid falling victim to the fraud. Notice received after you paid for the land does not prevent you from being a good-faith purchaser.

The best way to get a feel for the different effects of these kinds of statutes is to see how they yield different results for the same set of transactions.

Example

Ogre conveys Blackacre to Aisha at 11 am. Then at 11:15 am, Ogre conveys Blackacre to Bernie, telling Bernie "Aisha just bought the property, but she was going to go out to lunch to celebrate with her family so if you hurry, you can record before she does." Bernie rushes down to the county courthouse and records his deed at 12:30 pm. Aisha records her deed at 2 pm. Under a race statute, Bernie wins because he recorded first. Under a notice statute, Aisha wins because she was the last bona fide purchaser for value without notice of a prior conveyance. Ogre told Bernie about her so Bernie had notice. Under a race-notice statute, Aisha also wins because Bernie's notice of her purchase disqualifies him from the race, leaving Aisha to win.

Example

Odious conveys Greenacre to Arthur on Monday. Odious conveys Greenacre to Betty on Tuesday, not mentioning Arthur. On Wednesday, Arthur records his deed. On Thursday, Betty records her deed. Under a race statute, Arthur wins because he recorded first. Under a notice statute, Betty wins because she purchased later than Arthur and had no notice of Arthur. Under a race-notice statute, Arthur wins because he recorded before Betty and is a bona fide purchaser for value.

One peculiar feature of the recording statutes is the **Shelter Rule**. The Shelter Rule gives good title to someone who purchases from a person protected by the recording statute even if the subsequent purchaser would not herself be protected.

Example

Ohno conveys Redacre to Alice on Monday. Alice does not immediately record. On Tuesday, Ohno conveys Redacre to Bashir, who has no notice of Alice but records immediately. Alice records on Wednesday. On Thursday, Bashir can convey good title to Consuela even though Alice has already recorded—and even if Bashir tells Consuela about Alice. This is the result of the Shelter Rule, which allows him to convey good title to anyone because he is protected under the recording statutes.

Another feature of the recording system that surprises some students is that not every deed recorded at the Recorder of Deeds' office is sufficient to give prospective buyers constructive notice. To warn prospective victims of fraud that you have already purchased the property, they have to be able to find your deed. Most recorders of deeds maintain a **grantor-grantee index**: someone conducting a title search looks for a prior owner's name in the grantor index until they find the deed through which she or he conveyed away the property, then the title searcher looks for that grantee's name in the grantor index to find any conveyance that that person made, and so forth until they come to the most recent grantee of the property. A deed that cannot be found in this manner is called a **wild deed** and generally cannot give constructive notice to prospective buyers (and thus cannot give protection to the person who recorded it).

Example

Ahmed, the record owner of Grayacre, conveys the property to Belinda. Belinda records Ahmed's deed. Belinda then conveys Grayacre to Charles. Charles does not record Belinda's deed and subsequently sells to Deepak. Deepak records Charles's deed. Belinda then tries to sell Grayacre to Esther. Esther wisely performs a title search, tracing ownership up through Ahmed and Belinda, but no farther. Esther will have no reason to look for any conveyances from Charles because no recorded deed puts Charles in the chain of title. Charles's deed to Deepak is "wild" (unfindable) in the registry. To protect himself, and to prevent people like Esther from being defrauded, Deepak needed to have recorded not just Charles's deed to him but also Belinda's deed to Charles.

What You Need to Know:

1. Every state has title registries for land to help prospective purchasers determine whether the

person seeking to sell them land currently has good title to it.

2. Where these systems fail to prevent an unscrupulous seller from conveying the same property multiple times, state recording statutes determine which of the would-be buyers get the property and which are left to try to obtain damages from the seller.

3. Race statutes protect whichever buyer records first, whether or not that buyer knew of the other transactions. Notice statutes protect the last good-faith buyer not to have notice of prior transactions. And race-notice statutes protect whichever good-faith buyer records first.

4. The Shelter Rule allows persons protected by recording statutes to convey good title to other people, even those with notice of the original dispute.

5. Purchasers seeking to protect their title to property should record immediately upon buying the property and should take care that all deeds in their line of title are properly recorded and that all parties' names are spelled correctly in the registry of deeds.

LESSON 19: LAND PURCHASE FINANCING

Few aspects of property law mix old legal concepts with new ones to the extent that real estate financing does. The **mortgage** is many centuries old, yet its newer forms are frequently in the headlines, playing central roles in the 2007–08 financial crisis and earlier serving as a major force transforming metropolitan landscapes the country over.

Although the terminology here is not as arcane as in some other areas, it can be confusing. A mortgage is an interest in real property that a debtor gives to a creditor to help induce the creditor to lend the borrower money. As such, the mortgagor is the borrower (typically the property owner) while the mortgagee is the lender (typically a financial institution). Many people, even lawyers who ought to know better, get this backwards because they think of mortgages as something for which borrowers apply at banks. In fact, the prospective borrowers are applying for a loan; the mortgage is what they are offering to give the bank in order to get the loan.

The mortgage is separate from, although in service of, the actual loan, which is usually signified by a **note** in which the borrower promises to repay the loan. A mortgage gives the mortgagee rights if certain conditions are met, typically that the debtor fails to repay the loan that the mortgage was given to secure. This both gives the mortgagor an incentive to pay and protects the mortgagee's money should the mortgagor default.

You can think of the mortgage as a specialized form of a future interest. It is not very different from the mortgagor conveying the property "to myself, for so long as I make required payments on the note, and if I do not, to the mortgagee." Indeed, some states regard a homeowner's grant of a mortgage as a conveyance of an interest in the property. Other states view the mortgage only as a lien, giving the mortgagee no interest in the property unless the mortgagor defaults. This difference in interpretations can be important in determining, for example, whether one joint tenant's granting of a mortgage to a financial institution breaks the unity of title required to continue the joint tenancy.

The mortgage typically gives the mortgagee the right to take the property if the mortgagor defaults. In feudal England, just as today, some mortgagees took advantage of unsophisticated mortgagors to take away their property. The English **chancellor**, who was the head of the **equity** courts, would sometimes respond by forcing the mortgagees to give up the property the mortgagees had reclaimed and allow the mortgagors to **redeem** their right to the property by becoming current on their obligations. The threat that the equity courts would intervene made seized property difficult to plant or to sell. Accordingly, rather than wait for the mortgagor to go to the chancellor, the mortgagee took the initiative and filed an action to **foreclose** the mortgagor's rights. The mortgagee would try to prove to the chancellor that he had acted honestly and that he had given the mortgagor a reasonable opportunity to redeem his interest in the land. If the mortgagee's case satisfied the chancellor, he would approve the foreclosure, allowing the mortgagee to take the property free from any cloud on its title.

This procedure evolved into today's mortgage foreclosure action. Over the years, financial institutions have persuaded legislatures and courts to truncate greatly the old English foreclosure action. In fact, about half of the states no longer require the mortgagee to go to court at all to foreclose on a property.

A foreclosure cuts off the mortgagor's rights to the property, but it typically does not transfer clear title to the mortgagee. Instead, states commonly require the property to be auctioned off. If the auction brings more than the outstanding balance on the loan, the excess should be refunded to the mortgagor. In practice, however, mortgage auctions are rarely competitive, with the mortgagee often the only bidder and the prices often far below the true value of the property. Some courts have imposed duties on mortgagees to make good faith efforts to avoid foreclosures and to obtain fair value for the property if it is foreclosed and auctioned.

If the auction brings less than the amount outstanding on the loan, the mortgagee may want to seek a judgment against the mortgagor for the remainder. Although some states allow these **deficiency judgments**, others do not, in part because they doubt that the auction price is a fair representation of what the property was actually worth.

Until relatively recently, the same financial institution that loaned the mortgagor the money to purchase the house would receive the mortgagee's payments until the homeowner paid off the mortgage or suffered foreclosure. This had the effect of limiting the amount of money available for home loans in an area to the available assets of financial institutions in that area. After World War II, however, the federal government took steps to standardize mortgages around the country so that distant investors could buy mortgages from the financial institutions that made initial loans. Today, the functions associated with mortgage financing are commonly divided among several entities: one who processes the loan application and accepts the initial mortgage, another one or more entities that supply the capital to finance the loan, and yet another who services the mortgage (receiving payments and transferring them to whomever has bought the note from the institution that made the loan initially). Over the past two decades, this process became even more specialized, with some investors buying the rights to interest payments and others buying the rights to repayment of principal.

This specialization contributed considerably to the recent financial crisis. The entities granting loans knew they would immediately sell those loans to investors and hence faced little risk from approving unsound loans. They were paid primarily by the loan, so the more loans they could process—sound or not—the more fees they could collect. Some of these **mortgage originators** tried to behave responsibly, but others did not. The investors buying interests in mortgage-backed loans often had little realistic idea of how risky the loans were. Many thought they were protected by the large and supposedly diverse portfolio of loans in which they had invested, only to discover that a large fraction of those loans were unsound. When a slowing economy exposed the unsoundness of many of these loans, no one was sure who had how much exposure to losses and the financial system froze up.

Another, less prominent form of real estate financing is the installment sales contract or **land contract**. Under a typical land contract, the purchasers make a down payment to the seller and move in. The seller retains title, and the buyer pays off the balance of the sale price (plus interest) over time. If the buyer missed payments, the seller can bring an action to forfeit the buyer's interest and recover possession. Because few sellers can afford to finance the sale of their property in this manner, this approach is relatively rare. Land contract purchasers historically have had fewer rights than mortgagors.

What You Need to Know:

1. A mortgage is a right in real property that a borrower gives a lender to induce the lender to loan the borrower money.

2. If the borrower (called the mortgagor), fails to make the required payments, the lender (called the mortgagee) can foreclose on the mortgagor's interest and have the property sold at auction to repay the lender. Some states require foreclosures to be done in court; others allow self-help.
3. Some states allow deficiency judgments for loan balances unpaid after a foreclosure; others do not.
4. Some courts require mortgagees to show good-faith attempts to prevent foreclosures and to obtain fair value for the foreclosed property.
5. As the functions of approving, financing, and managing loans have been divided among multiple institutions, risk and uncertainty increased, culminating in the financial crises of 2007–09.
6. Some buyers who cannot obtain mortgages purchase homes on installment sales contracts.

LESSON 20: EASEMENTS

The right to take some action on land that would otherwise be a trespass is an **easement**. For example, if I have the right to cut across your land to get to the main road, I have an easement. Someone with an easement on the land of another does not have the right to possess that land, but she or he does have the right to be on that land for the specific purpose of the easement. Property law recognizes several different kinds of easements and several different ways of creating easements.

Perhaps the most common kind of easement is one to cross the land of another. If Steenberg Homes in the *Jacque* case discussed in Lesson 2 had had an easement, it could have delivered the mobile home across the plaintiffs' property without paying damages. An easement to cross someone else's land often can be quite important to the value of a property.

Some easements give rights to particular persons. For example, Imelda might give her brother Jiang the right to plant flowers in her back yard. This is called an **easement in gross**. Other easements give rights to the owners or occupants of particular nearby properties. For example, Ken might give the owner of the property on his right, who happens to be his sister Lakita, the right to draw water from his well. If the same rights would automatically flow to anyone to whom Lakita might sell the property, it is called an **easement appurtenant** to that property. When trying to decide whether an easement is in gross or appurtenant, ask yourself whom did the originator of the easement intend would have the rights if the neighboring landowner who currently has the rights were to sell her or his property and move away. The property on which an easement is imposed is the **servient tenement**. If an easement is appurtenant, the property whose owner holds the rights is the **dominant tenement**.

The clearest way to create an easement is by including it explicitly in a conveyance. This can be a freestanding conveyance or can be tied to another real estate transaction. For example, Mercedes might sell Norman the front part of her lot but in the deed **reserve** for herself the right to cross the land Norman is getting so that she can still get to the main road. Patty might sell Raul the back part of her lot but, to make the land useful to Raul, also **grant** him the right to cross the land she is retaining to get to the road. An old common law rule was skeptical about affirmative grants of easements, requiring elaborate transactions to accomplish the same thing; today, courts increasingly accept either grants or reservations of easements.

The law also will **imply** easements from the circumstances even without an express reservation or grant. A court may find an easement **implied from apparent and continuous use** if the grantor and grantee both act as if an easement exists after a piece of land has been subdivided. In the example above, if Mercedes did not explicitly reserve an easement over the land she is granting to Norman in her deed but continues to cross that land to get to the road and Norman does not object, the courts will imply that both Mercedes and Norman must have understood that she would have an easement. Where the facts are unclear, courts will often focus on whether the owner of the property subject to the purported easement had proper notice.

Courts may also find an easement **implied by necessity** if a transaction otherwise would leave the grantor's remaining property landlocked. Thus, even if the evidence of continuous use was unclear in the example above, if Mercedes would have no other lawful way to get to the road after granting the front of her lot to Norman, the law will imply that she must have reserved an easement for herself. The law disfavors easements by necessity and generally will not imply one if the grantor has any other way out, even an inconvenient one.

Easements may arise by **estoppel** if someone acts in a way that is inconsistent with denying the easement. For example, if Siegfried gives Tanya permission to cross his property to hers and she builds a home on her land in reliance on that permission, Siegfried may not withdraw her right to cross and render her house practically unusable.

Finally, easements can arise by prescription through a process very similar to that of adverse possession. But whereas an adverse possessor will have established her or his rights by taking full possession of a piece of property for the requisite period, someone obtaining an easement by prescription will only have undertaken the actions the eventual prescriptive easement permits (commonly crossing the property) without taking full possession.

Some easements are for a specific period of time and expire naturally. Otherwise, once an easement is established, it will continue until it is explicitly abandoned by the person holding the rights, until the easement goes unused so long that the courts regard it as abandoned, until it is seized by prescription (perhaps the owner of the servient property builds a wall blocking access and the easement holder fails to object effectively until the statute of limitations expires), or until ownership of the dominant and servient tenements come into the same hands.

A specialized form of easement that allows the easement holder to remove crops or other plants from a property is called a **profit**.

Although most easements convey the affirmative right to *do* something, the common law recognized four special negative easements giving the holder the right to *prevent* another landowner from doing something injurious to the easement-holder. These **negative easements** were for lateral support for land, for unimpeded access to traditional patterns of sunlight, for access to the flowing of water in an artificial stream, and for access to the flow of air in a defined channel. Thus, if I have an easement for lateral support from my next-door neighbor, she typically will not be allowed to excavate her property so close to the property line that dirt or buildings from my land fall into hers. Some jurisdictions reject some of these negative easements or have modified them; conversely, others recognize additional negative easements for conservation.

What You Need to Know:

1. Easements are rights to take actions that would otherwise be trespasses on the land of another.
2. Easements in gross create rights in particular persons; easements appurtenant give rights to the owner of a nearby property.
3. Land burdened by an easement is called the servient tenement; land whose owner enjoyed the right to an easement on someone else's land is called the dominant tenement.
4. Easements can arise by explicit grants or reservations in deeds, by implication, by estoppel, or by prescription.
5. Although most easements convey affirmative rights, a few easements prohibit neighbors from taking certain kinds of injurious actions.

LESSON 21: COVENANTS RUNNING WITH LAND

One of the most basic features of contract law is that it only binds persons who consent. As a principle of liberty, that has much to commend it. But contracts binding only the parties would be a wildly ineffectual means of controlling **negative externalities** (spillover effects) from nearby properties. Even if you and I sign a contract promising one another not to open taverns on our respective properties, neither one of us will have any real protection: either of us could sell our properties to someone who was not party to our contract and who is free to open a tavern there. Indeed, if a prospective tavern operator begins making inquiries in the area, you and I compete to be the one who gets to sell rather than the one who ends up stuck listening to boisterous patrons exiting at 2 a.m.

The tort of nuisance does not require individuals' consent, but its focus is a relative handful of highly offensive land uses: it may not help against uses that are appropriate in some locations but that can cause problems in others. And it certainly is no help in *preserving* beneficial land uses that provide **positive externalities** to neighbors (such as historic architecture). As noted in Lesson 20, easements generally create positive rights to include one's activities on someone else's property rather than negative rights to exclude undesirable actions there. Some other means of controlling private land seemed necessary.

Those means are **real covenants** and **equitable servitudes**. These are commitments in deeds that impose obligations on the present and future owners of one property to the benefit of present and future owners of another property.

Example

> *Kwami owns Redacre and Scarletacre. He gives Laura a deed to Scarletacre that forbids her or any subsequent owner from opening a tavern on Scarletacre.* Laura is bound by a real covenant. If Kwame then sells Redacre to Ming and Laura sells Scarletacre to Nadia, Ming will be able to sue Nadia if Nadia tries to open a tavern on Scarletacre.

The Third Restatement would relax some traditional rules concerning real covenants and equitable servitudes (and would combine them into a single body of law), but most states still follow traditional common law rules. Real covenants can only be created:

- When an **interest in real estate** is being transferred;

- If the language in the deed creating the obligation clearly binds subsequent owners; and
- If the obligation "**touches and concerns**" the property.

Thus, neighbors cannot simply agree to a real covenant between themselves and bind their successors unless they find some way to transfer interests in one of their property to the other of them. Language in a deed prohibiting a named grantee from undertaking a particular action is unlikely to be held to bind subsequent owners: courts will look for some clear intention that *all* owners of a particular piece of property are bound. And courts will not enforce as real covenants rules having little to do with the property (*e.g.*, one specifying which brand of orange juice the owners will drink). Real covenants that violate public policy, such as those imposing racial or other noxious forms of discrimination, are void and unenforceable.

In order to enforce a real covenant, the common law required both **horizontal privity** and **vertical privity**. Horizontal, or original, privity is a grantor-grantee relationship between the owners of the two properties—the one that is bound by the covenant and the one with the right to enforce the covenant—when it was first created. Without horizontal privity, no binding real covenant ever comes into existence. **Vertical privity** is a chain of title going back to the owner who was part of the transaction originally creating the real covenant. Traditionally, courts required vertical privity separately both for the **burden** (*i.e.*, the obligation to comply) and the **benefit** (*i.e.*, the right to sue) to run to subsequent owners. Thus, in the example above, if Abner took Redacre away from Ming through adverse position, he would not be able to enforce the real covenant against Nadia's tavern because he lacks vertical privity with Kwami: he just started his own chain of title. Some courts have begun to relax vertical privity requirements.

Similar to, but traditionally separate from, real covenants are equitable servitudes (occasionally called **reciprocal negative easements**). Equitable servitudes do not require privity. On the other hand, they do require that any party to be bound have notice—actual, constructive or inquiry—of the obligation. For example, in *Sanborn v. McLean*, 206 N.W.2d 496 (Mich. 1925), a developer sold off 91 lots in a luxury subdivision. The deeds to 53 of the properties, but not the one owned by the McLeans, referred to a master plan for the subdivision that allowed only residential uses throughout the subdivision. Prior to conveying away the property that ended up in the McLeans' hands, the developer had committed all of the properties he then owned to follow the restrictions in the deeds he granted to the earliest purchasers. When the McLeans tried to open a gas station on their land, their neighbors sued. The court held that the developer's commitment in the deeds to the other purchasers bound the land he later sold to the McLeans and that the McLeans had at least inquiry notice of those limitations because they should be able to see that the entire subdivision was conforming to some plan. Further research then would have revealed the references to the plan in the other deeds.

A plaintiff successfully enforcing a real covenant is entitled to money damages. A plaintiff successfully enforcing an equitable servitude is entitled to an injunction against the prohibited acts. Some restrictions function as both real covenants and as equitable servitudes and may be enforced as either if they meet the applicable requirements.

Once a real covenant or an equitable servitude is in place, courts are reluctant to declare it void even when circumstances change considerably from those that gave rise to the restriction in the first place. Only in extreme situations, where events frustrate the purpose of the covenant or servitude or where the covenant or servitude violates public policy, will courts declare it void. For example, in *Shelley v. Kramer*, 334 U.S. 1 (1948), the Court refused to enforce racially restrictive covenants in deeds. Of course, after some period of time a violation of a covenant or servitude may cease to be actionable under the statute of limitations.

Homeowners' associations and condominium associations often operate under, and enforce, extensive and complex systems of equitable servitudes. Courts are extremely deferential to restrictions on what individual owners can do with their properties when the original agreement establishing the community or condominium plan includes those restrictions. Even when the association's board adds new restrictions later, under rules in the original agreement allowing them to do so, courts often defer to the board and compel property owners to comply. This is true despite often-dubious impacts on other property owners.

What You Need to Know:

1. Real covenants and equitable servitudes are agreements that restrict the activities that owners can conduct on their land.
2. Unlike most contracts, real covenants and equitable servitudes bind subsequent owners who had no part in reaching the original agreement.
3. Property owners can create a real covenant only when they transfer an interest in land—creating privity of estate between the original parties—and even then only when it touches and concerns the property and does not violate public policy.
4. An equitable servitude does not require privity but does require notice to the owner against whom a court is enforcing the servitude.
5. Violations of real covenants result in awards of damages; violations of equitable servitudes result in injunctions against the forbidden activities.
6. Homeowners' associations and condominium associations rely heavily on equitable servitudes.
7. The Third Restatement would relax and simplify common law rules on covenants running with the land and end distinctions between real covenants and equitable servitudes.

LESSON 22: BASIC ZONING PRINCIPLES

In previous Lessons, we covered the restrictions private law places on owners' freedom to use their land. These restrictions can come in the form of nuisance suits, easements, real covenants, or equitable servitudes. In addition, however, governments can regulate how private property owners use their land. Although many forms of public land use regulation exist, the most pervasive is zoning. As its name implies, **zoning** involves a local government dividing its territory into different zones. For each zone, the local government's ordinance permits some land uses and prohibits others. As a result, a landowner's ability to use her or his property in a way that other owners might find objectionable depends not just on whether the intended land use is a nuisance or inconsistent with an easement, real covenant, or equitable servitude held by someone else but also whether that land use violates the zoning rules applicable to that property.

Early in the 20th century, when cities and towns first enacted zoning ordinances, some questioned whether they were constitutional. The U.S. Supreme Court resolved that question in *Euclid v. Ambler*, 272 U.S. 365 (1926). The zoning ordinance there cut the value of the plaintiff's property more than in half. Nonetheless, the Court held that the ordinance was not a public **taking** of private property without just compensation (and hence did not violate the Fifth and Fourteenth Amendments). The Court found that the ability to pass zoning ordinances was not very different from governments' power to remove nuisances (even though Ambler's property was not itself a nuisance). Because the ordinance in *Euclid* so dramatically reduced property values, and because the Court that decided the case was extraordinarily solicitous of property rights in its other cases, most observers concluded that the Court's failure to strike down the ordinance there eliminated any chance for a broad holding that zoning ordinances are takings, absent special circumstances. Subsequent cases have occasionally found constitutional violations where a particular city or town abused its zoning powers.

Zoning is typically carried out by cities and towns, although some states may allow counties and certain townships to zone as well. Cities and towns generally do not have inherent authority to zone: their zoning powers spring from state zoning enabling laws. Any attempt to zone that is inconsistent with the state's zoning enabling act is unlawful.

When a city decides to enact a zoning ordinance, most state zoning enabling acts require it first to develop a **comprehensive plan** for its territory. This plan ordinarily specifies what general kinds of uses the city would like to see occur in which parts of its territory. This typically includes both current uses and those the city would like to promote in the future; it can also involve reducing or removing certain uses in some parts of town. For example, a city might designate a decaying industrial area for redevelopment as residential lofts. The zoning enabling act may require the city to consult expert urban planners and seek public comment before finalizing its comprehensive plan.

Once the city approves its comprehensive plan, the zoning enabling act typically calls for the city to divide up its territory into zones and specify permitted and prohibited uses in each. Thus, for example, the zoning ordinance may provide that the area west of the river and north of Market Street should be limited to single-family homes, while the area west of the river but south of Market Street may be used for apartment buildings of up to four stories or for small stores. This kind of zoning, which aims to separate types of uses, is called "***Euclid*ian zoning**" because it was the kind the Supreme Court upheld in 1926. It aims to separate uses thought to be incompatible with one another (perhaps because one emits noise or odors that could interfere with the use and enjoyment of a neighboring piece of land being used in a different way). Other kinds of zoning might permit mixes of adjacent uses but try to limit the concentrations of more intensive, and disruptive, uses.

*Euclid*ian zoning typically relies on a hierarchy of land uses. Single-family residential homes are typically at the top of this hierarchy, essentially regarded as the least disruptive but most easily disrupted land use. At the bottom of the hierarchy—the "lowest" use—is typically heavy industry, which is relatively impervious to disruption by neighbors but most likely to create disturbing emissions. Under this approach, commonly called "**cumulative zoning**," higher uses are permitted in areas zoned for a lower use but not the other way around. Thus, for example, the owner of a property in an area zoned for heavy industry could put up an apartment building (or even a single-family home), but no one could open a factory in an area zoned for small stores.

Zoning authorities have broad authority to prevent new land uses that they disfavor but much less power to force the termination of existing uses. Limiting an owner's ability to develop a property as she or he would like strikes courts as far less of an imposition than forcing the owner immediately to stop what she or he is doing. Thus a zoning ordinance prohibiting bars from opening in a particular district likely will be effective against property owners there wishing to open a bar at some point in the future. But that ordinance could not immediately shut down bars already operating in the zone. Those bars could continue to operate as "**nonconforming uses**" even though no new ones could open. Some states' courts do, however, allow zoning ordinances to require nonconforming uses to phase out over a period of years. These courts reason that the nonconforming use's owners can still get a fair return on their investment in the property if they are allowed to "**amortize**" that investment over a number of years. Other courts regard "amortization" as an insufficient response to allegations that zoning ordinances effect unconstitutional takings when they require the termination of existing lawful activities.

Courts have allowed cities broad latitude in the criteria that guide their zoning ordinances. In addition to preventing nuisances and other polluters, they have allowed cities to enforce numerous aesthetic and cultural values through zoning ordinances.

What You Need to Know:

1. Zoning is a form of legislation, or public law, that seeks to achieve some of the same purposes as common law doctrines such as easements, covenants, and nuisance but operates separately under its own rules to govern relations between landowners and the government.
2. Zoning ordinances may restrict what landowners may do with their property even when nuisance

law, easements, real covenants, and equitable servitudes pose no barrier to that use.

3. Zoning generally can restrict property owners' choices of how to use their land without running afoul of the Takings Clause of the Fifth Amendment and the Fourteenth Amendment's Due Process Clause.
4. Zoning ordinances must comply with the state's zoning enabling act and must be consistent with the city or town's comprehensive plan.
5. Zoning ordinances typically treat single-family homes as the highest use of land and one permitted in any zone. By contrast, industrial production is considered the lowest land use and may only be initiated in areas zoned for it. Commercial uses and apartment buildings commonly are regarded as intermediate uses (between single-family homes and industry).
6. Zoning ordinances typically cannot require the immediate termination of existing nonconforming uses. Some states, however, allow zoning authorities to require removal of those uses after the owners have had a reasonable amount of time to recoup their investments.

NOTE: Many Property courses include a class or two on nuisance. Regulating nuisance was the original justification for zoning, and nuisance law is also relevant to other topics such as Easements and Covenants Running with the Land. Other schools cover nuisance in their Torts courses. Because we include a nuisance Lesson in our Torts chapter, we are not duplicating that here. Students who anticipate studying nuisance in Property should review that Lesson as it introduces the key concepts professors in either course are likely to cover.

LESSON 23: ZONING MECHANICS, FLEXIBILITY, AND EXCLUSION

Because zoning ordinances can sharply increase or decrease the value of property and can have a huge influence on the future development of a community, their application is often controversial. As noted in Lesson 22, owners whose property at present does not conform to a zoning ordinance may argue that they are entitled to preserve their **nonconforming use**. That doctrine is of little help, however, to those wanting to make changes to their property that violate zoning rules. And even owners whom the nonconforming use doctrine protects cannot expand the activities that violate the zoning ordinance.

One approach prospective developers can take is to argue that the zoning rules were not properly promulgated: that the zoning authority violated the **zoning enabling act**, that it failed to produce a proper comprehensive plan, that the zoning ordinance is inconsistent with that plan, or that it did not follow the required procedures in promulgating its zoning ordinance. These matters were discussed in Lesson 22.

Another possible challenge is that the municipal government is applying the zoning ordinance arbitrarily. *Anderson v. City of Issaquah*, 851 P.2d 744 (Wash. App. 1993), held an aesthetic zoning ordinance **unconstitutionally vague** as applied to a property owner who repeatedly submitted what seemed to be compliant plans to zoning authorities, only to have the authorities reject those plans for unclear and contradictory reasons.

If the zoning ordinance attempts to regulate expression, a property owner may be able to challenge it on constitutional grounds. *City of Ladue v. Gilleo*, 512 U.S. 43 (1994), struck down an ordinance restricting the placement of signs for violating the **First Amendment** both because it regulated too much protected speech and because it allowed exceptions that the Court held were unduly arbitrary. Attacks on zoning ordinances on **freedom of association** grounds have had mixed success: *Village of Belle Terre v. Boraas*, 416 U.S. 1 (1974), upheld an ordinance limiting the number of unrelated people who could live together as preserving a family-centered way of life in a town that feared an influx of college students, but *Moore v. City of East Cleveland*, 431 U.S. 494 (1977), struck down a single-family ordinance that was being applied to prevent a property owner from living with her grandsons.

Instead of challenging the zoning authorities, however, a property owner can ask those authorities for permission to carry out her or his plans despite the ordinance. Zoning authorities commonly grant dispensations for new, noncompliant uses in one of four ways:

1. Zoning **variances** are special administrative decisions that allow particular properties to fall out of compliance with zoning rules. For example, the zoning authorities might grant a variance to allow someone to open a small convenience store in an otherwise-residential community or to build a third story on their home in a community zoned for two-story dwellings.
2. **Special exceptions** are provisions in zoning ordinances that relax rules for properties that meet certain conditions. For example, a zoning ordinance might allow convenience stores to open in residential communities if they have no illuminated signs, do not sell alcohol, and have no more than a maximum amount of floor space or it might allow third stories on homes that are set back more than a specified number of feet from the curb.
3. **Zoning amendments** are changes to zoning laws that permit uses that prior law prohibited. For example, a city council might amend its zoning law to treat small convenience stores as permissible uses in residential neighborhoods or to allow homeowners to add third floors to their homes in certain parts of town.
4. **Floating zones** are relatively new devices that allow a certain number of uses of a particular nature but do not specify where those uses may occur. For example, a zoning ordinance might allow three small convenience stores to open in residential neighborhoods on the west side of town but not specify where. Once three such stores opened, the ordinance would bar all others.

Many zoning ordinances have the effect of requiring more expensive forms of development, such as single-family homes rather than apartment buildings (or homes with large yards rather than small ones). This can have the effect of preventing low- and moderate-income people from moving into the communities with these ordinances. Civil rights organizations, developers seeking to build multi-family housing, and people wanting to move into communities with such **exclusionary zoning** ordinances have sued to get these ordinances declared unconstitutional. Although the U.S. Supreme Court has declined to intervene absent proof of racially discriminatory motives, some state courts have held that these ordinances either violate state constitutions or are inconsistent with their zoning enabling acts. The best-known of these cases is *Southern Burlington Township NAACP v. Township of Mt. Laurel*, 336 A.2d 713 (N.J. 1975), in which the New Jersey Supreme Court struck down a zoning ordinance providing for minimum lot sizes that effectively allowed only affluent people to move into the community. The court went on to hold that all municipalities in New Jersey had to accept their "fair share" of low- and moderate-cost housing. The court subsequently had considerable difficulty enforcing its decision. Other courts have refused to enforce zoning ordinances that did not make adequate provision for low- and moderate-cost housing.

Courts also can strike down zoning ordinances under the Supremacy Clause if they violate federal civil rights laws that prohibit discrimination against people with disabilities and certain other vulnerable groups. For example, an ordinance that prohibits group homes might effectively discriminate against severely disabled people who cannot live independently on their own.

What You Need to Know:

1. Property owners and others may challenge zoning ordinances as unconstitutionally vague if they fail to give property owners clear guidance about what is and is not permissible.

2. Property owners and others may challenge zoning ordinances that restrict expression under the First Amendment.

3. Governments that enact zoning ordinances have the power to restrict unrelated people's right to live together unless the restrictions violate federal or state civil rights laws, but zoning ordinances may not prohibit family members from living together.
4. Zoning authorities can permit new development that does not comply with zoning ordinances by granting variances, including provision for special exceptions in the ordinance, amending the ordinance, or creating a "floating zone" that allows a certain number of potentially problematic uses without specifying the permissible location of those uses.
5. Zoning ordinances that drive up the cost of housing may be challenged as exclusionary under state constitutions and statutes.

LESSON 24: EMINENT DOMAIN, JUST COMPENSATION AND REGULATORY TAKINGS

As committed as our legal system is to the principle of private property, at times the government needs property that some private person owns for an important public function. In theory, we could simply require the government to negotiate to purchase that property; if the owner wishes not to sell, or is only willing to sell at a price the government will not pay, then under this hypothetical system the public function simply would not take place.

In fact, because some public activities are very important to the general welfare, our legal system has been unwilling to accept that possibility. We do, however, make the government pay for property it takes. This process is regulated by the **Takings Clause** of the Fifth Amendment of the U.S. Constitution, which provides: "nor shall private property be taken for public use, without just compensation." The Supreme Court has held the protection against takings to be an aspect of the liberty guaranteed by the Fourteenth Amendment's Due

Process Clause and hence fully applicable to state and local governments.

The main process by which the government takes full ownership of private property is called **condemnation**, and the power to condemn private property that the government needs is called **eminent domain**. Not all governmental bodies have the power of eminent domain, but the U.S. Government, the states, and most county and municipal governments do. Some governments have given certain private entities, such as railroads, similar powers for specified purposes.

A government entity with eminent domain powers can file a civil lawsuit against the property owner asking the court to give the government title to the property and to determine the compensation that the government must pay. Historically, the government need not take (and hence pay for) all of a property, and the piece it takes need not leave the remaining parts coherent or usable. After taking land for a highway or railroad down the middle of a farmer's land, the remaining pieces may be cut off from one another and not commercially viable to till. In addition, the values awarded in condemnation proceedings are typically much less than the private owner would have demanded to sell the property (if she or he were willing to sell at all).

Each of the major components of the Takings Clause has generated significant legal controversy. Specifically, courts have had to decide what property rights the clause protects from governmental intrusion, whether the government "takes" private property when it restricts that property's use but does not assume ownership, what is a permissible public use, and what is just compensation.

Although land, personal property, and intellectual property (such as patents, copyrights, and trademarks) all clearly are protected against government seizure, courts have been less sure whether the Takings Clause protects individuals against loss of benefits such as pensions or against changes in common law rules that benefited them.

Traditionally, the courts have found invasions of owners' right to exclude were takings that required just compensation while restrictions on the right to include only constituted takings in special circumstances. For example, in *Loretto v. Teleprompter Manhattan CATV Corp.*, 458 U.S. 419 (1982), the government required some property owners to allow cable television wires on their buildings. The Court held that, because this would otherwise be a trespass, it required compensation. Similarly, *Horne v. Department of Agriculture*, 135 S. Ct. 2419 (2015), held that a requirement that a requirement that raisin growers and handlers turn over a fraction of their crop to a government-organized marketing board was a taking requiring just compensation without regard to whether the original owners retained some contingent rights to those raisins. By contrast, in *Hadacheck v. Sebastian*, 239 U.S. 394 (1915), the Court found no taking in an ordinance that prohibited the owner of a brickyard from operating a kiln on his property despite the devastating impact on his business.

Nonetheless, regulations that sufficiently diminish the value of property could constitute a taking despite leaving ownership in private hands. *Pennsylvania Coal Co. v. Mahon*, 260 U.S. 393 (1922), addressed a state law that restricted coal companies' exploitation of mineral rights where doing so was likely to cause surface damage to property. Speaking through Justice Oliver Wendell Holmes, the Supreme Court held that this so reduced the practical value of mineral rights as to implicate takings analysis. Subsequent cases have sent mixed messages. *Lucas v. South Carolina Coastal Council*, 505 U.S. 1003 (1992), held that regulations that totally eliminated the value of property always constituted takings. But in *Penn Central Transportation Co. v. City of New York*, 438 U.S. 104 (1978), the Court held that courts should weigh many factors, including the utility of the property for other purposes and any features of a regulatory scheme that offset some of the property owner's losses, in deciding whether a taking occurred.

Where the government makes its approval of some use of land conditional on the private owner agreeing to provide an unrelated benefit to the public, the Court has regarded this arrangement as unduly coercive and found an **exaction**, which is a form of unconstitutional taking. In *Nollan v. California Coastal Commission*, 483 U.S. 825 (1987), land use authorities conditioned approval for replacement of a building on the private owners' land on their granting the public access across their land to the beach. While not questioning the authorities' ability to regulate construction near the beach, the Supreme Court struck down their attempt to extract a quid pro quo for their permission. Similarly, in *Dolan v. City of Tigard*, 512 U.S. 374 (1994), the Court refused to allow a city to condition approval of a building permit on the owner's dedication of a portion of her land to flood control.

As long as government entities exercising eminent domain powers pay compensation, the Supreme Court generally has been largely unwilling to second-guess whether the purpose of a taking is genuinely for "public use." In *Berman v. Parker*, 348 U.S. 26 (1954), the Court upheld the condemnation of a well-maintained structure as part of an urban renewal project in a decayed low-income neighborhood. Much more controversially, *Kelo v. City of New London*, 545 U.S. 469 (2005), found no constitutional objection to the condemnation of a healthy community to make way for a private industrial development that municipal officials believed was important for economic development. A number of states have passed laws prohibiting takings of the kind upheld in *Kelo*.

What You Need to Know:

1. The Takings Clause requires the government actions to pay just compensation when it takes private property for public purposes.

2. The power to take private land in exchange for just compensation is called condemnation or eminent domain.

3. Denying property owners the right to exclude unwelcome activities from their land generally requires just compensation; courts judge restrictions of the right to include on a case-by-case basis.

4. Government authorities cannot condition approvals of land uses on owners doing unrelated favors for the government or the public.

5. The courts generally will not question the purposes for which government takes private land.

CHAPTER 8

CONTRACTS

LESSON 1: INTRODUCTION; SOURCES OF LAW; OVERVIEW OF FIRST-YEAR CONTRACTS

Contracts professors sometimes say that they have the easiest job when it comes to teaching a first-year law course. The reason—so goes the (not-so-clever) joke—is that "the students' expectations are so low." The expectations often are low because students assume that the work of a contracts lawyer only involves the tedious line-by-line drafting of voluminous documents and that contracts all involve large transactions by big corporations and thus have little to do with the lives of average people.

You will discover in the first few weeks of your Contracts course that the truth is strikingly different. To be sure, contracts provide the foundation for large transactions by big corporations (mergers, acquisitions, etc.). But at its most basic, ***"contract" merely means a promise that is legally binding***. Thus, average people conclude contracts thousands of times in their lives. Indeed, in contrast to most of your other first-year courses, you certainly have been personally involved in contracts in the past and will be in the future. (With any luck, you will never commit nor be the victim of a crime or tort.)

Moreover, you will learn that *people can conclude contracts in a whole variety of unexpected ways*. To choose just a few examples, every time you eat at a restaurant, download an app, buy something at a store or on the Internet, rent a car, or take a job, you are concluding a contract. Thus, contracts affect the lives of nearly everyone nearly every day.

But why should the law be in the business of enforcing purely private deals between private parties? After all, government-provided courthouses, clerks, judges, etc., cost a great deal of money. The short answer is that *enforceable contract rights are essential to the functioning of a modern economy*. At a basic level, if the law did not enforce contracts—backed by the power of the government, acting through the courts—people would have to resort to "self-help" (often, violence) to get their contract partners to live up to agreed deals. (Why do loan sharks rely on violence to get paid back?—because their interest rates exceed the limits set by usury laws, and thus they cannot enforce their loan contracts through the courts.)

As a broader matter, enforcing promises facilitates the exchange of goods and services by willing participants. That is, contract law creates a structure within which private persons can acquire what they want. And by enforcing the deals private parties make about the future, contract law encourages the taking of risks. And entrepreneurship—the foundation of a growing economy—is all about the taking of risks by inventors and innovators. We all gain when the Apples, Googles, and Facebooks of the world create new and innovative products and services. If the founders of such enterprises could not rely on the contracts they conclude with others to get a new project off of the ground, they would have no incentive—well, at least substantially less incentive—to devote the time, money, and effort to build, create, innovate, modernize, and improve in the first place. (If they could not reap the benefits, why would they invest the costs?)

It is precisely because the economy as a whole benefits from encouraging entrepreneurs to engage in risky or large transactions, and average people to engage in run-of-the-mill deals, that all modern legal systems recognize and enforce contracts between private parties.

Sources of Law

In very large measure, contract law in the United States comes from the "common law." This distinctive feature of the Anglo-American legal system means that judges (not legislatures) have created the basic rules of contract law through a gradual process of resolving actual cases. Over time, a coherent body of rules has emerged from judicial opinions by the supreme courts in each state. Like your other common-law courses (*e.g.*, torts and property), therefore, you will learn the principles of contract law through reading judicial opinions.

Contract law as state law. In the federal system of the United States, each state is a "sovereign," which means that each has the authority to create law on its own. Contract law is a classic example of a subject that is left to the lawmaking power of the individual states (New York, Wisconsin, etc.). Although the federal government also has some authority to create contract law by statute, it has done so only on discrete subjects (*see*, for example, the CISG treaty below). Thus, the supreme court of each state—and *not* the U.S. Supreme Court—is the final authority on the common law of contracts for that state. That is why almost all of the cases you will read in Contracts are from state supreme or appellate courts (and if you read one from a federal court, it will be applying state law).

Similar to your other common-law courses, you frequently will run across the "***Restatement of Contracts***" in your Contracts course. The Restatement of Contracts, now in a second edition, is a distillation of the common law of contracts into a few hundred concise principles. (The term "blackletter law" comes from the fact that the Restatements set forth their rules in bold letters.) It is a product of the American Law Institute (ALI), an organization of distinguished lawyers, judges, and scholars, and thus is not binding law by itself; rather, it merely reflects the opinion of the ALI on what is common among the states and, on a few issues, on how the law should change. Nonetheless, you will see that in numerous cases the courts have adopted specific provisions of the Restatement as the law of their state.

The principal exception to the primacy of the common law in the field of contracts is the ***Uniform Commercial Code (U.C.C.)***. In certain areas of commerce in our modern economy, it is essential that the law be uniform throughout the country. To advance this goal, the legislatures of the states (except Louisiana) have enacted the U.C.C. into law as a uniform statute for the subjects within its scope. Although the U.C.C. governs a variety of specialized subjects, the one that you will encounter in first-year Contracts is Article 2 on transactions in "goods" (meaning moveable things, *see* § 2–105(1)). You also may encounter a few general principles, such as basic definitions, set forth in Article 1 of the U.C.C. In many cases the rules in U.C.C. Article 2 are the same as the common law (or are so specialized as to be beyond the scope of a basic contract law course). As a result, your Contracts professor likely will cover U.C.C. Article 2 only when it has rules on basic issues of contract law that differ from the common law.

A final source of contract law that your professor may mention is an international treaty that the U.S. has ratified, the ***United Nations Convention on Contracts for the International Sale of Goods ("CISG")***. Under the Constitution, the CISG operates as directly binding federal law and thus displaces both the state-law U.C.C. and the common law for international sales transactions. As accepted by the United States, the CISG applies when (a) the transaction involves a sale of goods (again, moveable things); (b) the parties have their respective "places of business" in different countries; and (c) both such countries have ratified the CISG. *See* Article 1(1)(a).

Overview of First-Year Contracts

Taken at a structural level, you will cover five principal subjects in first-year Contracts:

1. *Contract Formation.* Most first-year Contracts professors begin the semester with the rules governing how a contract is formed (*see* Part I below). The law recognizes two principal, and alternative, means of forming a contract: the first is the *traditional method*, which is based on the everyday notion of a "bargain" between two parties. Lessons 4 through 11 will cover this traditional method of contract formation. The second arises from a party's justified reliance on a promise and is known by the fancy term "*promissory estoppel.*" Lessons 12 and 13 will examine this alternative to the traditional method of contract formation.

2. *Contract Interpretation.* If the parties have formed a contract, a common question that arises is what, exactly, is the content and meaning of their deal. Such disputes of interpretation are among the most common in contract law cases. In this segment of your Contracts course (*see* Part II below), you will cover the principles of interpretation; the difficult subject of the "parol evidence rule" ("parol" is not a typo); and the implied obligation of good faith.

3. *Contract Defenses.* The next subject you will cover in Contracts is the defenses a party may have to the enforcement of a contract (*see* Part III below). In a whole variety of situations, our society (through the law) simply does not think that it is appropriate to hold a party to a contract even though all of the requirements for contract formation have been satisfied. Consider the example of a criminal who uses a gun to force another person to sign a contract ("duress"). In such cases, the law frees the disadvantaged party from the obligation to fulfill his otherwise-binding contractual promises.

4. *Performance and Breach.* If the parties have formed a contract and no defenses to enforcement exist, when and under what circumstances must they *perform* their contractual promises? This is important because the very definition of a "breach" is a failure to perform a contractual obligation when it is due. Part IV below will cover this important and sometimes difficult subject.

5. *Remedies.* If one party has breached a contract, what remedies are available to compensate the "injured party"? You will learn in this final segment of the course (*see* Part V below) that, as a basic proposition, an injured party may recover monetary damages measured by what she had a right to expect from the contract (the so-called "benefit of the bargain"). Because of the fundamental importance of this issue, a few professors begin the semester with the remedies for breach of contract. If your professor follows this approach, you should skip to Part V on contract remedies before returning to Part I on contract formation.

What You Need to Know:

1. Contract law involves a determination of when a promise is binding. This is a fundamental question because enforceable contract rights are essential to the functioning of a modern economy.

2. Contract law is found principally in the common law of each individual state. There are two

important exceptions: (1) the Uniform Commercial Code, and in particular its Article 2 governing transactions in "goods"; and (2) for international sales of goods, a specialized treaty, the United Nations Convention on Contracts for the International Sale of Goods ("CISG").

3. First-year Contracts covers five principal subjects: (a) contract formation; (b) contract interpretation; (c) defenses to enforcement; (d) performance and breach; and (e) remedies for breach.

LESSON 2: OVERVIEW OF CONTRACT FORMATION; MUTUAL ASSENT IN GENERAL

In this lesson we cover the basic definition of a "contract." We also begin the analysis of the traditional means of forming a contract, and especially the key concept of "mutual assent."

What Is a "Contract"? Before we get into the details of contract formation, let's begin with the overarching concept of a "contract." As stated in Restatement § 1, a contract merely is "***a promise or a set of promises for the breach of which the law gives a remedy***, or the performance of which the law in some way recognizes as a duty." In more direct words, a contract is a promise that the law says is binding in the sense that someone can sue you for not performing it. As you go through the first few weeks of Contracts, therefore, a fundamental concept for you to understand is "promise," and the key distinction for you to draw is between those promises that are binding (= a contract) and those that are not (= no contract).

Restatement § 2 defines a promise as "a manifestation of intention to act or refrain from acting in a specified way, so made as to justify a promisee in understanding that a commitment has been made." The key words in this definition are "manifestation" and "justify" (see below for more detail). You will see them repeatedly in first-year Contracts.

The definition of a contract also makes clear that not all promises are legally binding. (Adverbs like "legally" and adjectives like "binding" are very important in the law.) This makes sense: if your sweet Aunt Lilly promises to bake cookies for your birthday, but then forgets to do so, the law will not let you sue her for "breach of contract." But this seemingly obvious point raises a very important question: How should our legal system distinguish between such informal, unenforceable promises (= no contract) and the important, enforceable "contractual" promises on which a modern economy depends? Of course, Aunt Lilly may experience social sanctions for breaking her promise, such as your disappointed face in the sight of your birthday party guests. But you will have access to the courts of law only for those broken promises that are *legally* binding (= contracts). The rules of contract formation are here to draw the important distinction between these two kinds of promises.

The Traditional Method of Contract Formation. With this lesson we begin the analysis of the traditional method of contract formation, which goes back hundreds of years. Restatement § 17 states the basic test for this method: "[T]he formation of a contract requires a bargain in which there is a manifestation of mutual assent to the exchange and a consideration." You will see immediately that the central concept here is a "bargain" and this in turn requires two elements: (a) a *manifestation of mutual assent* and (b) *consideration*. We will see later that the courts also have recognized what is in effect a third element: (c) that the parties must define the *essential terms* of their deal.

Manifestation of Mutual Assent. In this first, fundamental "element" of the test, a great deal rides on the word "manifestation." Contract law determines whether people have assented to contractual obligations not on what they intend, but rather on what they "manifest." That is, the law focuses on the *external* meaning of a person's words and conduct. In the law, we call this the ***"objective" standard*** for determining intent—*i.e.*, whether a ***"reasonable person"*** in the position of the *other* party would understand her words and conduct, under the circumstances, to reflect an intent to be bound. The most common forms of such objective assent of course are express words ("I agree") or a signature on a contract document. But a manifestation of assent also may occur through a nod of a head, a wink of an eye, or really any word, gesture, or other action depending on the circumstances.

Thus, what a person *actually* means with her words or actions—her "subjective" intent—basically is irrelevant in determining assent to a contract. A famous judge (with, no kidding, the name "Learned Hand") once expressed the message this way: "A contract has, strictly speaking, nothing to do with the personal, or individual, intent of the parties. . . . If it were proved by twenty bishops that either party, when he used the words, intended something other than the usual meaning . . . he would still be held" to the contract. In short, if a person actually did not intend to agree to a contract, well, tough luck—for we all are bound by the reasonable, external meaning of what we say and do in the world.

Example

> Lucy owned some farmland and was discussing selling it to Zehmer at a bar over a friendly beer. Lucy then scribbled on a napkin an offer to sell the land to Zehmer at a stated price. Zehmer accepted, but later Lucy asserted that she meant the napkin as a joke. Upon suit by Zehmer, the court found that the parties formed a contract, reasoning that under the given circumstances a reasonable person in Zehmer's position would have understood that Lucy was sincere.

Unfortunately, sometimes you will read in court opinions that contract formation requires a "meeting of the minds." Taken literally, this is quite misleading. The law determines whether persons intend to be bound not on their "minds," but rather on externally observable evidence of their intent. (Everything depends on context. Bulgarians supposedly nod their head to say "no." But in the customs of U.S.-American society, the external meaning of a nod may well bind an unschooled Bulgarian to a contract in this country.)

When Subjective Intent May Prevail. The one (rare) exception to the rule that the parties' subjective intent is irrelevant involves situations in which one party knew or should have known of the other's true intent. The idea here is that if Party A actually *knew*, because of inside information, that Party B misspoke or otherwise did not intend what she appeared to say, Party A cannot retreat behind the objective rule to identify Party B's intent. The reason is that Party A knew more than what would appear to a reasonable person.

Example

> Helga and Jade have long had an inside joke to the effect that the phrase, "I totally agree," actually expresses *dis*agreement. At a company picnic, Helga offered to buy Jade's diamond ring for $400 and, in the presence of numerous witnesses, Jade said, "I totally agree." Because, notwithstanding the objective meaning of Jade's words, Helga knew Jade's true intent, the parties did not form a contract on the sale of the ring.

But what if *both* parties misspeak—that is, mistakenly communicate their true intent—such that their *objective* manifestations match but their respective *subjective* intents do not? The law calls this a "***misunderstanding***." Restatement § 20(1) has a very complicated rule to address this situation, but the simple idea is this: if, as discussed immediately above, one party either knew or should have known of the other party's true intent, that true intent prevails. But if both parties are *equally ignorant* about the true intent of the other, and the misunderstanding relates to a *material* aspect of their deal, no contract is formed at all.

Example

> Buyer and Seller agreed on a sale of a quantity of cotton to be delivered from India on the sailing ship "Peerless." Unknown to both parties, there were in fact two ships named "Peerless," one sailing in October and one in December. Buyer meant the October ship and Seller meant the December ship. (This is a real case and the irony of having two ships named "Peerless" is delicious.) The court found that because the parties were equally ignorant on the meaning intended by the other, and because the time of sailing was a material aspect of the deal, the parties had not formed a

contract at all—even though each had objectively manifested its intent to be bound to the deal.

The Mechanics: Offer and Acceptance. The traditional way in which mutual assent is expressed is through an "offer" (*see* Lessons 3–5) and an "acceptance" (*see* Lessons 6–8). In the standard case, the dance begins with one party (the "offeror") making a proposal to another (the "offeree") to conclude a contract on specified terms. If the offeree (objectively) declares her acceptance, then poof (!), the parties have formed a contract. In many cases, the dance is just that simple.

In other cases, however, the process is more prolonged and complicated. Think of a huge corporate merger. Each party may retain an army of lawyers to negotiate the deal. The sides may go back and forth for months, with each insisting on specific terms for inclusion in the contract. Ultimately, if they are able to agree on all terms, each side will "manifest" its assent by having an authorized representative sign a final, written contract. This example also shows, however, that not all contracts are formed through clearly identifiable offers and acceptances. Restatement § 22(2) thus declares that the required mutual assent may occur "even though neither offer nor acceptance can be identified and even though the moment of formation cannot be determined."

What You Need to Know:

1. A "contract" is merely a promise that law says is binding.

2. The traditional method of contract formation requires three elements: (a) mutual assent, (b) consideration, and (c) agreement on the essential terms.

3. On the first element, "mutual" assent means that both parties must manifest their intent to be bound. But the law determines a party's assent based on the objective standard—whether a "reasonable person" in the position of the other party would understand her externally observable words and conduct to reflect an intent to be bound.

4. The objective standard does not apply in the rare case in which one party knew or should have known of the other's true intent. If both parties inaccurately communicate their intent and both are equally ignorant about the true intent of the other, no contract is formed at all if the "misunderstanding" relates to a material aspect of the deal.
5. The traditional way in which mutual assent is expressed is through an "offer" and an "acceptance."

LESSON 3: OFFER

Lesson 2 explained that the traditional way parties manifest their "mutual" assent to a contract is through an "offer" and an "acceptance." This lesson and the two to follow delve into the concept of "offer" in more detail. Lessons 6–8 then analyze the concept of "acceptance."

Offer. Let's begin our review of "offer" with the basic definition in Restatement § 24: "An offer is a manifestation of willingness to enter into a bargain, so made as to justify another person in understanding that his assent to that bargain is invited and will conclude it." We see here again the key words "manifestation" and "justify"—and (again) both reflect the "objective" approach to intent. Thus, whether a proposal amounts to an "offer" depends on whether a reasonable person in the position of the recipient would understand the proposer's words and conduct to reflect an intent to be bound. In other words, ***an offer is simply the first—in a chronological sense—objective manifestation of intent*** (of the two required for "mutual" assent).

As always, everything depends on context. Whether a reasonable person in the position of the recipient of a proposal would understand it as a formal offer will depend on a whole variety of factors, including its wording (obviously); the level of detail; the time, place, and manner in which it is made; and the relationship between the parties.

The level of detail of a proposal often greatly affects whether it "objectively manifests" an intent to be a formal offer. That is, the less specific a proposal is about the terms of the deal the less likely it is that a reasonable person would understand it as an offer. Instead, the proposal may reflect merely an ***invitation to make an offer***. This is common in some lines of business: an interested buyer may send out a notice to many potential sellers inviting them to make an offer to provide the desired goods or services. The buyer then will be able to review the various offers and decide which one is best. Sellers also may engage in this practice. The classic example is a widely circulated advertisement or a "price quotation." Although (as always) the circumstances may indicate otherwise, these are generally understood only as an invitation to make an offer or to enter into negotiations. Even the use of the word "offer" may not be determinative.

Example

> A seller of salt, knowing the standard needs of buyers in the field, circulated a notice stating that it was "authorized to offer" a certain type of salt at a stated price. Upon suit by a buyer who declared an "acceptance," the court held that the notice was not an offer. The court reasoned that the notice both did not include certain terms commonly included in contracts in the salt industry and expressed a need to "discuss this proposal."

The next requirement for an offer is that it must ***"invite" acceptance*** by "another person." The idea here is, first, that the offer must be communicated to the offeree—for in general only those offerees who know of the existence of an offer may accept it. But as a more specific matter, the offer must empower acceptance by a specific offeree or set of offerees. And, again, we define that set of offerees on an objective basis. That is, only those persons may accept an offer who are "justif[ied] . . . in understanding" that *their* assent to the proposed contract "is invited."

Example

A man playing golf on an average day came upon a sign by a car dealership stating, "Hit a Hole-in-One and Win This Car." The sign then described a fancy new car. To the golfer's great surprise, he hit a hole-in-one. The car dealership then stated (accurately) that it intended the sign *only* for a tournament held the day before. The court nonetheless decided that the parties formed a contract, reasoning that under the circumstances the golfer was justified in understanding that the sign invited acceptance by him as well.

The final requirement for an offer is that the offeree must be justified in understanding that his acceptance of the proposed contract "will conclude it." The simple point here is that an offer must cover all things necessary for a contract *except for* a manifestation of acceptance by the offeree. But these words also carry a quite subtle message: that the offer must define the ***essential terms of a contract*** (the subject and price, for example). This reflects a third element of contract formation (beyond mutual assent and consideration), and is sufficiently important to justify a separate lesson. *See* Lesson 11. For now, you need merely understand that a valid offer must define the basic elements of a contract, for the courts are not in the business of creating contracts for private parties. (If your professor covers the "reasonable certainty" requirement here, you should read Lesson 11 before continuing.)

"Master of the Offer." A final important point about an offer is that the offeror retains (until an effective acceptance) all of the power over her proposed contracting process. That is, the offeror is the "master of the offer." At one level, this is an obvious point: the offeror proposes the deal and thus may define what the deal is. But this power of the offeror is, well, more powerful than might appear at first glance.

The concept of "master of the offer" extends to basically all aspects of the proposed deal. Indeed, the rule reminds us of our first-grade teacher describing the "who, what, where, when, and how" of a good story. Thus, the offeror may define the invited offerees (*who* may accept the offer); the substantive terms of the contract (*what* is offered); the circumstances for acceptance (including *where* the offeree must accept and perform); the allowed time for acceptance (until *when* the offeree may accept); and the means or method of acceptance (*how* the offeree may or must declare acceptance).

Indeed, the offeror retains her power over the offer even after it is made. The reason is straightforward: until the offeree declares his acceptance (thus forming a contract), the offeror's promises are not binding. In other words, until a contract is formed, the offeror can—through a corresponding declaration to the offeree—change the terms, time, or method of acceptance, and even terminate the very existence of the offer (a "revocation").

But this does not happen automatically, or even easily. Following the rule "use it or lose it," the offeror must exercise her "master of the offer" powers. Otherwise (you guessed it), our customary objective ("reasonable person") standard of interpretation applies. Another way to think about this is that the law will permit private parties to be demanding, exacting, or quirky—but it will not help them do so. Thus, if the offeror does not clearly define otherwise, a "reasonable" time, means, method, etc., will apply for the acceptance.

Bilateral vs. Unilateral Contracts. A final, powerful aspect of the "master of the offer" rule is that the offeror may define whether the offeree may accept merely by making a return promise or instead *only* by actually performing the defined actions. The legalistic way to describe this distinction—which some professors and the Restatement hate—is between an offer for a "bilateral" contract as opposed to one for a "unilateral" contract. These terms signify a contract with *two*, reciprocal promises ("*bi*-lateral") in contrast to a contract with *one* promise ("*uni*-lateral") and only performance on the other side.

The overwhelming majority of offers are for bilateral contracts. Most people who make offers are quite willing to form a contract based on the offeree's promise to perform in the future. In this common case, a contract is formed *as soon as* the offeree declares an acceptance through a *promise* to do the actions requested in the offer. Lessons 6 and 7 will examine acceptance for such a bilateral contract.

In some rare cases, however, the offeror is not interested in a mere promise. Instead, she is willing to be bound to a contract only *if and when* the offeree *performs* the requested act. The classic example is an offer of a reward for the return of a lost thing. Lesson 8 will examine acceptance for such a "unilateral" contract.

What You Need to Know:

1. An "offer" is an objective manifestation of an intent to enter into a bargain so made as to justify the recipient in concluding that an acceptance will form a contract.
2. An offer must invite acceptance by a defined set of offerees and state the essential terms of the proposed bargain. A proposal may, however, merely reflect an invitation to make an offer or to enter into negotiations, depending (as always) on the circumstances surrounding its making.
3. The offeror is "master of the offer." This means that she has the power to define all aspects of the proposed contract, including the invited offerees, the substantive terms, and the time, manner, and method of acceptance. If, however, she does not exercise this power expressly, a "reasonableness" standard will apply for these matters.

LESSON 4: TERMINATING THE OFFER

In the prior lesson, we saw that an offer is the first legal step in the contracting process. But after a valid offer, the focus shifts to the offeree. That is, all that remains to form a contract is a valid "acceptance" (*see* Lessons 6–8). Restatement § 35(1) thus describes the legal effect of an offer as giving to the offeree "a continuing power to complete the manifestation of mutual assent by acceptance of the offer." In this lesson, we examine how this "continuing power" could end *before* the offeree declares an acceptance.

In the most commonly used terminology, the offeree can no longer accept an offer after his power of acceptance has "***terminated***." Restatement § 36 states four separate ways in which this can occur: (a) rejection or counteroffer by the offeree; (b) lapse of time; (c) revocation by the offeror; or (d) death or incapacity of the offeror or offeree.

Rejection or Counteroffer. The most common way an offeree's power of acceptance terminates is through a rejection or counteroffer. A ***rejection*** is where the offeree responds to an offer with a simple "no." How do we know whether the offeree has said "no"? By now, you know the answer to such questions: the "objective" standard—*i.e.*, whether a "reasonable person" in the position of the offeror would understand the offeree's words and conduct as an intent not to accept the offer. The important point is that once the offeree makes such a "manifestation of intent" (in the negative, as it were) the power to accept the offer ends.

Example

> Sallie made a formal offer to sell her home to Bonzo for $500,000. Bonzo was not impressed with the proposed price and, being a bit impetuous, simply told Sallie, "no way." Because a reasonable person would understand these words as a rejection, Bonzo's power of acceptance terminated. Thus, any later attempt by Bonzo to declare an acceptance would *not* conclude a contract with Sallie (unless of course she were to reinstate her offer).

A ***counteroffer*** covers the situation in which the offeree proposes *any* additions or changes to the offer. Lesson 7 will explore this subject in more detail. What you need to know now is that a counteroffer has the same effect as a rejection: it terminates the power of the offeree to conclude a contract through a later attempt at acceptance.

Example

> Following our example above, assume that Bonzo instead replied to Sallie's $500,000 offer by saying, "$490,000 is all I can do." This is a counteroffer, with the effect that Bonzo's power of acceptance terminated.

Thus, if Bonzo later says, "Okay, come to think of it, $500,000 is fine with me," his attempted acceptance will *not* form a contract.

Lapse. The offeree also loses his acceptance power after the offer has "lapsed." Stated affirmatively, in order to form a contract the offeree must manifest his acceptance within the time allowed by the offer. The offeror may expressly define that time through her power as "master of the offer." But if she does not use that power, the offeree has a "reasonable" amount of time. How long is that? Well, everything depends on the circumstances. In the stock or bond trading business, a reasonable time may be only seconds; for an offer to build a nuclear power plant, in contrast, a reasonable time may be many months.

Example

Again following the example above, assume that Sallie made her $500,000 offer not only to Bonzo but also to three other people in a group, face-to-face meeting. Bonzo then waited two weeks before declaring his acceptance. It is quite likely that in these circumstances a "reasonable time" to accept Sallie's offer will long since have passed. The result again is that Bonzo's power of acceptance had already terminated by the time he tried to accept.

Under the traditional rule of the common law, an offer made in person (or, later, over the telephone) lapses at the end of the conversation. Stated as an absolute rule, this is too rigid. Though unlikely, special circumstances may indicate to a reasonable person that the offeror intended to keep the offer open beyond the end of the conversation.

Revocation. Lesson 3 already noted that until acceptance the offeror retains the power to "revoke" the offer. (The offeror can also "withdraw" the offer, which means to terminate it even before it reaches the offeree.) A revocation is merely a negative manifestation of intent communicated to the offeree. Restatement § 42 thus states that "[a]n offeree's power of acceptance is terminated when the offeree receives from the offeror a manifestation of an intention not to enter into the proposed contract." But there is more: whether a revocation has occurred is subject to our customary objective standard. Thus, the offeree's power to accept also terminates when the offeror "takes definite action inconsistent with an intention to enter into the proposed contract" and the offeree acquires, even from a third party, "reliable information to that effect." Restatement § 43.

Example

> Continuing with the above example, assume that after Sallie made her $500,000 offer, Bonzo said that he wanted "to think things over." A week later, a real estate agent told Bonzo, "Sallie sold her home to someone else—you snooze, you lose." Bonzo then tried to accept Sallie's offer. Because he had acquired reliable information that Sallie no longer intended to be bound to her offer to him, Bonzo lost his power of acceptance.

Death or Incapacity of Offeror or Offeree. The offeree's power of acceptance also terminates if either the offeror or the offeree dies or becomes mentally incapacitated. You might wonder how this could ever be relevant in the real world. (We likely care quite a bit less about things like contracts after we die.) Well, this rule is necessary because when we die our "estate" takes over all of our legal rights and obligations. The rule makes clear that the "personal representative" who oversees a deceased person's estate cannot accept any outstanding offers previously made to the deceased person. An offeree likewise cannot accept an outstanding offer made by the deceased person.

Example

> Returning to our example above, assume that Sallie died shortly after making her $500,000 home sale offer to Bonzo. (Poor Sallie!) Assume also that Sallie's home is worth $600,000, so that Bonzo would be thrilled to accept Sallie's offer. Because Sallie died first, Bonzo lost his power to accept Sallie's offer.

Beyond these four standard means by which the offeree's power of acceptance terminates, there is also a quite sophisticated concept of the *non*-occurrence of a "***condition of acceptance***." Your professor may or may not cover this concept along with contract formation. In any event, the idea is quite simple: if the offeror makes clear that the offer ends if a specific event does not occur, then—unsurprisingly—the offeree cannot accept if the event does not occur.

Example

> As a final spin on our above example, assume that Sallie offered to sell her house because her company planned to transfer her to the Paris, France, office. (Woo hoo for Sallie!) Because there was a small risk that the transfer would fall through, Sallie told Bonzo that approval of the transfer was a "prerequisite to my offer." Shortly thereafter, Bonzo learned that Sallie's company decided not to transfer her to Paris. (Poor Sallie.) Because this required "condition" has not occurred, Bonzo lost his power to accept Sallie's offer.

What You Need to Know:

1. An offeree has a "continuing power" to conclude a contract by making a manifestation of acceptance of the offer.
2. The offeree's power of acceptance "terminates" upon any one of five events: rejection or counteroffer by the offeree; lapse of time; revocation by the offeror; death or incapacity of the offeror or offeree; or, in a slightly different concept, a required "condition" of acceptance does not occur.

LESSON 5: IRREVOCABLE OFFERS AND OPTION CONTRACTS

Lessons 3 and 4 explained that the offeror has the power to revoke the offer at any time prior to a valid acceptance by the offeree. This lesson covers a variety of important exceptions to that basic rule.

As a bit of background, note that the offeror's power to revoke the offer exists even if she expressly promises not to do so. The reason for this (perhaps counterintuitive) rule is the same one that underlies the "master of the offer" rule: until a contract is formed by a valid acceptance, the offeror is not bound to *any* kind of promise.

"Option Contract." Well, you ask, is there any way that an offeree could hold an offeror to a promise not to revoke the offer? The answer is, "yes." Recall from Lesson 2 that the way to make a promise binding is to make a *contract*. Thus, the offeree can conclude a *separate* contract with the offeror under which he promises something in exchange for the offeror's promise not to revoke the principal offer. This mini-contract is called an "option contract." For this, we need—like any other contract—mutual assent, consideration, and essential terms. Thus, if the offeree promises something (usually, money) *separate from* the deal under discussion in order to "buy" the offeror's legal right to revoke her offer, then a subsidiary "option contract" is created that sort of hovers above the possible principal contract that the offeror is proposing.

Example

> Let's return to our example from Lesson 4 in which Sallie makes an offer to sell her home to Bonzo for $500,000. If Bonzo wants to bind Sallie *not* to revoke her offer while he "thinks things over for a week," he can propose an "option contract." This would require that Bonzo pay Sallie something separate (say, $500) in exchange for Sallie's promise not to revoke her offer for that one week. (This idea of an exchange of legal rights is the "consideration" doctrine we will cover in Lesson 9.) If the parties so conclude an option contract, then Sallie gets $500 and in return Bonzo gets one week to decide whether to accept Sallie's offer. During that time, Sallie would not have the power to revoke her principal $500,000 home sale offer to Bonzo.

Your professor may spend a bit of time on option contracts, because they can play an important role in a variety of circumstances. But the basic idea is that with such a "subsidiary" contract the offeror in effect sells her power of revocation for the agreed time. This is why the law calls this an "option" contract: it gives the offeree the option to conclude the principal contract, or not. Moreover, because during the period of the option the offeror cannot revoke the offer for the principal contract, the general rule that a rejection, counteroffer, or death terminates the offeree's power of acceptance does not apply.

Some states also have special rules that make option contracts particularly easy to create. A few states, for example, have adopted a rule in Restatement § 87(1) that recognizes an option contract if in a *writing* the offeror promises not to revoke the offer and merely states (but does not even expect to receive) a "purported" consideration for the option from the offeree.

Irrevocability Through Offeree Reliance. Another way that an offer can become irrevocable is through reliance by the offeree. With this rule, we confront for the first time the concept of "promissory estoppel." Lessons 12 and 13 will examine this doctrine in great detail. At this point, all you need to understand is that promissory estoppel is simply another way to form a contract—specifically, where the promisee takes actions in justifiable reliance on a promise and then will suffer harm if it is not enforced.

Justifiable reliance also can work to make an offer irrevocable through an "option contract" (which, again, is just one form of a contract). The idea is this: where an offeror expects that the offeree will take actions in reliance on the offer remaining open (*i.e.*, unrevoked), and the offeree in fact does so, the offer becomes irrevocable if justice so requires. This rule (*see* Restatement § 87(2)) thus has four elements: (1) an offer; (2) the offeror should reasonably expect that the offer will induce action or forbearance of a substantial character by the offeree before acceptance; (3) the offer in fact induces such action or forbearance; and (4) recognition of an option contract is necessary to avoid injustice.

The key thing to get here is that the offeree must rely specifically on the offer remaining open. As a practical matter, this arises only in bidding situations (such as with general contractors and subcontractors), although theoretically it can apply elsewhere as well. You likely will study two famous, contrasting cases on this subject (*Baird* and *Drennan*). The following example, based on the *Drennan* case, shows how this rule works in a real-world situation.

Example

> Drennan, a general contractor preparing a bid to build a public school, received an offer from Star Paving to perform the paving portion of the project. Because Star Paving's bid was the lowest for the paving subcontract, Drennan used it in calculating its overall bid, which ultimately was accepted by the school district. Unfortunately, before Drennan could inform the various subcontractors, Star Paving tried to revoke its offer. Upon suit by Drennan, the court found that because Star Paving expected Drennan to use its low bid, and because Drennan in fact did so, an option contract arose that precluded Star Paving from revoking its offer. Justice required this result because otherwise Drennan would have to pay some other paving subcontractor more than Star Paving had offered.

You should recognize that the option contract notion imposed by Restatement § 87(2) is a pure legal fiction. The law creates the option contract because justice requires this result in the narrow case in which an offeree takes action "of a substantial character" in reliance on the offer remaining open.

Firm Offers. A final way in which an offer may become irrevocable is through special rules governing "firm offers." For example, some states have specialized statutes that make offers irrevocable in bidding for public contracts. But the most well-known statute on firm offers is found in the Uniform Commercial Code (which, as noted in Lesson 1, governs transactions in movable things = "goods"). Under ***U.C.C. § 2–205***, an offer is irrevocable if it (1) is made by a "merchant" (a term § 2–104(1) defines basically as someone who regularly deals with the type of goods involved or otherwise acts like he has the required expertise); (2) is for the buying or selling of goods); (3) is made in a writing signed by the offeror; and (4) gives assurance that it will be held open. In such a case, the offer is irrevocable for the stated time, or if no specific time is stated for a "reasonable time," but in no event longer than three months.

Note that U.C.C. § 2–205 does not refer to this "merchant's firm offer" as an "option contract," nor does it require consideration or reliance by the offeree as discussed above. Rather, it just states that if the requirements are satisfied, the offer is not revocable. (Statutes can do that.)

What You Need to Know:

1. The general rule that an offeror may revoke the offer at any time before acceptance is subject to some important exceptions.
2. First, the offeror may not revoke if the parties separately form an "option contract," under which the offeree in essence "buys" the offeror's power of revocation for the agreed time.
3. Second, an option contract may come into being through expected and actual reliance by the offeree that the principal offer will remain open (the first form of the important contract law doctrine of "promissory estoppel").
4. Finally, an offer may become irrevocable through special rules governing "firm offers," the most notable of which is the "merchant's firm offer" rule in U.C.C. § 2–205.

LESSON 6: ACCEPTANCE IN "BILATERAL" CONTRACTS: IN GENERAL

After our extensive analysis of "offers" in the prior three lessons, now, at long last, we turn to the concept of "acceptance." We begin with what is by far the most common form—an acceptance in a "bilateral" contract.

Recall from Lesson 3 that this reflects the standard case in which the parties form a contract merely by making reciprocal *promises* (one in the offer and one in the acceptance). Indeed, this bilateral form so predominates in actual experience that the law has a *presumption* that an offeree may accept merely by making a *promise* to do—or to refrain from doing, as the case may be—the acts requested in the offer. Lesson 8 will analyze the alternative case of an offer for a "unilateral contract" under which a contract is not formed until the offeree completes the *performance* requested in the offer.

Let's begin our analysis of an acceptance with the simple definition in Restatement § 50(1): "Acceptance of an offer is a manifestation of assent to the terms thereof made by the offeree in a manner invited or required by the offer." At this point, much of this rule should not surprise you. But let's break it down into its elements.

Acceptance as Manifestation of Assent. First, as with all issues of intent, an objective standard applies to whether an offeree has accepted an offer. Thus—in an inverse of the rule on offers—an acceptance occurs when a reasonable person in the position of the offeror would understand the offeree's words and conduct as an intent to be bound. And again, the offeree's subjective—that is, "actual" or "real"—intent basically does not matter.

The result is clear where the offeree declares an acceptance with unambiguous words or a signature on a document (an ***"express" acceptance***). As you might imagine, however, most litigation arises from claims that an offeree has accepted the offer through his actions (an ***"implied" acceptance***). The reason for this (again) is that, under the objective standard, an offeree may make a promise through words, actions, or a combination of the two. In such a case, we have a bilateral contract: a promise in the offer and an implied promise (*i.e.*, acceptance) through the conduct of the offeree. A common example is where the offeree begins to do the thing requested in the offer.

Example

Pauline wanted her house painted and left a voice mail with Jamal (the owner of a painting business) saying, "I will pay you $8,000 to paint my house by next week." Jamal did not respond, but the next day he sent his employees to start painting Pauline's house. Under the circumstances, a reasonable person almost certainly would understand Jamal's conduct as saying, "I accept your offer."

As stated in Restatement § 62(1), where (as is standard) the offer permits the offeree to accept merely by making a promise, "the beginning of the invited performance . . . is an acceptance." The reason is that the offeree's conduct amounts to an implied manifestation to accept the offer and thus a *promise* to complete the performance.

The possibilities for an implied acceptance through conduct are almost endless. One controversial example involves a situation in which two people live together in a romantic relationship for a period of time, but never get legally married. In the common case, one gives up career opportunities to support the other. If the unmarried couple eventually has a falling out, the divorce statutes will not permit the "career sacrificer" to recover spousal support (formerly known as "alimony"). Nonetheless, a common claim in such situations is that, through their conduct, the parties formed an *implied contract* for an equitable division of financial assets. Some courts have allowed these claims (which pundits sarcastically have called "palimony"); but other courts have concluded that the marriage statutes reflect a public policy against recognizing implied contracts in such situations. (For more on the public policy defense, *see* Lesson 23.)

Generally, however, an offeree cannot manifest assent by pure ***silence or inaction***—for there would be no *objective* basis to indicate an intent to accept the offer. Restatement § 69 nonetheless recognizes three narrow exceptions: (a) where an offeree takes the benefit of offered services with a reasonable opportunity to reject them and reason to know that the offeror expected to get paid; (b) where the offeror gave the offeree "reason to understand" that silence means acceptance and the offeree actually intends to accept (which is very hard to prove); and (c) where because of previous dealings between the parties or otherwise, a reasonable person would expect the offeree to give notice of rejection under the circumstances.

Acceptance of the Terms of the Offer. The second requirement for an acceptance is that it must agree with the substantive terms proposed in the offer. This may seem obvious, but in the real world this rule is substantially trickier than it may seem. Indeed, this subject is so important that the entire next lesson (Lesson 7) is devoted to "Qualified Acceptances and Counteroffers." What you need to see now is simply that in order to form a contract the offeree's reply must unconditionally and completely accept the terms proposed in the offer. Otherwise, the reply is a rejection and a counteroffer.

Acceptance as Invited by the Offer. Recall from the "master of the offer" rule in Lesson 3 that the offeror may define, among other things, the *method or means* by which the offeree must express acceptance. In order to declare an effective acceptance and form a contract, therefore, the offeree must comply with any such requirements.

Example

> Ford made an offer to pay $50,000 to Servepro if it repaired a machine on Ford's assembly line. But the offer also stated, "You may accept this offer only by signing the enclosed copy and returning it to Ford's Vice President of Operations." Servepro sent an e-mail to Ford's factory manager declaring an express acceptance. Because Servepro did not follow the offer's clearly defined requirements, its attempted acceptance was not effective to form a contract.

Of course, the offeror nonetheless may disregard its own requirements and agree to the nonconforming acceptance. Thus, if in the example above Ford allowed Servepro to begin the repair work, its conduct almost certainly would reflect a manifestation that the "signed copy" requirement no longer applied.

Communication of Acceptance. Finally, an acceptance generally must be communicated to the offeror. But this general rule is subject to a very important exception, the so-called "***dispatched acceptance rule***" (aka "mailbox rule"). Under this rule, an acceptance becomes effective as soon as it is "put out of the offeree's possession" and even if it never reaches the offeror—provided that it is properly addressed and, of course, conforms to any method or means prescribed in the offer. If, therefore, an offer requires acceptance by a specified date, an offeree will form a contract by putting the acceptance in the mail, or sending it out by e-mail, by that date—even if it were to arrive much later or not at all. Electronic communications once threatened to make this rule irrelevant, but it is returning to prominence as spam filters become more aggressive.

What You Need to Know:

1. In the standard case of an offer for a "bilateral" contract, the offeree validly accepts merely by making a promise to perform as described in the offer. Because of the objective standard for issues of intent, the offeree's return promise may come through unequivocal words (express acceptance) or through conduct (implied acceptance).
2. In order to declare a valid acceptance, an offeree must do three things: (a) manifest its assent; (b) agree to the terms in the offer; and (c) follow any requirements in the offer as to the manner and means of acceptance.
3. Generally, an acceptance also must be communicated to the offeror; but under the "dispatched acceptance rule," an acceptance is effective as soon as it is put out of the offeree's possession.

LESSON 7: QUALIFIED ACCEPTANCES AND COUNTEROFFERS UNDER THE COMMON LAW

We saw in Lessons 6 and 9 that the offeror's status as "master of the offer" includes the power to define the terms of the proposed deal. But what happens if the offeree is not satisfied with those terms and instead wants to change some or add new ones? That is the subject we take up in this lesson.

Mirror Image Rule. The common law follows a quite strict rule for such a "qualified acceptance": in order to function as an acceptance and thus form a contract, a reply to an offer must unconditionally accept the exact terms proposed in the offer. In the traditional terminology, a valid acceptance must be a "mirror image" of the offer. If the offeree proposes changes or additions, however small, the law will treat the "acceptance" instead as a rejection and counteroffer (which "terminates" the offer, *see* Lesson 4). Indeed, the "mirror image" rule applies even if the reply states that it is an "acceptance." The substance, not the title or description, is what matters.

Example

> Fix-it, Inc. made an offer to Megaco to do some defined repair work for $10,000 "by next Tuesday." Megaco replied by saying, "We are pleased to accept your offer, but we really need the work done by Monday at the latest." Megaco's reply did not form a contract. Because it deviated from the terms of Fix-it's offer, Megaco's reply was not an acceptance, but rather was a rejection and a counteroffer.

Most often, a counteroffer impliedly incorporates the terms of the original offer, subject to the proposed changes. Thus, in the example above, if Megaco responded merely with, "OK, but we need the work by Monday," most likely a reasonable person would understand this counteroffer as impliedly including all of the *other* terms in Fix-it's offer.

Now, the fact that a reply to an offer merely *refers to* other terms does not mean that it necessarily is a "qualified" acceptance. Restatement § 59 states that the reply is a counteroffer only if it is "conditioned on the offeror's assent" to the proposed new terms. (Restatement § 61 suggests even more flexibility by stating that a deviating reply forms a contract "unless the acceptance is made to depend on an assent to the changed or added terms.") Thus, a reply could well operate as an acceptance if it makes clear that it is truly *unconditional*, and merely says something like, "Oh, by the way, here are some other things we can think about for later." Your professor may emphasize this possibility. But be aware that the courts generally have stuck quite closely to the "mirror image rule." That is, they commonly hold that a reply with changes or additions, however small, amounts to a counteroffer unless the offeree makes very clear that the new matters it raises do affect the *complete and unconditional* acceptance of the terms of the offer.

The Game Continues. With a counteroffer, the game starts all over again—but the terminology to describe the situation gets a little unwieldy: the original offeree becomes the "*counter-offeror*," and the original offeror becomes the "*counter-offeree*." If the counter-offeree (the original offeror) then accepts the counteroffer, bang (!) we have a contract. But if the counter-offeree in turn proposes changes or additions to the counteroffer, we have a new counteroffer (round three, as it were). And so the game continues, with each new change rejecting the prior offer and representing a new counteroffer. If you have the sense of a ping-pong game here, you are not far off: each time a counter-offeree makes a change to whatever proposal is then on the table, she is in essence saying, "Nope—but right back at you. How about these terms?"

"Battle of the Forms." In our modern electronic world, this game is all the more common because of the ease of creating form documents. Today, basically every commercial party has a lawyer-prepared form with dozens of favorable terms, typically on the back (or in an e-mail attachment). But business folks care about, well, business, not about all of the "lawyer-speak." As a result, they focus on the essential business aspects of their transaction—the subject of the deal, quantity, price, and time of performance. Almost no one reads the "fine print" (sometimes called "boilerplate," from terms stamped on lead boilers long ago) and obviously no two sets of fine print are exactly alike. Thus, once they agree on the business terms the parties typically carry out the transaction without noticing that they are still engaging in a "battle of the forms" with regard to all of the various terms in their competing form documents.

Well, you ask, how does this game *legally* end?

Last Shot Rule. The common law ends the game with the "last shot rule." Recall from Lesson 6 that, under our old friend the "objective manifestation of assent" rule, an offeree's conduct may manifest acceptance of an offer. And we noted there that a common example is where the offeree begins to do the thing requested in the offer. If you put this together with the mirror image rule, you get the last shot rule. In other words, where the parties are playing "counteroffer ping-pong," the last counter-offeree is deemed to accept whichever counteroffer is last on the table—in its entirety—if he begins to perform his part of the contemplated transaction. The "last shot," in short, totally wins the game.

Example

Let's go back to the Megaco and Fix-it example. Assume that Megaco replied to Fix-it's offer with an "Order Acceptance" form that agreed to the terms of the offer but also included dozens of "fine print" terms on the back. Under the mirror image rule, this would be a rejection and a counteroffer. Assume also that, after receiving the Order Acceptance form, Fix-it began to do the defined repair work. Under the last shot rule, Fix-it's conduct amounts to an acceptance of Megaco's counteroffer, including *all* of the terms on the back of Megaco's form (even if Fix-it never read, or even noticed, them).

There is much to criticize in these overly stylized and rigid rules for the contracting game. But the courts continue to adhere to them under the common law. We will see in Lesson 15, however, that the U.C.C. follows a completely different approach—one that rejects the mirror image and last shot rules in "battle of the forms" situations.

What You Need to Know:

1. Under the "mirror image" rule, a reply to an offer that changes or adds terms, however small, is not an acceptance, but rather a rejection of the offer coupled with a counteroffer.
2. Under the "last shot" rule, a counter-offeree that begins to perform the contemplated transaction is deemed to accept the entirety of the counteroffer last on the table.

LESSON 8: ACCEPTANCE IN "UNILATERAL" CONTRACTS

This lesson analyzes the rare case of an offer for a "unilateral contract." Whether an offer is for a bilateral contract or for a unilateral contract is within the power of the offeror (as "master of the offer"). But as noted in Lesson 7, the law presumes the former; as a result, the offeror must express her intent clearly if she does not want to be bound to a contract by a return promise of the offeree.

In an offer for a unilateral contract, the offeror makes clear that she wants something *done*, not merely promised. The ***classic examples*** are offers for a reward, for an employee bonus, or for the winner of a competition. Let's focus on the clearest case—an offer of a reward to anyone who finds a valuable lost thing (say, a ring). In such a case, the offeror is not interested in having hundreds of people declare an acceptance by merely promising to find the ring, thus forming hundreds of contracts. Rather, the offeror permits acceptance *only* by the one person who finds the ring, and no contract will come into being—that is, the offeror's promise to pay the reward will not become binding—unless and until the finder actually returns the ring.

For some reason, basically every Contracts professor in the country illustrates how an offer for a unilateral contract works through the example of a quirky offeror who likes to watch people walk across the Brooklyn Bridge.

Example

Quirky Quintina offers Wendell $500 if and only if he "walks all the way across the Brooklyn Bridge" and emphasizes, "I do not want your silly promises." This is an offer for a unilateral contract. Wendell can accept only by *doing* the requested act and—this is the key—no contract exists at all until Wendell *fully completes* his march across the bridge.

A further requirement is that the offeree must know of the offer's existence before completing the requested act.

Example

To generate buzz on the Internet, a resort in Wisconsin released a large-mouth bass, "Diamond Jim," into an adjacent lake and promised $10,000 to anyone who caught the fish. Curtis, who never has "surfed the web," went on his weekly fishing expedition and caught Diamond Jim, but (after taking a picture) he released the fish back into the lake. If Curtis in fact did not know of the resort's offer at the time, he did not accept the offer by catching the fish and thus is not entitled to the $10,000.

Revocation and Unilateral Contracts. Now, if you are carefully following all of the implications of the "master of the offer" power (*see*, again, Lesson 3), the traditional view of offers for a unilateral contract puts the offeree in a very delicate situation. Because a contract is not formed until the offeree *completes* the requested performance, the offeror retains her power to revoke the offer all along. Thus, in the Brooklyn Bridge example above, under the traditional approach Quintina could revoke her offer when Wendell is just one step short of completing his walk across the bridge. Because no contract yet exists, Quintina has no obligation to keep the offer open to allow Wendell to complete the requested performance.

Protection of Offerees. For those of you troubled by such a situation, have no fear—the law often pushes back when a strict application of a rule causes serious injustice. In this case, the "push back" came in the form of ***Restatement § 45***, which nearly all courts have adopted in some form. In relevant part, that section states: "Where an offer invites an offeree to accept by rendering a performance and does not invite a promissory acceptance, an option contract is created when the offeree . . . begins the invited performance[.]" (The same result applies when the offeree "tenders" the performance, that is, shows up with an intent and ability to perform.)

The key thing you will see in this rule is the reference to an ***option contract***. Recall from Lesson 5 that an option contract is a "subsidiary contract" that functions to make an offer of a principal contract irrevocable. And here again, the law creates a legal fiction to serve the interests of justice—specifically that the offeror of a unilateral contract makes a binding (implied) promise not to revoke the offer once the offeree *begins* performance. The result is an "option contract" to the effect that the offeror may not revoke the offer as long as the offeree continues his performance. If, then, the offeree completes the performance (although not obligated to do so), the principal contract is formed and both offeror and (obviously) offeree are bound.

Example

> Back to Quintina and Wendell: if Wendell *begins* to walk across the bridge—and for as long as he continues—an option contract exists that precludes Quintina from revoking her offer. If, but only if, Wendell completes his march across the bridge, Quintina will become obligated to perform her principal promise (*i.e.*, pay Wendell the $500).

The Key Distinction Between Bilateral and Unilateral Contracts. The one thing to be careful about here is the key distinction between an offer for a bilateral as opposed to one for a unilateral contract. Again, this is determined by looking at the offer. If, as the law presumes, an offer permits acceptance by a return promise (a bilateral contract), the offeree nonetheless may choose simply to perform (*i.e.*, not to make an express return promise). But—and this is important—the very *beginning* of the requested performance by the offeree functions as an *implied* promise to complete performance and thus *immediately* forms a contract (bing, bang, boom!). *See*, again, Lesson 6. This is yet another example of the objective standard of intent: That is, if an offeree actually begins the requested performance, a reasonable person would understand that conduct as an immediate acceptance of the offer (and thus as a *promise* to complete the performance).

If, in contrast, the offer makes clear that acceptance *only* may occur through and upon *complete* performance (*i.e.*, it is an offer for a unilateral contract), then the beginning of performance merely creates the subsidiary option contract as discussed above. That is, because the offeree may not accept by making a promise, the mere beginning of performance cannot reflect an acceptance. Moreover, although the offeror may not revoke the offer as long as the performance continues, the offeree retains the discretion to complete the performance (thus forming the principal contract)—*or not.*

A final word of caution: in many cases, the distinction we are discussing here is irrelevant to the analysis of a contract dispute. If the offeree has completed the performance, he has formed a unilateral contract (if that is what the offer required), but also certainly has objectively manifested a promissory acceptance to form a bilateral contract (if, as in the standard case, that is what the offer allowed). Which one the offer originally required simply does not matter anymore. The only situations in which the distinction really matters are (a) when the offeror tries to revoke the offer or (b) when the offeree begins, but then ceases, performance, but the offeror claims that this already reflected an acceptance of an offer for a bilateral contract.

What You Need to Know:

1. In the rare case of an offer for a "unilateral" contract, the offeree may accept *only* by full performance as described in the offer. Because the contract is not formed until that occurs, under the traditional view of the common law the offeror retained the power to revoke the offer at any time along the way.
2. The contemporary approach to an offer for a unilateral contract provides protection for the offeree in the form of an implied "option contract." Under this rule (as reflected in Restatement § 45), the offeror cannot revoke the offer once the offeree begins the requested performance. But the offeree can accept the principal offer—thus binding the offeror to fulfill its principal promise—only by completing the requested performance.
3. In many cases, whether the offer originally proposed a bilateral or a unilateral contract turns out not to matter. That is especially the case if the offeree in fact fully completes the requested performance prior to any attempted revocation by the offeror.

LESSON 9: CONSIDERATION: THE BASIC "BARGAIN" TEST

In this lesson, we analyze the second principal requirement to form a contract under the traditional method: the "consideration" doctrine. Recall from Restatement § 17 (in Lesson 2) that the formation of a contract requires "a bargain in which there is a manifestation of mutual assent to the exchange ***and a consideration***."

The Role of Legal "Formalities." We will get to the black-letter rules for consideration in a moment. But a bit of background might help you to understand the role "consideration" plays in contract law. In a sense, all of the law involves drawing lines—*i.e.*, separating *legally* significant events from the commonplace things that happen every day. The law cannot, and should not, get involved in every petty dispute. In contract law, the "consideration" doctrine draws the line between informal, non-legal promises (= no contract) and legally binding promises (= contract). (Thus, in contract law "consideration" does not have its commonplace meaning of thoughtfulness or kindness.)

A famous professor once called doctrines like this "formalities." By this he did not mean petty technicalities. Rather, he meant the important, "formal" rules that put people on notice of legally significant events. The consideration doctrine thus serves three principal functions: to warn people that they are about to form a contract; to provide proof when they have done so; and to guide them to do so effectively if that is what they want. Long ago (actually, very long ago), the law served these functions with the quaint requirement of a "seal." To form a contract, a person literally had to put a wax seal on a piece of paper as a signal of a legally significant event. (The well-known phrase "signed, sealed, delivered" comes from this old rule.) Over time, however, this quaint requirement—which was largely limited to aristocrats in any event—lost its meaning; as a result, nearly all states have eliminated the seal as a means of forming contracts. (Some retain a limited evidentiary effect.)

The Basic Test. Today, the consideration doctrine instead identifies legally significant promises through the concept of ***bargain***. The simple idea is that, with the backdrop of our individualistic and capitalistic society, people generally recognize that they are doing something serious when they promise to trade something they *legally* own for something another person *legally* owns. These reciprocal legal rights may come in the form of an actual, immediate performance or a promise to perform in the future. Restatement § 71 thus states that, "[t]o constitute consideration, a performance or a return promise must be bargained for." A performance or return promise is bargained for "if it is sought by the promisor in exchange for his promise and is given by the promisee in exchange for that promise."

The notion here is that, like the tango, it takes two to contract. Thus, *each side* must be willing to part with *its* legal rights "in exchange for" the legal rights traded by the other. This is the truest sense of the word "bargain." In contrast, think of a promise to give a gift and recall (from Lesson 2) sweet Aunt Lilly who promised to bake cookies for your birthday. Because Aunt Lilly did not ask for anything "in exchange for" her cookie promise, the law says that it "lacks consideration" and thus is not legally binding.

Now, the concept of "bargain" does not require *actual* negotiation (actual haggling or dickering between the parties). It merely requires a reciprocal "inducement"—that is, that each side is willing to *give* what it has because, *in exchange*, it wants to *get* what the other has. (For important notions like this, the law often falls back on Latin terms: the idea here is that we need a "***quid pro quo***," meaning a "this for that.")

The Legal Benefit/Legal Detriment Test. The traditional approach to the consideration doctrine also involves a requirement, in addition to the bargain element, known as the "legal benefit/legal detriment" test. The analysis above already reflects this element: to satisfy the consideration doctrine, each side must surrender a ***legal right*** in exchange for the ***legal right*** traded by the other. Unfortunately, courts often describe this requirement in quite convoluted terms. In the traditional terminology, each side's consideration must involve either a "detriment to the promisee" or a "benefit to the promisor." These words are unnecessarily confusing (and may seem like mumbo-jumbo to you). For this reason, the Restatement entirely dispenses with this element. The drafters reasoned that the simple requirement of a "bargained-for exchange" works so well that any separate requirement of a legal benefit or detriment tended merely to add confusion. Nonetheless, it is worth a bit of time to try to understand the benefit/detriment concept, for you will encounter it in many court opinions.

To begin, keep in mind that *each side* of the bargain must be "supported by consideration"—that is, each reciprocal promise must be *induced* by something "put on the bargaining table" as part of the deal. Therefore, you must analyze a potential "bargain" from both ends: once for Party A as promisor (with Party B as promisee), and once for Party B as promisor (with Party A as promisee).

With this background, the "benefit" and "detriment" ideas are merely alternatives for the "something" that may serve to induce each party's promise. In the great run of cases, each side's promise in the bargain is induced by a ***detriment to the promisee*** (the other side). This simply means that each side must make its promise because it wants the legal rights *given up by the other side (the promisee)*—which obviously is a "detriment" to the other side. The classic example is money exchanged for goods: The buyer's promise to give money is induced by the seller giving up the legal rights to the goods she owns (a detriment to the seller). In return, the seller's promise to transfer ownership of the goods is induced by the buyer giving up the legal rights to the money he owns (a detriment to the buyer). This may seem entirely obvious to you and, if so, good—don't overthink the point.

Note also that such a legal detriment does not require that the promisee suffer an actual *harm*—as long as, again, he gives up a *legal* right. It likewise does not require a formal *financial benefit* for the promisor (the person being induced). As one famous case observed, consideration merely means that each party "abandons some legal right in the present or limits his legal freedom of action in the future as an inducement for the promise" of the other party. That famous case is *Hamer vs. Sidway*, and it is in most Contracts casebooks.

Example

An uncle promised $5000 if his nephew would (among other things) refrain from drinking alcohol until he turned 21. The nephew complied, but when he turned 21 the uncle refused to pay. Upon suit by the nephew for breach of contract, the court held that even though the nephew might have been better off in some broad sense, he sustained a *legal detriment* because he refrained from doing something he had a *legal right* to do. (The legal drinking age was lower then.) For the same reason, it did not matter that the uncle did not get a financial benefit from the nephew not drinking. The deal also satisfied the bargain element: The uncle's $5000 promise induced the nephew to refrain from the stated acts and a desire for the nephew to do so induced the uncle to make the $5000 promise in the first place.

There is also an alternative, ***benefit to the promisor***, but it is almost never necessary to resort to this option in order to satisfy the consideration doctrine. Rarely, the promisor may be induced by a benefit that does not come from a legal right *given up by the promisee*. Most often, this requires that the benefit come from some third source. But in nearly all cases in the real world, a "benefit to the promisor" also involves a "detriment to the promisee." That is, in the standard example noted above, the *benefit* a buyer gets *also* results directly from the seller's *detriment* in giving up the legal rights to her goods; and the *benefit* the seller gets *also* results directly from the buyer's *detriment* in giving up the legal rights to his money. The two concepts come in the same package.

Nonetheless, in some rare cases one party's promise is not induced by a legal right (a "detriment") given up by the promisee.

Example

Jasmine wanted Neil's cool SUV, but she had no money. Neil nonetheless promised to give the SUV to

Jasmine if her rich Aunt Claydee gave him $25,000. Claydee did so (but later unfortunately died). Neil then realized that the SUV is worth more than $25,000 and tried to call off the deal with Jasmine. This transaction satisfies the consideration doctrine even though Jasmine gave up none of *her* legal rights—because Neil (the promisor) received a *benefit* in the form of Aunt Claydee's money "in exchange for" his promise to give the automobile to Jasmine (and Jasmine got what she wanted too).

You may spend a fair amount of time on the consideration doctrine because of the central role it plays in identifying legally binding promises. But as Lesson 10 will examine in more detail, most of the difficult cases for the doctrine arise in family or other non-commercial settings.

What You Need to Know:

1. The formation of a contract requires satisfaction of the consideration doctrine. This doctrine separates legally binding promises from routine social or gift promises.
2. To constitute consideration, a performance or a return promise must be "bargained for." This means that each side must seek the other's promise (or actual performance) "in exchange for" its own promise or performance.
3. In addition, under the traditional approach each party must give up a *legal detriment* as part of the bargain—that is, each side must promise (or actually do) something that it is not legally obligated to do in order to induce the return promise of the other. In rare cases, a transaction instead may satisfy the consideration doctrine if a promisor receives a *benefit* that does not result directly from the promisee giving up a legal right. The Restatement, however, dispenses with this element of the consideration doctrine.

LESSON 10: SPECIAL ISSUES FOR THE CONSIDERATION DOCTRINE

In most transactions—especially commercial transactions with "repeat players"—consideration is not an issue. Nearly all transactions involve an exchange of money for goods, services, real estate, intellectual property, etc., and you will see without using much brain power that each side is promising to give up its legal rights because it wants the legal rights the other side is promising in return.

The Difficulty of Family Cases. The difficult cases instead arise in family or other non-commercial settings. If a family member's gift promise is truly one-sided, it clearly does not satisfy the consideration doctrine and thus is not binding as a contract. But if the promise also is conditioned on some specific event or requirement, it can be quite difficult to tell whether the family member is motivated by a *quid pro quo* as opposed to simply a desire that the event or requirement occur before giving the gift (a so-called "***conditional gift***"). Assume, for example, that your Aunt Nia promises to give you $10,000 "if you get married." Is Aunt Nia just promising to make a gift out of the joy she would get from seeing you married? If this is the case, then Aunt Nia can change her mind at any time and take back her promise, even after you get married. Or have you instead formed a contract immediately upon your marriage, such that Aunt Nia is *obligated* to pay you the $10,000?

Of course, family members can and do make contracts (= legally binding promises) between them. But as one famous case observed, "the natural love and affection which is presumed to exist" between family members "is not sufficient consideration." The challenge in family and similar settings, therefore, is to tell the difference between "contractual" promises and those that are motivated by simple love and affection (even if they state a specific condition or requirement).

It is in such situations that the "bargain" requirement plays the decisive role. Using the above example, you must analyze whether Aunt Nia made her promise based on a *quid pro quo*—that is, because of something that she specifically wants out of you getting married (other than the "warm and fuzzies”). If the answer is “yes,” then the bargain satisfies the consideration doctrine and you have formed a contract. This is particularly likely to be true if the occurrence of the stated event (your marriage) would bring some specific ***benefit to the promisor*** (Aunt Nia). Assume, for example, that Aunt Nia stands to get $50,000 under the will of her deceased husband if all of her nieces and nephews get married, and you are the last one. In that case, it is more likely that Aunt Nia desires your marriage “in exchange for” her promise because she would get a specific, tangible benefit from that event occurring.

If, in contrast, the answer to the *quid pro quo* question is “no,” then Aunt Nia has merely made a promise of a conditional gift, which is not binding for lack of consideration.

Example

> A father promised to transfer ownership of his house to his daughter and (probably thinking that he knew something about contract law) made a big deal about a “requirement” that the daughter give him $1 “in return” (which she did). When the father died before transferring the house, a court held that the deal did not satisfy the consideration doctrine. The father’s promise to transfer the house and the daughter’s giving of $1 each reflected *something* of legal value. But the court found that the father did not seek the $1 “in exchange for” his house promise. Instead, the court held, the “house-for-$1” deal was a mere “sham” of a bargain.

Note that if Aunt Nia actually gives you the gift, even though she was not obligated to do so, she cannot demand it back. Such a “consummated gift” is binding as a matter of property law.

Nominal Consideration. What if one side’s “consideration” in a deal is something trivial (such as $1)? To be sure, $1 is *something*. But it would seem, well, a little fishy for someone to bargain away his valuable legal rights for only $1 (as in the father and daughter example above). The question in such cases, in other words, is whether the $1 is a mere pretense of consideration (*i.e.*, in name only = “nominal”). For such situations, the "bargain" requirement again does the decisive work. The classic example involves a promise to pay $1,000 to obtain a mere ***peppercorn***. Could this deal satisfy the consideration doctrine? Absolutely—but only if the buyer *really* was willing to part with his $1,000 "in exchange for" the peppercorn under the given circumstances (say, because it once was on George Washington's table).

"Adequacy" of Consideration. The law permits people to enter into whatever kinds of deals they want. Thus, as long as each party makes its promise in exchange for the legal rights it wants from the other under the circumstances (*i.e.*, a "bargained-for exchange"), a court will not second-guess their judgments and inquire into whether the bargain is "fair." That is, the courts will not examine whether the respective consideration provided by the two parties is "equal" or "adequate."

Example

> During World War II, a woman in Greece promised to pay $2000 after the war ended if a man gave her $25 immediately (which he did). After the war the woman refused to pay and the man sued her for breach of contract. The court held that the deal satisfied the consideration doctrine. Because the woman in fact was willing to make her $2000 promise in exchange for the immediate payment of $25 in those uncertain times, the court refused to inquire into the "adequacy" of the consideration that supported the deal.

For egregious cases (perhaps the above case is one), we will see in Lesson 23 a "defense" called "unconscionability," but this is not an issue of contract formation in the first place.

Past Consideration/Legal Duty Rule. As a corollary to the requirement of a bargained-for exchange of legal rights, a promise is not supported by consideration if the promisee already had conferred the "return" benefit ("***past consideration***") or otherwise merely does what it already was legally obligated to do ("***legal duty rule***"). This makes complete sense: an agreement cannot involve an exchange of legal rights if one side *already* had performed, or *already* was subject to a legal obligation to perform, its side of the deal.

Example

Frank is a firefighter employed by the local municipality. Upon being called to a burning house while on duty, Frank said to the homeowner, "I will fight the fire if you give me $1,000." Even if the homeowner agreed, the deal would not satisfy the consideration doctrine because Frank was *already legally obligated*—to the homeowner and to everyone else in the municipality—to fight the fire. But if Frank instead worked for a *different* municipality (and no other law required his involvement), his promise may well constitute consideration.

Your casebook may cover here the special rules for consideration regarding a modification of an existing contract. If so, consult the analysis of this issue at the end of Lesson 24.

Illusory Promises. Your professor almost certainly also will address the subject of "illusory promises." This is a fancy phrase, but the idea is quite simple. If I promise to sell you my car, "but only if I want to," I really have not made a promise at all. We have only the "illusion" of a promise, because I have not limited my legal rights in any way. This leads us to a rule: a promise does not satisfy the consideration doctrine if the promisor reserves ***unfettered discretion*** over whether he is obligated to fulfill the promise.

Example

Logger agreed to sell to Lumber Mill the timber on a specific plot of land then owned by a third party. But Logger promised to do so only "if Logger decides to buy the land." Because Logger has unfettered discretion over whether to buy the land, it really has not (yet) promised anything to Lumber Mill. As a result, Logger's promise to sell the timber really is not a promise at all and thus does not constitute consideration.

Even in such a case, however, a once-not-binding promise becomes binding if and when the condition is cleared away. Thus, in the above example, if Logger actually buys the land, then its discretion is gone and its now ***un***conditional promise becomes binding. The result is that the parties have formed a contract on the sale of the timber (assuming neither party revoked its promise before then, *see* Lesson 4).

In addition, if even the slightest limitation on discretion exists, and especially if the parties have agreed on an objective or third party standard, the promisor has given up *some* legal right to satisfy the consideration doctrine.

Example

> Under a land purchase transaction with Seller, Developer reserved a right to terminate the contract if it were not "satisfied" by a planned feasibility study. If both parties manifested their intent to be bound to this deal, they have formed a contract notwithstanding Developer's one-sided termination power. A slight limitation on Developer's discretion exists: it may exercise the termination power only if it honestly and in good faith were not to be satisfied by the study results—something a court could assess through testimony and other evidence. (For more on the doctrine of "good faith" *see* Lesson 21, and on the related subject of "conditions of satisfaction" *see* Lesson 25.)

Another, closely related issue involves ***alternative promises***. Assume that Gallery offers to Artie three paintings and says, "Choose one—$2,000." If Artie says, "agreed," have the parties formed a contract given that Artie retains discretion on which painting to choose? In such cases, you must analyze all of the alternatives offered. If *each* would be consideration if bargained for separately, then the parties have formed a contract. *See* Restatement § 77. In the painting example, Artie obviously is giving consideration with his promise to pay $2000 and he must choose one of the paintings; the Gallery is providing consideration as well, because *each of the alternatives* from which Artie must choose would require the Gallery to give up its legal right to the chosen painting.

Settlement of Claims. Public policy favors the settlement of legal disputes. How are settlements accomplished?—well, with contracts of course. If a person has a valid legal claim, her promise to surrender the claim certainly constitutes consideration for a promise by the other side to pay a sum of money in exchange.

But a special challenge arises when it turns out that the claim was not valid in the first place. Assume that Rosa agreed to pay Michael $25,000 in exchange for his promise not to sue her over a car accident, but *later* evidence surfaced to prove that Rosa was 100% free of fault (*i.e.*, that Michael did not have a valid claim against Rosa at all). Did Michael's promise not to sue Rosa constitute consideration for Rosa's promise (*i.e.*, must Rosa pay the $25,000 anyway)? This situation has caused headaches for the courts, because if the answer is "no," then every settlement could be upended by later investigation.

The traditional view on this issue, at least in some courts, nonetheless stuck closely to the "legal detriment" requirement (*see* Lesson 9). Under this view, a promise to release a legal claim through a settlement agreement constitutes consideration only if *both* (a) the claim has at least *some* foundation in law and fact, *and* (b) the releasing party believes in good faith that his claim is valid.

The Restatement has introduced a substantially more flexible view and this now seems to be the prevailing approach in the courts. ***Restatement § 74*** transforms the "and" in the traditional test into an "or": an agreement to surrender a claim that later is determined to be invalid nonetheless constitutes consideration if ***either*** (a) the claim has at least some foundation in law and fact, ***or*** (b) the surrendering party "believes [in good faith] that the claim . . . may be fairly determined to be valid." Thus, in our example, as long as Michael believed in good faith that he had a valid claim at the time of the settlement agreement, his promise not to sue Rosa constitutes consideration for Rosa's $25,000 promise. That is, Rosa and Michael formed a contract, even though—in law and fact—Michael did not have a valid claim in the first place.

What You Need to Know:

1. Most difficult cases under the consideration doctrine arise in family or non-commercial settings. In such cases, the requirement of a "bargain" (a *quid pro quo*) plays the decisive role in separating legally binding promises from mere promises to give a gift.
2. The bargain requirement also determines whether a promise reflects only "nominal" consideration. But if the parties entered into a bargained-for exchange of legal rights, the courts will not inquire into the adequacy of the exchange. In contrast, a promise to fulfill an already-existing legal obligation does not constitute consideration.
3. A promise that reserves unfettered discretion to the promisor (an illusory promise) does not satisfy the consideration doctrine.
4. Under the modern Restatement test, a promise to release a legal claim constitutes consideration even if the claim turns out to be invalid if *either* (a) at least some foundation exists for the claim *or* (b) the releasing party believes in good faith that the claim is valid.

LESSON 11: CERTAINTY/DEFINITENESS/ ESSENTIAL TERMS

Lessons 2 through 10 examined the two principal requirements to form a contract: mutual assent and consideration. Here we take up the final requirement, "reasonable certainty of terms."

Some professors do not examine this issue as a separate element of contract formation, but rather as a kind of "sub-element" of an offer (*see* Lesson 3). That is, they point out that an effective offer already requires an identification of the essential terms of that contract. Taken alone, this is well, fine, and good. But as noted in Lesson 2, not all contracts are formed through clearly identifiable offers and acceptances. As a result, there is value in pulling out the "reasonable certainty" issue and analyzing it as a *separate* requirement for contract formation.

This third requirement of contract formation goes by a number of different labels: "reasonable certainty of terms," "definiteness," and agreement on the "essential terms." The Restatement prefers the first formulation. Perhaps unfortunately, however, it provides only a fuzzy explanation of what "***reasonable certainty***" means. Section 33(2) requires only that a contract "provide a basis for determining the existence of a breach and for giving an appropriate remedy."

It might be helpful, therefore, to step back and figure out what the purpose of the "reasonable certainty" requirement is. The simple idea is that even if the parties have explicitly declared their assent to contractual obligations, a court will not make a contract for them if the indispensable, "essential" elements of the deal are missing. This does not mean that the parties must address all conceivable issues. But they must at a minimum agree on the essential aspects of a contract in order to enable the court to determine what their basic deal is.

Example

> Oprah and Abby expressly agreed on a "contract" under which Oprah would pay $10,000 for "one of Abby's rings" (she has dozens)—but which one was left "for later discussions." They have not formed a contract. Although both have objectively manifested an intent to be bound and an exchange of $10,000 for a ring satisfies the consideration doctrine, the parties' failure to agree on the very subject of the deal means that it is not "reasonably certain"—and a court will not invent that essential aspect of a contract for them.

As this example shows, another way to view the reasonable certainty requirement is that the parties must agree on the "***essential terms***" of a contract. And instead of the fuzzy rule in Restatement § 33(2), the courts traditionally have identified four specific items as falling in that category: ***the parties; the price; the subject matter (i.e., return performance for the price); and the time of performance***. The identity of the parties is rarely an issue. And in recent years courts have become increasingly willing to fill in a "reasonable time" for performance, but this is not always the case (see below). Most modern disputes instead arise when the parties have not sufficiently described the price or the subject matter of their agreement. (As Lesson 14 will explain, the U.C.C. is more flexible on this matter than is the common law. The Restatement supports a similarly flexible approach, but common law courts thus far have not broadly embraced that flexibility.)

With respect to the ***price***, the parties at least must agree on an ***objective means for determining*** the amount the buyer is obligated to pay. But they also may do so in a variety of implicit or indirect ways. This may occur through, for example, an agreement on the "market price" on a fixed date on a recognized market (such as on the New York Stock Exchange); on a formula or calculation method (such as with many adjustable rate mortgages); on an institution that regularly sets the price for similar contracts (such as the "blue book" for automobiles); or even on a specific person (such as a third-party expert). What is not sufficient, however, is a mere "***agreement to agree***" on the price at some later time.

Example

> A lease included a clause stating that at the end of its term "landlord and tenant shall agree on an appropriate rent" for a further term. At the end of the lease term, however, the parties could not agree on an "appropriate" rent and the landlord ordered the tenant to leave. Upon suit by the tenant, the court held that an "agreement to agree" on the rent does not suffice and thus that the parties had not formed a contract on a renewal of the lease. Because price is an essential term, it also refused to impose a "reasonable" rental amount.

The most important term is the very ***subject matter*** of the parties' agreement. This is what the seller must provide (*e.g.*, goods, services, lease rights) in return for the buyer's payment of the price. Included in the subject matter is also the *amount* of whatever it is that the seller must provide—how much space in a lease, the quantity in a sale of goods, etc. The subject of a contract can be as varied as human desires allow (although it cannot be illegal, *see* Lesson 23). Because of this, it is nearly impossible to state a fixed definition of a "reasonably certain" subject matter.

This is the reason for the Restatement's squishy standard that the parties must provide a court a basis "for determining the existence of a breach" and for determining an "appropriate remedy." This in turn may vary greatly depending on the type of contract and the relevant trade or business. For example, courts typically require considerable specificity for the sale of real estate, because they cannot order a transfer if the parties have not agreed on details of the land at issue. For loan transactions, the details of the credit (length of time, structure of repayment, etc.) commonly are essential terms. The place of performance may be an essential aspect for an excavation services contract, but not so for a software development contract.

A clear agreement on the ***time*** when the parties must perform their promises also can be an essential term for some contracts. This is especially true when a transaction involves a continuing relationship between the parties, as opposed to a one-time transfer of rights. Thus, for example, courts have insisted on more detail on the duration of lease contracts and of intellectual property licenses.

A final, and very important, point about the reasonable certainty doctrine is that it is ***closely related to mutual assent***. The more that the parties leave significant issues unresolved, the less likely it is that they have manifested their intent to be bound to contractual obligations in the first place. An often-contentious illustration of this is the common practice of a "***letter of intent***." Sophisticated parties engaged in long negotiations sometimes will draft such letters in order to set down in writing those subjects on which they have already agreed—even though they contemplate additional negotiations. If later negotiations fall apart, the frustrated party may claim that the letter of intent nonetheless *already* reflected a binding contract. Among the most significant factors the courts have looked to in such situations—beyond, of course, the express terms—is the extent to which the letter leaves significant issues unresolved. Other important factors include how detailed the letter of intent is, the size and significance of the transaction, and whether the letter expressly contemplates a further, final, and formal contract document.

A related issue arises when parties orally agree to a deal, but also discuss memorializing it in a formal document. Unless the circumstances show that they only were engaging in preliminary negotiations, the mere contemplation of a writing will not prevent their already-existing objective manifestations of assent from forming a contract. *See* Restatement § 27.

What You Need to Know:

1. As a third requirement of contract formation under the traditional method, the parties must sufficiently identify the essential elements of a contract. This doctrine is known by the various labels "reasonable certainty," "definiteness," and "essential terms."
2. Traditionally, the four essential terms are the parties, the price, the subject matter, and the time of performance. The degree of required certainty for each of these terms may vary greatly, however, depending on the type of contract and the relevant trade or business.

LESSON 12: PROMISSORY ESTOPPEL—BACKGROUND AND BASICS

With this lesson, we move from the traditional means of contract formation to an alternative means known as "promissory estoppel." This form of contractual liability arises in the case of a promise on one side and reliance on that promise by the other.

The Background in "Estoppel." In order to understand why promissory estoppel developed, it may help to see the problem it is designed to redress. At its most basic, the doctrine serves to avoid the injustice that may arise from an overly strict application of the consideration doctrine. The classic example is the 1845 case of *Kirksey v. Kirksey*:

Example

A man promised to give his widowed sister-in-law some land he owned if she moved from a distant state. In reliance on this promise, the woman moved her family, and in the process gave up a valuable homestead lease she had from the U.S. government. After a short time, however, the man revoked his promise and ordered the woman off his land. Upon suit by the woman, the court held that no contract existed that would preclude the man from revoking his promise—because there was no "bargained-for exchange" between the parties (*i.e.*, no consideration). (Recall, from Lesson 10, the presumption that deals between family members are motivated merely by "natural love and affection.")

This result may strike you as quite unfair, and eventually the courts saw it the same way. But the problem was that they had no doctrine that would allow them to enforce a promise based solely on the other party's reliance. What they did—following a long tradition of common law courts—was adapt a well-established doctrine to new circumstances. In this case, the doctrine was "***equitable estoppel***" (now known simply as estoppel). The basic idea of this defensive doctrine is that a party may be precluded ("estopped") from asserting a fact in court if he had previously represented the opposite to another party and that other party relied on the representation to her detriment. Traditionally, however, equitable estoppel may arise only from representations about *past* facts, not from *promises* about the future (*i.e.*, it could not be used to form a contract). But when confronted with injustices like that in *Kirksey v. Kirksey*, the courts stretched the estoppel concept to build an entirely new contract law doctrine.

"Promissory" Estoppel. As the name makes clear, the promissory estoppel method of contract formation is based on reliance on a *promise*. But what claim or argument is "estopped" when the doctrine applies?—well, any claim that a promise is not binding because of a lack of a "bargained-for exchange." Indeed, the now widely accepted formulation of promissory estoppel in Restatement § 90(1) appears in a subpart on "Contracts without Consideration."

The standard approach breaks Restatement § 90(1)'s promissory estoppel rule into four elements (although some courts cut the pie slightly differently): (1) a promise; (2) the promisor reasonably should have expected the promise to induce action or forbearance on the part of the promisee; (3) the promise in fact "induced such action or forbearance"; and (4) "injustice can be avoided only by enforcement of the promise."

Promise. You should now be well familiar with the basic concept of a promise. But as a reminder (from Lesson 2), a promise is founded on the notion of a "manifestation" of an intent to act and thus, again, is based on the objective ("reasonable person") test. As we have seen repeatedly, this test leaves much room for interpretation over whether a person's words and conduct reflect a "promise." Likely because of this, promissory estoppel claims became a small flood in the 1980s and 1990s—because disappointed people began seeing "promises" in any and all situations and then brought breach of contract claims based on "promissory" estoppel. To stem that flood, some courts began imposing higher standards for a valid promise to sustain a promissory estoppel claim. Some now require an "express" promise (*i.e.*, one made in words) or even an "explicit" promise (*i.e.*, one that leaves little room for doubt about the intention to act or refrain from acting in a specified way). Other courts, however, do not impose such heightened standards.

Expectation of Reliance. This element may be the most important. The promisor must reasonably expect that the promisee will go out and take actions in reliance on the promise without further conversation or negotiation. Notice, as an important matter, that the relevant party here is the promis***or***, not the promisee. Whether a particular promise is binding under promissory estoppel thus will depend on whether the promisor, under the circumstances, reasonably should have expected the promisee's reliance, in both its nature and extent. Promissory estoppel claims often fail on this element, especially for sophisticated parties.

Example

X-Corp and Y-Corp were engaged in negotiations over a major deal. To take stock of where they stood, they signed a "letter of intent" that set forth the terms thus far agreed and expressed their mutual desire for a favorable outcome. Unfortunately, the negotiations later broke down. X-Corp then filed a contract claim in promissory estoppel because it had passed up other valuable opportunities after the signing of the letter of intent. The doctrine should not apply on these facts. In the context of negotiations between sophisticated corporations, Y-Corp should not reasonably have expected any reliance on the letter of intent before the execution of a definitive contract document.

Actual Reliance. This third element of promissory estoppel often is the most straightforward. The simple idea is that the promisee must in fact take some action—or refrain from an action it otherwise would have taken—in reliance on the promise. (Some courts have added that the reliance must be "reasonable," but this tends to cause confusion with the second element discussed above.) The reliance can be of almost any nature and even may be based on a purely charitable promise.

Example

Rich Richie promised to donate ten million dollars to support the construction of a new wing at Mercy Hospital. With that promise in hand, Mercy engaged a construction firm and began building the wing. If Richie reasonably should have expected this action, Mercy's reliance made Richie's ten million dollar promise binding under promissory estoppel.

Avoidance of Injustice. As noted above, the promissory estoppel alternative for contract formation arose from a desire to avoid the injustice that sometimes can result from an overly strict adherence to the consideration doctrine. Most often, such an injustice arises from ***detrimental reliance*** by the promisee—that is, from the fact that the promisee will suffer harm if the court does not enforce the promise (as in the Mercy Hospital example above). With its flexible reference to injustice, however, this element leaves substantial discretion to the court. If a court finds that, under the given circumstances, justice does not require enforcement of the promise, it may refuse to recognize a contract on the basis of promissory estoppel.

Example

Knowing that his niece Jacqui needed transportation for a distant new job, Nanda said to her, "I promise to give you up to $20,000 to buy a car." Unknown to Nanda, Jacqui's mother had already bought her daughter a fancy new car for that purpose. Jacqui nonetheless went out and bought a second car in reliance on Nanda's promise. Jacqui is able to resell this second car without a loss. Under these circumstances, a court could well conclude that justice does not require enforcement of Nanda's promise to Jacqui.

What You Need to Know:

1. Promissory estoppel is an alternative method for enforcing a promise (*i.e.*, for concluding a contract). This doctrine arose out of a desire to avoid the injustice that may arise from an overly strict application of the consideration doctrine.
2. Under Restatement § 90(1), a party must prove four elements to form a contract under promissory estoppel: (1) a promise; (2) the promisor should reasonably have expected the promise to induce action in reliance on the part of the promisee; (3) the promise in fact induced reliance by the promisee; and (4) injustice can be avoided only by enforcing the promise.

LESSON 13: SPECIAL ISSUES FOR PROMISSORY ESTOPPEL

Lesson 12 covered the basic rationale and substance of promissory estoppel. In this lesson, we examine some special issues that arise in the application of that doctrine.

Possibility of a Limited Remedy for Breach. We saw in Lesson 12 that the result of a successful claim in promissory estoppel is a binding promise, and we have known since Lesson 2 that this means a contract. Thus, if promissory estoppel applies and the promisor does not fulfill his promise, the promisee has a claim for breach of contract. Generally, upon breach the injured party is entitled to the full value of the unfulfilled contractual promise (something we will cover in more detail in Lesson 27). Thus, if promissory estoppel makes a $10,000 promise binding, the promisee should be entitled to an award of $10,000.

But again promissory estoppel is fundamentally founded on avoiding injustice. As a result, a second sentence in Restatement § 90(1) expressly grants discretion to a court to tailor the remedy in promissory estoppel claims "***as justice requires***." A court may well conclude that the interests of justice require that the promisee recover the full value of the promise, and empirical studies indicate that this in fact occurs in about half of the promissory estoppel cases. But a court instead may decide that some other, more limited remedy is appropriate under the circumstances. Most often, this means merely an award to cover the money the promisee spent in reliance on the promise (the so-called "out of pocket" expenditures). (Lesson 28 below will explain this alternative "reliance" measure of damages in more detail.)

Example

> Knowing that a fire recently destroyed all of the belongings of her nephew Joe, rich Aunt Yolanda told him, "I'll give you $20,000 to replace your things." Joe then in fact was able to replace all of his lost belongings for $15,000. If Aunt Yolanda reneges on her promise, a court applying the promissory estoppel doctrine may well conclude that Joe's remedy should be limited to the $15,000 he actually spent.

Promissory Estoppel and Indefinite Promises. Because promissory estoppel is not founded on an actual agreement between two parties, special problems arise when negotiations fall apart before the parties can agree on the core aspects of their deal. But as a matter of emphasis, promissory estoppel requires a *promise*, not a full-blown offer. Thus, the "essential terms" doctrine (*see* Lesson 11) does not apply for promissory estoppel claims. This point may be especially important for business neophytes or other unsophisticated parties. The classic example is a Wisconsin case, *Hoffman v. Red Owl Stores*:

Example

Red Owl Stores, a grocery store chain, wanted a new franchise in northern Wisconsin. It sought out Hoffman, an unsophisticated small town baker, to convince him to open the franchise. Based on Red Owl's promise to grant him a franchise, Hoffman sold his own bakery at a loss, bought a small grocery store to gain experience, and moved his family to the proposed distant location. Ultimately, Red Owl refused to grant Hoffman the franchise. Upon suit by Hoffman for breach of contract, Red Owl pointed out that the parties had never even discussed the essential terms of a franchise (size of store, payments by Hoffman, etc.). The Wisconsin Supreme Court nonetheless held that promissory estoppel requires only a promise, not an offer with all essential terms, and thus ruled in favor of Hoffman.

In such cases, however, a court faces a substantial challenge in crafting an appropriate remedy: Without a party agreement on the subject matter (*e.g.*, size of the store) or the price (*e.g.*, Hoffman's franchise fee to Red Owl), the court simply cannot figure out what *future* profit the promisee expected from the deal under discussion (*e.g.*, a franchise). As a result, in such cases of an ***indefinite promise***, the best a court can do is compensate the promisee for his *past* losses—the amount of money spent or otherwise lost in reliance on the promise (see the nephew Joe example above). That was the case in *Hoffman*. The court awarded Hoffman only his losses on the sale of the bakery, the expenses in moving his family, etc.—*not* the amount of money he hoped to make from the promised Red Owl franchise in the future.

Such flexibility in promissory estoppel has led some courts to say, perhaps unthinkingly, that the doctrine is not based on a breach of *contract.* They seem to suggest that it is a free-floating category somewhere between contract and tort. This is both unnecessary and potentially confusing, and you are best advised to view the doctrine like the Restatement does: The application of promissory estoppel = a binding promise = a contract.

Charitable Subscriptions. We saw in Lesson 9 that one of the principal effects of the consideration doctrine is that promises to give a gift in the future are not enforceable. Under promissory estoppel, however, a promise to make a gift or donation may well become binding in the case of expected and detrimental reliance by the promisee. Restatement § 90(2) goes even further to make promises made in the context of charitable subscription campaigns binding without consideration *or* reliance. Thus far, however, very few courts have adopted the § 90(2) rule.

Nonetheless, as a descriptive matter courts have been quite open to claims that a gift promise to a charity either was based on an actual bargained-for exchange under the consideration doctrine or caused expected and detrimental reliance under promissory estoppel.

Example

> Rena Richie promised to donate $3 million to Bethel Hospital to buy an expensive new MRI machine, but also stipulated that the hospital rename the MRI room in her honor. Bethel agreed and then bought the new MRI machine. If Rena reneges on her promise, a court could well find that the parties formed a contract either through standard consideration ($3 million in exchange for the renaming of the MRI room) or through promissory estoppel (based on Bethel's expected and detrimental reliance).

What You Need to Know:

1. A court that recognizes a contract based on promissory estoppel has the discretion to limit the remedy as justice requires. Courts that do so most often limit the remedy to an award of the out-of-

pocket expenses incurred by the promisee in reliance on the promise.

2. Promissory estoppel also can apply to indefinite promises, that is, to promises that do not identify the essential terms otherwise required to form a contract. In such cases, however, a court can only award past "reliance" damages because it will lack information necessary to calculate the promisee's profit expected from the transaction in the future.

LESSON 14: CONTRACT FORMATION UNDER THE UNIFORM COMMERCIAL CODE

As noted in Lesson 1, the principal source of law for contracts in the United States is judge-made state common law. Nearly all of the rules discussed in the lessons to this point, therefore, are from the common law. But Lesson 1 also noted that the Uniform Commercial Code (U.C.C.) represents an important exception. The U.C.C. covers a whole variety of subjects, from negotiable instruments (Article 3) to Letters of Credit (Article 5) to Secured Transactions (Article 9). But in your first-year Contracts, you likely will review only U.C.C. Article 2, and then only its contract formation rules. In this lesson, we examine those rules of U.C.C. Article 2 (along with a few definitional rules from Article 1).

As a first reminder, ***U.C.C. Article 2 applies to "transactions in goods"*** (§ 2–102). Section 2–105 then defines "goods" as all "***things***" (*i.e.*, with a physical existence) that are "***movable***" at the time the seller is to transfer ownership (basically). Thus, for the multitude of transactions involving the sale of movable things, from pencils to tractor trailers, U.C.C. Article 2 provides the governing rules. And—contrary to a common misconception—Article 2 is not limited to transactions by merchants or other commercial parties (although it does have some special rules for merchants).

But before we get into the details, we need to note the legal nature of the U.C.C. Because it operates against the background of the common law, the U.C.C. can dispense with re-stating some fundamental rules of contract formation. Thus, the basic rule is that the principles of the common law continue to apply unless the U.C.C. has a contrary rule. *See* § 1–103(b). Perhaps the most prominent example of this is the basic notion of an offer. The U.C.C. does not define the term, with the result that ***the common law requirements of an offer continue to apply*** for transactions within U.C.C. Article 2. As a more general matter, the U.C.C. states only so-called "default rules." That is, the actual agreement of the parties comes first, such that the U.C.C. rules apply only to fill gaps. (The one unalterable exception, stated in § 1–302, is the basic requirement to adhere to good faith and reasonableness, etc.)

Following the same philosophy, U.C.C. Article 2 deliberately takes a flexible approach to the requirements for forming a contract. Its overall focus is on whether the parties *in fact* have agreed and as a result it rejects a variety of rigid rules traditionally applied in the common law. *See* §§ 1–201(a)(12) (defining a "contract" merely as the obligation that "results from the parties' agreement"); 1–201(a)(3)(defining "agreement" only as "the bargain of the parties in fact, as found in their language or inferred from other circumstances"). In addition, we will see in Lesson 20 that the U.C.C. in general embraces a more flexible approach to contract interpretation, especially with respect to a "course of performance," "course of dealing," or "usage of trade."

A number of contract formation rules in U.C.C. Article 2 reflect this flexibility. First, § 2–204(1) declares that a contract "may be made ***in any manner sufficient to show agreement***," and this expressly includes "conduct by both parties which recognizes the existence of such a contract." This rule explicitly rejects any fixation on a clearly identifiable offer or acceptance. Second, § 2–204(2) emphasizes in the same vein that a court may recognize a contract "***even though the moment of its making is undetermined***." Likewise, § 2–206(1) instructs the courts to interpret an offer "as inviting ***acceptance in any manner and by any medium reasonable in the circumstances***," unless the language and circumstances "unambiguously" indicate otherwise. The U.C.C. also has no formal "consideration" requirement because it is implied in the very application of Article 2 (a sale of "goods" in exchange for a "price").

The most important of the flexible formation rules in U.C.C. Article 2 is on the subject of definiteness ("essential terms"). In contrast to the common law (*see* Lesson 11), § 2–204(3) provides that a contract will not fail because of missing essential terms "***if the parties have intended to make a contract and there is a reasonably certain basis for giving an appropriate remedy***." When carefully considered, the last clause means that the U.C.C. requires an agreement only on one term: the very subject matter of the parties' agreement (*i.e.*, the goods to be bought and sold, including the quantity). Otherwise, U.C.C. Article 2 permits the court to apply a "reasonable" standard—provided that the parties (objectively) intend to be bound. *See* § 2–305 (providing for a "reasonable" price) and § 2–309 (providing for a "reasonable" time of performance).

Example

> Buyer and Seller enter into an agreement covering 2,000 specifically described stereo speakers, but leave the issue of the price for later discussions. If the parties have objectively manifested their intent to be bound, they have formed a contract under U.C.C. Article 2 on the basis of a reasonable price at the agreed time of delivery. (Recall from Lesson 11 that a court applying the common law very likely would *not* recognize a contract under similar circumstances.)

Contract Formation Under the CISG. Recall from Lesson 1 that a final source of important contract law is an international treaty ratified by the United States, the ***United Nations Convention on Contracts for the International Sale of Goods ("CISG")***. For international sale of goods transactions, the CISG generally follows the standard offer-acceptance scheme for contract formation (*see* Articles 14–24), but it entirely dispenses with a consideration requirement and has certain other special rules (such as on revocation of an offer).

What You Need to Know:

1. U.C.C. Article 2 applies to "transactions in goods," meaning all things with a physical existence that are "movable." Nonetheless, the rules of the common law continue to apply for gaps in the U.C.C. The most prominent example of this (for present purposes) is the concept of an offer, for which U.C.C. Article 2 has no rule.
2. U.C.C. Article 2 has very flexible rules on contract formation. The most prominent of these are that a contract may be made in any manner sufficient to show agreement; that an acceptance may come in any reasonable manner or medium; and that a contract generally will not fail for lack of essential terms as long as the parties intend to be bound. All that is required is an agreement on the subject matter (the goods and the quantity), and a court even can apply a "reasonable" time of performance and a "reasonable" price.

LESSON 15: THE BATTLE OF THE FORMS UNDER THE U.C.C.

Parties involved in contract negotiations rarely immediately agree on every issue. As a result, it is quite common that a purported acceptance does not fully agree with what the offer proposed. We saw in Lesson 7 that the common law applies the quite rigid "mirror image" and "last shot" rules for this common situation. These rules might have made sense in a quaint old time when parties negotiated in person over a limited set of issues. But they are quite clunky in an age of computers and form documents. Today, even small businesses hire a lawyer to create one standard "form contract" (the "fine print" or "boilerplate") and they send out that form in every transaction. (Less sophisticated parties think that a random form they find on the Internet will suffice.) The problem is that both sides commonly will use such pre-drafted standard forms. The result is a "battle of the forms."

In the real world, no one reads the small print terms in the forms the parties exchange. Businesspeople care about business terms, that is, the issues over which they actually negotiate in concluding a deal (our old friends from Lesson 11, the "essential terms"). And once they have agreed on those things, the parties commonly carry out the transaction—the seller ships the goods and the buyer pays for them—oblivious to the fact that the standard forms they *also* exchanged contain numerous conflicts. The parties think they have a contract before they perform, but each side assumes that *its* standard "terms and conditions" are part of the contract.

The common law's stylized "mirror image" and "last shot" rules—which award *total* victory to the side that happened to send the last form—make little sense in such situations. The drafters of U.C.C. Article 2 sought to address this problem with a new approach that is responsive to the reality of pre-drafted forms. Unfortunately, the result (in § 2–207) is poorly worded and can be quite confusing. Our goal in this lesson is to disentangle the rules in § 2–207 and hopefully clear away the potential for confusion. (Because of its complexity, some professors do not cover § 2–207 in first-year Contracts. If your professor follows this approach, you may skip this lesson.)

Offer. Even under the U.C.C., the first requirement in contract formation is an offer. But because the U.C.C. (as noted in Lesson 15) does not have a provision on this concept, we must fall back on the common law definition even for U.C.C. transactions.

Acceptance. Under the U.C.C. as well, a contract is formed if the offeree manifests an unconditional acceptance. *See* §§ 2–204, 2–206. Section 2–207 of the U.C.C. instead addresses the common situation in modern commerce in which a written reply to an offer indicates an "acceptance" but nonetheless includes additional or different terms. But before we get into the details, it is best to understand the overall structure of § 2–207.

You will see that § 2–207 has three subsections, and each addresses a separate subject: Subsection (1) provides the basic rules on when a written reply to an offer creates a contract. The second and third subsections then address the two alternatives: If the answer to the contract formation question under subsection (1) is "*yes*," then subsection (2) applies. If, in contrast, the answer under subsection (1) is "*no*," then subsection (3) applies.

Subsection § 2–207(1). The most fundamental purpose of § 2–207(1) is to ***reject the mirror image rule*** of the common law. It states this basic rule: "A definite and seasonable expression of acceptance . . . operates as an acceptance even though it states terms additional to or different from those offered[.]" (We will cover below the omitted words on a "written confirmation.") If you read the first phrase carefully, you will see that this rule states three requirements for an effective acceptance of the offer. It is easiest to work backward.

First, the written reply to the offer must contain an "***expression of acceptance***." If the reply states an *express* rejection or an *express* counteroffer (which is quite rare once the parties start exchanging formal business documents), we start all over. But if it indicates that it accepts the offer, then we stay in the world of § 2–207.

Second, the acceptance must be "***seasonable***," which simply means within a reasonable time of the offer (*see* § 1–205(b)).

Third, the acceptance must be "***definite***." By now, this should be a familiar term (from Lesson 11), and in it we find the heart of § 2–207(1). Businesspeople conclude deals on the basis of business issues—the goods (including quantity), the price for those goods, and the time of performance. These are the "definite" terms of a sale of goods contract (sometimes also called the "dickered terms"—the ones that are the common subject of actual negotiations). Under § 2–207(1), in other words, the key to contract formation is whether the reply agrees with the offer on these three fundamental business aspects of the deal.

If the reply satisfies these three requirements, it "operates as an acceptance"—that is, it immediately forms a contract. And for emphasis, § 2–207(1) contains an *express* rejection of the mirror image rule: an acceptance that satisfies the three requirements noted above concludes a contract "even though it states terms additional to or different from those offered." Thus, as long as the reply agrees with the offer on the essential terms, no other terms—even "material" ones such as on limitation of warranties or damages—preclude contract formation.

Example

> Buyco sent a "Purchase Order Form" offering to buy from Sellco "1,000 widgets at $4.00 per unit with delivery by June 1 of this year." Sellco promptly responded with an "Order Acknowledgement" form that stated, "We are pleased to accept your offer." The back of Sellco's form contained, however, dozens of fine print terms. Sellco's reply nonetheless formed a contract under § 2–207(1). Because it expressed acceptance, came promptly, and agreed with Buyco's offer on the "definite terms" of goods and quantity, price, and delivery time, it "operate[d] as an acceptance."

"Expressly Made Conditional" Clause. The final clause of § 2–207(1) nonetheless permits an offeree to insist on the application of *its* terms as a condition to contract formation. But following its basic philosophy, § 2–207(1) requires that the offeree declare this "expressly." Thus, most courts have imposed *very* high standards for an "expressly made conditional" clause.

Example

> Following the above example, assume that Sellco's Order Acknowledgement form also stated, "This acceptance is subject to the terms on the back page hereof." Nearly all courts have held that this ambiguous "subject to" language does not satisfy the final clause of § 2–207(1)—because it does not *expressly* declare that the offeree is unwilling to proceed with the transaction without the offeror's affirmative agreement on the offeree's proposed terms. Thus, even with the "subject to" clause, Sellco's reply formed a contract.

You will note that § 2–207(1) also refers to a "***written confirmation***." This refers to a situation in which the parties first agree on a basic deal through informal communications (such as telephone conversations) and then one of them follows up with a "confirmation." In such a situation, § 2–207(1) makes clear that any additional terms contained in the confirmation likewise do not prevent contract formation (nor, obviously, undo a contract previously concluded through the informal communications).

Subsection 2–207(2). The second subsection of § 2–207 applies when a reply to an offer "operates as an acceptance" under § 2–207(1) and thus immediately forms a contract. With a contract thus formed, ***§ 2–207(2) defines what terms are included in the contract***. It begins with a basic rule: "The additional terms are to be construed as proposals for addition to the contract."

The first point to notice is that this rule implicitly provides that the terms in the offer *automatically* are part of the contract. With this foundation, § 2–207(2) then states that the terms in the acceptance that would add to those in the offer "become part of the contract," but only if the transaction is "*between merchants*." The point here is that such terms can merge into the contract only between parties with business experience—and thus those parties who should pay attention to contract forms. (Consult Lesson 5 for a summary definition of merchant in U.C.C. § 2–104(1).)

But even if that is the case, § 2–207(2) contains a very powerful "unless." Under that subsection, *the additional terms do not become part of the contract* if any one of three separate things is true: (a) the offer "expressly limits acceptance to the terms of the offer"; (b) the additional terms would "materially alter" the contract; or (c) the offeror already had objected to the inclusion of such terms or does so later "within a reasonable time." The second of these limitations ("materially alter") is the most important. It basically says that if a proposed additional term in the acceptance is important—if the term would "result in surprise or hardship," as the Official Comments state—it does not become part of the contract under § 2–207(2).

Example

Keeping with the above example, assume that among the terms on the back of Sellco's Order Acknowledgement was this one: "Seller shall not be responsible for any consequential damages that exceed the total price of the goods sold." Because such a term almost certainly would "materially alter" the contract, it does not become part of the parties' contract. (But as an important reminder, such a "material" term does not prevent contract formation in the first place. The fact that the reference to "material terms" *first* appears in § 2–207(**2**) confirms the point.)

The second important thing you should notice about § 2–207(2) is that it does not expressly address what happens to ***"different terms"*** in the acceptance—*i.e.*, those that *conflict with* the offer's terms. The absence of a rule on "different terms" is more than a bit of a mystery. Nonetheless, the strong majority view in the courts is that the conflicting terms in *both* the acceptance *and* the offer are excluded from the contract (the so-called "knockout" rule).

Example

Keeping with the above example, assume that Buyco's original offer also had an express clause stating, "Seller shall be responsible for all consequential damages." Under the majority view, the conflict on this subject would mean that the damages clauses in both Buyco's offer and Sellco's acceptance would be excluded from the contract. The remaining default rules in U.C.C. Article 2—it has dozens of them—would then fill the gap.

A minority of courts take the view that § 2–207(2) treats different terms just like additional terms, but, by their very nature, they "materially alter" the contract. The result is that *only* the term in the acceptance is excluded and the offeror's term prevails.

Subsection 2–207(3). The third subsection of § 2–207 applies ***when "the writings of the parties do not . . . establish a contract"*** *under § 2–207(1).* From the above analysis, this occurs when the reply to the offer either (a) is not a "definite and seasonable expression of acceptance" or (b) contains an "expressly made conditional" clause. The second of these is substantially more common. In such a case, it is of course possible that the offeror would explicitly agree with the offeree's proposed standard business terms. But this is extremely rare—Why would the offeror do so?—and in any event, the courts have imposed a very strict standard of a "specific and unequivocal expression of acceptance on the part of the offeror." This is entirely consistent with § 2–207(3)'s rejection of the last shot rule (see immediately below).

Under § 2–207(3), if subsequent "conduct by both parties" recognizes the existence of a contract, then in fact a contract is formed. This commonly occurs through the seller shipping the goods and the buyer paying for them. But in such a case, § 2–207(3) declares that the contract includes only those terms "on which the writings of the parties agree." In other words, a contract formed solely through party conduct includes only the narrow set of terms on which ***the parties' forms overlap***. The default rules stated in U.C.C. Article 2 then fill the gaps. This is a pointed rejection of the "one side totally wins" approach of the last shot rule under the common law.

What You Need to Know:

1. U.C.C. § 2–207 is designed to address the modern reality of pre-drafted standard forms that the two parties commonly exchange, but neither actually reads.

2. Under § 2–207(1), a written reply to an offer forms a contract if it (a) expresses acceptance, (b) comes within a reasonable time of the offer, and (c) agrees with the offer merely on the "definite" terms of a sales contract. All other "additional or different terms" in the acceptance (even "material" ones) do not prevent contract formation. The offeree can prevent this result if its purported acceptance is "expressly made conditional" on the offeror's agreement to the additional or different terms.

3. Subsection 2–207(2) applies when a reply to an offer forms a contract under § 2–207(1). In such a case, "between merchants" the additional terms in the reply become part of the contract, unless the offeror already objected to them or does so within a reasonable time or they would materially alter the contract. For "different terms," the prevailing view "knocks-out" the terms in *both* offer and acceptance.
4. Subsection 2–207(3) applies when a reply to an offer does not form a contract under § 2–207(1). In such a case, the conduct of both parties nonetheless may recognize a contract and, if so, it includes only those terms on which the parties' respective forms overlap.

LESSON 16: ELECTRONIC AND "LAYERED" CONTRACTS

One modern development has posed special difficulties for courts applying both the U.C.C. and the common law: the sale of products to the public at large—including through the Internet—on the basis of standard form contracts. This subject remains one of the most controversial in modern contract law precisely because valid interests exist on the part of both mass-market sellers and consumers. A real-world situation will illustrate the tensions.

Example

Bennie buys a software program at Best Buy and pays the $25.99 price at the counter. When he opens the package at home, he finds a multi-page set of "contract" terms and a notice that if he does not agree he must return the product within ten days. One of the terms is absolutely necessary for a software seller: a limitation on liability for damage to the user's computer—because the seller does not know whether the buyer will install the program in a $500 laptop or a $50,000,000 mainframe. But dozens of other terms are there as well, some of which likely are very onerous for a consumer. If Bennie does not return the product in ten days, do all of the seller's terms become part of the parties' contract?

Similar challenges arise when consumers purchase goods or services over the telephone or, more commonly today, through the Internet. To address these new mass-market technologies and business practices, some courts have adopted new forms of contract analysis that are either efficient or unfair depending on your perspective. The goal of this lesson is to explore this modern legal controversy over the new technology-driven forms of contracting.

"Click-wrap" Contracts. The easiest of the modern mass-market contracting forms is the so-called "click-wrap" contract. This term addresses the increasingly common situation of contracts formed over the Internet. (Some of the folks who brought us the U.C.C. have proposed a uniform statute—known as "UCITA"—to govern all Internet contracting in this way, but only two states, Maryland and Virginia, have adopted it.) Unlike the example above, this form of contracting poses no problems for the traditional rules of contract formation. A buyer desiring to purchase a good, service, or software product is presented with all of the seller's proposed contract terms and must click on an "I Agree" box prior to concluding the transaction. In such a case, the buyer clearly manifests his assent to the seller's terms as part of the contracting process (and before his payment)—and there is no excuse based on a failure to read those terms.

"Browse-wrap" Contracts. This term addresses an increasingly rare circumstance: An Internet transaction where the seller does *not* require the buyer to click on an "I Agree" box covering the seller's contract terms. Without this express assent, the seller can argue only that the buyer implicitly accepted the seller's terms by browsing through the seller's Internet site. But courts generally have said that in order for the seller's terms to apply in this way, its website must unambiguously advise the buyer of that fact. As a practical matter, this is very hard for a seller to prove. Any reasonably sophisticated Internet seller today will avoid this difficulty simply by requiring a formal "click-wrap" contract as described above.

"Shrink-wrap" Contracts and the New "Layered" Contract Analysis. The most controversial modern contracting form has been the "shrink-wrap" contract. This term describes a situation in which the seller's standard contract terms are included inside the plastic "shrink-wrap" that surrounds a packaged product bought at a retail store. The Best Buy transaction above is an illustration. But the same situation can arise when a consumer buys a product over the telephone or when an Internet seller includes terms with a shipped product that are different from those in an original click-wrap contract. Under the traditional approach of the common law and the U.C.C., the analysis in such situations would seem to be straightforward: the parties formed a contract—through mutual assent, consideration, and an agreement on the essential terms—at the time of the original in-store, telephonic, or Internet purchase. With the contract thus concluded, the seller does not have a unilateral right to impose new terms later (even with buyer's supposed implicit "agreement").

Some courts, however, have recognized a new approach to this situation based on the "master of the offer" principle. As Lesson 3 described in detail, this principle holds the offeror has the power to define all aspects of the proposed contract, including the time, manner, and method of acceptance. Some courts have reasoned that this principle permits the seller/offeror in a mass-market transaction to delay the formation process until the point that the buyer/offeree begins to use the sold product. Thus, the seller's act of accepting the buyer's order, charging the buyer's credit card, and giving possession of the goods to the buyer does *not* (yet) form a contract. Instead, the seller's status as "master of the offer" permits it to state that the buyer may express its assent *later*, typically by either (a) clicking on an "I agree" box for later-delivered computer-based products, or (b) failing to return some other kind of product within a set time. At that point, all of the seller's proposed contract terms are available to the buyer in the "shrink-wrap" (or the new "click-wrap"). When, then, the buyer acts (or does not act) in the defined way, it manifests its assent to all of the seller's terms. This reflects a "rolling" or "layered" form of concluding a contract.

Example

Hill ordered a computer from one of Dell's call centers, and the representative charged Hill's credit card. Upon arrival, Hill found in the shrink-wrap packaging a form "contract" that stated at the top, "By retaining this product for thirty days, you agree to all of the terms and conditions set forth herein." Hill retained the computer for that time, but later discovered problems. When she filed suit, Dell pointed out that its "contract" contained a clause requiring private arbitration in the place of a lawsuit. The court adopted the "master of the offer" analysis and held that all of Dell's contract terms were binding on Hill because she manifested her acceptance of them by failing to return the computer within thirty days.

Other courts disagree with this "layered" contract analysis and continue to apply the traditional approach. For a sale of goods, these courts have held that the shrink-wrap terms at most reflect a "written confirmation" under U.C.C. § 2–207(1). *See* Lesson 15. In such a case, the terms are not effective under § 2–207(2) if they "materially alter" the contract formed in-store, on the telephone, or on the Internet (without a "click-wrap" contract)—and those are the terms that sellers care about. The controversy over the correct approach continues.

What You Need to Know:

1. The Internet and other modern technologies have created new forms of contracting, including "click-wrap," "browse-wrap," and "shrink-wrap" contracts. Click-wrap contracts pose little conceptual difficulty. They involve a buyer affirmatively clicking on an "I agree" box to accept an Internet seller's contract terms.

2. Browse-wrap contracts are more problematic for an Internet seller. Because they do not involve an "I Agree" box, the seller has the difficult task of

proving that the buyer otherwise manifested his assent to the seller's contract terms by browsing through the seller's website.

3. Some courts have recognized a new approach for shrink-wrap contracts. This "layered" contracting approach permits a seller, as "master of the offer," to delay contract formation until the buyer receives the product along with the seller's proposed contract terms contained in the shrink-wrap. At that point, the buyer may manifest his assent with notice of the seller's contract terms. Other courts disagree with this new approach.

LESSON 17: RESTITUTION ("UNJUST ENRICHMENT"); PROMISSORY RESTITUTION

Basically all of the lessons to this point have focused on the means by which a *promise* becomes binding—that is, how private parties create liability through a contract. But you also will cover in Contracts a separate body of law, Restitution (also known as "unjust enrichment"), which is not based on contractual promises. This lesson examines how this alternative form of liability nonetheless interacts with contract law in a variety of interesting ways.

Long ago, the common law recognized private claims only under the categories of contract, tort, and property. But then the courts started to run across cases like this one:

> Edward, a farmer, became suddenly ill, leaving his cows without care. Gilford, also a farmer, stepped in and paid substantial sums of money to care for Edward's cows during the illness. When Edward recovered, he refused to reimburse Gilford. Under such circumstances, the parties clearly did not form a contract—because Edward made no promise at all. Does Edward just get to keep (for free) the benefits Gilford conferred on him?

To address such obvious examples of injustice, common law courts began doing what they often do: they took an established doctrine and "stretched" it to cover a new situation. In this case, they recognized a claim based on a new term they simply created that made the situation *seem like a contract*: "implied-in-law contract" (or "quasi-contract"). To mask things further, they also used the Latin terms *quantum meruit* ("as much as was earned") and *quantum valebat* ("as much as it was worth").

Now, don't get confused here: these were just the words the courts used to find liability where in fact it did *not* exist based on an *actual* contract. Thus, ***an "implied-in-law contract" is NOT a contract***—it is an obligation imposed "by law." (In contrast, an "implied-in-fact" contract is, in fact, a contract—it is just one that arises from an implied agreement of the parties through their conduct by virtue of our old friend, the objective manifestation of assent rule, *see* Lesson 6.)

Starting about one hundred years ago, the courts began to see that what they were doing really represented a new, ***separate body of law: Restitution***. Today, an entire "Restatement of Restitution and Unjust Enrichment" exists that sets forth the rules in this field. Section 2 of this Restatement states the basic rule: "A person who is unjustly enriched at the expense of another is subject to liability in restitution." Because "unjust enrichment" best captures this basic premise, we will use that term below.

Why Study Unjust Enrichment in First-Year Contracts? A claim in unjust enrichment can arise whenever someone receives a benefit from another person under circumstances where it would be unjust to permit the recipient not to pay for it. For example, a claim may arise where someone gets possession of property owned by another or benefits from expenditures made by another (such as in the example above). This is true even though no possible contract claim exists.

But a claim founded in ***unjust enrichment also can become relevant to contract law in a variety of ways***. This occurs in three principal situations in which one party confers a benefit on another in the shadow of a contract: *first*, when the party had a justified belief that he had concluded a contract with the other person, but in fact no such contract existed (*see* the Hunter and Polly example below); *second*, when a contract existed, but the party exercised a power to "avoid" it based on a defense to enforcement (something Lessons 22–24 will cover in detail); *third*, when an enforceable contract existed, but the party exercised a power to "rescind" it due to a material breach by the other party (something Lesson 26 will cover in detail). In all these cases, the conferring party may bring a claim in restitution for the benefit that the recipient now "unjustly" has (*i.e.*, without legal justification). Another way to think about this is that the law of unjust enrichment sort of "lurks in the background" of contract law to clean up any messes left when contract liability goes away. On the other hand, no unjust enrichment claim exists for matters within the scope of a valid and enforceable contract.

The Basic Test of Liability. The Restatement of Restitution and Unjust Enrichment has a great number of highly detailed rules to govern specific situations. At bottom, however, a claim of unjust enrichment is based on this fundamental test: The plaintiff must prove (1) that she conferred a benefit on the defendant (some courts add that the benefit must be "measurable"); (2) that the defendant had knowledge of and retained the benefit; and (3) that it would be unjust under the circumstances to permit the defendant to retain the benefit without paying for it.

Example

> Hunter wanted his house painted and asked Polly, a painter, to do the work. Although they agreed on the details (color, etc.), they had not yet discussed the price when Hunter instructed Polly to "go ahead and paint the house." Polly did so, but then Hunter refused to pay, arguing that the parties had never agreed on a price (*see* the "essential terms doctrine," Lesson 11). Although she did not form a contract with Hunter, Polly likely has a claim in unjust enrichment for the reasonable value of her painting work for Hunter.

As you might imagine, the third element of the test is the one that causes the most problems. To assist in identifying an "unjust" enrichment, courts generally have recognized two important limitations. First, a person cannot assert a claim in unjust enrichment if she conferred the benefit as a ***gift*** (aka "gratuitously" or as a "volunteer"). This is the reason why a philanthropist who makes an unconditional donation cannot demand it back (and why you do not have to worry about returning birthday gifts). Second—in a term you can use to sound smart at parties—the person who conferred the benefit cannot have been an "***officious intermeddler***." The idea here is that the law will not recognize an unjust enrichment claim for someone who sticks her nose in other people's business by conferring benefits on unwilling recipients.

Example

> Misaki, an unemployed house painter, searched her neighborhood and found that Horace's house needed painting. While Horace was on vacation, Misaki swooped in and painted the house, and then demanded payment from Horace. Misaki does not have an unjust enrichment claim. Although she conferred a benefit on Horace and she expected compensation, she was an "officious intermeddler" because her intervention in Horace's affairs was not justified under the circumstances.

The amount of the recovery in unjust enrichment is ***the reasonable value of the benefit conferred***.

Promissory Restitution. A special problem at the border between contract law and unjust enrichment arises where one party first confers a benefit and the other later makes a *promise* to pay for it. This problem has bedeviled the courts. Consider the case of *Webb v. McGowin*, which is in most casebooks.

Example

> Webb risked his life to save his employer, McGowin, from a falling block of wood, but in the process was seriously injured. Thereafter, McGowin promised to pay Webb a defined pension for the rest of his life. When McGowin died, however, his estate refused to continue to honor the promise.

The problem with recognizing a contract in such a case is that Webb already had conferred the benefit at the time of McGowin's promise. And such "past consideration," as we saw in Lesson 10, cannot support a contract because of the absence of a bargained-for exchange. That is, McGowin's promise could not have "induced" Webb's action—as a matter of simple logic—because Webb had already completed the action long before the promise. No inducement = no consideration = no contract.

In the actual case, however, the court simply chose to look the other way. It found that McGowin's promise was binding based on a supposed "presumption" that Webb originally had acted at McGowin's request. This is permitted, the court held, if the act conferred a "material benefit" on the later promisor (McGowin). Although such cases do not arise often, a few other courts have followed this (quite suspect) reasoning.

The modern approach in Restatement § 86 addresses such cases based not on the notion of "material benefit," but instead on the possible existence of an unjust enrichment claim. It begins with a simple rule that empowers the courts to do justice: "A promise made in recognition of a benefit previously received by the promisor from the promisee is binding to the extent necessary to prevent injustice."

But § 86(2) then provides a clear limitation tied directly to the absence of an unjust enrichment claim by the promisee: "A promise is not binding under Subsection (1) . . . if the promisee conferred the benefit as a gift or for other reasons the promisor has not been unjustly enriched." If you think about it a bit, you will see that this rule tracks well with the consideration doctrine. It is based on the idea that when the promisee (Webb in the example) has a valid unjust enrichment claim (at least potentially so) he has a legal right to trade and thus induce the promise *at the very time it is made*. This is so because, as we saw above, unjust enrichment is a distinct legal right of recovery (a "cause of action"). This, then, is the "bargained-for exchange of legal rights": money from the promisor in exchange for a release of the potential unjust enrichment claim by the promisee.

For what reasons would a promisee in such a case *not* have an unjust enrichment claim? Section 86(2) expressly identifies one: if the promisee had conferred the benefit as a gift. Thus, for example, if a passerby—out of the goodness of her heart—puts out a smoldering fire on your lawn and you later promise to pay her $1,000 for saving your house, your promise likely is not binding under § 86. Another reason is in the case of an "officious intermeddler" as discussed above. But note that, depending on the interests of justice in a given circumstance, a court may well enforce a subsequent promise in such a case:

Example

Misaki, an unemployed house painter, painted Horace's house while he was on vacation, thinking that he would be pleased but also expecting compensation. When he returned, Horace promised to pay Misaki $10,000 for her work. A court may enforce Horace's promise under § 86 because concerns about a benefit being "forced onto" a recipient are less compelling when he later makes a voluntary promise to pay for it.

A final noteworthy situation in which an unjust enrichment might not exist is where the promisee was already legally obligated to confer the benefit. We saw in Lesson 10 that a promise to perform an already existing legal obligation is not consideration. On the same reasoning, a promise to pay for a benefit conferred due to an existing legal duty is not binding under § 86.

Example

Pursuant to a contractual obligation owed to Jim, Pia dug a ditch in Jim's yard. Jim was so pleased with Pia's work that he promised to pay her an *extra* $1,000. Jim's promise likely is not binding under § 86. The simple reason is that he has not been "unjustly" enriched by Pia doing what she was already legally obligated to do for him.

Restatement § 86 also ***limits recovery*** on promises made for a benefit already received in another way: the promise is not binding "to the extent that its value is disproportionate to the benefit." The "to the extent" language means that a court may limit the recovery to an amount reasonably close to the *value* of the benefit previously received. Thus, if the actual value of the painting job in the Horace and Misaki example above was only $5,000, a court may decide that justice requires the enforcement of Horace's later $10,000 promise only "to the extent" of $5,000.

What You Need to Know:

1. Restitution is a separate body of law founded on the principle that a person who is unjustly enriched at the expense of another is subject to liability to pay for the benefit received. Restitution is relevant to contract law in situations where a party confers a benefit because of a potential contract, but the contract never existed in the first place, is not enforceable, or is lawfully rescinded.
2. To recover in "unjust enrichment," a plaintiff must show (1) that she conferred a benefit on the defendant; (2) that the defendant had knowledge of and retained the benefit; and (3) that it would be unjust under the circumstances to permit the defendant to retain the benefit without paying for it. The third element is not satisfied if the plaintiff conferred the benefit as a gift or was an "officious intermeddler." The amount of the recovery in unjust enrichment is the reasonable value of the benefit conferred.
3. Under Restatement § 86 a promise made for a benefit already received is binding "to the extent necessary to prevent injustice." This is not the case if the promisee conferred the benefit as a gift or the promisor otherwise was not unjustly enriched.

LESSON 18: THE WRITING REQUIREMENT FOR SOME CONTRACTS

It is a common misconception among non-lawyers that all contracts must be in writing. In fact, generally speaking no such requirement exists under the common law. Nonetheless, every state has a general *statute* that creates a writing requirement, but only for specific categories of important contracts. Because we have a special concern about fraudulent claims for such contracts, the statute commonly is known as "the statute for the prevention of frauds," or, for short, "the Statute of Frauds."

For these specific categories of contracts, the writing requirement represents ***a second layer of protection***. That is, a party seeking to enforce such a contract must *both* satisfy the formation requirements covered in Lessons 2 through 15 *and* show that a satisfactory writing memorializes the contract. (As a formal matter, a failure to satisfy the writing requirement is a defense—like the others covered in Lessons 22 and 23—and thus must be raised by the defendant. Most casebooks nonetheless cover the statute of frauds immediately after contract formation.)

The Traditional Categories. The traditional version of the Statute of Frauds adopted by the individual states requires a writing for five categories of contracts. In the common terminology, these categories of contracts are "within the Statute."

1. A contract by an executor or administrator of an estate to assume a duty of the deceased person (the "***executor-administrator provision***").

Example

John died and in his will named Susan as the executor of his estate. If a creditor of John's claims that Susan agreed that *she* would pay John's debt (out of her own pocket), such a contract would have to be memorialized in a writing to be enforceable.

2. A contract to pay or guarantee the debts of a third person (the "***suretyship provision***").

Example

Tom wants a loan for a new business, but Citibank will grant him the loan only if Tom's rich Aunt Allegra gives a guarantee (*i.e.*, agrees to pay it if he does not). Such a guarantee contract by Allegra would have to be memorialized in a writing to be enforceable.

3. A contract made upon consideration of marriage (the "***marriage provision***").

Example

Lana promises to transfer land to Josiah in order to convince him to marry her. Such a contractual promise would have to be memorialized in a writing to be enforceable.

4. A contract for the sale of an interest in land, including leases and other kinds of real estate transfers (the "***land contract provision***").

Example

Cai concluded an oral contract to sell her house to Tyra. This contract is not enforceable unless it is memorialized in a writing.

5. A contract that cannot be performed within one year of its making (the "***one-year provision***").

   This may be the most difficult category. It applies to a contract only if the involved transaction cannot, *under any circumstances*, be performed within one year of when the contract is made. Thus, for example, a "lifetime" employment contract does not need a writing because the employee could, possibly, die within one year. Likewise, a construction contract that usually would take two years to complete is not "within the Statute" because the construction company could, theoretically, hire thousands of additional workers and complete the project in less than one year. But if the performance is *measured by* a time beyond one year—*e.g.*, a contract of "employment for two years"—the contract must be memorialized in a writing to be enforceable.

In addition, every state has a variety of other statutes that create a writing requirement for specialized subjects. A common example is real estate broker contracts. U.C.C. § 2–201 also creates a writing requirements for ***contracts for the sale of goods over $500***.

Satisfying the Writing Requirement. If a contract is "within the Statute of Frauds," what, exactly, must the parties do to "satisfy" the writing requirement? Restatement § 131 in essence identifies *three requirements*:

First, there must be a ***writing*** (or a set of interrelated writings, see below). Law professors love to play around with this requirement, because it does not mean *only* something made of wood pulp. Rather, any tangible form will suffice (writing on a wall, for example). In addition, effectively all states—spurred by a 2001 federal "E-SIGN Act"—have adopted a uniform statute (the Uniform Electronic Transactions Act–UETA) declaring that electronic records (*e.g.*, e-mails) may satisfy any writing requirement and that signatures made in electronic form may satisfy any signature requirement.

Second, the writing must reasonably identify the essential elements of the contract. In essence, this requirement has two subparts: (1) The writing must contain at least our four familiar ***essential terms*** of a contract (from Lesson 11). U.C.C. § 2–201, however, is very flexible in this regard: the writing need *only* contain the *quantity* of the involved goods. (2) The writing must indicate that a contract "has been made." But note here that *the writing does not have to* ***be*** *the contract itself*—any old writing, including one well after the contract transaction, may satisfy the Statute of Frauds, as long as it indicates that the parties at some point concluded a binding deal. Note also that these content requirements may come in more than one writing if "the circumstances clearly indicate that [the writings] relate to the same transaction," *see* Restatement § 132.

Finally, at least one writing must be "***signed by the party to be charged***." This phrase has tripped up law students from the beginning of time (well, from the first Statute of Frauds in England in the 1600s). The key is not to get confused by the terminology. The idea is simply that a contract within the Statute of Frauds is enforceable *against* a party only if *she* has signed a satisfactory writing. Thus, we care only about the party that wants out of the deal (typically, the defendant as a civil procedure matter). So here is what you must do: identify the party that does *not* want to be held to a contract and (voilà!) that is the "party to be charged," and thus the one whose signature on a writing is required in order to enforce the contract against her.

Example

> Cai and Tyra concluded an oral house sale contract, but *only* Cai signed a writing with the essential terms. If Cai wants out of the deal (and thus is the "party to be charged"), the Statute of Frauds *is* satisfied, and Tyra could enforce the contract against Cai. But if Tyra wants out of the deal (and thus is the "party to be charged"), the Statute is *not* satisfied, with the result that Cai could not enforce the contract against Tyra.

In the case of a set of writings that collectively satisfy the writing requirement, the party to be charged need merely sign one—provided again that the various writings "relate to the same transaction."

Finally, note that the ***CISG***—the treaty we mentioned in Lesson 1 that governs international sale of goods contracts—has no writing or other form requirements *at all*, unless a particular country has declared a specific reservation (and the U.S. has not). *See* CISG Articles 11–12.

What You Need to Know:

1. Each state has a general statute—commonly known as "the Statute of Frauds"—that lists certain categories of contracts that must be memorialized in a writing to be enforceable. When this Statute applies, it creates a second requirement in order to enforce a contract, that is, one in addition to the basic requirements for contract formation.
2. The most common form of the Statute of Frauds applies to five specific categories of contracts. Other specialized statutes also impose a writing requirement, the most prominent of which is a contract for the sale of goods over $500 under U.C.C. Article 2.

3. Three requirements apply to "satisfy" the Statute of Frauds: (1) a writing (or set of interrelated writings); (2) the writing(s) must indicate that a contract "has been made" and contain the essential terms of the contract; and (3) at least one writing must be signed by the "party to be charged," which merely means the party that does not want to be bound to the claimed contract.

LESSON 19: EXCEPTIONS TO THE WRITING REQUIREMENT

Like nearly everything in the law, the law recognizes certain exceptions to the writing requirement discussed in Lesson 18. This lesson examines those exceptions.

Part Performance Exception for Land Contracts. The common law always has had a bit of a fixation on land contracts. As an illustration, courts very early on recognized an exception to the Statute of Frauds where one party has partially performed a land purchase transaction. This is a classic example:

> Sonny entered into an oral contract to buy land from his father, Franco. Sonny paid the purchase price and, with Franco's consent, built a house on the land with his own money. When Franco later died, his other heirs claimed an interest in the land (and the house on it) arguing that because the Sonny-Franco contract was not memorialized in a writing, it was not enforceable due to the Statute of Frauds.

Seeing the injustice of such a situation, the courts in every state recognize a "part performance exception" to the writing requirement for land sale contracts. In general, a claimant (such as Sonny) must satisfy two requirements to rely on this exception: *First*, he must show that he took definite actions in reliance on the oral contract. To assess this, courts commonly focus on the extent to which the buyer has already taken possession of and made valuable, permanent, and substantial improvements. Another way to see this is that, as more such evidence piles up of the existence and terms of a contract, the parties' performance serves the evidentiary function at the core of the writing requirement. *Second*, most courts say that the claimant must be seeking an order for a formal transfer of the land (so-called "specific performance," *see* Lesson 28), as opposed to an award of money damages. This makes enforcement easier, because it avoids potentially messy valuation issues.

The Broader "Reliance" Exception. The drafters of the Restatement very much liked the idea behind the part performance exception for land contracts. They thus took that idea and constructed a general reliance exception applicable to all types of contracts within the Statute of Frauds. The result in § 139 is ***another version of "promissory estoppel"*** (*see* Lessons 12–13). In this case, the claim that is "estopped" is that a contract is not enforceable because of a failure to satisfy a writing requirement. Section 139 states four familiar requirements—*see* Lesson 12 for more detail—for this exception: (1) a promise; (2) the promisor should reasonably have expected the promise to induce reliance by the promisee; (3) the promise in fact induced such reliance; and (4) injustice can be avoided only by enforcement of the promise "notwithstanding the Statute of Frauds."

But § 139(2) also instructs the courts to consider the following ***circumstances in assessing the issue of avoiding injustice***: (a) whether other remedies—such as restitution—are available to protect the promisee (Sonny in the above example); (b) the extent to which the promisee's actions in reliance were "definite and substantial"; (c) the extent to which the promisee's actions "corroborate" the existence and terms of the contract or "clear and convincing evidence" otherwise exists to that effect; (d) the reasonableness of the promisee's reliance; and (e) the extent to which the promisee's reliance was "foreseeable by the promisor."

Example

> By oral contract, ADP in Alaska hired Kathleen Rice in Maryland to assume an important post for two years. In reliance on this, Rice quit her job and moved to Alaska. Shortly thereafter, ADP terminated Rice and, citing the writing requirement for contracts over one

year, refused to pay her for the remaining time on her two-year oral contract. The court applied § 139 and enforced ADP's promise notwithstanding the Statute of Frauds. After applying the relevant factors of § 139, the court found that Rice otherwise "would be a victim of injustice."

However, the various state courts are all over the map—if you excuse the pun—on acceptance of Restatement § 139's general reliance exception. Some state courts have *adopted it for all contracts* within the Statute of Frauds. Some states *reject it for some categories* (such as employment contracts). Other courts *reject it for all contracts*, reasoning that the courts should not create an exception that would trump a statute passed by the legislature.

U.C.C. § 2–201 also recognizes a set of exceptions for its own writing requirement. The first is the ***merchant's confirmation exception*** in § 2–201(2), which has five requirements: (a) following an oral contract, one party sent a written confirmation that was "sufficient against the sender" (*i.e.*, was signed by the sender and otherwise satisfied the content requirements noted above); (b) both parties to the transaction were "merchants" (*see* the summary definition from § 2–104(1) in Lesson 5); (b) the confirmation was sent within a reasonable time of the oral contract; (d) the recipient received it and had "reason to know of its contents"; and (e) the recipient did not object to it within ten days of receipt. In such a case, the contract is enforceable against the recipient even though he did *not sign* a satisfactory writing.

In-Court Admission Exception. U.C.C. § 2–201(3)(b) recognizes an exception where a party "admits in his pleading, testimony or otherwise in court" that the parties concluded a contract. This "in-court admission exception" creates a delicate ethical problem for a lawyer: If a client admits that she concluded an oral contract, the lawyer may not make contrary factual claims in court. Nonetheless, the Statute of Frauds is a separate legal defense, and thus it is widely acknowledged that the lawyer properly may seek to preserve it in a legal proceeding.

Finally, the U.C.C. also has its own ***part performance exception*** in § 2–201(3)(c). This exception disregards the writing requirement with respect to goods "for which payment has already been made and accepted" (which runs in favor of a buyer) *or* "which have been received and accepted" (which runs in favor of a seller).

(U.C.C. § 2–201(3)(a) also has a quite detailed specially manufactured goods exception that your professor likely will not cover in any detail.)

What You Need to Know:

1. The courts have recognized exceptions to the writing requirement in the Statute of Frauds. By far the most common is the part performance exception for land contracts.
2. Restatement § 139(1) also recognizes a general reliance exception that parallels the promissory estoppel doctrine for the formation of contracts. Section 139(2) instructs the courts to consider specific factors in weighing whether justice requires enforcement of a contract notwithstanding the Statute of Frauds. Nonetheless, not all states have adopted this general reliance exception.
3. The U.C.C. recognizes exceptions for its Statute of Frauds. The most important ones are (a) the merchant's confirmation exception, (b) the in-court admission exception, and (c) the part performance exception.

LESSON 20: PRINCIPLES OF CONTRACT INTERPRETATION

The subject we take up in this lesson is what happens when the parties clearly formed a contract but then disagree about the meaning of one or more of its terms. Such disputes of interpretation are among the most common contract law cases in the case reporters. Unfortunately, on this subject it is very hard to summarize the law because the various state courts sometimes follow quite different approaches and often use quite different terminology in describing the rules. Our goal here thus will be to review the structure of analysis that most courts follow and to point out where the courts diverge within this structure.

The Meaning of Contract Terms. Let's start with a basic principle that all courts seem to follow: the fundamental rule of contract interpretation is to give effect to the parties' shared intent. This may seem to violate our standard objective approach to issues of intent—and in a certain sense it does. The idea, however, is not all that strange: if *both* parties agreed at the time of contract formation that a term has an idiosyncratic or specialized meaning different from what might appear to an external observer, then that agreed meaning prevails. As one court has explained, "parties, like Humpty Dumpty, may use words as they please. If they wish the symbols 'one Caterpillar D9G tractor' to mean '500 railroad cars full of watermelons,' that's fine—provided [the] parties share this weird meaning." But as you might imagine, most often it is *very* difficult for a party to prove this shared meaning if it differs from the ordinary meaning of the words the parties actually used in their contract.

The Restatement **(§ 201(2))** takes this notion even further in a situation where the parties attached *different* meanings to a term. It states that one side's meaning prevails if the other party had "reason to know" of that meaning. This is a version of the traditional objective standard of interpretation and it may have relevance in some special situations. But for most contract interpretation disputes, the courts generally follow the structure described below.

Written Contracts and the Special Role of the Judge. Most disputes over interpretation arise because the parties failed to agree expressly at the time of contract formation and now disagree over the meaning of the contract's terms. But in order to analyze this common situation, we must step back and review the respective roles of judges and juries. You certainly will have heard repeatedly by this point in the first semester of law school that the judge (aka "the court") decides issues of *law* and the jury decides issues of *fact*. In this allocation of responsibility, the judge may resolve a case as a matter of law and without a jury only if there are no disputed issues of material fact ("summary judgment" from your lessons on civil procedure). For a contract that is entirely oral, issues of fact will abound (who said what and when, etc.) and thus most often a jury will have to resolve disputes over contract interpretation.

Things are different, however, when the parties put down some or all of their contractual agreements in a *final writing*. (The formal term for this is an "integrated" writing, *see* Lesson 21.) This is so because the fundamental rule in most (if not all) of the states is that the formal ***interpretation of a written contract is an issue of law*** for the court. But what if one party argues that the written words are ambiguous, such that issues of fact arise about what happened during the parties' negotiations? Such a situation in essence requires a two-stage analysis:

Step One: Is the Contract Ambiguous? In the first stage, the judge must decide whether the disputed contract term is "ambiguous." Courts most often say that language in a written contract is ambiguous if it is "reasonably susceptible to more than one meaning." If the judge concludes that the contractual language is *un*ambiguous, then it will decide the case on that basis as a matter of law and on its own (*i.e.*, without a jury). Most often, this happens by "summary judgment" long before a trial could begin. Unfortunately, the states diverge substantially on exactly *how* a judge should make such a determination.

One camp follows the traditional ***"plain meaning" approach*** (as supported by the "four corners" rule). It is here that the objective standard of interpretation plays its most potent role. Under this view, the judge must read *only* the words in the writing (*i.e.*, within its "four corners"). The judge may consider the entire writing, not only the specific words in dispute; but it will not allow the parties to submit other, so-called "extrinsic" evidence—that is, evidence outside of the writing—in deciding whether the disputed contractual language is ambiguous. (Some law professors are highly critical of this approach; they argue that language is never so fixed and precise that it can convey a "plain meaning" without consideration of the context in which it was used.)

Another camp instead follows the ***"contextual" approach***. Under this view, in deciding whether disputed language is ambiguous the court also must consider (in the words of a Maryland court) "the character of the contract, its purpose, and the facts and circumstances of the parties at the time of execution." This means that the court will allow the parties to submit—beyond arguments about the meaning of the contractual writing—other evidence about the intent of the parties such as affidavits of persons involved in the negotiations, other documents, etc. This approach obviously leaves much more room for argumentation about whether terms in a writing that appear to have a "plain meaning" in fact are ambiguous. Many courts in this camp nonetheless limit the allowable evidence at this stage to objective evidence (and thus not evidence about one party's subjective intent or understanding).

Three forms of extrinsic evidence are particularly potent for the contextual approach: (a) If a contract involves repeated occasions for performance—say, a painting contract that covers ten successive houses—a "***course of performance***" by one party without objection by the other may provide strong evidence of their shared understanding about a disputed term (and may even reflect a formal contract modification). (b) Similarly, if the parties had done similar deals in the *past*—say, if they had performed nine separate house painting contracts before their latest one—a "***course of dealing***" regarding a particular issue may provide a common understanding for interpreting their latest deal. (c) Finally, if the parties are knowledgeable about the practices or methods in a particular industry—say, a house builder and a house painting company—a regularly observed "***usage of trade***" in that industry may provide a context for interpreting a disputed term in their contract. Indeed, these forms of interpretive evidence are so powerful that U.C.C. § 2–202 instructs a court to consider them *regardless* of whether it thinks the parties' contract is ambiguous. *See* § 2–202, Official Comment 1(c).

But as a matter of emphasis, under either the "plain meaning" or the "contextual" approach if the judge finds that the disputed language is *un*ambiguous, it will resolve the case as a matter of law (*i.e.*, without a jury) on the basis of the objective meaning of the words in the contractual writing.

Stage Two: Interpretation of Ambiguous Contracts. If, however, the judge determines that disputed contractual language is ambiguous, then the issue becomes one of *fact* for the jury in a trial (or in the case of an agreed "bench trial," for the judge as a finder of fact). At the trial, the parties may submit any evidence (including, of course, extrinsic evidence beyond the writing) that sheds light on their intention at the time the writing was executed. This does not become a free-for-all, however. The judge will permit the parties to present only evidence that sheds light on a meaning to which the disputed language is "reasonably susceptible." Some courts say in this vein that the parties may present only evidence that is within a "zone of reasonableness."

Example

> A buyer and seller entered into a contract covering a quantity of "chickens." Unfortunately, a dispute arose when the buyer contended that the term meant only "young" chickens, but the seller contended it meant less valuable "stewing" chickens. The court found that the term "chicken" was ambiguous. It then permitted the parties to submit evidence within the bounds of the meaning of "chicken" (but not that the term meant, for example, bowling balls).

Canons of Construction. Over time, the courts also have developed certain "canons of construction" that function as a "rule of thumb" for interpretation. There is a whole raft of them, and some even conflict with others. The most commonly used ones (often accompanied by Latin terms) are the following:

1. If one party was entirely responsible for drafting a contract or a particular provision, a court will interpret any ambiguity against that drafter (*contra proferentem*);

2. Handwritten terms are preferred over pre-printed terms;
3. Specific terms are given greater weight than general language;
4. The meaning of a term in a list is affected by theme of the others on the list (*noscitur a sociis*);
5. A general term associated with specifically enumerated items is presumed to be limited to things of same nature as those specifically enumerated (*ejusdem generis*). An example might be a contract to sell "oil, gas, and other minerals" on a plot of land: given that "oil and gas" are fossil fuels, the general term "other minerals" would not include gold or silver; and
6. If a contract specifies certain things, it impliedly excludes other things of the same nature (*expressio unius exclusio alterius*). An example might be a contract to sell "all gold and silver ores" on a plot of land—the inclusion of only "gold and silver" would preclude any argument that the parties agreed to sell other ores (such as platinum).

As a descriptive matter, when a court applies such a "canon of construction" it usually does so to conclude that a disputed term is not ambiguous (and thus that it can resolve the dispute over contract interpretation as a matter of law).

What You Need to Know:

1. If *both* parties agreed at the time of contract formation on the meaning of a specific term (even one that differs from the objective interpretation), that agreed meaning prevails. This is very difficult to prove, however.
2. The interpretation of a written contract is an issue of law for the court (judge).
3. Under a first stage of interpretation, the judge must decide whether a disputed term is ambiguous. Some courts follow a "plain meaning" rule on this issue; others, however, also consider

other evidence from the circumstances surrounding the execution of the writing. If—under either approach—the court concludes that the disputed term is unambiguous, it will apply that objective meaning as a matter of *law*.

4. If, in contrast, the court concludes that the disputed term is ambiguous, then the issue becomes one of *fact* for the jury—to determine, based on all relevant evidence, what the actual shared intent of the parties was.

5. Courts sometimes apply a variety of "canons of construction" to determine whether contractual language is ambiguous.

LESSON 21: THE PAROL EVIDENCE RULE; IMPLIED TERMS AND GOOD FAITH

Lesson 20 reviewed the interpretation of terms actually in a contract, especially one in writing. Here we address a related situation: where the parties have put their agreement in writing but one of them argues that *another* promise, understanding, etc., exists that is *not* in the writing. This is the subject of the "parol evidence rule" (the absent "e" in parol is not a typo)—or PER for short. Unfortunately, the PER is among the most confusing and misunderstood rules in all of contract law. (Because of the related subject matters, some casebooks cover both contract interpretation and the PER under the general heading, "Effects of Adopting a Writing.")

The Purpose of the PER. Let's begin with the basic purpose of the PER: if the parties have gone to the hassle of putting some or all of their agreement down in a final writing, the law ought to protect that writing against attacks based on prior evidence from the outside. The purpose, in short, is to advance the certainty and predictability of contracts by permitting the parties to rely on the terms they reduce to a final writing. The law achieves this result by having the judge decide *in advance* whether a party even may present evidence that would contradict, or in some cases even add to, the terms of the writing. Thus, effectively all subjects in this lesson on the PER are issues of law for the judge to decide.

Unfortunately, the very title of the "parol evidence rule" is misleading. First, the word "parol" means something that is oral. But the PER protects a final writing against *all* evidence—whether oral or written—that is prior to or contemporaneous with the creation of the writing. Second, the PER is not really a rule of "evidence"; rather, it is a substantive rule of contract law that governs the definition of the parties' contractual rights and obligations. Well, now that we have cleared that away, let's get to what the PER says and does.

The Three Layers of PER Analysis. The PER in essence has three layers of analysis depending on the force of the writing at issue. The *first layer* just asks whether the writing is relevant *at all*. The PER does not protect all written agreements, only those that are "***integrated***." But don't trip over this fancy word—it just means that the parties have reduced at least part of their agreement to a ***final writing***. Restatement § 209 thus defines an "integrated agreement" merely as "a writing or writings constituting a final expression of one or more terms of an agreement."

Thus, a mere proposal for, or a draft of, a contract most often will not represent a *final* writing that would trigger the PER. In such a case, the writing will not preclude either party from offering evidence that their *real* contractual deal is entirely different.

Example

> In May, in connection with negotiations over a painting contract, Remod Inc. sent Hotelco a proposed "deal terms" document which, among other things, had a section on "scope of work." At some later point the parties in fact concluded an oral contract. But Hotelco now wants to introduce evidence from April that Remod also agreed to repair the plasterwork in the hotel rooms, even though the "scope of work" section of the May document did not mention this. If the court concludes that the May document was not a *final* expression of any part of the parties' deal, the PER

> rule would not preclude Hotelco from introducing evidence of the supposed other agreement from April.

Another way to see this issue is that if a writing is not an agreed *final* expression by the parties on anything, then the PER does not apply *at all*.

The *second layer* of PER analysis kicks in when a writing reflects the parties' final agreement on at least *part* of their contractual deal. The law calls this a "***partially integrated***" agreement. (In a real sense, this second layer follows directly from the first, and in fact some professors collapse the two into one layer of analysis because, by definition, a final writing reflects at least a partially integrated agreement.) As one court has explained, "A partially integrated writing is one that the parties intended to be a final expression as to the terms in the writing, but not as to all the terms of their agreement." If a writing is at least partially integrated, the PER applies to protect the final writing. It does so by prohibiting a party from introducing evidence of an alleged prior or contemporaneous promise, understanding, agreement, etc., that would conflict with the unambiguous terms that are in the writing—but only those terms. *See* Restatement § 215.

Example

> Following the example above, assume that the judge instead concludes that the May "deal terms" document in fact expressed the parties' final agreement on the specific subject of the "scope of work." In such a case of a "partially integrated" agreement, the PER would preclude Hotelco from introducing evidence of any claimed prior agreement that would conflict with the "scope of work" section of the May document.

Substantial disputes nonetheless can arise about what, actually, is a "conflict." In the above example, Hotelco may argue that the scope of work section only covered *painting* work, and thus that the claimed agreement on *plasterwork* does not conflict with the "scope of work" section of the May document.

The *third layer* of PER analysis addresses whether the final writing also covers the *entirety* of the parties' contractual deal. Restatement § 210(1) defines such a "***completely integrated***" agreement as a writing "adopted by the parties as a complete agreement and exclusive statement of the terms of the agreement." You might view such a writing as saying, "Our entire deal is in this writing—and there are no other agreements between us." In such a case, a party may not introduce evidence even of a claimed *additional* agreement that is *consistent* with the terms of the writing. A completely integrated agreement thus represents the totality of the contract to the exclusion of all prior claimed promises, understandings, agreements, etc.

Example

> Following the above example, assume that the judge also concludes that Remod and Hotelco assented to the May "deal terms" document as the final agreement on their *total* contractual deal. In such a case of a "completely integrated" agreement, the PER also would preclude Hotelco from introducing evidence even of a consistent additional term (*i.e.*, on a subject not addressed in the writing at all).

The challenge is *how* to determine whether a final writing reflects a completely integrated agreement (as opposed to merely a partially integrated one). Unfortunately, the courts diverge on this issue—but they generally do so along the lines discussed for contract interpretation in Lesson 20: (a) Some courts follow the four corners rule, and thus decide the issue of complete integration based solely on reading the writing at issue. Such courts are especially influenced by an "integration" (or "merger") clause in the writing (*e.g.*, "The Parties agree that this writing reflects the entirety of their agreement on the subject matter hereof.") (b) Most courts and the Restatement in contrast also consider the surrounding circumstances—such as how complete and detailed the writing is; the relationship between the parties; how sophisticated the parties are; whether lawyers were involved; and the formality of the setting in which the writing was executed. Separately, Restatement § 216 says that a court should conclude that a writing reflects only a partial integration to the extent that the claimed extrinsic agreement is one that, under the circumstances, "might naturally be omitted from the writing." The idea here is that the parties likely would not put in a final writing covering one subject (say, a land sale contract) an agreement that is part of the overall deal but nonetheless is on an entirely different subject (say, to deliver flowers to the seller's grandmother).

A full understanding of the PER nonetheless requires four important clarifications. First, the PER rule does not apply if the language in the writing itself is ambiguous. In such a case we have an issue of interpretation as covered in Lesson 20. Second, the PER does not block evidence designed to show that the parties had no contract in the first place, or that a defense to enforcement exists (*see* the next two lessons), or that a party is entitled to a particular remedy for breach of the contract (*see* Lessons 27 and 28). Third, the PER only addresses agreements that were prior to or contemporaneous with the creation of the writing. Any *later* agreements may serve to explain the meaning of terms in the writing or even reflect an agreed modification of the contract (*see* Lesson 24). Finally, the PER reflects only a threshold question for a judge about whether a party may *introduce evidence* about a prior agreement outside of a final writing. If the judge determines that the PER does not preclude such evidence, the proponent must still *prove*, as a matter of fact, that the parties actually had such a prior extrinsic agreement.

The U.C.C. and the PER. The approach of U.C.C. § 2–202 to the PER is essentially the same as the common law. In two respects, however, the U.C.C. is more flexible than the common law. First, § 2–202 states that even a final writing may be supplemented by the three potent forms of extrinsic evidence noted in Lesson 20: course of performance, course of dealing, and usage of trade. Second, the official comments to § 2–202 observe that evidence of a prior consistent additional agreement should be excluded if the agreement "certainly" would have been included in the writing under the circumstances (as compared to "naturally" under the Restatement).

The CISG and the PER. For international sale of goods, the CISG—the international treaty noted in Lesson 1—entirely rejects any form of a parol evidence rule. *See* Articles 8(3), 11.

Implied Terms and Good Faith. Another challenge courts confront in resolving interpretation disputes arises from the fact that, as a practical matter, the parties to a future contract do not have the time, money, or even desire to negotiate over every petty detail that may be relevant to their deal. And some understandings are so routine or obvious that the parties do not even discuss them, nor certainly put them down in writing.

The most famous case in which a court confronted this issue is *Wood v. Lucy, Lady Duff Gordon*. There, a famous designer (Lady Duff Gordon—incidentally, a survivor of the Titanic) granted to Wood the exclusive right to market her designs. A dispute then arose over the scope of Wood's obligations. The court held that, although Wood made no express promise, the circumstances of the parties' deal, and especially the grant of *exclusive* rights, reflected an "implication of a promise" by Wood to make "reasonable efforts" to market the designs. (In the same vein, the U.C.C. imposes a "best efforts" obligation for exclusive dealing arrangements. *See* § 2–306.)

Over time, the courts began to see that similar notions are at the foundation of most deals. Thus, every state (and the U.C.C., *see* § 1–304) now recognizes in some form an "implied covenant of good faith and fair dealing" in every contract. Though easily stated, the nature of this implied term is subject to substantial controversy. Nonetheless, a broad consensus holds that the implied duty of good faith does not create a free-standing obligation of charity or kindness, and that it may not trump a carefully negotiated, express term of a contract. Rather, it prohibits a party from taking affirmative steps to frustrate the right of the other party to receive the benefits of the contract. It also has special relevance when a contract gives one party a discretionary power during performance; in such a case, the duty of good faith operates—unless carefully negated in express contract terms—to require the exercise of such discretion in a way that is consistent with the other party's reasonable expectations at the time the contract was formed.

Example

A franchise contract for a local restaurant required the franchisor's approval for any relocation. When the franchisee began losing money, the franchisor refused both to grant a relocation request and to communicate with a potential buyer of the franchise at the same location. It turned out that the franchisor secretly wanted to replace the existing franchisee with a "company store" and was looking for an excuse to do so. The court held that these actions frustrated the reasonable expectations of the franchisee and thus reflected a violation of the implied covenant of good faith and fair dealing, with the result that the franchisor breached the contract.

[Your professor also may mention—though likely will not—the implied warranties imposed by the U.C.C. for sale of goods contracts. "Warranty" is merely a fancy term for a promise about the quality of goods. The U.C.C. automatically imposes (unless negated in the contract, *see* § 2–316) an implied warranty by the seller that sold goods are of at least average quality ("merchantability," *see* § 2–314) and that they are fit for any "particular purpose" for which the buyer requires them if the buyer justifiably relied on the seller's expertise in choosing them (*see* § 2–315).]

What You Need to Know:

1. The parol evidence rule (PER) advances certainty in contract law by protecting a final writing against claims of prior promises, understandings, agreements, etc. (a) But it only applies in the case of a writing that is a *final* expression of at least part of the parties' agreement. (b) In the case of such a "partially integrated" agreement, the PER precludes the introduction of evidence of any claimed prior agreement that would *conflict* with the terms of the writing. (c) In the case of a "completely integrated" agreement, the PER *also* precludes the introduction of evidence of a prior *consistent* additional agreement.

2. However, the PER (a) does not apply if the language in the writing itself is ambiguous; (b) does not block evidence that no contract existed in the first place or that supports a defense or remedy; (c) does not apply to later agreements; and (d) is only a threshold evidentiary question on whether a party may *try* to prove a prior agreement not set forth in the writing.

3. All states and the U.C.C. recognize a "covenant of good faith and fair dealing" in every contract. This implied contract term prohibits a party from frustrating the right of the other party to receive the benefits of the contract and also precludes the exercise of discretionary powers in a way that is inconsistent with the reasonable expectations of the parties at the time the contract was formed.

LESSON 22: PRE-FORMATION DEFENSES, PART I

With this lesson we turn to an entirely new subject matter: the situations in which the law precludes the *enforcement* of a contract even though all of the requirements for contract *formation* have been satisfied. We begin in this lesson with contract "defenses"—*i.e.*, those based on events that existed at the time of contract formation (because there are so many, they spill over to Lesson 23).

The analysis for each defense is quite straightforward: you need merely identify the elements of the test and then see whether the facts of a particular case satisfy that test. The result for all is essentially the same: where a party has a defense, the other party may not enforce the contract. Stated in an affirmative way, a party with a defense has a power to "avoid" the contract by asserting the defense. But because defenses are protective, the reverse is not true: the party with a defense may choose to enforce the contract *against* the other party. If a party asserts a valid defense, each side will have a restitution claim against the other for any benefit previously conferred. *See* Lesson 17.

The Statute of Frauds (a Reminder). As a quick reminder, the statute of frauds (*see* Lesson 18) also is a defense. That is, where the statute applies the defendant must raise the issue in its "answer" to the plaintiff's "complaint." Only then must the plaintiff prove that the statute of frauds is satisfied for the contract at issue.

Minority. This is perhaps the easiest of the defenses: someone who concludes a contract while under the age of eighteen has a right of "disaffirmance" (which equates to a right to avoid the contract). An exception is for contracts that involve "necessaries" (food, clothing, etc., when not provided by parents). Again, because this is a defense, the "infant" may enforce a favorable contract against the other party (whether through her parents or, after turning eighteen, through her own "ratification" of the contract). Some dispute exists, however, over whether, upon such a disaffirmance, the minor must return only that which she then has (the traditional view) or instead must account for any broader benefits she gained from the prior use of the subject matter of the contract.

Mental Incapacity. The defense of mental incapacity is a bit more complicated because of the broad range of relevant conditions. Nonetheless, the trend seems to be in favor of the approach in Restatement § 15. Under this approach, if a person enters into a transaction "by reason of mental illness or defect" he will incur only "voidable contractual duties" in two situations: The first is if he is "unable to understand in a reasonable manner the nature and consequences of the transaction." This is the traditional notion of a person who lacks the mental capacity to know that he is entering into a contract at all. The second situation is where a person "is unable to act in a reasonable manner" in deciding to enter into the transaction. The idea here is person who has the requisite understanding but enters into a contract under a mental compulsion (*e.g.*, bipolar disorder, formerly "manic-depressive illness"). For this latter category, however, the person will have a defense only if the other party had "reason to know of [the] condition" at the time the contract was made. (The Restatement test for a defense based on intoxication is basically the same, *see* § 16.)

Restatement § 15 also recognizes, however, that unfairness might arise if the other party in fact did not *know* of the mental illness. If that is true, no defense will exist "to the extent that the contract has been so performed in whole or in part or the circumstances have so changed that avoidance would be unjust." In such a case in which the "*status quo*" cannot be restored, the court has the power to craft a remedy "as justice so requires."

Duress arises where a person uses a threat to compel another to enter into a contract. A defense on this basis has two elements: (a) an improper threat; and (b) the threat induces assent by the victim because she had no reasonable alternatives (*i.e.*, the threat precludes the exercise of free will). The word "improper" (some courts say "wrongful") is the most difficult aspect of this test. In the long ago past, the only threats that supported a duress defense were those that involved death or bodily harm. Today, however, "improper" is understood to mean almost any threat of a crime or tort; of criminal prosecution; or of bad faith use of civil process or breach of an existing contract.

This more modern approach makes clear that "***economic duress***" also is a defense. The idea here is that a threat to cause extreme economic hardship also may leave the victim with no reasonable choice but to enter into a contract with the wrongdoer. A standard example is where a contract already exists, but one party uses the other's financial distress to extract a favorable contract modification or some other contractual advantage. Often, this involves a bad faith threat to withhold a scheduled payment or other needed goods or services. This does not mean that the law now bans hard bargaining; rather, the victim must prove that under the circumstances it had no reasonable alternative but to accede to the wrongdoer's bad faith demands—and often simply filing a breach of contract lawsuit (or just saying "no") is a viable alternative.

Undue Influence. The defense of "undue influence" is similar in some respects to duress but does not require a wrongful threat. The idea here is that someone knowingly takes undue advantage of another's weakness in order to secure a favorable contract. It is generally understood to require two elements: (1) lessened capacity by the weaker party to make a free contract, even if only temporary. This may be due to age, physical condition, emotional anguish, or a combination of these or similar factors; and (2) intentional application of excessive strength by the dominant party, including based on an existing relationship with the weaker party. On this element, the courts have considered a variety of factors surrounding the making of the contract, such as whether the negotiation or conclusion of the contract took place at an unusual time or place; insistent demands for prompt action; extreme emphasis on the consequences of delay; the use of multiple persuaders; and the absence of third-party advisors for the weaker party.

Mutual Mistake. The defense of mutual mistake arises where both parties wrongly assume some important background fact is true at the time the contract was formed. The standard test has four elements: (a) a mistake of fact by both parties (that is, both parties knew that the deal was based on a particular fact (later determined to be untrue), even if one of them would benefit from the situation); (b) the mistake was about "a basic assumption on which the contract was made"; (b) the mistake turns out to have a "material," adverse effect on one party; and (d) the adversely affected party did not bear the risk of the mistake.

The last element very often is the most important one. Obviously, a party bears a risk if the contract itself so provides. But a party also bears the risk in a case of so-called "conscious ignorance"—that is, where the party knew of a particular risk at the time of contract formation but did nothing to protect itself. Finally, Restatement § 154 states that a party bears a risk when it is allocated to him by the court "on the ground that it is reasonable in the circumstances to do so," such as when that party is an expert on the subject matter of the risk or otherwise was in the best position to investigate that risk.

Example

> Lumberco contracted to buy a tract of land from Owner. Both parties knew that Lumberco's principal reason for concluding the deal was to harvest valuable

lumber on the land. But they did not know that a forest fire had destroyed all of the lumber the day before. Lumberco likely has a defense of mutual mistake if the fire was completely unexpected and the contract said nothing about the subject. But this would not be the case if Lumberco knew, for example, that dry conditions in the area had already caused a number of forest fires—for then a strong argument would exist that Lumberco assumed the risk that such a forest fire would occur.

A separate, but related claim arises where both parties are mistaken about the *contents of a writing*. This is quite rare and, as a practical matter, only comes up when a third party prepares the writing (such as a surveyor who errs in the technical description of sold land). In such a case, the disadvantaged party may request the court to "reform" the writing to say what *both parties* thought it said in the first place.

Unilateral Mistake. The defense of "unilateral" mistake arises where only one party is mistaken about a basic assumption of the deal. The courts are substantially more skeptical about this defense than about mutual mistake. The first four elements are the same (other than, of course, the first): (a) a mistake of one party; (b) the mistake is about "a basic assumption on which the contract was made"; (c) the mistake has a "material" adverse effect on the mistaken party; and (d) that party did not bear the risk of the mistake. Again, such claims commonly founder on this fourth element. But the test for unilateral mistake also has another important element: (e) The mistaken party must prove that either (i) enforcement of the contract would be unconscionable, or (ii) the other party had "reason to know" of the mistake (or caused the mistake).

Example

In a bidding contest for the building of a house, Contractor made a calculation error and submitted a bid that was 25 percent lower than the others. Not surprisingly, Owner accepted that bid. Contractor should be able to satisfy the first three elements of a unilateral mistake defense: (a) it made a mistake (although unknown to Owner) in calculation; (b) this was a basic assumption of Contractor's bid; and (c) the 25 percent underbid likely has a material effect on the transaction. But Contractor may have difficulty proving (d) that it did not assume the risk of the mistake. (e) It also would have to prove either (i) that enforcement of the contract would be unconscionable (which may be difficult) or (ii) that the Owner had "reason to know" of the mistake (which may be true from the fact of the 25 percent lower bid) or that the mistake was the Owner's fault (which is very unlikely).

What You Need to Know:

1. In some situations the law recognizes a defense to the enforcement of properly concluded contracts. But only the protected party may raise the defense and she thus may choose to enforce a favorable contract. If a contract is so "avoided" based on a defense, each party will have a restitution claim for any benefit previously conferred on the other.

2. The recognized defenses include: the statute of frauds (*see* in Lesson 18); minority; mental incapacity; duress; undue influence; mutual mistake; and unilateral mistake. Lesson 23 will cover more such defenses.

LESSON 23: PRE-FORMATION DEFENSES, PART II

This lesson continues the examination of pre-formation "defenses" to the enforcement of a contract.

Misrepresentation. The defense of misrepresentation arises where one party makes a factually inaccurate statement that convinces the other party to enter into a contract. The defense has three elements: First, the party must make a misrepresentation = "an assertion that is not in accord with the facts" (Restatement § 159). But be careful here. The assertion must be about an existing *fact*. A statement of opinion or a prediction about the future does not suffice. Thus, a salesperson's general claim that a Range Rover is "awesome" is not a statement of fact. Also, a person's statement about what she intends to do in the future is not a misrepresentation unless she in fact does not have that intent at the time (something that is very difficult to prove).

Second, the misrepresentation must have induced the other party to enter into the contract (in the words of Restatement § 167, it must have "substantially contribute[d]" to the other party's decision to manifest his assent). Some courts explain this element as requiring that the other party believed the statement of fact to be true and relied on it in entering into the contract.

Finally, the misrepresentation must have been *either* "fraudulent" *or* "material." Under Restatement § 162(1), a ***fraudulent misrepresentation*** exists if the maker both (a) intends the assertion of fact to induce the other party to enter into the contract *and* (b) (i) "knows or believes" that the assertion is not true; (ii) "does not have the confidence that he states or implies in the truth of the assertion"; *or* (iii) "knows that he does not have the basis that he states or implies for the assertion." If this test is satisfied, a defense to enforcement of the contract arises *irrespective* of the importance of the misrepresented fact (although some courts unthinkingly state that even here the misrepresented fact must be "material"). Note also that, beyond this consequence in contract law, fraud may subject the wrongdoer to tort liability (including punitive damages) and even criminal liability (such as jail time—ouch!).

An entirely innocent misrepresentation also creates a defense if it involves a ***material*** fact. Restatement § 162(2) defines a misrepresentation as "material" if "it would be likely to induce a reasonable person to manifest his assent, or if the maker knows that it would be likely to induce the recipient to do so." The important point here is that a party's misrepresentation of a material fact may create a defense even if he did not know of its falsity and did not intend to defraud.

Example

In negotiating over a sale of her house to Bridget, Innocent stated that the foundation had "no problems." Unknown to Innocent, the foundation in fact had hidden structural flaws. Bridget likely may avoid the contract based on the defense of misrepresentation. Although Innocent knew nothing of the flaws in the foundation, that fact likely was "material" under the circumstances (*i.e.*, would have caused a reasonable buyer not to conclude the house sale contract). This would not be the case, however, if Bridget did not reasonably rely on the statement (such as if Bridget actually hired a structural engineer who negligently missed the foundation problems).

Nondisclosure. In some cases, a failure to disclose a known fact can have the same effect as an affirmative misrepresentation. The law thus recognizes a defense for nondisclosure as well. This defense comes in two flavors. The first, *concealment*, is easy: where a party takes affirmative steps to prevent the other party from learning about a fact. This might arise, for example, if a house seller intentionally paints over cracks to conceal structural flaws in the foundation. Restatement § 160 states that such an action "is equivalent to an assertion that the fact does not exist" (*i.e.*, a misrepresentation).

The second flavor, a mere nondisclosure of a fact, presents a more challenging problem. A basic principle of contract law is *caveat emptor*—the buyer beware. Thus, the law does not require that contract parties disclose every potentially relevant fact or otherwise constantly look out for the interests of the other party. Rather, contract law recognizes a defense for nondisclosure only in narrow, important categories: (1) where a party made a representation that was true at the time but because of subsequent events it has become a misrepresentation (or fraudulent or material); (2) where a party knows that the other is making a mistake as to a "basic assumption" of the deal and the non-disclosure "amounts to a failure to act in good faith and in accordance with reasonable standards of fair dealing." In its essence, this rule creates a duty to disclose where one party knows that the other is operating under a mistake and basic norms of honesty and fairness require disclosure. (Note the parallel—though not an exact one—with the defense of unilateral mistake covered in

Lesson 22.); (3) where a party knows that disclosure would correct a mistake of the other party as to the contents or effect of a writing; or (4) where a party is obligated to disclose a fact "because of a relation of trust and confidence" with the other party. *See* Restatement § 161.

The final situation is closely related to a separate defense, "***constructive fraud***." (The law uses the word "constructive" when it knows a situation does not meet a particular legal test, but nonetheless wants to treat it the same way.) This defense arises where someone fails to disclose a fact in breach of a fiduciary or confidential relationship. A fiduciary relationship is one imposed by *law* as automatically requiring trust and protection (such a lawyer to her client or a guardian to his ward). A confidential relationship arises as a matter of *fact* where one person does not look out for her own interests because she justifiably places "trust and confidence" in the judgment of the other party. Close family relations are the most common example. In either situation, if the two parties conclude a contract and the obligated party does not disclose all relevant facts, the protected party will have a defense to the enforcement of any disadvantageous contract.

Contract of Adhesion. In general, a party cannot escape his obligations by arguing that he did not read the contract document. But many courts have recognized what is in effect a separate defense for unexpected terms in a "contract of adhesion." (Restatement § 211(3) classifies this doctrine as a question of contract formation, but the courts have treated it as they would a defense.) A contract of adhesion is a standardized form offered to consumers on a "take it or leave it" basis and thus with no realistic chance to bargain over its terms. In such a case, a court will not enforce the terms of the contract that were "beyond the reasonable expectations" of the adhering (that is, the weaker) party at the time of formation. The classic example of a contract of adhesion is an insurance contract—and indeed, with very few exceptions, the courts have applied this doctrine only for such contracts.

Unconscionability. Despite this fancy word, the defense of "unconscionability" basically means that a court will not assist in enforcing a contract that "shocks its conscience." A much more flexible defense than contract of adhesion, unconscionability applies based on a composite consideration of unequal bargaining power and substantively unfair terms. Thus, the courts consider two factors: (1) "procedural" unconscionability, which focuses on the extent to which the weaker party's assent resulted from unequal bargaining power (which in turn means that this defense rarely succeeds in contracts between experienced commercial parties); and (2) "substantive" unconscionability, which focuses on the extent to which the contract's terms are "overly harsh and one-sided" for the weaker party. The prevailing view is each factor must be true, at least a little bit. (You might think of this as requiring that the two factors together equal 100 percent, but that as little as 1 percent can come from one of them.)

Example

> In connection with a sale of a chair, a furniture company had an unsophisticated woman with little formal education sign a standardized form contract. Included in the "legalese" of the form was a complicated clause providing that, if the woman did not pay in a timely manner, the company could seize not only the chair but *everything* purchased from the store *at any time in the past*. The court found that because of the combined force of the unequal bargaining power (the procedural factor) and the oppressiveness of the term (the substantive factor) the seizure clause was "unconscionable" and thus unenforceable.

Unconscionability may preclude enforcement of the entire contract or (unlike most other defenses) merely a specific contract term.

Public Policy (and Illegality). In rare circumstances, a court will refuse to enforce a contract (or, here again, merely one contract term) based on "public policy." In the extreme version, this defense applies where a contract involves an illegal act (such as a contract for murder), or where specific legislation forbids a particular kind of contract (such as a loan contract with a usurious interest rate). Beyond these clear examples, however, an overly expansive public policy defense can undermine the certainty of contractual deals. The Restatement test (§ 178(1)) also is quite open-ended. It states that a contract term is unenforceable based on public policy if "the interest in its enforcement is clearly outweighed in the circumstances by a public policy against the enforcement of such terms."

Precisely because the test is so vague, the courts have been quite hesitant to invalidate voluntary deals on public policy grounds. Nonetheless, four examples from recent cases will give you a sense of where courts have found that fundamental public interests outweigh the benefits of private bargaining: (a) contracts that unreasonably restrain free trade (such as an overly broad restriction on an employee's right to compete with her former employer—your professor may explore such contracts in great detail); (b) contracts that affect close family relations (such as surrogacy contracts where a woman is paid to carry a child); (c) contracts that release a person from tort liability for his own intentional or "grossly negligent" acts—although courts generally permit such "exculpatory clauses" for simple negligence; and (d) contracts that unreasonably affect the rights of third parties (such as, in a small but growing number of states, where parents conclude contracts for their children that release third parties from liability even for simple negligence).

What You Need to Know:

1. The law also recognizes these other defenses to the enforcement of contracts: misrepresentation; nondisclosure; contract of adhesion; unconscionability; and illegality and public policy.
2. Unlike the other defenses, the defenses of contract of adhesion, unconscionability, and public policy empower a court to invalidate only the specific objectionable term(s) and leave the rest of the contract intact.

LESSON 24: POST-FORMATION EXCUSES; CONTRACT MODIFICATIONS

The prior two lessons examined defenses to the enforcement of a contract based on a fact or action that affected the parties' bargaining process right from the beginning. This lesson takes up the "excuses" to performance—that is, based on events that occur *after* contract formation. (The Restatement describes this notion as a "discharge" of a duty to render performance.) This lesson also reviews the special rules for contract modifications.

In general, the law considers contracts as a form of "strict liability." Thus, a party is liable for failing to perform a contractual promise (*i.e.*, a breach) even if she made every reasonable effort to perform (that is, even if the non-performance was not her fault). Long ago, however, courts began to open the door a bit with the excuse of "impossibility" of performance. Today, the law recognizes two related excuses in the same vein: (1) impossibility/impracticability of performance; and (2) frustration of purpose.

Impossibility/Impracticability of Performance. In its most fundamental form, this excuse is based on the simple notion that a party should not be held liable for breach of contract if some unexpected event after contract formation makes it impossible for her to perform. Consider as an extreme example a singer who dies and thus is unable to perform at a scheduled concert. In this vein, the Restatement recognizes as examples of actual impossibility the death or incapacity of a necessary person (§ 262); the destruction, etc., of a necessary thing (§ 263); and prevention due to an unexpected governmental regulation or order (§ 264)

Originally, the law recognized such an excuse only where performance became *literally* impossible. If, for example, a contract required delivery of a large product to a remote area, no excuse arose if a freak flood destroyed the only bridge to that area—because it would still be *possible* to deliver (using boats, etc.). Today, however, the courts recognize a bit (but only a bit) more flexibility with the doctrine of "impracticability of performance." This term covers situations in which performance is possible but only with "extreme and unreasonable difficulty, expense, injury, or loss." But again, the words "extreme and unreasonable" leave a very high bar.

With this background, we can turn to the general four-part test for an excuse based on impossibility/impracticability (*see* Restatement § 261 and U.C.C. § 2–615): (a) An event occurs after contract formation that makes performance impracticable ("extreme and unreasonable," *see* above); this is not the case, however, if the affected party is able to overcome the effects of the event through the exercise of reasonable efforts. (b) That this event would *not* occur was a "basic assumption on which the contract was made." This element reflects the principle that the law only provides protection for unexpected events that affect a material aspect of the parties' contractual bargain. (c) The adversely affected party was not at fault in causing the event. (d) The adversely affected party did not bear the risk that the event would occur.

Like the pre-formation defense of mistake, the last element often is the most important one. The courts have phrased the underlying principle in a variety of ways. Some say that the event must not have been reasonably "foreseeable" at the time of contract formation. Restatement § 261 uses the more flexible phrase "unless the language or the circumstances indicate the contrary." In any event, this element captures the notion that a party will not have an excuse if it reasonably was aware at the time of contract formation that the event could occur, but it failed to protect itself.

Example

> Builder contracted to construct a house for Owner. Unfortunately, shortly before Builder was able to complete construction a fire destroyed the entire structure. Builder likely does not have an excuse for impracticability. It likely could prove (a) that the fire made timely performance "extreme and unreasonable"; (b) that the non-occurrence of the fire was a "basic assumption" of the parties' contract; and (c) that it was not at fault for causing the fire. But it likely would have difficulty proving (d) that it did not bear the risk—because it controlled the construction site and

should have taken greater precautions against such a fire. Thus, it would be liable to Owner for not completing construction on time.

A common way for a party to protect itself in this regard is through a so-called *force majeure* clause in the contract itself. Such a clause says, for example, that a party does not have to perform in the event of fires, floods, "Acts of God" (weather), war, civil unrest, labor strikes, etc. But the danger of crafting such a list is that a court will find that the party impliedly assumed the risk of anything *not* stated there (*see* the "*expressio unius*" principle in Lesson 20).

Frustration of Purpose. This excuse is similar to impracticability, except that the relevant event does not affect *performance* of a contract but instead a party's *purpose* for concluding the contract. The classic example is *Krell v. Henry*, which involved a contract to rent a room to view the king's coronation parade. Unfortunately, the parade was postponed when the king became ill. The postponement did not affect the renter's *performance* at all (he still could pay); but it took away the fundamental *purpose* for renting the room at the specific time scheduled for the parade.

Beginning with *Krell v. Henry*, the courts saw that this was another appropriate situation for an excuse from performance. Frustration of purpose requires essentially the same four elements as impracticability. The only difference is the first element: an event occurs after contract formation that "substantially frustrates" one party's "principal purpose" for concluding the contract. The words "principal" and "substantial" are important. As Restatement Comment (d) to § 265 explains, (a) "[t]he object must be so completely the basis of the contract that, as both parties understand, without it the transaction would make little sense," and (b) the frustration "must be so severe that it is not fairly to be regarded as within the risks that [the party] assumed under the contract." Again, the remaining three elements are the same as for impracticability.

Example

Roadco concluded a contract to rent from Leaseco a concrete mixing machine. Both parties knew that Roadco only needed the machine because the government had just awarded it a contract to build a highway. The government then cancelled the highway project. Although the cancellation does not affect Roadco's ability to pay for the machine, it may have excuse for frustration of purpose based on the test described above—provided especially that it did not assume the risk of the government's cancellation (*i.e.*, that the cancellation was not reasonably foreseeable at the time it concluded the contract with Leaseco).

Contract Modification. Subsequent developments often cause parties to modify, or even fully terminate, their contracts. To do so, they need a new, separate contract—because again to change their legal relationship they must make new, legally binding promises. Thus, the parties need a mutual manifestation of assent (*see* Lessons 2 through 8), new consideration (*see* Lessons 9 and 10), and an agreement on essential terms (*see* Lesson 11, although this rarely is an issue because modifications commonly build on the essential terms of the original deal).

The consideration doctrine nonetheless poses special challenges where an agreed modification changes the obligations of only one side. Under the "legal duty rule" discussed in Lesson 10, such a deal would lack consideration, because the other side is merely promising to do what it is already legally obligated to do under the original contract. (No such issue should arise for a complete termination contract because each side gives up its legal rights under the existing contract in exchange for the reciprocal rights of the other.)

Nonetheless, agreed one-sided modifications can facilitate valuable adjustments to later developments. As a result, both the U.C.C. and the Restatement relax the consideration requirement for contracts that modify existing contracts. Indeed, for sale of goods contracts, ***U.C.C. § 2–209(1)*** declares categorically that a modification "needs no consideration to be binding." To protect against unfounded claims on this basis, however, § 2–209(2) validates contractual agreements that prohibit oral modifications of written contracts (so-called "no oral modifications" (NOM) clauses) and § 2–209(3) requires a writing if, as modified, the contract involves goods over $500 (*see* Lesson 18).

Restatement § 89 states more generally that a promise to modify a contract not yet fully performed "is binding" (that is, without additional consideration) if it is "fair and equitable in view of circumstances not anticipated by the parties when the contract was made." This rule often comes up in construction contracts when the parties encounter unexpected obstacles:

Example

> Excavator concluded a contract with Developer to clear a lot for a building project. Shortly after beginning, Excavator discovered a substantial amount of previously unknown hazardous waste. Developer then promised Excavator $50,000 extra (a fair amount) to complete the excavation work. After Excavator did so, however, Developer—citing the consideration doctrine—refused to pay the extra $50,000. The parties likely concluded a binding modification contract under Restatement § 89. Because (a) they had not anticipated the hazardous waste and (b) the modification deal was fair, Developer's $50,000 promise is binding notwithstanding the "legal duty rule."

Some states also have a general statute that dispenses with the consideration requirement for contract modifications that are in writing.

What You Need to Know:

1. The law grants an excuse from the duty to perform a contract based on impracticability where an event occurs after formation that is contrary to a basic assumption on which the contract was made and makes performance "extreme and unreasonable." The adversely affected party also must not have been at fault for the event and must not have assumed the risk that it would occur.

2. The law recognizes a separate excuse based on frustration of purpose where an event occurs after formation that "substantially frustrates" one party's "principal purpose" for entering into the contract. The other three elements are essentially the same as the test for impracticability of performance.

3. For an agreement to modify an already existing contract, the U.C.C. abolishes and the Restatement substantially relaxes the consideration requirement.

LESSON 25: EXPRESS CONDITIONS TO PERFORMANCE

If the parties have formed a contract and no defenses to enforcement exist, the parties obviously must *perform* their contractual promises. And as we saw in Lesson 24, contract law imposes "strict liability," with the result that *any* failure to perform, however small, is a breach. But note the obvious point that a party generally cannot breach her promise until the time that she is obligated to perform it. (If I promise to mow your lawn tomorrow, I cannot breach that promise until, well, tomorrow.) Thus, a breach is any failure to perform "when performance . . . is due." Restatement § 235(2). This lesson begins our analysis of this fundamental "when" question with the ability of a party to include in her contract an "express condition to performance."

Express Conditions. Assume that Bertha wants to buy a horse from Sheng, but *only* if it is fully free of disease. Bertha of course can get a *promise* from Sheng that this will be true. But consider what happens if Sheng breaches the promise: Bertha must take and pay for the diseased horse—subject to something we will cover in the next lesson—and then sue Sheng to recover the damages due to the disease. That of course can be a costly and hassle-filled problem for Bertha.

This is where the notion of an "express condition" comes in: Bertha can put in her contract with Sheng a clause stating that she does not have to perform her part of the deal *at all* if the horse has any disease. Restatement § 224 defines such an "express condition" as "an event, not certain to occur, which must occur . . . before performance under a contract becomes due." Notice again the connection with whether a party's performance "becomes due." If a party's performance is subject to an express condition, then her duty to perform "cannot become due unless the condition occurs." Restatement § 225(1).

Example

> Bertha included the following clause in her contract with Sheng: "Bertha's obligation to perform under this contract is subject to the condition that veterinarian Ann Vetter certify that the horse is free of all disease before noon on our closing date in one month." If this event does not occur, then Bertha will have no obligation to perform her contractual promises (take and pay for the horse) *at all*.

Express conditions are powerful tools, for the law ***strictly enforces*** them. That is, for express conditions "close" is not enough. Thus, in the above example, Bertha would have no obligation to take and pay for the horse if veterinarian Vetter finds even the *slightest* disease. This point also is illustrated by a "***time is of the essence clause***" (a common express condition). If Bertha's condition also included such a clause, she could refuse to buy the horse if the veterinarian missed the noon deadline by as little as one minute. And once the stated time has passed such that the condition cannot ever occur, Bertha's duty to perform is forever "discharged." Restatement § 225(2).

But express conditions also can be valuable tools that permit deals to happen in the first place—for they allow the parties to conclude contracts even under substantial uncertainty. They are particularly common in complicated corporate deals, such as mergers and acquisitions: The parties enter into a binding contract, but each states expressly the conditions that must be satisfied before the scheduled "closing date" set some months later. In the interim—this is very important—both parties *remain bound* to the contract. This, also, is where lawyers come in. After signing the contract each side sends out its lawyers to do "due diligence" on whether the stated conditions are satisfied. If any stated condition is not satisfied (say, the buyer's lawyers find fraud in the seller's accounting books), the beneficiary of the condition (the buyer in the example) may refuse to close the deal.

Because a condition is so powerful, however, the law requires that it be stated explicitly. Most often, courts require clear conditional language, such as "if," "unless," "provided that," or "on the condition that." A mere statement of obligation or expectation—*e.g.*, "the horse shall be free of disease"—will not suffice. In such a case, the language reflects not a condition, but rather a promise by the other party that the event will occur.

But this again highlights the significant ***difference between promises and conditions***. A failure to fulfill a promise results in liability for breach; the non-occurrence of a condition does not have this effect, however, because no one promised that the event would occur. Thus, in the horse example, if the veterinarian finds a disease, Sheng is not liable for breach. Bertha merely has the right to walk away from the deal. However, if a party (say, Bertha) has enough bargaining power, she can demand *both* an express condition tied to the future event *and* a separate promise by the other party (Sheng) that the event will occur. In such a case, Bertha would be in a very powerful position if the veterinarian does not make the required certification: She can either (a) completely walk away from the deal because of the non-occurrence of the condition, or (b) waive the condition (see below) and sue Sheng for breach of contract.

Conditions of Satisfaction. A special issue arises where one party's performance is conditioned on being satisfied with some event, most often the performance of the other party (a "condition of satisfaction"). An example is where a person commissions an artist to paint a "satisfactory" portrait. Without some limitation, a strict interpretation of "satisfaction" would put the artist at the mercy of the portrait buyer. It is here that the implied duty of "good faith" discussed in Lesson 21 plays an important role, for it requires that the beneficiary of the condition exercise good faith in deciding on whether she is satisfied.

But what does "good faith" mean? Well, it depends. The law divides such conditions into two categories: (1) For those conditions that involve "aesthetics, taste, or fancy" (*e.g.*, a portrait as above), a "subjective satisfaction" test applies. Good faith here means only whether the person *honestly* was dissatisfied (and it is *very* hard to prove otherwise). (2) In contrast, for those conditions that involve "commercial quality, operative fitness, or mechanical utility" (*e.g.*, a machine or a building) an "objective satisfaction" test applies. Good faith in this context means whether a *reasonable person* under the circumstances would have been satisfied (a standard subject to examination by expert witnesses).

Excuse of Conditions. Because, again, express conditions can be so harsh (with the strict enforcement rule), the law recognizes a few "excuses" for non-occurrence. The first is if the beneficiary acts in bad faith to prevent the occurrence ("prevention" or "interference"). This would be the case, for example, if Bertha kidnapped veterinarian Vetter and held her hostage until after the closing date. Second, the beneficiary may "waive" the condition, that is, knowingly and voluntarily give up its benefit. This commonly occurs if the beneficiary decides that she nonetheless wants to go ahead with the deal. Third, the beneficiary may be "estopped" to enforce the condition. This occurs where her words or conduct cause the other party justifiably to take detrimental actions on the belief that the beneficiary would not enforce the condition. (*See* Lesson 12 for more on the doctrine of estoppel.) Fourth, under Restatement § 229 a court may excuse non-occurrence if the other party would suffer a "disproportionate forfeiture," provided that the condition was not a "material part" of the parties' deal. The idea here is that a court may excuse the non-occurrence of a condition if it is only minor or technical in nature (*e.g.*, a simple notification requirement under an insurance contract) and the other party would suffer a major loss if the condition is enforced (*e.g.*, the loss of the entire insurance payment). Finally, in rare cases a court may excuse a condition if its occurrence becomes impracticable (say, veterinarian Vetter dies) and the other party would otherwise suffer a forfeiture—provided again that the condition is not a material aspect of the parties' deal (*see* Restatement § 271).

What You Need to Know:

1. An express condition permits a party to make its performance contingent on the occurrence of a specified event. The law strictly enforces such "express conditions." If the event does not occur precisely as stated, the party's duty to perform does not become due at all.
2. Generally, courts require that an express condition be stated clearly. In the case of doubt, the clause at issue is interpreted only as a promise by the other party that the event will occur.
3. For "conditions of satisfaction," a subjective (personal satisfaction) test applies for contracts that involve "aesthetics, taste, or fancy," but an objective (reasonable person) test applies for contracts that involve "commercial quality, operative fitness, or mechanical utility."
4. The law recognizes a variety of "excuses" for the non-occurrence of a condition. These include prevention, waiver, estoppel, disproportionate forfeiture, and impracticability.

LESSON 26: CONSTRUCTIVE CONDITIONS; MATERIAL BREACH; ANTICIPATORY REPUDIATION

This lesson continues with the "when" question first examined in Lesson 25. If all express conditions have occurred (or been excused), how do we know when a party's performance "is due," such that a failure to perform amounts to a breach of contract? That is the question we examine in this lesson.

Constructive Conditions of Exchange. The parties of course can expressly define in their contract when each is obligated to perform, and commonly they do so. But what rule applies if the parties' contract identifies a date, but does not state the order (*i.e.*, which party must perform first). In such a case, each side likely will say to the other, "You go first," because neither wants to stick its neck out and be forced to trust that the other will perform later. In such a situation, the law creates a "default" rule: (a) If it is *possible* for both parties to perform at the *same time* (say, exchanging money for a deed to real estate), then they *must* perform at the same time; (b) if, in contrast, one party's performance takes longer (say, building a house), then that party must perform *first*. *See* Restatement § 234.

But precisely because this is such an important question, the law also "constructs" a ***conditional relationship*** between the parties' respective performance obligations. (That sentence is a mouthful, but don't give up.) The idea is simply this: the law assumes that each party enters into the contractual deal on the basis, "I don't have to perform if you don't perform." In fancier terms, the law assumes that each party's duty to perform is conditioned on the other party timely performing its obligations (a "condition of exchange"). And recall from Lesson 25 that a "condition" is something that must occur before a party's performance obligation becomes due. Thus, if the parties are obligated to perform at the same time, Restatement § 238 states that "it is a condition of each party's dut[y] to render [her] performance" that the other party perform "his part of the simultaneous exchange" (or at least make a "tender" of it = offer to perform with a present intent and ability to do so).

Example

> Petra contracted to sell her house to Sylvia for $250,000 "free of all mortgages and liens" on October 1. Because the two performances can occur at the same time (delivery of deed and payment of money), each party's duty to perform is conditioned on the other party performing her obligations at the same time. Thus, if Petra shows up on October 1 with a deed encumbered by a mortgage (or does not show up at all), Sylvia is not obligated to pay the purchase price. The reverse is true if Silvia does not show up with the proper amount of money.

If, in contrast, one party must perform some or all of its obligations first—based on the terms of the parties' contract or the fact that one performance takes longer (see above)—then the other party's duty to perform is conditioned on that longer performance in a timely manner occurring first. This also is true for complicated deals where each party has a variety of performance obligations at different times. In such a case, each party's duty to perform at any given time is conditioned on the other party having timely performed in a timely manner any required earlier obligations. *See* Restatement § 237.

Example

> Archie contracted to design a house for Kalinda for $25,000. Because designing a house takes longer than paying money, it is a condition to Kalinda's obligation to pay the $25,000 that Archie *first* complete the design (subject to the *very* important point about material breach immediately below).

But—and this is important—these "constructive" conditions created by law are ***not strictly enforced*** (in contrast to the express conditions created by the parties' express agreement, see Lesson 25). Instead, they are subject to a test of reasonableness. As stated in a famous case, *Jacob & Youngs v. Kent*, "Intention not otherwise revealed may be presumed to hold in contemplation the reasonable and probable." Thus, a condition constructed by the law is satisfied—with the result that the other party's performance obligation "becomes due"—if a party comes reasonably close to fulfilling her contractual obligations.

Material Breach vs. Partial Breach. We noted in Lesson 25 that *any* failure to perform fully and on time is a breach. But how much of a delay or defect in performance will fail to satisfy the "reasonably close" (these are our words) standard of a constructive condition of exchange? The law answers this question with the concept of "material" breach. That is, if a party commits a material breach and does not cure it in a timely manner, then the constructive condition to the other party's duty to perform is *not* satisfied. The result is that the other party is "discharged" from her duty to perform the contract (but nonetheless retains a right to damages for breach, see below). If, in contrast, the non-performance amounts only to a "partial" breach, then the condition *is* satisfied and the other party must perform his part of the deal (but again retains a right to damages).

Example

> Returning to the Petra and Sylvia example above, assume that a search on September 30 revealed a $500 lien on the house by an unpaid plumber. This lien reflects a breach of contract by Petra. But it is so small that Petra's performance satisfies the constructive condition to Sylvia's obligation to perform (*i.e.*, is only a "partial" breach). Thus, Sylvia would be obligated to take and pay for the house (but may of course withhold $500 as damages).

Whether a breach is material is an intensely factual question that depends on each specific contract and situation. But courts have identified a variety of ***factors to consider*** (*see* Restatement § 241): whether the injured party has received the substantial benefit of what he was entitled to expect under the contract; the extent to which damages would adequately compensate for the harm; the extent to which the breacher would suffer a forfeiture; the extent of uncertainty about the breacher's ability to cure; and the extent to which the breacher acted in good faith. Of these, however, the most important typically is the first—whether the performance fulfilled the essential purpose of the contract, such that the injured party substantially received what he was entitled to expect under the contract. If the breacher then does not cure a material breach in a timely manner—including with reference to the importance of delay under the parties' contract and the ability of the injured party to make substitute arrangements—the injured party's duty to perform under the contract is "discharged." Restatement § 242.

The law also uses the term "***substantial performance***" as a sort of opposite for material breach. That is, if a party has "substantially" completed her performance obligation, then no material breach has occurred. Courts especially like to use the "substantial performance" terminology in construction contracts.

Example A

Developer contracted to construct a house for Buyer. Upon completion, Buyer discovered defective carpeting in a guest bedroom. Although this represents a breach, the house still may be used for its intended purpose (human habitation). Thus, very likely Developer has "substantially performed" (*i.e.*, the carpet breach is not material). As a result, Buyer must take and pay for the home (but has a right to damages).

Example B

Assume, instead, that the defects were in the roof and the house is now exposed to damaging elements such as rain and snow. This likely would not reflect "substantial performance" (*i.e.*, would be a "material" breach) because Buyer is not able to live in the house. Unless Developer cures within a reasonable time, Buyer has a right to refuse to perform its part of the deal (*i.e.*, has a right not to buy the house).

Most often, the question of material breach arises when a dispute has thrown the deal entirely off track and both parties have refused to continue with performance. Thus, one of them clearly has committed a material breach and the opportunity for a timely cure is lost. When the dispute reaches court, each side in effect will say, "Mommy, he hit me (materially) first"—that is, each will argue he was justified in ceasing his performance because the other party committed and failed to cure an earlier material breach.

The Consequences of Breach. As the above examples show, the consequences differ fundamentally if a breach is only partial as opposed to material. In the case of a *partial breach* (*i.e.*, the breacher nonetheless has substantially performed such that the constructive condition of exchange is satisfied) the injured party must perform her part of the deal and her only remedy is a claim for damages (as examined in Lesson 27).

A uncured *material breach*, in contrast, gives the injured party an important choice among three options: (a) She may declare an immediate material breach, withhold her own performance, and seek full contract damages (again, *see* Lesson

27). (The Restatement refers to a right to damages for "total breach," but—except for subtleties—the concept is the same.) (b) She instead may elect to treat the breach as partial only and continue with her own performance (in essence thus waiving the materiality of the breach), but nonetheless reserve her right to damages for the breach. She would do this if, for example, the contract is part of a broader transaction, time is short, and no viable alternatives exist. (c) Finally, she may choose to rescind the contract entirely and sue in restitution. The idea here is that, because the breacher in effect has destroyed the contract through his material breach, the injured party has a right to rescind it as a formal matter. Lesson 28 will examine this alternative in more detail.

Anticipatory Repudiation. We noted in Lesson 25 that a party "generally" cannot breach his promise until the time that he is obligated to perform it. The concept of an "anticipatory repudiation" addresses the situation in which a breach can occur *before* a duty to perform "becomes due."

An anticipatory repudiation is a ***"definite and unequivocal manifestation" of an intent to commit a material breach*** when the performance comes due. Like all manifestations, this may occur either through a statement by the obligated party or "a voluntary affirmative act," in this case one that "renders [him] unable or apparently unable to perform without such a breach." Restatement § 250. If this test is met, the other party may treat the words or conduct as an immediate material breach (with all the related rights, see above) even though the obligated party's duty to perform has not yet become due.

A party who believes that her contract partner may have committed an anticipatory repudiation must be very careful, however—for the words "definite and unequivocal" set a high bar. If this test is *not* met, and the party nonetheless withholds or ceases her own performance, then *she* has committed the first material breach—giving the contract partner all of the related rights noted above.

Example

Constructo Corp. contracted to build a shed for Bernie for $5,000 by July 1. In early June, Constructo e-mailed Bernie stating, "We are having some scheduling challenges." When nothing happened in the next two weeks, Bernie on June 20 wrote a letter declaring that Constructo had committed an anticipatory repudiation and that "our contract is terminated." If Constructo's lack of progress and early June e-mail amounted to a "definite and unequivocal" manifestation of an intent to commit a material breach on July 1, then Bernie's June 20 letter was justified. But if Constructo did not so manifest an anticipatory repudiation (say, because it only takes five days to build the shed), then Bernie committed an anticipatory repudiation (the first material breach) with his letter.

Moreover, a repudiator may ***"retract" the repudiation*** by notification, provided that the other party has not previously (a) "materially change[d] his position in reliance on the repudiation" or (b) "indicate[d] to the [repudiator] that he considers the repudiation to be final." Restatement § 256(1). Finally, courts generally require that, in order to recover damages for material breach based on an anticipatory repudiation, the injured party prove that *she* would not have committed a material breach when *her* performance came due.

Right to Request Adequate Assurance of Performance. Because of the high bar, a party may have substantial doubt about whether the other party's words and conduct amount to an anticipatory repudiation. This can leave her in a delicate situation, especially if timely performance is particularly important under the circumstances. In such a case, the law provides a little bit of relief in the form of a "right to request adequate assurance of performance." Specifically, Restatement § 251 provides that if "reasonable grounds arise to believe" that the other party will commit a material breach when performance comes due, then a party "may demand adequate assurance of due performance." If reasonable, she also may suspend her own performance pending such an assurance. A failure by the other party "to provide within a reasonable time such assurance of due performance as is adequate under the circumstances," then constitutes an actual anticipatory repudiation (even if the original words or conduct did not).

What You Need to Know:

1. The law constructs a conditional relationship between the parties' respective performance obligations. Unlike express conditions, however, these "constructive conditions of exchange" are not strictly enforced.
2. Rather, such conditions are not satisfied only in the case of a "material" breach (aka non-substantial performance). Courts have identified a variety of factors to assess whether a breach is material, but the most important typically is whether the performance fulfilled the essential purpose of the contract.
3. The consequences differ fundamentally depending on the degree of the breach. In the case of a "partial" breach, the injured party's only remedy is a claim for damages. A uncured "material" breach, in contrast, gives the injured party an important choice: She may (a) cease her own performance, declare an immediate material breach, and seek full contract damages, (b) treat the breach as partial only and proceed to perform (but nonetheless seek damages), or (c) rescind the contract and sue in restitution.
4. A party can commit a material breach before his performance becomes due through an "anticipatory repudiation." In the event of uncertainty, the other party may have a "right to request adequate assurance of performance."

LESSON 27: THE STANDARD REMEDY—RECOVERY OF EXPECTATION DAMAGES

In this lesson, we examine the standard "expectation" measure of damages for breach of contract as well as the recognized limitations on the recovery of such damages. Lesson 28 then will cover the two alternative measures of damages: "reliance" and "restitution."

The Basic Test. As we noted in our very first lesson, enforceable contract rights are essential to the functioning of a modern economy. Through contract law, our society creates a structure within which private persons can enforce the beneficial deals that they make with others. This principle also is at the foundation of the measure of damages in the event of a breach: the law seeks to put an injured party in the positions he would have been if the contract had been performed as promised—that is, it gives him the "benefit of the bargain" that he was entitled to expect under the contract.

Restatement § 347 sets forth the standard test for such "expectation" damages: A person injured by a breach of contract is entitled to recover (a) "the loss in the value to him" from the other's party's failure to perform, *plus* (b) "any other loss" caused by the breach, *less* (c) "any cost or other loss that he has avoided by not having to perform." Distilled to simpler ideas, this rule is pretty straightforward: The injured party is entitled to recover the lost *benefits* he was entitled to receive under the contract, plus any *other losses* he sustained because of the breach, less any losses he *avoided* from not having to perform his side of the deal.

(a) "Loss in Value." In its essence, the expectation measure of contract damages is "forward-looking"—for it seeks to put the injured party in the position he *would have been* (in the future) if the contract had been performed as promised. The core part of this concept is the "loss in value" from the other party's failure to perform. The classic example is a 1929 case from New Hampshire, *Hawkins v. McGee*:

Example

> Hawkins had a damaged hand from an accident. McGee (a doctor) promised a "100% perfect hand" if Hawkins would permit him to try out a new skin-grafting procedure. The surgery was a failure, and in fact left the hand worse than before. The trial court awarded Hawkins only an amount corresponding to

the *negative* effects of the surgery, but the state supreme court reversed. The proper measure for breach of contract, the supreme court held, was expectation damages. Under this measure, Hawkins was entitled to damages measured by the difference between the value of his hand in its present state and the value it would have had to Hawkins if McGee had fulfilled his "100% perfect hand" promise.

In most cases, the basic "loss in value" measurement thus involves comparing, as a monetary matter, (a) the value of the breached contractual promise in the relevant market (often called the fair market value) with (b) the injured party's actual position after the breach. Expectation damages are measured by the difference. Thus, for example, if Shawn breaches a contract to sell his SUV to Brianna for $10,000 and the SUV actually is worth $12,000, Brianna recovers $2,000 in expectation damages (the "benefit of her bargain"). But this example also emphasizes a fundamental message: the injured party only recovers her ***net expectation***. That is, when the law speaks of "putting the injured party in the position she would have been if the contract had been performed as promised," we must take into account what *she* was obligated to do under the contract as well.

Example

Tanya had a contract with Eric to paint his house for $10,000 and she expected to spend $9,000 to do so. Eric then breached the contract even before Tanya could begin. Tanya's expectation damages are $1,000. She was entitled to expect $10,000 from Eric; but because of the breach, she avoided $9,000 in costs that she expected to incur. Thus, she recovers only her *net* expectation of $1,000.

The same result obtains if, to replace the non-performance by the breacher, the injured party must conclude a substitute transaction with a third party. In such a case, expectation damages correspond to the difference between (a) the price in the original contract and (b) the amount the injured party had to pay in the required substitute transaction.

Example

> Seller breached a contract to supply a quantity of gasoline to Buyer for $50,000. To cover its own commitments, Buyer then had to pay a third-party supplier $60,000 to obtain that quantity of gasoline in a timely manner. Buyer's expectation damages are $10,000 = the difference between what it would have paid if the original contract had been performed as agreed ($50,000) and what it had to pay the substitute third-party supplier ($60,000).

(If, as in this example, the transaction involves the sale of goods, the U.C.C. has its own damages rules. *See* §§ 2–701 through 2–715. But these rules track the basic principles discussed here.)

"Diminution in Value" vs. "Cost of Performance." In some cases (especially construction cases), the "loss in value" calculation can be tricky. The problem is illustrated by this situation:

Example

> Under a mining lease with Groves, the John Wunder Company promised to restore Groves's land to a level state at the end of its operations. It failed to do so. When Groves brought a claim for his expectation damages, however, he confronted this problem: if the land were leveled as promised, its value would increase by $12,000 at most. But the cost of getting another company to do the leveling work was $60,000. What are Groves's expectation damages: the *lost market value* of his land from John Wunder failing to perform ($12,000) or the *cost* of actually getting the promised performance from a third party ($60,000)?

Restatement § 348 addresses such situations by letting the injured party choose (within limits): he may recover *either* the "diminution in value" *or* the "cost of performance" as long as the latter "is not clearly disproportionate to the probable loss in value." The *Groves vs. John Wunder Co.* case is in many casebooks because this "clearly disproportionate" test could go either way.

(b) "Other Losses." The basic "loss in value" test only relates to the non-performance of the contract at issue. But what if a breach of that contract causes the injured party to sustain losses from *other* transactions? The term for such losses is "consequential damages," and they can be much, much larger than the core "loss in value." But the law permits the injured party to recover these as well.

Example

> Seller breached a $100,000 contract to deliver pistons to Buyer, an engine manufacturer. Because of this breach, Buyer was not able to perform dozens of downstream contracts with *its* engine-buying customers, who then asserted total damages claims against Buyer of $5 million. When it sues Seller for breach of the piston contract, Buyer may be able to recover as "consequential damages" the $5 million in losses that it sustained from having to pay the claims by its downstream customers.

Because the stream of such damages may be almost unending, however, the four limitations discussed below are particularly important for the recovery of consequential damages.

Another term you will run across is "*incidental damages*" (although they tend to be much less important than consequential damages). These are any extra costs the injured party incurs in the performance of the core contract. Assume, for example, that Buyer and Seller are in the same town and Seller breaches their contract. If Buyer then incurs extra expenses to pick up the contract goods from a distant supplier, it may recover these "incidental" damages as well.

(c) "Losses and Costs Avoided." As a matter of fairness, expectation damages should be *reduced* if the injured party gets some benefit from not having to perform its part of the contract. Assume, for example, that an employee earning $100,000 under a three-year contract is wrongfully terminated after two years, but then gets a one-year job with another employer at $95,000. That $95,000 is a loss that the employee *avoided* after the breach. Not surprisingly, the law takes this benefit into account by reducing the recoverable damages to the net amount of $5,000. Separately, the "costs avoided" part of this rule is a reminder that the injured party may recover only her *net* expectation. (Recall the Tanya and Eric example above.)

The law also recognizes ***four limitations on the recovery of contract damages***. These apply to all damages, but are principally relevant to consequential damages.

(1) The first is so obvious that it sometimes is not even emphasized (or is rolled into the second limitation below): the damages claimed by the injured party must have been ***caused*** by the breach. (If your landlord breaches your lease, you may not recover as "damages" the money you lost at a casino that day.)

(2) The second limitation relates to proof: the injured party's recovery is limited to the damages that she is able to ***prove to a reasonable degree of certainty***. This requirement extends to both the fact and the amount of damages. Nonetheless, courts tend to be quite flexible on this rule; often, if the injured party is able to prove that it sustained *some* damages, courts instruct juries—who ultimately decide on damages—that the *amount* need not be proven with "mathematical certainty" as long as the damages are not "speculative." In contrast, courts are more exacting on the proof requirement regarding *new businesses*, whose future profits and prospects tend to be more uncertain.

(3) The third limitation is that an injured party may recover only those damages that were ***reasonably foreseeable*** at the time of contract formation. The classic example is an English case from the 1800s, *Hadley v. Baxendale.*

Example

> A mill contracted with a transportation company to deliver a broken crankshaft to its manufacturer to construct a replacement. The transportation company delayed in delivering the crankshaft, and as a result the mill was forced to stop production for a number of extra days. When the mill sued for its lost profits for those extra days (*i.e.*, consequential damages), the court held that the transportation company was not

liable. It reasoned that the idling of the mill for those extra days was not a loss reasonably within the contemplation of the parties at the time they concluded their contract.

The modern rule in Restatement § 351 is essentially the same: a party may not recover damages that the breacher "did not have reason to foresee as a probable result of the breach when the contract was made." Notice that the test is not whether the breacher *knew* of the possible damages, but rather whether it had "reason to know" that they might occur (*i.e.*, whether the losses were foresee***able***) at the time of contract formation. But the Restatement rule also emphasizes that losses may be foreseeable either because they follow "in the ordinary course of events" or "as a result of special circumstances . . . that the party in breach had reason to know."

(4) The fourth limitation goes by the name "***mitigation principle***." It has a special connection to the final element of the basic test—that an injured party may not recover damages that it avoided after the breach. The mitigation principle simply extends this notion to cover damages that the injured party *could have avoided* through the exercise of reasonable efforts after the breach. Thus, Restatement § 350(1) states that damages are not recoverable "for loss that the injured party could have avoided without undue risk, burden or humiliation."

Example

A mall tenant breached its four-year lease by leaving after three years. The next day, however, another potential tenant offered to lease the same space on the same terms for one year. The landlord rejected the offer. Under the mitigation principle, the landlord likely will not be able to recover from the original tenant the lost lease payments for the remaining year, because it reasonably could have avoided those losses by accepting the new tenant.

Nonetheless, the notion of "reasonable" efforts is important. In the above example, the landlord's damages would not be reduced if the possible new tenant had been unsuitable in some objective way. A famous example involved a movie studio that breached a film contract with a star but offered her another film role at the same compensation. The court found that the second role was not reasonably comparable to the first, and thus allowed the star to recover the full payment for the first film (in addition to the payment for the second). The mitigation principle also does not apply if the injured party has made reasonable but unsuccessful efforts to avoid a loss.

What You Need to Know:

1. The standard remedy for breach of contract is to grant damages that put the injured party in the position it would have been if the contract had been performed as promised (expectation damages). Under the standard test, the injured party is entitled to recover the loss in value from non-performance of the contract, plus any other loss caused by the breach ("consequential damages"), less any costs or losses avoided because of the breach.

2. Where an injured party's expectation damages are uncertain (especially in construction cases), the law permits her to recover either the *market value* of the loss she sustained or the *cost* of obtaining the promised performance from a third party, provided that the latter is not "clearly disproportionate" to the former.

3. The law recognizes four limitations on the recovery of contract damages: (1) causation; (2) proof to a reasonable degree of certainty; (3) the damages must have been reasonably foreseeable at the time of contracting; and (4) the injured party may not recover damages it could have avoided through the exercise of reasonable efforts ("mitigation principle").

LESSON 28: RELIANCE AND RESTITUTION; SPECIFIC PERFORMANCE; LIQUIDATED DAMAGES

This final lesson will explore the alternative remedies of "reliance" and "restitution" damages. It also will analyze the "extraordinary" remedy "specific performance" as well as the ability of the parties to agree on the recoverable damages through a so-called "liquidated damages" clause.

Reliance Damages. In contrast to expectation damages, the reliance measure of damages for breach of contract merely compensates the injured party for any money he *actually spent* in preparing for or performing the contract (so-called ***"out-of-pocket" damages***). In this sense, the reliance measure is "backward-looking"—for it seeks, in the words of Restatement § 344(b), to put the injured party "in as good a position as he would have been in had the contract not been made." You might think of this measure as an amount of money necessary to get the injured party "back up to zero" (where he was before concluding the contract with the breacher).

Why, you ask, would an injured party ever want this measure of recovery instead of full expectation damages? Well, he would do so if he entered into a bad deal in the first place, and thus had a *negative* expectation under the contract.

Example

> Mary contracted to pay John $10,000 to construct a fountain on her lawn. After John spent $7,000 building the fountain, Mary breached the contract. Unfortunately, John is a bad businessman and he later figured out that he would have spent $11,000 to construct the fountain. He would not want to pursue his expectation interest, because if the deal had been performed as promised he would have sustained a loss. Instead, he will seek only his reliance damages = the $7,000 he spent performing the contract before Mary's breach.

An injured party also may be limited to recovering reliance damages if he is not able to prove his expectation damages to a reasonable degree of certainty (*see* Lesson 27).

The primary standard of recovery nonetheless remains expectation. Thus, Restatement § 349 permits the breacher to try to prove that the injured party would have lost money on the deal. If the breacher succeeds, the reliance recovery is ***reduced by the amount of the expected loss***. Thus, in our example above, if Mary is able to prove that John would have suffered the $1,000 loss from full performance of the contract, his reliance recovery would be reduced from $7,000 to $6,000.

Restitution Damages. A party may have a right to recover, instead, restitution damages in certain situations relevant to contract law. As Lesson 17 explained, this can occur when she conferred a benefit on the other party but has a defense to the enforcement of the contract (*see* Lessons 22–24) or no contract existed in the first place (*see* Lessons 2–11).

But here we are concerned in particular about the third situation referred to in Lesson 17: where a breach by one party permits the other to rescind the contract. As Lesson 26 explained, such a right arises in the event of a "material" breach of contract (aka non-substantial performance by the breacher). In such a case, the injured party may rescind the contract and—with the contract now out of the picture—bring claim in restitution to recover any benefit she had previously conferred on the breacher. The measure of such a recovery is the ***reasonable (market) value of the benefit conferred***.

Example

> To tweak the above example, assume that Mary committed a material breach of contract. Assume also that as of that time, John's partially constructed fountain on Mary's lawn was already worth $8,000. In such a case, John could decide to rescind the contract and bring a claim in restitution for the $8,000 benefit he conferred on Mary in the form of the partially constructed fountain (and without a reduction for any negative expectation as discussed above for reliance damages!).

However, the injured party's right to recover in restitution in such a case is subject to two important limitations: First, he may not seek restitution if he already has performed *all* of his duties under the contract and the breacher merely owes a payment of money. Second, he otherwise may not recover in restitution an amount in excess of the total compensation defined in the parties' contract (although the Restatement disagrees with this limitation).

Summary of the Interaction of the Three Measures of Recovery. It may be helpful at this point to summarize how the three alternatives to measuring damages fit together in the system: In the event of a breach of contract, the injured party may be able to choose any one of the three measures. First, she may seek his full expectation damages (*see* Lesson 27). Second, she instead could seek to recover only reliance damages for any money she expended in performance of the contract. Again, she likely would choose this measure only if she entered into a bad deal in the first place, and thus had a negative expectation under the contract (*see* above). Third, provided that the other party committed a material breach of contract, she may choose to rescind the contract entirely and bring a restitution claim for the reasonable value of any benefit previously conferred on the breacher (*see* above).

Restitution for the Breacher. Although this may surprise you, even a material breacher may have a right to recovery in restitution. The modern view grants him this right, provided that his breach did not involve fraud or other bad faith conduct. But of course, any such recovery by the breacher will be reduced by the damages the injured party is entitled to recover for breach of the contract in the first place.

As a final note, contract law (decidedly unlike tort law) does not permit the recovery of *punitive damages*. Similarly, an injured party may not recover *damages for emotional distress* (except in a very narrow set of highly personal matters, such as contracts for funerals).

Specific Performance. What if the injured party does not want money damages at all, but instead wants the court to *order*—in the form of an injunction—the breacher to *do* what was promised? This is known as "specific performance," but the common law traditionally has viewed it as an "extraordinary remedy." Thus, courts generally will grant such an order only if the standard remedy of damages (the so-called "remedy at law") would be "inadequate."

Example

> Adana breached a contract to sell to Johann for $3 million a unique painting by Claude Monet. John's standard remedy for this breach would be a monetary award for the difference between the purchase price and the fair market value of the painting. But because the joy of possessing a unique Monet painting really cannot be measured in monetary terms, a court likely would order Adana to deliver the painting to Johann (for which of course he must pay the $3 million).

Traditionally, in assessing claims for specific performance the common law focused on whether the subject of the contract was "unique." The standard example was a contract to sell land. Modern courts instead consider specific performance in light of whether an award of monetary damages would be adequate to protect the full expectation interest of the injured party. Restatement § 360 identifies three factors for a court to consider: (a) "the difficulty of proving damages with reasonable certainty"; (b) "the difficulty of procuring a suitable substitute" with an award of monetary damages (which tracks with the idea of whether the subject is unique); and (c) "the likelihood that an award of damages could not be collected" (given that a damages award is of little value if the breacher has no money or has deviously hidden it away).

An order of specific performance nonetheless is an "***equitable remedy***" within the sound discretion of the court. As a result, courts will take into account issues beyond compensation. Thus, courts generally will not issue such an order if it would (a) compel an individual to perform personal services; (b) impose excessive administrative burdens on the court; (c) impose excessive hardship on the breacher or third parties; or (d) otherwise be against the public interest.

A ***liquidated damages clause*** is one in which the parties agree in their contract on the damages that are recoverable in the event of a breach. The common law traditionally does not favor such clauses and refuses to enforce them if they function not as compensation, but instead as a "***penalty***." (As noted above, contract law does not allow the recovery of punitive damages.) Under the traditional test, such a clause is enforceable only if two separate requirements are met: (a) the damages that might arise on breach must have been *difficult to estimate* at the time of contracting, *and* (b) the *amount* of the agreed damages must have been a *reasonable estimate* of just compensation for the likely harm from a breach. Traditionally, if either of these elements is not satisfied, the court will refuse to enforce the liquidated damages clause, and thus force the injured party to prove its actual damages. (Some courts also inquire into the intent of the parties, and specifically whether the purpose of the liquidated damages clause from the beginning was to impose a penalty upon breach.)

The modern test in Restatement § 360 is a more flexible. It permits enforcement of a liquidated damages clause based on a general test of reasonableness. Specifically, such a clause must be "reasonable" in consideration of "the anticipated or actual loss caused by the breach and the difficulties of proof of loss." The "or" in the first part of this test is quite important. It permits a court to consider the "reasonableness" of the amount of agreed damages in light of *either* what the parties originally anticipated *or* what the actual damages turned out to be.

What You Need to Know:

1. Reliance and restitution are alternative measures of recovery in breach of contract cases. An injured party that chooses to seek reliance damages is entitled to compensation for the money she spent in preparing for or performing the contract (but this amount will be reduced by any loss the breacher can show that the injured party would have sustained from full performance). In the event of a material breach of contract, the injured party instead may seek restitution damages measured by the reasonable value of any benefit previously conferred on the breacher.

2. A court will order a party to perform a contract ("specific performance") only if monetary damages would be inadequate to compensate the injured party. The modern view instructs a court to consider three factors in making such a determination. A court also will consider broader equitable factors in exercising its discretion to issue such an order.

3. Under the modern view, courts will enforce a liquidated damages clause only if it is reasonable in light of (a) the anticipated or actual loss caused by a breach and (b) the difficulties of proof of loss.

TABLE OF CASES

INDEX

References are to Pages